W9-CSA-061

W-85 Bus 201 2995B

Introduction to Management Science

Introduction

SECOND EDITION

THOMAS M. COOK / ROBERT A. RUSSELL

Arthur Young & Company   The University of Tulsa

to Management Science

PRENTICE-HALL, INC., Englewood Cliffs, New Jersey 07632

Library of Congress Cataloging in Publication Data

COOK, THOMAS M.   (date)
    Introduction to management science.

    Includes bibliographies and index.
    1. Management—Mathematical models. 2. Operations
research. I. Russell, Robert A., 1946– joint author.
II. Title: Management science. III. Title
HD30.25.C67 1981   658.4′034   80–28810
ISBN 0-13-486092-6

Editorial/production supervision by *Linda Stewart*
Interior and cover design by *Wanda Lubelska*
Interior Design Supervision by *Lee Cohen*
Manufacturing buyers: *Gordon Osbourne, Ed O'Dougherty*

© **1981, 1977 by Prentice-Hall, Inc., Englewood Cliffs, N.J. 07632**

All rights reserved. No part of this book
may be reproduced in any form or
by any means without permission in writing
from the publisher.

Printed in the Unites States of America

10   9   8   7   6   5   4   3

Prentice-Hall International, Inc., *London*
Prentice-Hall of Australia Pty. Limited, *Sydney*
Prentice-Hall of Canada, Ltd., *Toronto*
Prentice-Hall of India Private Limited, *New Delhi*
Prentice-Hall of Japan, Inc., *Tokyo*
Prentice-Hall of Southeast Asia Pte. Ltd., *Singapore*
Whitehall Books Limited, *Wellington, New Zealand*

Contents

PART II
DETERMINISTIC MODELS

2 LINEAR PROGRAMMING: FORMULATION AND APPLICATIONS 32

3 SOLVING LP PROBLEMS: GRAPHICAL AND SIMPLEX METHODS 66

4 SENSITIVITY ANALYSIS   114

5 TRANSPORTATION AND ASSIGNMENT PROBLEMS   148

6 NETWORK MODELS 200

Scenario: General Motors Corporation 201

7 PROJECT SCHEDULING 232

Scenario: The Army Corps of Engineers 233

8 OTHER MATHEMATICAL PROGRAMMING TOPICS   270

Scenario: Bechtel, Inc.   271

PART III
STOCHASTIC MODELS   313

9 PROBABILITY CONCEPTS AND DISTRIBUTIONS   314

Scenario: Las Vegas, Nevada   315

10 DECISION THEORY 354

11 FORECASTING 400

PART IV
CONCLUSION

16 MIS AND DECISION SUPPORT SYSTEMS   626

17 MANAGEMENT SCIENCE: PRESENT AND FUTURE   642

PART V
APPENDIXES   661

APPENDIX A
GLOSSARY   663

APPENDIX B

APPENDIX C
TABLE AREAS OF A STANDARD NORMAL
DISTRIBUTION   724

APPENDIX D
SELECTED VALUES OF THE BINOMIAL
CUMULATIVE DISTRIBUTION FUNCTION   726

APPENDIX E
THE CUMULATIVE POISSON
DISTRIBUTION   732

APPENDIX F
THE CHI-SQUARE DISTRIBUTION   736

Preface

The second edition of *Introduction to Management Science* is designed to introduce the reader to the field of operations research/management science. It contains the basic philosophy and many of the features of the first edition, but is truly a significant revision in that much has been added.

Like the first edition, the revision presents a general introduction to the field. Although the book can be used by students of any discipline, it is aimed at the business students who will most likely pursue a career in an organization requiring some managerial ability and decision-making skill. It is written at a level that is appropriate for both the undergraduate and graduate student.

The second edition continues the effort at being a very student-oriented text. It is designed so that readers without a rigorous mathematical background can learn about and gain appreciation of quantitative methods for decision making. A course in college algebra or finite mathematics is sufficient mathematical preparation. An introductory course in statistics is recommended, but certainly not a necessity. As a further aid to students, important terms are italicized in the text and highlighted as key words in the margin at the point of definition. Review questions and problems are presented at the end of each chapter as well as answers to selected problems which are given in Appendix J.

Since the revised edition contains some very significant changes, we should point out the major enhancements as follows:

1. Broader coverage of OR/MS topics. Five new chapters have been added as well as expansions of previous chapters. An emphasis on

interpretation of computer output has been added to the linear programming chapters; the transshipment model has been included in the transportation and assignment chapter; PERT/COST has been added to the project scheduling chapter; and a brief discussion of materials requirements planning (MRP) has been added to the inventory chapter. In order to present coverage of additional mainstream OR/MS topics, we have added chapters on network models, other mathematical programming topics (which include integer, goal, and dynamic programming), forecasting, Markov processes, and the emerging new field of decision support systems (DSS).

2. Reorganization of topics—We have organized the topics of the second edition in two basic parts. The first part of the text deals with deterministic decision models, and the second part addresses stochastic decision models. We felt that this organization provides a common foundation for the topics and a logical progression from deterministic to stochastic problems.

3. Emphasis on real world applications—In order to motivate the reader and give him an appreciation of OR/MS, we have provided real company success stories at the beginning of each chapter. These scenarios pertain to the topics covered in the associated chapter and highlight dollar savings and other benefits derived from OR/MS. Moreover, applications from the literature and the authors' consulting experience are presented in the text as well as in the end of chapter problems which are labeled with the nature of the application.

4. Solved problems—At the end of each chapter, we present the complete solution of several problems which illustrate the techniques developed in the chapter.

5. Cases—In the second edition, we continue the tradition of presenting OR/MS cases which are more involved than ordinary problems. In this edition, however, we place them at the end of the book so that (a) those instructors who prefer not to use them can delete them without loss of continuity, and (b) the student will not know immediately which chapter is associated with the case, and therefore must decide on an appropriate approach to the case solution.

6. Expanded problems—There are approximately 60 percent more problem exercises provided at the end of the chapters. These problems span the public and private sector as well as service and manufacturing industries.

7. New pedagogical aids—In addition to solved problems, we have added a glossary in Appendix A at the end of the text. The student will thus have a single convenient source for the definition of technical terms. A *Study Guide* will also be available in this edition.

The separate paperback guide will include a summary of the key points of each chapter as well as a review of key terms, worked out problems, and sample exams with solutions.

Several people deserve a special mention for their contributions to this revision. We would like to thank the reviewers, whose comments and suggestions led to an improved manuscript: Donald Adolphson, University of Washington; Leonidas Charalamuides, Marquette University; Jim Courtney, Texas Tech University; Kathy Corriher, International Paper Company; G. H. Mashayekhi, Central Michigan University; and William James Zavoina, Loyola College.

We would like to thank the staff at Prentice-Hall for their assistance, particularly Executive Editor Ron Ledwith for his creative ideas and support, Quantitative Editor Doug Thompson, and Production Editor Linda Stewart.

Our thanks also to Margaret Carpenter and Beverly Teague who typed the manuscript as well as the Instructor's Manual.

PART I
Introduction

1

Introduction to Management Science

HERTZ RENT-A-CAR

Hertz Rent-A-Car is number one in the car rental business and trying hard to stay that way. Hertz operates a substantial fleet of vehicles in more than 100 cities in the United States and Canada. Most of the major Hertz field operations are organized as pools consisting of from 2 to 10 cities with fleets of 2,000 to 6,000 cars.[1] The major benefit of the pool arrangement is the potential for improving fleet utilization through the shifting of cars from cities with surplus to cities with shortages.

Imagine though the complexity of Hertz's short-term planning problem. How would you allocate cars to each city on a daily basis? Keep in mind the dual and conflicting goals of the Hertz management—assuring adequate vehicle availability for the customer and, at the same time, maintaining a high degree of utilization for each car in the fleet.

The distribution problem has both a "city dimension" and a "time dimension." City demand for cars can vary significantly and the planning horizon must extend well beyond the current day. Arrangements for transfers of cars must be made days in advance. A further complication is that the capacity or available number of cars is highly complex and uncertain. New cars are always being installed and other cars retired; some are moving to and from the maintenance shop. Finally, the Hertz Rent-It-Here, Leave-It-There policy means that future rentals can occur anywhere and return anywhere.

The complexity and importance of the short-range planning problem has long been recognized by the Hertz management. However, until recently their decisions were based on "gut feelings," with heavy reliance on sometimes distorted hand-computed averages and statistics. Spurred by competition and the desire to be more profitable, Hertz decided to turn to a sound analytical approach to the short-range planning problem.

The Hertz Operations Research group responded by developing the Pool Control System (PCS). PCS is an interactive model-oriented management tool.

---

[1]Martin Edelstein and Myron Melnyk, "The Pool Control System," *Interfaces,* 8 (November 1977), 21–36.

It is a descriptive rather than a prescriptive analytical tool, whose purpose is to clarify and evaluate alternatives. Ultimate decision making is left to the manager. (PCS provides the information and reports to aid in the decision.) The PCS system uses a model (a system of equations) to calculate estimates for key variables, such as capacity and demand. It is a time-sharing-based system that answers the following kinds of questions for each city: How many cars will be needed? How many cars will be available or can be moved in from other pool cities? How many reservations can be accepted? How will the actions taken for any city on any day affect future days and other cities?

PCS is an example of a successful decision support system that combines an analytical model with a computerized information system. All levels of management at Hertz have attributed dramatic improvements in both customer service and fleet utilization to PCS. Approximately 50 cities representing over 60% of Hertz's car fleet use PCS daily. Those cities using the system have realized an increase of at least 10 percent in the average number of rentals per car. This directly affects bottom-line performance. This is all accomplished by a system whose total operating cost for each pool city never exceeds $10 a day.

PCS has been used most successfully in handling the Florida winter season, the Olympics, the Super Bowl, the summer peak on the West Coast, the presidential inauguration, and major conventions as well as normal business periods. The next time you find yourself walking (not running) through an airport, you might have the Pool Control System to thank.

INTRODUCTION

Prior to the twentieth century, business and other organizations functioned in a less complex environment than that of today. Managers of contemporary organizations (such as Hertz Rent-A-Car) must cope with a dynamic world of increased population, inflation, recession, social consciousness, and shortages of energy resources such as crude oil. Consequently, the decision-making task of modern management is more demanding and more important than ever.

Fortunately, we human beings can use our ingenuity to find new ways to handle the problems that confront us. Even though contemporary institutions face an increasingly complex and uncertain environment, they also have available innovative approaches to dealing with decision problems. This book is concerned with some of the new tools and technology that have been developed specifically to help management in the decision-making process.

management science   *Management science* is the discipline devoted to studying and developing procedures to help in the process of making decisions. It is also commonly called *operations research*. The two terms have come to be used interchangeably, and we shall use both throughout the text. The principal characteristic of operations research/management science (OR/MS) is its use of the scientific method for decision making. Management can approach complex decision problems in several ways. Managers may resort to intuitive or observational approaches that depend on subjective analyses. Or, putting faith in "proven" procedures, they may simply repeat other managers' solutions. Such attempts at handling problems are sometimes called *seat-of-the-pants* approaches. They may not attack the problems in a systematic manner, and they do little to improve or advance the managerial decision process. On the other hand, a management science approach provides a rational, systematic way to handle decision problems. Using a systematic approach, the decision maker has a better chance to make a proper decision.

operations research

Our greatest technical accomplishments have been achieved by utilizing the scientific method. Only recently, however, have we begun to apply this methodology outside the laboratory environment of physics and chemistry. Even though these new environments are less controlled, the operations of organizations and their decision-making processes still lend themselves to analysis through scientific methodology.

How did scientific methodology come to be applied to decision problems? The answer to that question will further your comprehension of the field of management science.

HISTORICAL OVERVIEW

Operations research/management science is an interdisciplinary field comprising elements of mathematics, economics, computer science, and engineering. Its specific content expanded enormously after the twentieth-century invention of electronic computers. Its fundamental philosophical principle, however—the use of scientific methodology to solve problems—was a recorded management technique much earlier. Venetian shipbuilders of the fifteenth century, for example, are known to have used an assembly line of sorts in outfitting ships.

Progress was not consistent until the Industrial Revolution, however. Based on his analysis of the manufacture of straight pins, Adam Smith proclaimed the merits of division of labor in 1776. Charles Babbage, an English mathematician and mechanical genius, wrote a seminal treatise titled *On Economy of Machines and Manufactures* (1832). In it, Babbage discussed such issues relevant to management science as skill differential in wages and concepts of industrial engineering.

In the late nineteenth century, an American engineer, Frederick Taylor, formally advocated a scientific approach to the problems of manufacturing. Taylor, sometimes called the father of scientific management, was largely responsible for developing industrial engineering as a profession. It was his philosophy that there was one "best way" or most efficient way to accomplish a given task. He used time studies to evaluate worker performance and to analyze work methods.

Henry L. Gantt, a contemporary of Taylor's, refined the content of early scientific management by bringing into consideration the human aspect of management's attitude toward labor. He espoused the importance of the personnel department to the scientific approach to management. Perhaps his greatest contribution, however, was his scheduling system for loading jobs on machines. Basically a recording procedure, Gantt's system was devised to minimize job completion delays; it permitted machine loadings to be planned months in advance.

The early scientific management era was an important stage of development for OR/MS. However, its progress was mostly limited to establishing or improving efficient performance of specific tasks in the lower levels of organizations. It may not be possible to pinpoint the first true application of management science, but several pioneers should be noted. As early as 1914, an Englishman named Frederick W. Lanchester attempted to predict the outcome of military battles based on the numerical strength of personnel and weaponry. Lanchester's predicting equation may represent the first attempt to model an organizational decision problem mathematically. In 1915, Ford W. Harris published a simple lot-size formula that constituted the basis for inventory control for several decades and still finds wide use today. Just as Harris helped establish inventory control theory, a Danish mathematician, A. K. Erlang, founded modern waiting-line, or queuing, theory. He developed mathematical formulas to predict waiting times for callers using automatic telephone exchanges.

One of the first to apply sophisticated mathematical models to business problems in the United States was Horace C. Levinson, an astronomer by training. In the 1930s, Levinson studied such market-oriented applications as the relationship between advertising and sales and the effect of income and residential location upon customer purchases.

Despite such advances in the scientific approach to quantitative management problems before 1940, OR/MS did not emerge as a recognized discipline until World War II. In the late 1930s, the British assembled a team of specialists to investigate the effective use of radar. Subsequently, the British military establishment increasingly called upon the British scientific establishment to study other problems, such as antisubmarine warfare, civilian defense, and the optimal deployment of convoy vessels to accompany supply ships.

This approach to military problem solving called upon experts from various areas of specialization. Perhaps the most famous British group was headed by the distinguished physicist P. M. S. Blackett. Blackett's Circus, so-called, consisted of three physiologists, two mathematical physicists, an Army officer, a surveyor, two mathematicians, an astrophysicist, and a general physicist. This multidiscipline team approach has become a characteristic of OR/MS. The highly successful British operational research was credited with helping to win the Battle of Britain and the Battle of the North Atlantic.

Such successes influenced the United States military establishment to include "operations analysis" groups on its staff. During World War II, the United States gathered mathematicians, statisticians, probability theorists, and computer experts to work on operations analysis. During the period, John von Neumann made immense contributions in the area of game theory and utility theory, and George Dantzig worked on the simplex method of linear programming.

After the war, the military establishment increased its research programs and retained some operations research personnel, but industry largely ignored the methodology of the discipline. Many operations research ideas naturally had a military orientation, and nonmilitary managers tended to regard the techniques either as irrelevant to their problems or impossible to implement. Two events helped to bring operations research to industry. In 1947, George Dantzig developed *linear programming*, a technique that uses linear algebra to determine the optimal allocation of scarce resources. Obviously, such a method could be applied profitably to many business problems. Operations research began to be regarded as sometimes relevant to industry.

linear
programming

The second, and more important, occurrence to enhance the acceptability of nonmilitary operations research was the development and production of high-speed electronic computers. Some operations research techniques entailed long, complex calculations to solve real-world problems. Computers, capable of performing such calculations millions of times faster than people, were invaluable tools for the operations research profession. With the advent of electronic instruments to perform functions that were previously impossible or unprofitable, OR/MS could be perceived as valid to, and valuable for, business and industry. The dependence of OR/MS methodology on computers cannot be overemphasized. Even today, certain large-scale problems cannot be solved with current techniques and existing computer hardware. Research will undoubtedly improve the methodology; but it is ultimately the future generations of computers that will allow operations researchers and management scientists to extend the successful applications of their discipline.

Given the favorable climate engendered by industry's acceptance of OR/MS in the 1950s, the discipline developed rapidly. One measure of its formalization was the establishment of professional associations. Chief among these are: Operational Research Society (British, 1950); Operations Research Society of America (1952); The Institute of Management Science (United States, 1953); and American Institute of Decision Sciences (1969).

By the end of the 1950s, many of the standard tools of OR/MS, such as linear programming, dynamic programming, inventory control theory, and queuing theory, were relatively well developed. However, in the 1950s most of the OR/MS applications focused on specialized and very well defined problems. Since the early 1960s, formal OR/MS endeavors have dealt increasingly with planning problems that are less well structured and less realistic. Decision analysis emerged as a process for dealing with decisions associated with much uncertainty. Goal programming and multiobjective linear programming were developed to deal with decision problems that have multiple and sometimes conflicting goals.

During the 1970s and into the 1980s, OR/MS has become increasingly concerned with the interface with management information systems (MIS). Computerized data bases play a vital role in supporting OR/MS models as well as in everyday decision making. The marriage of OR/MS and MIS has resulted in a special kind of information system called a decision support system (DSS). This type of system holds great promise for the enhancement of the decision-making process at all levels of management. It will be interesting to observe future developments in this exciting new area.

Since 1950, the field of OR/MS has progressed steadily. Currently more than 20,000 people are involved in applying, teaching, or researching the field. Most *Fortune 500* companies practice OR/MS. Smaller companies may not require full-time OR/MS programs and personnel, but they often hire management consultants for OR/MS projects. Given such exposure, business is finding increasingly desirable the employee who has OR/MS training. As a result, many universities offer undergraduate and graduate degrees in the field, and most business schools have requirements in the subjects of operations research, management science, decision science, or quantitative methods.

THE NATURE OF MANAGEMENT SCIENCE

You have probably gained some insight into the nature of management science from the preceding brief historical overview. In this section we define the actual content of this discipline more specifically. Harvey Wagner, past president of The Institute of Management Sciences, has described OR/MS simply and yet precisely. Wagner states that operations research is a scientific approach to problem solving for executive management. The Operations Research Society of America amplifies this basic definition by calling operations research an experimental and applied science devoted to observing, understanding, and predicting the behavior of purposeful human/machine systems. It is logically applied, therefore, to the practical problems of government, business, and society.

As the foregoing definitions suggest, the fundamental characteristic of OR/MS is its scientific or systematic approach to decision making. But how can we apply the scientific method to the often uncontrollable and imprecise environment of the real world? In laboratory experiments, data are rejected unless they are demonstrably accurate, and all conditions are strictly controlled. In modern organizations, data are often imperfect, and the outside world exerts a significant influence on many of the variables under study. Factors relevant to a management science experiment are often impossible to manipulate. Furthermore, the functioning and profitability of the firm usually take precedence over artificial changes induced for the sake of experimentation. For example, a company would not temporarily close its warehouses in order to determine the exact shortage costs for its inventory.

Even though the management scientist usually cannot perform a "pure" scientific experiment, this does not preclude using a scientific approach. The management scientist works in a situation analogous to an astronomer's: Each has little control over a constantly changing universe and yet each performs scientific experiments and builds mathematical models to account for the observed phenomena.

THE SCIENTIFIC METHOD

In order to see how the management scientists may use a scientific approach, you must recall the basic steps of the scientific method. These are

1. Observation
2. Definition of the problem
3. Formulation of a hypothesis
4. Experimentation
5. Verification

As you would suppose, the first three steps of the scientific method can be carried out by the management scientist much as they would be by a chemist or a biologist. However, experimentation and verification can pose special problems in real-world applications.

Let us consider a hypothetical problem for the manager of a manufacturing firm to see how the scientific method can be applied to the analysis of a business problem. The first step of the scientific method requires the recognition of a particular phenomenon. Suppose that the manager of the manufacturing firm has observed a significant rise in inventory costs over the past year. This observation suggests the existence of a problem that can perhaps be treated, yielding benefits to the firm.

Thus, it is necessary to pinpoint the exact nature of the problem. The manager has observed rising costs. These may simply be due to inflation. Some observations may be directly related to the symptoms of the problem rather than to the problem itself. It is important that the decision maker formulate the problem precisely and address the truly relevant issues. Much time, effort, and money can be wasted looking at the wrong problem.

In our example, suppose that the manager has determined that inventory costs have risen even faster than the national rate of inflation. The manager suspects that a significant part of the increased cost is caused by the firm's current inventory policy and thus is potentially amenable to change. The manager's problem can now be clearly defined: It is necessary to determine a new inventory policy that will reduce inventory costs.

The inventory costs of the company are comprised primarily of inventory holding costs (costs of carrying and storing) and inventory replenishing costs (costs of ordering and restocking). A closer examination by the manager yields the fact that replenishing costs have increased more rapidly than holding costs. This is true primarily because transportation costs and the clerical costs of placing orders have risen sharply. The manager now has a hypothesis: Ordering larger quantities fewer times per year will decrease overall inventory costs. This new policy will increase holding costs somewhat, but it will lower replenishing costs at the same time.

Now the manager needs to determine how much larger the orders should be. A trial-and-error approach can be implemented by changing the order quantity and observing the effects on total inventory costs. Observations will then confirm or disprove the initial hypothesis. Another approach is to use a mathematical inventory model (Chapter 14) that "fits" the particular problem. This approach, if applicable, eliminates the need for trial and error, for the model determines the order quantity. A third approach is computer simulation (Chapter 13). In any of these situations, the manager ultimately determines whether the hypothesis is valid by comparing the cost of the new solution with the cost before experimentation. Higher costs may indicate that the original hypothesis is incorrect. In that case, further experiments are called for to try to develop a better hypothesis.

Verification of the conclusions of the experiment can be made in several ways. The most accurate, of course, is actually to implement the new solution within the company and then observe its effects. This procedure can be very dangerous in practice, and it may have far-reaching consequences throughout the organization. Usually, it is best to try to forecast the success of the new solution by applying it to hypothetical data or data that represent past transactions of the firm. However, since costs, prices, and demand are constantly changing, success on past data does not necessarily guarantee success in future inventory transactions for the company. Thus, complete verification in the real world is not always possible.

A SYSTEMS APPROACH

The scientific method is extremely useful for trying to solve certain very specific problems the management scientist encounters. It is usually applied, however, within a much broader context known as the *systems approach*. The word *system* is much used in our society. We hear of computer systems, solar systems, nervous systems, political systems, and systems we usually cannot beat. In this book, we shall refer to a system as a whole comprising interrelated parts intended to accomplish a specific objective. Thus, a computer system is made up of hardware components (such as the central processing unit, card reader, and disk and tape drives) and software components (such as the operating system software and various compilers). These components interact to accomplish the objective of processing computer jobs.

systems approach

Organizations, too, conform to our definition of a system. One kind of organization that can use management science to its advantage—the kind with which we will be concerned primarily—is a human/machine system comprising components such as machinery, departments, divisions, and individual people. The main purpose of the management scientist is to aid in the achievement of the goals of the organization as a whole. Viewing the organization as a system permits us to consider the individual components in relation to the entire organization.

This perspective is essential, for the good of the whole may not necessarily derive from the greatest good for each of the parts. In other words, concentrating only on a particular component of the organizational system may result in *optimization,* or best achievement of goals, for that component but a less than optimal solution or *suboptimization,* for the organization as a whole. Optimizing the organization's goals is sometimes accomplished by optimizing its subsystems. In other cases, however, suboptimization of various components is necessary for the sake of the organization's greatest good. A systems approach best equips the decision maker to determine which alternative actually will maximize the realization of the goals of the organization.

Just as a systems approach helps us to have a balanced perspective concerning an organization's components, it also helps us to view the organization as a component, or subsystem, of the environment in which it exists. Today's human/machine organizations operate under conditions of rapid change and ever-increasing complexity. Good decision making, therefore, requires that management take a broad view. Just as an inventory problem, for example, within a single component may affect an organization's production, finance, accounting, and personnel functions, so too the organization's inventory decisions can affect external supply, demand, and prices in the general market.

Usually, no single decision maker is sufficiently multitalented to understand the ramifications of proposed solutions on all aspects of the organization, including its internal and external environments. Often, a team of specialists is formed to attack quantitative management problems. The concept of the team approach to decision making is a key characteristic of the OR/MS approach. You may recall that one of the first operations research teams, Blackett's Circus, consisted of 11 different specialists. Depending on the type of application, an OR/MS team might include experts in mathematical programming, accounting, finance, marketing research, engineering, mathematics, behavioral science, statistics, computer programming, and other fields. This interdisciplinary approach tends to treat the individual phases of a problem most effectively; consequently, the success of the entire project is enhanced.

To summarize, management science applications include any approach to problem solving that incorporates all, or most of, the following characteristics:

1. Viewing the problem within a systems perspective
2. Applying the scientific method to develop the solution methodology
3. Using a team, or interdisciplinary, approach
4. Using a mathematical model
5. Using a high-speed electronic computer

We have not yet said much about the fourth essential characteristic of management science, model building. Your introduction to mathematical models is in the following section. Most of the topics you will encounter in this text involve some use of a mathematical model.

MODELS IN MANAGEMENT SCIENCE

In general terms, a model is a representation or an abstraction of an object or a particular real-world phenomenon. A good model accurately displays the key properties of the entity it represents. Many different dis-

FIGURE 1.1 The three types of models

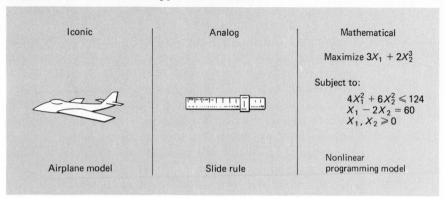

Iconic	Analog	Mathematical
		Maximize $3X_1 + 2X_2^3$
		Subject to:
		$4X_1^2 + 6X_2^2 \leqslant 124$ $X_1 - 2X_2 = 60$ $X_1, X_2 \geqslant 0$
Airplane model	Slide rule	Nonlinear programming model

ciplines employ the use of models. For example, aeronautical engineers use scale-model airplanes in wind tunnels, and civil engineers may use scale models of bridges, buildings, or river systems. More abstract models are used by economists to predict future economic activity and by ecologists to estimate potential effects on the environment. In each of these applications, the model represents an abstraction of reality; and the purpose of the model is to gain specific information about, and general insight into, the phenomenon it represents. By using models, we may investigate certain cause-and-effect relationships and the interaction between key variables.

iconic model   Many different models exist, but each may be classified as belonging to one of three types. (Figure 1.1) An *iconic* model is a physical representation that actually looks like the object it represents. Examples of iconic models include model airplanes and cars, or photographs.

analog model   An *analog* model substitutes one property for another; it can represent dynamic situations statically. For example, a slide rule is an analog model because it substitutes physical distances for numerical quantities. A frequency polygon is an analog model in statistics because it represents numerical data pictorially. Why is a flow chart an analog model in computer programming? The third class of model consists of *symbolic,* or *symbolic or* *mathematical,* models. This type of model is important to the management *mathematical model* ment scientist. Mathematical models attempt to represent nonmathematical reality by means of equations and other mathematical statements. These models translate the essential features of a given situation into mathematical symbols. Then, the symbols can be manipulated in ways that the actual personnel, production, inventory, and so on, cannot. A mathematical model is thus a formal structure that creates a framework within which a problem can be analyzed.

Building useful models for management science applications requires a delicate balance between accuracy and simplicity. The model must be detailed enough to represent the essential realities of the problem and yet manageable in terms of computation and implementation. No mathematical model can capture all characteristics, properties, and uncertainties of a real situation. Attempting to build such a total model results in outright failure or in a model that is too cumbersome to use.

Some management science models involve relationships that cannot be expressed as a system of equations. An example is a model based on properties of mathematical group structures. (A group is a collection of elements having certain properties; matrices and real numbers are examples of groups.) However, most models created for management science applications do consist of a system of equations. A single equation, *objective* called the *objective function,* is used to measure the effectiveness of pro-*function* posed solutions. The remaining equations, called the *constraints,* ensure *constraints* that the solution satisfies certain requirements dictated by the nature of the problem. To illustrate the nature of a mathematical model, let us consider a small mathematical model that has an objective function and only one constraint.

Our problem is well known in OR/MS literature. It is called the knapsack problem, or sometimes the cargo-loading problem, and it has many applications. Let us consider seven items that we would like to take on a camping trip. Table 1.1 lists the weight and the subjective value we have assigned to each item. We further assume that our knapsack has a 10-pound capacity, which means that we cannot take all seven items on the camping trip. The problem is to choose the items that maximize the sum of their values to us and yet do not exceed the 10-pound limit.

Before we create a mathematical model of this problem, we need to define some decision variables. Decision variables have two characteristics: They are the variables whose solution values actually indicate the solution to the problem and those variables over which the decision

TABLE 1.1   Knapsack problem data

Item	Weight (lbs)	Value
1 Water	3.00	60
2 Tent	5.00	60
3 Food	4.00	40
4 Matches	.01	10
5 Fishing tackle	4.00	20
6 Sleeping bag	3.00	10
7 Snake bite kit	.50	3

maker has control. Our problem is to decide which items to take on the trip. Therefore, let

$$x_i = \begin{cases} 1 & \text{if we take item } i, \text{ for } i = 1, 2, \ldots, 7 \\ 0 & \text{otherwise} \end{cases}$$

Thus $x_4 = 1$ means that we take item 4 and $x_4 = 0$ means that we do not take item 4. Our measure of effectiveness is total value; therefore, our objective function is to maximize $60x_1 + 60x_2 + 40x_3 + 10x_4 + 20x_5 + 10x_6 + 3x_7$. Our only restraint is our weight capacity, which can be represented by $3x_1 + 5x_2 + 4x_3 + .01x_4 + 4x_5 + 3x_6 + .50x_7 \leq 10$. Our final mathematical model is thus

Maximize $60x_1 + 60x_2 + 40x_3 + 10x_4 + 20x_5 + 10x_6 + 3x_7$ (value)
subject to $3x_1 + 5x_2 + 4x_3 + .01x_4 + 4x_5 + 3x_6 + .50x_7 \leq 10$ (weight)
where $x_i = 0$ or 1 for $i = 1, 2, \ldots, 7$.

Solving the foregoing mathematical model is not so easy as deriving it, but this time the answer is given to you. The best solution is to take items 1, 2, 4, and 7, and the associated value is 133. This means that we would take water, a tent, matches, and a snake bite kit on the camping trip. Once the model and a solution procedure are established, we can investigate various properties of the problem if we want. For example, we can study the effect of capacity on maximum value by changing the capacity from 10 to other values (such as 9 or 11) and re-solving the model. In this way, a model can be manipulated to reveal various relationships among key variables in the problem.

Although model building is an integral part of OR/MS procedures, it is still more an art than a science. Successful model-building comes with experience and practice at relating situations to mathematical equations. A few standard models have been created that can be used in certain commonly occurring problem situations. However, most quantitative problems are unique simply because every organization has its own restrictions, limitations, and goals. Most of the time, therefore, models have to be built from scratch.

No model is perfect, and no model can truly represent the situation it symbolizes. Thus, successful management science projects do not depend solely upon models and scientific techniques. As the discipline becomes more sophisticated, greater emphasis is being placed on human factors. There is awareness of the need to balance purely quantitative approaches with the experience, judgment, and insight provided by management. This is a progressive step.

BASIC STEPS IN THE OR/MS APPROACH

Not all OR/MS projects follow the exact steps shown in Figure 1.2, but most do approximate the general process. First is the problem-formulation step. We have already mentioned this important step in conjunction with the scientific method. Even though problem formulation sounds easy, it is a critical and nontrivial step. Defining the real problem and not just the symptoms of the problem requires insight, some imagination, and time.

It is general practice (although not required) to use a model in the quantitative analysis process. Once the problem has been well defined, we might find a model that has previously been developed to solve that kind of problem. If one is not available, it will be necessary to develop a model that will accurately reflect the essence of the decision-making problem.

The next step is to solve or manipulate the model in order to obtain a solution and hopefully a prescription for the problem. The model solution requires the necessary input data. The preparation of data to make it usable to the model often requires a major effort. Often the data are not readily available, and must be obtained from the accounting, production, or engineering departments. Even when available, the data often have to be transformed to a different form to be usable by the model.

FIGURE 1.2 Flow diagram of a typical six-stage OR/MS study (after Ackoff)

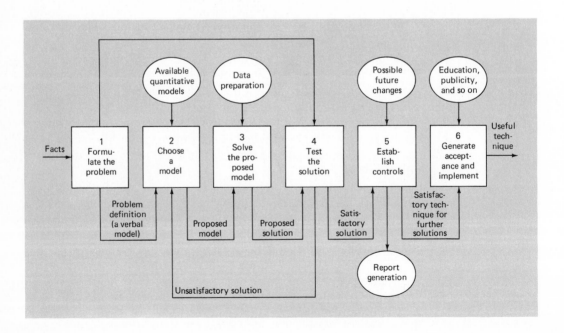

The actual solution of the model is usually accomplished by a solution procedure called an *algorithm*. The calculations are usually performed on a high-speed computer, although small problems can sometimes be solved by hand. Once the solution is obtained, it must be tested for accuracy. Generally, tests of reasonableness are applied and the solution is checked to see if it really "solves" the decision problem. An inaccurate or unreasonable solution usually implies that the model used does not accurately reflect the true nature of the problem. In this case the model must be modified or replaced by a more appropriate choice.

Given a satisfactory solution, the next step is to establish controls for the use of the model. Guidelines as to the assumptions and limitations of the model need to be established as well as procedures to guarantee input data integrity and solution quality. Another important consideration is the design of flexibility within the model and entire OR/MS process. The model and general procedure should not only be useful in solving today's problem but also future problems with some variations in problem characteristics. This "flexibility planning" will ensure the usefulness of the model for a much longer period of time.

The last step of the OR/MS process is often the most difficult. Implementing and generating acceptance for a new procedure often meets with resistance to change. There are many stories concerning potentially useful models that were never implemented because of politics, lack of communication between analyst and user, or fear of change. This is why education, publicity, and documentation of the new procedure are important in implementation. A close working relationship and involvement on the part of the model user as well as an understanding of human and organizational behavior are invaluable prerequisites to the emergence of a useful technique.

MANAGEMENT SCIENCE AND THE FUNCTIONAL AREAS OF BUSINESS

Most of you reading this book are majoring in business and have interests in one of its primary functional areas. In this section, we relate management science to each of these areas. As you will see, these are basically two-way relationships: Management science needs information, policy, and other guidance from the functional areas, and each area has specific problems for which management science can help to generate solutions.

ACCOUNTING

Management science models and techniques are virtually useless without accurate data. An organization's accounting department can be vital in providing the necessary data. Woolsey and Swanson have advised the practicing management scientist to make friends with a cost accountant, who "can be the greatest ally for which the up-and-coming OR man can hope."[2]

Management science, in return, can make significant contributions to the field of accounting. The study of management information systems (MIS) has been applied to automate and improve various accounting procedures. An MIS is a formal system (usually computerized) for collecting, analyzing, and reporting information to managers. Statistical sampling theory has been used to improve the reliability and systematization of auditing procedures. Linear programming has been used to assign audit staff personnel to audit engagements, and goal programming has been used for broad planning purposes in CPA firms. Management science procedures have also been used to resolve transfer-pricing and by-product-costing and to develop standard costs. Other applications include inventory control and forecasting future transactions.

FINANCE

The management scientist needs the financial analyst to provide input concerning cash-flow restrictions and policies. The OR/MS practitioner also needs data about the cost of capital and facts concerning long-range capital requirements. Successful management science applications in the financial realm include capital-budgeting, a procedure that assesses various projects requiring cash outlays in order to maximize net benefits in limited-budget situations. Computer simulation models have been used to build corporate financial-planning models. These simulation models are manipulated to answer various "what if" questions concerning the future of the firm. Management science has also been used to design investment portfolios. Portfolio selection procedures are used primarily to choose investment vehicles and mixes that will interact to minimize risk or maximize gain. Other financial applications include equipment-replacement analysis and determination of dividend policies.

MARKETING

Marketing-research applications are numerous. They include determination of product mix, product selection, and forecasting future demand. Advertising applications include the selection of media in order to maximize a product's effective exposure to a particular market segment at

---

[2]R. E. D. Woolsey and H. S. Swanson, *Operations Research for Immediate Application: A Quick and Dirty Manual* (New York: Harper & Row Publishers, Inc.), 1975, p. 168.

lowest cost. Management science techniques have also been used to assign salespeople to territories, to determine the appropriate number of
accounts for them to serve, and to establish their travel routes in order to
minimize the distances they must cover. Physical distribution problems
are especially suited to resolution by management science techniques.
Models have been developed to determine least-cost shipping patterns
from plant to market. Location theory has been used to determine optimal
locations and sizes for warehouses so that the cost of the distribution of
goods is minimal. Other marketing applications include assessing competitive marketing strategies and analyzing packaging effectiveness.

MANAGEMENT

Management is a general term, and almost any application of management science can be viewed as an aid to management since one of management's primary functions is decision making. If we focus on the functional area of production or operations management, we find applications
to production scheduling, aggregate planning, forecasting, scheduling,
assembly line balancing, plant layout and location, distribution, inventory
control, quality control, and more.

In some circles, management science and behavioral management are
contrasted as quantitative and qualitative management, respectively.
By behavioral management, we mean the body of knowledge devoted
to understanding human and organizational behavior. Each mode, however, is less effective without the other. Behavioral scientists utilize quantitative techniques in order to draw conclusions concerning observed
human or organizational behavior. Management science relies upon the
fundamentals of behavioral management in order to solve real-world
problems successfully. The solutions proposed by management scientists
almost always require some changes within the organization. These
changes often have behavioral ramifications. In fact, it is entirely accurate
to describe the management scientist as an agent of change.[3]

Management science exists ultimately for people. As a collection of
techniques and models isolated from a human context, the discipline is
meaningless. If management science is to be implemented successfully,
human factors and behavioral aspects must receive careful consideration.
After all, what good is an optimally balanced assembly line if the workers
are poorly motivated or on strike?

---

[3]M. Radnor and R. Neal, "The Progress of Management-Science Activities in Large U.S.
Industrial Corporations," *Operations Research,* 21 (March–April 1973), 427–450.

MANAGEMENT SCIENCE IN ACTION

There are obviously multitudes of management science applications, ranging from traditional military and production concerns to more contemporary ones in the fields of environmental engineering, the social sciences, and even sports. In this section, we discuss three specific applications of management science in which concrete results were achieved.

VEHICLE-ROUTING PROBLEM

Many organizations are faced with the problem of how to route a fleet of vehicles efficiently. This problem is particularly common among wholesale and retail distributers (who schedule deliveries), refuse collection companies (which schedule collections), and the U.S. Postal Service (which does both).

Let's consider the actual industrial refuse collection problem experienced by a private firm in a large southwestern city.[4] The firm had roughly 740 scheduled pickups during a 6-day work week. The accounts were scattered throughout an entire city and its outlying areas, situated within a 20-mile radius from the central truck depot. Between 120 and 160 accounts were serviced daily Monday through Friday, and certain accounts were serviced 2, 3, or 6 times a week. The firm used four large hoist-compactor trucks to collect the refuse. These large trucks are quite uneconomical to operate; management estimated that it cost $25 per hour to operate each of them.

The problem was to sequence these four trucks. Each morning, the trucks would leave the depot, collect the refuse at the various accounts, visit dump sites whenever necessary, and ultimately return to the depot. Management's approach to sequencing the trucks had been basically intuitive rather than scientific and methodical. As a result, fuel costs were high, and the drivers often earned overtime pay by working late to finish their rounds.

This problem is generically related to the classical traveling salesman problem in operations research literature. Basically, how can a single salesman, vehicle, or other entity be sequenced among n points, visiting each one only once so as to minimize total distance traveled? The complexity of the problem will be clearer if you consider how many possible sequences there are. In general, for n points to be visited, there are $(n - 1)!$ possible sequences. Thus, for $n = 11$ there are 3,628,800 possible sequences, but for $n = 21$ there are 2,432,900,000,000,000,000 possible se-

---

[4]Thomas Cook and Robert Russell, "A Simulation and Statistical Analysis of Stochastic Vehicle Routing with Timing Constraints," *Decision Sciences*, 9 (October 1978), 673–687.

quences. Can you imagine how many sequences there are for $n = 160$?

The management science approach to this problem does not attempt to find the one best (optimal) sequence. Technology does not yet exist to consistently find the optimal solution to sequencing problems with more than 150 points in the sequence. In addition, this vehicle-routing problem has complicating factors, such as the need to have all four truck routes reasonably evenly balanced with respect to workload and the fact that some accounts have time constraints. (That is, several of the accounts must be serviced at specified times of the day.)

algorithm To develop a more efficient routing system, a systematic solution procedure, more often called an *algorithm*, was developed and coded for use on a computer. Solutions were generated that attempted to minimize the distance traveled while meeting time constraints and balancing the routes. The computerized procedure generated four well-balanced routes with significant improvements in the distances traveled. The new routes were implemented by management, and the drivers then made a few refinements in the routes that had been generated by computer. After implementing the new routes, each truck's travel time was reduced by roughly 2 hours each day. The reduction in distance traveled per day by the four trucks averaged 25 percent.

In a very similar application to school bus routing in Tennessee, a management science approach enabled a school district to save approximately $250,000 annually. The number of buses needed dropped from 13 to 9, and the total distance traveled by the buses was reduced by 50 percent.[5]

TAR SANDS MINING OPERATIONS

If you have tried to buy gasoline recently, you are probably painfully aware that the energy crisis is upon us. It is critical that we find new sources of energy that can be harnessed. The Athabasca tar sands in Alberta, Canada, are estimated to have 600 billion barrels of crude oil, of which 300 are believed recoverable.[6] This represents approximately one-fourth of Saudi Arabia's presently known oil reserves.

Unfortunately, 2 tons of acceptable-grade tar sand are required to produce 1 barrel of crude oil. The amount of raw material that has to be moved and the mining machinery required to do it are prodigious. The cost of the overall project is estimated at $2 billion; the capital cost of the mining alone is $500 million.

---

[5]P. Krolak, "Empirical and Theoretical Bounds on Generalized Vehicle Scheduling," paper presented at the ORSA/TIMS meeting, Las Vegas, Nevada, November 1975.
[6]F. Paul Wyman, "Simulation of Tar Sands Mining Operations," *Interfaces*, 8, Part 2 (November 1977), 6–20.

Syncrude of Canada Limited was charged by the Alberta Government to develop and execute the engineering plan for mining the tar sand, extracting the bitumen and upgrading it to crude oil. Given a contract deadline, Syncrude had to determine whether the project was feasible and what type of equipment would have to be designed and ordered. The equipment selection decision was particularly critical because production feasibility and economics were at stake, and a lead time of 3 to 4 years existed between equipment ordering and project startup.

Canadian Bechtel Limited, an engineering firm, was called in to estimate system availabilities and production levels of several mining methods. The decision was complicated by the severe winter conditions and the many types of mining equipment. Draglines and bucketwheel excavators, however, are the main alternatives for large-scale surface mining.

Bechtel decided to use computer simulation to investigate the total system availability and production level of the various mining alternatives. The simulation model was organized into five modules, pertaining to mining, transportation, storage, extraction, and weather.

The value of the simulation model lies in the fact that many alternatives and conditions could be "simulated" on a computer without actually conducting the experiments in the real world. The simulation showed that a feasible scheme actually did exist for meeting production using either draglines or bucketwheels. It also showed that the bucketwheel scheme resulted in higher capital and operating costs; this difference had not been anticipated prior to the simulation analysis.

After the simulation analysis Syncrude decided to order the dragline-type equipment. The decision resulted in a new state-of-the-art scheme for mining tar sand. The impact for Syncrude was most significant because the selection of equipment worth $500 million is an irreversible decision once it is made. The simulation was also useful in estimating production capability and in showing the most economical balance of equipment sizes to achieve that production. The simulation model continues to be used for planning the details of balancing the operations.

INVENTORY CONTROL SYSTEM

Now, let us consider a computer-oriented inventory control system that was successfully applied to the centralized control of inventory in several branch warehouses.[7] The purpose of the branch, or satellite, warehouses was to increase the firm's competitive advantage by offering quick delivery times to customers. The satellite warehouses were managed by

[7]J. Bishop, Jr., "Experience with a Successful System for Forecasting and Inventory Control," *Operations Research,* 22 (November–December 1974), 1224–1231.

a centralized inventory control group whose objective was to maintain adequate levels of inventories to provide good customer service at least cost.

Prior to a management science approach (in 1968), the inventory manager's policy was to restock each major warehouse once a week. The manager reviewed each inventory item daily and ordered approximately a 2-month supply of any product for which the current level was below 1 month's estimated sales. In an effort to improve upon the manual inventory system, the company decided to computerize certain tasks, such as the production of inventory forms, and, at the same time, to investigate other possible changes.

Other improvements in inventory policy were slow to evolve, however, because management was basically skeptical about radically innovative management science techniques. One of the first changes was the development of a more accurate procedure for forecasting each satellite warehouse's transactions. An exponential smoothing procedure was used to forecast sales; then, based on these sales forecasts, new reorder points, and order quantities were calculated by means of inventory control models. Daily ordering reports were generated by the computer, which provided relevant data for each product. Included in the report were suggested order quantities. However, the report had a unique feature: It allowed management to override the computer on any items whose inventory levels were below the reorder point. Thus, management had the option of accepting the computerized order quantities or of suggesting order quantities of its own. This manual override feature turned out to be the key to implementing the management science approach successfully. It gave management an awareness of its participation in, and essential control over, decision-making processes. Initially, management was reluctant to accept the computer output, and it countermanded 80 percent of the computer's decisions. Confidence was gained, and overridden output had dropped to 10 percent a year later.

Several other reports were generated for the firm, including a monthly out-of-stock analysis and a final report that summarized the month's transactions and the status of satellite warehouse operations. The management science approach was successful in that manual errors were reduced by 75 percent, inventories by 30 percent, and out-of-stock situations by 25 percent. The first-year return on investment was approximately 150 percent, all development costs included.

The experience was so positive that the firm undertook further systematic investigations. The second phase included a computer simulation model of the inventory system. With the aid of the simulation model, the firm studied different inventory policies, review periods, and levels of the production planning horizon. The practice of management science has become an ongoing function in this firm.

SUMMARY

You have been introduced to operations research/management science in this chapter. As an interdisciplinary field, OR/MS has existed only a little more than 35 years, but its body of knowledge draws upon related fields as old as human communication. Earliest formal OR/MS activities were military applications by the British during World War II. The field has grown greatly since the early 1940s, and OR/MS is now widely practiced in business and government.

In principle, OR/MS is the application of scientific or systematic methods to improve the decision-making process. The OR/MS approach assumes a systems viewpoint from which scientific procedures can be applied to various aspects of an entire problem. The advantage of the systems approach is that it allows the optimization of an organization's overall goals, not just those of isolated departments or components of the human/machine system.

The characteristic most distinguishing the OR/MS approach is its use of mathematical models. Mathematical models attempt to translate the essential qualities of real-world situations into systems of equations. Manipulating or solving the mathematical models can engender effective strategies or courses of action for the decision maker.

The real-world applications of OR/MS are numerous. In this chapter, we presented three applications in which specific improvements over previous operations were achieved. OR/MS procedures are distinguished from other theoretical scientific endeavors in that they must ultimately be useful or implementable in the real world. OR/MS must eventually serve the end to which it is directed—namely, human needs.

LOOKING AHEAD

In the chapters to follow we shall examine certain basic OR/MS methods. These methods include some of the most widely used OR/MS techniques today. That is the main reason for your exposure to them in an introductory text. For example, a recent survey of 260 of *Fortune's* top 500 corporations and 160 of the largest California-based firms yielded some interesting facts about the usage of OR/MS in large companies.[8] Table 1.2 reflects the percentage of use of the listed techniques by the 150 responding firms. As you can see, the main topics of this text are widely used among large U.S. corporations.

---

[8]George Thomas and Jo-Anne DaCosta, "A Sample Survey of Corporate Operations Research," *Interfaces,* 9 (August 1979), 102–111.

TABLE 1.2   Usage of OR/MS techniques among large corporations

Technique	Percent of firms using technique
Statistical analysis	93
Simulation	84
Linear programming	79
PERT/CPM	70
Inventory theory	57
Queuing theory	45
Nonlinear programming	36
Heuristic programming	34
Bayesian decision analysis	32
Dynamic programming	27
Risk analysis	3
Integer and mixed programming	2
Delphi	1
Financial methods	1

The techniques listed above and all other OR/MS procedures fall into one of three categories. These three categories are defined according to the nature of the environment in which a decision must be made. The environment or the data for a problem can be either

1. Deterministic
2. Stochastic
3. Uncertain

deterministic problems *Deterministic problems* are those in which data are known with certainty. For example, the knapsack problem we examined earlier is a deterministic problem since all values, weights, and capacities were known exactly. *stochastic problems* *Stochastic problems* are those in which the data are not known with certainty, but a probability distribution is known. For example, consider an inventory problem in which the customer demand for a product each month is not known exactly. However, past records for the company indicate a reliable frequency distribution for this stable product. Thus, we can specify the probability that future demand will exceed a specified amount. *uncertain problems* Problems that must be dealt with when data are *uncertain* are the most difficult of all. An example of this type of problem is the determination of a bid in a competitive bidding situation. In bidding for a contract, the uncertainty hinges around the bids to be submitted by the competition. Future demand or future sales are often uncertain quantities, too.

25

In subsequent chapters we first look at deterministic decision models. Beginning with linear programming, we then examine transportation and assignment models along with other network-type models. Next, we study project scheduling, and finally some more advanced mathematical programming topics, such as goal and integer programming.

The remainder of the book deals with stochastic decision models. We begin this part of the text with a review of probability concepts and then move to decision analysis or decision making under uncertainty. Forecasting comes next, followed by queuing theory or the analysis of waiting lines. We next study the very valuable tool of computer simulation, then inventory control and Markov processes. Following this we deal with the management information system interface and the emerging decision support systems. Finally, we examine current trends and the future of OR/MS, as well as discussing the problem of implementation and some future challenges.

Each chapter will begin with a scenario featuring a well-known company and its experience in applying OR/MS to its real-world problems. We hope these scenarios will stimulate your interest in and appreciation of OR/MS. Each of the following chapters will end with a solved problem section. In this section, additional problems are solved to further illustrate the techniques presented in the chapter and to help you with the homework problems. At the end of the text you will find cases dealing with most of the topics covered in the text. The cases are more involved and more challenging than the typical homework problems. They do, however, provide you the opportunity to develop your realistic problem-solving skills and to apply the newly learned techniques from the text.

REVIEW QUESTIONS

1. Management science attempts to apply scientific methodology in solving decision problems. How does this methodology differ from the scientific method used in the physical science laboratory?

2. What characteristics distinguish the OR/MS approach to problem solving?

3. In what ways does management science contribute to the functional areas of business? In what ways does it borrow from these areas?

4. What are the advantages of adopting a systems perspective in making decisions for an organization?

5. Several applications of management science are mentioned in this chapter. List as many others as you can.

6. Recall the story of the three blind men who each examined a different part of an elephant. Draw an analogy between their conclusions and the systems approach.

7. List some applications of OR/MS to your major field of interest.

8. What does it mean to "solve" a model?

9. Explain how data can be a serious problem in the application of OR/MS methodology.

10. In the context of decision making, explain the difference in the terms *deterministic, stochastic,* and *uncertain.*

11. In order for management science applications to be successful in the real world, more than just a good mathematical model is necessary. What else is needed?

12. What are some of the factors responsible for the rapid growth of OR/MS after 1950?

13. Does management science benefit all levels of management? Explain.

14. Pick some organization with which you are familiar and describe the organization as a whole and its related components.

15. What are some advantages of using mathematical models? What are some potential pitfalls?

PROBLEMS

1.1 *Simple sales forecasting model.* An appliance manufacturer has developed a small mathematical model that forecasts potential sales given price and advertising expenditures. Let y represent sales and x_1 and x_2 represent advertising expenditures and price, respectively. Then the model predicts that $y = 8.14 + .66x_1 - .17x_2$. Determine the sales forecast if the price is $250 and advertising expenditures are $40,000. Comment on the possible accuracy or inaccuracy of the model. What variables or relationships may have been omitted?

1.2 Three OR/MS applications are listed as follows. In each case, state the variables relevant to the problem, the data that are required, and what form the output, or answer to the problem, should take.

  a. Scheduling commercial airlines between major U.S. cities

  b. Determining the location and size of regional warehouses for a retail manufacturer

  c. Selecting an investment portfolio for an insurance company

1.3 Recall the knapsack example from Table 1.1. Suppose that it will not be necessary to take water on the trip. Formulate the new model and determine a solution.

1.4 Is your model in Problem 1.3 deterministic or stochastic? Explain.

1.5 *Newsboy problem.* Consider an example of the classical newsboy problem. Suppose that you manage a newstand which buys papers for 12 cents and sells them for 20 cents. The demand for newspapers is variable each day, but past sales records reveal the relative frequencies of demand shown in the table.

Demand	Probability
50	.10
75	.40
100	.35
125	.15

How many papers should you stock considering that leftover papers are worthless the next day? What kind of systematic decision procedure can you think of to solve the problem?

1.6 Is the newsboy problem (Problem 1.5) deterministic or stochastic?

1.7 *Econometric model.* Consider the following econometric model for forecasting national income:

$$C_t = cY_{t-1} + b \qquad (1)$$

$$I_t = k(Y_{t-1} - Y_{t-2}) + A \qquad (2)$$

$$Y_t = C_t + I_t \qquad (3)$$

where the subscripts refer to time periods. Equation 1 says that consumption equals the marginal propensity to consume c times the income in the preceding period Y_{t-1}, plus a constant b. Equation 2 says that current investment I_t equals the product of the accelerator k and the change in income that occurred in the preceding period, $(Y_{t-1} - Y_{t-2})$ plus autonomous investment, A. Equation 3 simply defines current income as the sum of consumption and investment.

Using the model requires collecting data on the past values of C, I, and Y. Furthermore, it is necessary to estimate the constants or parameters of the model, c, b, and k. Comment on the accuracy of the model in estimating national income.

1.8 Which is preferable, a simple model that is a relatively good approximation of the problem or a very complex and large model that captures nearly all the relevant aspects of the decision problem?

1.9 *Demand model.* The marketing analyst for a company has determined that the price–demand relationship for their product is linear for a price between $12 and $20. That is,

demand $D = 1,500 - 30p$ where p = price

a. How many units can they expect to sell with a price of $15?

b. Given a variable cost of $10 for each unit, what price will maximize profit?

1.10 *Location model.* Three work stations are located along an assembly line as indicated below. All three stations use the same type of parts from an in-process inventory bin that is to be located somewhere along the line. Develop a model to determine the optimum location in order to minimize the sum of the square of the distances from the bin to each work station. Solve your model.

	Station 1		Station 2		Station 3	
0	5		13		22	Distance (ft)

1.11 *Purchase decision.* An airlines company is considering the purchase of a sophisticated inspection machine to help identify structural defects in their airplanes. The device will cost $1,000,000 a year to own and operate but will make the airplanes approximately 10 percent more safe. If the average value of a jet airliner is $6 million and the limits of liability per passenger are $75,000, should the airlines purchase the device considering that airliners very rarely crash?

1.12 *Car rental model.* Recall the Hertz Rent-A-Car problem from the scenario at the beginning of the chapter. One of the equations in their PCS model relates to estimation of completed rentals in city n on day d. This variable CR_{nd} is estimated by

$$CR_{nd} = \overline{CR}_{nd} + \min{(CAP_{nd}, DMHD_{nd})} \cdot LFE_{nd}$$

$$\text{where } \overline{CR}_{nd} = \sum_{i=1}^{28} RNT_{n,d-i} \cdot LFE_{in,d-i}$$

$RNT_{in,d-i}$ = number of rentals in city n on day $d - i$
$LFE_{in,d-i}$ = percentage of rentals due back on day $d - i$
CAP_{nd} = rental capacity of city n on day d
$DHMD_{nd}$ = estimated demand at city n on day d

Some of the assumptions of the model are that no car will be rented more than twice on a given day and that LFE data supplied by the customer are a good estimate of rental life.

a. Do you think that these assumptions significantly reduce the usefulness of the model?

b. Can you think of any other implicit assumptions or limitations of the portion of the model shown?

BIBLIOGRAPHY

Ackoff, Russell L., and Patrick Rivett, *Manager's Guide to Operations Research.* New York: John Wiley & Sons, Inc., 1963.

———, and Maurice W. Sasieni, *Fundamentals of Operations Research.* New York: John Wiley & Sons, Inc., 1968.

Anderson, D. R., D. J. Sweeney, and T. A. Williams, *An Introduction to Management Science: Quantitative Approaches to Decision Making,* 2nd ed. St. Paul, Minn.: West Publishing Company, 1979.

Churchman, C. West, Russell L. Ackoff, and E. L. Arnoff, *Introduction to Operations Research.* New York: John Wiley & Sons, Inc., 1957.

Eck, R. D., *Operations Research for Business.* Belmont, Calif.: Wadsworth Publishing Company, Inc., 1976.

Hillier, F. S., and Gerald J. Lieberman, *Introduction to Operations Research.* San Francisco: Holden-Day, Inc., 1974.

Levin, Richard I., and Charles A. Kirkpatrick, *Quantitative Approaches to Management,* 4th ed. New York: McGraw-Hill Book Company, 1978.

Littauer, S. B., "What's OR/MS?" *Management Science, Application Series,* 17 (October 1970).

Miller, David W., and Martin K. Starr, *Executive Decisions and Operations Research,* 2nd ed. Englewood Cliffs, N.J.: Prentice-Hall, Inc., 1969.

Simon, Leonard S., "What Is a Management Scientist?" *Interfaces,* 1 (February 1971).

Waddington, C. H., *OR in World War II: Operational Research Against the U-Boat.* London: Paul Elek Ltd., 1973.

Wagner, Harvey M., "The ABC's of OR," *Operations Research,* 19 (December 1969).

PART II
Deterministic Models

2

Linear Programming: Formulation and Applications

SHELL OIL COMPANY[1]

Shell

Shell Oil Company in the United States is comprised of two systems, known as the East of the Rockies region and the West of the Rockies region; the two systems are essentially independent. The East of the Rockies system has three refineries, which service over 100 terminal demand points. The company markets over a dozen grades of liquid petroleum products. These products can be shipped by pipelines, barges, or tankers. Shell's product distribution problem is complicated by the fact that the terminals can be served by more than one refinery, via different modes of transportation (with different routes), each having different throughput costs and capacities. Therefore, getting the final product to the customer involves large amounts of capital and operating expenses; approximately 10 percent of Shell's revenues go to pay for transportation costs.

The people at Shell realize that a total systems approach is far more suitable than intuition alone or than looking at only a small part of the total distribution network. They have utilized linear programming codes together with model builders and report generators to better manage their distribution system. The linear programming model that they developed consists of 575 constraints and approximately 1,700 variables. Applications of the model have included studies on opening and closing of terminals, expansion of facilities, and tanker and barge requirements.

The linear programming model took about 8 months to develop; one-fourth of this time was for getting acquainted with the people involved, the system, and sources of data. The cost of running the complete system using IBM's MPSX LP package on an IBM 370/168 computer varies from only $15 to $30, depending on the time of day. There are over 10 optional reports that management can access from the analysis. The most widely used are: Refinery Supply Demand Summary, Product Distribution Volumes, and Tanker Reports.

---

[1]T. K. Zierer, W. A. Mitchell, and T. R. White, "Practical Applications of Linear Programming to Shell's Distribution Problems," *Interfaces*, 6 (August 1976), 13–26.

Between September 1973 and 1976, Shell used the model in over 15 projects. Although the model is not without its limitations, it has been quite valuable in helping to manage the East of the Rockies distribution system.

WHAT IS LINEAR PROGRAMMING?

Of all the available techniques and decision tools in management science, linear programming (LP) is one of the most widely used. It is primarily concerned with the determination of the best allocation of scarce resources. Usually, a firm's scarce resources include capital, labor, raw materials, finished goods, or time. For instance, a marketing department may suggest several new products that its firm can sell successfully. However, each new product contributes a different amount to profit and requires a different amount of each of the scarce resources. Furthermore, there are not enough resources to produce all the new products suggested. Which new products and how much of each one should the firm produce? Linear programming can be used to aid in this decision process. In this case, it would probably be used to show what product mix will maximize profits but not exceed the available resources.

mathematical programming
Linear programming is a component of the more general technique of *mathematical programming*. Mathematical programming is concerned with the development of modeling and solution procedures for the purpose of maximizing the extent to which the goals and objectives of the decision maker are realized. Very special conditions must hold before a general mathematical programming problem is actually an LP problem. These special linearity conditions will be described later in the chapter.

Despite the implication of its name, LP has little to do with computer programming. In LP, the word *programming* is related to planning. Specifically, it refers to modeling a problem and subsequently solving it by mathematical techniques. As we shall see, LP is very similar to setting up and solving a system of linear equations.

Even though LP is quite different from computer programming, computer development has played an integral part in the successful application of LP. Real-world LP problems often involve hundreds of variables and equations. These problems would be impossible to solve without a high-speed computer.

Historically, significant contributions to LP were Leontief's input-output analysis in 1936 and the publication, in 1947, of George Dantzig's technique for, and mathematical proof of, the simplex solution procedure.

Today, LP is one of the most widely used mathematical programming and optimization techniques. In surveying *Fortune 500* companies, the authors found that of those responding 95 percent claimed to use LP at least to some extent. More specifically, 37.5 percent claimed to use it very frequently, 32.5 percent used it frequently, 25 percent used it rarely, and only 5 percent never used it. Undoubtedly, smaller companies use LP less. In some cases, it is simply not needed; in other cases, managers may not understand LP nor realize its potential. In appropriate situations, LP can be a very powerful tool.

GENERAL AREAS OF APPLICATION

As you can imagine, LP has many business applications. But LP is also often used as a tool for developing economic theory and for the systematic analysis of problems both in the physical and social sciences. When a problem can be looked at as a matter of effectively allocating scarce resources, LP can often be used in its solution.

Industrial, agricultural, and military applications of LP are the most extensive. Some of these include scheduling military and industrial oil tanker fleets, dietary planning, agricultural land use and farm management, urban traffic control, oil refinery operation, scheduling blast furnace operations, and minimizing trim losses in paper mills.

Each of the functional areas of business has its own relationship to LP. In accounting, this relationship is multifaceted. In an LP analysis, the accountant supplies required data. Some public accounting firms employ teams of management consultants as advisors to clients. These consultants sometimes use LP to help solve clients' problems. Moreover, certain LP applications are directed to the accounting function itself. These are usually in the areas of budgeting and financial planning. One particularly interesting example is an accounting system in the petroleum industry that is structured on an LP model.[2] Applications in finance include portfolio selection models and financial mix strategies in which LP is used to select the best means for financing company projects.

Marketing applications of LP are numerous and include effective media selection for advertising strategies, development of least-cost distribution patterns, warehouse location, and optimal allocation of sales forces. Management applications of LP include production scheduling, human resource planning, and other kinds of resource allocation.

The list of applications is continually growing as more decision makers

---

[2]J. Demski, "An Accounting System Structured on a Linear Programming Model," *The Accounting Review,* 42 (October 1967), 701–712.

are becoming aware of the utility of LP and the availability of computers increases. The development of more powerful computers will also pave the way for applications that are currently beyond the capability of existing hardware.

PROBLEMS LP CAN BE USED ON

In this section, we discuss some of the general problem situations to which LP can be applied. The following five areas represent the kinds of problems for which LP is now widely used. Can you think of other examples, perhaps innovative ones?

Blending   In blending problems, several raw ingredients are mixed into a final product that must fulfill certain specifications. Each of the raw ingredients contributes certain properties to the final product and entails a given cost. Examples of blending problems are blending petroleum products, mixing cattle feed, mixing meats to make sausage, and mixing paint. Many different combinations of these ingredients will result in satisfactory end products; the objective is to determine the blend of ingredients that does not exceed available supply, meets all technical specifications, and minimizes costs.

Determining product mix   In these problems, it is necessary to determine the kinds and quantities of products to be manufactured in order to maximize profits. A firm can almost always manufacture several different products; each of these requires the use of limited production resources and contributes a certain amount toward profit. The final product mix must take into consideration the limited resources, expected demand for each product, and various management policies.

Physical distribution and assignment   In physical distribution problems it is necessary to ship goods from supply points or production facilities to warehouses or centers of customer demand. Each supply point has a specified capacity, and each point of demand has a specified level of demand. Furthermore, shipping and/or production costs vary for the different plant-to-market alternatives. The problem is to determine the shipping pattern that minimizes shipping costs, meets all demand, and does not exceed available supply. In assignment problems, the objective is to assign facilities or people to specified jobs in order to maximize performance or minimize costs or time.

Production scheduling and inventory planning   Many firms produce products that are subject to fluctuations in demand. Widely varying production rates have proven to be very costly. The problem is basically to determine a production schedule that meets anticipated demand and yet maintains reasonable inventory levels and minimizes the overall costs of production and carrying inventory.

Purchasing   Linear programming can be used to help confront the kind of purchasing decisions in which products are available at different quantities, qualities, and prices. The objective is profit maximization, and the purchase decision must take into consideration the output requirements and specifications as well as budget limitations. Linear programming can also be used in "make-or-buy" situations. In these cases the problem is whether to produce a product or purchase it from an outside source.

THE LP MODEL

Linear programming is a mathematical technique that will maximize or minimize a linear function subject to a system of linear constraints. This linear function, together with the system of linear constraints, forms what is called the *linear programming model*. The canonical form of an LP model is as follows:

linear programming model

Maximize $c_1x_1 + c_2x_2 + \cdots + c_nx_n$ [2.1]

subject to the restrictions $a_{11}x_1 + a_{12}x_2 + \cdots + a_{1n}x_n \leq b_1$ [2.2]

$$a_{21}x_1 + a_{22}x_2 + \cdots + a_{2n}x_n \leq b_2$$

$$\vdots$$

$$a_{m1}x_1 + a_{m2}x_2 + \cdots + a_{mn}x_n \leq b_m$$

and $x_1 \geq 0, x_2 \geq 0, \ldots, x_n \geq 0$ [2.3]

Any problem whose mathematical formulation fits this general model is an LP problem.

An LP model consists of two basic parts—an objective function and a set of constraints. The function, 2.1, being maximized, $c_1x_1 + c_2x_2 + \cdots + c_nx_n$, is called the *objective function*. It is simply a mathematical expression that measures the effectiveness of a particular solution for the LP problem. The restrictions, 2.2, in the foregoing model are called *constraints*. These mathematical statements specify such elements of the problem as the limitations of available resources or the demand that must be met. Conditions 2.3 are called the *nonnegativity conditions*.

objective function

constraints

nonnegativity conditions

decision variables

The x_j variables are *decision variables;* that is, they are the variables whose value is determined when the LP model is solved. Their values provide the answers that are being sought in the LP analysis. In order to *parameters*

determine the values of the decision variables, the LP model needs data. The input data constants are often referred to as *parameters*. The a_{ij}, c_j, and b_i in the general model are all parameters of the model.

Not all valid LP models fit the exact form of the standard model. Variations include an objective function that is to be minimized and constraints that are equations rather than inequalities.

FORMULATING LP MODELS

There are many different types of models. You may be familiar with econometric models, civil engineering prototype models, iconic and analog models, even models of the world. In this section, we shall deal with mathematical models. Before any problem can be solved by LP analysis, it must be formulated as a mathematical model that fits the general form set forth in the preceding section. In any mathematical model, the decision maker is attempting to represent the essence of some problem in terms of relationships between symbols. In LP formulations, the real-world problem is translated into mathematical equations.

Model building is more an art than a science; thus, formulating successful models depends greatly upon the decision maker's own ingenuity and experience. Formulation can often be the most difficult part of an LP analysis. It is also the most important, for once the problem has been formulated correctly, it can be solved on a computer by an LP computer code. We shall state several business problems and show how to formulate them as LP models. In this way, you will begin to gain a feeling for how to approach the formulation of an LP model.

[PRODUCT MIX EXAMPLE]   The Faze Linear Company is a small manufacturer of high-fidelity components for the discriminating audiophile. It currently manufactures power amplifiers and preamplifiers; it has the facilities to produce only power amps, only preamps, or a combination of both. Production resources are limited, and it is critical that the firm produce the appropriate number of power amps and/or preamps in order to maximize profit. Currently, the power amp is selling for $799.95 and is contributing $200 toward profit. The preamp sells for $1,000 and contributes $500 to profit. Figure 2.1 illustrates the product mix problem.

We shall assume that the firm can sell all the components that it can produce and that plant equipment and labor skills are interchangeable between the power amps and preamps.

Constructing the objective function   Given its limited production capacities, Faze Linear would like to produce the exact number of power amps and/or preamps each day that maximize its profits. The objective function of the LP model must evaluate the profit potential of any proposed product mix. The first step in the construction of the objective function is the determination of the appropriate decision variables. What is the manufacturer trying to decide? Specifically, the answer to the question, How many power amps and how many preamps should be produced each day? Thus, let the decision variable x_1 equal the number of power amps to be produced each day, and let x_2 equal the number of preamps to be produced each day. Since x_1 and x_2 contribute $200 and $500, respectively, to profit, we may state the objective function as: Maximize $200x_1 + 500x_2$. Preamps contribute more to profit; so it may seem that only preamps should be produced. However, this may not be true since preamps also require more production resources.

Constructing the constraints   In this simplified example, we shall assume that there are only three production resources. The production process is limited by scarcity of high-quality transistors for the preamps, assembly worker hours, and inspection and testing worker hours. Because of a shortage of high-quality transistors, at most 40 preamps can be manufactured on a daily basis; all other electronic components are in adequate supply. There are only 240 hours of assembly worker time available each day. Furthermore, each power amp requires 1.2 hours for assembly and each preamp requires 4 hours. Finally, there are 81 worker hours available for inspection and testing each day, and the two components require .5 and 1 hour, respectively.

Since power amps do not require the transistor that is in short supply, the limited availability of these transistors will directly affect only the number of preamps produced each day. This constraint may be expressed as $x_2 \leq 40$.

Both components require assembly time; thus, the assembly time constraint must ensure that the combined assembly time of both components

FIGURE 2.1   Faze Linear product mix problem

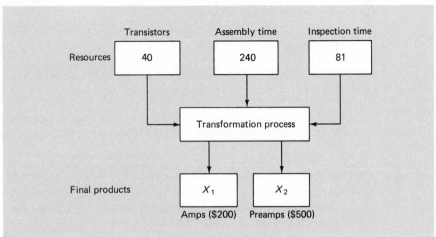

must not exceed 240 hours. This may be expressed as $1.2x_1 + 4x_2 \leq 240$. For inspection and testing time, the constraint is $.50x_1 + 1x_2 \leq 81$. Since it is impossible to produce a negative number of components, we impose the nonnegativity conditions $x_1, x_2 \geq 0$.

The final LP formulation is thus

$$
\begin{array}{ll}
\text{Maximize} & 200x_1 + 500x_2 \\
\text{subject to} & x_2 \leq 40 \\
& 1.2x_1 + 4x_2 \leq 240 \\
& .50x_1 + 1x_2 \leq 81
\end{array}
$$

$$x_1, x_2 \geq 0$$

This problem is simple, and LP is not necessary to solve it. However, product mix problems involving hundreds of products and constraints are impossible to solve intuitively, and the use of LP is necessary. As an exercise, try to solve the Faze Linear problem intuitively. How high is your profit? Later, we shall determine the optimum product mix by LP.

GUIDELINES FOR CONSTRUCTING LP MODELS

In order to formulate an LP model successfully, the decision maker must:

1. Understand the problem
2. Identify the decision variables
3. Choose a numerical measure of effectiveness for the objective function
4. Represent this measure of effectiveness as a linear expression involving the decision variables
5. Identify and represent all constraints as linear expressions involving the decision variables
6. Collect data or make appropriate estimations for all parameters of the model

It is not possible to give a magic formula for success in LP model formulation, but the following suggestions can help.

Understand the problem   Make sure that you understand the problem fully. Is the objective clear? Is the problem a maximization or a minimization?

Determine variables   Decide what the decision variables should be. What, precisely, is being sought in the problem? Is it a production schedule, a resource allocation, a shipping pattern, or something else? Remember that the optimum values of the decision variables must provide the answers to the problem. The most common error beginning students make is defining decision variables incorrectly and thus developing invalid models.

Identify and represent all constraints   A constraint must be constructed for each limited resource. Be certain that each decision variable that affects the given resource is included in the constraint. Formulate constraints for all technical specifications or requirements, such as usage or production in fixed proportions. Finally, check for other types of constraint, such as management policies, demand, or other pertinent conditions.

Collect relevant data   All parameters of the model must be defined as numerical constants. Are all relevant data available? In LP analysis, the collection and estimation of relevant data is often the most time-consuming part of the project.

[DIET PROBLEM EXAMPLE]   In this example, we present a simplification of the classical diet problem. This is a minimization, rather than a maximization, problem. The objective is to determine the type and amount of foods to include in a daily diet in order to meet certain nutritional requirements at minimum cost. The foods we include are tuna fish, milk, spinach, and whole-wheat bread; the only nutrients we consider are vitamins A, C, and D, and iron. We are given the nutritional and cost data shown in Table 2.1. Figure 2.2 illustrates the diet minimization problem.
The decision to be made is simply to determine the amount of each type of food to include in the daily diet. Thus, let x_1 = number of gallons of milk, x_2 = number of pounds of tuna fish, x_3 = number of loaves of bread, and x_4 = number of pounds of spinach. The objective function, therefore, is to minimize $1.95x_1 + 1.80x_2 + .75x_3 + .80x_4$.

The constraints must ensure that the RDA for each vitamin is met. For vitamin A, each gallon of milk contains 6,400 IU, each pound of tuna fish

TABLE 2.1   Nutrition and cost data for diet problem

Nutrient	Gallon of milk	Pound of tuna fish	Loaf of bread	Pound of spinach	Recommended daily allowance (RDA)
Vitamin A	6,400	237	0	34,000	5,000 IU
Vitamin C	40	0	0	71	75 mg
Vitamin D	540	0	0	0	400 IU
Iron	28	7	13	8	12 mg
Cost	$1.95	$1.80	$.75	$.80	

FIGURE 2.2   The diet problem

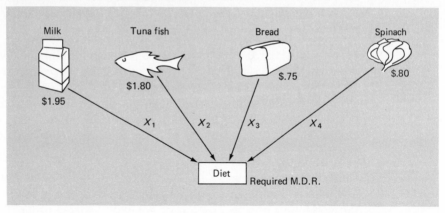

contains 237 IU, bread contains none, and each pound of spinach contains 34,000 IU. Hence, the RDA constraint for vitamin A is written $6,400x_1 + 237x_2 + 0x_3 + 34,000x_4 \geq 5,000$.

The other three constraints and nonnegativity conditions are written:

$$40x_1 + 0x_2 + 0x_3 + 71x_4 \geq 75$$

$$540x_1 + 0x_2 + 0x_3 + 0x_4 \geq 400$$

$$28x_1 + 7x_2 + 13x_3 + 8x_4 \geq 12$$

$$x_1, x_2, x_3, x_4 \geq 0$$

[PRODUCTION/DISTRIBUTION EXAMPLE]   In this example, two production plants located in different parts of the country must produce and distribute a product to three regional warehouses. The three warehouses have demands of 500, 2,000, and 900, respectively. The cost of shipping, based primarily on distance, is given in Table 2.2. The labor and power costs are less at plant 1; each unit is produced at a cost of $1.50. Each unit at plant 2 is produced at a cost of $2.

The objective in this problem is to meet all demand and minimize the combined cost of production and distribution. The decision to be made

TABLE 2.2   Cost ($) of shipping one unit

From plant	To warehouse		
	1	2	3
1	.30	.90	.80
2	.70	.20	.40

concerns how much should be shipped from each plant to each warehouse. Figure 2.3 depicts the combined production and distribution problem.

It is more meaningful (although not essential) to represent these decision variables as variables with two subscripts. Let

$$x_{ij} = \text{amount shipped from plant } i \text{ to warehouse } j$$

where $i = 1, 2$
$j = 1, 2, 3$

Since each unit that is shipped must first be produced, we develop an objective function to minimize $(1.50 + .30)x_{11} + (1.50 + .90)x_{12} + (1.50 + .80)x_{13} + (2 + .70)x_{21} + (2 + .20)x_{22} + (2 + .40)x_{23}$.

The only restriction in this model is that demand must be met. In order to meet the demand at warehouse 1, all the shipments sent to warehouse 1 must sum to 500. Thus, the first constraint is $x_{11} + x_{21} = 500$. The other two demand constraints are $x_{12} + x_{22} = 2,000$ and $x_{13} + x_{23} = 900$. The nonnegativity condition is $x_{ij} \geq 0$ for all i and j. The complete formulation of the model is thus

$$\text{Minimize} \quad 1.80x_{11} + 2.40x_{12} + 2.30x_{13} + 2.70x_{21} + 2.20x_{22} + 2.40x_{23}$$
$$\text{subject to} \quad x_{11} + x_{21} = 500$$
$$x_{12} + x_{22} = 2,000$$
$$x_{13} + x_{23} = 900$$

$$x_{ij} \geq 0 \text{ for all } i \text{ and } j$$

FIGURE 2.3 The production and distribution problem

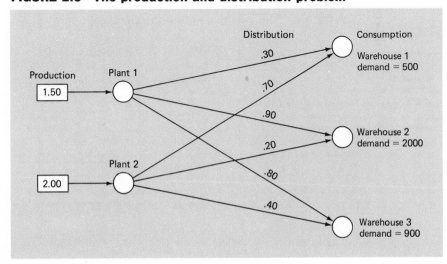

TABLE 2.3   Cost and composition of fertilizer components

Mixing component	Cost	Nitrogen (%)	Phosphorus (%)
1	$.20	60	10
2	.30	10	40

[BLENDING EXAMPLE]   The Green Turf Lawn and Garden Store is trying to sell its own brand of lawn fertilizer this year. It plans to sell two types of fertilizer, one high in nitrogen content and the other an all-purpose fertilizer. The fertilizers are mixed from two different components that contribute nitrogen and phosphorus in different amounts. The composition of each component and cost per pound is given in Table 2.3. Figure 2.4 shows the blending problem.

This season's demand is estimated to be 5,000 25-pound bags of high-nitrogen fertilizer and 7,000 25-pound bags of all-purpose fertilizer. The fertilizer high in nitrogen is to contain between 40 and 50 percent nitrogen, and the all-purpose fertilizer is to contain, at most, 20 percent phosphorus. How many pounds of each mixing component should Green Turf purchase in order to satisfy estimated demand at minimum cost?

Let x_1 and x_2 be the number of pounds of mixing component 1 that are purchased for the high-nitrogen and all-purpose fertilizers, respectively. Similarly, let y_1 and y_2 be the number of pounds of mixing component 2 that are obtained for the high-nitrogen and all-purpose fertilizers. The objective function is then formulated to minimize $.20x_1 + .30y_1 + .20x_2 + .30y_2$.

Assuming that Green Turf wants at least to meet its estimated demand, we can specify the demand on high-nitrogen fertilizer by $x_1 + y_1 \geq 25$

FIGURE 2.4   The fertilizer blending problem

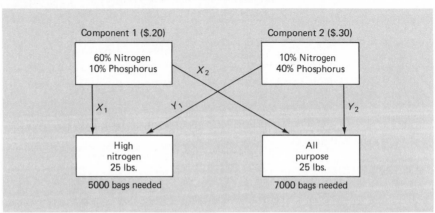

44

(5,000). Similarly, the demand for all-purpose fertilizer is specified by $x_2 + y_2 \geq 25$ (7,000).

Since the different mixing components contribute different amounts of nitrogen and phosphorus, we must calculate a weighted average to represent the content of a particular blend. The high-nitrogen fertilizer must contain at least 40 percent nitrogen. Thus, $(.60x_1 + .10y_1)/(x_1 + y_1) \geq .40$. This constraint is not a linear expression, but it can be turned into one by eliminating the fraction, thus:

$$.60x_1 + .10y_1 \geq .40 (x_1 + y_1)$$

$$.20x_1 - .30y_1 \geq 0$$

The upper limit of 50 percent nitrogen can be written $(.60x_1 + .10y_1)/(x_1 + y_1) \leq .50$, or $.10x_1 - .40y_1 \leq 0$.

Finally, the 20 percent phosphorus restriction on the all-purpose fertilizer is represented $(.10x_2 + .40y_2)/(x_2 + y_2) \leq .20$, or $-.10x_2 + .20y_2 \leq 0$.

The final LP model, then, is stated:

$$\text{Minimize} \quad .20x_1 + .30y_1 + .20x_2 + .30y_2$$
$$\text{subject to} \quad x_1 + y_1 \geq 125{,}000$$
$$x_2 + y_2 \geq 175{,}000$$
$$.20x_1 - .30y_1 \geq 0$$
$$.10x_1 - .40y_1 \leq 0$$
$$-.10x_2 + .20y_2 \leq 0$$

$$x_1, x_2, y_1, y_2 \geq 0$$

[CONSTRAINED BREAK-EVEN ANALYSIS]   The Braden Co. has decided to add one new product line and is considering the addition of two other products. Part of their decision process is to perform a standard break-even analysis to determine what volume of sales is needed in order for revenue to equal total fixed and variable costs.

One of the firm's accountants has determined the break-even point for product x to be 1,000 units. The graph in Figure 2.5 illustrates the calculation of the break-even point given the following data on product x:

Product	Selling price per unit	Variable cost per unit	Fixed cost
x	$20	$10	$10,000
y	25	12	10,000
z	15	8	10,000

FIGURE 2.5 Break-even graph for product x

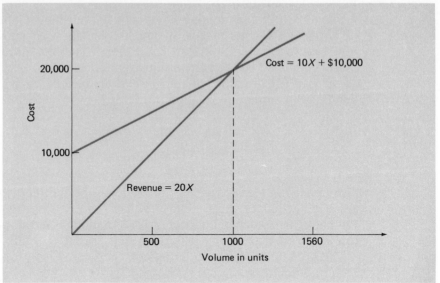

In considering the addition of product lines y and z, management would like to know what sales volumes of x, y, and z would be necessary to break even and furthermore minimize total capital outlay. Braden currently has contracted to provide 750 units of product x. The same customer has also requested 400 units of z if the product is produced. Braden management is reluctant to produce over 300 units of product y initially, as the market for this product is unproven.

It is not possible to graph the break-even chart for this problem in two dimensions, and the constraints on the sales volume of products x, y, and z preclude using standard break-even analysis. However, linear programming can be used to solve the problem.

Since management is interested in determining the break-even quantities of x, y, and z (given the stated restrictions), let

$$x_1 = \text{number of units of product x to produce}$$
$$x_2 = \text{number of units of product y to produce}$$
$$x_3 = \text{number of units of product z to produce}$$

The objective function must represent total variable and fixed costs and can be written as

$$\text{Minimize } 10x_1 + 12x_2 + 8x_3 + 30,000$$

46

Since the 30,000 fixed cost is independent of the decision variables, it can be omitted from the objective function, yielding

$$\text{Minimize } 10x_1 + 12x_2 + 8x_3$$

The first constraint forces the total revenue to equal total costs and can be stated as

$$20x_1 + 25x_2 + 15x_3 = 10x_1 + 12x_2 + 8x_3 + 30{,}000$$

or

$$10x_1 + 13x_2 + 7x_3 = 30{,}000$$

The other constraints reflecting sales contracts and demand limitations are expressed as

$$x_1 \geq 750$$

$$x_2 \leq 300$$

$$x_3 \geq 400$$

The complete model with nonnegativity conditions is thus

$$
\begin{aligned}
\text{Minimize} \quad & 10x_1 + 12x_2 + 8x_3 \\
\text{subject to} \quad & 10x_1 + 13x_2 + 7x_3 = 30{,}000 \\
& x_1 \qquad\qquad\qquad \geq 750 \\
& \qquad\quad x_2 \qquad\quad \leq 300 \\
& \qquad\qquad\quad x_3 \geq 400
\end{aligned}
$$

$$x_1,\ x_2,\ x_3 \geq 0$$

The solution to the problem is left as an exercise in Chapter 3.

[MACHINE LOADING EXAMPLE]   Nickleson Machine Shop wants to develop a math model to help decide which jobs should be processed on which machines so as to minimize total cost. Initially, the manager wants to try LP on a small example to see if the results are satisfactory. The first consideration, then, is loading three jobs; two machines are available for processing. The jobs correspond to producing 3, 7, and 4 units, respectively, for products 1, 2, and 3. Machine 1 has 8 hours available during each day, but machine 2 has only 6. Table 2.4 gives relevant cost and production time data, and Figure 2.6 illustrates the jobs queuing up for processing on the two machines.

TABLE 2.4 Machine loading cost and production time data

Machine	Product	Cost of producing one unit of product j on machine i ($)			Time required to produce one unit of product j on machine i (hr)		
		1	2	3	1	2	3
1		13	9	10	.4	1.1	.9
2		11	12	8	.5	1.2	1.3

If we let x_{ij} = the amount of product j to be allocated for production to machine i, then we can formulate the objective function to minimize $13x_{11} + 9x_{12} + 10x_{13} + 11x_{21} + 12x_{22} + 8x_{23}$. The time constraints on machine availability are

$$\text{Machine 1} \quad .4x_{11} + 1.1x_{12} + .9x_{13} \leq 8$$

$$\text{Machine 2} \quad .5x_{21} + 1.2x_{22} + 1.3x_{23} \leq 6$$

The production requirements specify that the appropriate number of units be produced for each product. These constraints are

$$\text{Product 1} \quad x_{11} + x_{21} = 3$$

$$\text{Product 2} \quad x_{12} + x_{22} = 7$$

$$\text{Product 3} \quad x_{13} + x_{23} = 4$$

The final LP model is

$$
\begin{aligned}
\text{Minimize} \quad & 13x_{11} + 9x_{12} + 10x_{13} + 11x_{21} + 12x_{22} + 8x_{23} \\
\text{subject to} \quad & .4x_{11} + 1.1x_{12} + .9x_{13} \leq 8 \\
& .5x_{21} + 1.2x_{22} + 1.3x_{23} \leq 6 \\
& x_{11} + x_{21} = 3 \\
& x_{12} + x_{22} = 7 \\
& x_{13} + x_{23} = 4 \\
& x_{ij} \geq 0; \, i = 1, 2; \, j = 1, 2, 3
\end{aligned}
$$

MATHEMATICAL ASSUMPTIONS AND LIMITATIONS OF LP

Now that you are more familiar with LP, we can discuss the requirements for an LP model. It is tacitly assumed that there is a single goal we can represent by a linear objective function and that all restrictions are lin-

FIGURE 2.6 Three jobs to be processed on two machines

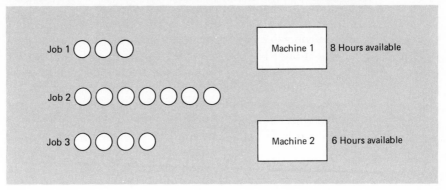

ear in nature. Given these prior conditions, any LP model has two basic properties: certainty and linearity.

certainty   *Certainty* requires that all parameters of the model be known. In the realm of decision-making problems, LP falls into the class of decision making under certainty. In other words, the objective function coefficients, c_j, the coefficients of the constraints, a_{ij}, and the right-hand-side numbers, b_i, must all be known constants. When a decision maker cannot determine exact values for some of these parameters, specific numerical values must be estimated and assigned, nonetheless, in order to use LP. This requirement bears repeating: Specific numerical values are necessary in order to solve an LP model. By using sensitivity analysis (a technique discussed in Chapter 4), the decision maker can explore the effects of changing some parameters over a range of values. This capability is particularly important when some parameters have been estimated or are known to change over time.

linearity   *Linearity* is a property of mathematical functions. The term denotes the stable relationship between dependent and independent variables that are graphically expressed by straight lines. Suppose that y is a variable whose value depends on the value of an independent variable x. If y is linearly related to x, the graph of y versus x results in a straight line.

In LP, we generally use more than two variables. Suppose that we have n variables $x_1, x_2, \ldots, x_n$. Then a linear expression in terms of these variables is of the form $a_1x_1 + a_2x_2 + \ldots + a_nx_n$. Note that in a linear expression the coefficients are constants, all variables have an exponent of 1, and no variables are multiplied together.

The linearity assumption of LP means that it is necessary for the objective function and the left-hand side of every constraint to be a linear expression. For example, $8x_1 + 17x_2$ is a linear expression, but $8x_1^2 +$

$17x_2x_3$ is nonlinear since x_1 has an exponent of 2, and x_2 and x_3 form a product.

Three properties of linearity help to clarify the implications of linearity. These properties are proportionality, additivity, and divisibility.

proportionality   *Proportionality* requires that the amount of each resource used must be proportional to the value of the decision variable. This must be true over the entire range of values for the decision variable. Thus, there can be no special costs that raise a decision variable's value above zero, such as a fixed, or startup, charge associated with beginning an activity. In the objective function, the contribution to profit must also be proportional to the value of the decision variable. For example, in an objective function to maximize $3x_1 + 7x_2$, each unit of x_1 contributes \$3 (a proportional amount) to the value of the objective function.

additivity   *Additivity* postulates that the value of the objective function and the amount of resource used is equal to the sum of the contributions of all decision variables. Using the same objective function, maximize $3x_1 + 7x_2$, suppose that $x_1 = 1$ and $x_2 = 1$. Additivity asserts that the contributions of 3 and 7, respectively, must add together to form a sum of 10.

divisibility   *Divisibility* simply means that the decision variables are allowed to assume a continuous range of values. Thus the decision variable values may be fractional or any decimal value. The point here is that LP generally will not provide integer, or whole number, solutions. Of course, we know that it is impossible to manufacture a fractional number of automobiles. In problems where integer solutions are required, LP may be used to provide approximate answers by rounding off the solution to integers. However, doing so may cause significant departure from optimality. If optimal integer solutions are required, you must resort to another, more difficult, *integer* branch of mathematical programming known as *integer programming*.

programming   Obviously, then, conditions compatible with linear expression must exist before LP can be used. Many mathematical programming models are nonlinear, and other techniques must be used to solve these types of problem. In some cases, however, LP is used to get approximate solutions to nonlinear problems. This is done since LP is generally much faster and can solve much larger problems than the nonlinear techniques.

SUMMARY

Linear programming is a method for dealing with decision problems that can be expressed as constrained linear models. The primary assumptions of all linear programming models are certainty of the parameters and linearity of the objective function and all constraints.

In this chapter, we have focused on how to formulate LP models and the many applications of linear programming. Even though model building is more of an art than a science, you can gain competence through practice and the following of the six steps listed in the chapter. The formulation of models is still one step that requires human insight and is not solvable by a computer.

We have seen how Shell Oil Co. has used linear programming to their advantage in managing their product distribution system. Several other prototype examples have been presented in the chapter; these examples have application to the functional areas of business, including production, marketing, finance, and accounting. Specifically, these examples have dealt with product mix, diet, blending, production/distribution, break-even analysis, and machine loading. In the solved problem section that follows we examine a portfolio selection problem. Additionally, the problems at the end of the chapter deal with several other types of applications.

SOLVED PROBLEM

PROBLEM STATEMENT

Portfolio selection is a financial decision problem in which specific investment alternatives must be selected given a certain budget. The alternatives generally consist of common stocks, bonds, and other securities. The objectives are usually to maximize return or minimize risk or the variation in return. Several mathematical programming approaches have been used in designing portfolios. Some of these approaches are beyond the scope of this book; however, linear programming can be applied when the relationships involved are linear.

The United Credit Union has $500,000, which has accrued from previous investments. The management at United would like to reinvest the $500,000 in a portfolio that would maximize yield while maintaining an acceptable level of risk. The investment opportunities, rates of return, and risk measurements are shown in the table.

Investment alternative	Expected rate of return	Estimated variation (σ) in rate of return
Municipal bonds	7.5	.2
Government bonds	6.5	0
Midland Oil stock	11.9	6.0
Western Coal stock	8.8	4.5
Northern Automotive stock	10.0	5.0

The management has decided that the weighted average risk factor (σ) for the entire portfolio should not exceed 3.0. They also want to invest at least 20 percent in bonds, but at least 30 percent of bond investment must be in government bonds. Their final policy is to invest no more than $250,000 in Western Coal stock.

SOLUTION

The formulation of the portfolio selection problem as a linear programming model requires the expression of the objective and all policies and restrictions as linear relationships. The first step is to determine the decision variables; these should reflect the basic question that needs to be answered: How much should United invest in each of the five alternatives?

Therefore, let

$$x_1 = \text{amount invested in municipal bonds}$$
$$x_2 = \text{amount invested in government bonds}$$
$$x_3 = \text{amount invested in Midland Oil stock}$$
$$x_4 = \text{amount invested in Western Coal stock}$$
$$x_5 = \text{amount invested in Northern Automotive stock}$$

The linear programming model can be written as

Maximize $\quad 7.5x_1 + 6.5x_2 + 11.9x_3 + 8.8x_4 + 10.0x_5$

subject to $\quad .2x_1 + 0x_2 + 6x_3 + 4.5x_4 + 5x_5 \leq 3.0(500,000)$

(average risk constraint)

$$x_1 + x_2 \qquad\qquad\qquad \geq 100,000$$

(total bond requirement)

$$-.3x_1 + .7x_2 \qquad\qquad\qquad \geq 0$$

(government bond percentage)

$$x_4 \qquad \leq 250,000$$

(coal restriction)

$$x_1 + x_2 + x_3 + x_4 + x_5 = 500,000 \quad \text{(total budget)}$$

$$x_1, x_2, \ldots, x_5 \geq 0$$

The first and third constraints perhaps require some explanation. The coefficients of the first constraint are obtained by dividing each associated standard deviation of return σ by 500,000 (the total weight) to ensure that the weighted average is ≤ 3.0. The third constraint is formed by $x_2 \geq .3(x_1 + x_2)$, or $-.3x_1 + .7x_2 \geq 0$.

REVIEW QUESTIONS

1. How does LP differ from just solving a system of equations?

2. Interpret the difference between an equality, and an inequality constraint.

3. The nonnegativity conditions are not always imposed in every LP model. Give some situations in which they might not be enforced.

4. What does "linearity" mean?

5. Can you think of any LP applications other than those discussed in the chapter?

6. What are three properties of linearity?

7. Explain what is meant by the phrase, "Model building is more an art than a science."

8. What assumptions must be satisfied in order for a problem to be solved by LP?

PROBLEMS

2.1 *Product Mix.* The Ace Manufacturing Company produces two lines of its product, the super and the regular. Resource requirements for production are given in the table. There are 1,600 hours of assembly worker hours available per week, 700 hours of paint time, and 300 hours of inspection time. Regular customers will demand at least 150 units of the regular line and 90 of the super. Formulate an LP model that will determine the optimal product mix on a weekly basis.

Product line	Profit contribution	Assembly time (hr)	Paint time (hr)	Inspection time (hr)
Regular	$50	1.2	.8	.2
Super	75	1.6	.9	.2

2.2 *Product Mix.* The Crazy Nut Company wishes to market two special nut mixes during the holiday season. Mix 1 contains $\frac{1}{2}$ pound of peanuts and $\frac{1}{2}$ pound of cashews. Mix 2 contains $\frac{3}{5}$ pound of peanuts, $\frac{1}{4}$ pound of cashews, and $\frac{3}{20}$ pound of almonds. Mix 1 sells for $1.49 per pound, and mix 2 sells for $1.69 per pound. The data pertinent to the raw ingredients appear in the table. Assuming that Crazy can sell all cans of either mix that it produces, formulate an LP model to determine how much of mixes 1 and 2 to produce.

Ingredient	Amount available (lb)	Cost per lb
Peanuts	30,000	$.35
Cashews	12,000	.50
Almonds	9,000	.60

2.3 *Break-even Analysis.* A firm is considering the production of two new products. Data pertaining to sales price and costs are shown in the table. The firm has already contracted to provide 500 units of product A and would like to calculate the break-even quantities for products A and B. Formulate an LP model to determine the break-even points for products A and B at minimal total capital outlay.

Product	Selling price per unit	Variable cost per unit	Fixed cost
A	$30	$16	$10,000
B	35	18	12,000

2.4 *Portfolio Selection.* Western Trust Co. invests in various types of securities. They have $5 million for immediate investment and wish to maximize the interest earned over the next year. Risk is not a factor. There are four investment possibilities, as outlined in the table. To further structure the portfolio, the Board of Directors of Western has specified that at least 40 percent of the investment must be placed in corporate bonds and common stock. Furthermore, no more than 20 percent of the investment can be in real estate. Formulate an LP model to meet their objectives.

Investment	Expected interest earned (%)	Maximum allowable investment (000,000's)
Corporate bonds	8.5	$3
Common stock	9.0	3
Gold certificates	10.0	2
Real estate	13.0	1

2.5 *Investment and Budget Allocation.* The Viscus Oil Company must decide how to allocate its budget from windfall profits. The government grants certain tax breaks if the company invests funds in research concerned with energy conservation. However, the government stipulates that at least 60 percent of the funds must be funneled into research for automobile efficiency. Viscus has a $1 million budget for energy research and development this year; the research proposal data are shown in the table. Assuming Viscus wants to maximize return on its investments and receive the government tax break, how should the budget be allocated? Formulate as an LP model.

Project	Management policy on upper limit of expenditures	Forecast return on investment (%)
Methanol fuel research	$300,000	4.0
Electrically operated cars	100,000	0.1
Emission reduction	300,000	3.0
Solar cells	200,000	2.0
Windmills	100,000	1.0

2.6 *Production and Distribution.* The Leiz Manufacturing Company produces small chips for use in pocket calculators. Leiz has two plants that produce the chips and then distribute to five different wholesalers. The cost of production at plants 1 and 2 is $2.19 and $2.38, respectively. Forecast demand indicates that shipments will have to be 2,000 to wholesaler 1; 3,000 to wholesaler 2; 1,000 to wholesaler 3; 5,000 to wholesaler 4; and 4,000 to wholesaler 5. The distribution costs of shipping a chip from plant to wholesaler are shown in the table. Production capacity at each plant is 8,000 units. Formulate an LP model to determine how many chips each plant supplies each wholesaler.

From plant	To wholesaler				
	1	2	3	4	5
1	.03	.02	.05	.04	.02
2	.06	.04	.02	.03	.05

2.7 *Loan Planning.* Mydlend Mortgage Company makes four types of loans, as listed in the table. The company is trying to decide how to allocate $5 million in funds. The company president has decided that the average risk must not exceed 3.7 percent. Formulate an LP model to maximize yield in allocating the $5 million.

Type of loan	Yield (%)	Risk (%)
First mortgage	7	3.5
Remodeling	1	2.0
Auto	8	3.8
Signature	14	4.0

2.8 *Diet Planning.* An agriculture student wants to determine what quantities of various grains to feed cattle in order to meet minimum nutritional requirements at lowest cost. The student is considering the use of corn, barley, oats, and wheat. The table relates the relevant dietary information per pound of grain. Formulate an LP model to determine the dietary mix that minimizes cost.

Nutrient	Corn	Barley	Oats	Wheat	Recommended daily allowance
Protein	10	9	11	8	20 mg
Calcium	50	45	58	50	70 mg
Iron	9	8	7	10	12 mg
Calories	1,000	800	850	9,000	4,000
Cost per lb	$.55	$.47	$.45	$.52	

2.9 *Marketing Media Selection.* A manufacturer of tennis rackets would like to introduce its new line of poly-play rackets. The firm may advertise in leading tennis magazines or on television during the World Championship Tennis pro tour and major international tournaments. The feeling is that those players whose annual income exceeds $15,000 will be 1.8 times more likely to buy this new racket. The objective in the advertising scheme is to maximize potential sales. One unit of TV advertising costs $35,000 and reaches approximately 2 million people, half of whom make more than $15,000 annually. One unit of advertising in tennis magazine 1 costs $25,000 and reaches 1 million people, three-fourths of whom are in the higher income bracket. One unit of advertising in tennis magazine 2 costs $15,000 and reaches 600,000 people, two-thirds of whom have incomes exceeding $15,000. The total advertising budget is $250,000. Formulate the problem as an LP model.

2.10 *Purchasing.* McKisson Co. purchases two components for the assembly of their block-and-tackle sets. A total of four suppliers are available that can supply the components. However, each supplier has a different per unit purchase price, distribution cost, and available supply. Purchase prices and freight costs are given in the table. Additionally, suppliers 1, 2, 3, and 4 have the capacity to supply 2,000, 3,000, 4,000, and 4,000 components, respectively. (Their production capacity is equally taxed by either component.) McKisson has a demand of 5,000 units for component 1 and 6,000 units for component 2. How many units of each component should McKisson order from each supplier in order to minimize costs?

	Purchase price			
	Supplier 1	Supplier 2	Supplier 3	Supplier 4
Component 1	$5	$7	$6	$4
Component 2	8	8	9	7
	Freight cost			
	Supplier 1	Supplier 2	Supplier 3	Supplier 4
Component 1	$1.65	$1.25	$ .95	$1.10
Component 2	1.75	1.35	1.10	1.15

2.11 *Financing Decisions.* Consider the problem faced by a major city of financing various capital improvement projects. Of highest priority are the renovation of existing sewage treatment plants and the development of a water pipeline from another region to ensure a good-quality water supply. The projects will cost $200 million and will be funded by the sale of a proposed bond issue, and loans from an insurance company and a bank. Underwriters in Chicago have stated that no more than $110 million in bonds can be sold at the proposed rate of 10%. The bank will loan no more than $100 million at a rate of 13 percent and insists that its loan be no larger than one-half the bond debt. Finally, the insurance company will loan up to $80 million but at a rate of 15 percent. Formulate a linear programming model to determine the best financing strategy for the city.

2.12 *Transportation.* The Normal Distribution Company supplies five major metropolitan areas from three of its regionally located warehouses. It would like to minimize the transportation cost of shipping from warehouse to market. Transportation costs are shown in the table. Formulate an LP model to meet all demand at minimum transportation cost.

From warehouse	To city					Supply
	1	2	3	4	5	
1	$ 7	$ 5	$12	$11	$ 9	500
2	13	12	6	3	8	300
3	7	6	5	4	14	350
Demand	150	200	100	300	400	

2.13 *Production/Product Mix.* A manufacturer of office equipment would like to optimize the company's product mix. Currently, the firm produces desks, chairs, tables, and filing cabinets. Each product's resource requirements are given in the table. The desks, chairs, tables, and cabinets contribute $150, $45, $100, and $40 to profit, respectively. The minimum monthly demand requirements are 75 desks, 120 chairs, 100 tables, and 50 filing cabinets. Additionally, management does not want the number of filing cabinets to exceed 10 percent of the total number of items produced. Formulate as an LP model.

Product	Wood (board ft)	Plastic (sq ft)	Steel alloy (lb)	Administrative worker hours
Desks	0	6	9	2.5
Chairs	3	1	1	1.2
Tables	5	2	2	2.2
Cabinets	0	0	15	1.9
Availability	1,000	1,200	1,000	1,500

2.14 *Blending.* The Smelly Oil Company produces all three major types of gasoline: regular, premium, and unleaded. Its gasoline is produced by blending two petroleum components and a high-octane lead additive. Minimum octane ratings must be met as provided in the following table of data:

Gasoline	Minimum octane	Selling price per gal.
Regular	89	$1.50
Premium	94	1.57
Unleaded	87	1.55

Cost and availability data for the ingredients in the blends are shown in the next table:

Blending ingredients	Octane	Cost per gal	per month (gal)
Component 1	130	$1.24	76,000
Component 2	75	$1.18	95,000
Lead additive	1,100	$2.50	60,000

Formulate an LP problem to determine the blends that maximize profits and meet all technical specifications. Assume that octane values mix linearly.

2.15 *Capital Rationing.* The Zink Fuel Company is confronted with five projects competing for the firm's fixed budget of $300,000. The net investment and estimated present values of future cash inflows for each project are listed in the table. Each of the projects are of the type that can be funded partially. That is, it is not necessary to fund all or none of the project (as is often the case). Formulate an LP model to maximize the total present value of the projects selected.

Project	Net investment	Present value of inflows at 10 percent
1	$ 80,000	$115,000
2	100,000	150,000
3	70,000	85,000
4	90,000	110,000
5	120,000	133,000

2.16 *Shopping Center Design.* Lincoln Properties has invested in the development of an indoor shopping center mall in the Kansas City suburbs. They must now plan for the size and quantity of stores to lease to in the mall. Smaller stores having 2,500 square feet are more profitable, but large "anchor" stores (approximately 250,000 square feet) are necessary to attract sufficient volumes of traffic. Medium-sized stores average around 100,000 square feet. The mall will contain 1 million square feet, and Lincoln Properties want at least one large anchor store in the mall. Furthermore, they want a 3:1 ratio of medium to large stores, and they want the total square footage of small stores to be 1.5 times that of medium and large stores combined. Leasing rates are anticipated to be $265,000, $170,000, and $20,000 per year for large, medium-size, and small stores, respectively. Formulate an LP model to determine the most profitable store configuration in the new mall.

2.17 *Production and Inventory Planning.* The Coldman Company has a production planning problem. Management wants to plan production for the ensuing year so as to minimize the combined cost of production and inventory storage costs. In each quarter of the year, demand is anticipated to be 65, 80, 135, and 75, respectively. The product can be manufactured during regular time at a cost of $16 per unit produced, or during overtime at a cost of $20 per unit. The table gives data pertinent to production capacities. The cost of carrying one unit in inventory per quarter is $2. The inventory level at the beginning of the first quarter is zero. Formulate an LP model to minimize the production plus storage costs for the year.

	Capacities (units)		
Quarter	Regular time	Overtime	Quarterly demand
1	80	10	65
2	90	10	80
3	95	20	135
4	70	10	75

2.18 *Machine Loading.* Jiffy Job Shop would like to try a quantitative approach to its machine loading problem. There are three machines in the shop, and they are used to produce five different products. Each machine has an 8-hour time availability each working day. Today, the demand is 6, 3, 2, 1, and 5 for products 1 through 5, respectively. The table gives relevant cost and production time data. Formulate an LP model to determine the amount of product j to be allocated for production on machine i.

		Cost of producing one unit of product j on machine i					Time required to produce one unit of product j on machine i (hr)				
Machine	Product	1	2	3	4	5	1	2	3	4	5
1		$12	$10	$13	$ 9	$8	1	.8	1.5	.5	.6
2		7	6	12	11	9	1.5	.9	.7	.4	.9
3		14	8	5	3	2	1.2	1.1	.9	.8	.5

2.19 *Refinery Operation.* An American oil company uses crude oil from around the world to produce its final petroleum products. The different input mixes of the crude oils are shown in the table. The fractions indicate the optimal usage of each crude as a component of each final product. Thus, the input of Gulf crude is best utilized when 15 percent is used for regular gas, 40 percent for unleaded, and so on. The price per barrel of the crudes are $34, $35, $33, $34, and $37, respectively, for the Gulf, North Atlantic, Alaskan, Mexican, and OPEC oil. The objective is to meet market demand at minimum cost. Formulate the refinery optimization problem as a linear optimization model.

Crude oil	Optimal fraction of allocation				
	Regular	Unleaded	Premium	Diesel	Fuel oil
Gulf	.15	.40	.30	.10	.05
North Atlantic	.20	.30	.20	.15	.15
Alaskan	.40	.10	.10	.20	.20
Mexican	.25	.30	.30	.10	.05
OPEC	.10	.40	.40	.10	—
Demand (barrels/day)	30,000	50,000	20,000	25,000	35,000

2.20 *Personnel Scheduling.* Ma-Bell Corporation has a scheduling problem. Operators are needed according to the schedule shown in the table. Operators work 8-hour shifts and can begin work at either midnight, 4 A.M., 8 A.M., noon, 4 P.M. or 8 P.M. Let x_j equal the number of operators beginning work in time period j, $j = 1, 2, \ldots, 6$. Formulate an LP model to hire the minimum number of operators the company needs.

Time period	Operators needed
Midnight to 4 A.M.	4
4 A.M. to 8 A.M.	6
8 A.M. to noon	90
Noon to 4 P.M.	85
4 P.M. to 8 P.M.	55
8 P.M. to midnight	20

2.21 *Cutting Stock (Trim Loss).* Potluck Forests, Inc., produces paper products. In one of their processes, reels of 100-inch-wide paper are cut into smaller width reels of the same length. Each week, orders for different width reels are received. Currently, the cutting patterns are manually estimated by an experienced operator. Potluck wishes to apply linear programming to this classical OR problem. This week the company has orders for 30, 50, 25, and 90 reels, respectively, of the 60, 48, 36, and 24-inch widths. The objective is to cut the original 100-inch reels to meet demand and minimize waste. Waste is defined as both trim loss and surplus. Trim loss is the leftover portion of a 100-inch reel. For example, if a 100-inch reel is cut into two 36-inch reels and a 24-inch reel, there is 4 inches of leftover trim loss, as shown.

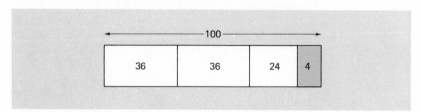

Surplus waste is generated when more reels of a certain type are cut than are demanded. For example, if there are 5 extra 24-inch reels cut, there is a waste of $5 \times 24 = 120$. Determine all possible ways to cut the 100-inch reels to yield reels of sizes 60, 48, 36, and 24. Let x_j represent the number of 100 inch reels to be cut in pattern j. Calculate the trim loss for each pattern and formulate an LP model to minimize total trim and surplus waste.

2.22   *Production Scheduling.* The Akron Tire Company currently produces four lines of tires: the economy, glass-belted, snow tire, and the steel radial. Recent recessionary trends have caused a decline in demand, and the company is laying off workers and discontinuing its third shift.

The problem it faces is that of rescheduling production during the first and second shifts for the remaining quarter of the year. The production process primarily involves the use of vulcanization, fabrication, and plastometer machines. However, the limiting resource in production is the availability of machine hours on the vulcanization machines. The economy, glass-belted, snow tire, and steel radial require 4, 5, 5, and 7 hours, respectively, of vulcanizing time.

The sales manager has forecast the expected sales for each of the four tires in the last quarter of the year. These estimates are shown in the following table:

	Forecast sales			
Month	*Economy*	*Glass-belted*	*Snow tire*	*Steel radial*
October	8,000	19,000	4,000	7,000
November	7,000	19,000	15,000	7,000
December	6,000	18,000	17,000	7,000

The production capacity in terms of vulcanizing hours available is expressed by month and shift in the next table:

	Vulcanizing hours available	
Month	Shift 1	Shift 2
October	110,000	100,000
November	130,000	120,000
December	115,000	116,000

The labor cost of operating the vulcanizing machines is $10 per hour during the first shift. The shift differential requires that the wages be $12 per hour during the second shift. The other relevant cost is storage: It costs $4 per month to store a tire, regardless of its type. Note that it will be necessary to store some tires in the problem, as there is not enough labor available during December to meet December demand.

Assuming that the company wishes to produce exactly as many tires as the sales manager has forecast, formulate an LP model to determine a production schedule that will meet demand at minimum total cost.

2.23   *Air Cleaner Design.* A tractor manufacturer in Bombay, India, needs to design an air cleaner for their 60-hp tractor. The limiting specifications are that the diameters of the main body (x_2) and the exit duct (x_1) should not exceed $6\frac{1}{4}$ and $2\frac{1}{2}$ inches, respectively. In order to maintain pressure drop, these same diameters should not go below $3\frac{3}{4}$ and $1\frac{1}{2}$ inches, respectively. The tractor manufacturer has contracted to supply a minimum of 50 air cleaners per month. There is a national shortage of sheet metal, as the Indian government will only sanction 15,000 square inches of material per month. Other technical air cleaner requirements dictate that the total amount of metal per air cleaner should be no less than 250 square inches. Other parts and scrap require that all areas must be multiplied by 1.6 to obtain total metal requirements. The area of metal required by each air cleaner (including scrap) is given by $1.6(2.75\pi x_1 + 10\pi x_2)$, where $\pi = 3.1416$. Formulate an LP model to minimize the metal used in each air cleaner and to determine diameters x_1 and x_2.

2.24   *Agricultural Land Allocation.* Agricultural applications of LP are numerous. The optimal use of agricultural land resources is becoming increasingly important in order to feed the world's people. This case is based on an actual model used to allocate land optimally given a set of agronomic and institutional constraints specific to the foreign country.

We consider a group of 11 possible crops and 8 agricultural regions in which the crops may be cultivated. Each region is currently supporting a certain acreage of one or more of the 11 crops. However, a reallocation of the land may result in more efficient utilization, and also a higher net revenue per acre of crop, in each region.

The 11 crops are categorized as follows:

Winter crops	Summer crops
1 Wheat	5 Cotton variety 1
2 Barley	6 Cotton variety 2
3 Broad beans	7 Rice
4 Lentils	8 Corn
	9 Millet
	10 Sesame
	11 Sugar cane

The following variables are relevant to the model:

i = region number (8)
j = crop number (11)
r_{ij} = net revenue factor per acre of crop j in region i
x_{ij} = acreage to be assigned to crop j in region i
y_{ij} = actual current acreage of crop j in province i
w_i = total area in winter crops in region i
s_i = total area in summer crops in region i
y_i = total cultivated area in region i
    (note that $w_i < y_i$ and $s_i < y_i$)
y_{i11} = actual acreage of sugar cane in region i

The objective function of the model defines net revenue in terms of crop yield, a_{ij}, crop price, p_j, and cultivation costs, c_{ij}. Thus $r_{ij} = a_{ij}p_j - c_{ij}$. Assuming that all parameters a_{ij}, p_j, and c_{ij} are known, we can then calculate the r_{ij} for the objective function.

The constraints relate to the following restrictions:

The total acreage of winter crops must equal w_i.

The total acreage of summer crops must equal s_i.

The total acreage of cotton crops in each region i must not exceed one-third of the total cultivated area in region i.

Even though the objective is to maximize net revenue, there exists a constraint that the new acreage of the staple crops wheat, broad beans, and corn must be at least .3, .3, and .85, respectively, as large as the current acreage of these three crops.

Each region must cultivate the exact same amount of sugar cane as is currently being cropped.

Formulate an LP model to maximize the net revenue, subject to the foregoing constraints.

BIBLIOGRAPHY

Anderson, David, Dennis Sweeny, and Thomas Williams, *Linear Programming for Decision Making: an Applications Approach.* New York: West Publishing Co., 1974.

Daellenbach, Hans G., and Earl J. Bell, *User's Guide to Linear Programming.* Englewood Cliffs, N.J.: Prentice-Hall, Inc., 1970.

Dano, Sven, *Linear Programming in Industry: Theory and Applications,* 2nd ed. Vienna: Springer-Verlag, 1965.

Gass, Saul I., *Illustrated Guide to Linear Programming.* New York: McGraw-Hill Book Company, 1970.

Hadley, George, *Linear Programming.* Reading, Mass.: Addison-Wesley Publishing Co., Inc., 1962.

Henderson, A., and R. Schlaifer, "Mathematical Programming: Better Information for Better Decision Making," *Harvard Business Review,* 32 (May–June 1954), 73–100.

Lee, Sang M., *Linear Optimization for Management.* New York: Mason/Charter Publishers, Inc., 1976.

Naylor, Thomas H., Eugene T. Byrne, and John M. Vernon, *Introduction to Linear Programming: Methods and Cases.* Belmont, Calif.: Wadsworth Publishing Company, Inc., 1971.

Stockton, R. Stansbury, *Introduction to Linear Programming.* Homewood, Ill.: Richard D. Irwin, Inc., 1971.

Strum, Jay E., *Introduction to Linear Programming.* San Francisco: Holden-Day, Inc., 1972.

3

Solving LP Problems: Graphical and Simplex Methods

CANADIAN FOREST PRODUCTS LTD.[1]

Prior to 1967 the Canadian Forest Products Ltd. based their plywood production choices on past experience, "gut feelings," and intuition. In 1967, rising costs prompted them to consider a linear programming approach to their production plan.

The plywood production process was more complicated than you might think. There were 7 grades of peelable logs available from 5 sources which can be peeled into 4 veneer thickness (140 possible combinations). Peeling results in veneer of 4 thicknesses, 2 species, and 12 grades (96 combinations). Plywood can be made into 10 thicknesses, 12 grades, 3 widths, and 5 lengths, and may be sold in 2 separate markets (3600 possible combinations). Also, the production process involves 4 different lathes, 7 dryers, and 5 presses!

The company decided that its objective was to: maximize contribution margin = sales income − wood costs. A linear programming model was developed that included input from raw materials, production, sales, and the different operating strategies. The computer output from the model, then, is the basis for the annual operating plan, detailing most profitable products, and annual targets for raw materials, and production and sales by item, grade, and market.

The annual plan is implemented by scheduling on a biweekly basis. The biweekly schedule is then implemented in turn on a day-to-day basis by scheduling the mill on a daily and a shift basis. Since changes in sales, production, and costs do occur, actual production and inventories are monitored against the targets specified by the annual operating plan. The daily tracking and biweekly performance reports show how well the annual plan is being implemented. However, the plan is not a gospel, and whenever market and operating conditions change significantly, the operations plan is revised by reoptimizing the LP model with new data.

---

[1]D. B. Kotak, "Application of Linear Programming to Plywood Manufacture," *Interfaces*, 7 (November 1976), 56–68.

In addition to the biweekly schedule, a financial variance report is generated monthly. This report measures the dollar variance between the budget and the actual performance and breaks it down into how much variance was caused by price, mix, and volume. The financial variance report, together with the financial statement prepared by the accounting department, forms the key management information system. It measures in dollars the effect of achieving or exceeding the biweekly and daily volume targets.

As a result of using the scientific approach, the contribution margin of the Plywood and Hardboard Division has increased by an average of $1 million per year between 1970 and 1975 as compared to the base year, 1969.

INTRODUCTION

In Chapter 2, we examined some of the mathematical assumptions of LP, how to formulate LP problems, and typical areas of application. In this chapter, we investigate how these formulated LP models can be solved. We look first at the graphical method of solution; it yields insight into the nature of an LP problem. The graphical method is limited to problems with no more than three variables since we cannot draw graphs in more than three dimensions. Therefore, our second subject, the simplex method, is the technique used for solving most real-world LP problems. It is a relatively efficient solution procedure, and with the aid of a computer, it enables us to solve LP problems that have many variables and constraints.

THE GRAPHICAL METHOD

The graphical method of LP solution simply involves plotting each of a problem's constraints to form a region of possible solutions. We then examine this region to select the best alternative. To illustrate the graphical method, let us return to the Faze Linear product mix example of Chapter 2. Recall that the objective is to produce the appropriate number of power amplifiers and preamplifiers in order to maximize the profit. The two components contribute $200 and $500, respectively, to profit. The model we derived is

$$
\begin{aligned}
\text{Maximize} \quad & 200x_1 + 500x_2 && \text{(profit)} \\
\text{subject to} \quad & x_2 \leq 40 && \text{(transistor availability)} \\
& 1.2x_1 + 4x_2 \leq 240 && \text{(assembly time)} \\
& .5x_1 + 1x_2 \leq 81 && \text{(inspection/testing time)} \\
& x_1, x_2 \geq 0
\end{aligned}
$$

The next step in the graphical method is to plot the constraints on a graph. Since the constraints are inequalities rather than equations, their graphs are regions rather than lines. However, the easiest way to graph an inequality is first to graph it as an equality, then simply shade in the appropriate area.

The first constraint $x_2 \leq 40$ can be located on the graph by first locating its x_1 and x_2 intercepts on the x_1 and x_2 axes, respectively. Since the first constraint does not involve x_1, it does not have an x_1 intercept. The x_2 intercept is determined by treating the constraint as an equation yielding $x_2 = 40$. The graph of $x_2 = 40$ is shown in Figure 3.1.

The inequality $x_2 \leq 40$ is graphed from $x_2 = 40$ (as shown in Figure 3.1) by simply observing on which side of the line the origin is located. Substituting $x_1 = 0$ and $x_2 = 0$ into the inequality $x_2 \leq 40$, we find that 0 is smaller than 40, and the origin is thus included in the inequality. Thus the graph of $x_2 \leq 40$ is the region established by the line $x_2 = 40$, and it contains the origin. The graph of $x_2 \leq 40$ is shown in Figure 3.2. Notice that the shaded area is bounded by the x_1 and x_2 axes as a result of the non-negativity conditions. That is, the conditions $x_1, x_2 \geq 0$ restrict the expression of the constraint to the first quadrant of the plane.

In the second constraint, we determine the x_1 intercept by letting $x_2 = 0$ and solving $1.2x_1 + 4(0) = 240$, from which we obtain $x_1 = 200$. Setting $x_1 = 0$, we obtain the x_2 intercept by solving $1.2(0) + 4x_2 = 240$; thus, we have $x_2 = 60$. Plotting the second constraint with the first, we obtain the graph in Figure 3.3. The third constraint is plotted in the same way, and finally we have established the region of possible solutions, as indicated in Figure 3.4.

FIGURE 3.1   Graph of $x_2 = 40$

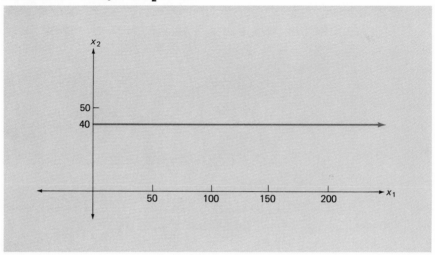

FIGURE 3.2 Graph of $x_2 \le 40$

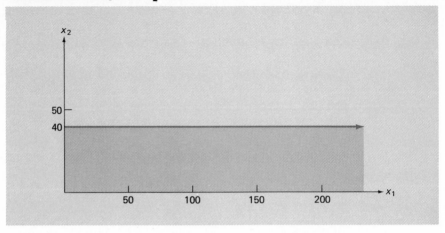

Any proposed solution to the Faze Linear problem is possible only if it falls within the shaded region. Called the *feasible* region, this area encompasses all points that satisfy all constraints and the nonnegativity *feasible and* conditions. Any solution that satisfies all constraints is said to be *feasible*, *infeasible* and a solution that violated any one of the constraints is *infeasible*. For *solutions* example, Faze Linear may want to produce $x_1 = 100$ power amps and $x_2 = 20$ preamps. Such a solution is feasible (as you can see in Figure 3.5). However, if the company wants to produce $x_1 = 100$ power amps and $x_2 = 50$ preamps, this is not feasible, since it violates the third constraint. To calculate this, substitute $x_1 = 100$ and $x_2 = 50$ into the third constraint; then, you have $.5(100) + 1(50) = 50 + 50 = 100 > 81$. The production of 100 power amps and 50 preamps daily requires 100 hours of inspection and testing time daily, and only 81 hours is available. From

FIGURE 3.3 Graph of $x_2 \le 40$ and $1.2x_1 + 4x_2 \le 240$

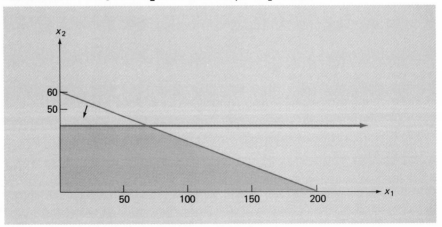

FIGURE 3.4 Graph of Faze Linear constraints

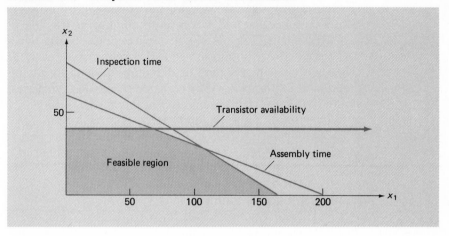

Figure 3.5, you can see that the point (100, 50) does not fall in the feasible region.

optimal
solutions   An *optimal* solution is a solution that is not only feasible but achieves the *best possible* value for the objective function. If we are trying to increase profit, an optimal solution is a feasible solution that maximizes profit. Similarly, if we are minimizing, an optimal solution is a feasible solution that minimizes whatever criterion of effectiveness the objective function measures. The goal of LP is to determine an optimal solution. Therefore, let us proceed to find the optimal solution to the Faze Linear problem.

At first, the determination of an optimal solution may seem to be almost impossible. You see that the feasible region in Figure 3.5 encom-

FIGURE 3.5 Graph of Faze Linear feasible, infeasible, and extreme points

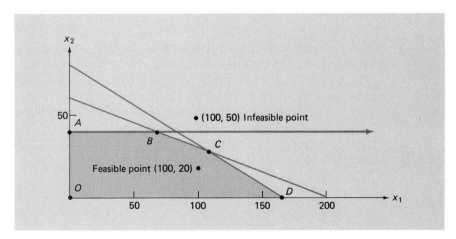

passes an infinite number of feasible solutions. How, then, can we find the one or ones that are optimal? Fortunately, LP provides a result that allows us to exclude all but a finite number of feasible points.

extreme
points

In Figure 3.5, notice that the feasible region contains five vertices. These vertices, or corner points, are called *extreme points* of the feasible region. They play an integral part in the simplex method, as the fundamental theorem of LP describes. The *extreme point theorem* states: If an optimal solution to a linear programming problem exists, then at least one such optimal solution must be an extreme point solution.

extreme
point
theorem

The importance of the extreme point theorem is that it restricts our search for an optimal solution from an infinite number of possibilities to a finite number of extreme points, no matter how large the problem. Of course, really large LP problems have an astronomical (although finite) number of extreme points.

In our small example with the Faze Linear Company, we have only five extreme points. One of these includes the origin (0, 0). One approach to determining the optimal solution is to find the coordinates of the other four extreme points and then simply find the profit associated with each of these. The point with the highest profit is the optimal solution to the Faze Linear problem.

Finding the coordinates of all five extreme points, however, is laborious and unnecessary. The following procedure can be used to single out an extreme point that is the optimum. The objective function is the measuring device we use to determine the relative worth of any proposed solution. Let P = profit; then we wish to maximize $P = 200x_1 + 500x_2$. The objective function is now in the form of a linear equation. If we let $P = \$20,000$, we can then plot the graph of $20,000 = 200x_1 + 500x_2$ on the graph of Figure 3.5. Doing this, we get the result shown in Figure 3.6.

Any point on the line $20,000 = 200x_1 + 500x_2$ within the feasible region is feasible and will yield a profit of \$20,000. If we convert the objective function to slope-intercept form, we obtain $x_2 = -.4x_1 + .0020P$. Thus, the slope of the objective function is $-.4$ regardless of the profit P. Letting $P = \$30,000$, we again plot a profit line shown in Figure 3.6. Any point on the line and in the feasible region will yield a profit of \$30,000. We can see that moving the profit line with slope $-.4$ away from the origin toward the northeast increases profit. We must move the line as far as we can and still have at least one point on the line be in the feasible region. Clearly, this is accomplished at the extreme point C. Thus, the point C is the optimum solution to the Faze Linear problem.

Precisely how does point C yield the optimum solution? The point C consists of an x_1 coordinate and an x_2 coordinate. Evaluating these two coordinates then yields a production level for x_1 and x_2, that is, the optimal number of power amps and preamps to produce each day. In order

FIGURE 3.6 Graph of Faze Linear profit lines and optimal solution

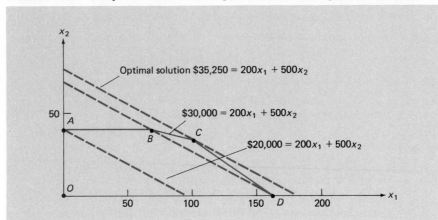

to determine the coordinates of the point C, we notice that the point C occurs at the intersection of the two lines $1.2x_1 + 4x_2 = 240$ and $.5x_1 + 1x_2 = 81$. Thus, the coordinates can be determined by solving these two equations simultaneously.

$$1.2x_1 + 4x_2 = 240$$
$$\underline{-2.0x_1 - 4x_2 = -324}$$
$$-.8x_1 = -84$$
$$x_1 = 105$$

Substituting 105 for x_1 in the first equation, we obtain $x_2 = [240 - 1.2(105)]/4 = 28.5$. Thus, optimal product mix is to produce 105 power amps and 28.5 preamps each day. The profit associated with the optimal solution is found by substituting into the objective function to yield $200(105) + 500(28.5) = \$35,250$.

Did you notice that the LP solution suggests the production of 28.5 preamps daily? As we have said before, LP does not necessarily generate integer solutions. It is impossible to manufacture 28.5 preamps per day unless a unit is half-completed one day and then finished the next day, and so on. If whole-number solutions are sought, what is wrong with trying to produce 105 power amps and 29 preamps? Alternatively, we could round off the LP optimal solution and produce 105 and 28, respectively, for a profit of $35,000 per day. This solution, however, might not be the optimal integer solution.

THE SIMPLEX METHOD

As you can probably imagine now, it is impossible to use the graphical method of solution on problems that are at all complex. The greatest importance of the graphical method is as an aid to understanding the simplex method. We will discuss the simplex method in its basic form here. For large-scale, real-world applications of LP, more sophisticated variants of the simplex method are actually used; however, the principles are essentially the same.

The simplex method is similar to solving a system of linear equations. In fact, the simplex method does solve a system of equations, and the solution derived not only solves the equations but also optimizes an objective function. In this sense, the simplex method is a straightforward generalization of various methods for solving a system of equations with which you may be familiar, such as Gauss–Jordan elimination.

iterative technique The simplex method is an *iterative technique*. That is, it establishes an initial feasible solution, then repeats the solution process, making successive improvements, until the optimal solution is found. It is sometimes *adjacent* referred to as an *adjacent extreme point solution procedure* because it *extreme* generally begins at a feasible extreme point, then successively evaluates *point* adjacent extreme points until the one representing the optimal solution *solution* is found. Recall from the extreme point theorem that an optimum (if it *procedure* exists) may always be found at an extreme point. This can be illustrated by considering the feasible region of the Faze Linear problem we previously solved by the graphical method. Figure 3.7 shows the five extreme points and their respective coordinates. When we solve the Faze Linear problem by the simplex method, we shall find that the simplex method starts at the origin (0, 0), proceeds to the adjacent extreme point (0, 40), goes to (66.7, 40), and finally arrives at the next adjacent extreme point (105, 28.5), which is the optimal solution.

FIGURE 3.7   Faze Linear feasible region and associated extreme points

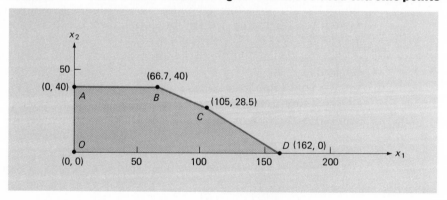

74

SIMPLEX PROCEDURES

In order to use the simplex method, it is necessary to state all the constraints as equations rather than inequalities. Mathematically, it is easier to solve systems of equations than systems of inequalities. Therefore, we shall have to convert less-than-or-equal-to and greater-than-or-equal-to constraints into equations. First we shall learn how to convert $\leq$ constraints.

Suppose that we have the constraint $x_1 + x_2 \leq 5$. We may convert this inequality to an equation by adding an additional variable, called *slack variable* a *slack variable*. Thus, we have

$$x_1 + x_2 + s_1 = 5 \qquad \text{where } s_1 \geq 0$$

A slack variable, as the name implies, represents unused resources. In the foregoing equation, if $x_1 = 2$ and $x_2 = 1$, then s_1 must equal 2. Thus, $x_1 + x_2 < 5$ and s_1 represents two units of the right-hand-side resource that are left over.

Notationally, we distinguish between slack and decision variables. The x_i represent decision variables and refer to actual activities; the s_i denote slack variables that represent unused capacity.

Now to convert the LP formulation of the Faze Linear problem to standard form by adding a slack variable for each $\leq$ constraint:

Maximize $200x_1 + 500x_2$

subject to
$$x_2 \leq 40$$
$$1.2x_1 + 4x_2 \leq 240 \rightarrow$$
$$.5x_1 + 1x_2 \leq 81$$
$$x_1, x_2 \geq 0$$

Maximize $200x_1 + 500x_2 + 0s_1$
$$+ 0s_2 + 0s_3$$

subject to
$$x_2 + s_1 = 40$$
$$1.2x_1 + 4x_2 + s_2 = 240$$
$$.5x_1 + 1x_2 + s_3 = 81$$
$$x_1, x_2, s_1, s_2, s_3 \geq 0$$

We have thus transformed a system of inequalities into a system of equations ready to be solved by the simplex method. Notice that the slack variables are given an objective function coefficient of zero. Thus, the slack variables affect the profit only indirectly through their values in the constraints.

basic feasible solutions The simplex method is only concerned with solutions that correspond to extreme points of the feasible region. These extreme point solutions are also called *basic feasible solutions*. In general, an LP problem in standard form has more variables than constraints. For instance, let n = the number of decision variables and m = the number of inequality constraints; then m slack variables must be added to convert the inequality constraints to equations in standard form. Thus, we generally have $m + n$

variables and m constraints. This actually gives us n *degrees of freedom* (choices) in solving the $m \times (m + n)$ system of equations. That is, we may set n particular variables equal to zero and then solve the m equations in terms of the remaining m variables. To illustrate, let us take a small 2×3 example. Suppose that we wish to solve

$$2x_1 + 3x_2 + 8x_3 = 11$$

$$4x_1 + 6x_2 + 7x_3 = 13$$

We have one degree of freedom in the foregoing 2×3 system, since we have one more variable than equation. Actually, the number of solutions to the system is infinite, since we can set x_1 equal to any number and solve in terms of x_2 and x_3. For example, x_1 can be set equal to zero, in which case we get $x_2 = 1$ and $x_3 = 1$ as the solution. However, we can set $x_2 = 0$ and we get $x_1 = \frac{3}{2}$ and $x_3 = 1$. We can even set $x_3 = 0$, but if we do in this system, we get no solution at all.

nonbasic variables   In general, the variables set to zero are called *nonbasic variables* and those that are nonzero are called *basic variables*. In the example above, *basic variables* one solution is $x_1 = 0$, $x_2 = 1$, and $x_3 = 1$; in this case, x_1 is a nonbasic variable and x_2 and x_3 are basic variables. In the simplex method, with $m + n$ variables and m constraints, there will be, at most, m variables not equal to zero. A solution derived by setting n of the variables equal to *basic* zero is called a *basic solution*. If all nonzero variables are also nonneg- *solution* ative, the basic solution is also feasible and thus corresponds to an extreme point.

There are potentially

$$\binom{m + n}{m} = \frac{(m + n)!}{m!n!}$$

basic solutions to an LP problem. For large m and n, then, you can see that the number of possible solutions becomes astronomical. Fortunately, the simplex method only examines basic feasible solutions. In the Faze Linear problem, we have five variables and three constraints. There are potentially $5!/(3!2!) = 10$ basic solutions to this problem. However, only five of these are basic feasible. To illustrate the solution values of all five variables associated with each extreme point, look at Table 3.1. Notice that the values of all the variables, including the slack, are nonnegative.

BASIC STEPS IN THE SIMPLEX PROCEDURE

Now that you have some (perhaps vague!) idea of how the simplex method works, let us look closer at the details of the procedure. In successively

TABLE 3.1 Basic feasible solutions for the Faze Linear problem

Extreme point (in Fig. 3.6)	Power amps x_1	Preamps x_2	Transistor slack s_1	Assembly slack (hr) s_2	Inspection slack (hr) s_3	Profit
A	0	40.0	0	80.0	41.0	$20,000
B	66.7	40.0	0	0	7.7	33,333
C	105.0	28.5	11.5	0	0	35,250
D	162.0	0	40.0	45.6	0	32,400
O	0	0	40.0	240.0	81.0	0

examining adjacent extreme points, the simplex method continually finds improved solutions. That is, it only examines points that are not only feasible but yield at least as good a value in the objective function as the previous point. In short, the simplex method encompasses the following basic steps:

1. An initial basic feasible solution is established.

2. An optimality check is next performed to determine whether the solution is yet optimal. If the solution is optimal, stop, for no further calculations are needed. However, if the solution is not optimal, a new variable must be found that will improve the solution. This new *entering variable* is always a nonbasic variable whose value is currently zero.

entering variable

3. The value of the entering variable is increased until the value of some basic variable is forced down to zero. This basic variable is called the *leaving variable*.

leaving variable

4. The entering variable now takes the place of the leaving variable; at any iteration there are only m variables that are in the solution. The next step is to update all relevant information required in the simplex procedure. This updating process is called *pivoting*. After updating, the procedure returns to step 2.

pivoting

THE SIMPLEX TABLEAU

iteration   Each repetition of steps 2 through 4 is called an *iteration* in the simplex method. The computer can execute such iterations by merely storing the appropriate information and then operating on it whenever it is needed. When you execute the simplex method by hand, the calculations are more conveniently dealt with in tabular form. This table is called a *simplex tableau*; the form of a starting tableau is shown in Tableau 3.1. The c_j row at the top of the tableau is the coefficients of the respective

simplex tableau

77

TABLEAU 3.1 Form for initial simplex tableau

c_B	c_j	decision variables c_1 c_2 ... c_n	slack variables 0 0 ... 0	Solution values
	Basic variables	x_1 x_2 ... x_n	s_1 s_2 ... s_m	
0	s_1	a_{11} a_{12} ... a_{1n}	1 0 ... 0	b_1
0	s_2	a_{21} a_{22} ... a_{2n}	0 1	b_2
.	.	.	. . .	.
.	.	.	. . .	.
0	s_m	a_{m1} a_{m2} ... a_{mn}	0 0 1	b_m
	z_j			
	$c_j - z_j$			

solutions of basic variables

variables in the objective function. The variables in the *Basic variables* column are those m variables currently in the solution. All other variables are assumed to be zero. The solution value for these basic variables is found under the *Solution values* column at the far right. The c_B column at the far left is those c_j coefficients associated with the basic variables. The a_{ij} terms correspond to the coefficients in the original set of constraints. The bottom row of the tableau is very important, for this row indicates whether the solution is optimal. These $c_j - z_j$ numbers under each column indicate the per-unit increase in the value of the objective function for every unit of x_j brought into solution. The z_j numbers represent the amount of profit that is lost for each unit of variable x_j that is brought into solution. These $c_j - z_j$ indicators are often called *oppor-* *opportunity* *costs* *tunity,* or *relative costs*.

To further illustrate the simplex tableau and the simplex calculations, let us return to the Faze Linear problem. In this problem we have two decision variables, three constraints, and three slack variables. The initial tableau for this problem is found in Tableau 3.2. Notice that the numbers under the columns headed by the variables (such as x_1, x_2, s_3) are simply the columns of the constraint coefficients we established in the original model in standard form. Similarly, the solution column is simply the original right-hand side.

THE BASIC STEPS APPLIED

Step 1: Establish initial basic feasible solution   To complete the initial tableau requires no calculation (except possibly the z_j values). The tableau always contains as many basic variables as there are constraints. To determine which variables are in the initial solution, we scan the original col-

TABLEAU 3.2   Initial simplex tableau for Faze Linear

objective function coefficients of basic variables →

	c_B	Basic variables	c_j 200	500	0	0	0	Solution	
			x_1	x_2	s_1	s_2	s_3		
	0	s_1	0	1	1	0	0	40	← value of s_1
	0	s_2	1.2	4	0	1	0	240	← value of s_2
	0	s_3	.5	1	0	0	1	81	← value of s_3
		z_j	0	0	0	0	0	0	← profit
		$c_j - z_j$	200	500	0	0	0		of solution

objective function coefficients

opportunity costs

umn of coefficients of the constraints in standard form and pick those variables that have a +1 coefficient and all other coefficients of 0.

For example, in the Faze Linear example, the slack variables satisfy this condition. Notice the columns of the slack variables in the equations below.

$$\text{Maximize } 200x_1 + 500x_2 + 0s_1 + 0s_2 + 0s_3$$
$$\text{subject to} \quad 0x_1 \quad 1x_2 + \boxed{1}\,s_1 + \boxed{0}\,s_2 + \boxed{0}\,s_3 = 40$$
$$1.2x_1 + 4x_2 + \boxed{0}\,s_1 + \boxed{1}\,s_2 + \boxed{0}\,s_3 = 240$$
$$5x_1 + 1x_2 + \boxed{0}\,s_1 + \boxed{0}\,s_2 + \boxed{1}\,s_3 = 81$$

These starting variables are always either slack variables or *artificial variables*, which we discuss later in the chapter. Setting up the initial tableau completes the first step of the simplex method.

Step 2: Check solution for optimality   In the lower right-hand side of the initial Faze Linear tableau (Tableau 3.2), the profit of the current solution is 0. This is because only slack variables are in solution. The *Solution* column indicates that $s_3 = 81$ (that is, we have 81 hours of inspection time left over) and s_1 and s_2 are equal to 40 and 240, respectively. In the tableau, the decision variables x_1 and x_2 are nonbasic and equal to zero; thus, we are producing nothing and, consequently, making zero profit. This basic feasible solution corresponds to extreme point O in Figure 3.7.

The $c_j - z_j$ opportunity costs indicate whether the current solution is optimal or not. In this case, they indicate that it is not optimal because they are not all less than or equal to zero.

The z_js represents the amount of profit that is given up for each unit of variable x_j that enters the solution. The c_js indicate the amount of profit gained for each unit of x_j brought into solution. The $c_j - z_j$, then, represents the net profit for bringing x_j into solution. Thus, we can improve our profit by bringing in either x_1 or x_2. Normally, you will choose the variable whose $c_j - z_j$ is largest. This choice of entering variable gives the fastest rate of improvement, though not necessarily the greatest degree of improvement. Hence, x_2 is chosen as the entering variable.

The z_js can be calculated by observing how much of each of the current basic variables must be given up in order for x_j to have its value increased and enter the solution. The coefficients in the column of the tableau that *substitution* are directly under any variable x_j are called *substitution rates or substi-* *rates or* *tution coefficients*. They indicate how much of the current solution must *coefficients* be changed for every unit of x_j brought into solution. Thus, from Tableau 3.2, we can see that if 1 unit of x_2 enters the solution (that is, if one preamp is produced), then we must give up 1 unit of transistor slack, 4 units of assembly slack, and 1 unit of inspection slack time. Furthermore, each of the three basic variables s_1, s_2, and s_3 is worth zero. It costs nothing to give them up! Thus, each $z_j = 0$.

The calculations for z_1 and z_2 are shown below.

c_B		x_1					c_B		x_2		
0	×	0	=	0	↙sum these		0	×	1	=	0
0	×	1.2	=	0	to get z_1		0	×	4	=	0
0	×	.5	=	0			0	×	1	=	0
		z_1	=	0					z_2	=	0

to get z_2 appears at right of second block with ↙sum these

Each $c_j - z_j$ for the nonbasic variables is calculated.

$$c_1 - z_1 = 200 - [0(0) + 0(1.2) + 0(.5)] = 200$$
$$c_2 - z_2 = 500 - [0(1) + 0(4) + 0(1)] = 500$$

The $c_j - z_j$ for all basic variables is always zero.

For every unit of x_1 brought into solution, we can increase profits by 200; for every unit of x_2, we can increase profits by 500. Therefore, because when we are maximizing, we normally bring in the nonbasic variable that has the largest $c_j - z_j$ value, x_2 now enters the solution.

Step 3: Increase value of entering variable until some basic variable reaches zero Since only m variables can be basic (in this case $m = 3$), we must now determine a variable to leave the basis. Our resources are limited; so increasing the value of x_2 forces at least some of the other basic variables to decrease in value. We must be careful not to increase x_2 so much that some basic variable becomes negative. Happily, there is a simple test to determine which variable should leave the solution and *ratio test* how much of x_2 should enter. This *ratio test* consists of dividing each number in the *Solution* column by its associated coefficient in the column under x_2. This ratio is formed only for those rows in which the coefficient under x_2 is positive. Negative and zero coefficients are excluded. Hence, for row 1 we form the ratio $^{40}/_1$; for row 2, $^{240}/_4$; for row 3, $^{81}/_1$. We get 40, 60, and 81, respectively. Tableau 3.3 illustrates the calculations.

The row that has the smallest ratio shows the variable to leave the solution. Since row 1 has the smallest ratio, s_1 leaves the solution. The value of the minimum ratio gives the amount of x_2 that enters the solution. On the basis of these operations, we are now in business producing 40 preamps a day!

If you view the simplex tableau as a representation of a system of equations, it is easier to understand why the ratio test determines the maximum amount of x_2 that can enter the solution. Rewriting the elements in Tableau 3.1 as coefficients, we have

$$0x_1 + 1x_2 + 1s_1 + 0s_2 + 0s_3 = 40$$

$$1.2x_1 + 4x_2 + 0s_1 + 1s_2 + 0s_3 = 240$$

$$.5x_1 + 1x_2 + 0s_1 + 0s_2 + 1s_3 = 81$$

Since x_1 and x_2 are nonbasic in the initial tableau, their values are zero. However, as we consider increasing the value of x_2, we can express the basic variables s_1, s_2, and s_3 in terms of the value of x_2 as

TABLEAU 3.3 Illustration of columns involved in ratio test

	c_B	Basic variables	c_j 200 x_1	500 x_2	0 s_1	0 s_2	0 s_3	solution column Solution	Ratio	
leaving variable $s_1 \rightarrow$	0	s_1	0	①	1	0	0	40	$^{40}/_1$	← minimum
	0	s_2	1.2	4	0	1	0	240	$^{240}/_4$	mum
	0	s_3	.5	1	0	0	1	81	$^{81}/_1$	ratio
		z_j	0	0	0	0	0	0		
		$c_j - z_j$	200	500	0	0	0			

column of entering variable

$$s_1 = 40 - x_2$$
$$s_2 = 240 - 4x_2$$
$$s_3 = 81 - x_2$$

From the three foregoing equations, we can see that increasing the value of x_2 to a sufficiently high value causes some slack variable to become negative. We want to find the largest possible value for x_2 so that a basic variable becomes zero but not negative. We could solve the three inequalities for x_2, so that

$$40 - x_2 \geq 0$$

$$240 - 4x_2 \geq 0$$

$$81 - x_2 \geq 0$$

However, these simply imply that $x_2 \geq {}^{40}\!/_1$, $x_2 \geq {}^{240}\!/_4$, and $x_2 \geq {}^{81}\!/_1$. Thus, the largest possible value for x_2 is 40, and the ratio test is a shortcut for determining this value.

Step 4: Bring new variable into solution and revise tableau for new iteration   In the last basic step of the simplex method, we must bring x_2 into the solution and revise all the numbers in the tableau so that we may return to step 2 and begin a new iteration. The procedure used to do this is *pivoting*. All rows in the tableau (including the $c_j - z_j$ row), are updated by this procedure with the exception of the z_j row. The z_j values are always calculated by summing the products of the c_B column times the column of substitution coefficients of variable j. It is not necessary to calculate the z_j row in the tableaus following the initial tableau, but for completeness we shall calculate the z_j row in all tableaus.

There are two steps to the pivoting process. In one step, we update the *pivot row* pivot row; this is the row in which the minimum ratio occurred. In the other step, we update all remaining rows.

The number in the tableau that occurs at the intersection of the leaving *pivot* row and entering column is called the *pivot element*. In Tableau 3.3, the *element* circled number is the pivot element, and the arrows indicate the entering column and leaving row. The entire pivot row is updated by dividing all entries in the pivot row by the pivot element. Thus, we divide the pivot row by 1, yielding $({}^0\!/_1 \quad {}^1\!/_1 \quad {}^1\!/_1 \quad {}^0\!/_1 \quad {}^0\!/_1 \quad {}^{40}\!/_1)$. Tableau 3.4 shows the partially completed tableau. The pivot row did not change, for the pivot element was 1. Naturally, for any pivot element other than 1, the row changes. For every row other than the pivot row and the z_j row, we can update by using the formula:

New row = old row − pivot intersection number × new pivot row

TABLEAU 3.4 First iteration with pivot row updated

c_B	Basic variables	c_j 200 x_1	500 x_2	0 s_1	0 s_2	0 s_3	Solution
500	x_2	0	1	1	0	0	40
0	s_2						
0	s_3						
	z_j						
	$c_j - z_j$						

← updated pivot row

pivot
intersection where the *pivot intersection number* is the number in the row that is in
number the pivot column. To demonstrate the formula, let us update the remaining rows in the tableau:

New row 2
$$
\begin{array}{rrrrrrl}
(1.2 & 4 & 0 & 1 & 0 & 240) & = \text{old row 2} \\
-(4)(0 & 1 & 1 & 0 & 0 & 40) & = -4 \text{ times updated pivot row} \\
\hline
1.2 & 0 & -4 & 1 & 0 & 80 & = \text{new row 2}
\end{array}
$$

New row 3
$$
\begin{array}{rrrrrrl}
(.5 & 1 & 0 & 0 & 1 & 81) \\
-(1)(0 & 1 & 1 & 0 & 0 & 40) \\
\hline
.5 & 0 & -1 & 0 & 1 & 41
\end{array}
$$

New $c_j - z_j$ row
$$
\begin{array}{rrrrrl}
(200 & 500 & 0 & 0 & 0) \\
-(500)(0 & 1 & 1 & 0 & 0) \\
\hline
200 & 0 & -500 & 0 & 0
\end{array}
$$

Once these rows have been updated, we can calculate the z_j values as:

$$z_1 = 500(0) + 0(1.2) + 0(.5) = 0$$
$$z_2 = 500(1) + 0(0) + 0(0) = 500$$
$$z_3 = 500(1) + 0(-4) + 0(-1) = 500$$
$$z_4 = 500(0) + 0(1) + 0(0) = 0$$
$$z_5 = 500(0) + 0(0) + 0(1) = 0$$
$$\text{profit} = 500(40) + 0(80) + 0(41) = 20,000$$

In Tableau 3.5, the completed tableau for the second solution is presented.
The solution corresponds to extreme point A in Figure 3.7. The current solution value in the lower right-hand side of the tableau is calculated by

TABLEAU 3.5 Updated tableau after first iteration

	c_j	200	500	0	0	0		
c_B	Basic variables	x_1	x_2	s_1	s_2	s_3	Solution	Minimum ratio
500	x_2	0	1	1	0	0	40	—
0	s_2	1.2	0	−4	1	0	80	$^{80}/_{1.2} = 66.67$
0	s_3	.5	0	−1	0	1	41	$^{41}/_{.5} = 82$
	z_j	0	500	500	0	0	20,000	
	$c_j - z_j$	200	0	−500	0	0		

taking the c_B column times the *Solution* column to yield: profit $= 500(40)$ $+ 0(80) + 0(41) = 20,000$.

The pivoting process merely involves multiplying one equation by a constant and adding it to another equation. However, certain rules involving elementary row operations are observed so that the solution to the updated system of equations is the same as the original LP model. Thus, the rows in the tableau of Tableau 3.5 still represent equations.

Returning to our calculations, we can see that the second solution in Tableau 3.5 is not optimal since $c_1 - z_1 = 200$. Thus, x_1 will be the entering variable, and the leaving variable is calculated by forming the minimum ratios $^{80}/_{1.2}$ and $^{41}/_{.5}$. No ratio is formed for row 1 since it has a zero in the x_1 column. Row 2 yields the minimum ratio, and s_2 becomes the leaving variable. Thus, 1.2 becomes the pivot element.

In updating the rows of the tableau, we first calculate the new pivot row:

$$\left(^{1.2}/_{1.2} \quad ^{0}/_{1.2} \quad ^{-4}/_{1.2} \quad ^{1}/_{1.2} \quad ^{0}/_{1.2} \quad ^{80}/_{1.2}\right)$$
$$= (1 \qquad 0 \qquad ^{-10}/_{3} \quad ^{5}/_{6} \qquad 0 \qquad 66^{2}/_{3})$$

The remaining rows are updated:

New row 1
$$\begin{array}{ccccccl}
(0 & 1 & 1 & 0 & 0 & 40 &) = \text{old row 1} \\
- 0(1 & 0 & ^{-10}/_{3} & ^{5}/_{6} & 0 & 66^{2}/_{3}) & = -0 \text{ times updated pivot row} \\
\hline
0 & 1 & 1 & 0 & 0 & 40 & = \text{new row 1}
\end{array}$$

New row 3
$$\begin{array}{ccccccl}
(.5 & 0 & -1 & 0 & 1 & 41 &) \\
- (.5)(1 & 0 & ^{-10}/_{3} & ^{5}/_{6} & 0 & 66^{2}/_{3}) \\
\hline
0 & 0 & ^{2}/_{3} & ^{-5}/_{12} & 1 & 7^{2}/_{3}
\end{array}$$

New $c_j - z_j$ row

$$
\begin{array}{ccccc}
(200 & 0 & -500 & 0 & 0) \\
(-200)(\ 1 & 0 & -10/3 & 5/6 & 0) \\
\hline
0 & 0 & 166\tfrac{2}{3} & -166\tfrac{2}{3} & 0
\end{array}
$$

The z_j values are

$$z_1 = 500(0) + 200(1) + 0(0) = 200$$
$$z_2 = 500(1) + 200(0) + 0(0) = 500$$
$$z_3 = 500(1) + 200(-10/3) + 0(2/3) = -166\tfrac{2}{3}$$
$$z_4 = 500(0) + 200(5/6) + 0(-5/12) = 166\tfrac{2}{3}$$
$$z_5 = 500(0) + 200(0) + 0(1) = 0$$
$$\text{profit} = 500(40) + 200(66\tfrac{2}{3}) + 0(7\tfrac{2}{3}) = 33,333\tfrac{1}{3}$$

The value of the new solution is $33,333\tfrac{1}{3}$. The basic feasible solution corresponds to extreme point B in Figure 3.7. The updated tableau is shown in Tableau 3.6.

One more iteration is required before optimality is reached. The next, and final, solution is presented in Tableau 3.7. This solution corresponds to the optimal extreme point C in Figure 3.7. The tableau indicates optimality since all solution values are nonnegative and all $c_j - z_j$ are less than, or equal to, zero, which indicates that no higher profit can be achieved. The feasibility of the solution may be checked by substituting this tableau's values back into the original constraints of the model.

From Tableau 3.7, we can see that variables x_2, x_1, and s_1 are in the final solution at values 28.5, 105, and 11.5, respectively. This corresponds to real conditions of producing 28.5 preamps and 105 amps and having 11.5 surplus transistors. The optimal profit is found in the lower right-hand corner

TABLEAU 3.6   Updated tableau after second iteration

	c_j	200	500	0	0	0		
c_B	Basic variables	x_1	x_2	s_1	s_2	s_3	Solution	Minimum ratio
500	x_2	0	1	1	0	0	40	$40/1 = 40$
200	x_1	1	0	$-10/3$	$5/6$	0	$66\tfrac{2}{3}$	—
→ 0	s_3	0	0	$2/3$	$-5/12$	1	$7\tfrac{2}{3}$	$7\tfrac{2}{3}/2/3 = 11.5$
	z_j	200	500	$-166\tfrac{2}{3}$	$166\tfrac{2}{3}$	0	$33,333\tfrac{1}{3}$	
	$c_j - z_j$	0	0	$166\tfrac{2}{3}$	$-166\tfrac{2}{3}$	0		

TABLEAU 3.7 Optimal tableau for Faze Linear problem

c_B	Basic variables	c_j	200 x_1	500 x_2	0 s_1	0 s_2	0 s_3	Solution
500	x_2		0	1	0	$5/8$	$-3/2$	$28\frac{1}{2}$
200	x_1		1	0	0	$-5/4$	5	105
0	s_1		0	0	1	$-5/8$	$3/2$	$11\frac{1}{2}$
	z_j		200	500	0	$62\frac{1}{2}$	250	35,250
	$c_j - z_j$		0	0	0	$-62\frac{1}{2}$	-250	

at the value of \$35,250. This solution is precisely the same solution as determined by the graphical method.

Which of the three resources are being fully utilized? From the optimal tableau, we can see that slack variables s_2 and s_3 are nonbasic and therefore have value zero. Consequently, there is no surplus assembly or inspection time, and these two resources are being fully utilized.

MINIMIZATION PROBLEMS AND OTHER TYPES OF CONSTRAINTS

In the preceding section, we examined the maximization of an *LP* problem with only $\leq$ constraints. In this section, we consider minimization and equality as well as $\geq$ constraints. We should point out that equality and $\geq$ constraints occur as frequently in maximization as in minimization problems. We started out examining only $\leq$ constraints for simplicity and convenience.

There are two approaches to solving a minimization problem. First, we can simply formulate the minimization problem, then change the signs of all coefficients in the objective function and solve the problem as a maximization problem. The resulting values of the decision variables will be correct, and multiplying the final objective function value by -1 yields the correct minimum value. Many computer codes only maximize (or minimize), and the decision maker must sometimes use this reversing trick to solve an *LP* problem on the computer.

Another approach to minimization involves changing the simplex solution procedure. Again, the alteration is simple; it involves only a change in the selection criterion for the entering variable. Instead of picking the variable with the most positive $c_j - z_j$ to enter the solution, we simply pick the variable with the most negative $c_j - z_j$. Such a selection lowers rather than raises the value of the objective function. The minimization procedure terminates when all $c_j - z_j \geq 0$. Before we illustrate this minimization procedure, however, you must learn how to handle equality and $\geq$ constraints. These constraints often occur in maximization problems; they are not restricted to minimization problems.

Consider the constraint $7x_1 + 5x_2 = 10$. This equality constraint is already an equation, and it appears to be ready for the simplex method. However, it is not clear what the starting value of x_1 and x_2 should be in the initial solution. To answer this would require solving the system of constraints. We can avoid having to solve the system if we add a *artificial* dummy variable, called an *artificial variable*. Thus, we convert the initial *variable* equality to

$$7x_1 + 5x_2 + A_1 = 10$$

In the initial solution, we shall let $A_1 = 10$. Unlike slack variables, artificial variables are not allowed to assume a nonzero value in the optimal solution. For example, if A_1 were to equal 2 in the preceding equation, then $7x_1 + 5x_2$ would equal 8 rather than 10.

Artificial variables are used only to obtain a starting (*pseudofeasible*) solution for the simplex method and must eventually be forced out of the solution. We shall do this by assigning artificial variables extremely low objective function coefficients in maximization problems and extremely high objective function coefficients in minimization problems.

In a $\geq$ constraint, the idea is to add an artificial and subtract a slack. If we have the constraint $7x_1 + 5x_2 \geq 10$, we convert this to an equation by subtracting a slack to yield $7x_1 + 5x_2 - s_1 = 10$. In order to obtain a starting feasible solution, we then add an artificial to obtain $7x_1 + 5x_2 - s_1 + A_1 = 10$. In this case, A_1 allows us to determine a starting solution easily, and s_1 allows the value of $7x_1 + 5x_2$ to exceed 10.

In the following minimization example, you will encounter constraints of all three types.

EXAMPLE   Consider an oil company that produces a petroleum product requiring the input of crude oil A and crude oil B. Each barrel of the final product must contain at least 50 gallons. In this final mix, at least 20 gallons must be crude oil A and, at most, 30 gallons can be crude oil B. Crude oil B costs $.75 per gallon, and crude oil A costs $1.00 per gallon. How many gallons of crude A and B should be in each barrel of the petroleum product in order to meet specifications and minimize costs?

If we let x_1 equal the number of gallons of crude B in a barrel of final product and x_2 the number of gallons of crude A, then the problem is formulated thus:

$$\text{Minimize} \quad .75x_1 + 1.00x_2$$
$$\text{subject to} \quad x_1 + x_2 \geq 50$$
$$x_1 \leq 30$$
$$x_2 \geq 20$$
$$x_1, x_2 \geq 0$$

Converting the constraints to standard form, we have

$$x_1 + x_2 - s_1 + A_1 = 50$$

$$x_1 + s_2 = 30$$

$$x_2 - s_3 + A_3 = 20$$

The subscripts of the slacks and artificials are chosen to correspond to the number of the constraint in which they appear.

In the objective function, we must penalize the artificial variables so that they will not appear in the final solution. Assigning the artificials an arbitrarily high cost accomplishes this for a minimization problem. For a maximization problem we would assign the artificials an arbitrarily low profit. If we let M ($-M$ for a maximization) represent a very large number (say, 999,999,999 on the computer), we can write the objective function as

$$\text{Minimize} \quad .75x_1 + 1.00x_2 + 0s_1 + 0s_2 + 0s_3 + MA_1 + MA_3$$

The problem is now in standard form and can be solved by the simplex method. The big M is simply treated as a number; thus, the basic simplex procedure does not change.

To help you visualize the nature of the minimization problem, let us consider a brief graphical analysis. In Figure 3.8, the oil company's minimization problem is graphed. The constraints $x_1 \leq 30$, $x_2 \geq 20$, and $x_1 + x_2 \geq 50$ each define a half-space in the plane. The set of points satisfying all three constraints and defining the feasible region is indicated by the shaded area in the graph.

The objective function, cost $= .75x_1 + 1.00x_2$, is represented by the dashed line in Figure 3.8. Points A and C are the only extreme points of the feasible region. The direction of decreasing costs is toward the southwest; thus point $C = (30, 20)$ is the optimal extreme point. The associated solution is to mix 30 gallons of crude B and 20 gallons of crude A per barrel for a minimum cost of $42.50.

Now let us solve the same problem with the simplex method. Since some variables that have coefficients of zero are not shown in each constraint, we rewrite the initial LP model in order to demonstrate the existence of each variable in each constraint. The problem is thus restated as

FIGURE 3.8 Graphical solution of oil company's minimization problem

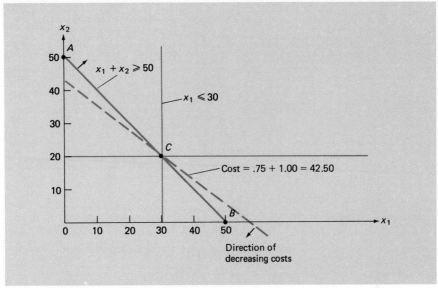

Minimize $\quad .75x_1 + 1.00x_2 + 0s_1 + 0s_2 + 0s_3 + MA_1 + MA_3$
subject to $\quad 1x_1 + 1x_2 - 1s_1 + 0s_2 + 0s_3 + 1A_1 + 0A_3 = 50$
$\qquad\qquad 1x_1 + 0x_2 + 0s_1 + 1s_2 + 0s_3 + 0A_1 + 0A_3 = 30$
$\qquad\qquad 0x_1 + 1x_2 + 0s_1 + 0s_2 - 1s_3 + 0A_1 + 1A_3 = 20$
$\qquad\qquad x_1, x_2, s_1, s_2, s_3, A_1, A_3 \geq 0$

In developing the initial tableau, it is important to remember that those variables with a coefficient of $+1$ in one row and 0 in all other rows will be in the initial solution. Hence, A_1, s_2, and A_3 are the initial basic variables. Notice that their position in the basic solution column is dictated by the position of the 1 in their column of substitution coefficients. That is, A_1 is first with $\begin{pmatrix}1\\0\\0\end{pmatrix}$, s_2 is second with $\begin{pmatrix}0\\1\\0\end{pmatrix}$, and A_3 is third with $\begin{pmatrix}0\\0\\1\end{pmatrix}$.

The initial simplex tableau is shown in Tableau 3.8. The M's are treated simply as numbers; thus, a sample z_j calculation yields

$$z_1 = M(1) + 0(1) + M(0) = M$$

The current cost is calculated as

$$\text{cost} = M(50) + 0(30) + M(20) = 70M$$

As far as procedure goes, the only change from our maximization example is that we pick the variable with the most negative $c_j - z_j$ to enter

TABLEAU 3.8   Initial tableau for minimization problem

	c_j	.75	1.00	0	0	M	0	M		
c_B	Basic variables	x_1	x_2	s_1	s_3	A_1	s_2	A_3	Solu-tion	Minimum ratio
M	A_1	1	1	−1	0	1	0	0	50	$^{50}/_1$
0	s_2	1	0	0	0	0	1	0	30	—
M	A_3	0	①	0	−1	0	0	1	20	$^{20}/_1$
	z_j	M	2M	−M	−M	M	0	M	70M	
	$c_j - z_j$	.75 − M	1.00 − 2M	M	M	0	0	0		

the solution. In this case, $1.00 - 2M$ is more negative than $.75 - M$; thus, x_2 is the entering variable. The minimum ratios of $^{50}/_1$ and $^{20}/_1$ are calculated for rows 1 and 3, respectively. Since $20 < 50$, we find that A_3 will leave the solution.

From Tableau 3.8, we can see that the pivot element is 1; thus, the updated pivot row becomes

$$(0/1 \quad 1/1 \quad 0/1 \quad -1/1 \quad 0/1 \quad 0/1 \quad 1/1 \quad 20/1)$$

$$= (0 \quad 1 \quad 0 \quad -1 \quad 0 \quad 0 \quad 1 \quad 20) \qquad \text{updated pivot row}$$

The other rows are updated thus:

New row 1:
```
    (1   1  −1    0   1   0    0   50) = old row 1
 − (1)(0   1    0  −1   0   0    1   20) = −1 times updated pivot row
      1   0  −1    1   1   0   −1   30) = new row 1
```

New row 2:
```
    (1   0   0    0   0   1   0   30)
 − (0)(0   1   0   −1   0   0   1   20)
      1   0   0    0   0   1   0   30
```

New $c_j - z_j$ row:
```
              (.75 − M   1.00 − 2M   M    M    0   0   0)
 − (1.00 − 2M)(  0          1        0   −1    0   0   1)
               .75 − M    0   M   1.00 − M   0   0   −1.00 + 2M
```

The completed tableau is shown in Tableau 3.9. Note that we have succeeded in driving one of the artificials from the solution.

In the next iteration, x_1 has the most negative $c_j - z_j$. Its $c_j - z_j$ value

TABLEAU 3.9   Tableau after first iteration for minimization problem

		c_j	.75	1.00	0	0	M	0	M		
c_B	Basic variables	x_1	x_2	s_1	s_3	A_1	s_2	A_3	Solution	Minimum ratio
M	A_1	①	0	−1	1	1	0	−1	30	$^{30}/_1$
0	s_2	1	0	0	①	0	1	0	30	$^{30}/_1$
1.00	x_2	0	1	0	−1	0	0	1	20	—
	z_j	M	1.00	−M	M − 1.00	M	0	1.00 − M		
	$c_j − z_j$	.75 − M	0	M	1.00 − M	0	0	−1.00 + 2M	30M + 20	

is .75 − M, meaning that for every unit of x_1 brought into solution, we can increase our cost by .75 − M; actually, this is a decrease since .75 − M < 0. The minimum ratio test provides an interesting situation. We have ratios of $^{30}/_1$ and $^{30}/_1$ in rows 1 and 2. Why isn't a ratio for row 3 calculated? The fact that both ratios for rows 1 and 2 are the same means that either A_1 or s_2 may be chosen as the leaving variable. This tie also means that one of the basic variables will assume a zero value in the updated tableau. *degeneracy* This situation is referred to as *degeneracy*. We shall discuss it later in the chapter. For the moment, we chose A_1 as the leaving variable. The pivot element is 1, and the updated pivot row is

$$(1 \quad 0 \quad −1 \quad 1 \quad 1 \quad 0 \quad −1 \quad 30) = \text{updated pivot row}$$

The other rows are

New row 2:

$$
\begin{array}{l}
(1 \quad 0 \quad 0 \quad 0 \quad 0 \quad 1 \quad 0 \quad 30) = \text{old row 2} \\
\underline{- (1)(1 \quad 0 \quad −1 \quad 1 \quad 1 \quad 0 \quad −1 \quad 30)} = -1 \text{ times updated pivot row} \\
0 \quad 0 \quad 1 \quad −1 \quad −1 \quad 1 \quad 1 \quad 0 = \text{new row 2}
\end{array}
$$

New row 3:

$$
\begin{array}{l}
(0 \quad 1 \quad 0 \quad −1 \quad 0 \quad 0 \quad 1 \quad 20) \\
\underline{- (0)(1 \quad 0 \quad −1 \quad 1 \quad 1 \quad 0 \quad −1 \quad 30)} \\
0 \quad 1 \quad 0 \quad −1 \quad 0 \quad 0 \quad 1 \quad 20
\end{array}
$$

New $c_j − z_j$ row:

$$
\begin{array}{l}
(.75 − M \quad 0 \quad M \quad 1.00 − M \quad 0 \quad 0 \quad −1.00 + 2M) \\
\underline{- (.75 − M)(\quad 1 \quad \quad 0 \quad −1 \quad\quad 1 \quad\quad 1 \quad 0 \quad −1 \quad\quad\quad)} \\
0 \quad\quad 0 \quad .75 \quad\quad .25 \quad\quad −.75 + M \quad 0 \quad −.25 + M
\end{array}
$$

91

TABLEAU 3.10 Optimal tableau for minimization problem

c_B	c_j / Basic variables	.75 x_1	1.00 x_2	0 s_1	0 s_3	M A_1	0 s_2	M A_3	Solution
.75	x_1	1	0	−1	1	1	0	−1	30
0	s_2	0	0	1	−1	−1	1	1	0
1.00	x_2	0	1	0	−1	0	0	1	20
	z_j	.75	1.00	−.75	−.25	.75	0	.25	42.50
	$c_j - z_j$	0	0	.75	.25	−.75 + M	0	−.25 + M	

In Tableau 3.10 we find the updated, and optimal, tableau. All the $c_j - z_j$ values are greater than or equal to zero, all basic variable values are nonnegative, and the constraints are satisfied; the solution is optimal. The solution indicates that we should mix 30 gallons of crude oil B and 20 gallons of crude oil A in each 50-gallon barrel of the petroleum product. The total cost per barrel is $42.50. In this example, all artificials have been driven from the solution. If any artificials remain at nonzero value in a final solution, they indicate that the original problem does not have a feasible solution.

SUMMARY OF SIMPLEX PROCEDURE

The following steps summarize the procedures we have discussed for solving LP problems by the simplex method.

1. Assuming that the LP model has been correctly formulated, it must first be converted to standard form.

2. Convert $\leq$ constraints to standard form by adding a slack variable, equality constraints by adding an artificial variable, and $\geq$ constraints by adding an artificial, and subtracting a slack, variable.

3. Choose the initial basic feasible solution by placing in solution those slack and/or artificial variables that have a +1 coefficient in the original column of constraints in standard form.

4. Fill in the initial tableau by simply entering the constraint equations as they appear in standard form. Calculate the $c_j - z_j$ values for the solution.

5. Check the $c_j - z_j$ values for the solution. If the problem is a maximization and all $c_j - z_j$ values are ≤ 0, stop, for the solution is optimal. (If the problem is a minimization and all $c_j - z_j$ values are ≥ 0, stop, for the solution is optimal.)

6. Otherwise, determine the entering variable by selecting the variable whose $c_j - z_j$ value is most positive (or most negative in a minimization).

7. Determine the variable to leave the solution by forming the ratios between the entries in the solution column and associated positive entries in the column of the variable entering the solution. The row in which the minimum ratio occurs designates the basic variable that is to leave the solution.

8. Bring the entering variable into solution and update the tableau by pivoting. Divide the pivot row by the pivot element and update all other rows by the formula on page 82. Go to step 5.

SPECIAL CASES IN THE SIMPLEX METHOD

In most applications of LP, a unique optimal solution is obtained. However, variations do exist. Next, we show you how to approach certain of these special cases.

UNBOUNDED SOLUTION

It is possible for an LP problem to have a nonempty set of feasible solutions and yet have no finite optimal solution. This can occur whenever the feasible region extends infinitely in the direction of improvement for the objective function. Consider the example

$$\text{Maximize} \quad x_1 + x_2$$
$$\text{subject to} \quad 5x_1 - x_2 \geq 10$$
$$3x_1 - 2x_2 \leq 9$$
$$x_1, x_2 \geq 0$$

The graph of this problem is shown in Figure 3.9.

As you can see, the feasible region is unbounded. We can pick arbitrarily large values of x_1 and x_2 in order to make the objective function as high as desired. Thus, there exists no finite optimum. Note however, that an infinite feasible region does not imply an unbounded solution. In this example, if we were minimizing the same objective function, the finite optimum would occur at $x_1 = 2$ and $x_2 = 0$.

The simplex method can detect the existence of an *unbounded solution* during the process of selecting the entering variable. If a variable with a promising $c_j - z_j$ opportunity cost has been chosen, the next step is to calculate the minimum ratio in order to determine the leaving variable. However, if no entries in the pivot column are positive, no positive ratio can be formed and the problem is identified as unbounded. To visualize

FIGURE 3.9   Unbounded feasible region

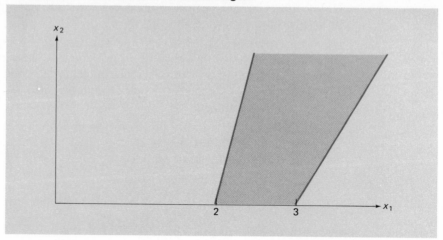

this situation, look at the second simplex tableau in standard form as shown in Tableau 3.11. At this iteration, it would pay $^6\!/_5$ for every unit of x_2 brought into solution, but the solution is unbounded since the entries $-^1\!/_5$ and $-^7\!/_5$ are both negative in the potential pivot column under x_2.

The detection of unbounded solutions in the simplex tableau can be explained by reinterpreting the meaning of tableau elements in a given column. We have called these elements substitution coefficients, for they represent the per-unit decrease of the solution values for every unit of the associated variable brought into solution. For example, the $-^1\!/_5$ and $-^7\!/_5$ under variable x_2 in Tableau 3.11 represent the reduction in the solution values 2 and 3 for every unit of x_2 brought into solution. Since $-^1\!/_5$ and $-^7\!/_5$ are negative, this means that the solution values 2 and 3 will actually increase by $^1\!/_5$ and $^7\!/_5$, respectively, for every unit of x_2 brought into solution. Thus, no matter how much of x_2 is brought into solution, the solution

TABLEAU 3.11   Unbounded solution

c_j		1	1	0	$-M$	0	
c_B	Basic variables	x_1	x_2	s_1	A_1	s_2	Solution
1	x_1	1	$-^1\!/_5$	$-^1\!/_5$	$^1\!/_5$	0	2
0	s_2	0	$-^7\!/_5$	$^3\!/_5$	$-^3\!/_5$	0	3
	z_j	1	$-^1\!/_5$	$-^1\!/_5$	$^1\!/_5$	0	2
	$c_j - z_j$	0	$^6\!/_5$	$^1\!/_5$	$-M-^1\!/_5$	0	

TABLEAU 3.12 Modified Faze Linear problem at optimality

c_B	c_j Basic variables	200 x_1	400 x_2	0 s_1	0 s_2	0 s_3	Solution
400	x_2	0	1	0	$5/8$	$-3/2$	28.5
200	x_1	1	0	0	$-5/4$	5	105
0	s_1	0	0	1	$-5/8$	$3/2$	11.5
	z_j	200	400	0	0	400	32,400
	$c_j - z_j$	0	0	0	0	-400	

values of the basic variables will never become negative or infeasible. Therefore, an unlimited amount of x_2 can enter the solution, causing the problem to be unbounded.

Unbounded solutions usually mean that the LP model has been formulated incorrectly. No meaningful real-world LP problems exist in which the decision variables can assume infinite values.

NO FEASIBLE SOLUTION

It is also possible to have an LP problem in which *no feasible solution* exists. This situation corresponds to a problem that is formulated incorrectly or has conflicting restrictions within the constraint set. Consider the example

$$
\begin{aligned}
\text{Minimize} \quad & x_1 + x_2 \\
\text{subject to} \quad & x_1 - x_2 \geq 1 \\
& -x_1 + x_2 \geq 1 \\
& x_1, x_2 \geq 0
\end{aligned}
$$

It is obvious from inspecting the model that the two constraints are inconsistent. The graph in Figure 3.10 shows the nature of the inconsistency. No point satisfies both constraints simultaneously. In the simplex method, an infeasible problem is indicated whenever the final solution contains an artificial variable at nonzero value.

DEGENERACY

We have already run across the notion of *degeneracy* in the minimization example. In a nondegenerate solution, the nonbasic variables have zero values and the m basic variables in solution have positive values. In a

FIGURE 3.10 No feasible region

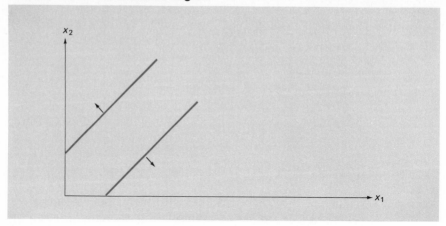

degenerate solution, at least one basic variable has a zero value. This does not really pose a problem. If you check back to Tableau 3.12, you will see that the basic variable s_2 has a zero value, and therefore the solution is degenerate. All this means is that there is no slack in the second constraint.

Theoretically, degeneracy does pose a potential problem. Early researchers were afraid that *cycling* could occur in a degenerate solution. In cycling, a degenerate basic variable is removed from the solution at zero value only to return at a later iteration with no improvement, thereby creating a cycle and an infinite loop. Techniques were established to assure that cycling would never occur. Practically speaking, remedies are virtually unnecessary, for cycling almost never occurs in real-world applications.

ALTERNATIVE OPTIMA

The optimal solution to an LP problem is not necessarily unique. It is possible that an adjacent extreme point will yield the same profit (or cost). Graphically, this happens whenever the slope of the objective function equals the slope of a constraint equation that passes through an optimal extreme point. In Figure 3.11, we show a modified version of the Faze Linear problem. The problem was modified by changing the profit of x_2 (preamps) to 400 rather than 500. With this modification, both the points (105, 28.5) and (162, 0) yield a profit of $32,400, which is optimal. In Figure 3.11, if the dashed line representing the objective function were moved toward the feasible region it would eventually intersect the entire line segment between points (105, 28.5) and (162, 0) rather than at a single extreme point.

Alternative optima are also easy to detect in the simplex tableau. Let us consider the modified Faze Linear problem in Tableau 3.12. The solution remains unchanged from Tableau 3.7; only the $c_j - z_j$ values have changed. The $c_j - z_j$ row indicates that the solution is still optimal. But since the $c_j - z_j$ for s_2 is zero, we may pivot in s_2 for x_2 and change the profit by zero. The resulting solution also yields a profit of \$32,400 and thus is an alternative optimum.

In general, if a nonbasic variable has a $c_j - z_j$ of zero at optimality, it indicates an alternative optimal solution exists and can be obtained by simply bringing this nonbasic variable into the solution.

COMPUTERS AND LINEAR PROGRAMMING

Applications of LP in the real world inevitably involve the use of electronic digital computers. In these cases, extensive information, data manipulation, and numerical computation require high-speed computers.

Major computer manufacturers can usually provide computer software packages that perform LP on their machines. For example, IBM, Control Data Corporation, Univac, and Honeywell, among others, have standard LP packages. However, it is not necessary to have your own computer in order to use LP. Commercial computer time-sharing companies with available software packages have made it rather easy to use a computer without having to own one. Data input and program output will vary slightly from one software package to another, but are relatively standardized. Listed in Table 3.2 is sample input and output from a relatively standard LP computer program. The problem solved is the now familiar Faze Linear product mix example. Note the slight degree of numerical round-off error in some of the answers.

Performing LP analysis can be relatively cost-effective. For example, an LP problem with 62 variables and 32 constraints was run on a Xerox Sigma 6 computer, and the total cost of the job was around \$1. This cost is based on computer execution time, computer memory required, and

FIGURE 3.11   Faze Linear problem with alternative optima

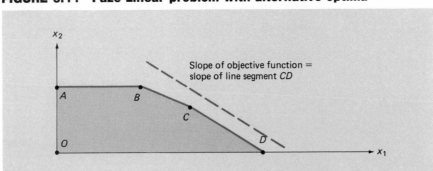

TABLE 3.2 Computer solution to Faze linear problem

FAZE LINEAR PROBLEM

THE ORIGINAL COEFFICIENTS OF THE CONSTRAINTS
```
        CODE 0 ==> <OR= CONSTRAINT
        CODE 1 ==> >OR= CONSTRAINT
          CODE 2 ==> = CONSTRAINT
```

```
  CODE CONSTANT A(I,1)   A(I,2)
  TYPE OF CONSTRAINT
1  0     40.00     .00    1.00
2  0    240.00    1.20    4.00
3  0     81.00     .50    1.00
```
R'HS COEFFICIENTS   COEFFICIENTS OF THE CONSTRAINTS
THE COEFFICIENTS IN THE ORIGINAL OBJECTIVE FUNCTION TO BE MAXIMIZED ARE:
```
            200.00   500.00
```

OPTION SELECTED -- PRINT SENSITIVITY ANALYSIS

BASIC SOLUTION   4
```
    X( 2)=     28.499969
    X( 1)=    105.000061  ←—OPTIMAL VALUES OF THE BASIC VARIABLES
    S( 1)=     11.500018
```

CURRENT VALUE OF OBJECTIVE FUNCTION IS   35250.00

THE LAST BASIC FEASIBLE SOLUTION IS OPTIMAL   OPTIMAL SOLUTION VALUE
    OPTIMAL VALUE OF THE ORIGINAL OBJECTIVE FUNCTION IS   35250.00 ←
CONSTRAINT   SHADOW PRICE
```
    1          .0000
    2        62.5000   SHADOW PRICES
    3       249.9999
```
                   FAZE LINEAR PROBLEM
              *** SENSITIVITY ANALYSIS ***

                  OBJECTIVE FUNCTION RANGING

VARIABLE	DECREASE	INCREASE	* RANGE * MINIMUM	MAXIMUM
X(1)	50.0000	50.0000	150.0000	250.0000
X(2)	99.9999	166.6665	400.0000	666.6663

                  RIGHT HAND SIDE RANGING

CONSTRAINT	DECREASE	INCREASE	* RANGE * MINIMUM	MAXIMUM
1	11.5000	NO LIMIT	28.5000	NO LIMIT
2	45.5999	18.4000	194.4001	258.3999
3	7.6667	19.0000	73.3333	100.0000

other factors. Of course, really large industrial applications cost considerably more, but it has been shown, for example, that a medium-size oil refinery saves approximately $2,000 daily after its operation has been analyzed with LP.[2]

---

[2]Harvey M. Wagner, *Principles of Management Science* (Englewood Cliffs, N.J.: Prentice-Hall, Inc., 1975), p. 585.

Naturally, LP analysis requires resources other than computer hardware and software. Two other necessary ingredients are a source of reliable data (which is harder to come by than you might realize!), and personnel who know how to model the problem, load it on the computer, and interpret the computer output. The interpretation of computer output is sometimes facilitated by using report generators to summarize the information that is to be conveyed to management. This step alone requires personnel who are adept at LP and, possibly, computer programming.

SUMMARY

In solving LP problems, the graphical method, because it can solve problems with only three or fewer variables, is useful only for illustrative purposes. The simplex method, or a variation of it, is actually used in real applications. On a computer, the simplex method is capable of solving problems that have hundreds of decision variables and constraints. Though real problems are never solved by hand, you should have gained an understanding of how the simplex method works from this chapter. Iterative procedures are common among the many techniques used in OR/MS.

Understanding the principles of the simplex method will also enhance your understanding of postoptimality analysis. In Chapter 4, we look at some of the questions that can be answered once the optimal solution has been obtained.

SOLVED PROBLEMS

PROBLEM STATEMENT

Solve the following minimization problem graphically:

$$
\begin{aligned}
\text{Minimize} \quad & 2x_1 + 3x_2 \\
\text{subject to} \quad & x_2 \geq 2 \\
& 4x_1 + 3x_2 \geq 12 \\
& x_1 + 2x_2 \leq 8 \\
& x_1, x_2 \geq 0
\end{aligned}
$$

SOLUTION

Plotting each of the constraints, we obtain the region shown. The feasible region is the shaded triangular area defined by the constraints. It contains

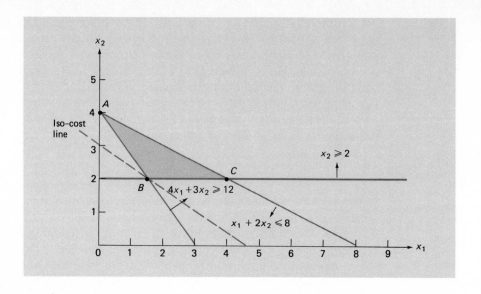

only three extreme points A, B, and C. The slope of the objective function is $-\frac{2}{3}$ and sliding the isocost line up toward the "northeast" from the origin, we find that extreme point B is the optimum. The coordinates for B are found by solving simultaneously the two equations that represent the two lines defining point B.

$$x_2 = 2$$
$$4x_1 + 3x_2 = 12$$
$$x_2 = 2$$
$$x_1 = \tfrac{3}{2}$$

Thus, the optimal solution is $x_1 = \frac{3}{2}$, $x_2 = 2$ with an objective function value of 9.

PROBLEM STATEMENT

Solve the following maximization problem by the simplex method:

$$
\begin{aligned}
\text{Maximize} \quad & 3x_1 + 5x_2 + 4x_3 \\
\text{subject to} \quad & x_2 + 2x_3 \le 6 \\
& 3x_1 + 2x_2 + x_3 \le 18 \\
& x_1, x_2 \ge 0
\end{aligned}
$$

SOLUTION

We first convert the problem to standard form:

$$\text{Maximize} \quad 3x_1 + 5x_2 + 4x_3 + 0s_1 + 0s_2$$
$$\text{subject to} \quad x_2 + 2x_3 + s_1 \quad = 6$$
$$3x_1 + 2x_2 + x_3 \quad + s_2 = 18$$
$$x_1, x_2, x_3, s_1, s_2 \geq 0$$

The problem now has five variables and two equations; there will be two variables in solution. Placing the two slack variables in the initial tableau, we obtain

	c_j	3	5	4	0	0		
c_B	Basic variables	x_1	x_2	x_3	s_1	s_2	Solution	Minimum ratio
0	s_1	0	①1	2	1	0	6	$6/1$
0	s_2	3	2	1	0	1	18	$18/2$
	z_j	0	0	0	0	0	0	
	$c_j - z_j$	3	5	4	0	0		

In the next tableau, x_2 replaces s_1 in the solution:

	c_j	3	5	4	0	0		
c_B	Basic variables	x_1	x_2	x_3	s_1	s_2	Solution	Minimum ratio
5	x_2	0	1	2	1	0	6	—
0	s_2	③3	0	-3	-2	1	6	$6/3$
	z_j	0	5	10	5	0	30	
	$c_j - z_j$	3	0	-6	-5	0		

In the final tableau, x_1 replaces s_2:

101

c_j		3	5	4	0	0	
c_B	Basic variables	x_1	x_2	x_3	s_1	s_2	Solution
5	x_2	0	1	2	1	0	6
3	x_1	1	0	-1	$-2/3$	$1/3$	2
	z_j	3	5	7	3	1	36
	$c_j - z_j$	0	0	-3	-3	-1	

The optimal solution is $x_1 = 2$, $x_2 = 6$, and the maximal objective function value is 36.

REVIEW QUESTIONS

1. Under what conditions can you use the graphical method to solve an LP problem?

2. What does every basic feasible solution correspond to, geometrically?

3. What characterizes an iterative procedure?

4. Why are slack variables added to ≤ constraints? What is the purpose of artificial variables?

5. Given an LP problem with $m + n$ variables and n constraints, how many basic variables (variables in solution) will there always be?

6. What is the meaning of a $c_j - z_j$, and what is the rationale for picking the nonbasic variables with the largest positive $c_j - z_j$ to enter the solution when maximizing?

7. Why are slacks and/or artificial variables used in the starting solution?

8. What is the purpose of the minimum ratio test in the simplex method?

9. How does the simplex method detect when the optimal solution has been achieved?

10. What is the difference between a degenerate and a nondegenerate solution?

11. Can there be more than one optimal solution to an LP problem?

12. How does the simplex method detect an unbounded solution?

13. Why are some nonlinear problems solved approximately by the use of LP?

PROBLEMS

3.1 Solve the following problem graphically.

$$\text{Maximize} \quad 6x_1 + 8x_2$$
$$\text{subject to} \quad x_1 \leq 12$$
$$x_2 \leq 10$$
$$2x_1 + 3x_2 \leq 36$$
$$x_1, x_2 \geq 0$$

3.2 Solve Problem 3.1 by the simplex method.

3.3 Solve the following minimization problem by the graphical method.

$$\text{Minimize} \quad x_1 + x_2$$
$$\text{subject to} \quad x_2 \geq 2$$
$$2x_1 - x_2 \geq 0$$
$$3x_1 + 2x_2 \leq 12$$
$$x_1, x_2 \geq 0$$

3.4 Consider the problem

$$\text{Maximize} \quad 2x_1 + 6x_2 + 5x_3$$
$$\text{subject to} \quad x_1 + x_2 + x_3 = 3$$
$$x_1 + 2x_2 + 3x_3 \leq 10$$
$$2x_1 + 6x_2 + 1x_3 \geq 5$$
$$x_1, x_2, x_3 \geq 0$$

a. Convert this system to standard form.

b. What is the maximum number of possible basic solutions?

3.5 Use the simplex method to solve the following problem.

$$\text{Maximize} \quad 3x_1 + 5x_2 + 4x_3$$
$$\text{subject to} \quad x_2 + 2x_3 \leq 6$$
$$3x_1 + 2x_2 + x_3 \leq 24$$
$$x_1 + x_2 + x_3 \leq 12$$
$$x_1, x_2, x_3 \geq 0$$

3.6 Solve Problem 2.1 (product mix) by the graphical method.

3.7 *Sales Territory Assignment.* The marketing manager of Computate, a manufacturer of minicomputers, is trying to decide how to assign his sales staff to three market regions. Region 1 is an industrial area of a large city and can be expected to yield sales of 8 minicomputers per salesperson per week. Regions 2 and 3 yield approximately 7 and 5 sales per salesperson per week. Because of turnover, only 7 salespeople are available for assignment. The travel budget is set at $700 per week, and travel plus selling expenses in the three regions are $90, $70, and $60, per salesperson per week, respectively. The profit contribution per computer is $250.

a. Formulate an LP model to determine the optimal allocation of salespeople to regions.

b. Solve the model by the simplex method.

3.8 Solve by the simplex method.

$$\text{Maximize} \quad 8x_1 + 7x_2$$
$$\text{subject to} \quad 3x_1 + 4x_2 \leq 15$$
$$7x_1 + 5x_2 \leq 20$$
$$x_1, x_2 \geq 0$$

3.9 Solve Problem 2.2 (product mix) by the graphical method.

3.10 Solve the following minimization by the simplex method.

$$\text{Minimize} \quad 12x_1 + 18x_2$$
$$\text{subject to} \quad 2x_1 + 3x_2 \geq 6$$
$$5x_1 + x_2 \geq 10$$
$$x_1, x_2 \geq 0$$

3.11 Given the following incomplete simplex tableau for a maximization problem, answer questions a–d.

| c_B | Basic variables | c_j | 6 | 8 | 10 | 0 | 0 | |
			x_1	x_2	x_3	s_1	s_2	Solution
			.10	.25	0	1	0	120
			.50	.75	1	0	2.50	650
	z_j							
	$c_j - z_j$							

a. Which variables are basic?

b. Complete the partial tableau.

    c. Is the solution optimal? If not, which variable should enter?

    d. Finish solving the problem.

3.12 Use the simplex method to solve the following minimization problem.

$$\text{Minimize} \quad 40y_1 + 240y_2 + 81y_3$$
$$\text{subject to} \quad 1.2y_2 + .5y_3 \geq 200$$
$$y_1 + 4y_2 + y_3 \geq 500$$
$$y_1, y_2, y_3 \geq 0$$

3.13 Convert the following problem to standard form.

$$\text{Maximize} \quad 2x_1 + 4x_2$$
$$\text{subject to} \quad 3x_1 + x_2 = 3$$
$$4x_1 + 3x_2 \geq 6$$
$$x_1 + 2x_2 \leq 3$$
$$x_1, x_2 \geq 0$$

3.14 Solve Problem 3.13 by the simplex method.

3.15 Determine the optimal solution to the following problem.

$$\text{Maximize} \quad 3x_1 + 2x_2 + 5x_3$$
$$\text{subject to} \quad 5x_1 + 4x_2 + x_3 \leq 40$$
$$11x_1 - 4x_2 = 0$$
$$-4x_1 + 5x_2 + 3x_3 \geq 10$$
$$x_1, x_2, x_3 \geq 0$$

3.16 Use the simplex method to determine the optimal solution to the problem in the production distribution example in Chapter 2.

3.17 Consider the following problem with only one constraint:

$$\text{Maximize} \quad 5x_1 + 2x_2 + 3x_3 + x_4$$
$$\text{subject to} \quad 4x_1 + 3x_2 + 3x_3 + x_4 \geq 7$$
$$x_i \geq 0 \quad \text{for all } i$$

    a. How many variables will be in any basic solution?

    b. Find the optimal solution by inspection.

    c. Verify your results with criteria from the simplex method.

3.18 Consider the LP problem:

$$\text{Maximize} \quad 2x_1 + 3x_2 + 5x_3 + 1x_4$$
$$\text{subject to} \quad 3x_1 + 1x_2 + 1x_3 + 3x_4 = 5$$
$$2x_1 - 1x_2 + 1x_3 + 1x_4 = 3$$
$$5x_1 + 2x_3 + 3x_4 \le 8$$
$$x_1,\ x_2,\ x_3,\ x_4 \ge 0$$

After the model has been converted to standard form, the optimal tableau is:

	c_j	2	3	5	1	$-M$	$-M$	0	
c_B	Basic variables	x_1	x_2	x_3	x_4	A_1	A_2	S_3	Solution
1	x_4	0	0	0	1	1	1	−1	0
5	x_3	2.5	0	1	0	−1.5	−1.5	2	4
3	x_2	.5	1	0	0	−.5	−1.5	1	1
	$c_j - z_j$	−12	0	0	0	$8 - M$	$11 - M$	−12	23

a. What is the optimal solution?

b. Is it degenerate?

c. Are there any alternative optima?

d. Is the solution unbounded?

3.19 *Product Mix.* Home Products, Inc., specializes in home cooking devices. They are trying to plan production for their electric skillets and crock pots. The company works a 40-hour week and has its production limited only by productive capacity. The table indicates production capacity in terms of units of final product. The profit contribution is $5 for a skillet and $7 for a crock pot. Formulate and solve the product mix problem. You may want to convert the capacity values to hours of production capacity required per unit.

	Weekly capacity (units)	
Department	Skillets	Crock pots
Casting	400	—
Wiring	250	250
Assembly	500	400

3.20 *Petroleum Blending.* The Slik Oil Company produces two lines of motor oil and a special engine additive called *Motor Honey.* All three products are produced by blending two components. These components contribute various properties, including viscosity. The viscosity in the product is proportional to the viscosities of the blending components. The pertinent data appear in the tables below. Assuming no limitation on the demand, determine how many barrels of each oil product Slik should produce each week.

Blending Component	Viscosity	Cost per barrel	Availability per week (bbl)
1	20	$36.50	10,000
2	60	41.00	4,000

Product	Viscosity required	Revenue per barrel
30W oil	30	$38
40W oil	40	39
Motor Honey	50	41

3.21   *Inventory/purchasing.* A stereo mail-order warehouse has 8,000 feet available for storage of loudspeakers. The jumbo speakers cost $295 each and require 4 square feet of space; the midsize speakers cost $110 and require 3 square feet of space; and the economy speakers cost $58 and require 1 square foot of space. The demand for the jumbo speakers is, at most, 20 per month. The wholesaler has $10,000 to invest in loudspeakers this month. Assuming that the jumbo speakers contribute $105 to profit, the midsize contribute $50, and the economy contribute $28, how many units of each type should the wholesaler buy and stock?

3.22   *Product Mix.* The Green Country Lumber Company produces two wood products, interior wood paneling and plywood. The resource requirements for each product are provided in the table. Assuming that production time is limited to 4,000 hours per week, use the simplex method to maximize Green Country's profit.

Wood product	Production time per sq yd (hr)	Demand	Profit contribution per sq yd
Plywood	.025	At least 6,000 sq yd per week	$.30
Paneling	.040	At most 4,000 sq yd per week	.45

3.23 Consider the following maximization problem and an associated simplex tableau.

$$\begin{aligned}
\text{Maximize} \quad & 4x_1 + 5x_2 + 6x_3 + 5x_4 \\
\text{subject to} \quad & 2x_1 + 5x_2 + 4x_3 + 3x_4 \le 224 \qquad \text{resource 1} \\
& 5x_1 + 4x_2 - 5x_3 + 10x_4 \le 280 \qquad \text{resource 2} \\
& 2x_1 + 4x_2 + 4x_3 - 2x_4 \le 184 \qquad \text{resource 3} \\
& x_1,\, x_2,\, x_3,\, x_4 \ge 0
\end{aligned}$$

c_B	c_j Basic variables	4 x_1	5 x_2	6 x_3	5 x_4	0 s_1	0 s_2	0 s_3	Solution
5	x_4	0	$1/5$	0	1	$1/5$	0	$-1/5$	8
6	x_3	0	$3/5$	1	0	$1/5$	$-1/15$	$-1/30$	20
4	x_1	1	1	0	0	$-1/5$	$2/15$	$11/30$	60
	z_j	4	$43/5$	6	5	$7/5$	$2/15$	$8/30$	400
	$c_j - z_j$	0	$-18/5$	0	0	$-7/5$	$-2/15$	$-8/30$	

a. What is the solution? Is it optimal?

b. Which constraints are binding; that is, which are being met exactly?

c. Which resources are fully utilized?

d. What would happen to the value of the objective function if one unit of x_2 were brought into solution?

e. Which special cases in the simplex method apply here: degeneracy, alternative optima, no solution, unbounded?

3.24 Solve Problem 2.21 (cutting stock) on a computer using an LP computer code.

3.25 Each of the following tableaus represent a possible solution to a maximization problem. Label each tableau with each of the following conditions that apply: (a) feasible; (b) optimal; (c) unbounded; (d) no feasible solution; (e) degeneracy; (f) alternative optima.

a.

c_B	Basic variables	c_j 9 x_1	7 x_2	0 s_1	0 s_2	Solution
9	x_1	1	$\frac{1}{2}$	$\frac{1}{4}$	0	15
0	s_2	0	3	$-\frac{1}{2}$	1	18
	z_j	9	4.5	2.25	0	135
	$c_j - z_j$	0	2.5	-2.25	0	

b.

c_B	Basic variables	c_j 6 x_1	12 x_2	16 x_3	0 s_1	0 s_2	0 s_3	Solution
16	x_3	0	0	1	$\frac{1}{2}$	0	$-\frac{1}{3}$	200
0	s_2	0	0	0	$-\frac{3}{2}$	1	$-\frac{1}{3}$	200
12	x_2	$\frac{1}{2}$	1	0	$-\frac{1}{2}$	0	$\frac{2}{3}$	200
	z_j	6	12	16	2	0	2.67	5600
	$c_j - z_j$	0	0	)	-2	0	-2.67	

c.

c_B	Basic variables	c_j 4 x_1	12 x_2	16 x_3	0 s_1	0 s_2	0 s_3	Solution
16	x_3	0	0	1	$\frac{1}{2}$	0	$-\frac{1}{3}$	200
0	s_2	0	0	0	$-\frac{3}{2}$	1	$-\frac{1}{3}$	200
12	x_2	$\frac{1}{2}$	1	0	$-\frac{1}{2}$	0	$\frac{2}{3}$	0
	z_j	6	12	16	2	0	2.67	3200
	$c_j - z_j$	-2	0	0	-2	0	0	

d.

c_B	Basic variables	c_j 4 x_1	10 x_2	0 s_3	0 s_1	$-M$ A_2	$-M$ A_3	Solution
0	s_1	0	24	24	1	-12	0	24
4	x_1	1	1	1	0	1	0	0
$-M$	A_2	0	-1	-1	0	0	1	1
	z_j	4	$4 + M$	$4 + M$	0	4	$-M$	$-M$
	$c_j - z_j$	0	$6 - M$	$-4 - M$	0	$-4 - M$	0	

e.

c_B	Basic variables	c_j 9 x_1	7 x_2	0 s_1	0 s_2	Solution
9	x_1	1	$-\frac{1}{2}$	$\frac{1}{4}$	0	15
0	s_2	0	-3	$-\frac{1}{2}$	1	18
	z_j	9	-4.5	2.25	0	135
	$c_j - z_j$	0	11.5	-2.25	0	

f.

c_B	Basic variables	c_j 9 x_1	7 x_2	0 s_1	0 s_2	Solution
9	x_1	1	0	$\frac{1}{3}$	$-\frac{1}{6}$	-15
7	x_2	0	1	$-\frac{1}{6}$	$\frac{1}{3}$	18
	z_j	9	7	$\frac{11}{6}$	$\frac{5}{6}$	-9
	$c_j - z_j$	0	0	$-\frac{11}{6}$	$-\frac{5}{6}$	

3.26 *Concrete Mix.* The McMichael Concrete Co. is trying to optimize its concrete mix. Different hardening qualities are needed for various applications. Their primary ingredients are limestone and clay, which cost $8 and $11 per ton, respectively. McMichael mixes their concrete in 20-ton batches. For their hardest mix, they need at least 8 tons of clay and no more than 14 tons of limestone. Formulate the problem, and use the simplex method to determine the optimal blend for the hard mix.

3.27 Solve Problem 2.9 (media selection) by the simplex method.

3.28 Listed below is the computer solution of the following problem:

$$\text{Maximize} \quad 5x_1 + 2x_2 + 8x_3$$
$$\text{subject to} \quad x_1 - 2x_2 + x_3 \leq 440$$
$$2x_1 + 3x_2 - x_3 \leq 600$$
$$6x_1 - x_2 + 3x_3 \leq 120$$
$$x_1, x_2, x_3 \geq 0$$

a. Which variables are basic?

b. What is the solution and its objective function value?

c. Which constraints are binding?

PROBLEM 3.28

THE ORIGINAL COEFFICIENTS OF THE CONSTRAINTS
```
              CODE 0 ==> <OR= CONSTRAINT
               CODE 1 =-> >OR= CONSTRAINT
                CODE 2 ==>  =  CONSTRAINT
```

```
  CODE CONSTANT  A(I,1)   A(I,2)   A(I,3)
1   0   440.00    1.00    -2.00    -1.00
2   0   600.00    2.00    -3.00    -1.00
3   0   120.00    6.00    -1.00     3.00
```

THE COEFFICIENTS IN THE ORIGINAL OBJECTIVE FUNCTION TO BE MAXIMIZED ARE:
```
              5.00     2.00     8.00
```

OPTION SELECTED == PRINT SENSITIVITY ANALYSIS

BASIC SOLUTION   3
```
   S( 1)=    799.999756
   X( 2)=    240.000046
   X( 3)=    120.000000
```

CURRENT VALUE OF OBJECTIVE FUNCTION IS   1440.00

THE LAST BASIC FEASIBLE SOLUTION IS OPTIMAL
OPTIMAL VALUE OF THE ORIGINAL OBJECTIVE FUNCTION IS   1440.00
```
CONSTRAINT    SHADOW PRICE
     1            .0000
     2           1.7500
     3           3.2500
```
                PROBLEM 3.28

            *** SENSITIVITY ANALYSIS ***

            OBJECTIVE FUNCTION RANGING

			* RANGE *	
VARIABLE	DECREASE	INCREASE	MINIMUM	MAXIMUM
X(1)	NO LIMIT	18.0000	NO LIMIT	23.0000
X(2)	4.6667	NO LIMIT	-2.6667	NO LIMIT
X(3)	7.2000	NO LIMIT	.8000	NO LIMIT

            RIGHT HAND SIDE RANGING

			* RANGE *	
CONSTRAINT	DECREASE	INCREASE	MINIMUM	MAXIMUM
1	799.9998	NO LIMIT	-353.9998	NO LIMIT
2	640.0000	NO LIMIT	-40.0000	NO LIMIT
3	320.0000	6399.9922	-200.0000	6519.9922

d. What are the $c_j - z_j$ values of slack 2 and slack 3? (Refer to shadow prices of constraints 2 and 3.)

e. How many complete iterations did the simplex method require to reach optimality?

3.29 Solve the constrained break-even analysis problem that was formulated in Chapter 2, page 47.

3.30 Assuming that you have formulated the LP model for Problem 2.22 about the Akron Tire Company, solve the model by the use of an LP computer code. What is the optimum production schedule and its associated minimum quarterly cost?

3.31 *Land allocation.* Using an LP computer code, find the optimum land allocation for Problem 2.24 based on the data in the two tables that follow.

Net revenue factor (r_{ij})

Region	Crop										
	Wheat	Barley	Broad beans	Lentils	Cotton type 1	Cotton type 2	Rice	Corn	Millet	Sesame	Sugar cane
1	1.4	2.9	2.8	4.1	.2	.7	1.0	2.3	.7	1.7	.8
2	1.1	2.7	2.9	3.9	.1	.8	1.1	2.1	.6	1.8	.9
3	1.3	2.8	3.0	2.8	.1	.6	.9	2.2	.5	2.0	1.1
4	1.5	2.6	2.9	4.3	.1	.8	1.2	2.3	1.0	2.7	1.2
5	1.1	2.9	3.1	4.4	.2	.8	.8	2.0	1.3	2.2	.8
6	1.2	3.0	2.8	4.4	.1	.9	.7	2.0	1.2	2.5	1.7
7	1.3	2.6	2.7	5.0	.1	.8	.9	2.1	.7	2.6	1.0
8	1.1	2.6	2.6	4.5	.2	.8	.8	1.9	.9	2.1	1.9

Area presently cropped (1,000's of acres)

Region	Winter crops				Summer crops						
	Wheat	Barley	Broad beans	Lentils	Cotton type 1	Cotton type 2	Rice	Corn	Millet	Sesame	Sugar cane
1	201		17		230		216	103			
2	94	10	4				138	76			
3	106		9		143		201	41			
4	8		38			55		42		27	
5	15		76			89		13	133		
6	21	98	8			108		15			
7	30		51	80		58		97			
8	105		13					13	123	6	62

3.32 Solve the air cleaner design problem 2.23.

BIBLIOGRAPHY

Charnes, Abraham, and W. W. Cooper, *Management Models and Industrial Applications of Linear Programming.* New York: John Wiley & Sons, Inc, 1961.

Daellenbach, Hans G., and Earl J. Bell, *User's Guide to Linear Programming.* Englewood Cliffs, N.J.: Prentice-Hall, Inc., 1970.

Dantzig, George B., *Linear Programming and Extensions.* Princeton, N.J.: Princeton University Press, 1963.

Gass, Saul I., *Illustrated Guide to Linear Programming.* New York: McGraw-Hill Book Company, 1970.

Hadley, George, *Linear Programming.* Reading, Mass.: Addison-Wesley Publishing Co., Inc., 1962.

Haley, K. B., *Mathematical Programming for Business and Industry.* New York: St. Martin's Press, Inc., 1967.

Hamilton, William F., et al., *Linear Programming for Management.* Newburyport, Mass.: Entelek, 1969.

Hillier, Frederick, and Gerald J. Lieberman, *Introduction to Operations Research.* San Francisco: Holden-Day, Inc., 1974.

Kwak, No Kyoon, *Mathematical Programming with Business Applications.* New York: McGraw-Hill Book Company, 1973.

Lee, Sang M., *Linear Optimization for Management.* New York: Mason/Charter Publishers, Inc., 1976.

Orchard-Hays, William, *Advanced Linear Programming Computing Techniques.* New York: McGraw-Hill Book Company, 1968.

Stockton, R. Stansbury, *Introduction to Linear Programming.* Homewood, Ill.: Richard D. Irwin, Inc., 1971.

Taha, H. A., *Operations Research: An Introduction.* New York: The Macmillan Company, 1971.

Teichroew, Daniel, *An Introduction to Management Science: Deterministic Models.* New York: John Wiley & Sons, Inc., 1964.

Wagner, Harvey M., *Principles of Management Science with Applications to Executive Decisions.* Englewood Cliffs, N.J.: Prentice-Hall, Inc., 1970.

113

4
Sensitivity Analysis

NATIONAL AIRLINES[1]

In 1973, the world fuel crisis had a drastic effect on the airline industry. Monthly fuel supplies became limited and fuel prices soared from 14 cents to 22 cents per gallon in the 5-month period from December 1973 to May 1974. In June 1974, National Airlines implemented their Fuel Management and Allocation Model, which utilizes linear programming to solve this problem. In its first month of use, the model enabled National to realize an 11.75 percent drop in fuel costs, although the average cost for domestic truck airlines increased by 2.87 percent.

In its first two years of usage, the model enabled National Airlines to save several million dollars. Just as important, it helped minimize the effect of price increases and fluctuating allocation levels as well as to maintain a planned flight schedule.

The LP model itself deals with quantities of fuel that should be purchased from various vendors. Flight schedules consist of a chain of flights or legs that each aircraft must follow. Each city and vendor has a different fuel price structure and quantity discount system. The decision process is complicated by the fact that cheaper fuel loaded to the maximum adds weight to the aircraft, causing more fuel to be burned and possibly even requiring higher-priced fuel to be purchased later in the flight schedule. The LP model contains approximately 2,400 variables and 800 constraints for a flight schedule of 350 flight segments, 50 station/vendor combinations, and multiple aircraft types. CPU time on an IBM 360-65 computer is approximately 15 minutes.

The output from the model consists of four reports: Optimal Fueling Policy Cost Report, Total Vendor Data Report, Station/Vendor Data Report, and Flight Operations Fueling Report. Given fuel purchase decisions, optimal flight altitudes can also be determined to minimize fuel consumption.

With rapidly changing fuel costs and availabilities, it is very important for National Airlines to be able to respond to weekly or monthly changes.

---

[1]D. Wayne Darnell and Carolyn Loflin, "National Airlines Fuel Management and Allocation Model," *Interfaces*, 7 (February 1977), 1–16.

Through the use of sensitivity analysis (to be discussed in this chapter) it is possible for National to immediately evaluate a price or supply change. The analysis determines how much the costs and purchase quantities can vary from their optimal values without affecting the decisions, and at what point a new solution is necessary. In addition, alternative flight schedules can be analyzed quickly to determine the effect on current fuel contracts and allocation levels at each station. Thus, the model not only impacts economically, but helps National to maintain normal schedule operations even with erratic supply changes.

THE NATURE OF SENSITIVITY ANALYSIS

In preceding chapters, we have studied how to model an LP problem and how to calculate an optimal solution by using the simplex method. These two phases, however, generally do not complete an LP analysis; a third phase, called *sensitivity analysis* or *postoptimality analysis,* is usually undertaken. In this chapter we discuss sensitivity analysis and the kinds of questions it allows the decision maker to answer. We look first at an LP model called the *dual problem* to learn what information it can provide concerning the value of our limited resources. Then, we examine some basic procedures in sensitivity analysis and explore the sensitivity of an optimal LP solution to changes in the data or parameters of the model.

sensitivity analysis

If all the parameters for LP models were perfectly accurate or never changed over time, there would be little need for sensitivity analysis. However, the parameters (the c_j, a_{ij}, and b_i) used in real-world LP models are often only estimates. These parameters are often arrived at by means of subjective estimates, limited sampling, or observations subject to human error. Even if the parameters are accurately measured or predicted at a particular time, they may be subject to change. Businesses operate in a dynamic environment, and data pertaining to demand, prices, or resource availability may change significantly in short periods of time. Thus, management and the quantitative decision maker should not consider the original, computer-generated simplex solutions to be final or sacred in any sense. A problem's "optimal" solution is only as accurate as the original data from which it is derived. Thus, it is important to be able to investigate the possible effects on the optimal solution as the various a_{ij}, b_i, and c_j parameters change.

Some LP models may be relatively insensitive to changes in the parameters. In these cases, the original solution may remain optimal even as the parameters are varied over a wide range of values. On the other hand, some models are acutely sensitive to even minor changes in a single parameter. For these models, it is very important to identify the critical parameters so that special care may be taken in estimating their values and investigating their total effect on the optimal solution.

Through the use of sensitivity analysis, new insights can be obtained from the LP model without its having to be re-solved. For example, management may ask, "If the net profit on our deluxe product were to drop 20 percent in the next year, would our current production schedule remain optimal, and, if so, by how much would our total profit change?" Or, a firm may want to know by how much it can reduce the availability of a particular resource before endangering its ability to meet next month's demand. Or, the manager of a product development division might ask, "Given our current limited resources, if we were to introduce a new product, how much must it contribute to profit and overhead in order to make it worthwhile to produce?"

Answers to these questions and many others can be investigated through sensitivity analysis. There are some who claim that there is really no such thing as "the optimal solution." Given limiting assumptions, imperfect data, and the inability to totally anticipate the future, one solution is unlikely to cover all possibilities. What is really needed, they say, is a range of alternatives (with advantages and disadvantages of each alternative), so that management or the decision maker can make a logical choice. Sensitivity analysis can aid in generating alternatives and in planning for responses to unpredictable changes. In this way, sensitivity analysis is a direct tool to aid in flexibility planning. Recall from Chapter 1 that there is a need for management scientists to generate not only models and solutions that are currently effective, but also solutions that are flexible and adaptable to future conditions.

To illustrate the need for sensitivity analysis and flexibility planning, let's return to the National Airlines scenario. Given a pricing structure and fuel allotments, the LP model specifies purchase quantities from each vendor at various locations. What happens if a particular vendor cannot meet the planned allotment? Fuel must be purchased from another vendor at a higher cost. Sensitivity analysis can be used to determine what fueling decision should be made to keep the additional cost at a minimum.

Suppose now that a particular vendor can meet his allotment but raises his price per gallon for fuel. How much can the price vary before the previous fueling decisions are no longer optimal? At National Airlines, sensitivity analysis has proven valuable in day-to-day operations by allowing management to evaluate the effect of price changes and respond immediately.

Management should be aware of the types of question it can pose and reasonably expect to answer through sensitivity analysis. It is more important for you to understand the nature of sensitivity analysis than to be able to work through the calculations of the simplex method in this respect: Once the model is established, the simplex method is completely computerized in real-world applications. Sensitivity analysis, however, is valueless unless you understand what kinds of insight it can yield. With such understanding, you can perceive decision problems in terms of questions sensitivity analysis can answer.

DUALITY

Every LP problem has a counterpart problem called the *dual*. We shall discuss the dual problem and duality primarily as they apply to *shadow prices*, which tell us something about the value of limited resources. But you should be aware that the notion of duality is central to optimization theory, not only for LP but for all mathematical programming. Duality provides the theoretical basis for many sophisticated solution procedures and algorithms for solving special classes of mathematical programming problems. Indeed, duality provides the foundation for sensitivity analysis.

In the next section, you will learn how the dual is formed from the original, or *primal*, LP problem. You will also discover that solving the original LP model yields the optimal solution to the dual problem, and vice versa. Thus, in solving any LP problem, we can solve either the primal or the dual, whichever is computationally easier. (Generally, the problem with fewer constraints is easier to solve.)

THE DUAL PROBLEM

Let us explore the dual problem for an LP problem that has all inequality constraints. Consider the primal problem

$$
\begin{aligned}
&\textit{Primal}\\
&\text{Maximize}\quad 5x_1 + 4x_2 + 9x_3\\
&\text{subject to}\quad 7x_1 + 6x_2 + 3x_3 \le 20\\
&\qquad\qquad\quad\ \ 1x_1 + 4x_2 + 8x_3 \le 15\\
&\qquad\qquad x_1,\ x_2,\ x_3 \ge 0
\end{aligned}
$$

The associated dual is stated

$$
\begin{aligned}
&\textit{Dual}\\
&\text{Minimize}\quad 20y_1 + 15y_2\\
&\text{subject to}\quad 7y_1 + 1y_2 \ge 5\\
&\qquad\qquad\quad\ \ 6y_1 + 4y_2 \ge 4\\
&\qquad\qquad\quad\ \ 3y_1 + 8y_2 \ge 9\\
&\qquad\qquad\quad y_1,\ y_2 \ge 0
\end{aligned}
$$

TABLE 4.1   Relationship between primal and dual coefficients

Primal		Dual
ith primal constraint	$\leftrightarrow$	ith dual variable y_i
Objective function coefficient c_j	$\leftrightarrow$	Right-hand-side coefficient for jth dual constraint

Can you determine how the dual was formed from the primal problem? All the coefficients in the dual are derived from the primal. Actually, the dual constitutes something of a flip-flopped version of the primal. In order to take the dual of a primal problem that has all inequalities in the same direction, we follow these steps:

1. Form the dual objective function from the primal right-hand-side coefficients.

2. Form the ith dual constraint from the ith column of coefficients in the primal constraints.

3. Form the dual right-hand-side coefficients from the primal objective function coefficients.

4. If the primal is a maximization, form the dual as a minimization (and vice versa), and reverse the direction of the inequalities in the constraints.

We associate a dual variable y_i with the ith primal constraint. Thus, the number of variables in the dual problem depends upon the number of primal constraints, not the number of primal variables. The one-to-one correspondence between entries in the dual problem and those in the primal is further illuminated by Table 4.1.

Let us take the dual of the Faze Linear example of previous chapters. Its primal problem is

$$\begin{aligned}
\text{Maximize} \quad & 200x_1 + 500x_2 \\
\text{subject to} \quad & x_2 \leq 40 \quad \text{(transistors)} \\
& 1.2x_1 + 4x_2 \leq 240 \quad \text{(assembly hours)} \\
& .5x_1 + x_2 \leq 81 \quad \text{(inspection hours)} \\
& x_1, x_2 \geq 0
\end{aligned}$$

The dual problem is

$$\begin{aligned}
\text{Minimize} \quad & 40y_1 + 240y_2 + 81y_3 \\
\text{subject to} \quad & 1.2y_2 + .5y_3 \geq 200 \\
& y_1 + 4y_2 + y_3 \geq 500 \\
& y_1, y_2, y_3 \geq 0
\end{aligned}$$

If you understand the economic situations represented by the primal and dual problems, you will better understand the conceptual relationship between the two. Recall that x_1 represents the number of power amps, and x_2 the number of preamps, to produce each day. The y_i variables of the dual represent the marginal value of primal resource i. Thus, y_1 represents the amount by which profit in the primal objective function can be increased per *additional* unit of transistors made available. Likewise, y_2 measures the potential contribution of an additional assembly hour, and y_3 measures the potential contribution of each additional inspection hour. In the primal problem, the objective function maximizes the total contribution to profit. In the dual problem, the objective function minimizes the total marginal value of all resources.

Similarly, a primal constraint insures that the availability of a primal resource is not exceeded, and a dual constraint insures that the marginal value of the required resources for each product must be at least that of the product's profit contribution. For example, in the first dual constraint to the Faze Linear problem, we have $0y_1 + 1.2y_2 + .5y_3 \geq 200$. This constraint specifies that the number of transistors required to produce a power amp (zero) times the marginal value of a transistor (y_1) plus the time required to assemble a power amp (1.2) times the marginal value of assembly hours (y_2) plus the time required to inspect a power amp (.5) times the marginal value of inspection hours (y_3) must be greater than or equal to 200, which is the profit contribution of a power amp. The second dual constraint is interpreted in a similar manner.

SHADOW PRICES

Earlier in the chapter, we stated that it is possible to solve an LP problem in either its primal or dual form. As a matter of fact, an optimal simplex tableau contains the solution to both the primal and its associated dual. To see this, refer to the optimal tableau for the Faze Linear problem that is reconstructed in Tableau 4.1. The optimal primal solution is found in the *Solution* column; the optimal values of x_2, x_1, and s_1 are 28.5, 105, and 11.5, respectively. But where is the optimal dual solution? If you enjoy working puzzles, you may want to explore Tableau 4.1 a bit before reading further.

Recall that there are as many dual variables as there are primal constraints. If there are m primal constraints, we seek m dual variable values. In Tableau 4.1, there are three primal constraints, and we seek the values of the dual variables y_1, y_2, and y_3. You will always find the optimal dual variable values in the $c_j - z_j$ row corresponding to m particular variables. These variables are precisely those m variables that are in solution in the initial tableau. In this example, s_1, s_2, and s_3 were initially in solution.

TABLEAU 4.1 Optimal tableau for Faze Linear problem

c_B	Basic variables	c_j					Solution
		200	500	0	0	0	
		x_1	x_2	s_1	s_2	s_3	
500	x_2	0	1	0	$5/8$	$-3/2$	$28\frac{1}{2}$
200	x_1	1	0	0	$-5/4$	5	105
0	s_1	0	0	1	$-5/8$	$3/2$	$11\frac{1}{2}$
	z_j	200	500	0	$62\frac{1}{2}$	250	35,250
	$c_j - z_j$	0	0	0	$-62\frac{1}{2}$	-250	

negatives of the optimal dual variables y_i
(also called shadow prices)

In order to determine the optimal value of y_1, y_2, and y_3, we simply change the signs of the $c_j - z_j$ values associated with s_1, s_2, and s_3. Thus, $y_1 = 0$, $y_2 = 62.5$, and $y_3 = 250$. You can check the feasibility of these values by substituting them into the dual constraints.

Whenever an artificial variable is in the initial solution, an M coefficient may appear in the $c_j - z_j$ row. For example, suppose that an artificial has a $c_j - z_j$ value of $-1.6 - 3M$ in the final tableau. In order to obtain the optimal dual variable associated with the constraint in which the artificial appears, we simply change the sign and ignore the M coefficient. Thus, the associated dual variable is 1.6. In Chapter 3, Tableau 3.10 contains two artificial variables and depicts the optimal solution to the primal. The associated dual solutions are $y_1 = .75$, $y_2 = 0$, and $y_3 = .25$.

shadow prices The values of the optimal dual variables are quite important; they are called *shadow prices*. At optimality, the *i*th shadow price (y_i) measures the per-unit contribution of the *i*th primal resource to the value of the objective function as long as the current basis remains optimal. The *i*th shadow price y_i is meaningful only so long as changes in the availability of primal resources do not cause some current basic variable to be pivoted out of solution. To illustrate, let us return to Tableau 4.1. We have already found that $y_1 = 0$, $y_2 = 62.5$, and $y_3 = 250$. Thus, an additional unit of assembly time is worth $62.50 to the value of the objective function. The manager, however, must be aware that a shadow price measures gross contribution, not net contribution. The net value of assembly time also has to reflect the cost of procuring that additional hour. Assuming that you were production manager at Faze Linear and that additional assembly and inspection hours cost roughly the same, which department would you choose to expand? Why?

To answer that question knowledgeably, you would require an analysis to determine how much each department could be expanded before the basis would change and the shadow prices become meaningless. Such an investigation is called sensitivity analysis, and it is the topic to which we now turn.

SENSITIVITY ANALYSIS

Now that you have some idea of the kinds of information conveyed by the primal and dual aspects of an LP problem, let us explore how the optimal solution changes with respect to changes in the various parameters of the model. We have already seen how useful shadow prices can be in giving insight into the economic aspects of the LP model. Using sensitivity analysis, we can determine the range over which shadow prices remain valid as well as answer many other meaningful questions.

Specifically, we address three types of basic sensitivity analysis:

1. Right-hand-side ranging
2. Adding a new variable
3. Changes in the objective function coefficients

Other kinds of analysis, which we shall not address in this introductory text, include changes in the constraint coefficients and adding another constraint.

RIGHT-HAND-SIDE RANGING

The objective of *right-hand-side ranging analysis* is to determine how much the right-hand side of a particular constraint can be increased or decreased; thus, we establish the range over which the associated shadow price is valid. The analysis is relatively straightforward if the effect of slack in a constraint is understood.

Consider the constraint $x_1 + x_2 \leq 10$. If we introduce a slack variable s_1, we obtain $x_1 + x_2 + s_1 = 10$. If $s_1 = 0$, then $x_1 + x_2$ must sum to 10. On the other hand, if $s_1 = 2$, then the sum of $x_1 + x_2$ is 8, and, effectively, their sum has been reduced. The point to be made is that introducing positive slack in a constraint is tantamount to decreasing the right-hand side. Likewise, introducing negative slack is equivalent to increasing the right-hand side. [A negative slack $(-s_i)$ variable is one that is subtracted in a constraint equation, whereas a positive slack is added $(+s_i)$.] For example, if $s_1 = 3$ in the equation $x_1 + x_2 - s_1 = 10$, then $x_1 + x_2$ must sum to 13 in the equation. This is equivalent to allowing the right-hand-side 10 to increase. To summarize:

In a constraint equation

increasing positive slack $(+s_i)$ = decreasing the right-hand side by the same amount

increasing negative slack $(-s_i)$ = increasing the right-hand side by the same amount

---

Given the fact that introducing positive or negative slack is equivalent to decreasing or increasing the right-hand side, then right-hand-side ranging for a particular constraint simply boils down to determining the maximum amount of positive and negative slack that can be introduced. To see how to do this, refer to Tableau 4.1, the optimal simplex tableau associated with the Faze Linear problem.

The right-hand side of the second constraint in the original primal model is 240, indicating that 240 hours of assembly time is available. Let us investigate how much the 240 can be decreased before some variable currently basic is pivoted out of the basis. As we have said, this amounts to determining how much positive slack can be brought into the second constraint.

In Tableau 4.1, the second slack s_2 is associated with the second constraint. How much of positive s_2 can be introduced in the second constraint without changing the basis? The maximum amount is easily determined in exactly the same manner that we determined how much of the entering variable could be brought into solution in the simplex procedures of Chapter 3. To do so, we must simply perform the minimum ratio test!

Consider Tableau 4.2, which is a shortened version of Tableau 4.1. The maximum amount of s_2 we can introduce is found by determining the minimum ratio between the entries in the *Solution* column and their associated positive entries in the s_2 column. Since $\frac{5}{8}$ is the only positive entry, the minimum ratio, by default, is $28\frac{1}{2} \div \frac{5}{8} = 45\frac{3}{5}$. Hence, we may

TABLEAU 4.2 Short version of Faze Linear optimal tableau

c_B	Basic variables	Positive slack, s_2	Solution	Minimum ratio	minimum ratio yields
500	x_2	$\frac{5}{8}$	$28\frac{1}{2}$	$28\frac{1}{2} \div \frac{5}{8} = 45.6$	← max RHS
200	x_1	$-\frac{5}{4}$	105	—	decrease
0	s_1	$-\frac{5}{8}$	$11\frac{1}{2}$	—	for positive slack

decrease the right-hand side by a maximum of $45\frac{3}{5}$; any larger decrease causes basic variable x_2 to have a negative value. In terms of the Faze Linear problem, this means that the 240 assembly hours can be reduced to $194\frac{2}{5}$ before the basis changes and the shadow price y_2 becomes invalid.

To determine how much the right-hand-side entry of 240 can be increased, we consider introducing $-s_2$ into the solution (see Tableau 4.3). You should be aware that the variable $-s_2$ is not actually a part of the simplex tableau; it is introduced at this point only as a means of performing right-hand-side ranging. Notice that the signs on the entries in the s_2 column have also been changed. The minimum ratio is clearly $11\frac{1}{2} \div \frac{5}{8} = 18\frac{2}{5}$. Thus, we may increase the right-hand side of 240 by $18\frac{2}{5}$ before the basis changes. In terms of the Faze Linear problem, this means that the assembly hours can be increased to $258\frac{2}{5}$ before s_1 is forced to a negative value.

We have now determined the total range over which the shadow price $y_2 = 62.5$ is valid. As long as the amount of assembly hours is between $194\frac{2}{5}$ and $258\frac{2}{5}$, the y_2, or marginal value of assembly hours, is $62.50 per unit.

We can also perform right-hand-side ranging for the other two constraints in the Faze Linear problem. For the first constraint, the analysis is even simpler. The decrease is determined by $11\frac{1}{2} \div 1 = 11\frac{1}{2}$. The amount of increase is unbounded since no minimum ratio can be formed with nonpositive entries from the s_1 column. This makes sense intuitively, for slack s_1 is already in solution; that is, we already have $11\frac{1}{2}$ transistors left over. It should not affect the current solution no matter how many transistors might be made available; they would only be surplus. For the third constraint, the range or inspection time over which the shadow price remains valid is $73\frac{1}{3}$ to 100. Table 4.2 summarizes our right-hand-side ranging analysis.

TABLEAU 4.3   Tableau with $-s_2$ introduced for right-hand-side ranging

c_B	Basic variables	Negative slack, $-s_2$	Solution	Minimum ratio	minimum ratio yields maximum right-hand-side increase for negative slack
500	x_2	$-\frac{5}{8}$	$28\frac{1}{2}$	—	
200	x_1	$\frac{5}{4}$	105	$105 \div \frac{5}{4} = 84$	
0	s_1	$\frac{5}{8}$	$11\frac{1}{2}$	$11\frac{1}{2} \div \frac{5}{8} = 18.4$ ←	

TABLE 4.2 Analysis of right-hand-side ranging summarized

Resource	Original right-hand-side value	Shadow price	Range Minimum	Range Maximum
Transistors	40	$ 0	$28\frac{1}{2}$	No limit
Assembly time	240	62.50	$194\frac{2}{5}$	$258\frac{2}{5}$
Inspection time	81	250.00	$73\frac{1}{3}$	100

ADDING A NEW VARIABLE

It is not unusual to want to introduce a new variable into an existing LP model. It is very helpful to know whether such a variable (or product) will be active in the solution or what its objective function coefficient must be in order for it to be in solution. Given the new variable's resource requirements, it is possible to determine such information without having to re-solve the problem.

Since the shadow prices give us the marginal value of each scarce resource, we may use them to calculate the opportunity cost of bringing a new variable into solution. That is, we can use the shadow prices to calculate the total value in terms of resources that must be given up in order to bring each unit of the new variable into solution.

Let us return to the Faze Linear example and introduce a new, high-quality digital tuner that is sure to tickle the fancy of many an audiophile. Suppose that, in addition to the power amp (x_1) and the preamp (x_2), the management at Faze Linear is also considering the production of a new tuner (x_3). In terms of the scarce resources, the new tuner would require 1 high-quality transistor, 5 hours of assembly, and 2 hours of inspection. The marketing department forecasts that this tuner should enter the market with a price of approximately $1,500. If markup is 100 percent—that is, profit contribution is $750—should Faze Linear produce this product?

The opportunity cost of producing the tuner can be calculated by multiplying the shadow price of each scarce resource times the amount of the resource required by the production of the tuner. Summing these opportunity costs gives us the amount of profit that must be forfeited in order to produce the tuner. This is equivalent to the z_j we used in the simplex calculations. The analysis is not completed until the c_j, or the amount of profit gained, is also considered.

For the tuner, we have an opportunity cost of

TABLE 4.3 New product analysis

Resource	Shadow price		Amount of resource required		Opportunity cost
Transistors	$ 0	×	1	=	$ 0
Assembly hours	62.5	×	5	=	312.50
Inspection hours	250.0	×	2	=	500.00
Total opportunity cost (z_3)					$812.50

$$z_3 = 0(1) + 62.5(5) + 250(2) = \$812.50$$

If the profit contribution is only $750, then the $c_j - z_j$ for the tuner is

$$c_3 - z_3 = \$750 - \$812.50 = \$-62.50$$

and it should not be produced and sold at this price.

Table 4.3 summarizes the analysis. It is clear from Table 4.3 that if Faze Linear wants to produce the tuner, its profit contribution must be raised from $750 to over $812.50. This could be accomplished by cutting corners on production costs or raising the selling price.

CHANGES IN THE OBJECTIVE FUNCTION COEFFICIENTS

The objective function coefficients (usually profits or costs) may change over time, or they may originally have been rough estimates. In either case, it may be necessary for management to investigate the effects that changes in the objective function coefficients have on the optimal solution. Unlike changes in the right-hand side, changes in the objective function coefficients do not change the values of the basic variables so long as the basis does not change. Thus, changes in the objective function coefficients can only affect the optimality of the current solution and the objective function value itself. Changes in optimality are signaled by the $c_j - z_j$ values.

We will separate this analysis into two parts: first, we deal with nonbasic objective function coefficients; and then, we approach basic objective function coefficients.

Nonbasic objective function coefficient   Such a coefficient is one whose associated decision variable is nonbasic and not in solution. Thus, the decision variable associated with a nonbasic objective function coefficient is automatically zero; and its $c_j - z_j \leq 0$ if we are maximizing or $c_j - z_j \geq 0$ if we are minimizing. This must be true, for otherwise we could pivot the decision variable into solution and improve the objective function value.

Changing a nonbasic objective function coefficient, then, affects the value of the $c_j - z_j$ indicator. The basis does not change unless $c_j - z_j$ becomes greater than zero if maximizing and less than zero if minimizing. The amount that c_j can change is governed by the current $c_j - z_j$ value. Thus, we have the following rules:

---

1. If you are maximizing, you may decrease the value of any non-basic c_j to minus infinity. You may increase c_j up to the value of z_j.

2. If you are minimizing, you may increase the value of any non-basic c_j to infinity. You may decrease c_j down to the value of z_j.

To illustrate these rules, refer again to Tableau 4.1. The only nonbasic variables are s_2 and s_3. Currently, the objective function coefficients of s_2 and s_3 are both zero. Let us denote the objective function coefficients as c_{s2} and c_{s3}, respectively. Then, the first rule specifies that c_{s2} may decrease to $-\infty$ and may increase to 62.5. If c_{s2} were to increase to, say, 63, then its associated $c_j - z_j$ would become $+.5$, and s_2 would be brought into solution, thus changing the current basis. Similarly, we may decrease c_{s3} to $-\infty$ and increase c_{s3} to 250.

Basic objective function coefficient   If we consider changing an objective function coefficient whose associated decision variable is basic, the same principles apply as in the case of a nonbasic. However, changing a basic objective function coefficient can affect the $c_j - z_j$ of all nonbasic variables. Thus, a more lengthy analysis is required when the objective function coefficient is basic. To begin with, let us consider changing the profit contribution of preamps in the Faze Linear example. Presently, the objective function coefficient $c_2 = 500$. Let us denote the change in c_2 by Δ. Incorporating this change into Tableau 4.1, we establish the values of Tableau 4.4.

In Tableau 4.4, notice the new $c_j - z_j$ values for the nonbasic variables s_2 and s_3. These new values are determined by calculating a new z_j value in precisely the same manner that we did in Chapter 3 in the section headed, *The basic steps applied*.

TABLEAU 4.4 Changed preamp profit contribution

		c_j	200	$500 + \Delta$	0	0	0	
c_B	Basic variables		x_1	x_2	s_1	s_2	s_3	Solution
$500 + \Delta$	x_2		0	1	0	$\frac{5}{8}$	$-\frac{3}{2}$	$28\frac{1}{2}$
200	x_1		1	0	0	$-\frac{5}{4}$	5	105
0	s_1		0	0	1	$-\frac{5}{8}$	$\frac{3}{2}$	$11\frac{1}{2}$
	z_j		200	$500 + \Delta$	0	$62\frac{1}{2} + \frac{5}{8}\Delta$	$250 - \frac{3}{2}\Delta$	
	$c_j - z_j$		0	0	0	$-62\frac{1}{2} - \frac{5}{8}\Delta$	$-250 + \frac{3}{2}\Delta$	$35{,}250 + 28\frac{1}{2}\Delta$

this change in the c_B affects the z_j value of all nonbasic variables having a nonzero entry in row 1 of the tableau

The value of Δ may vary so long as no $c_j - z_j$ for a nonbasic variable becomes greater than zero. Thus, we need to solve for Δ such that

$$-62\frac{1}{2} - \frac{5}{8}\Delta \leq 0$$

$$-250 + \frac{3}{2}\Delta \leq 0$$

The first inequality yields $\Delta \geq -100$, and the second one requires that $\Delta \leq 166\frac{2}{3}$. Thus, the allowable range on Δ is $-100 \leq \Delta \leq 166\frac{2}{3}$. The c_2 coefficient that was originally 500 may vary from 400 to $666\frac{2}{3}$ before the basis changes.

If there were many nonbasic variables, the foregoing analysis would become tedious. Fortunately, there is an equivalent shortcut procedure. This procedure refers to the optimal tableau and simply forms ratios between the $c_j - z_j$ row and the tableau entries in the row associated with the current basic variable whose objective function coefficient is being analyzed. Suppose that we are considering changes in a basic objective function coefficient c_j. Let i denote the tableau row in which the associated basic variable x_j appears. Let a_{ij} denote the entries in the tableau. Then for i fixed, we find

Minimum $(c_j - z_j)/a_{ij} > 0$ for the maximum positive change

and

Minimum $|(c_j - z_j)/a_{ij} < 0|$ for the maximum negative change

Thus, in the previous example where we considered changing c_2, we divide the $c_j - z_j$ row by the tableau row in which x_2 (associated with c_2) is the basic variable. Thus, we get

$$\frac{c_j - z_j \text{ row}}{x_2 \text{ row}} = \frac{0 \; 0 \; 0 \quad -62.5 \quad -250}{0 \; 1 \; 0 \quad \frac{5}{8} \quad -\frac{3}{2}}$$

We ignore any fractions with a zero in the numerator or the denominator. We have only one fraction > 0, so that the maximum positive change is

$$\frac{-250}{-3/2} = 166\tfrac{2}{3}$$

We have only one negative fraction, so that the maximum negative change is

$$\left|\frac{-62.5}{5/8}\right| = \left|-100\right| = 100$$

Note that if there were more than one positive or negative fraction, we would have to choose the minimum value among the positive fractions for the maximum positive change, and the minimum absolute value among the negative fractions for the maximum negative change.

In Table 4.4, this analysis, together with an analysis on basic objective function coefficient c_1, is summarized. When you are sure you understand the analysis for c_2, work through the analysis for $c_1 = 200$ to see if your results agree with those in Table 4.4.

In the special case of alternative optima, the shortcut method needs to be slightly modified. Under conditions of alternative optima, some nonbasic variable, say variable r, has a zero $c_j - z_j$ value. If its associated $a_{ir} > 0$ then the maximum negative (positive) change for the basic objective function coefficient in question is zero when maximizing (minimizing). On the other hand, if $a_{ir} < 0$, then the maximum positive (negative) change is zero when maximizing (minimizing). Remaining upper and lower limits are calculated as in Table 4.4.

TABLE 4.4   Sensitivity analysis for basic objective function coefficients*

	Basic variables	
	Power amps, x_1	Preamps, x_2
Tableau row i	2	1
Original c_j	200	500
Minimum $(c_j - z_j)/a_{ij} > 0$	50	$166\tfrac{2}{3}$
Upper limit for c_j	250	$666\tfrac{2}{3}$
Minimum $|(c_j - z_j)/a_{ij} < 0|$	50	100
Lower limit for c_j	150	400
Range for c_j	150 to 250	400 to $666\tfrac{2}{3}$

*This shortcut method is not necessarily valid for the special case of alternative optima. (See explanation in the above paragraph.)

INTERPRETATION OF COMPUTER OUTPUT

The types of sensitivity analysis that we have discussed (with the exception of adding a new variable) are often standard LP computer code output, or at least a report option. In order to illustrate the interpretation of sensitivity analysis output, let us look again at the computer output for the Faze Linear product mix problem. Table 4.5 shows the computer solution and sensitivity analysis output.

TABLE 4.5   Computer sensitivity analysis for Faze Linear problem

```
FAZE LINEAR PROBLEM

   THE ORIGINAL COEFFICIENTS OF THE CONSTRAINTS
            CODE 0 ==> <OR= CONSTRAINT
             CODE 1 ==> >OR= CONSTRAINT
              CODE 2 ==>   = CONSTRAINT

   CODE CONSTANT  A(I,1)  A(I,2)
 1   0    40.00    .00    1.00
 2   0   240.00   1.20    4.00
 3   0    81.00    .50    1.00

   THE COEFFICIENTS IN THE ORIGINAL OBJECTIVE FUNCTION TO BE MAXIMIZED ARE:
             200.00   500.00

   OPTION SELECTED == PRINT SENSITIVITY ANALYSIS

   BASIC SOLUTION   4
    X( 2)=    28.499969
    X( 1)=   105.000061
    S( 1)=    11.500018

   CURRENT VALUE OF OBJECTIVE FUNCTION IS     35250.00

        THE LAST BASIC FEASIBLE SOLUTION IS OPTIMAL
        OPTIMAL VALUE OF THE ORIGINAL OBJECTIVE FUNCTION IS      35250.00
   CONSTRAINT      SHADOW PRICE
        1               .0000
        2             62.5000
        3            249.9999
                        FAZE LINEAR PROBLEM
                    *** SENSITIVITY ANALYSIS ***

                    OBJECTIVE FUNCTION RANGING
                                                              * RANGE *
   VARIABLE      DECREASE       INCREASE            MINIMUM            MAXIMUM
    X( 1)        50.0000        50.0000            150.0000           250.0000
    X( 2)        99.9999       166.6665            400.0000           666.6663

                    RIGHT HAND SIDE RANGING
                                                              * RANGE *
   CONSTRAINT    DECREASE       INCREASE            MINIMUM            MAXIMUM



        1        11.5000       NO LIMIT             28.5000           NO LIMIT
        2        45.5999        18.4000            194.4001          258.3999
        3         7.6667        19.0000             73.3333          100.0000
```

130

Constraint	Sensitivity of right-hand-side coefficients		
	Maximum decrease	Maximum increase	Range
1	11.5	Infinite	28.5 to infinity
2	45.6	18.4	194.4 to 258.4
3	7.67	19.0	73.33 to 100

The shadow prices can be determined by observing the numbers printed under the heading SHADOW PRICE. Notice that there is a shadow price associated with each constraint.

The right-hand-side ranging analysis for each constraint is located at the bottom of Table 4.5. The range specified indicates the range over which the right-hand-side coefficient can vary (while holding all others constant) without changing the basic variables, that is, without causing the current solution to be infeasible.

The analysis of changes in the objective function coefficients is shown near the middle of the output. Here the MINIMUM and MAXIMUM values determine the range over which each c_j can vary without changing the basic variables. This analysis is performed only for the decision variables, x_j, and not the slack variables.

Even though the output does not include the analysis of adding a new variable, it does provide the shadow prices, thereby enabling the user to easily analyze the addition of a new variable by hand calculations.

SUMMARY

In this chapter, we have examined the closely related topics of the dual problem and sensitivity analysis. In more advanced topics, duality plays a very important role in the development of optimization techniques. We studied the dual problem primarily as a means for understanding shadow prices better. Shadow prices provide valuable information about the marginal value of scarce resources.

Sensitivity analysis allows us to determine the range over which these shadow prices are valid. A sensitivity analysis can actually be more useful to management than the optimal LP solution itself. It can help management make better decisions regarding such problems as capacity expansion, adding new products, changes in resource availabilities, and price fluctuations. In general, it is a technique that helps management to better relate the economics of the firm to the LP model being analyzed.

In right-hand-side ranging, we determined the range over which a right-hand side can be varied without causing the basis to change. In adding a new variable, we determined whether the variable is worthwhile to introduce to the solution or what its objective function must be in order to make it worthwhile. The final kind of sensitivity analysis involved a ranging analysis on the objective function coefficients. In two separate procedures, we determined the range over which nonbasic and basic objective function coefficients can change before the basis changes.

Right-hand-side ranging and objective coefficient analysis are often times standard output of available LP computer codes. The addition of a new product, however, generally requires individual analysis.

SOLVED PROBLEMS

PROBLEM STATEMENT

The Faze Linear Company abandoned the idea of producing an expensive state of the art digital tuner, but decided to produce a high-quality and more reasonably priced tuner which sells for $795. The profit contribution of this tuner is $400. The manufacture of this tuner requires no special high-quality transistors, but requires 2 hours of assembly and 1 hour of inspection. In order to determine an optimal product mix, Faze Linear reformulated their model as follows:

$$\text{Maximize} \quad 200x_1 + 500x_2 + 400x_3$$
$$\text{subject to} \quad x_2 \leq 40$$
$$1.2x_1 + 4x_2 + 2x_3 \leq 240$$
$$.5x_1 + 1x_2 + 1x_3 \leq 81$$
$$x_1, x_2, x_3 \geq 0$$

where x_1, x_2, and x_3 represent the numbers of amps, preamps, and tuners to be produced, respectively.

Solving the model yields the following optimal tableau:

	c_j	200	500	400	0	0	0	
c_B	Basic variables	x_1	x_2	x_3	s_1	s_2	s_3	Solution
500	x_2	$1/10$	1	0	0	$1/2$	-1	39
400	x_3	$2/5$	0	1	0	$-1/2$	2	42
0	s_1	$-1/10$	0	0	1	$-1/2$	1	1
	z_j	210	500	400	0	50	300	36,300
	$c_j - z_j$	-10	0	0	0	-50	-300	

a. What is the new solution and its profit?

b. Which resources are fully utilized?

c. How much would the profit contribution of amplifiers have to increase before they would be produced?

d. The management at Faze Linear is concerned about the availability of the special high-quality transistors. How much could the availability of transistors change before the current product mix is no longer optimal?

e. Determine the new product mix if the number of inspection hours decreases from 81 to 80.

SOLUTION

a. The new solution is to produce 39 preamps and 42 tuners per day for a profit contribution of $36,300. It is no longer profitable to produce the amplifiers.

b. Resources 2 and 3, or the assembly and inspection time. This is evident by the fact that only slack s_1 (transistors) is in solution at a positive value (therefore having excess or underutilized resources).

c. Currently, the $c_1 - z_1$ value of amplifiers (x_1) is -10. Therefore, the profit contribution of amplifiers would have to increase by more than $10 to be profitable to produce.

d. Transistor availability comprises the first constraint. Slack s_1 is associated with the first constraint; thus consider the s_1 column and the solution column:

s_1	Solution	Minimum ratio	$-s_1$	Solution	Minimum ratio
0	39	—	0	39	—
0	42	—	0	42	—
1	1	1	−1	1	—

Forming the minimum ratio with the positive slack s_1 yields a value of 1. Thus, the 40 available transistors can decrease to 39 without changing the basic variables. Changing the sign of s_1 and its column creates a column of zero and negative numbers. The minimum ratio cannot be calculated as the amount of $-s_1$ that could be brought into solution is unbounded. No amount of extra transistors will affect the solution. The range for transistors is 39 to ∞.

e. The long way to solve this part would be to solve the entire problem from scratch. However, by using the definition of the substitution coefficients, we can easily determine the new solution. Consider the slack s_3 associated with inspection hours. Since s_3 is a positive slack, bringing it into solution is equivalent to decreasing the right-hand side. Consider the s_3 column and the solution column:

s_3	Solution	New solution
-1	39	$39 - (-1)1 = 40$
2	42	$42 - 2(1) = 40$
1	1	$1 - 1(1) = 0$

The substitution coefficients in the s_3 column tell us how much of the solution value for each basic variable we must sacrifice for each unit of s_3 brought into solution. Thus, the new solution is $x_2 = 40$, $x_3 = 40$, and $s_1 = 0$.

PROBLEM STATEMENT

The management of the Faze Linear Company in the previous problem would like to systematically explore other questions and options in their product mix problem. However, they prefer the convenience of a computer output and its various reports. Listed below is the computer solution and sensitivity analysis of the new product mix problem of the previous problem.

a. What are the shadow prices?

b. The management at Faze Linear has earmarked some funds for capital expansion. Which of the three resources in the LP model are recommended for expansion?

c. They are also considering the marketing of a new graphic equalizer. This unit would require no special transistors and 1 hour each of assembly and inspection. It would contribute $320 to profit. Should it be produced?

d. In order to meet the price cuts of competition, Faze Linear may have to drop the prices on their preamp and tuner. How much could each of these profit contributions decrease (holding all other prices fixed) before the current product mix is no longer optimal?

e. The right-hand-side ranging analysis suggests that the allowable range on inspection time is 80 to 120 hours per day. What does this mean? That is, what if labor shortages reduced the total number of inspection hours per day to less than 80?

```
EXPANDED FAZE LINEAR PROBLEM

    THE ORIGINAL COEFFICIENTS OF THE CONSTRAINTS
              CODE 0 ==> <OR= CONSTRAINT
              CODE 1 ==> >OR= CONSTRAINT
              CODE 2 ==>   =  CONSTRAINT

    CODE CONSTANT  A(I,1)  A(I,2)  A(I,3)
  1   0    40.00    .00   1.00    .00
  2   0   240.00   1.20   4.00   2.00
  3   0    81.00    .50   1.00   1.00

    THE COEFFICIENTS IN THE ORIGINAL OBJECTIVE FUNCTION TO BE MAXIMIZED ARE:
              200.00   500.00   400.00

    OPTION SELECTED == PRINT SENSITIVITY ANALYSIS


    BASIC SOLUTION   4
      X( 2)=     39.000000
      X( 3)=     42.000000
      S( 1)=      1.000000

    CURRENT VALUE OF OBJECTIVE FUNCTION IS     36300.00

      THE LAST BASIC FEASIBLE SOLUTION IS OPTIMAL
        OPTIMAL VALUE OF THE ORIGINAL OBJECTIVE FUNCTION IS      36300.00
    CONSTRAINT     SHADOW PRICE
         1            .0000
         2          50.0000
         3         300.0000


                    EXPANDED FAZE LINEAR PROBLEM
                  *** SENSITIVITY ANALYSIS ***

                  OBJECTIVE FUNCTION RANGING

                                                  * RANGE *
    VARIABLE     DECREASE      INCREASE      MINIMUM        MAXIMUM

    X( 1)      NO LIMIT      10.0000      NO LIMIT      210.0000
    X( 2)       99.9999     300.0000      400.0000      800.0000
    X( 3)       25.0000     100.0000      375.0000      500.0000


                  RIGHT HAND SIDE RANGING

                                                  * RANGE *
    CONSTRAINT   DECREASE      INCREASE      MINIMUM        MAXIMUM

       1          1.0000      NO LIMIT      39.0000      NO LIMIT
       2         78.0000       2.0000      162.0000      242.0000
       3          1.0000      39.0000      80.0000      120.0000
```

SOLUTION

a. The shadow prices may be found under the heading SHADOW PRICE. The first slack s_1 (transistors) is basic, so that the associated dual variable $y_1 = 0$. The slacks s_2 (assembly) and s_3 (inspection) have shadow prices of 50 and 300, respectively.

b. As seen by the shadow prices in part a, the marginal value of inspection time is highest (300), followed by assembly time (50). Since there are surplus transistors, their marginal value is 0. Therefore, the in-spection hours should first be considered for expansion, followed by assembly hours.

c. The equalizer should be produced only if its profit contribution ex-ceeds the value of the current production it would replace. In calcu-lating its $c_j - z_j$ value, we first determine its z_j value by multiplying its resource requirements times their marginal values at optimality.

$$
\begin{array}{lr}
\text{transistors} & 0 \times 0 \\
\text{assembly} & 1 \times 50 \\
\text{inspection} & \underline{1 \times 300} \\
& z_4 = \$350
\end{array}
$$

Thus, $c_4 - z_4 = \$320 - \$350 = -\$30$ and the equalizer should not be produced at a profit contribution of only $320.

d. Looking at the sensitivity of the objective function coefficients, we see that the profit contribution of preamps can decrease to $400 and the profit contribution of tuners can decrease to $375 before the cur-rent basic variables would no longer be optimal and some nonbasic variable would enter the solution, replacing a basic variable and changing the product mix.

e. If the number of inspection hours drops below 80, the current three basic variables can no longer be used to comprise a feasible solution to the product mix problem. The three variables could be used to solve the constraint equations, but at least one of the basic variables would assume a negative value (infeasible). This does not mean, how-ever, that the problem has no solution; it just means that some other combination of variables and a different product mix must be used to provide a solution that is meaningful.

REVIEW QUESTIONS

1. What is a shadow price?
2. Explain why a shadow price is valid only for a specified range of values of the right-hand side.
3. If a primal LP model has m constraints and n variables, how many constraints and variables will its dual have?
4. In what ways can sensitivity analysis be more valuable to manage-ment than the optimal solution alone?
5. For any nonbasic variable in an optimal LP solution, how much would its objective function coefficient have to change in order for it to enter the solution?

6. Explain whether each kind of change in a, b, and c, below, **prior to** a change of basis can affect (1) solution, (2) solution value, (3) $c_j - z_j$ values, or (4) other entries in the tableau.

   a. Changes in the right-hand side

   b. Changes in the objective function coefficients

   c. Adding a new variable

PROBLEMS

4.1 Formulate the dual problem for the following linear programming model.

$$\text{Maximize} \quad 16x_1 + 10x_2 + 9x_3$$
$$\text{subject to} \quad 3x_1 - 4x_2 + 8x_3 \leq 52$$
$$14x_1 + 7x_2 + 4x_3 \leq 40$$
$$x_1, x_2, x_3 \geq 0$$

4.2 The LP problem following is the dual to a problem. Find the primal problem to which it corresponds.

$$\text{Minimize} \quad 3x_1 + x_2 + 5x_3$$
$$\text{subject to} \quad x_1 + x_2 + x_3 \geq 40$$
$$2x_1 + 3x_2 \qquad \geq 50$$
$$3x_1 + 2x_2 + 4x_3 \geq 20$$
$$x_1, x_2, x_3 \geq 0$$

4.3 Given the primal problem

$$\text{Minimize} \quad 15x_1 + 40x_2$$
$$\text{subject to} \qquad x_1 \geq 13$$
$$x_2 \geq 10$$
$$3x_1 + 4x_2 \geq 15$$
$$-5x_1 + 17x_2 \geq 19$$
$$x_1, x_2 \geq 0$$

From a computational point of view, would you rather solve this primal or its associated dual? Why?

4.4 You are given the following product mix problem:

$$\text{Maximize} \quad 4x_1 + 5x_2$$
$$\text{subject to} \quad x_1 + 2x_2 \leq 8 \quad \text{(machine } A \text{ hours)}$$
$$3x_1 + 2x_2 \leq 12 \quad \text{(machine } B \text{ hours)}$$
$$x_1, x_2 \geq 0$$

    a. Write the dual of this problem.

    b. Solve the primal and the dual.

    c. Interpret the primal and the dual.

4.5 Solve Problem 4.4 (primal) graphically.

    a. Show the new solution when the objective function changes to max $2x_1 + 5x_2$.

    b. Show the new feasible region when the right-hand side changes from (8, 12) to (6, 8).

    c. Describe verbally what happens to the feasible region when an additional variable x_3 is added to the model.

4.6 Solve the following primal problem graphically, and solve its associated dual by inspection.

$$\text{Maximize} \quad 4x_1 + 8x_2$$
$$\text{subject to} \quad 8x_1 + 4x_2 \le 8$$
$$x_1, x_2 \ge 0$$

4.7 Consider the model below that corresponds to a manufacturing problem with two products and three resources.

$$\text{Maximize} \quad 3x_1 + 8x_2$$
$$\text{subject to} \quad 2x_1 + 4x_2 \le 1000 \quad \text{(resource 1)}$$
$$6x_1 + 2x_2 \le 1200 \quad \text{(resource 2)}$$
$$x_2 \le 200 \quad \text{(resource 3)}$$
$$x_1, x_2 \ge 0$$

The optimal simplex tableau is

c_B	c_j Basic variables	3 x_1	8 x_2	0 s_1	0 s_2	0 s_3	Solution
3	x_1	1	0	$1/2$	0	-2	100
0	s_2	0	0	-3	1	10	200
8	x_2	0	1	0	0	1	200
	z_j	3	8	$3/2$	0	2	1900
	$c_j - z_j$	0	0	$-3/2$	0	-2	

    a. What is the optimal solution?

    b. What are the shadow prices?

    c. Which resource has the highest marginal value at optimality?

    d. Over what ranges in each of the right-hand-side constants are these shadow prices valid?

4.8 In Problem 4.7:

    a. Formulate the dual problem from the stated primal.

    b. Obtain the optimal dual solution from the optimal primal tableau.

    c. Compare the values of the optimal primal and dual objective functions.

4.9 Refer again to Problem 4.7.

    a. Determine the permissible ranges over which the objective function coefficients can vary for variables s_1 and s_3.

    b. Repeat part a for variables x_1, s_2, and x_2.

    c. Consider the addition of a new variable x_3. This variable will require 2 units of each of the three resources. What must x_3's minimal profit contribution be in order for it to be profitable to produce?

4.10 The following primal problem has two variables and three constraints. Solve it indirectly by solving the dual problem by the simplex method.

$$\begin{aligned}
\text{Maximize} \quad & 2x_1 + x_2 \\
\text{subject to} \quad & x_2 \le 10 \\
& 2x_1 + 5x_2 \le 60 \\
& 2x_1 + 2x_2 \le 18 \\
& x_1, x_2 \ge 0
\end{aligned}$$

4.11 The optimal simplex tableau for a maximization problem with all $\le$ constraints is as shown.

	c_j	4	2	0	0	0	
c_B	Basic variables	x_1	x_2	s_1	s_2	s_3	Solution
2	x_2	0	1	1	-1	0	4
4	x_1	1	0	$-\tfrac{1}{4}$	$\tfrac{3}{4}$	0	3
0	s_3	0	0	2	-4	1	8
	$c_j - z_j$	0	0	-1	-1	0	20

    a. Which of the three resources are being fully utilized?

    b. Suppose that the resources could be obtained at no cost. Which right-hand side would you recommend for expansion, and why?

    c. How much can each right-hand-side coefficient be increased before the basis changes?

4.12 Refer to the optimal tableau in Problem 4.11.

    a. How many variables are contained in the dual of this problem?

    b. What are the optimum dual variable values?

    c. How much can each right-hand-side coefficient be decreased before the basis changes?

    d. Without reworking the problem, predict the new objective function value and solution values for x_2, x_1, and s_3 when the first right-hand-side coefficient is increased by 6. *Hint:* Use the column of substitution coefficients under s_1.

4.13 Try to give an economic interpretation of the dual to the example concerning production distribution in Chapter 2.

4.14 Consider the diet problem example in Chapter 2. Try to give a possible economic interpretation of its dual. *Hint:* The dual variables can be thought of as values or "prices" associated with each nutrient.

4.15 Below you will find the optimal tableau of the diet problem example in Chapter 2.

c_j		1.60	1.00	.65	.30	0	0	0	0	M	M	M	M	
c_B	Basic variables	x_1	x_2	x_3	x_4	s_1	s_2	s_3	s_4	A_1	A_2	A_3	A_4	Solution
1.60	x_1	1	0	0	0	0	0	−.0018	0	0	0	.0018	0	.740
0	s_1	0	−237	0	0	1	−47.89	23.62	0	−1	47.89	−23.62	0	28200.48
.30	x_4	0	0	0	1	0	−.014	.0010	0	0	.014	−.001	0	.639
0	s_4	0	−7	−13	0	0	−.112	−.0435	1	0	.112	.0435	−1	13.851
$c_j - z_j$		0	1.00	.65	0	0	.0042	.0026	0	M	M − .0042	M − .0026	M	$1.39

    a. What is the optimal solution? Is it palatable to you? How much does it cost to feed each individual on a daily basis? Do you think the constraints covered everything that should be considered in a daily diet?

    b. Which nutritional requirements are being met exactly? Which nutrients are being given in overdoses?

c. Determine the range over which the vitamin C requirement can vary before the basis changes.

d. For all four foods, determine the range over which their prices can vary without changing the basis.

4.16 Listed below is the formulation and optimal computer solution to the Ace Manufacturing Company of Problem 2.1. Let

$$x_1 = \text{units of regular produced}$$
$$x_2 = \text{units of super produced}$$

Maximize $50x_1 + 75x_2$
subject to $1.2x_1 + 1.6x_2 \leq 1600$ assembly
$.8x_1 + .9x_2 \leq 700$ paint
$.2x_1 + .2x_2 \leq 300$ inspection
$x_1 \geq 150$ regular demand
$x_2 \geq 90$ super demand

```
ACE MANUFACTURING COMPANY

    THE ORIGINAL COEFFICIENTS OF THE CONSTRAINTS
         CODE 0 ==> <OR= CONSTRAINT
           CODE 1 ==> >OR= CONSTRAINT
             CODE 2 ==>   =  CONSTRAINT

   CODE CONSTANT  A(I,1)   A(I,2)
 1   0   1600.00   1.20     1.60
 2   0    700.00    .80      .90
 3   0    300.00    .20      .20
 4   1    150.00   1.00      .00
 5   1     90.00    .00     1.00

   THE COEFFICIENTS IN THE ORIGINAL OBJECTIVE FUNCTION TO BE MAXIMIZED ARE:
                      50.00    75.00

   OPTION SELECTED -- PRINT SENSITIVITY ANALYSIS

   BASIC SOLUTION   4
       S( 1)=    388.888672
       S( 5)=    554.444336
       S( 3)=    141.111160
       X( 1)=    150.000000
       X( 2)=    644.444336

   CURRENT VALUE OF OBJECTIVE FUNCTION IS      55833.32

       THE LAST BASIC FEASIBLE SOLUTION IS OPTIMAL
         OPTIMAL VALUE OF THE ORIGINAL OBJECTIVE FUNCTION IS      55833.32
   CONSTRAINT     SHADOW PRICE
         1            .0000
         2          83.3333
         3            .0000
         4         -16.6667
         5            .0000
```

OBJECTIVE FUNCTION RANGING

VARIABLE	DECREASE	INCREASE	* RANGE * MINIMUM	MAXIMUM
X(1)	NO LIMIT	16·6667	NO LIMIT	66·6667
X(2)	18·7500	NO LIMIT	56·2500	NO LIMIT

RIGHT HAND SIDE RANGING

CONSTRAINT	DECREASE	INCREASE	* RANGE * MINIMUM	MAXIMUM
1	388·8887	NO LIMIT	1211·1113	NO LIMIT
2	499·0000	218·7500	201·0000	918·7500
3	141·1112	NO LIMIT	158·8888	NO LIMIT
4	150·0000	623·7498	·0000	773·7498
5	NO LIMIT	554·4443	NO LIMIT	644·4443

a. What is the marginal value of the right-hand-side coefficient of the regular demand (fourth) constraint? Remember that this is a $\geq$ constraint!

b. Ace Manufacturing is faced with declining profit contribution in the face of inflation and would like to know the effect of declining profit on the optimal product mix. From the computer printout, determine the range over which the profit contributions of the regular and super products can vary before the current product mix is no longer optimal.

c. Over what range can each of the right-hand-side coefficients vary while maintaining the optimality of the current product mix?

d. Ace Manufacturing is considering the release of a regular demand contract for 50 units in order to produce more super product. How much should they be willing to pay to break the contract?

4.17 Consider the 2 × 2 example in Problem 4.4. Find three feasible solutions for the primal problem and three feasible solutions for the dual problem. Plug these feasible solutions into their respective objective functions and observe their respective solution values. Are the values of the objective function of the maximization problem (this is often called the *max* objective function) always less than or equal to those of the minimization (the *min*)? Observe their two optimal values.

dual theorem   A fundamental result in duality theory is the *dual theorem*. It states that if both the primal and dual are feasible, then the solution value of any feasible solution of the max problem is always less than or equal to any feasible solution of the min problem. Furthermore, the optimal solution values of the two problems are equal.

complemen- **4.18**   Another fundamental property in duality theory is called *comple-*
tary slackness   *mentary slackness.* Basically, this is a statement of the fact that if a constraint in an LP problem is not tight, its associated shadow price must be zero. A constraint is tight if the solution variable values equal the right-hand side when they are substituted into the constraint. Thus, a nontight constraint is simply one in which some slack exists. Consider the optimal solution to the Faze Linear problem (Tableau 4.1). Which constraints are tight? Which shadow prices are zero?

Complementary slackness is intuitively reasonable, for if a constraint is not tight, some of the associated resource is left over and should have a marginal value (shadow price) of zero.

4.19   Refer to Tableau 3.10, which is the optimal tableau for the minimization problem solved in Chapter 3.

a.   What are the shadow prices?

b.   What is the new minimum cost if the cost per gallon of crude oil B is dropped by $.02?

c.   How much can the right-hand-side restriction of 20 on crude oil A change before the basis changes?

d.   Over what range can the cost for crude oil A vary without changing the basis?

4.20   Refer to the simplex solution of Solved Problem 2 at the end of Chapter 3.

a.   Perform a sensitivity analysis for both right-hand-side coefficients

b.   State the value of the shadow prices.

c.   Perform a sensitivity analysis on the objective function coefficients of s_1, x_1, and x_2.

4.21   *Product Mix.* The Southeastern Textile Mill produces four different styles of cotton cloth. The four basic materials are a bleached style, a printed style, and two dyed styles, red and blue. The profit contributions of these four products are $.80, $1.20, $1.50, and $1.60 per square yard, respectively. The company is committed to produce at least 6,000 square yards of the printed style for next week. The maximum possible sales for the bleached style is 100,000 square yards.

Southeastern's production involves five basic processes. These processes and their available capacity in millions of process hours are: desizing, 15; bleaching, 150; printing, 180; dyeing, 15; and calendering, 45. The resource requirements of each of the four products are stipulated in Southeastern's LP model. Let

x_1 = number of square yards of bleached material produced
x_2 = number of square yards of printed material produced
x_3 = number of square yards of red dyed material produced
x_4 = number of square yards of blue dyed material produced

$$
\begin{aligned}
\text{Maximize} \quad & .80x_1 + 1.20x_2 + 1.50x_3 + 1.60x_4 \\
\text{subject to} \quad & 7.7x_1 + 11.1x_2 + 7.7x_3 + 8.3x_4 \le 15{,}000{,}000 \\
& 100.x_1 + 95.x_2 + 91.x_3 + 83.x_4 \le 150{,}000{,}000 \\
& 33.x_2 \le 180{,}000{,}000 \\
& 2.5x_3 + 2.9x_4 \le 15{,}000{,}000 \\
& 2.5x_1 + 3.3x_2 + 3.1x_3 + 2.9x_4 \le 45{,}000{,}000 \\
& x_1 \le 100{,}000 \\
& x_2 \ge 6{,}000 \\
& x_1, x_2, x_3, x_4 \ge 0
\end{aligned}
$$

After adding the required slack and artificial variables, the optimal simplex tableau is as presented on the opposite page.

a. What is the optimal solution and the total profit?

b. Is the solution degenerate? Are there alternative optima?

c. Which of the five departments appears to be most promising in terms of expansion? What else would you have to take into consideration?

d. What is the incremental profit associated with adding one more process hour of bleaching capacity? Over what range is this valid?

e. Consider another new printed style x_5 which requires 9.1 hours of printing and 4.0 hours of calendering. What does its profit contribution have to be in order for it to be profitably produced?

f. Suppose that an additional 10 hours of bleaching capacity is made available. What are the new values for x_1, x_2, x_3, and x_4? *Hint:* Use the appropriate substitution coefficients in the optimal tableau.

c_B	Basic variables	x_1	x_2	x_3	x_4	s_7	s_1	s_2	s_3	s_4	s_5	s_6	A_7	Solution
c_j		.80	1.20	1.50	1.60	0	0	0	0	0	0	0	$-M$	
1.60	x_4	−.60	0	0	1	2.38	.78	−.06	0	0	0	0	−2.38	1,792,837
1.50	x_3	1.64	0	1	0	−1.14	−.71	.07	0	0	0	0	1.14	6,862
0	s_3	0	0	0	0	33.00	0	0	1	0	0	0	−33.00	179,802,000
0	s_4	−2.38	0	0	0	−4.10	−.48	.01	0	1	0	0	4.10	9,783,616
0	s_5	−.86	0	0	0	−.11	−.06	−.03	0	0	1	0	.11	39,759,680
0	s_6	1	0	0	0	0	0	0	0	0	0	1	0	100,000
1.20	x_2	0	1	0	0	−1	0	0	0	0	0	0	1	6,000
$c_j - z_j$		−.71	0	0	0	−.92	−.18	−.001	0	0	0	0	$-M + .92$	2,886,032

4.22 Refer to the portfolio selection problem in the Solved Problem section at the end of Chapter 2. The United Credit Union has done an LP analysis of their model and have the following LP computer output with sensitivity analysis.

```
UNITED CREDIT UNION PORTFOLIO SELECTION PROBLEM

   THE ORIGINAL COEFFICIENTS OF THE CONSTRAINTS
         CODE 0 ==> <OR= CONSTRAINT
           CODE 1 ==> >OR= CONSTRAINT
             CODE 2 ==>  =  CONSTRAINT

   CODE CONSTANT  A(I,1)  A(I,2)  A(I,3)  A(I,4)  A(I,5)
  1   0 1500000.00    .20     .00    6.00    4.50    5.00
  2   1  100000.00   1.00    1.00     .00     .00     .00
  3   1       .00    .00    -.30     .70     .00     .00
  4   0  250000.00    .00     .00     .00    1.00     .00
  5   0  500000.00   1.00    1.00    1.00    1.00    1.00

   THE COEFFICIENTS IN THE ORIGINAL OBJECTIVE FUNCTION TO BE MAXIMIZED ARE:
             .075    .065    .119    .088    .100

   OPTION SELECTED == PRINT SENSITIVITY ANALYSIS

   BASIC SOLUTION    5

      X( 3)= 44027.250000
      X( 1)= 79181.000000
      X( 2)= 76791.812500
      S( 4)= 50000.000000
      S( 2)= 55972.812500

   CURRENT VALUE OF OBJECTIVE FUNCTION IS      47469.28

      THE LAST BASIC FEASIBLE SOLUTION IS OPTIMAL
        OPTIMAL VALUE OF THE ORIGINAL OBJECTIVE FUNCTION IS      47469.28
   CONSTRAINT    SHADOW PRICE
         1          .0080
         2          .0000
         3          .0084
         4          .0000
         5          .0709
```

*** SENSITIVITY ANALYSIS ***

OBJECTIVE FUNCTION RANGING

VARIABLE	DECREASE	INCREASE	* RANGE * MINIMUM	MAXIMUM
X(1)	.0082	.0671	.0668	.1421
X(2)	.2145	.0085	-.1495	.0735
X(3)	.0132	.2460	.1058	.3650
X(4)	NO LIMIT	.0190	NO LIMIT	.1070
X(5)	NO LIMIT	.0110	NO LIMIT	.1110

RIGHT HAND SIDE RANGING

CONSTRAINT	DECREASE	INCREASE	* RANGE * MINIMUM	MAXIMUM
1	.0000	914001.0000	1500000.0000	2414001.0000
2	NO LIMIT	155972.8125	NO LIMIT	255972.8125
3	77586.2500	175000.1250	-77586.2500	175000.1250
4	250000.0000	NO LIMIT	.0000	NO LIMIT
4	NO LIMIT	999999.0000	NO LIMIT	999999.0000
5	152333.4375	.0000	347666.5625	500000.0000

a. What is the composition of their optimal portfolio?

b. What is the average rate of return on their portfolio?

c. What is the marginal value of their capital?

d. Over what range can the rate of return for each investment vary without changing the optimal basis?

e. Over what range can the available capital vary without affecting the optimal basis?

4.23 Refer to the Akron Tire Co. (Problem 2.22). Solve this rather large problem (48 variables and 18 constraints) with an LP computer code that has a sensitivity analysis output report in order to answer the following questions.

a. During which months and which shifts is the marginal value of vulcanizing time the highest?

b. In the month of October, over what range can the cost of steel-belted radials and glass-belted tires vary before the production schedule is no longer optimal?

c. Suppose there was a 10 percent reduction in the level of forecasted demand for all tires in each of the three months. Would this invalidate the optimal basic feasible solution?

d. What would be the effect of an increase in the cost of inventory from $4 to $5 per month per tire?

BIBLIOGRAPHY

Charnes, Abraham, and W. W. Cooper, *Management Models and Industrial Applications of Linear Programming*. New York: John Wiley & Sons, Inc., 1961.

Dantzig, George B., *Linear Programming and Extensions*. Princeton, N.J.: Princeton University Press, 1963.

Gass, Saul I., *Illustrated Guide to Linear Programming*. New York: McGraw-Hill Book Company, 1970.

Lee, Sang M., *Linear Optimization for Management*. New York: Mason/Charter Publishers, Inc., 1976.

Orchard-Hays, William, *Advanced Linear Programming Computing Techniques*. New York: McGraw-Hill Book Company, 1968.

Taha, H. A., *Operations Research: An Introduction*. New York: The Macmillan Company, 1976.

Teichroew, Daniel, *An Introduction to Management Science: Deterministic Models*. New York: John Wiley & Sons, Inc., 1964.

Wagner, Harvey M., *Principles of Management Science with Applications to Executive Decisions*. Englewood Cliffs, N.J.: Prentice-Hall, Inc., 1975.

5

Transportation and Assignment Problems

Agrico AGRICO CHEMICAL COMPANY[1]

The Agrico Chemical Company is a subsidiary of The Williams Companies, one of the nation's 350 largest industrial companies. Agrico is one of the largest manufacturers of chemical fertilizers in the United States. Led by progressive management, Agrico had grown from a relatively small firm to a company with sales exceeding $500 million in less than a decade.

By the mid-1970s, however, sharply escalating distribution costs, together with the highly seasonal demand pattern of chemical fertilizers, was creating a complex problem that standard techniques involving charts and cost figures could not handle. The complexity of the situation affected the three major segments of the company's operation—production, distribution, and inventory. In response to their problems, management decided to develop an integrated computer-based planning system.

To aid in their problem solution, Agrico enlisted an outside team of management science consultants. The consultants brought on board the knowledge of advanced network methodology to deal with the multiple-time-period distribution problem. The Agrico distribution problem was indeed large in scale, as it consisted of 4 production plants, 78 distribution centers, and approximately 2,000 customers.

An integral part of the production, distribution, and inventory (PDI) system is a transshipment network model (a model very similar to the transportation model used here in Chapter 5). A state-of-the-art transshipment algorithm enabled the production, distribution, and inventory problem, with approximately 2,400,000 decision variables, to be solved in less than 1 minute of CPU time. The efficiency of the algorithm enabled the PDI system to be used extensively to evaluate the benefit/cost impact of alternative capital investments.

---

[1]Fred Glover, Gene Jones, David Karney, Darwin Klingman, and John Mote, "An Integrated Production, Distribution, and Inventory Planning System," *Interfaces*, vol.9, no. 5 (November 1979), 21–35.

Some of the areas of cost savings uncovered by use of the model include:

1. The early completion of a distribution center would save $175,000.

2. The location of a distribution center on the upper Ohio River would save $100,000 per month in transportation costs.

3. Changing the capacity of some distribution centers while doubling the capacity of a nitrogen chemical plant would save $12,000 annually.

However, the most significant impact of the PDI system is in the increased planning capability and the rescheduling of all production and distribution activities. During 1977 and 1978, the PDI system has resulted in a savings of $4 million. When all decision alternatives suggested by the system have been implemented, it is expected that Agrico's $70 million annual distribution and inventory costs will be reduced by more than $8 million.

SPECIALIZED LP MODELS

In this chapter, we explore two very special LP models. These models have a special type of structure that lend themselves to ease in computational analysis. These models, called transportation and assignment models, are also widely used in OR/MS applications. Both of these models fall into the category of network models, which we discuss further in Chapters 6 and 7. A network is a collection of nodes or points connected by links. (Figure 5.2 on page 166 depicts a simple network.)

Transportation or distribution models are particularly useful in determining the best distribution or allocation of a product from origin to destination. We have just learned how such a model is useful to the Williams Companies in marketing and distributing their chemical products. We shall also see how the transportation model is useful in production scheduling and the allocation of productive capacity to various time periods.

The assignment problem is a special case of the transportation model. It is concerned with the one-to-one assignment of one set of objects to another. The assignment model is useful in the matching of workers to jobs, jobs to machines, salesmen to territories, and so on. It is often used as a submodel to more complex OR/MS models. Since both transportation *special* and assignment models can be solved by general-purpose LP codes, let us *purpose* see why *special-purpose methods* have been developed and refined for *methods* solving this class of problems.

RATIONALE FOR SPECIAL-PURPOSE ALGORITHMS

The transportation and assignment models we shall examine in this chapter are two of the more common network models. They have many applications, both directly and as subproblems of even larger problems. They are both LP models and thus can be solved by using a general-purpose LP computer code. However, transportation and assignment models have a special mathematical structure that can be exploited to yield streamlined versions of the general simplex method. Taking advantage of special network structure can yield not only cost savings in terms of computation but also solutions to large-scale problems that are otherwise too large to be solved on contemporary computers by the general simplex method. These streamlined versions of the simplex method are *algorithm* special-purpose algorithms. An *algorithm* is a systematic procedure for arriving at a solution for a problem. The primary benefits of these special-purpose algorithms for transportation and assignment problems are as follows:

1. Computations are generally 100 to 150 times faster than the general simplex method.

2. Significantly less computer memory is required, thus permitting even larger problems to be solved.

3. Transportation and assignment problems that have integer (whole-number) data yield integer solutions when solved by special-purpose algorithms.

This third factor is particularly important. Many real-world applications require whole-number solutions. For example, it is hard to ship half a car from Detroit or to build one-third of an airplane. Furthermore, general LP can yield noninteger solutions that deviate significantly from optimality when they are rounded off. Other general management science techniques that guarantee an integer solution, moreover, are usually inefficient and unable to solve large-scale problems.

ADVANTAGES AND DISADVANTAGES OF HEURISTICS

In this chapter, we develop special-purpose algorithms to solve the transportation and assignment models. In the case of the transportation problem, we also consider *heuristic* solution approaches.

heuristic   A *heuristic* is a rule-of-thumb procedure that determines a good, but not necessarily optimal, solution to a problem. The simplex method, for example, is not heuristic since it is an optimization technique that guarantees the optimal solution, provided one exists. Heuristic solutions are usually obtained much faster and thus at lower cost. These simple rules of thumb can also be performed by hand sometimes, thus eliminating the need to use a computer. On the other hand, heuristics cannot be considered as accurate as optimization techniques since an optimal solution is not guaranteed. A good heuristic is generally within 10 percent of optimality, but the great disadvantage of using a heuristic is that the amount of error is not known. That is, if you use a heuristic that has not been thoroughly tested, you do not know whether your answer is 5, 10, or even 30 percent from the optimal solution.

Management science techniques have made significant progress in helping to solve medium and large-scale operational problems. Sometimes, however, it is said that little has been done to help management with the small or daily problems of operation. It is in this area that heuristics can be most beneficial. Their simplicity and ease of calculation make it possible for management to use these decision rules on a short-term basis without having to undertake extensive preparations.

Do not gain too simple a notion of heuristics, however. Sophisticated heuristics have been developed for certain very difficult problems for which there are no effective optimization techniques. For these problems, heuristics are not a convenience but a necessity. Among problems of this type are warehouse location models, vehicle-routing problems, airline scheduling, job shop scheduling, network design problems, and others.

THE TRANSPORTATION PROBLEM

The particular model we address in this section is called the *Hitchcock–Koopmans transportation problem,* after its two formulators. As you have probably guessed, the model can be used to determine optimal shipping patterns. The model has many other applications, however; it is sometimes called the distribution problem.

EXAMPLE   The Faze Linear Company is very progressive and has already used LP to determine its optimal product mix (see Chapter 3). The company is now faced with the problem of how to distribute its electrical components from plants to regional warehouses. Faze Linear has plants located in Washington, D.C., Denver, and Los Angeles; regional warehouses are located in New York, Chicago, Dallas, and San Francisco (see Figure 5.1). This month, the company has available 50 units at Washington, 80 units at Denver, and 120 units at Los Angeles. In order to meet predicted demand, Faze Linear must ship 90 units to New York, 70 to Chicago,

FIGURE 5.1 Location of plants and warehouses for Faze Linear

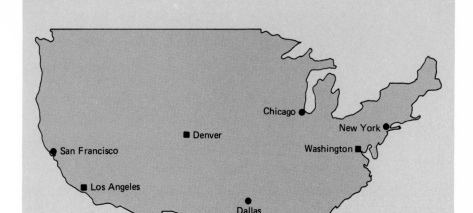

40 to Dallas, and 50 to San Francisco. Relevant per-unit transportation costs for each component as well as demand-and-supply data are given in Table 5.1. Faze Linear wants to determine the shipping pattern that meets all demand at minimum transportation cost.

The Faze Linear distribution problem is actually an LP problem. To formulate it let x_{ij} denote the amount to be shipped from plant i to warehouse j where $i = 1, 2, 3$ and $j = 1, 2, 3, 4$. In this notation, x_{23} represents the number of units to be shipped from Denver to Dallas. Notice that the first subscript refers to the row (plant) in Table 5.1 and the second subscript refers to the column (warehouse). The problem may be formulated as

$$\text{Minimize} \quad 8x_{11} + 9x_{12} + 11x_{13} + 16x_{14} + 12x_{21} + 7x_{22} + 5x_{23} + 8x_{24}$$
$$+ 14x_{31} + 10x_{32} + 6x_{33} + 7x_{34}$$

$$\text{subject to} \quad x_{11} + x_{12} + x_{13} + x_{14} = 50$$
$$x_{21} + x_{22} + x_{23} + x_{24} = 80$$
$$x_{31} + x_{32} + x_{33} + x_{34} = 120$$
$$x_{11} + x_{21} + x_{31} = 90$$
$$x_{12} + x_{22} + x_{32} = 70$$
$$x_{13} + x_{23} + x_{33} = 40$$
$$x_{14} + x_{24} + x_{34} = 50$$
$$x_{ij} \geq 0; \ i = 1, 2, 3; \ j = 1, 2, 3, 4$$

TABLE 5.1 Data for Faze Linear distribution problem

| | Shipping costs | | | | |
| | To warehouse | | | | |
From plant	New York	Chicago	Dallas	San Francisco	Supply
Washington, D.C.	$ 8	$ 9	$11	$16	50
Denver	12	7	5	8	80
Los Angeles	14	10	6	7	120
Demand	90	70	40	50	

The foregoing model may be solved directly by the general simplex method. However, streamlined simplex procedures are available that offer the three benefits described earlier in this chapter. Charnes and Cooper developed the stepping-stone method, which was one of the first specialized simplex procedures for transportation problems. Later, Dant- *modified* zig developed the *modified distribution, or MODI, method,* which remains *distribution* the best approach for solving transportation problems. Computational *(MODI)* researchers have further refined the MODI method so that really signifi- *method* cant computational savings can be achieved. For instance, transportation problems that have 1,000 plants and 1,000 warehouses (that is, 1 million decision variables) have been solved in 14 seconds or so on a CDC 6600 computer. Problems of this size are not even solvable without using special-purpose algorithms.

We can generalize transportation problems to include more than plants and warehouses. We may so interpret any situation in which a homo-geneous product is available in the amounts $a_1, a_2, \ldots a_m$ at m sources 1, 2, ..., m, respectively. Furthermore, demands $b_1, b_2, \ldots, b_n$ are present at n destinations 1, 2, ..., n, respectively. The transportation cost per unit from the ith source to the jth destination is a known constant, c_{ij}, and directly proportional to the amount shipped. Letting x_{ij} again repre-sent the amount shipped from source i to destination j, we obtain the general transportation model

$$\text{Minimize} \quad \sum_{i=1}^{m} \sum_{j=1}^{n} c_{ij} x_{ij} \tag{5.1}$$

$$\text{subject to} \quad \sum_{j=1}^{n} x_{ij} = a_i, \; i = 1, 2, \ldots, m,$$

$$\sum_{i=1}^{m} x_{ij} = b_j, \; j = 1, 2, \ldots, n,$$

$$x_{ij} \geq 0 \text{ for } i = 1, 2, \ldots m; \; j = 1, 2, \ldots, n$$

It is assumed that total supply equals total demand; that is,

$$\sum_{i=1}^{m} a_i = \sum_{j=1}^{n} b_j.$$

We shall find that this assumption can easily be circumvented by adding a dummy source or destination.

SOLVING TRANSPORTATION PROBLEMS HEURISTICALLY

In this section, we consider two heuristics methods as well as the MODI optimization method for the transportation problem. The heuristics we discuss in this section are intuitive; hopefully, they will give you some insight into possible approaches to other types of problems. The heuristics are also helpful in providing a starting point for the calculations in the MODI method.

ROW MINIMUM METHOD

The row minimum heuristic is a very quick way to obtain a feasible solution to the transportation problem. Computational investigations have shown that it is one of the best heuristics with which to start the MODI method for optimizing. That is, the row minimum heuristic coupled with the MODI method can solve transportation problems faster than any other procedures.

To explain the row minimum procedure, we need a transportation tableau. A table of this type is helpful in solving transportation problems, just as the simplex tableau is helpful in solving LP problems. Tableau 5.1 illustrates a transportation tableau for the Faze Linear problem. The usual practice in these tableaus is to list the sources as rows and the destinations as columns. The available supply for each source is listed in the far right column, and the required demands at each destination are summarized in the bottom row. The per-unit transportation cost for shipping from source to destination is found in the upper left-hand corner of the square in the row associated with the source and the column associated with the destination. For example, the per-unit transportation cost from the Los Angeles source to the Chicago destination is $10. The 12 squares *cells* (or *cells*) formed by the three sources and four destinations correspond to direct routes over which shipments can take place. In any feasible solution, the sum of the shipments across any row must not exceed the supply available, and the sum of the shipments down any column must satisfy the demand required.

TABLEAU 5.1 Transportation tableau for Faze Linear

To / From	New York	Chicago	Dallas	San Francisco	Supply
Washington	8	9	11	16	50
Denver	12	7	5	8	80
Los Angeles	14	10	6	7	120
Demand	90	70	40	50	250

Unlike some other "quick and dirty" transportation heuristics, the row minimum rule does not ignore the costs for the various shipments. As the name implies, the row minimum heuristic proceeds by trying to assign shipments to the minimum-cost cell in each row. The process starts in row 1, continues to row 2, and so on, until all supply is exhausted and all demand is satisfied. To summarize the procedure:

1. Find the minimum-cost cell in row 1. If there is a tie, make an arbitrary choice. Allocate as much supply as possible to this cell. The maximum allocation is determined by the supply available and the demand required by the source and destination associated with this minimum-cost cell.

2. Delete the row (or column) whose supply (or demand) has just been exhausted by the allocation in the previous step.

3. Proceed to the next row that has not been deleted and find the minimum-cost cell. Again, make an allocation and delete the appropriate row or column.

4. Repeat step 3 until all supply is exhausted and all demand is satisfied. Whenever the last row in the tableau is reached, the process returns to the first row in the tableau for the next execution of step 3.

For the Faze Linear problem, the row minimum solution is shown in Tableau 5.2. The number added to a cell represents the shipment to be made from the associated source to destination. In this example, the row minimum procedure started in row 1 and made an allocation of 50 to the minimum-cost cell (1, 1). We shall use the notation (i, j) to denote the cell

TABLEAU 5.2   Row minimum solution for Faze Linear

To (j) / From (i)	New York	Chicago	Dallas	San Francisco	Supply
Washington	8 / 50	9	11	16	50
Denver	12	7 / 40	5 / 40	8	80
Los Angeles	14 / 40	10 / 30	6	7 / 50	120
Demand	90	70	40	50	250

associated with source i and destination j. Row 1 has its supply exhausted and is deleted. Proceeding to the second row, we find that cell (2, 3), with a cost of 5, is minimal. Thus, 40 units is allocated to cell (2, 3), and column 3 is deleted. Proceeding to the third row, we find cell (3, 3), at a cost of 6, is minimal, but it is not available since column 3 has been deleted. Thus we allocate 50 units to the next minimal-cost cell (3, 4). Since row 1 is deleted, we return to row 2 and allocate 40 units to cell (2, 2). This deletes row 2, and we again proceed to row 3, allocating 30 units to cell (3, 2) and then 40 units to cell (3, 1). This deletes all three rows and also satisfies all required demand. The cost of the row minimum solution is found by multiplying each shipment by its per-unit transportation cost. The row minimum cost is $8(50) + 7(40) + 5(40) + 14(40) + 10(30) + 7(50) = \$2,090$.

VOGEL'S APPROXIMATION METHOD (VAM)

Vogel's approximation heuristic is generally (though not always) more accurate than the row minimum rule. However, more calculations are involved, and thus more total computation time is required when VAM is used with the MODI method to obtain an optimal solution. VAM can be used when the decision maker is satisfied with obtaining a good heuristic solution that is not necessarily optimal.

VAM is an interesting heuristic that can be applied to problems other than transportation problems. The basic idea in VAM is to avoid shipments that have a high cost. The row minimum method is somewhat shortsighted in that it simply assigns to the lowest-cost cell available *in a particular row*; this can cause high costs to be incurred in other rows.

VAM looks at the opportunity cost of not assigning to the minimum-cost *opportunity* cell in a row or column of the transportation tableau. The *opportunity* *loss* *loss* is conservatively estimated to be the difference in cost between the lowest and next lowest-cost cells in that particular row or column. Then, assignment is made to the minimum-cost cell in the row or column that has the highest potential opportunity loss. If we view the opportunity loss as a possible penalty, the idea is to avoid a high penalty. This assignment then avoids incurring the highest opportunity loss. The details of VAM are presented as follows:

1. For each row, calculate the potential opportunity loss as the difference between the minimum-cost cell and the next lowest-cost cell in that row.

2. For each column, calculate the potential opportunity loss as the difference between the minimum-cost cell and the next lowest-cost cell in that column.

3. Find the highest potential opportunity loss from among all rows and columns, and find the minimum-cost cell associated with that row or column. If a tie exists in opportunity losses among rows and columns, break the tie arbitrarily.

4. Allocate the maximum possible amount of supply to the minimum-cost cell in step 3; this will delete a row or column. Reduce the supplies and demands appropriately.

5. If a row has been deleted, recalculate the column opportunity losses. If a column has been deleted, recalculate the row opportunity losses.

6. If all allocations have been made, stop. Otherwise, begin another iteration by returning to step 3.

Let us apply the VAM procedure to the Faze Linear distribution problem. The VAM heuristic begins by calculating the potential opportunity losses of not assigning to the lowest-cost cell in each row and column. The beginning calculations are shown in Tableau 5.3. There you see that the highest opportunity loss is 4, which is associated with column 1. This means that if we do not ship in the least-cost cell in this column ($8 per unit), we will have to ship in a cell that has a cost of at least $4 per unit more. In fact, the additional cost would be either $4 or $6 per unit. Thus, we allocate all the supply possible, which is 50 units, to cell (1, 1), which has the minimum cost of $8. The supply for row 1 is exhausted; so we draw a line through the costs in row 1 as a reminder that these costs are no longer usable in calculating opportunity losses.

Tableau 5.4 shows the results we get when we recalculate the column opportunity losses for the next iteration. The highest opportunity loss is

TABLEAU 5.3 Initial VAM calculations for Faze Linear

	Column opportunity costs	4	2	1	1	
Row opportunity costs	From \ To	New York	Chicago	Dallas	San Francisco	Supply
1	Washington	~~8~~ 50	~~9~~	~~11~~	~~16~~	~~50~~
2	Denver	12	7	5	8	80
1	Los Angeles	14	10	6	7	120
	Demand	~~90~~ 40	70	40	50	250

TABLEAU 5.4 Second iteration for Faze Linear VAM

	Column opportunity costs	~~4~~ 2	~~2~~ 3	1	1	
Row opportunity costs	From \ To	New York	Chicago	Dallas	San Francisco	Supply
~~1~~	Washington	~~8~~ 50	9	~~11~~	~~16~~	~~50~~
2	Denver	12	7 70	5	8	~~80~~ 10
1	Los Angeles	14	10	6	7	120
	Demand	~~90~~ 40	~~70~~	40	50	250

now 3 and is associated with column 2. Thus, we allocate all we can to the lowest-cost cell (2, 2); this allocation is 70 units, which is all the demand that is required in column 2. We adjust the supplies and demands, delete column 2 by drawing a line through its costs, and update the row opportunity losses in Tableau 5.5.

This time, the largest opportunity loss is the 3 associated with row 2. Allocating the available 10 units deletes row 2 and leaves only row 3 with available supply. Three more iterations are required to reach the final VAM solution. The final tableau is shown in Tableau 5.6.

The distribution cost of the VAM solution is 8(50) + 7(70) + 5(10) + 14(40) + 6(30) + 7(50) = \$2,030, which is \$60 lower than the row minimum solution. Usually, VAM provides at least as good a solution as row minimum, although not always.

SOLVING TRANSPORTATION PROBLEMS BY THE MODI METHOD

Even though the VAM solution to the Faze Linear problem is better than the row minimum solution, it is still not optimal. The MODI method can be used to take any basic feasible solution to a transportation problem and determine an optimal solution from it. MODI is a streamlined version of the simplex method that takes advantage of the special mathematical structure of the transportation model.

One advantage of the MODI method is that it does not require the use of slack or artificial variables to get a starting feasible solution. It can also take advantage of the advanced starting feasible solutions provided by row minimum or VAM. The calculations in the MODI method are aimed at making successive improvements in a feasible solution until the optimal solution is reached. The method parallels the simplex method in that the following steps are executed:

1. A variable is found that can reduce transportation costs when brought into solution.
2. This variable's maximum allowable value is determined.
3. The variable that must leave the solution is determined, then all other variables in solution are updated.

Fortunately, it is not necessary to store and update a large number of entries in a simplex tableau as you must do in the general simplex method. The corresponding amount of storage space and computation is thus eliminated.

Consider the row minimum heuristic solution to the Faze Linear distribution problem that we restate in Tableau 5.7. Notice that there are six

TABLEAU 5.5 Third iteration for Faze Linear VAM

		New York	Chicago	Dallas	San Francisco	Supply
	Column opportunity costs	~~4~~ 2	~~2 3~~	1	1	
Row opportunity costs	From \ To					
~~1~~	Washington	~~8~~ 50	~~9~~	~~11~~	~~16~~	~~50~~
3 ~~2~~	Denver	~~12~~	~~7~~ 70	~~5~~ 10	~~8~~	~~80~~ 10
1	Los Angeles	14	10	6	7	120
	Demand	~~90~~ 40	~~70~~	~~40~~ 30	50	250

TABLEAU 5.6 Final solution for Faze Linear VAM

		New York	Chicago	Dallas	San Francisco	Supply
	Column opportunity costs	~~4 2 0~~	~~2 3~~	~~1 0~~	~~1 0~~	
Row opportunity costs	From \ To					
~~1~~	Washington	8 50	9	11	16	~~50~~
~~3 2~~	Denver	12	7 70	5 10	8	~~80 10~~
~~7 1~~	Los Angeles	14 40	10	6 30	7 50	~~120 80 40~~
	Demand	~~90~~ ~~40~~	~~70~~	~~40~~ ~~30~~	~~50~~	~~250~~

TABLEAU 5.7   Row minimum solution for Faze Linear distribution problem

From \ To	K_1 New York	K_2 Chicago	K_3 Dallas	K_4 San Francisco	Supply
R_1 Washington	8 50	9	11	16	50
R_2 Denver	12	7 40	5 40	8	80
R_3 Los Angeles	14 40	10 30	6	7 50	120
Demand	90	70	40	50	250

cells in which shipments occur. For a transportation problem that has m sources and n destinations, a basic feasible solution always involves $m + n - 1$ cells. Even though there are $m + n$ functional constraints, one of them is redundant since all the constraints are equalities and it is assumed that total supply equals total demand. This can be illustrated by showing that a demand constraint equals the sum of all the supply constraints minus the sum of the remaining demand constraints. In using any starting solution from the row minimum or VAM heuristics, we must be sure that the solution contains $m + n - 1$ cells.

In order to improve any feasible transportation solution by means of the MODI method, we need to determine which cells need to have their shipments increased and which need to have their shipments decreased. As in the regular simplex method, we make these improvements one variable at a time. Thus, initially, we need to find a cell whose shipments we can increase and, by doing so, reduce transportation costs.

In the regular simplex method, cost-reducing variables are recognized by having a negative $c_j - z_j$ value. The same $c_j - z_j$ indicators are used in the MODI method but are calculated in a much easier way. The first step in determining $c_j - z_j$ values for all nonbasic cells (those that have no shipments) is to assign row and column indicators to each row and column of the transportation tableau. In our example, we let R_1, R_2, and R_3 represent row indicator values and K_1, K_2, K_3, and K_4 represent column indicator values. Refer to Tableau 5.7 to see these indicators associated with their appropriate rows or columns. For those of you who have already studied Chapter 4, these indicators are simply the dual variables of the dual problem.

In general, for an $m \times n$ transportation problem we let

R_i = indicator value assigned to row i, $i = 1, 2, \ldots, m$

K_j = indicator value assigned to column j, $j = 1, 2, \ldots, n$

As we have stated previously, x_{ij} represents the shipment from source i to destination j, and c_{ij} represents the associated per-unit transportation cost.

In order to compute values for the R_i and K_j indicators, we use a result from duality theory that states

$$R_i + K_j = c_{ij} \qquad \text{whenever } x_{ij} > 0 \qquad \text{[5.2]}$$

Thus, $R_i + K_j = c_{ij}$ for any cell (i, j) in which a positive shipment occurs. Since we have m supply constraints and n demand constraints for a total of $m + n$ constraints, we might expect to have $m + n$ basic cells. However, since one constraint is always redundant in transportation models, we actually have $m + n - 1$ cells with positive shipments in any non-degenerate solution. Thus, condition 5.2 yields $m + n - 1$ equations, which we can solve to determine the R_i and K_j values. In Tableau 5.7, the cells (1,1), (2,2), (2,3), (3,1), (3,2), and (3,4) have positive shipments. Thus we obtain the following six equations:

$$R_1 + K_1 = c_{11} = 8 \qquad \text{[5.3]}$$

$$R_2 + K_2 = c_{22} = 7 \qquad \text{[5.4]}$$

$$R_2 + K_3 = c_{23} = 5 \qquad \text{[5.5]}$$

$$R_3 + K_1 = c_{31} = 14 \qquad \text{[5.6]}$$

$$R_3 + K_2 = c_{32} = 10 \qquad \text{[5.7]}$$

$$R_3 + K_4 = c_{34} = 7 \qquad \text{[5.8]}$$

Notice that we have six equations in seven unknowns. Since we have one more unknown than equation, we have one degree of freedom and can set any one of the R_i or K_j equal to an arbitrary value. It is simplest to set R_1 equal to zero and then to solve for the other indicator values. Solving such a system of equations may sound tedious, but the special structure of the transportation problem makes the system of equations trivial to solve. This system of equations is triangular once R_1 is set equal to zero, and the other R_i and K_j may be determined without any calculations.

For example, once $R_1 = 0$, then in equation 5.3 we have

$$R_1 + K_1 = 8 \qquad\qquad [5.3]$$
$$0 + K_1 = 8$$
$$K_1 = 8$$

Now that $K_1 = 8$, in 5.6 we have that

$$R_3 + K_1 = 14 \qquad\qquad [5.6]$$
$$R_3 + 8 = 14$$
$$R_3 = 6$$

And now that $R_3 = 6$, we have

$$R_3 + K_2 = 10 \qquad\qquad [5.7]$$
$$6 + K_2 = 10$$
$$K_2 = 4$$

$$R_3 + K_4 = 7 \qquad\qquad [5.8]$$
$$6 + K_4 = 7$$
$$K_4 = 1$$

With $K_2 = 4$, equation 5.4 becomes

$$R_2 + K_2 = 7 \qquad\qquad [5.4]$$
$$R_2 + 4 = 7$$
$$R_2 = 3$$

And finally, given $R_2 = 3$

$$R_2 + K_3 = 5 \qquad\qquad [5.5]$$
$$3 + K_3 = 5$$
$$K_3 = 2$$

We have solved the entire system of equations by merely setting $R_1 = 0$ and substituting for the remaining R_i and K_j values. Even though the R_i and K_j values are all nonnegative in this example, they may be positive, negative, or zero.

Recall that our purpose in calculating the R_i and K_j values was to determine which variables (cells), if any, can have their shipments increased and thereby reduce transportation costs. In the regular simplex method discussed in Chapter 3, we used the $c_j - z_j$ indicators to measure potential improvements. We can use precisely the same approach in the MODI method because the sum of $R_i + K_j = z_{ij}$ for any transportation variable x_{ij}. Thus, we can calculate the opportunity cost of increasing the shipments through any nonbasic cell (those with no shipments) as

$$c_{ij} - (R_i + K_j) \tag{5.9}$$

Since we are trying to minimize costs, we achieve the optimal solution whenever all the $c_{ij} - (R_i + K_j)$ are zero or positive. We indicate the value of each $c_{ij} - (R_i + K_j)$ in the lower right-hand part of each nonbasic cell. See Tableau 5.8 for the R_i and K_j values for the initial row minimum solution of the Faze Linear distribution problem. Notice the $c_{ij} - (R_i + K_j)$ values in the enclosed portion of each empty nonbasic cell. (The $c_{ij} - (R_i + K_j)$ numbers were derived as shown in Table 5.2.) The only nonbasic cell that reduces transportation cost is cell (3, 3). This is so because it is the only cell that has a negative opportunity cost. For each unit that we can ship through cell (3, 3) (that is, from Los Angeles to Dallas), we can reduce the total transportation cost by \$2. This assumes that some of the existing shipment determinations we have made already will be reduced appropriately.

Increasing the shipments through cell (3,3) actually causes a chain reaction in some of the other shipments from sources to destinations. For instance, if we increase the shipment through cell (3,3) by, say, 10 units, then we must reduce the sum of the previous shipments out of source 3 by 10 units. This is true since source 3 (that is, Los Angeles) has only 120 units available. Likewise, if we ship 10 units through cell (3,3) into destination 3 (Dallas), we must decrease the sum of the previous ship-

TABLEAU 5.8   Initial transportation tableau with R_i and K_j values for Faze Linear

		$K_1 = 8$ New York	$K_2 = 4$ Chicago	$K_3 = 2$ Dallas	$K_4 = 1$ San Francisco	Supply
	To / From					
$R_1 = 0$	Washington	8 / 50	9 / 5	11 / 9	16 / 15	50
$R_2 = 3$	Denver	12 / 1	7 / 40	5 / 40	8 / 4	80
$R_3 = 6$	Los Angeles	14 / 40	10 / 30	6 / −2	7 / 50	120
	Demand	90	70	40	50	

TABLE 5.2 $c_{ij} - (R_i + K_j)$ **values for Faze Linear second solution**

Nonbasic cell	$c_{ij} - (R_i + K_j)$		Opportunity cost
(1,2)	$9 - (0 + 4)$	$=$	5
(1,3)	$11 - (0 + 2)$	$=$	9
(1,4)	$16 - (0 + 1)$	$=$	15
(2,1)	$12 - (3 + 8)$	$=$	1
(2,4)	$8 - (3 + 1)$	$=$	4
(3,3)	$6 - (6 + 2)$	$=$	-2

ments into destination 3 by 10 units. The overall chain reaction is illustrated in Figure 5.2.

The black lines in Figure 5.2 represent shipments that currently exist; the dashed brown line represents the upcoming shipment through cell (3,3). The solid brown lines indicate the shipments that are affected by the chain reaction caused by increasing shipments through cell (3,3). The *closed loop* brown lines, including the dotted one, form a *closed loop*. It is only around the closed loop that adjustments need to be made when the shipment from Los Angeles to Dallas is increased. Thus, if we increase the shipment through cell (3,3), we must decrease the shipment through cell (2,3), increase the shipment through cell (2,2), and, finally, decrease the shipment through cell (3,2). These adjustments meet all demands without exceeding any of the supply available.

FIGURE 5.2 Graph of current solution for Faze Linear problem

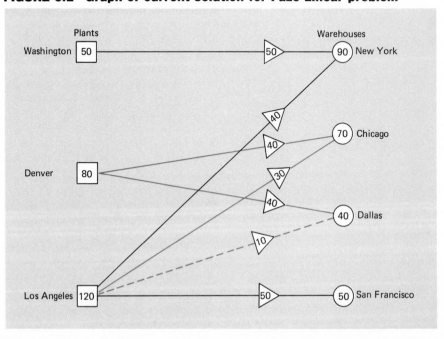

It is easier to determine the chain reaction that occurs whenever a nonbasic cell's shipments are increased by finding the closed loop in the transportation tableau itself. This closed loop is established by a labeling process that assigns plus and minus signs to the appropriate cells. The general idea is to leave the nonbasic cell and make a rook's tour of the basic cells, creating a closed loop that returns to the nonbasic cell. For those of you who do not play chess, a rook's tour consists of only horizontal and vertical movements.

Only one closed loop exists in the tableau, and it can be determined and labeled by the following process: Begin by placing a plus sign (+) in the empty nonbasic cell that is to have its shipments increased. Trace a closed path consisting of basic cells (those with positive shipments) back to the nonbasic cell. The path may skip over some basic cells, but corners of the closed path must occur only at basic cells. After placing a plus sign in the nonbasic cell, alternate minus and plus signs in the basic cells that comprise the closed loop. Only label the basic cells necessary to complete the loop. Skip over any other basic cells. The number of labeled cells is always an even number.

To illustrate the process of identifying and labeling the closed loop, refer to Tableau 5.9, in which the closed loop for cell (3,3) is shown. The loop was determined by placing a plus sign in cell (3,3), a minus sign in cell (3,2), a plus in cell (2,2), and finally a minus in cell (2,3). Notice that the plus and minus signs are placed only in basic cells.

TABLEAU 5.9   Closed loop for cell (3,3)

		$K_1 = 8$	$K_2 = 4$	$K_3 = 2$	$K_4 = 1$	
	From \ To	New York	Chicago	Dallas	San Francisco	Supply
$R_1 = 0$	Washington	8 50	9	11	16	50
$R_2 = 3$	Denver	12	7 40 +	5 40 −	8	80
$R_3 = 6$	Los Angeles	14 40	10 30 −	6 +	7 50	120
	Demand	90	70	40	50	250

   Sometimes the closed loop is not immediately identifiable from looking at the transportation tableau. Fortunately, there is a systematic procedure for determining the cells in the loop. The procedure for finding the loop is as follows:

1.   Place a plus sign (+) in the empty nonbasic cell that is to have its shipments increased.

2.   Cross off any row or column that contains only one cell with a positive shipment. (*Note:* The plus sign counts as a "shipment.")

3.   Successively cross out rows and columns until the only rows and columns left contain two shipments. The uncrossed cells define the closed loop.

The wide lines in Tableau 5.9 illustrate the crossed out rows and columns. Initially, row 1 and column 4 can be crossed out, since they contain only one positive shipment. Once the shipment of 50 is crossed out in row 1, the shipment of 40 is alone in column 1. We can then cross out column 1, but all other rows and columns contain two shipments and cannot be crossed out.

   Once the closed loop has been traced, it is necessary to determine the amount of supply that can be shipped through cell (3,3). The labels on the closed loop indicate the chain reaction caused by increasing the shipment through cell (3,3). Thus, increasing shipments in cell (3,3) also increases shipments in cell (2,2) but decreases shipments through cells (2,3) and (3,2). Since no shipment can be negative, we can increase the shipment in cell (3,3) no more than the minimum of shipments in the negatively labeled cells (2,3) and (3,2). The shipment of 30 units in cell (3,2) is the smaller; thus, we can increase the shipment through cell (3,3) by 30 units.

   The new solution and adjustments in shipments is shown in Tableau 5.10. Notice how the shipments in the cell labeled with pluses have been increased by 30 and the shipments in the cells labeled with minuses have been decreased by 30. Effectively, variable x_{33} has entered the solution at a value of 30, and variable x_{32} has become a nonbasic variable and left the solution. The total cost of the original row minimum solution was $2,090. The total cost of the second solution obtained by the MODI method is calculated in Table 5.3. Its total cost, $2,030, represents a savings of $60. Coincidentally, this second solution is the same as the solution obtained by the VAM heuristic. This solution is not optimal; another iteration of the MODI method is required before optimality is achieved.

   To see where further improvements can be made, we must calculate new values of the R_i and K_j indicators. These values must satisfy equations based on the general statement in [5.2] for the new solution. Since

TABLEAU 5.10 Second solution for Faze Linear based on closed-loop adjustments

		$K_1 = 8$ New York	$K_2 = 2$ Chicago	$K_3 = 0$ Dallas	$K_4 = 1$ San Francisco	Supply
	To From					
$R_1 = 0$	Washington	8 50	9 7	11 11	16 15	50
$R_2 = 5$	Denver	12 −1	7 70	5 10	8 2	80
$R_3 = 6$	Los Angeles	14 40	10 2	6 30	7 50	120
	Demand	90	70	40	50	250

cells (1,1), (2,2), (2,3), (3,1), (3,3), and (3,4) are basic, we obtain the system

$$R_1 + K_1 = 8$$
$$R_2 + K_2 = 7$$
$$R_2 + K_3 = 5$$
$$R_3 + K_1 = 14$$
$$R_3 + K_3 = 6$$
$$R_3 + K_4 = 7$$

Setting R_1 equal to zero and substituting, we obtain $K_1 = 8$, $R_3 = 6$, $K_3 = 0$, $K_4 = 1$, $R_2 = 5$, and $K_2 = 2$ as the solution to the foregoing system of equations.

Now we can use the R_i and K_j values with expression 5.9 to calculate the opportunity cost of increasing the shipment in any nonbasic cell. The calculations of the $c_{ij} - (R_i + K_j)$ values are shown in Table 5.4, as are the R_i and K_j values and opportunity costs. Since nonbasic cell (2,1) is the only cell with negative opportunity costs, we must increase shipments through it to make any improvements.

TABLE 5.3   Total cost of second solution

Route	Shipment	Cost per unit	Total cost
Washington/New York	50	$ 8	$ 400
Denver/Chicago	70	7	490
Denver/Dallas	10	5	50
Los Angeles/New York	40	14	560
Los Angeles/Dallas	30	6	180
Los Angeles/San Francisco	50	7	350
			$2,030

TABLE 5.4 $c_{ij} - (R_i + K_j)$ values for Faze Linear third solution

Nonbasic cell	$c_{ij} - (R_i + K_j)$		Opportunity cost
(1,2)	$9 - (0 + 2)$	=	$ 7
(1,3)	$11 - (0 + 0)$	=	11
(1,4)	$16 - (0 + 1)$	=	15
(2,1)	$12 - (5 + 8)$	=	-1
(2,4)	$8 - (5 + 1)$	=	2
(3,2)	$10 - (6 + 2)$	=	2

The next step is to determine the closed loop for cell (2,1) so that the appropriate shipment adjustments can be made. Tableau 5.11 shows the part of the second-solution tableau that contains the closed loop. The loop was traced by assigning a plus to cell (2,1), skipping basic cell (2,2) because it is not needed, assigning a minus to cell (2,3), a plus to cell (3,3), and finally a minus to cell (3,1). The smallest shipment in a cell with a minus label is 10 units in cell (2,3). Thus, we adjust the labeled cells by 10 units and obtain the third solution in Tableau 5.12.

TABLEAU 5.11   Closed loop for cell (2,1)

12 +	7	5 −
	70	10
14 −	10	6 +
40		30

170

TABLEAU 5.12   Third solution (optimal) for Faze Linear problem

From \ To	New York	Chicago	Dallas	San Francisco	Supply
	$K_1 = 8$	$K_2 = 3$	$K_3 = 0$	$K_4 = 1$	
Washington $R_1 = 0$	8 — 50	9	11	16	50
Denver $R_2 = 4$	12 — 10	7 — 70	5	8	80
Los Angeles $R_3 = 6$	14 — 30	10	6 — 40	7 — 50	120
Demand	90	70	40	50	250

To find out whether this third solution is optimal, again we calculate the R_i and K_j indicators. Since cells (1,1), (2,1), (2,2), (3,1), (3,3), and (3,4) are basic, we obtain the equations

$$R_1 + K_1 = 8$$
$$R_2 + K_1 = 12$$
$$R_2 + K_2 = 7$$
$$R_3 + K_1 = 14$$
$$R_3 + K_3 = 6$$
$$R_3 + K_4 = 7$$

Setting R_1 equal to zero and backsubstituting, we obtain $K_1 = 8$, $R_2 = 4$, $K_2 = 3$, $R_3 = 6$, $K_3 = 0$, and $K_4 = 1$.

TABLE 5.5 $c_{ij} - (R_i + K_j)$ values for Faze Linear optimal solution

Nonbasic cell	$c_{ij} - (R_i + K_j)$		Opportunity cost
(1,2)	$9 - (0 + 3)$	=	$ 6
(1,3)	$11 - (0 + 0)$	=	11
(1,4)	$16 - (0 + 1)$	=	15
(2,3)	$5 - (4 + 0)$	=	1
(2,4)	$8 - (4 + 1)$	=	3
(3,2)	$10 - (6 + 3)$	=	1

FIGURE 5.3 Optimal shipping pattern for Faze Linear

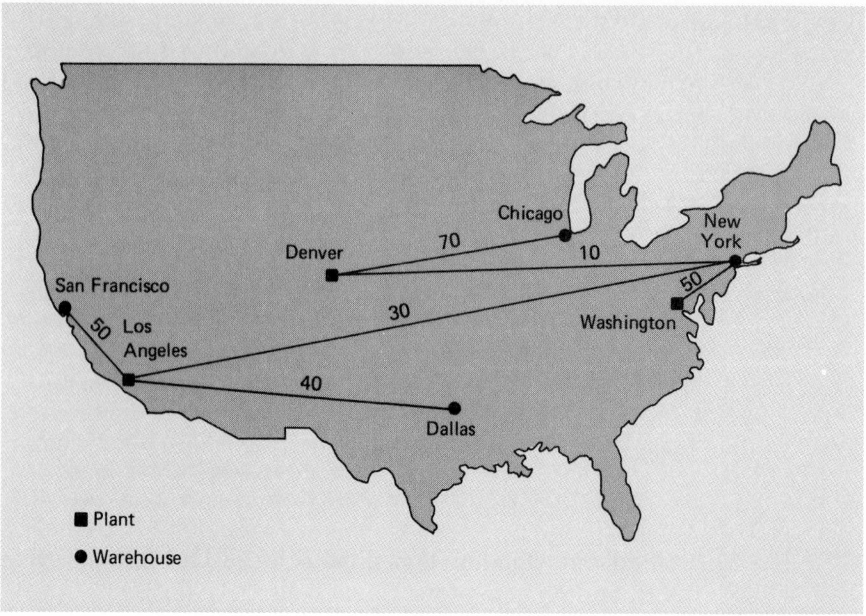

Again, we use expression 5.9 to determine the $c_{ij} - (R_i + K_j)$ opportunity costs (see Table 5.5). Since none of the opportunity costs is negative, no further improvement can be made and the third solution is optimal. Its minimum cost is calculated as $8(50) + 12(10) + 7(70) + 14(30) + 6(40) + 7(50) = \$2{,}020$. The optimal shipping pattern is shown in Figure 5.3.

SUMMARY OF MODI METHOD

1. Generate a starting feasible solution by using a heuristic such as the row minimum rule or VAM. Make sure that the starting feasible solution contains $m + n - 1$ basic cells.

2. Compute the R_i and K_j indicator values for the current solution by using the formula $R_i + K_j = c_{ij}$ for each basic cell (i,j). Solve the resulting $m + n$ equations by setting R_1 equal to zero and backsubstituting for the remaining R_i and K_j values.

3. Calculate the opportunity costs of increasing shipments through each nonbasic (unused) cell using the formula $c_{ij} - (R_i + K_j) =$ opportunity cost for nonbasic cell (i,j).

4. Select the nonbasic cell with the most negative $c_{ij} - (R_i + K_j)$ value. If no nonbasic cell has a negative $c_{ij} - (R_i + K_j)$, stop, for the solution is optimal.

5. Trace the closed path for the nonbasic cell that has the most negative $c_{ij} - (R_i + K_j)$ value. Place a plus sign in this nonbasic cell and sub-

sequently alternate minus and plus signs in labeling the basic cells around the closed loop.

6. Determine the smallest shipment Δ (the delta symbol, Δ, usually represents amount of change) in all cells with a minus label. Adjust the shipments around the closed loop by subtracting Δ from minus-labeled cells and adding Δ to all plus-labeled cells.

7. Return to step 2.

It should be noted that the MODI method can be used to maximize transportation models as well as to minimize them. The modification is the same as in the simplex method for general LP. In order to maximize, we can change the signs of the objective function and minimize, or we can choose the nonbasic cell with the most positive $c_{ij} - (R_i + K_j)$ to enter the solution; all other steps remain the same. A maximization example is solved in the solved problem section at the end of this chapter.

TOTAL SUPPLY AND DEMAND NOT EQUAL

In using the MODI method, we assume that total supply and demand are equal. This is generally not the case in real-world transportation applications. Usually, the problems are unbalanced in that supply exceeds demand, or vice versa. However, unbalanced transportation problems are easily balanced for the MODI method by simply adding a fictitious source or destination to absorb the excess demand or supply.

SUPPLY EXCEEDS DEMAND

dummy destination   Whenever supply exceeds demand, we simply add a fictitious, or *dummy*, destination whose demand equals the excess supply. Doing so artifically balances the transportation problem. To illustrate the technique, consider the Faze Linear problem with an additional 20 units of supply at the Washington plant. This makes total supply equal to 270 units, whereas total demand equals 250. Adding an additional destination is analogous to adding a slack variable in the simplex method. The cost of all shipments to the dummy destination must be zero. This is obviously the case since these shipments are never actually made. In developing a transportation tableau with excess supply, we add a dummy column with zero per-unit transportation costs. The optimal tableau for the Faze Linear problem with excess supply is shown in Tableau 5.13.

The solution to a transportation problem that has a dummy destination is obtained by the exact same MODI procedures. The only difference is in interpreting the optimal solution. In Tableau 5.13, we find that 20 units are allocated to cell (3,5). This simply means that these 20 units are not

TABLEAU 5.13   Balanced tableau when supply exceeds demand

To From	New York	Chicago	Dallas	San Francisco	Dummy	Supply
Washington	8 70	9	11	16	0	70
Denver	12 10	7 70	5	8	0	80
Los Angeles	14 10	10	6 40	7 50	0 20	120
Demand	90	70	40	50	20	270

shipped from Los Angeles. Thus, Los Angeles is the plant that stores the excess supply. We have determined not only the optimal shipping pattern but also which plant is not utilized at full capacity.

DEMAND EXCEEDS SUPPLY

dummy source

Whenever demand exceeds supply, it is, of course, impossible to meet all demand requirements. The question becomes, Which destinations shall receive shipments in order to minimize the distribution cost of the supply that is available? The trick is similar to the case in which supply exceeds demand, except that a *dummy source* is added. Consider the Faze Linear problem with 20 additional units of demand at Dallas. Adding the dummy source to absorb the 20 extra units of demand requires an additional row in the transportation tableau. See Tableau 5.14 for the optimal tableau for the Faze Linear problem with excess demand.

In making accommodations for demand exceeding supply, more than one destination might fail to have all its demand requirements met. In this case, we can see in Tableau 5.14 that the 20 fictitious units at the dummy source are assigned to New York. This means that only 70 of the 90 units in demand at New York are shipped. However, the solution does allocate the 250 units of available supply at minimum transportation cost.

DEGENERACY

Recall from Chapter 3 that degeneracy occurs whenever a basic variable assumes a zero value. In the regular simplex method, degeneracy causes no problem, but it can in the MODI method if not handled properly. The

174

MODI method, with m sources and n destinations, requires $m + n - 1$ basic cells. If fewer than $m + n - 1$ cells are designated as basic, then the R_i and K_j values cannot be calculated and closed loops do not exist. Degeneracy is easily handled by always maintaining $m + n - 1$ basic cells even though some may have zero shipment and be degenerate. Degeneracy can arise in the following situations:

1. In determining a feasible starting solution, fewer than $m + n - 1$ cells are used.

2. In working toward optimality, the MODI method may have more than one basic cell leave the solution at an iteration. This results in fewer than $m + n - 1$ cells being basic.

In the first situation, degeneracy is easily handled by never deleting a row and a column of the transportation tableau at the same time. For instance, in using either row minimum or VAM, we may assign to a cell whose associated source has 50 units of supply and associated destination has 50 units of demand. Allocating the maximum amount (50 units) to this cell would delete its row and column at the same time. However, $m + n - 1$ cells can be preserved if the associated row is not deleted but rather has its supply adjusted to be zero! That is, we delete the column but not the row and actually allocate the zero units of supply to another cell at another step in the heuristic. This results in some cell's receiving a zero shipment, but the trick preserves the necessary number of $m + n - 1$ cells.

TABLEAU 5.14   Balanced tableau when demand exceeds supply

To / From	New York	Chicago	Dallas	San Francisco	Supply
Washington	8 / 50	9	11	16	50
Denver	12 / 10	7 / 70	5	8	80
Los Angeles	14 / 10	10	6 / 60	7 / 50	120
Dummy	0 / 20	0	0	0	20
Demand	90	70	60	50	270

TABLEAU 5.15   Degeneracy in the MODI method

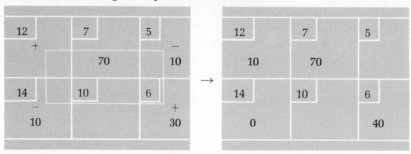

In the second case, degeneracy arises whenever there is more than one basic cell in the closed loop that is minus-labeled and has the minimum shipment amount. In this situation, care must be taken to delete only one of these cells. For example, consider Tableau 5.15, which is an altered version of Tableau 5.11. Both cells (2,3) and (3,1) have shipments of 10 units and are labeled with minus signs. In making the shipment adjustments, we can maintain $m + n - 1$ cells if we only delete one of these two cells, either (2,3) or (3,1). Arbitrarily deleting one and placing a zero shipment in the other maintains $m + n - 1$ basic cells. This same procedure extends to cases where more than two minus-labeled cells in the loop have the same minimal shipment.

FURTHER APPLICATIONS OF TRANSPORTATION MODELS

The utility of the transportation problem is that it may be applied to more than just transportation and distribution problems. Other fruitful areas of application are production scheduling and inventory storage problems. For illustrative purposes, let us consider the following case of the El Paso Slacks Company.

EXAMPLE   The El Paso Slacks Company produces a particular pair of pants that is subject to demand fluctuations throughout the year. In order to smooth production costs, the company produces some excess during seasons when demand volume lessens and stores the pants as inventory for the season when demand is high. The production capacity is 120,000 pairs of pants per season except summer, when employee vacations reduce production capacity to 110,000 pairs. The marketing department has forecast sales for each season; figures are shown in Table 5.6. There are two types of cost: production and inventory storage. The per-unit production cost is $5 per pair of pants during the first two seasons, but inflation is expected to raise production cost to $6 in fall and winter. As inventory,

TABLE 5.6 El Paso slacks sales forecast data (thousands)

Season	Forecast demand	Production capacity
Spring	110	120
Summer	90	110
Fall	140	120
Winter	115	120
	455	470

the pants can be stored for several months. However, it costs $1 per quarter to store them, and due to style changes, all pants should be delivered to retailers by the end of the year. No backlogging is allowed. The company is planning ahead and wants to know which production schedule minimizes combined production and inventory costs for the year.

The problem is legitimately modeled as a transportation problem, and the particulars are shown in Tableau 5.16. The rows of the tableau indicate quarterly production capacity, and the columns indicate quarterly demand. The costs in each cell indicate per-unit production costs plus whatever unit storage costs apply. For instance, in cell (1,4), which represents spring production for winter consumption, the cost is $8 = $5 production cost + $3 storage cost (for three quarters). Cell (3,3) has a cost of $6 = $6 production cost + 0 storage cost. The crossed-out cells are impermissible cells because consumption cannot possibly precede production.

Solving this transportation model yields an optimum production and

TABLEAU 5.16 El Paso Slacks Company problem

Season	Spring	Summer	Fall	Winter	Excess capacity	Production capacity
Spring	5	6	7	8	0	120
Summer	✕	5	6	7	0	110
Fall	✕	✕	6	7	0	120
Winter	✕	✕	✕	6	0	120
Demand	110	90	140	115	15	470

inventory storage schedule for the El Paso Slacks Company. The solution would be rendered in production and storage amounts rather than shipments from sources to destinations.

THE ASSIGNMENT PROBLEM

The assignment problem is another special LP problem. It has a wide range of applications and, like the transportation problem, is solvable by a special-purpose algorithm that is much more efficient than the regular simplex method.

The assignment problem is closely related to the transportation problem; in fact, it is a special case of the transportation problem. However, the basic idea is to assign n single elements rather than many units from each source to destination. Some typical applications of the assignment problem include the least-cost or least-time assignment of jobs to machines, workers to tasks, salesmen to territories, and contracts to contractors. The assignment method is also used to solve subproblems of even larger and more involved management science models.

To illustrate the assignment problem, let us consider the Ace Machine Shop problem, whose data are presented in Table 5.7. Three jobs (1, 2, and 3) must be processed by the machine shop. Any of the three jobs can be processed on any of the three machines. However, each job is to be processed on only one machine, and each machine can be assigned only one job. Thus a solution will define a one-to-one correspondence between jobs and machines. The processing costs vary from machine to machine, as indicated in Table 5.7. The optimal solution is shown in Tableau 5.17. As indicated by the white, boldface numbers in Tableau 5.17, the least-cost solution is to assign job 1 to machine B, job 2 to machine C, and job 3 to machine A. The total cost of the assignment is $42 + 46 + 43 = \$131$. The Ace Machine Shop problem illustrates the characteristics of assignment problems. Notice in Tableau 5.17 that precisely one assignment

TABLE 5.7   Cost data ($) for assigning jobs to machines

	Machine		
Job	A	B	C
1	57	42	65
2	39	48	46
3	43	72	53

TABLEAU 5.17 Optimal solution for Ace Machine Shop problem

Job	Machine		
	A	B	C
1	57	42	65
2	39	48	46
3	43	72	53

occurs in each row and each column. Also, the problem is square in that there are an equal number of rows and columns. We can describe the assignment model as a transportation model with an equal number of sources and destinations and all supplies and demands equal to 1.

In general, if we have n jobs to be assigned to n machines, we can state the mathematical model of the assignment problem as

$$\text{Minimize} \quad \sum_{i=1}^{n} \sum_{j=1}^{n} c_{ij} x_{ij} \qquad [5.10]$$

$$\text{subject to} \quad \sum_{j=1}^{n} x_{ij} = 1, \quad i = 1, 2, \ldots, n$$

$$\sum_{i=1}^{n} x_{ij} = 1, \quad j = 1, 2, \ldots, n$$

$$x_{ij} \geq 0 \quad \text{for all } i \text{ and } j$$

where c_{ij} equals the cost of assigning job i to machine j. In solving the assignment model, n of the x_{ij} variables are in solution at a value of 1 and all other x_{ij} equal 0.

The assignment model is a special case of the transportation model; this can be seen by comparing systems 5.1 and 5.10. The assignment problem can be solved by using a transportation method such as the MODI method. However, the resulting solution would be highly degenerate (it would contain $n - 1$ degenerate cells), and even faster and more efficient techniques are available for solving assignment problems.

THE HUNGARIAN METHOD

The Hungarian method for solving the assignment problem is named in honor of the Hungarian mathematician, D. König, who proved a theorem required for its development. Our version of this method can be calculated by hand, and it may seem rather simplistic. But properly executed, the Hungarian method yields optimal solutions to the assignment problem. Our procedure is based on a mathematically proven algorithm for arriving at an optimal solution.

The method is founded upon the concept of opportunity losses. You have encountered opportunity losses before in calculations for the VAM heuristic. In the assignment method, the optimal solution incurs zero opportunity loss. Any other solution with a higher cost incurs an opportunity loss that is equal to its increase in cost over the minimum cost obtainable in the optimal solution. The basic idea in the Hungarian method is to avoid opportunity losses.

A fundamental principle underlying the Hungarian method is that a constant may be subtracted from any row or column in the assignment cost tableau without changing the optimal assignments. Changing the costs in such a manner changes the cost of the solution, of course, but not the actual assignments.

To develop the Hungarian method, let us consider the 4 × 4 assignment problem of the Research & Development Corporation, which is subcontracting four energy-related projects to four independent bidders. For political reasons, each of the bidders has been promised one project. The management at Research & Development wants to minimize the total expenditure for contracts. In Tableau 5.18, the bid amounts are indicated.

The Hungarian method has three basic steps: The first is to calculate an assignment tableau of opportunity losses; the second step is to determine whether an optimal assignment can be made. If an optimal assignment cannot be made, then we must revise the opportunity loss tableau and return to the second step. We repeat steps 2 and 3 until an optimum is achieved.

In solving the 4 × 4 assignment problem for the Research & Development Corporation, we must first calculate the opportunity loss tableau. We make use of the principle that subtracting a constant from any row or column does not change the location of the optimal assignments. In calculating the total opportunity loss tableau, we first calculate row opportunity losses, then column opportunity losses. The row opportunity losses are calculated by subtracting the least cost in each row from all other costs in that row. For instance, in Tableau 5.18, the lowest cost in row 1 is 17. Thus, making an assignment in cell (1,4) incurs zero opportunity loss. However, since cell (1,1) has a cost of 20, an assignment in cell (1,1) incurs an opportunity loss of 20 − 17 = 3. Subtracting the lowest cost in a particular row from the other costs in that row yields at least one zero-cost cell in each row. This step is called a row reduction and is shown in Tableau 5.19. The row reduction does not change the solution to the problem, only the costs in the assignment tableau.

The next step is to perform a column reduction. This involves subtract-

TABLEAU 5.18 Contract bid amounts (thousands of dollars) for Research & Development Corporation

Bidder	Project 1	2	3	4
A	20	36	31	17
B	24	34	40	12
C	22	40	38	18
D	36	39	35	16

ing the lowest number in each column from all other numbers in that column. For example, Research & Development Corporation incurs a zero opportunity loss in assigning project 1 to bidder A. Referring to Tableau 5.19, we can see that the opportunity loss is $12 - 3 = 9$ if the assignment is made to cell (2, 1) (that is, if project 1 is assigned to bidder B). Performing the column reduction for each column from Tableau 5.19, we obtain the total opportunity loss tableau in Tableau 5.20.

The total opportunity loss tableau has the same assignment solution as the original problem, and it also has a zero in each row and each column. The zero-cost cells show where an assignment can be made that incurs no opportunity loss. An optimal solution is found whenever all assignments can be made in unique cells that have zero opportunity losses. Sometimes this is possible after determining the total opportunity loss tableau. However, this is not the case in Tableau 5.20, for only two assignments can be made in zero-cost cells.

TABLEAU 5.19 Row reduction of Research & Development tableau

Bidder	Project 1	2	3	4	Least cost subtracted from row
A	3	19	14	0	17
B	12	22	28	0	12
C	4	22	20	0	18
D	20	23	19	0	16

TABLEAU 5.20   Total opportunity loss tableau for Research & Development Corporation

Bidder	Project				
	1	2	3	4	
A	0	0	0	0	
B	9	3	14	0	
C	1	3	6	0	
D	17	4	5	0	least cost subtracted
	3	19	14	0	← from column

We need a systematic procedure for determining whether an optimal solution has been found. One such procedure entails crossing out all zero costs by drawing as few horizontal and vertical lines as possible through the assignment tableau. If the number of lines necessary to accomplish this is less than the number of rows or columns in the assignment tableau, the problem is not optimal and the total opportunity cost tableau must be revised further. If, however, n lines in an $(n \times n)$ assignment problem are required to cross out all zero costs, then the problem is solved and optimal assignments can be made. The only weakness in this procedure is that it depends upon human judgment for determining the minimum number of lines.

This test for optimality is applied to the total opportunity loss tableau (Tableau 5.20). Only two lines are required (as is shown in Tableau 5.21)

TABLEAU 5.21   Crossing out all zero costs with only two lines

Bidder	Project			
	1	2	3	4
A	0	0	0	0
B	9	3	14	0
C	1	3	6	0
D	17	4	5	0

**TABLEAU 5.22 Revised opportunity
loss tableau**

Project			
1	2	3	4
0̶	0̶	0̶	1̶
8	2	13	0
0̶	2̶	5̶	0̶
16	3	4	0

to cover all zero costs. Since the problem has four rows, an assignment is not yet possible.

The next step is to revise the opportunity loss tableau in order to generate more zero-cost cells without altering the solution to the original problem. We do this in the following way: (1) we select the smallest number from each number not covered by a straight line; (2) we add this smallest number to each cost that lies at the intersection of two straight lines, and we subtract it from each cost that is not covered by a line. Note that costs covered by only one line are unchanged by this procedure.

In Tableau 5.21, we find that the smallest number not covered by a straight line is 1. Subtracting 1 from each cost not covered by a line and adding 1 to the point of intersection gives us the situation shown in Tableau 5.22. It is possible to cross out all zero costs in Tableau 5.22 with only three lines; thus, we must revise the opportunity loss tableau further. The smallest cost not covered is a 2; subtracting this from each cost not covered by a line and adding it to each point of intersection, we obtain the facts of Tableau 5.23.

Since four lines are required to cross out all zero costs, we can make an optimal assignment. The optimal assignment is to assign project 1 to bidder C, 2 to B, 3 to A, and 4 to D. The solution is indicated by the white, boldface numbers in Tableau 5.23. To calculate the total cost of the optimal solution, we refer to the original costs from Tableau 5.18 and calculate the data shown in Table 5.8.

Although we have determined that an optimal assignment can be made it may not be obvious where these assignments should occur. A systematic approach to making the assignments is called for. One procedure is to find

TABLEAU 5.23   Optimal opportunity loss tableau

Bidder	Project			
	1	2	3	4
A	0	0	0	3
B	6	0	11	0
C	0	2	5	2
D	14	1	2	0

TABLE 5.8   Cost (thousands of dollars) of Research & Development Corporation optimal solution

Assignment	Cost
1 to C	$ 22
2 to B	34
3 to A	31
4 to D	16
Total cost	$103

a row or column with only one zero-cost cell and no previous assignments. An assignment must be made in this cell. For example, column 3 in Tableau 5.23 has only one zero; it appears in cell (A, 3). Since no more assignments can be made in column 3 or row A, we draw a line through column 3 and row A. Then, we again seek a row or column with a single zero and find row D. We make an assignment in cell (D, 4) and draw lines through column 4 and row D. The procedure is repeated until all assignments are made. If the remaining rows or columns all have two or more zero-cost cells, an assignment can be made in any zero-cost cell that has not been covered by a straight line.

SUMMARY OF THE HUNGARIAN METHOD

1. Determine the total opportunity loss tableau:
   a. Select the least cost in each row and subtract it from each cost in that row.

     b.   Using the row-reduced cost tableau that has been generated, select the least cost in each column and subtract it from every cost in that column.

2.   Determine whether an optimal assignment can be made by drawing the minimum number of horizontal and vertical lines through the total opportunity loss tableau that will cover all zero-cost cells. If the number of lines required is less than the number of rows (columns), go to step 3. Otherwise, stop and make the optimal assignments.

3.   Revise the total opportunity loss tableau:

     a.   Select the smallest number not covered by a line and subtract this number from every number not covered by a line.

     b.   Add this same number to any number at the intersection of two lines. Go to step 2.

Note that the Hungarian method can also be used to maximize objectives in assignment problems. To accomplish this, we simply change the signs of the profit coefficients and minimize; or, alternatively, we may calculate the total opportunity loss tableau based on the largest profit, rather than the lowest cost, in each row or column.

SUMMARY

Network models are very important to, and have widespread applications among, management science techniques. Transportation and assignment models are linear network models with a special structure that considerably simplifies their computation.

Transportation problems can be solved by heuristics methods, such as row minimum or VAM (Vogel's approximation method), that are fast and yield good, but not necessarily optimal, solutions. The MODI method can be used to take a starting feasible solution from row minimum or VAM and improve it to optimality. Degeneracy is easily handled in the MODI method by ensuring that the tableau has $m + n - 1$ basic cells at all times. An important characteristic of transportation-type models is that integer (whole number) parameters yield integer solutions. Applications other than physical distribution exist for transportation models; among these are production scheduling and inventory storage problems.

The assignment problem is a special case of the transportation problem. The Hungarian method is an efficient procedure for determining optimal solutions to assignment problems. With minor modifications, the Hungarian method can be used to maximize, as well as minimize, assignment objectives.

SOLVED PROBLEMS

PROBLEM STATEMENT

From warehouse	To city					
	1	2	3	4	5	Supply
1	1.50	1.65	2.05	1.40	1.35	800
2	1.60	2.10	1.80	1.65	2.00	1000
Demand	500	200	300	600	800	

The Burgraf Co. distributes its product from 2 warehouses to 5 major metropolitan areas. Next month's anticipated demand exceeds warehouse supplies and the management at Burgraf would like to know how to distribute their product in order to maximize revenue. Their distribution costs per unit are shown in the table. To be competitive Burgraf must charge a different price in the different cities. Selling prices are $9.95, $10.50, $9.50, $11.15, and $10.19 in cities 1, 2, 3, 4, and 5, respectively. The tableau of revenue = selling price − distribution cost is given as

From warehouse	To city					
	1	2	3	4	5	Supply
1	8.45	8.85	7.45	9.75	8.84	800
2	8.35	8.40	7.70	9.50	8.19	1000
Demand	500	200	300	600	800	

SOLUTION

Since this problem is a maximization rather than a minimization, we compute the opportunity costs for VAM as the difference between the most-profitable cell and next-most-profitable cell in a row or column.

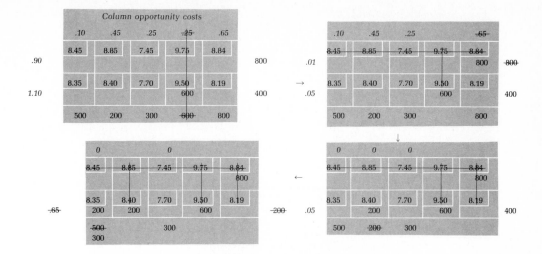

The VAM solution provides a feasible solution that is also optimal. In order to prove optimality through the MODI method it is necessary to add a dummy warehouse and ensure that we have $m + n - 1$, or $3 + 5 - 1 = 7$ basic cells that form no closed loops. Examining the tableau below establishes the optimality of the solution.

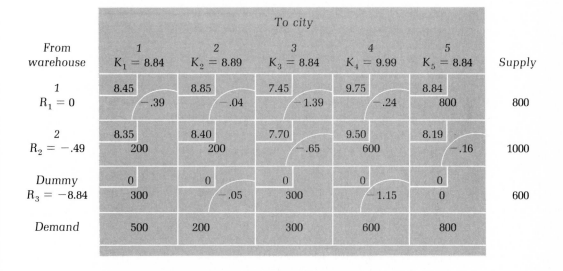

From warehouse	To city 1 $K_1 = 8.84$	2 $K_2 = 8.89$	3 $K_3 = 8.84$	4 $K_4 = 9.99$	5 $K_5 = 8.84$	Supply
1 $R_1 = 0$	8.45 $-.39$	8.85 $-.04$	7.45 -1.39	9.75 $-.24$	8.84 800	800
2 $R_2 = -.49$	8.35 200	8.40 200	7.70 $-.65$	9.50 600	8.19 $-.16$	1000
Dummy $R_3 = -8.84$	0 300	0 $-.05$	0 300	0 -1.15	0 0	600
Demand	500	200	300	600	800	

PROBLEM STATEMENT

The assignment model is often used as a subproblem of more complex problems. It is useful in the solution of the well-known traveling salesman problem, which is a classical combinatorial problem that is very difficult to solve optimally. In the traveling salesman problem, a "salesman" must leave a home base, visit each of n locations once, and return to the home base. The objective is to determine the sequence of locations in order to minimize the distance traveled. For n locations there are $(n - 1)!$ possible sequences, called tours.

For an example, let us consider a delivery truck routing problem in which a truck must leave a warehouse and visit four customer delivery points and then return to the warehouse. The matrix of distances is shown below; point 1 is the warehouse.

	Distance (miles)				
To From	1	2	3	4	5
1	—	10	7	5	5
2	11	—	4	6	8
3	7	4	—	7	8
4	5	5	7	—	3
5	3	8	8	3	—

SOLUTION

In unusual cases, the solution of the distance matrix as an assignment problem yields an optimal sequence or tour for the traveling salesman problem. The vast majority of the time, however, the optimal assignment solution does not form a tour. It is possible to solve a sequence of properly constructed assignment problems that will eventually solve the traveling salesman problem. To illustrate, we solve the 5 × 5 distance problem as an assignment problem.

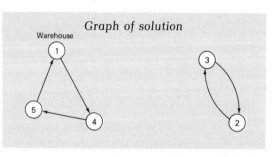

Row reduction					
	1	2	3	4	5
1	—	5	2	0	0
2	7	—	0	2	4
3	3	0	—	3	4
4	2	2	4	—	0
5	0	5	5	3	—

After the row reduction the optimal assignment is 1–4, 2–3, 3–2, 4–5, and 5–1. This assignment does not form a single connected tour, as shown in the graph.

In order to preclude the infeasible subtour 3–2, 2–3, let us set the distance from 2 to 3 equal to infinity in the distance matrix. This will prevent 2 being assigned to 3.

Row reduction					
	1	2	3	4	5
1	—	5	2	0	0
2	5	—	—	0	2
3	3	0	—	3	4
4	2	2	4	—	0
5	0	5	5	3	—

2 subtracted

Column reduction					
	1	2	3	4	5
1	—	5	0	0	0
2	5	—	—	0	2
3	3	0	—	3	4
4	2	2	2	—	0
5	0	5	3	3	—

2 subtracted

After a row and column reduction, the total opportunity loss matrix yields a new optimal assignment. This time the assignment is 1–3, 3–2, 2–4, 4–5, and 5–1. This assignment yields the optimal tour of length $7 + 6 + 4 + 3 + 3 = 23$. The second graph shows the optimal tour.

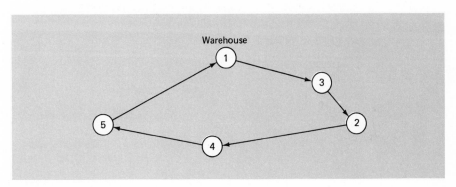

REVIEW QUESTIONS

1. Explain why transportation and assignment models are part of the category of network models.

2. What are the advantages of using special-purpose algorithms to solve transportation and assignment problems?

3. What are the advantages and disadvantages of using heuristics versus optimization techniques?

4. Why would you expect VAM usually to yield a better heuristic solution than the row minimum method?

5. Briefly discuss the theoretical basis of VAM.

6. List some applications of transportation models other than distribution of a commodity from plant to market.

7. Specifically, how does the assignment math model differ from the transportation math model?

8. How is degeneracy handled in the MODI method?

9. Discuss whether the Hungarian method is heuristic or an optimization technique.

10. List some applications of the assignment model.

PROBLEMS

5.1 *Product Distribution.* The P & R Company distributes its product from three plants to four regional warehouses. The monthly supplies and demands along with per-unit transportation costs are given in the table. Using the row minimum heuristic, find a feasible shipping pattern and total transportation cost.

From plant	To warehouse				
	1	2	3	4	Supply
1	2	12	6	10	20
2	14	6	2	12	10
3	18	8	10	8	25
Demand	11	13	17	14	55

5.2 Use VAM to solve Problem 5.1.

5.3 Use the row minimum starting solution and the MODI method to determine an optimal solution to Problem 5.1.

5.4 *Stock Redistribution.* The Reasor Department Store chain has excess stock of a particular product at two stores, and shortages at four others. The objective is to redistribute the stock at minimum transportation cost. Given the following stock and cost information, find the optimal distribution pattern at minimum cost.

Store	Excess	Shortage
1	50	
2	75	
3		20
4		30
5		45
6		30

	Cost data			
		To store		
From store	3	4	5	6
1	$7	$3	$5	$8
2	6	4	2	9

5.5   Solve the El Paso Slacks Company's production scheduling problem in Tableau 5.16 by the MODI method.

5.6   *Physical Distribution.* Nationwide Distributors is trying to determine the most effective way to distribute their product in order to maximize profits. Their distribution costs from their 3 plants to their regional warehouses is shown in the table.

	To warehouse					
From plant	1	2	3	4	5	Supply
1	2.25	1.50	3.00	2.00	1.25	1000
2	3.15	2.75	1.00	1.95	1.60	1500
3	2.00	2.50	3.35	2.15	2.20	1200
Demand	800	600	1000	500	800	

The average selling price for the product at each warehouse is $9.75, $10.15, $9.95, $9.50, and $9.85, respectively. Determine the shipping pattern that maximizes revenue.

5.7 Refer to Problem 2.12. Find an initial feasible solution using VAM and then solve by the MODI method.

5.8 Solve the following transportation problem using VAM.

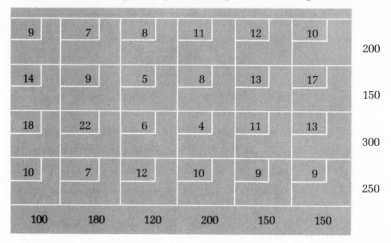

9	7	8	11	12	10	200
14	9	5	8	13	17	150
18	22	6	4	11	13	300
10	7	12	10	9	9	250
100	180	120	200	150	150	

5.9 Determine the optimal solution to Problem 5.8 by using the MODI method.

5.10 *Court Docket Assignments.* A city government wants to improve the efficiency of the local court system. They have collected data on the average length of time a particular judge requires to handle each type of case. Given the composition of the types of cases scheduled on each docket, the times shown in the table were estimated for each judge to process each different docket. Determine the assignment of judges to dockets to minimize the time required to complete all dockets.

| | | Docket | | |
	1	2	3	4
1	13	20	17	18
2	15	19	18	13
Judge 3	16	14	16	15
4	14	15	18	17

5.11   *Rental Trailer Relocation.* The Continental Trailer Rental Company has a problem in trying to relocate rented trailers. Currently, its supply exceeds the demand, and it is necessary to relocate trailers at minimum transportation cost. There are surplus trailers at locations 1, 2, 3, and 4, whereas trailers are in demand at locations 5, 6, and 7. The relevant data are given in the table. Determine the optimum relocation of trailers.

	Location						
Trailer status	1	2	3	4	5	6	7
Surplus	6	7	8	3			
Shortage					5	4	9

	Cost per trailer transported		
From \ To	5	6	7
1	$ 8	$11	$8
2	12	10	6
3	15	7	9
4	12	12	7

5.12   *Production and Distribution.* Consider a variation of the production/distribution example of Chapter 2. In this problem, it is necessary to address production, as well as transportation, costs in the transportation model. Assume that two plants have production capacities of 2,600 and 1,800, respectively. The three warehouses have demands of 1,500, 2,000, and 900. The product is produced at plant 1 at a per-unit cost of $1.50, whereas the per-unit cost at plant 2 is $2. Transportation costs are given in the table. Set up and solve a transportation model that determines the amount to produce at each plant and the resulting shipping pattern.

	To warehouse			
From plant	1	2	3	Supply
1	$.30	$.50	$.80	2,600
2	$.70	$.20	$.40	1,800
Demand	1,500	2,000	900	4,400

5.13   *Traveling Salesman.* A salesman must fly from city to city to maintain his major accounts. This week he has to leave his home base and visit each of 4 cities and return home. The table shows the air fare between the various cities. The home city is city 1. Use the assignment method to determine the tour that will minimize the total air fare of visiting all cities and returning home.

To *From*	1	2	3	4	5
1	—	375	600	150	190
2	375	—	300	350	175
3	600	300	—	350	500
4	150	350	350	—	300
5	190	175	500	300	—

5.14   *Aggregate Production Planning.* The Yuba Manufacturing Co. is planning its aggregate production levels for the last quarter of the year and would like to minimize the combined cost of production and inventory. Production capacities for October, November, and December are 6,000, 6,000, and 4,000, respectively. The demand for the firm's product is expected to be 3,000, 7,000, and 5,000 during the last quarter. Given that per-piece production cost is $3.00 and storage cost per month is $1.00, find a low-cost production/inventory schedule.

5.15   *Job Assignment.* Three jobs must be processed. There are three machines available, but each job must be done on only one machine. Jobs may not be split between machines. The cost of processing each job on each machine is given in the table. Determine the minimum-cost assignment for each job.

	Machine		
Job	X	Y	Z
1	10	16	8
2	8	6	4
3	16	12	8

5.16 *Production Scheduling.* The American Products Corporation must decide on its production schedule for the next four months. It has contracted to supply a special part for the months of October, November, December, and January at the rates of 12,000, 10,000, 15,000, and 17,000 units, respectively. American can produce each part at a cost of $6 during regular time or $9 during overtime. Each month, American has a production capacity of 10,000 units during regular time and 6,000 units during overtime. The part can be stored at a cost of $2 per month; however, there is zero inventory on hand at the beginning of October and there must be zero inventory at the end of January. American can thus overproduce in some months and store the excess to help meet future demand in other months. Construct a transportation model (tableau) to solve American's production scheduling and inventory storage problem. *Hint:* Define the sources as the modes of production in each month, and define the destinations as the demand required during each month.

5.17 *More-for-less Paradox.* Is it actually possible to ship more for less? Assuming no quantity discounts and the same transportation costs, is there ever a situation in which shipping more units will lower costs? Consider the following 3 × 4 transportation problem with optimal solution as shown in the first tableau. Suppose that we add an additional unit of supply to source 2 and an additional unit of demand to destination 1. The results are shown in the second tableau.

		To destination				
		$K_1 = -1$	$K_2 = 3$	$K_3 = 1$	$K_4 = 3$	
	From source	1	2	3	4	Supply
$R_1 = 2$	1	1 — 11	6	3 — 9	5	20
$R_2 = 0$	2	7	3 — 2	1 — 8	6	10
$R_3 = 1$	3	9	4 — 11	5	4 — 14	25
	Demand	11	13	17	14	55

minimum cost $152

To destination					
From source	1	2	3	4	Supply
1	1	6	3	5	20
2	7	3	1	6	11
3	9	4	5	4	25
Demand	12	13	17	14	56

minimum cost $151?

Obviously, shipping the additional unit through cell (2,1) raises costs by $7. Without solving the problem from scratch, can you find an alternative shipping schedule that will lower costs?

5.18 *Least-Time Transportation Model.* In the least-time transportation problem the objective is to minimize the maximum time required to complete any shipment. In a least-time transportation tableau the numbers in the cells represent times. The standard transportation objective function (5.1) is rewritten for the least time model as minimize $z = \max \{t_{ij}\}$ such that $x_{ij} > 0$. The least-time problem corresponds, for example, to a military airlift operation in which it is desired to complete all operations as soon as possible.

Assume that the cost figures of the 4×6 tableau in Problem 5.8 correspond to times. Devise your own procedure (heuristic or otherwise) to come up with a feasible solution that minimizes the maximum time of all cells with a positive shipment.

5.19 *Automobile Distribution.* The Missan Sports Car Company produces several lines of automobiles, among which is its super racer, the 290ZX. These specialty cars are hand-assembled at each of four plants, in Boston, Cleveland, Denver, and Detroit. Missan currently has custom orders for one 290ZX at Chicago, Wichita, Tulsa, and Dallas. Each plant currently has one model ready for shipping. The transportation cost data are given in the table.

a. Which method is best for solving this problem?

b. Determine the optimal solution.

	Transportation cost per 290ZX			
To From	Chicago	Wichita	Tulsa	Dallas
Boston	$130	$240	$250	$300
Cleveland	40	210	220	270
Denver	150	110	115	125
Detroit	35	190	300	250

5.20 *Assignment of Contracts.* The Concrete Construction Company has requested bids for subcontracts on five different projects. Five companies have responded; their bids are represented below. Determine the minimum cost assignment of subcontracts to bidders, assuming that each bidder can receive only one contract. If each bidder could receive any number of contracts, then what would be the optimal assignment?

	Bid amount				
			Project		
Bidder	1	2	3	4	5
1	$41,000	$72,000	$39,000	$52,000	$25,000
2	22,000	29,000	49,000	65,000	81,000
3	27,000	39,000	60,000	51,000	40,000
4	45,000	50,000	48,000	52,000	37,000
5	29,000	40,000	45,000	26,000	30,000

5.21 *Plant Location.* The TDW Production Company is unable to meet its increased yearly demand because of production capacities. It is thinking about building a new factory to meet this new demand and also decrease transportation cost. The current production and distribution system is summarized below. The costs in the table indicate per-unit transportation costs. The proposed new factory, C, would have a capacity of 2,000 and would have transportation costs of $3, $2.50, $4, and $2 to warehouses 1, 2, 3, and 4, respectively.

	Warehouse				
Factory	1	2	3	4	Factory capacity
A	$2.90	$2.60	$3.50	$4.00	2,500
B	3.10	3.30	3.70	3.00	1,500
					4,000
Demand	1,000	1,500	2,000	500	5,000

The company is currently losing $20 per unit on unsatisfied demand, since this is the profit they net on each unit that is sold (not including transportation costs). However, the new factory would cost $21,000 per year over the life of the factory. Evaluate TDW's proposal to add the new factory.

5.22 *Applicant Selection.* The Psychological Testing Agency has recently tested seven applicants for five jobs that are available at the Coldman Company. Each job has a primary skill, and Coldman's objective is to pick the five applicants whose aptitude test scores will maximize total performance. Only one worker can be assigned to only one job. The aptitude test scores are listed below. Determine the five best applicants for the five jobs.

	Job				
Applicant	1	2	3	4	5
1	95	110	103	115	98
2	89	95	100	87	92
3	120	132	118	128	121
4	107	119	112	108	96
5	75	83	99	100	85
6	113	115	98	111	120
7	102	73	95	70	94

BIBLIOGRAPHY

Bazaraa, Mokhtar S., and John J. Jarvis, *Linear Programming and Network Flows.* New York: John Wiley & Sons, Inc., 1977.

Charnes, Abraham, and W. W. Cooper, *Management Models and Industrial Applications of Linear Programming,* Vol. 1. New York: John Wiley & Sons, Inc., 1961.

Daellenbach, Hans G., and Earl J. Bell, *Users' Guide to Linear Programming.* Englewood Cliffs, N.J.: Prentice-Hall, Inc., 1970.

Gupta, Skiv K., and John M. Cozzolino, *Fundamentals of Operations Research for Management.* San Francisco: Holden-Day, Inc., 1975.

Hillier, Frederick S., and Gerald J. Lieberman, *Introduction to Operations Research.* San Francisco: Holden-Day, Inc., 1974.

Hu, T. C., *Integer Programming and Network Flows.* Reading, Mass.: Addison-Wesley Publishing Co., Inc., 1969.

Kwak, N. K., *Mathematical Programming with Business Applications.* New York: McGraw-Hill Book Company, 1973.

Loomba, N. P., and E. Turban, *Applied Programming for Management.* New York: Holt, Rinehart, and Winston, Inc., 1974.

Simmons, Donald M., *Linear Programming for Operations Research.* San Francisco: Holden-Day, Inc., 1972.

Wagner, Harvey M., *Principles of Management Science: With Application to Executive Decisions.* Englewood Cliffs, N.J.: Prentice-Hall, Inc., 1975.

6

Network Models

GENERAL MOTORS CORPORATION[1]

A company the size of General Motors would understandably have a very large and complex production planning and distribution problem. To help in the management of production planning and distribution, GM decided to use a specialized network model. The objective of the analysis was to determine the number and type of each model of car to produce at each plant and then to determine the distribution center to which each model should be shipped.

The type of network model used is called a transshipment model, and Figure 6.27 illustrates a simplified network model of the problem. The transshipment model can be used to incorporate the various production costs at each plant, as well as the transportation costs from plant to distribution center. The model also reflects the bounded production capacities at each plant and the limits for each type of car model at each plant.

A typical application for the Pontiac or Buick division involves a transshipment model with approximately 4,000 network arcs and 1,200 network nodes. Recently developed network algorithms enable a network model of this size to be solved on a computer in less than 10 seconds. This kind of speed enabled GM to develop an on-line computer capability. The network model is linked to a graphics display terminal and an English-language input processor. Thus, the manager need not be an OR/MS expert to use the system. Management can feed in relevant data using the English language and within seconds observe the optimal solution on the display terminal. The system is a successful decision support system that is currently being used by the executive division for planning purposes. If the model is slightly modified for other settings, it can be used in production and distribution of products other than cars. The model can also be used to handle decisions relevant to various stages of a production process.

---

[1]F. Glover and D. Klingman, "Network Application in Industry and Government," *AIIE Transactions*, 9, No. 4 (1977), 363–376.

INTRODUCTION

In this chapter we continue our study of network models. In Chapter 5 we looked at transportation and assignment models and in Chapter 7 we will look at PERT/CPM, a network approach to project scheduling.

network   Recall that a *network* is a collection of nodes or points connected by arcs. Figure 6.1 depicts a simple network. Why are networks important and why are three chapters in this text related to network models? The answer is twofold. First, network models arise frequently in management science applications. Many real-world problems have a network structure or can be modeled in network form. Table 6.1 provides several common examples of systems that can be represented as networks. In addition to the physical systems listed in Table 6.1, there are some problems that do not appear physically to be a network but can be modeled as a network in the abstract. Some of these examples include scheduling problems, inventory problems, and even financial applications, including cash management.

A second reason for the importance of network models is their solution efficiency. Network models are at the problem-solving frontiers in terms of problem size and solution speed. Network decision models having as many as 62.5 million variables have been tackled by network models. Network models can also be solved in reasonable amounts of computer time where other approaches are impractical. These properties have led *netform* some researchers to advocate a "*netform concept*," whose philosophy is *concept* to extract network structure from a problem whenever possible.[2] Some problems are not purely network problems, but have some network substructure. Exploiting the network substructure by embedding a network algorithm in the overall solution procedure can possibly yield significant computational efficiency and in some cases can yield solutions to previously unsolvable problems.

FIGURE 6.1   A simple network

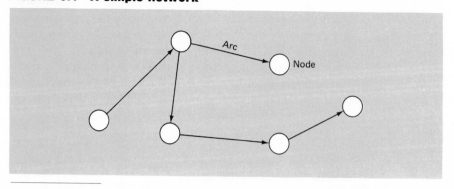

[2]F. Glover, J. Hultz, and D. Klingman, "Improved Computer-Based Planning Techniques, Part II," *Interfaces*, 9 (August 1979), 12–20.

TABLE 6.1 Examples of networks

Physical distribution systems	City streets and traffic signals
Communication networks	Airline flight legs
Pipeline systems	Production assembly line systems

THE SHORTEST-ROUTE PROBLEM

shortest route

In this chapter we examine four network models. All have interesting applications and are also often used as subproblems of larger or more complex decision problems. The first model we consider is the shortest route problem. In this problem the objective is to find the *shortest route* along arcs from one node to one or more other nodes in the network. The arcs usually represent distances, but can represent times or costs.

To illustrate the problem and an algorithm for solving it, let us consider the problem faced by a sales representative who has to visit each of her six main accounts each month. Figure 6.2 contains the network graph of the sale rep's problem. Node 1 is her home city and the other six nodes represent the cities she must visit. The arcs represent the existing highways and the numbers on the arcs indicate distances between nodes. The arcs are *nondirected*; that is, they permit flow in either direction. In solving the shortest-route problem, we will determine the shortest route from the home base to each other city. The algorithm we use assumes that none of the distances are negative. In actual practice this is not a limiting assumption.

FIGURE 6.2 Graph of sales rep's problem

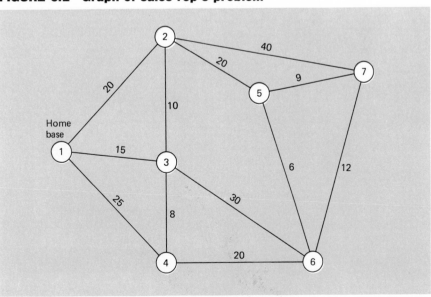

203

SHORTEST-ROUTE ALGORITHM

The algorithm to solve the shortest-route problem is iterative in nature. At each step the shortest distance to one node is determined; thus, after $n - 1$ steps the procedure is finished, where n = number of nodes in the network.

The algorithm consists of two parts, a *labeling procedure* to determine the shortest distance from node 1 to every other node, and a *backtracking procedure* to determine the actual route from node 1 to any other node.

Labeling Procedure   The labels for the nodes consist of an ordered pair of numbers, where the first number indicates the distance from node 1, and the second number indicates the preceding node on the route from node 1 to the node in question. The labels will initially be called temporary labels, but as the shortest distance is found, they will become permanent labels.

The labeling process begins by labeling all nodes that can be reached directly from node 1. In our example these are nodes 2, 3, and 4. We temporarily label each node with the direct distance from node 1 and the previous node on the route which is node 1. These labels are shown in Figure 6.3. Notice that the first component of each label is simply the distance from node 1; these labels are 20, 15, and 25 for nodes 2, 3, and 4, respectively. Of these three nodes, node 3 is closest to node 1. Since all

FIGURE 6.3   Initial labels in shortest-route algorithm

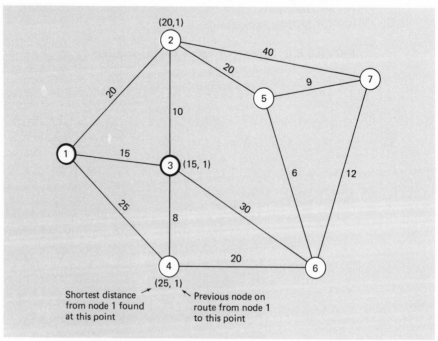

Shortest distance from node 1 found at this point

Previous node on route from node 1 to this point

other arcs have positive distance, we can conclude that there is no shorter route to node 3 than directly from node 1. (Note that we cannot conclude this about node 4.) Thus, we can permanently label node 3 with the label (15,1). Permanently labeled nodes are indicated by a darker line around the node. Node 1 is permanently labeled at the beginning of the labeling process. We now have two classes of nodes; those that are permanently labeled and those that have temporary labels or no labels at all.

The next iteration in the algorithm begins by labeling "outward" from the newest permanently labeled node. We check all nodes that are reachable by a direct arc from node 3. These are nodes 2, 4, and 6. Passing through node 3 on the way from node 1 to node 2 offers no improvement to the direct route from node 1. Thus, node 2's label is unchanged. However, passing through node 3 does offer a distance reduction of $25 - (15 + 8) = 2$ miles for node 4. Thus, we change node 4 label to (23,3) to reflect the distance and previous node of the best route found so far in traveling from node 1 to node 4. Node 6 can also be labeled now with the label (45,3). The forty-five is obtained from the shortest distance to node 3, $15 + 30$, which is the length of the arc from node 3 to node 4. The updated labels are shown in Figure 6.4. Node 2, with a distance of 20, has the smallest distance from node 1 among all temporarily labeled nodes. Thus, the shortest distance from node 1 to node 2 is 20, and node 2 can be permanently labeled.

In the third iteration we can label nodes 5 and 7 from node 2. Node 4, however, has the smallest distance label and can be permanently labeled (see Figure 6.5).

In the fourth iteration we can branch out from node 4 to improve the label on node 6 from (45,3) to (43,4). Node 5 has the lowest temporary distance label and can be fixed permanent (see Figure 6.6).

In the next two iterations we fix nodes 6 and 7 permanently in that order. The final labels are shown in Figure 6.7.

From Figure 6.7 we can determine the shortest distances from node 1 to every other node by looking at the distance component of each label. For instance, we can look at the label for node 7 and determine that the length of the shortest route from 1 to 7 is 49 miles. To determine the route that achieves that shortest distance requires a backtracking process.

Backtracking Procedure   The backtracking procedure simply uses the second component of the node label to determine the predecessors along the shortest route. For example, in starting at node 7, the second label tells us that node 5 is the node that precedes node 7 along the shortest route from node 1 to node 7. Moving to node 5, we find that node 2 precedes it and finally, node 1 precedes node 2. Thus, the backtracking sequence yields

$$7 \rightarrow 5 \rightarrow 2 \rightarrow 1$$

FIGURE 6.4   Node labels after second iteration

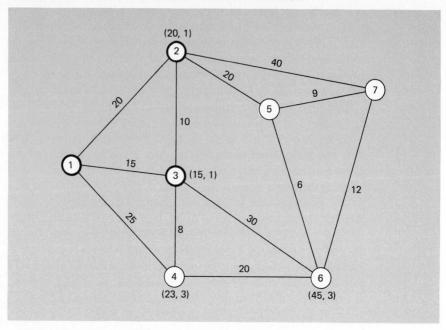

FIGURE 6.5   Node labels after third iteration

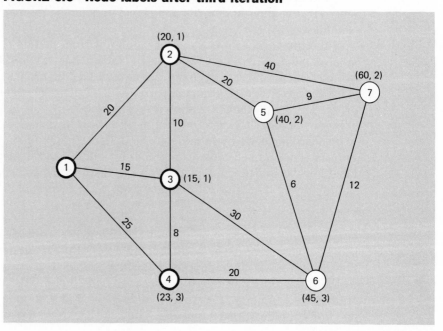

FIGURE 6.6   Node labels after fourth iteration

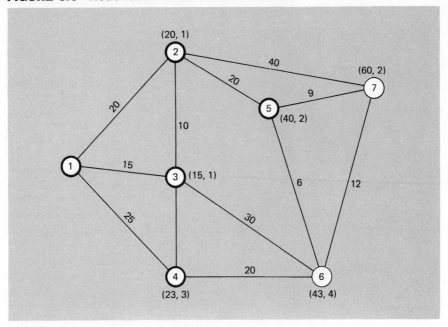

FIGURE 6.7   Final labels for sales rep example

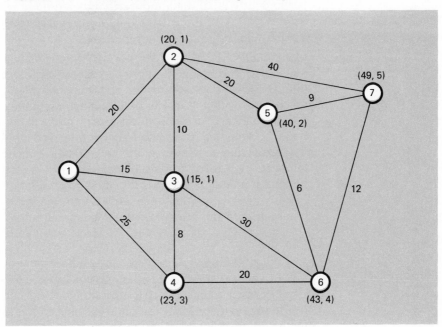

Using the same backtracking procedure, we can determine the shortest route from node 1 to all other nodes.

Node	Shortest route	Distance
2	1–2	20
3	1–3	15
4	1–3–4	23
5	1–2–5	40
6	1–3–4–6	43
7	1–2–5–7	49

The algorithm may seem to require a lot of steps for such a simple problem, which you can probably solve by inspection. However, for larger problems with hundreds or thousands of nodes and even more arcs, the algorithm is necessary and easily implemented on a computer. We summarize the shortest-route algorithm as follows:

LABELING

Step 1: Compute the distance from node 1 to all other nodes that are connected directly to node 1. Set the distance portion of their labels equal to the distance to node 1. Set the predecessor portion of their labels equal to node 1.

Step 2: Permanently label the temporarily labeled node whose distance from node 1 is minimal. Break ties (if any) arbitrarily. If all nodes are permanently labeled, go to step 4.

Step 3: Identify all unlabeled or temporarily labeled nodes that can be reached directly from the new permanently labeled node. Compute the new distance for the node reached by adding the distance label of the permanently labeled node to the distance from the permanently labeled node to the node in question. If the node in question is unlabeled, temporarily label it with the newly calculated distance. If the node in question is already temporarily labeled, update its current distance label only if the newly calculated distance is less than its previous distance label. For any node whose distance label is updated, set its predecessor label equal to the new permanently labeled node. Go to step 2.

BACKTRACKING

Step 4: After the labeling process, each node other than node 1 will have a permanent distance and predecessor label. To determine the shortest route from node 1 to any other node, say node j, refer to the predecessor label for node j. Move to the node specified by the predecessor label and examine its predecessor label. Then move to the node specified and so on until node 1 is reached. The

FIGURE 6.8 Network for equipment replacement decision

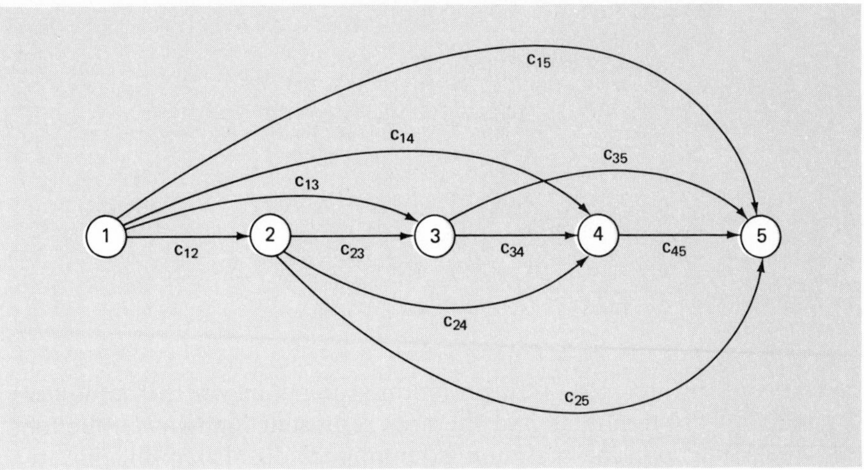

sequence of nodes traced in the backtracking process constitutes the shortest route from node 1 to node j.

SHORTEST-ROUTE APPLICATION— EQUIPMENT REPLACEMENT ANALYSIS

Consider a capital equipment leasing decision in which a company must choose between leasing new equipment at higher leasing costs or maintaining old equipment at higher operating and maintenance costs. For the example, let us assume a 4-year planning horizon. One alternative available to the company is to lease a new piece of equipment at the beginning of year 1 and keep it until the end of year 4. The alternative is represented by the arc from node 1 to node 5 in Figure 6.8.

The cost c_{15} is associated with arc (1,5) and represents the combined leasing, operating, and maintenance costs for four years. Another alternative is to lease a new piece of equipment each year. This alternative would cost $c_{12} + c_{23} + c_{34} + c_{45}$. Thus, the cost c_{ij} represents the cost of leasing and maintaining the equipment from the beginning of year i to the beginning of year j. The minimum-cost solution to the problem is obtained by simply finding the shortest route from node 1 to node 5.

THE MINIMUM SPANNING TREE PROBLEM

The minimum spanning tree problem involves the selection of a set of arcs that will span (connect) all nodes of a network and will minimize the sum of the arc lengths. The problem differs from the shortest route problem in that the arcs of the network do not yet exist and are to be selected.

The problem has applications in several areas. It is particularly useful

FIGURE 6.9 A tree and a nontree

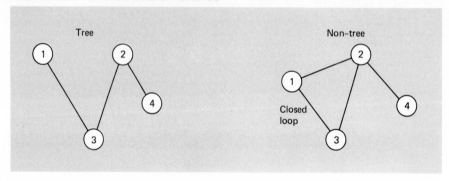

in designing transportation systems in which the nodes of the network are terminals and the arcs represent highways, pipelines, airways, and *minimum* so on. The *minimum spanning tree* is also applicable to communication *spanning tree* and teleprocessing systems, as we shall see later.

The type of structure that will connect all nodes in a network and be of minimal length is a tree. A *tree* is a graph in which the arcs connect all nodes (that is, provide paths along which one node can eventually reach any other node) and form no closed loops. A tree has the property that if it spans a network graph with n nodes, the tree will always contain $n - 1$ arcs. Figure 6.9 illustrates a tree and a graph that is not a tree.

To illustrate the minimum spanning tree problem, let us consider a pipeline design problem in which the objective is to lay as little pipe as possible in order to enable the terminals to send fluid to any other terminal. Figure 6.10 shows the seven terminals, their possible pipeline connections, and the length of the pipeline in miles.

GREEDY ALGORITHM
FOR MINIMUM SPANNING TREE

Given the 7 nodes in the pipeline network, we wish to select a tree consisting of 6 arcs that will connect all nodes and be of minimal length. The procedure for solving the problem is very straightforward and ranks among the simplest optimization techniques in all of OR/MS!

"greedy" The minimum spanning tree algorithm is a type of *"greedy"* algorithm *algorithm* because at each step being greedy, that is, selecting the minimal-length arc, will lead to an optimal solution. To start the procedure simply begin at any node and select the shortest arc leading to another node. This forms a connected segment of 2 nodes and an unconnected segment of the remaining nodes. Next, select the shortest arc leading from a node in the connected segment to a node in the unconnected segment. Repeat this process until all nodes are connected. This procedure will construct the

FIGURE 6.10 Potential pipeline connections

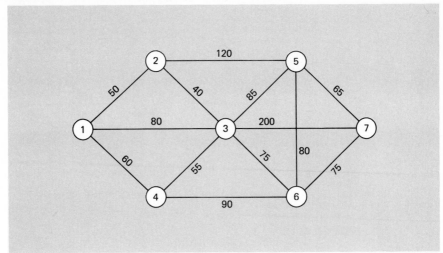

minimum spanning tree. We can summarize the greedy algorithm procedure as follows:

1. Start with any node and select the shortest arc leading to any other node. This forms a connected segment of 2 nodes.

2. Select the shortest arc leading from the connected segment to the unconnected segment of arcs.

3. Add the unconnected node of the newly selected arc to the list of connected nodes and delete it from the list of unconnected nodes. If all nodes are connected, STOP; otherwise, go to step 2.

The greedy algorithm can be executed using the matrix of distances between nodes or the network graph. Let us use the graph of the pipeline network to illustrate the greedy algorithm.

Since we can start with any node, let us start with node 1. The shortest arc leading out of node 1 is arc (1,2), with a length of 50. Nodes 1 and 2 now become connected as indicated by the heavy line in Figure 6.11.

The shortest arc connecting node 1 or node 2 to the remaining arcs is arc (2,3). Add arc (2,3) to the tree (Figure 6.12).

The unconnected node closest to node 1, 2, or 3 is node 4. Connect 4 to 3 (Figure 6.13).

The next node to be connected is node 6, as it is closer than 5 or 7 (Figure 6.14).

Node 7 is closer than node 5 to the connected segment, so add arc (6,7) to the tree (Figure 6.15).

Finally, connect node 5 to node 7, which is the closest node in the connected segment (Figure 6.16).

FIGURE 6.11

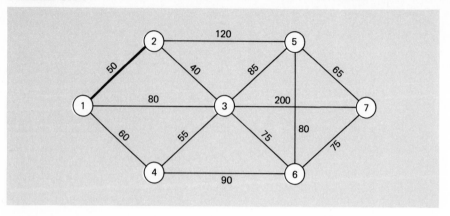

FIGURE 6.12

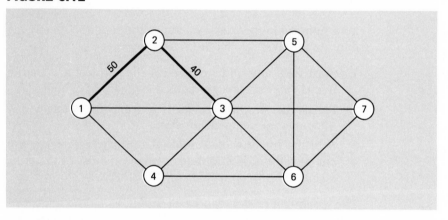

FIGURE 6.13

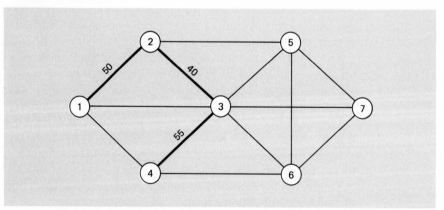

FIGURE 6.14

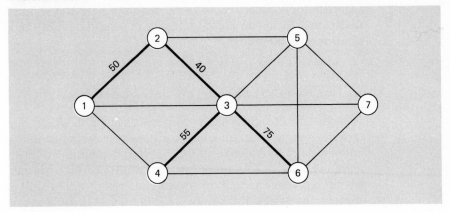

FIGURE 6.15

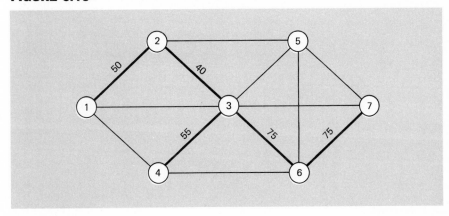

FIGURE 6.16

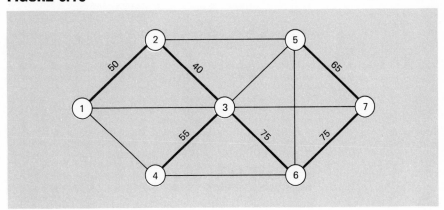

The spanning tree consists of the heavy arcs in the graph shown in Figure 6.16. Notice that the tree requires precisely 6 arcs, connects all nodes, and forms no closed loops. The total length of the minimal spanning tree is 360 miles.

MINIMUM SPANNING TREE APPLICATION— TELEPROCESSING SYSTEM DESIGN

Consider the design of a teleprocessing system in which remote computer terminals must be connected to a data processing center and associated computer. The objective is to establish communication lines with sufficient capacity at minimal cost. The solution to this design problem is a tree if expensive switching equipment is not used to split signals passing through the nodes of the network. Figure 6.17 illustrates the relative loca-

FIGURE 6.17 Layout of teleprocessing design problem

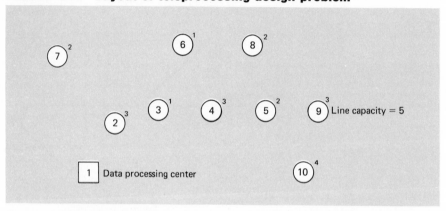

TABLE 6.2 Matrix of distances

	1	2	3	4	5	6	7	8	9	10
1	—	28	57	72	81	85	80	113	89	80
2	28	—	28	45	54	57	63	85	63	63
3	57	28	—	20	30	28	57	57	40	57
4	72	45	20	—	10	20	72	45	20	45
5	81	54	30	10	—	22	81	41	10	41
6	85	57	28	20	22	—	63	20	28	63
7	80	63	57	72	81	63	—	80	89	113
8	113	85	57	45	41	20	80	—	40	80
9	89	63	40	20	10	28	89	40	—	40
10	80	63	57	45	41	63	113	80	40	—

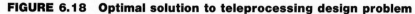

FIGURE 6.18 Optimal solution to teleprocessing design problem

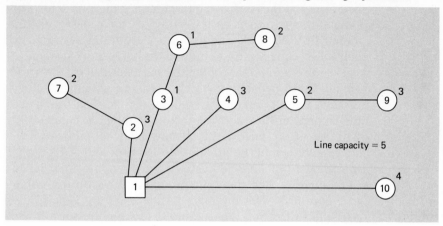

tions of 9 terminals which need to be connected to the central computer. The numbers beside the nodes represent the amount of information that is generated at that terminal.

Table 6.2 contains the matrix of distances between all 10 nodes. Note that the cost of a line is proportional to its length.

If the communicated lines to be established have no capacity limitations, the optimal solution to the teleprocessing design problem would be the minimal spanning tree. However, all lines have a finite capacity. Assume a line capacity of 5 in Figure 6.17. The solution to the problem then becomes a "capacitated minimum spanning tree." This problem is much more difficult to solve, but heuristic and optimization procedures do exist for solving it.[3] One approach is a branch-and-bound optimization procedure (see Chapter 8) which utilizes the minimum spanning tree as a subproblem. We will not discuss the method here; however, the optimal capacitated minimum spanning tree is shown in Figure 6.18.

THE MAXIMAL FLOW PROBLEM

In the maximal flow problem the objective is to determine the maximum amount of flow (that is, fluid, traffic, information, etc.) that can be transmitted through the nodes and arcs of a network. We assume a single input

---

[3]K. M. Chandy and R. A. Russell, "The Design of Multipoint Linkages in a Teleprocessing Tree Network," *IEEE Transactions on Computers*, C-21 (October 1972), 1062–1066.

source sink node called the *source* and a single output node called the *sink*; all flows commence at the source and terminate at the sink. The problem has applications in such areas as the study of traffic flow, pipeline design, communication network design, and distribution systems. It is particularly helpful in capacity planning for these types of systems.

maximal flow The *maximal flow* problem is characterized by the arcs of the network having finite capacities which limit the amount of flow that can pass through the arc in a given amount of time. The problem is to determine the amount of flow across each arc (subject to capacity restrictions) that will permit the maximal total flow from source to sink.

Let us return to the pipeline design problem of Figure 6.10 and assume that all the pipelines indicated have been laid in order to meet demand *arc capacities* requirements. The same pipeline network with *arc capacities* is shown in Figure 6.19. The numbers beside each arc specify the capacity in a particular direction. For example, looking at arc (1,2), we have

The 3 by node 1 indicates a capacity of 3 in the direction of node 1 to node 2; the 0 on the arc indicates a 0 capacity in the reverse direction of node 2 to node 1.

Obviously, there are many possible ways to send various flow quantities along the paths from source to sink. One rule we must remember is *conservation* the *conservation of flow*, which means that whatever flows into a node *of flow* must flow out. Solving the maximal flow problem is almost as simple as

FIGURE 6.19   Arc capacities for pipeline flow problem

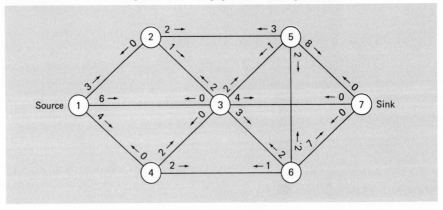

FIGURE 6.20 Before and after arc capacities

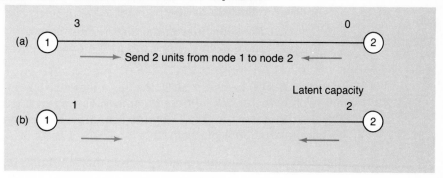

repeatedly finding paths from source node to sink node with available capacity. For this procedure to work, there are two other guidelines that must be followed.

The first guideline is that the maximum amount that can flow from source to sink along a given path is equal to the minimum available capacity on any arc in the path. (This is similar to the weakest link in the chain analogy.) Second, we need a way of changing flows along paths to achieve a better flow assignment. Our arbitrary assignment of flows along paths does not guarantee that we will achieve the optimal solution. The mechanism by which we can eventually achieve the optimal flow pattern is as follows: When assigning a flow to an arc, (1) reduce the capacity in the direction of the flow by the amount of the flow, and (2) increase the capacity in the opposite direction of the flow by the amount of the flow. Step 2 might seem strange, but it allows us to "undo" a flow that is not optimal.

For example, consider arc (1,2) in Figure 6.19. Before the assignment of any flows, the capacities of the arc are as shown in Figure 6.20(a). After an assigned flow of 2 units, the capacity of 3 is reduced by 2 units and the capacity of 0 is increased by 2 units in the opposite direction. This "artificial capacity" of 2 units is simply a latent capacity which gives us the opportunity to later "take back" the 2 units of flow from node 1 to node 2 and send them somewhere else in order to get more flow to the sink node.

A MAXIMAL FLOW ALGORITHM

Given the guidelines described above, we can now formalize a maximal flow algorithm.

1. Find a path from source node to sink node with positive flow capacity. If no paths with positive flow capacity exist, STOP, for the current flows are optimal.

2. Determine the arc in the path with minimum flow capacity, c_{min}. Increase the flow along the path by c_{min}.

3. Decrease the capacities in the direction of flow by c_{min} for all arcs in the path. Increase the capacities in the opposite direction by c_{min} for all arcs in the path. Go to step 1.

Step 1 leaves the choice of paths up to the decision maker; thus, different people might make different choices. However, if properly executed, the algorithm will provide an optimal solution. Let us apply the algorithm to the pipeline flow problem.

Iteration 1:   Choosing path 1–2–5–7, the minimum capacity c_{min} is 2. Assigning a flow of 2 to the path and revising the network in Figure 6.19 yields the network shown in Figure 6.21.

Iteration 2:   Selecting path 1–2–3–5–7 yields $c_{min} = 1$. Updating the network capacities, we have the network shown in Figure 6.22.

Iteration 3:   Select path 1–3–7. $c_{min} = 4$. The resulting network is shown in Figure 6.23.

Iteration 4:   Assign flow of 2 along path 1–3–6–7 as shown in Figure 6.24.

Iteration 5:   Assign flow of 1 along path 1–4–3–5–7.

Iteration 6:   Assign flow of 1 along path 1–4–3–6–7.

Iteration 7:   Assign flow of 2 along path 1–4–6–7.

The final network is shown in Figure 6.25.
The maximal flow through the network is 13 units. That no more flow is possible can be verified by observing that there is no positive capacity

FIGURE 6.21

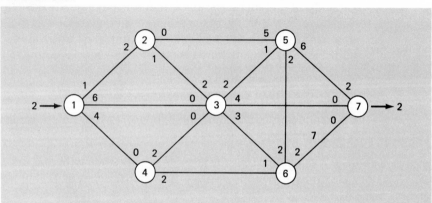

FIGURE 6.22

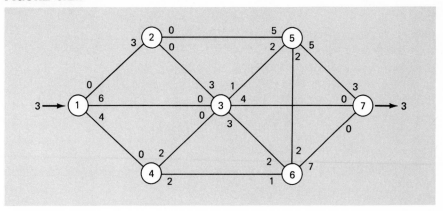

FIGURE 6.23

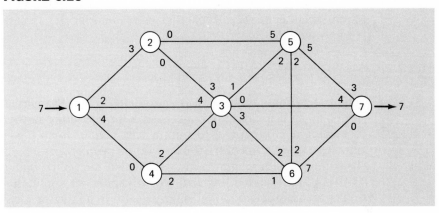

FIGURE 6.24

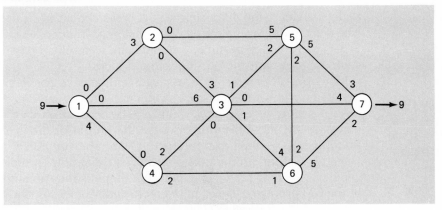

FIGURE 6.25

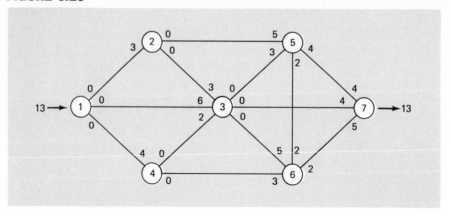

in any of the arcs leading out of the source node. The actual flow quantities can be determined by keeping track of the flow assignments or by comparing the final arc capacities with the original capacities; the difference equals the flow.

THE TRANSSHIPMENT PROBLEM

The transshipment problem is sometimes called the max flow/min cost problem, as it is not only concerned with allocating flows but also with achieving a minimum distribution cost. The transshipment model is a direct generalization of the transportation problem presented in Chapter 5. Its solution methodology is very similar to the MODI method and hence will not be discussed. Instead, we will focus on applications.

The transshipment model is very useful in analyzing physical distribution systems, as it allows for points which are neither supply nor demand points. These so called transshipment points are illustrated in Figure 6.26. *transshipment* Node 5 is a *transshipment point,* since no supply or demand is present at *point* node 5; nodes 1 and 4 are sources, whereas nodes 2, 3, 6, and 7 are sinks. The objective is to ship the 36 units of supply from nodes 1 and 4 to nodes 2, 3, 6, and 7 in the required amounts and at minimal cost. The c_{ij} along each arc represent the per unit shipping cost.

Many operations research/management science problems can be formulated as network-flow-type problems. This is another reason for at least discussing this model. Additionally, capacities can be accommodated for any arc, reflecting physical limitations or the decision maker's preference. As a final example, let us look at a simplified version of the General Motors production/distribution planning problem from the chapter's opening scenario. Figure 6.27 depicts the transshipment model of the GM problem. The c_{ij} in the rectangular boxes on the arcs represent per unit distribution costs, and the U_i and L_j in the semicircles represent

FIGURE 6.26 Warehouse distribution problem

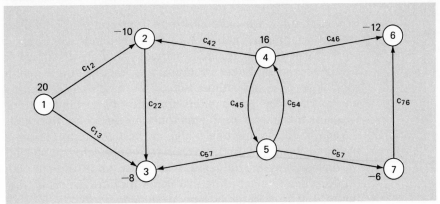

upper and lower bounds, respectively. The U_i represent production capacity for a given model at a plant and the L_i represent minimum demand for the specified model at the regional distribution centers.

Standard transportation and transshipment models assume a homogenous commodity to be shipped. A unique feature of this model is that it handles multicommodities (multicar models) in a single-commodity framework.

FIGURE 6.27 Production planning and distribution network model

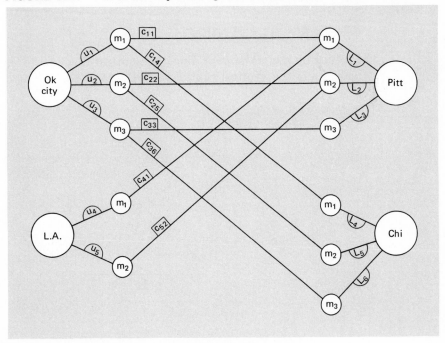

SUMMARY

In this chapter, we have continued our study of network models. They are important since many real-world problems can be modeled as a network. Even though the four network models discussed in the chapter can be solved by linear programming, this has been avoided in favor of special-purpose algorithms which are much easier, more intuitive, and much faster. Network models are currently at the frontiers of OR/MS in terms of the size of problems that can be solved optimally.

Each of the four models—the shortest route, minimum spanning tree, maximal flow, and transshipment—is applicable to specialized kinds of problems. They are, in general, however, applicable to physical distribution problems, scheduling problems, and design problems such as pipeline or teleprocessing systems design.

The transshipment problem represents a general network flow problem and contains the transportation and assignment problems as special cases. Since network models yield integer solutions and are efficiently solved, they are often exploited as subproblems of larger or more complex problems, to make them easier to solve.

SOLVED PROBLEMS

PROBLEM STATEMENT

Given the network shown, find the shortest distance to all nodes from node 1 and the shortest route to node 6.

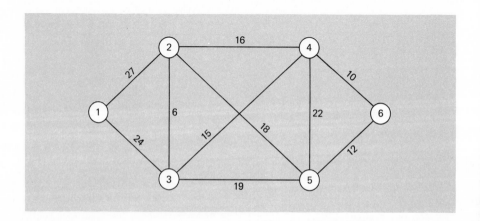

SOLUTION

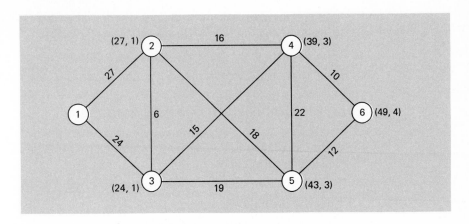

The shortest route from node 1 to node 6 is 1-3-4-6.

PROBLEM STATEMENT

Determine the minimum spanning tree for the network in the preceding problem.

SOLUTION

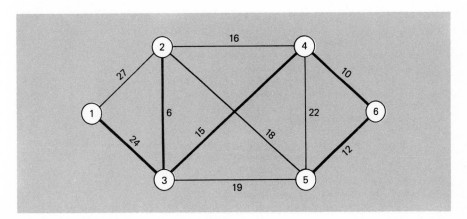

REVIEW QUESTIONS

1. Why are network models an important part of OR/MS?
2. List three specific applications of network models.
3. What determines whether a model is a linear network model?
4. How does the transshipment model generalize the transportation model?
5. Explain what is meant by a greedy algorithm.
6. Briefly discuss the English language processor function and General Motors management's use and acceptance of the production planning/distribution model.
7. Why won't the shortest-route algorithm always work if we allow negative arc lengths?
8. The maximal flow algorithm assumed a single source and sink. How might you handle the case of multiple sources or multiple sinks?
9. Are any of the three network algorithms in this chapter a heuristic?
10. Are both the transportation and assignment models of Chapter 5 special cases of the transshipment model?

PROBLEMS

6.1 Find the shortest route from node 1 to all other nodes in the network shown.

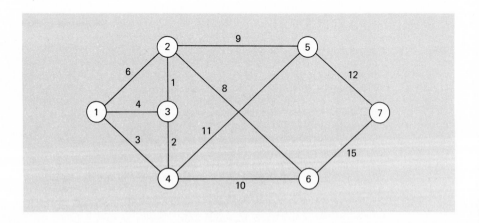

6.2 Find the minimum spanning tree for the network in Problem 6.1.

6.3   Given the following arc capacities on the network from Problem 6.1, determine the maximum flow from node 1 to node 7. Specify the flows on each arc.

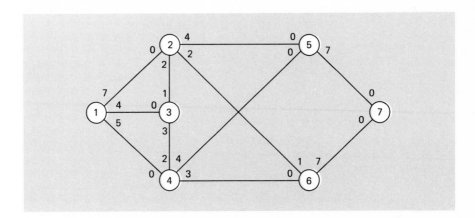

6.4   *Equipment Replacement Strategy.* An enterprising marketing student has decided to operate a single-plane commuter service between a major city and a resort area during his 4 years of college. Having limited funds, he is trying to determine the optimal replacement strategy. Assuming that year 0 is now, the following table gives the total net discounted cost associated with purchasing an airplane (purchase price minus trade-in allowance, plus running and maintenance costs) at the end of year i and trading it in at the end of year j.

	j			
i	1	2	3	4
0	8	15	20	30
1		9	17	22
2			10	18
3				12

a.   Formulate a shortest route model to determine at which times the airplane should be replaced in order to minimize total cost over 4 years.

b.   Solve the problem.

6.5   *Air Conditioning System Design.* A contractor is trying to plan the air-conditioning system for a new single-level office building. The required air-conditioning outlets are shown in the diagram. The arcs represent feasible runs for the air-conditioning ducts. The numbers on the arcs represent linear feet. What duct layout will service all outlets and use the least amount of duct length?

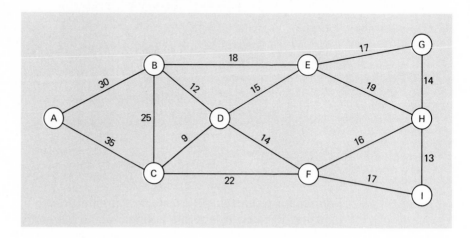

6.6   *Traffic Flow.* The east-west freeway system passing through a metropolitan area can accommodate traffic flows with capacities in thousand vehicles per hour as shown. What is the peak traffic load in vehicles per hour that the freeway system could handle?

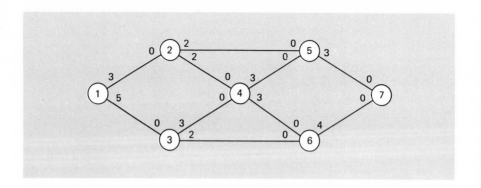

6.7   *Telephone Cable Layout.* The Rural Telephone Co. is developing plans to connect six outlying towns with underground cable in order that any one town can communicate with another. The matrix of distances between towns is given below. Determine the cable connections that will result in minimal total length.

From town	To town					
	A	B	C	D	E	F
A	—	10	9	30	27	20
B	10	—	15	18	17	20
C	9	15	—	25	21	16
D	30	18	25	—	8	17
E	27	17	21	8	—	13
F	20	20	16	17	13	—

6.8 *Telecommunication System Design.* In a telecommunication network, reliability is sometimes defined as the maximum number of users to be "down" due to a single telecommunication cable failure. Given the 7 terminals and one computer center shown, draw the network tree that is most reliable. Is it likely to be a minimum spanning tree?

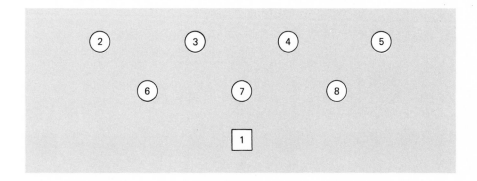

6.9 *Tire Redistribution.* The Bottom Dollar Discount store chain has an excess supply of radial tires at some warehouses and a shortage at others. In order to get ready for their upcoming sale, they want to redistribute their tire stock at minimum cost. Use your own ingenuity (rather than an algorithm) to solve the Bottom Dollar transshipment problem.

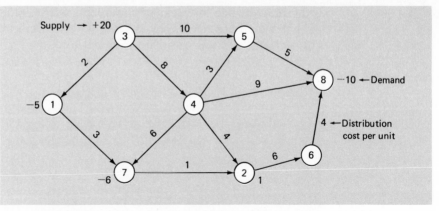

6.10 In the sales rep's routing problem of Figure 6.2, suppose that a new turnpike has been developed to connect node 1 to node 5 at a distance of 35 miles. Does this change the shortest route from node 1 to node 7? Determine the new shortest routes to all nodes.

6.11 *Parts Routing.* Reliable Airlines maintenance base has a state-of-the-art materials handling system for their shop. Computerized "auto pickers," computer terminals, and a pneumatic tube system enable mechanics to obtain parts through the tube system from another building, where the warehouse is located. Assuming that time is proportional to distance, specify the pneumatic-tube routings from each department to the warehouse in order to minimize parts travel time.

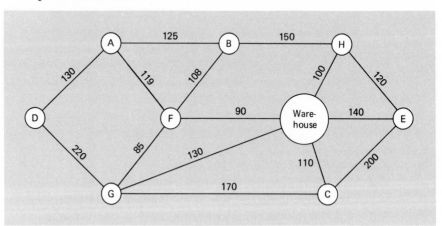

6.12 *Max Flow/Min Cut Theorem.* Suppose that we partition the set of network nodes into two sets c and its complement $\bar{c}$. Those arcs that have one node in c and the other node in $\bar{c}$ comprise a network cut. Removing the cut arcs from the network completely disconnects the sink node from the source node and thus eliminates any flow.

The capacity of the cut equals the sum of the arc capacities in the cut. A cut is illustrated below and is comprised of arcs (1,2) and (1,3). The cut capacity is 38.

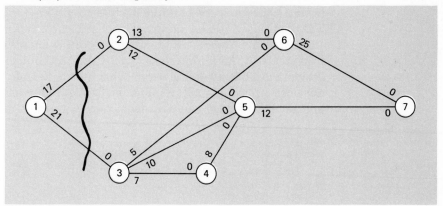

The max flow/min cut theorem states that the maximal flow from source to sink is equal to the minimal cut capacity. That is, of all possible cuts, the one with minimal capacity yields the value of the maximal flow. Find the minimum cut in the network shown and verify its minimal cut capacity by determining the maximal flow.

6.13 *Sprinkler System Design.* Reba Manufacturing will have to install a sprinkler system in their plant in order to get fire insurance. The plant manager has sketched possible pipe routings, distances, and the required outlets in the various departments. He would like to

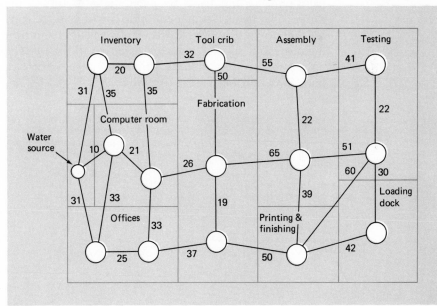

use as little piping as possible in servicing the various areas. Design the optimal sprinkler system for Reba.

6.14 *Crude Oil Shipping.* Far Eastern Freight Lines has an opportunity to ship crude oil from a Middle Eastern country to the United States. The contract would be lucrative, but Far Eastern has made previous freight commitments of other commodities in other ports. The freighter will have some capacity to ship oil, but the question is, how much? The available cargo capacities in barrels between various ports are shown below. What is the maximum amount of crude oil that Far Eastern can ship from port A to the United States?

From \ To		Capacities (1000 bbl)						
		A	B	C	D	E	F	U.S.
A		—	—	30	25	10	—	—
B		—	—	15	8	—	12	15
C		—	5	—	25	18	13	—
D		—	—	12	—	17	9	—
E		—	14	—	15	—	16	—
F		—	—	—	6	11	—	16

6.15

Purchasing. A private refuse collection company must purchase a front-end-loading truck to meet demand on its newly acquired routes. The truck has an economic life of 4 years. A new truck costs $48,000 now but will cost $54,000 two years from now. The operating costs and salvage values are shown in the table. Determine the optimum purchase plan for providing a truck for 4 years. Consider both new and used truck options.

Number of years used	Salvage value end of year	Annual operating and maintenance costs
1	$30,000	$ 6,000
2	22,000	8,000
3	15,000	12,000
4	8,000	15,000

BIBLIOGRAPHY

Bazaraa, M. S., and J. J. Jarvis, *Linear Programming and Network Flows*. New York: John Wiley & Sons, Inc., 1977.

Ford, L. R., Jr., and D. R. Fulkerson, *Flows in Networks*. Princeton, N.J.: Princeton University Press, 1962.

Hillier, F. S., and G. J. Lieberman, *Introduction to Operations Research*, 3rd ed. San Francisco: Holden-Day, Inc., 1980.

Hu, T. C., *Integer Programming and Network Flows*. Reading, Mass.: Addison-Wesley Publishing Co., Inc., 1969.

Wagner, H. M., *Principles of Operations Research*. Englewood Cliffs, N.J.: Prentice-Hall, Inc., 1975.

7

Project Scheduling

THE ARMY CORPS OF ENGINEERS

**US Army Corps
of Engineers**

The Army Corps of Engineers is responsible for managing large construction projects for the federal government. In 1979, the Army Corps of Engineers was responsible for 760 different projects nationwide. The 1979 expenditure for these projects was in excess of $2,600,000,000. In a recent interview with the Assistant Chief of the Engineering Division for the Corps of Engineers in Tulsa, Oklahoma, the importance of project scheduling methods such as work breakdown structure, PERT/CPM, PERT/Cost, and other network modeling techniques was emphasized. Here are excerpts from the interview with Don Henderson.

QUESTION: Does the Army Corps of Engineers use project scheduling techniques such as PERT/CPM and PERT/Cost?

ANSWER: Yes, there is no other way you can manage a large construction program such as we have here in the district without some kind of management tools that will tell you who is working on what and make it timely in both design, acquisition, and construction.

QUESTION: How large do you feel the project should be before you implement such a management tool?

ANSWER: Well, I would say $100,000 or larger. We use PERT/CPM methods internally. We use it on studies. We use it on just about everything, every major study we have. It's the only way we can do our job. There is no other way I know of. You must have some kind of network that identifies the activities and the sequence of activities that you are trying to perform.

QUESTION: Do you feel that you have saved time by using it?

ANSWER: Oh yes. I don't think you can do the job without some kind of network tool. What will happen is that you won't get all your activities scheduled properly and the one that you forgot will hold up the whole job until you can actually execute it.

QUESTION: On a relatively small job ($100,000), how much time is saved by using PERT/CPM techniques?

ANSWER: Oh, I'd say at least 10 percent. The more complex the job is, the more essential it is to have some kind of planning system. There is no way you could do a $100 million job without some kind of network analysis system to show you when everything has to fit together and how they fit together.

INTRODUCTION

Project scheduling is one of the few applications of management science that is widely accepted among both large and small organizations. Project managers must know how long a specific project will take to finish, what the critical tasks are and, very often, what the probability is of completing the project within a given time span. In addition, it is often important to know the effect on the total project of delays at individual stages. For these and other reasons, several techniques have been created upon which project managers rely. This chapter examines how the manager can integrate the use of a work breakdown structure (WBS), Gantt charts, and program evaluation and review technique (PERT) to solve the problems of scheduling and controlling projects.

The scheduling techniques we discuss in this chapter can be applied to a wide variety of projects. Government contractors are almost always required to use scheduling techniques such as PERT for projects of even moderate size. Construction companies often use these techniques for scheduling moderate to large-scale projects. One construction company, for example, applies PERT to all projects with a cost greater than $150,000. Designers of computerized information systems are using analytical scheduling techniques more and more. In short, almost any project is a likely candidate because the cost of using these techniques is often outweighed by the benefit.

WORK BREAKDOWN STRUCTURE

When confronted with the task of scheduling and controlling a project of significant size and scope, you must identify each of the tasks involved. In addition, time estimates for each task must be developed, and the necessary resources, both human and nonhuman, must be identified. To accomplish this primary task, it is often desirable to use a WBS. WBS is

FIGURE 7.1   General form of work breakdown structure (WBS)

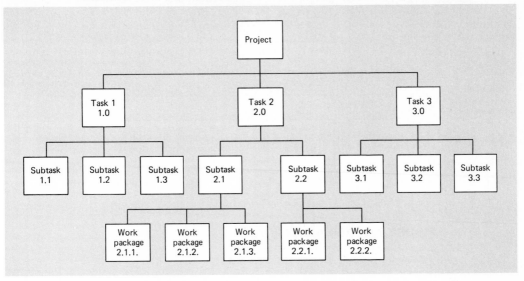

actually a graphical representation of the tasks involved in a particular project. This technique constitutes a way to classify individual tasks by a natural breakdown of the project in a manner analogous to an organization chart. Indeed, WBS is the organizational structure of the project. It starts with a word description of the project and then breaks the project down into major tasks. These major tasks are reduced to tasks, then to

work package minor tasks, and so on. Finally, the smallest element in the WBS, the *work package,* is defined in detail. Each work package identifies the resources and time it requires, all important precedent relationships, and the individual who is responsibile for that work package. When all work packages are completed, the project is complete. Figure 7.1 illustrates the general form of the WBS.

Let us use the construction of an apartment building to illustrate the use of WBS. As you can see in Figure 7.2, the entire project can be broken down into six major tasks. These major tasks can then be broken into subtasks, as shown in Figure 7.3. Finally, these subtasks can be broken into work packages, as shown in Figure 7.4. It should be emphasized that WBS is not a solution to the project-scheduling problem but rather a preliminary, structured approach to collecting the data necessary for use with one of the more sophisticated techniques, such as PERT. Once the project has been broken down using WBS, the next step is to choose a way to schedule and control the project.

FIGURE 7.2 Second-level WBS

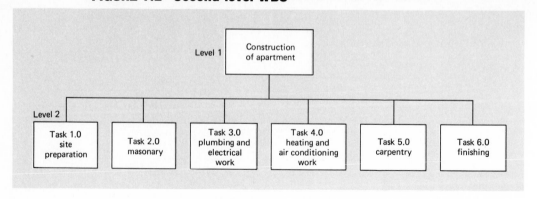

FIGURE 7.3 Third-level WBS

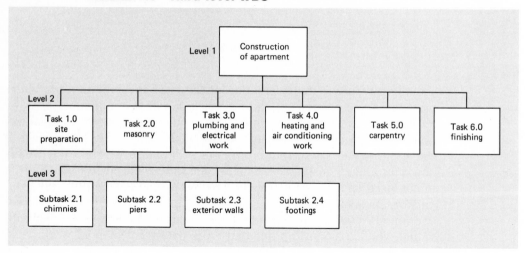

GANTT CHARTS

For relatively small projects, a simple Gantt milestone chart, or a series of them, may be the best scheduling tool. A Gantt chart is simply a bar chart that plots tasks against time. Once the project manager has created the WBS for a project, the *Begin* and *Finish* dates for the various tasks, subtasks, and work packages can then be scheduled. A single Gantt chart for major tasks and subtasks might be designed for management review, but any real scheduling must be done at the lowest level in the WBS. Each work package must have beginning and ending dates.

236

FIGURE 7.4 Fourth-level WBS

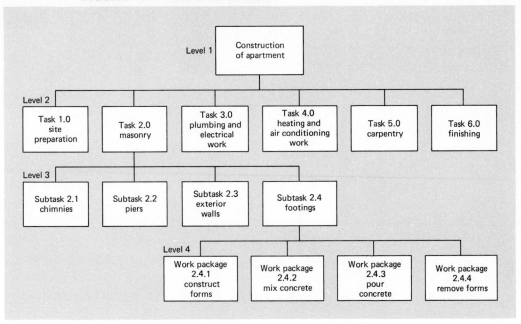

A relatively small project, such as building a house, might be effectively scheduled and controlled by means of a Gantt chart. Ordinarily, however, Gantt charts are primarily record-keeping tools for monitoring projects. They are limited in that they cannot generate information about the interrelationships among various tasks nor about the minimum possible completion times for various tasks. Figure 7.5 shows a typical Gantt chart for an apartment construction project at the major task level.

DETERMINISTIC PERT

PERT (program evaluation and review technique) evolved from Gantt charts in the late 1950s and was first applied to the U.S. Navy's Polaris submarine project. This project was so large that it was actually a necessity to create a planning and control technique such as PERT. The Polaris project, for instance, had more than 3,000 contractors, many of whom were performing multiple functions. Because of PERT's success in this and subsequent programs, major federal contracting agencies, such as the Department of Defense and NASA, require contractors to utilize PERT in scheduling and controlling their projects.

What, specifically, can PERT do for the project manager? PERT can be

FIGURE 7.5 Gantt chart for construction project

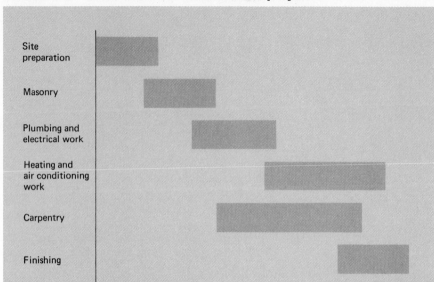

used as a planning tool as well as a controlling tool. In its planning function, PERT can be used to compute the total expected time needed to complete a project, and it can identify "bottleneck" activities that have a critical effect on the project completion date. Stochastic PERT, to be discussed later in this chapter, allows the project manager to estimate the probability of meeting project deadlines. One of PERT's greatest benefits is that it forces the project manager to plan the project in explicit detail.

Once a project has been scheduled using PERT, you might think that the technique is of no further use. This is not the case; PERT is typically used throughout the project as a control technique. Used periodically during the project, PERT monitors progress and calls attention to any delays that threaten the success of the project as a whole. In addition, PERT and similar techniques such as the *critical path method (CPM)* can be used to evaluate and make decisions concerning time and cost trade-offs of specific project activities.

Before we examine PERT as a methodology for scheduling and controlling a project, it is important for you to know certain terminology that we shall relate to a specific example.

activity   An *activity* is a task the project requires. Because of the nature of PERT, *time*   an activity corresponds to the smallest task in the WBS, namely, the work *estimate*   package. Each activity must have associated with it a *time estimate,* and

238

TABLE 7.1 Project table

Activity	Immediate predecessor	Time estimate (days)
A	—	3
B	A	4
C	A	5
D	B, C, F	7
E	—	3
F	E	6

precedence relationships any *precedence relationships* must be defined. Table 7.1 depicts this pertinent information for a small project.

As these data show, work on activities A and E can begin immediately. Activities B and C cannot be started until activity A has been completed. Activities B, C, and F must be completed before activity D can be started.

One of the problems that PERT addresses is the determination of the *network diagram or PERT chart* minimum time required to complete the project. In order to analyze our project more completely, a *network diagram*, or *PERT chart*, is introduced. The PERT chart (Figure 7.6) is a graphical representation of the entire project. An arrow represents an activity and a circle represents *event* an *event*, which is defined as the completion of an activity. The network depicts the precedence relationships involved in the project. As the project table states, the PERT chart shows graphically that it is necessary to *dummy activity* finish activity A before beginning activities B and C. The *dummy activity* depicted in Figure 7.6 is a way to indicate diagrammatically that both B *path* and C must be finished before D can be started. A *path* through a PERT network is a sequence of connected activities. In our example, there are three paths, A–B–D, A–C–D, and E–F–D. The length of each path can be

FIGURE 7.6 PERT chart showing critical path E–F–D

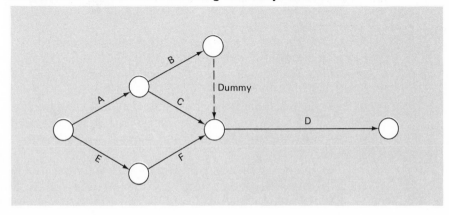

computed by adding the times for each activity on the path. Thus, the length of path A–B–D is $3 + 4 + 7 = 14$ days, and the lengths of paths A–C–D and E–F–D are 15 and 16 days, respectively. The longest path *critical* through the network is called the *critical path*. The length of the critical *path* path corresponds to the minimum time required to complete the project— thus the critical nature of the longest path. The activities on the critical *critical* path are *critical activities* because a delay in any of these results in a *activities* delay of the entire project. In other words, there is no slack time in the *slack* activities on the critical path. *Slack time* is defined as the latest time an *time* activity can be completed without delaying the project minus the earliest time the activity can be completed. In other words, slack time is the amount of time an activity can be delayed without delaying the entire project.

Returning to our example, it is a simple process to identify the critical path by comparing the lengths of each path. Path E–F–D has a length of 16 days. Hence, the minimum time in which the project can be completed is 16 days from the start of the project; delay of activities E, F, or D will delay the entire project. Path A–B–D has a total of 2 days of slack time, and path A–C–D has 1 day of slack time.

As the number of activities increases, drawing a chart and finding the critical path by inspection or complete enumeration becomes more and more impractical. Therefore, we need an algorithm (a systematic approach) to find the critical path. To explain the algorithm, four variables must be defined. Let

ES_i = earliest start time for activity i assuming all predecessor activities
    started at their earliest start time
EF_i = earliest finish time for activity i
    $= ES_i + t_i$ where t_i is the time estimated for activity i
LF_i = latest finish time for activity i without delaying the project
LS_i = latest start time for activity i without delaying the project
    $= LF_i - t_i$

Let us return to our example to illustrate how these four variables are calculated and how the critical path is identified. The algorithm to find the critical path is basically a three-step process. The first step is to calculate the earliest start time (ES_i) and the earliest finish time (EF_i). The second step is to calculate the latest start time (LS_i) and the latest finish time (LF_i) for each activity. Finally, the slack time is calculated for each activity, and the critical path is the sequence of activities that has zero slack time.

To calculate the earliest start time, let all activities that don't have any predecessors start at time zero. To calculate the earliest finish time for these initial activities, merely add the time it takes to complete the activities. Hence, the earliest start time for activities A and E of our example is zero, and the earliest finish time for both activities is $ES_i + t_i$, or $0 + 3$. To calculate the earliest start and earliest finish times for the other activities, it is necessary to add the largest earliest finish time of all immediate predecessor activities to the time for that activity. In our example, activity A has to be finished before B and C are started. Therefore, the earliest start time for activities B and C is 3 (which is the earliest finish time for predecessor A). The earliest finish time for B is $ES_B + t_B$, or $3 + 4 = 7$. Similarly, the earliest finish time for C is 8, and the earliest finish time for F is 9. Consequently, because activity D cannot be started until B, C, and F are finished, the earliest start time for D is 9 (the largest earliest finish time of all immediate predecessors).

Calculating the latest finish times and latest start times is a similar procedure, but to do it we must start at the other end of the PERT network. For all ending activities, set the latest finish time equal to the largest earliest finish time. In our example, there is only one ending activity; hence, the latest finish time is equal to the earliest finish time for activity D. Subtracting the end activity's time from its latest finish time yields the latest start time. The latest finish time for the other activities is equal to the smallest latest start time for all immediate successor activities. Therefore, the latest finish time for activities B, C, and F is 9. The latest start time for activity B is $9 - 4 = 5$.

The latest start time for activity C is $9 - 5 = 4$. Activity A has two successor activities, B and C. Remember, activity A's latest finish time is the minimum latest start time for its successor activities. Hence, the latest time activity A can finish is 4. If activity A finishes after the fourth day, the project will be delayed.

Once the four times have been calculated for each activity, it is a simple procedure to identify the critical path. Slack time is calculated by subtracting the earliest finish time from the latest finish time. Activities with zero slack time are on the critical path. In other words, a delay in any activity on the critical path results in a delay of the entire project. Table 7.2 indicates that the critical path is comprised of activities E-F-D. (See Figure 7.7 for the graphical representation of this situation.) Any activity that has a nonzero slack time is not critical and can be delayed as much as the slack time without delaying the project.

STOCHASTIC PERT

Until now, we have treated PERT as a deterministic technique in which all activity times are known with certainty. It is obvious that for most projects these activity times are random variables. If these random times take on values significantly different from those point estimates used in the PERT analysis, the output from PERT (that is, the critical path, project

TABLE 7.2 Data for PERT algorithm

Activity	Immediate predecessor	Time	ES	EF	LS	LF	Slack
A	—	3	0	3	1	4	1
B	A	4	3	7	5	9	2
C	A	5	3	8	4	9	1
D	B, C, F	7	9	16	9	16	0
E	—	3	0	3	0	3	0
F	E	6	3	9	3	9	0

completion time, and so on) is rendered invalid. To compensate for the lack of certainty in many of the time estimates, the project manager is often asked to give three subjective time estimates for each activity. These time estimates are

a_i = most optimistic time required for activity i
m_i = most likely time required for activity i
b_i = most pessimistic time required for activity i

These three time estimates are used to define a probability distribution of time for each activity. The distribution used almost exclusively is the *beta distribution*. There is no rigorous mathematical proof that the beta distribution is most appropriate, but three properties make the beta a logical choice. First, it is a continuous probability distribution; second, it is not necessarily symmetrical; and finally, it has a bounded range of values. In addition, empirical investigations support the use of the beta

beta distribution

FIGURE 7.7 Evaluated PERT chart

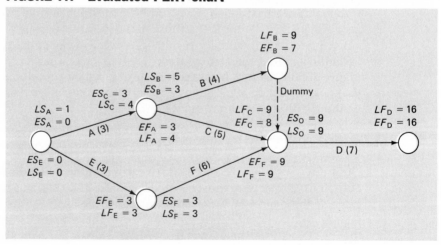

FIGURE 7.8 The beta distribution

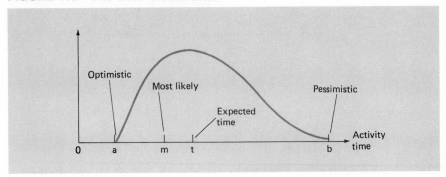

distribution for PERT times. Figure 7.8 depicts a beta-distributed activity time.

The mean of the distribution, the expected time for an activity, is calculated using the following function:

$$\bar{t}_i = \frac{a_i + 4m_i + b_i}{6}$$

where $\bar{t}_i$ = the expected time for activity i.

The standard deviation of the beta distribution can be approximated using

$$\sigma_i = \frac{b_i - a_i}{6}$$

Suppose, for example, the three time estimates for activity 5 are $a_5 = 2$ days, $m_5 = 6$ days, and $b_5 = 10$ days. Then the expected time for activity 5 is $\bar{t}_5 = (2 + 24 + 10)/6 = 6$ days. The standard deviation of time required for activity 5 is $\sigma_5 = (10 - 2)/6 = 8/6 = 1.33$.

The reason for calculating the standard deviation is to provide a means of computing the probability of completing the project on or before the scheduled completion date. To explain how this probability is computed, let us look at a stochastic version of our original problem. The first step is to calculate the expected time and standard deviation for each activity using the formulas specified by the beta distribution. This is accomplished in Table 7.3. The next step is to find the *expected critical path*. (Since the calculated critical path may not, in fact, be the actual critical path, we can only refer to it as an expected critical path.) Finding the expected critical path is done by using the algorithm previously developed for deterministic PERT. The only difference is that in this situation you use the expected activity time instead of the single time estimate. As you can see in Table 7.4, the expected critical path is E-F-D.

expected critical path

TABLE 7.3 Stochastic PERT table

Activity	Immediate predecessor	a_i	m_i	b_i	$\bar{t}_i$	σ_i	σ_i^2
A	—	1	3	5	3.00	.67	.45
B	A	1	4	5	3.67	.67	.45
C	A	3	5	7	5.00	.67	.45
D	B, C, F	3	7	12	7.16	1.50	2.25
E	—	2	3	4	3.00	.33	.11
F	E	2	6	9	5.83	1.17	1.37

Once the expected critical path has been identified, it is often useful to know the probability of completing the expected critical path within a given length of time. For example, what is the probability that the tasks on the expected critical path will all be complete by the end of the project's seventeenth day? To compute a probability of this type, it is necessary to calculate the variance (σ_i^2) for each activity's time. This is done by simply squaring the standard deviation. If we assume that the activities on a given path are independent (that is, that the duration of one task has no effect on the length of time necessary to complete another task), then the variance related to an entire path's length is the sum of the variances of the individual activities on that path. Therefore, assuming independence, the variance for path E-F-D is .11 + 1.37 + 2.25 = 3.73. In addition, if there are many activities on a given path (that is, more than 30), the distribution of the total time of the path is often assumed to be normally distributed.

Given the mean and variance of a normally distributed random variable (path length), it is possible to determine the probability of completing that path within a certain length of time. For example, what is the probability of completing path E-F-D within 17 days? The standard deviation of the total time that it takes to complete path E-F-D is $\sqrt{3.73}$, or 1.93, and the mean is 15.99. Given these facts, the distribution of times necessary to complete path E-F-D is shown in Figure 7.9. The probability of completing path E-F-D within 17 days is represented by the shaded portion of the normal curve in Figure 7.10.

TABLE 7.4 Data for stochastic PERT algorithm

Activity	Immediate predecessor	Expected Time	ES	EF	LS	LF	Slack
A	—	3.00	0	3.00	0.83	3.83	0.83
B	A	3.67	3.00	6.67	5.16	8.83	2.16
C	A	5.00	3.00	8.00	3.83	8.83	0.83
D	B, C, F	7.16	8.83	15.99	8.83	15.99	0
E	—	3.00	0	3.00	0	3.00	0
F	E	5.83	3.00	8.83	3.00	8.33	0

FIGURE 7.9 Normal distribution of days necessary to complete path E–F–D

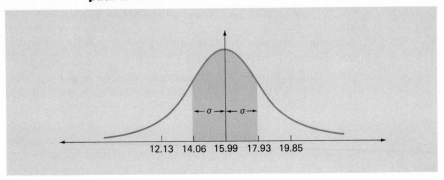

12.13 14.06 15.99 17.93 19.85

To compute this probability, it is necessary to transform our normal distribution into the standard normal with a mean of 0 and a standard deviation of 1. This is done by using the following Z transformation:

$$Z = (x - \mu)/\sigma$$

where μ = mean of the nonstandard normal
σ = standard deviation of the nonstandard normal
x = nonstandardized normal variate

Therefore, the probability of completing path E-F-D is calculated by first calculating Z. Thus, $Z = (17 - 15.99)/1.93 = .5233$. Once Z has been computed, finding the probability of $Z \leq .5233$ is accomplished by using a standard normal table such as Appendix C at the back of this book. The probability that path E-F-D will be finished within 17 days is approximately .699. (To find this, you look up $Z \leq .5233$ in the table. Be sure to verify it for yourself.) In other words, $P(x \leq 17) = P(Z \leq .5233) = .699$. It is important to remember that the normality assumption postulates the

FIGURE 7.10 Normal distribution showing probability of completing E–F–D within 17 days

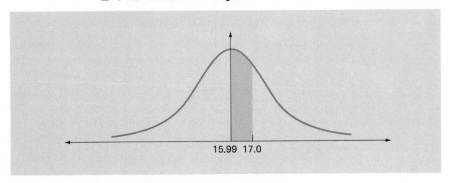

15.99 17.0

existence of a large number of random variables (that is, activities on a path). For rough approximations, 30 random variables is usually acceptable; for more rigorous applications, however, an n closer to 100 is preferable.

Having computed the probability of completing the expected critical path within 17 days, can you then conclude that this probability is the probability of completing the project in 17 days or less? The answer is no. Since activity times are random variables, it is possible that a path different from the expected critical path might cause the project to last longer than 17 days. To illustrate this idea, let us consider path A-C-D. The expected time for path A-C-D (t_{A-C-D}) is $3 + 5 + 7.16 = 15.16$, and the standard deviation for path A-C-D is $\sqrt{.45 + .45 + 2.25} = 1.775$. Thus, $Z = (17 - 15.16)/1.775 = 1.037$. Therefore, $P(t_{A-C-D} \leq 17) = P(Z \leq 1.037) \cong .849$. Similarly, the probability of completing path A-B-D within 17 days is approximately .963. Now, if we assume that the length of the paths are independent random variables, we can compute the probability of completing the project within 17 days as the joint probability of completing each path within 17 days. In other words, P(project time $\leq$ 17 days) = P(path A-B-D $\leq$ 17 and path A-C-D $\leq$ 17 and path E-F-D $\leq$ 17). If independence is assumed, P(project time $\leq$ 17) = $(.963)(.849)(.699) = .5715$.

If the various assumptions necessary to compute the probability of project completion cannot be made (that is, if the individual paths are not independent or do not have a large number of activities), *discrete digital simulation* is often used to estimate the probability of project completion within a specific time period. For each activity, the computer merely samples from a beta distribution for which the parameters have been established as previously described. On each iteration, a project completion time is computed and is added to a frequency distribution of project lengths. Given enough iterations, it is reasonable to use this frequency distribution to describe the probabilities of various project durations.

EVALUATING TIME-COST TRADE-OFFS

So far, we have discussed two variations of PERT that emphasize time factors in project evaluation. Deterministic PERT is useful when a project's time parameters are known with a good degree of certainty. Stochastic PERT, on the other hand, allows uncertain times to be estimated so that probabilities concerning such activities' duration and completion *critical* can be computed. In a third technique, the *critical path method* (CPM), *path* cost was introduced as a companion factor to time for project evaluation. *method* In their early use, PERT and CPM actually differed in two ways. First, *(CPM)* PERT allowed for stochastic times, using the three-point estimate discussed in the preceding section. CPM, however, assumed that times are known with certainty. This distinction is still valid to some extent. When a project is rather uncertain in nature (as, for example, a research project or an out-of-the-ordinary undertaking), PERT is the logical technique to use for planning and control. For more common projects, such as certain construction projects in which the times necessary to complete individual tasks can be closely estimated, deterministic PERT or CPM may be more desirable.

As we have mentioned, the second distinction between PERT and CPM lay in the area of project costs. CPM made use of a dual perspective: time and cost. You should realize, however, that this difference between PERT and CPM has faded as both techniques have evolved. In fact, most PERT software packages now include provisions for evaluating time–cost trade-offs. For that reason, the discussion of time and cost factors that follows refers to using "versions of PERT and CPM," because, in fact, both methods have been used to make valid analyses of the kind to be discussed.

Until now, we have talked about these project-evaluating techniques primarily as descriptive and predictive tools. Versions of PERT and CPM, however, are used to make decisions concerning how best to shorten a project's completion time. A project manager often has the prerogative of increasing resource allocation to specific tasks so that the project can be finished at an earlier date. In other words, a project manager may have such options as hiring additional workers or working personnel overtime to expedite the completion of a task. To give you an idea of how these time–cost trade-off decisions are made, let us consider our previous deterministic example. Table 7.5 reflects the costs of feasible reductions in each activity's completion time.

The crash time estimate in Table 7.5 represents the amount of time it would take to complete an activity if management wished to allocate additional resources to that activity. The incremental cost of crashing an activity is also reflected in Table 7.5. Remember that there were three paths in the PERT network of our original problem. These paths are summarized in Table 7.6.

TABLE 7.5   Time-cost trade-off data

Activity	Normal time estimate (days)	Crash time estimate (days)	Incremental cost of crash time
A	3	2	$150
B	4	3.5	100
C	5	4	200
D	7	5	300
E	3	3	—
F	6	5	75

TABLE 7.6   PERT paths

Path	Length (days)
A-B-D	14
A-C-D	15
E-F-D	16

In terms of shortening the total project, it is clear that to shorten paths A-B-D or A-C-D without shortening path E-F-D does no good. Remember, the minimum length of the project is the length of the longest individual path. Therefore, we must look at path E-F-D to determine how to expedite the completion of the total project. Table 7.7 indicates that we have two alternatives for shortening path E-F-D. Because of the lower per day cost, it seems logical to add resources to activity F (that is, activity F is crashed) so that the length of the project is reduced from 16 days to 15 days at a cost of $75.

TABLE 7.7   Alternatives for shortening E–F–D

Activity	Days saved by crashing	Cost of crash per day	Cost of crash
E	0	—	—
F	1	$ 75	$ 75
D	2	150	300

To shorten the project further, paths A–C–D and E–F–D must both be shortened. Since D is the only activity that can still be shortened on path E–F–D, there is no alternative. Fortunately, D is common to all three paths, and a reduction in D results in shortening all three paths. For $300, D can be reduced from 7 days to 5 days, and each path can be reduced 2 days. Therefore, paths E–F–D and A–C–D would take 13 days and path A–B–D would take 12 days. Further reduction in paths A–B–D or A–C–D would not be fruitful because the length of path E–F–D cannot be reduced. To summarize, we can reduce the project schedule from 16 days to 13 days at a cost of $375.

PERT/COST

Every project manager has two major problems when managing a large project. First, he or she must be concerned with the time and schedule aspect of the project. We have seen that PERT/CPM can be a very useful tool for scheduling the project and continually monitoring the schedule. A second major problem the project manager is concerned with is that of cost budgets. PERT/Cost can be used to aid in planning, scheduling, and controlling the cost of the project. Specifically, once the various work packages have been identified in the WBS and their costs have been estimated, the project manager must predict the cash flow for the project. In addition, the project manager must periodically review expenditures to determine if actual costs are exceeding budgeted cost so that he or she can take the necessary corrective action to reduce or eliminate cost overruns. Our discussion of PERT/Cost is divided into two sections, the prediction of cash flows and the monitoring and control of project costs.

The estimation of a project's cash flow using PERT/Cost is a five-step process. This five-step process is depicted in the flow chart in Figure 7.11.

Let us illustrate how PERT/Cost estimates monthly cash flows by using the example shown in Table 7.8. The first step in the cash flow analysis

FIGURE 7.11   Steps in project cash flow analysis

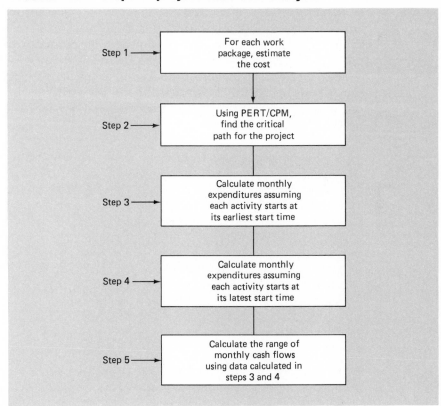

TABLE 7.8 Project table

Activity	Time (months)	Immediate predecessors
A	2	—
B	3	—
C	3	A
D	2	A
E	2	B
F	7	B
G	4	C
H	3	D, E
I	2	H
J	4	G, I

is to estimate or budget each activity. In many applications, the cost of a work package or individual task is assumed to be linear (constant). Thus, if activity A is estimated to cost $10,000, the per-month cost is assumed to be $5,000 ($10,000/2 months). With many PERT/Cost software packages, however, this simplifying assumption is not necessary. In our example, however, costs are assumed to be linear. The estimated costs for each activity are shown in Table 7.9.

The next step is to find the critical path for the network depicted in Figure 7.12. Using the PERT algorithm discussed earlier in this chapter, we can identify the critical path as path B–E–H–I–J. See Table 7.10 for the necessary calculations.

TABLE 7.9 Project budget

Activity	Total estimated cost	Estimated monthly cost
A	$ 10,000	$ 5,000
B	24,000	8,000
C	30,000	10,000
D	20,000	10,000
E	40,000	20,000
F	140,000	20,000
G	160,000	40,000
H	90,000	30,000
I	100,000	50,000
J	100,000	25,000
	$714,000	

FIGURE 7.12 PERT network

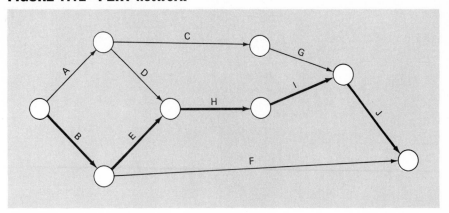

Step 3 says to calculate expected monthly expenditures based on the assumptions that each activity starts as soon as possible and that cost expenditures are at a uniform rate. Given these two assumptions, the monthly expenditures are calculated in Table 7.11.

The next step is to calculate the expected monthly cash outflows based on the assumption that activities start at their latest starting times. These outflows are calculated in Table 7.12.

The final step in predicting the monthly cumulative cash requirements for a project is to examine the range between the expected monthly cumulative cash outflow assuming an earliest start time and the expected cumulative cash outflow assuming a latest start time. This information is

TABLE 7.10 Data for the PERT algorithm

Activity	Time	ES_i	EF_i	LS_i	LF_i	Slack
A	2	0	2	1	3	1
B	3	0	3	0	3	0
C	3	2	5	3	6	1
D	2	2	4	3	5	1
E	2	3	5	3	5	0
F	7	3	10	7	14	4
G	4	5	9	6	10	1
H	3	5	8	5	8	0
I	2	8	10	8	10	0
J	4	10	14	10	14	0

TABLE 7.11 Budgeted monthly cash expenditures assuming earliest start time

Activity	\<th colspan=14\>Month													
	1	2	3	4	5	6	7	8	9	10	11	12	13	14
A	5,000	5,000												
B	8,000	8,000												
C			8,000											
D			10,000	10,000	10,000									
E			10,000	10,000										
F				20,000	20,000									
G				20,000	20,000	20,000	20,000	20,000	20,000	20,000				
H						40,000	40,000	40,000	40,000					
I						30,000	30,000	30,000						
J									50,000	50,000	25,000	25,000	25,000	25,000
Monthly cost	13,000	13,000	28,000	60,000	50,000	90,000	90,000	90,000	110,000	70,000	25,000	25,000	25,000	25,000
Accumulated project cost	13,000	26,000	54,000	114,000	164,000	254,000	344,000	434,000	544,000	614,000	639,000	664,000	689,000	714,000

TABLE 7.12 Budgeted monthly cash expenditures outflows assuming latest start time

Activity	Month													
	1	2	3	4	5	6	7	8	9	10	11	12	13	14
A	8,000	5,000	5,000											
B		8,000	8,000											
C				10,000	10,000									
D				10,000	10,000									
E				20,000	20,000									
F						10,000		20,000	20,000	20,000	20,000	20,000	20,000	20,000
G							40,000	40,000	40,000	40,000				
H						30,000	30,000	30,000						
I									50,000	50,000				
J											25,000	25,000	25,000	25,000
Monthly cost	8,000	13,000	13,000	40,000	40,000	40,000	70,000	90,000	110,000	110,000	45,000	45,000	45,000	45,000
Accumulated project cost	8,000	21,000	34,000	74,000	114,000	154,000	224,000	314,000	424,000	534,000	579,000	624,000	669,000	714,000

TABLE 7.13 Range of expected cash requirements by month

Month	Cumulative expected cash outflows assuming LS_i	Cumulative expected cash outflows assuming ES_i
1	$ 8,000	$ 13,000
2	21,000	26,000
3	34,000	54,000
4	74,000	114,000
5	114,000	164,000
6	154,000	254,000
7	224,000	344,000
8	314,000	434,000
9	424,000	544,000
10	534,000	614,000
11	579,000	639,000
12	624,000	664,000
13	669,000	689,000
14	714,000	714,000

FIGURE 7.13 Feasible region for cumulative expected cash outflows

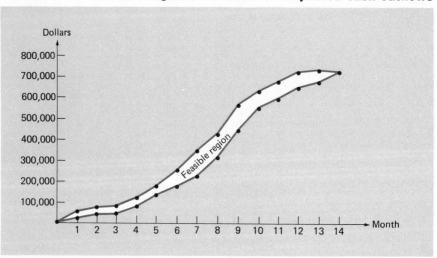

summarized in Table 7.13. The feasible region of cumulative expected cash outflows is graphed in Figure 7.13.

From our example, it should be obvious that the project manager faces a dilemma in scheduling activity starting times when he or she considers project costs as well as project schedules. If activity times are not known with certainty, then starting at the earliest possible times provides the project manager with a hedge. This hedge, however, is not without a cost. The cost is obviously derived from the time value of money. In other words, in addition to the direct budgeted cost of the project, the cost of financing the project must be considered. This cost of financing can be a significant factor in persuading a project manager to delay the start of a task as long as is possible.

In addition to predicting the monthly cash needs for a project, a primary responsibility of the project manager is to monitor and control costs. It is extremely important for a project manager to identify cost overruns and cost underruns so that appropriate action can be taken. Typically, monitoring of project costs is facilitated by a PERT/Cost report produced periodically (monthly or biweekly), which identifies activities that are projected to have a cost overrun or underrun. Let us examine how this critical report is produced. Periodically, a project manager reviews the status of the various work packages to ascertain the actual expenditure to date and the work package's percentage completion. This information, together with the original detailed budget for the project, allows the project manager to identify cost overruns and underruns. Let us illustrate the process of producing a PERT/Cost report by using our previous example. If we assume that we are at the end of the sixth month and the expenditures and activity completion percentages are as shown in Table 7.14, it is

TABLE 7.14   Activity cost and completion data after 6 months

Activity	Expenditures to date	Percent completion
A	$12,000	100
B	24,000	100
C	30,000	80
D	18,000	100
E	45,000	95
F	60,000	50
G	40,000	25
H	30,000	25
I	0	0
J	0	0

possible to calculate a value of work completed for each activity using the formula

$$V_i = \frac{P_i}{100} B_i$$

where V_i = value of the work completed
P_i = percentage of work completed for activity i
B_i = budget for activity i

Once V_i has been calculated for each activity, it is possible to calculate the amount of the cost overrun or underrun by subtracting the value of the work completed from the actual cost of the work completed using the formula

$$D_i = C_i - V_i$$

where D_i = difference between the actual cost and the value of the work on activity i; if this difference is positive we have a cost overrun, and if it is negative we have a cost underrun
C_i = actual cost of activity i

It is apparent from the PERT/Cost report in Table 7.15 that several activities have overruns and several have underruns, and that these overruns and underruns nearly balance each other. The prudent project manager, however, would look closely at activities C, E, and H to determine the cause of the overrun and see if some type of corrective action might be appropriate.

TABLE 7.15   PERT/Cost report

Activity	Budget, B_i	Expenditures to date, C_i	Value V_i	Differences, D_i
A	$ 10,000	$12,000	$10,000	$ 2,000
B	24,000	24,000	24,000	0
C	30,000	30,000	24,000	6,000
D	20,000	18,000	20,000	−2,000
E	40,000	45,000	38,000	7,000
F	140,000	60,000	70,000	−10,000
G	160,000	40,000	40,000	0
H	90,000	30,000	22,500	7,500
I	100,000	0	0	0
J	100,000	0	0	0

SUMMARY

The management of large complex projects is a significant problem in today's modern industrial society. Fortunately, management science has provided several tools such as WBS, PERT/CPM, and PERT/Cost that greatly aid the project manager in scheduling and controlling large projects. WBS is a necessary first step in organizing any project, as it represents the organizational structure of the project in hierarchical form. Once the WBS has been completed, PERT or CPM can be used to schedule the project, identify critical tasks, and estimate project completion times with various degrees of confidence. PERT is typically used during the life of the project for schedule monitoring and control purposes. This monitoring function is necessary so that the consequences of various delays can be predicted and corrective action in the form of additional resources can be applied to keep the project on schedule. In addition, PERT/Cost enables the project manager to estimate cash outflows and monitor the project's cost to identify cost overruns early enough to take the appropriate action.

SOLVED PROBLEMS

PROBLEM STATEMENT

Consider the project information in the table below.

Task	Immediate predecessor	Time estimate (days)
A	—	5
B	—	4
C	A	6
D	A	3
E	B	3
F	B	6
G	E	2
H	F	5
I	C, D	8
J	G, H	5

1. Draw the PERT network for the project.
2. Use the PERT algorithm to find the critical path.
3. What is the minimum project completion time?

SOLUTION

1. Add PERT chart:
2. To find the critical path, it is necessary to compute the slack time for each task. This is done below using the PERT algorithm.

Task	Time	ES	EF	LS	LF	Slack time
A	5	0	5	1	6	1
B	4	0	4	0	4	0
C	6	5	11	6	12	1
D	3	5	8	9	12	4
E	3	4	7	10	13	6
F	6	4	10	4	10	0
G	2	7	9	13	15	6
H	5	10	15	10	15	0
I	8	11	19	12	20	1
J	5	15	20	15	20	0

The critical path consists of those activities that have zero slack time. Therefore, the critical path is B–F–H–J.

3. The minimum project completion time is the length of the critical path. The length of the critical path is the latest finish time for activity J, which is 20 days.

PROBLEM STATEMENT

Consider the project information in the table on the following page.

1. Draw the PERT network for this project.
2. Compute the mean and variance in time for each activity.
3. Find the expected critical path.
4. What is the expected length of the critical path?
5. Assuming normality and path independence, what is the probability of completing the project in less than 22 days?

Task	Immediate predecessor	Time estimates		
		a_i	m_i	b_i
A	—	4	5	7
B	A	2	3	5
C	A	5	7	11
D	B	2	2	2
E	B	3	4	6
F	D	3	5	6
G	C	3	3	3
H	C	2	2	2
I	G, H	3	4	6
J	E, F	4	6	7

SOLUTION

1. The PERT network is

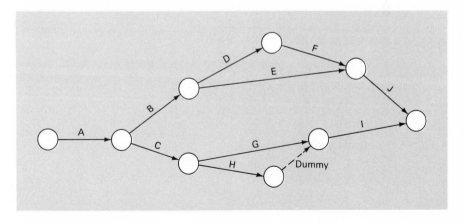

2. The mean time for task A is computed as follows:

$$\bar{t}_A = \frac{4 + 4(5) + 7}{6}$$

$$= \frac{31}{6} = 5.167$$

The standard deviation for task A is computed:

$$\sigma_A = \frac{7 - 4}{6} = \frac{3}{6} = \frac{1}{2}$$

Therefore, the variance for task A is

$$\sigma_A^2 = \left(\frac{1}{2}\right)^2 = \frac{1}{4} = .25$$

The mean time and variances for the remaining tasks are shown in the table.

Task	Mean time	Variance
A	5.167	.25
B	3.167	.25
C	7.333	1.0
D	2.000	0
E	4.167	.25
F	4.833	.25
G	3.000	0
H	2.000	0
I	4.167	.25
J	5.833	.25

3. The expected critical path is composed of all those activities whose slack time is zero. Slack times are computed in the table.

Task	Expected time	ES	EF	LS	LF	Slack time
A	5.167	0	5.167	0	5.167	0
B	3.167	5.167	8.333	5.167	8.333	0
C	7.333	5.167	12.500	6.500	13.833	1.333
D	2.000	8.333	10.333	8.333	10.333	0
E	4.167	8.333	12.500	11.000	15.167	2.667
F	4.833	10.333	15.167	10.333	15.167	0
G	3.000	12.500	15.500	13.833	16.833	1.333
H	2.000	12.500	14.500	14.833	16.833	2.333
I	4.167	15.500	19.667	16.833	21.000	1.333
J	5.833	15.167	21.000	15.167	21.000	0

Therefore, the expected critical path is A–B–D–F–J.

4. The expected length of the critical path is the latest finish time of the ending activity (activity J), which is 21 days.

5. The probability of completing the project in 22 days is the probability completing all paths within 22 days. If we make the necessary assumptions, the probability of completing path A–B–D–F–J in 22 days is found as follows:

$$Z = \frac{X - \mu}{\sigma}$$

$$= \frac{22 - 21}{\sqrt{.25 + .25 + 0 + .25 + .25}}$$

$$= \frac{1}{1} = 1$$

$$P(\text{path A–B–D–F–J} \leq 22) = P(Z \leq 1) = .8413$$

Similarly, $P(\text{path A–B–E–J})$ is computed as

$$Z = \frac{22 - 18.334}{\sqrt{.25 + .25 + .25 + .25}} = 3.667$$

$$P(\text{path A–B–E–J} \leq 22) \cong 1.0$$

$P(\text{path A–C–G–I} \leq 22)$ is

$$Z = \frac{22 - 19.667}{\sqrt{.25 + 1.0 + 0 + .25}}$$

$$= 1.905$$

$$P(\text{path A–C–G–I} \leq 22) = P(Z \leq 1.905)$$

$$= .9713$$

$P(\text{path A–C–H–I} \leq 22)$ is

$$Z = \frac{22 - 18.667}{\sqrt{.25 + 1.0 + 0 + .25}}$$

$$= 2.72$$

$$P(\text{path A–C–H–I} \leq 22) = P(Z \leq 2.72)$$

$$= .9967$$

The probability of all paths being complete in 22 days, assuming independence of paths and normality, is the product of the individual probabilities, or

$$P(\text{project time} \leq 22) = (.8413)(1)(.9713)(.9967)$$

$$= .814$$

REVIEW QUESTIONS

1. Distinguish between Gantt charts and PERT.
2. What are the basic elements in a work package?
3. What is the basic purpose of using WBS?

4. On what kinds of project would you use deterministic PERT rather than stochastic PERT?

5. What can PERT do for the project manager?

6. Define "critical path."

7. How is slack time computed?

8. Why is the beta distribution used for PERT times?

9. Why compute σ_i?

10. What assumptions are made in order to make probabilistic statements about project completion schedules?

11. Explain in your own words how and why simulation is used with PERT.

12. What does PERT/Cost do for the project manager?

PROBLEMS

7.1 Prepare the WBS for a project with which you are familiar. In addition to identifying each task and subtask, prepare the necessary work packages.

7.2 Draw Gantt charts for the various task levels of the WBS prepared for Problem 7.1.

7.3 Consider the information in the table.

Task	Immediate predecessor	Estimated time (days)
A	—	5
B	—	4
C	A	3
D	B	7
E	C	2
F	D, E	1

a. Draw the PERT network diagram for this project.

b. Use the PERT algorithm for finding the critical path.

c. What is the minimum project completion time?

d. Would the critical path change if F were to take 5 days rather than 1? Explain.

7.4 Consider the project information in the table.

Task	Immediate predecessor	Estimated time (weeks)
A	—	5
B	—	6
C	A	4
D	B	3
E	B	5
F	C, D	2
G	E	2
H	E	4
I	F, G	3
J	H	2
K	I, J	5

a. Draw the PERT network diagram for the project.

b. Use the PERT algorithm for finding the critical path.

c. What is the minimum project completion time?

7.5 Consider the project information in the table.

Task	Immediate predecessor	Estimated time (weeks)		
		a_i	m_i	b_i
A	—	3	5	6
B	A	3	4	7
C	A	1	3	5
D	B	2	4	7
E	C	2	5	8
F	D	1	2	4
G	E	2	3	4

a. Draw the PERT network diagram for this project.

b. Compute the mean and variance in time for each activity.

c. Find the critical path by inspection.

d. What is the expected length of the expected critical path?

e. Assume that the time required to complete a path is normally distributed. What is the probability of completing the critical path in less than or equal to 15 weeks?

f. Again assuming normality and path independence, what is the probability of completing the entire project in less than or equal to 15 weeks?

    g. If you wanted to be at least 95 percent sure of completing the project on time, what schedule would you quote?

7.6   Consider the information in the table.

    a. Draw the PERT network diagram for this project.

    b. Compute the mean and variance in time for each activity.

    c. Find the critical path using the PERT algorithm.

    d. What is the expected length of the expected critical path?

    e. Assuming that the time required to complete a path is normally distributed, what is the probability of completing the critical path in less than or equal to 50 weeks?

    f. Again assuming normality and path independence, what is the probability of completing the entire project in less than or equal to 50 weeks?

    g. If you wanted to be at least 95 percent sure of completing the project on time, what schedule would you quote?

		Estimated time (weeks)		
Task	Immediate predecessor	a_i	m_i	b_i
A	—	4	5	7
B	—	5	9	11
C	A	5	10	15
D	A	4	5	8
E	A	5	7	12
F	D, C	3	4	7
G	D, C	2	3	4
H	D	7	12	18
I	B, E	6	11	14
J	F	5	6	9
K	G	5	7	9
L	H, I	2	3	5
M	J, K	7	8	9
N	L	1	3	4
O	M, N	15	17	22

7.7   *Sports Scheduling.* State University is planning a holiday basketball tournament and has decided to use PERT to schedule the project. The tasks and time estimates have been identified as set forth in the table.

Task	Description	Immediate predecessors	a_i	m_i	b_i
			Estimated time (days)		
A	Team selection	—	1	3	5
B	Mail out invitations and receive acceptances	A	4	5	10
C	Arrange accommodations	—	8	10	15
D	Plan promotional strategy	B	2	3	5
E	Print tickets	B	4	5	8
F	Sell tickets	E	15	15	15
G	Complete arrangements	B, C	7	8	10
H	Develop practice schedules	C	2	3	4
I	Practice sessions	H	2	2	2
J	Conduct tournament	F, I	3	3	3

a. Draw the PERT diagram and identify the expected critical path.

b. If the tournament is to be held starting December 27, when should team selection begin to assure 98 percent certainty that the tournament will be held as scheduled?

7.8 Consider the project in Problem 7.3. Assume crash times and crash costs as set forth in the table.

Activity	Normal time estimate (days)	Crash time estimate (days)	Incremental cost of crash time
A	5	4	$100
B	4	3.5	100
C	3	2.5	150
D	7	5	400
E	2	2	—
F	1	1	—

a. What is the shortest time in which the project can be completed?

b. What is the total incremental cost of achieving the shortest completion time?

c. What is the minimum incremental cost of completing the project in 10 days?

7.9   Consider the project in Problem 7.4. Assume the crash times set forth in the table.

Activity	Normal time estimate (weeks)	Crash time estimate (weeks)	Incremental cost of crash time
A	5	4	$100
B	6	4	400
C	4	3.5	100
D	3	3	—
E	5	4	100
F	2	1.5	150
G	2	2	—
H	4	3	175
I	3	2	125
J	2	2	—
K	5	2	500

   a.   What is the shortest time the project can be completed?

   b.   What is the total incremental cost of achieving the shortest completion time?

   c.   What is the incremental cost of completing the project in 18 days?

7.10   Consider the information in the table.

Task	Immediate predecessor	Time estimates a_i	m_i	b_i
A	—	3	4	7
B	—	4	9	12
C	A	5	11	15
D	A	3	5	8
E	B	5	7	12
F	D, C	3	4	7
G	D, C	2	3	4
H	E	7	11	18
I	E	7	10	14
J	F	4	6	9
K	G	5	7	9
L	H, I	2	3	5
M	J, K	7	8	9
N	L	1	3	4
O	M, N	14	17	23

a. Draw the PERT network diagram for this project.

b. Compute the mean and variance in time for each activity.

c. Find the critical path using the PERT algorithm.

d. What is the expected length of the expected critical path?

e. Assuming the time required to complete a path is normally distributed, what is the probability of completing the critical path in 50 days or less?

f. Again assuming normality and path independence, what is the probability of completing the entire project in 50 days or less?

g. If you wanted to be at least 95% sure of completing the project on time, what schedule would you quote?

7.11 Consider the project in Problem 7.4, assuming the normal times and the crash times set forth in the table.

Activity	Normal time estimate	Crash time estimate	Incremental cost of crash time
A	5	4	$100
B	6	4	400
C	3	2.5	100
D	5	5	—
E	4	3	100
F	2	1.5	150
G	1	1	—
H	4	3	175
I	3	2	125
J	1	1	—
K	7	4	500

a. What is the shortest time in which the project can be completed?

b. What is the total incremental cost of part a?

c. What is the incremental cost of completing the project in 18 days?

7.12 Apply PERT to the project described in your WBS for Problem 7.1.

7.13 Consider the project in Problem 7.4. The budgeted costs for the various activities are shown in the table. Develop a total cost budget based on both an earliest start time and a latest start time schedule.

Activity	Budgeted cost
A	$70,000
B	85,000
C	27,000
D	43,000
E	45,000
F	50,000
G	15,000
H	25,000
I	32,000
J	48,000
K	79,000

7.14 Again using the project in Problems 7.4 and 7.13, prepare a cost report that reflects overruns and underruns at the end of 6 weeks. Progress on the project and actual costs incurred through 6 weeks are shown in the table.

Activity	Cost incurred	Percentage complete
A	$75,000	100
B	77,000	90
C	20,000	10
D	10,000	5
E	0	0
F	0	0
G	0	0
H	0	0
I	0	0
J	0	0
K	0	0

7.15 Consider the project in Problem 7.6. After 6 months of working on the project, top management has requested a detailed cost report that would reflect total cost overruns and cost overruns by various tasks or work packages. To comply, the data shown in the table have been collected. You are to prepare a report that reflects the total cost overruns or underruns and the individual work package overruns and underruns.

Activity	Cost incurred to date	Budget	Percentage complete
A	$ 22,000	$ 25,000	100
B	48,000	45,000	90
C	75,000	100,000	10
D	20,000	20,000	95
E	14,000	20,000	50
F	94,000	85,000	100
G	47,000	40,000	100
H	125,000	120,000	100
I	109,000	100,000	100
J	97,000	100,000	100
K	87,000	100,000	70
L	0	25,000	0
M	0	75,000	0
N	0	73,000	0
O	0	197,000	0

BIBLIOGRAPHY

Bierman, Harold, Jr., Charles P. Bonini, and Warren H. Hausman, *Quantitative Analysis for Business Decisions,* 5th ed. Homewood, Ill.: Richard D. Irwin, Inc., 1977.

Buffa, Elwood S., *Operations Management: The Management of Productive Systems.* New York: John Wiley & Sons, Inc., 1976.

Evarts, Harry F., *Introduction to PERT.* Boston: Allyn and Bacon, Inc., 1964.

Levin, Richard I., and Charles A. Kirkpatrick, *Planning and Control with Pert/CPM.* New York: McGraw-Hill Book Company, 1966.

Murdick, Robert G., and Joel E. Ross, *Information Systems for Modern Management.* Englewood Cliffs, N.J.: Prentice-Hall, Inc., 1975.

Wiest, J., and F. K. Levy, *Management Guide to PERT/CPM.* Englewood Cliffs, N.J.: Prentice-Hall, Inc., 1969.

8

Other Mathematical Programming Topics

BECHTEL, INC.[1]

Bechtel, Inc., is an engineering firm that has clients all over the world. In one of their overseas projects, Bechtel contracted with the Algerian government to bring water to the inland region of Setif. The project involves pumping water 27 kilometers south, up over mountains, directing it by pipelines, tunnels, and pumping stations to a set of retention reservoirs, and then distributing it to an agricultural irrigation system. If the project is successful, 200 square miles of land could be brought under cultivation. The Setif region could then be developed as a long-term food source for Algeria and neighboring countries.

A manually derived water-conveyance system had been designed, but Bechtel wanted to check the design against a scientifically optimized design. For this purpose, a mathematical programming model employing geometric programming was developed. The model would estimate the optimal pipe diameter and the optimal number of pumping stations, given a specified flow rate, for selected segments of the pipeline system.

The manually derived system was constrained so as to not exceed a pipe diameter of 54 inches; this limitation was imposed in order to use locally manufactured pipe and to reduce construction difficulties. Under the 54-inch constraint, the mathematical programming model confirmed the accuracy of the manual system design. However, a consultant at Bechtel took the liberty to perform some sensitivity analysis with the mathematical model. He found that by relaxing the 54-inch restriction and incorporating a 69-inch-diameter pipe and one extra pumping station, the annualized cost of the system was reduced $1,250,000 per year.

Given the huge cost savings, the Algerian government adopted the larger-diameter design and the project in 1978 had entered the detailed engineering design phase. Depending on future prices of energy in Algeria, the ultimate

[1]F. Paul Wyman, "The Use of Geometric Programming in the Design of an Algerian Water Conveyance System," *Interfaces*, 8 (May 1978), 1–6.

cost savings could be several times the estimated million dollars per year. Given a 50-year project life, the present value of cost savings resulting from the design improvement should easily exceed $50 million.

As a result of the success of the Algerian water-conveyance project, Bechtel is exploring the use of geometric programming with other projects in other areas.

INTRODUCTION

Even though linear programming is a very useful technique, there are many business decision problems that do not satisfy the LP linearity or certainty assumptions. Many of these same decision problems, however, can generally be represented as another type of mathematical model. These other types of mathematical models are classified as integer, goal, dynamic, or nonlinear programming problems.

Just how do these mathematical models differ from linear programming models? Integer programming models differ only in that they require some or all decision variable values to be integer (whole numbers). Recall the divisibility assumption of LP, which allows LP solutions to be fractional or noninteger. Goal programming is different in that it addresses the existence of more than one objective or goal. The objective in goal programming is to develop a solution that satisfies as many goals as possible. However, these goals are often incompatible, so that the goals must be ranked in order of importance. Dynamic programming is significantly different from LP in that it takes a serial approach to solving the problem. It breaks the main problem into a series of smaller subproblems. Additionally, dynamic programming can be applied to stochastic problems and problems whose parameters change over time. Finally, nonlinear programming addresses all models whose objective function or constraints contain a nonlinear expression. This is an area of mathematical programming in which special cases have been solved, but no general procedure exists for solving all types of nonlinear problems.

INTEGER PROGRAMMING

integer programming Integer programming has grown in importance for two basic reasons. One reason is that many real-world problems require whole-number solutions. The other reason is that integer programming enables us to formulate or structure problems that otherwise could not be modeled.

That is, certain modeling "tricks" can be employed using integer-valued variables.

Most mathematical models do not yield integer solutions, naturally. However, we should point out again that certain network models, such as transportation, assignment, and transshipment, do yield integer solutions.

TYPES OF INTEGER MODELS

All integer models require some or all of the decision variables to be *all-integer* integer. The *pure-integer* or *all-integer* model requires all variables to *mixed-integer* be integer. *Mixed-integer* models require some variables to be integer but allow the remaining variables to be continuous (noninteger). Finally, *0–1 integer* *0–1 integer* models require all variables to assume a value of either 0 or 1. To illustrate these three types of models, consider the three models below:

$$
\begin{aligned}
\text{Maximize} \quad & 35x_1 + 20x_2 \\
\text{subject to} \quad & 4x_1 + 7x_2 \le 28 \\
& 9x_1 + 12x_2 \le 50 \\
& x_1, x_2 \text{ integers}
\end{aligned}
$$

all-integer model

$$
\begin{aligned}
\text{Maximize} \quad & 35x_1 + 20x_2 \\
\text{subject to} \quad & 4x_1 + 7x_2 \le 28 \\
& 9x_1 + 12x_2 \le 50 \\
& x_1 \ge 0 \\
& x_2 \text{ integer}
\end{aligned}
$$

mixed-integer model

$$
\begin{aligned}
\text{Maximize} \quad & 35x_1 + 20x_2 \\
\text{subject to} \quad & 4x_1 + 7x_2 \le 28 \\
& 9x_1 + 12x_2 \le 50 \\
& x_1, x_2 \text{ 0 or 1}
\end{aligned}
$$

0–1 integer model

The three models differ only in the nature of the integer requirements on the decision variables. However, the solution of each type of integer model benefits by the use of different solution procedures. The 0–1 models are easiest to solve because they present fewer combinations of decision-variable values.

SOLUTION OF INTEGER PROGRAMMING MODELS

Of all the approaches to integer programming, none is nearly as efficient as the simplex method for linear programming. Thus, the size of the integer models that can be solved optimally is generally much smaller. The primary approaches to obtaining integer solutions to otherwise linear models are:

1. Linear programming with rounding
2. Complete enumeration
3. Cutting-plane techniques
4. Partial enumeration via branch and bound

Rounding off LP solutions to linear models with integer restrictions is probably the most common or practical approach. It is convenient and often results in optimal or near-optimal solutions. However, the approach has two pitfalls. First, the rounded solution can be far from optimal. Examples have been contrived to show that this is true, although in most real-world problems the rounded solutions are close to optimal. Second, and more seriously, it may be impossible, or at least extremely difficult, to round off the variables and satisfy all the constraints.

Complete enumeration involves the evaluation of all possible combinations of decision-variable values. As you can imagine, the number of combinations can grow astronomically large for even medium-size problems. Even though complete enumeration will provide an optimal solution, it is a viable approach only for relatively small problems (usually for $n \leq 20$, where n equals the number of possible decision variable values).

Cutting-plane techniques were the focus of early attempts to derive integer solutions. The basic idea was to ignore the integer restrictions and solve the model as an LP. Noninteger optimal solutions were "cut off" by adding an additional constraint to the model which would exclude the noninteger point, but would not exclude any integer points. Figure 8.1 *cut* shows a *"cut"* that defines a new feasible region and excludes the previous LP optimum. In actual practice, cutting-plane methods worked but required the successive solution of many LP solutions before an integer

FIGURE 8.1 A cutting plane

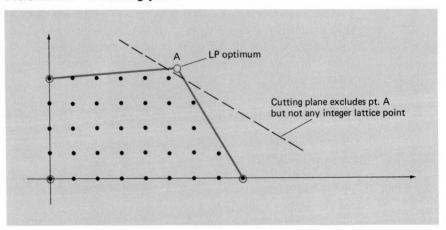

extreme point was generated. The slowness of cutting-plane methods encouraged research in the direction of partial enumeration procedures.

partial
enumeration   *Partial enumeration* determines the optimal solution by examining only a portion of all possible combinations of integer values. The procedure basically divides the set of all solutions into subclasses and searches only among promising subclasses of solutions. One means of performing partial enumeration is called branch and bound. This procedure appears to be the most promising of the four approaches. One of its disadvantages is that it must be tailored for the specific problem to be solved; it is unlike the simplex method, which is a general method applicable without modification to all LP models.

GRAPHICAL EXAMPLE   To illustrate the nature of integer programming problems, let us look at a two-variable graphical example. Consider the maximization problem

$$\begin{aligned}
\text{Maximize} \quad & 6x_1 + 4x_2 \\
\text{subject to} \quad & x_2 \le 3 \\
& 4x_1 + 1.5x_2 \le 12 \\
& 2x_1 + 2x_2 \le 8 \\
& x_1, x_2 \ge 0 \text{ and integer}
\end{aligned}$$

The feasible region for the foregoing problem consists of the integer (lattice) points shown in Figure 8.2. Notice that the feasible region consists of 12 points, not an infinite number as in the LP case. The LP optimal solution to the model ignoring the integer restriction is $x_1 = 2.4$ and $x_2 = 1.6$. Rounding off this solution yields (2,1), which is not the optimal integer solution. Evaluating all the integer points yields $x_1 = 2$, $x_2 = 2$

FIGURE 8.2   Feasible integer points

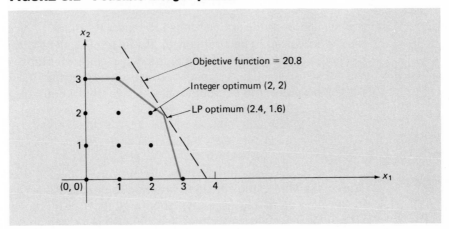

as the optimal integer solution. Evaluating all integer points is not difficult for this small problem, but it becomes impossible with large problems. We turn now to a systematic procedure for evaluating integer points more efficiently.

BRANCH-AND-BOUND METHOD

The simplex method is an adjacent-extreme-point procedure that moves along extreme points successively, making improvements until an optimum is found. Unfortunately, in integer programming the optimum is not necessarily at an extreme point of the convex hull of the feasible region. Furthermore, we have no systematic procedure such as the simplex method that will take us directly to the optimum. Thus, we are restricted to intelligent search-type procedures.

branch-and-bound   *Branch-and-bound* procedures partition the set of all solutions into smaller subsets and search among promising subsets. Initially, the method breaks the set of all solutions into two mutually exclusive subsets. Subsequently, these two subsets are partitioned into two smaller subsets and so on. Fortunately, not all subsets are further subdivided, as some are *bounding* determined not to contain an optimal solution. The *bounding* aspect of branch and bound determines upper and/or lower bounds of the best solution contained in any subset of solutions. In a maximization problem, a subset whose upper bound is less than the value of a known feasible solution will be excluded from further consideration. It is in this manner that partial enumeration is achieved. The process of determining how to *branching* partition the subsets is called *branching*. Branch and bound is a general approach rather than a specific procedure for a given problem. The branching-and-bounding rules will differ for each type of problem. We now look at how the rules are developed for a 0–1 integer programming problem called the knapsack problem.

Branch and Bound Applied to the Knapsack Problem   We first encountered a knapsack-type problem in Table 1.1. Recall that the objective is to choose, among a set of items, the subset that maximizes the value of the subset subject to a capacity constraint. Consider the following 0–1 integer programming formulation of a five-item knapsack problem:

$$\text{Maximize} \quad 60x_1 + 54x_2 + 32x_3 + 18x_4 + 13x_5$$
$$\text{subject to} \quad 30x_1 + 36x_2 + 32x_3 + 24x_4 + 26x_5 \leq 90$$
$$x_i = 0 \text{ or } 1, \quad i = 1, 2, \ldots, 5$$

The coefficients in the objective function represent values, the coefficients in the constraint represent weights, and the right-hand-side value, 90, represents a weight capacity. Each item must be selected in its entirety

FIGURE 8.3   Set of IP solutions as a subset of LP solutions

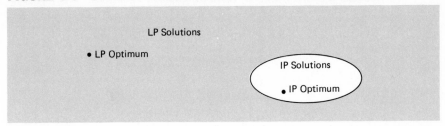

LP Solutions

● LP Optimum

IP Solutions

● IP Optimum

or not at all; fractional parts are not allowed. If fractional parts were allowed, the problem would have a trivial solution via linear programming.

The bounding part of branch-and-bound algorithms is often accomplished by model relaxation. Before you go to sleep solving the problem, however, we should point out that relaxation in this context refers to loosening or dropping restrictive assumptions. The most common relaxation is the *LP relaxation,* in which the integer restriction is dropped and *LP relaxation* the variables are treated as continuous. The LP relaxation of this knapsack problem is accomplished by replacing

$$x_i = 0 \text{ or } 1 \qquad \text{with } 0 \le x_i \le 1$$

Solving the relaxed problem yields an objective function value that is greater than or equal to (less than or equal to for a minimization problem) the optimal integer objective function value. This principle is illustrated in Figure 8.3, in which the set of integer programming solutions is contained within the set of linear programming solutions. Thus, if the optimal LP solution to the relaxed problem happens to be integer, it will be the optimal solution to the integer problem. The reverse is not generally true; that is, the optimal integer solution is not generally optimal for the relaxed LP.

Solving the relaxed knapsack problem (sometimes called the cheesecake problem because we can now take fractional pieces) is particularly simple and does not require the simplex method. If we form the ratio of value to weight, the optimal LP solution is obtained by simply loading the knapsack with highest-ratio items first until the capacity is depleted. Using this biggest "bang for the buck" approach, the last item placed in the knapsack might be fractional. Listing the items in order of value/weight, we have

Item	Value/weight
1	2
2	1.5
3	1
4	.75
5	.50

FIGURE 8.4 First level in branch-and-bound tree

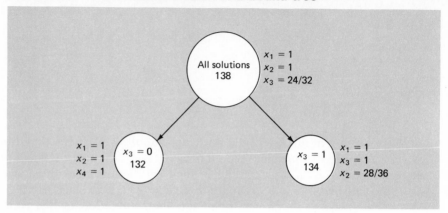

Thus, the optimal LP solution to the relaxed LP is to enter item 1, item 2, and $^{24}/_{32}$ of item 3. We cannot place all of item 3 in the 90-pound knapsack, since it weighs 32 pounds and items 1 and 2 together weigh 66 pounds. Substituting $x_1 = 1$, $x_2 = 1$, and $x_3 = {}^{24}/_{32}$ into the objective function yields an upper bound $= 60 + 54 + 24 = 138$ on the value of the optimal integer solution.

We now need to implement a branching process to partition the set of all solutions into the smaller subsets. Since the knapsack problem involves 0–1 variables, the partitioning process will create a binary tree. The first partition is shown in Figure 8.4. Since the decision variable with a fractional value is the one in question, we will partition the set of all solutions into two classes—those in which the fractional variable $= 0$ and those in which the fractional variable $= 1$. In Figure 8.4 we have created two nodes in the tree—one representing the set of all solutions in which $x_3 = 0$ and the other representing the set of all solutions in which $x_3 = 1$. Fixing $x_3 = 0$ in the relaxed LP and solving for the remaining variables, we obtain $x_1 = 1$, $x_2 = 1$, and $x_4 = 1$; the bound is shown in the node as 132. Fixing $x_3 = 1$ and solving the relaxed LP, we obtain $x_1 = 1$, $x_3 = 1$, and $x_2 = {}^{28}/_{36}$; the bound is 134.

Notice in the $x_3 = 0$ node of the branch-and-bound tree that the LP solution is integer. This means that we found the optimal solution in the *lower* $x_3 = 0$ class of solutions. Since the $x_1 = 1$, $x_2 = 1 x_4 = 1$ solution is feasi-*bound* ble, its value of 132 constitutes a *lower bound* on the optimal solution to the *upper* knapsack problem. Thus, given the *upper bound* of 134 in the $x_3 = 1$ node, *bound* we can conclude that the value of the optimal solution is bounded within 132 to 134. Also, there is no further need to branch from the $x_3 = 0$ node in the branch-and-bound tree; we say that this node is fathomed. In the other $x_3 = 1$ node, however, we have a decision to make regarding the value of x_2; hence, we will branch from this node. Normally, when there are several nodes from which we could branch, we choose the node with the highest upper bound.

Branching from the $x_3 = 1$ node yields the binary tree shown in Figure 8.5. In solving the cheesecake problem for the second-level nodes of the tree, we must include the restrictions specified by all predecessor nodes. Thus, in determining a bound for the $x_2 = 1$ node, we must fix $x_3 = 1$ and $x_2 = 1$ in the relaxed LP.

In examining the three terminal nodes of the tree, we can see that the highest upper bound is associated with the $x_3 = 0$ node. Thus, the $x_2 = 0$ *fathomed* and $x_2 = 1$ nodes are *fathomed* because we have already found a feasible solution whose value is higher than the upper bounds of these two nodes. Since all terminal nodes are fathomed, we conclude that the optimal solution is the integer solution $x_1 = 1$, $x_2 = 1$, $x_3 = 0$, $x_4 = 1$, $x_5 = 0$ with value 132 found at the $x_3 = 0$ node. (Note that if the $x_3 = 0$ node had not generated an integer solution in the bounding process, we would have to branch from it.)

We can summarize the branch-and-bound technique for an integer maximization problem as follows:

1. Establish an upper bound on the set of all solutions by using LP relaxation or some other bounding procedure.

2. Branch from the unfathomed terminal node in the branch and bound tree that has the largest upper bound. (This will create two more nodes in 0–1 integer problems.)

3. Calculate an upper bound for each new node created in step 2.

FIGURE 8.5   Second level in branch-and-bound tree

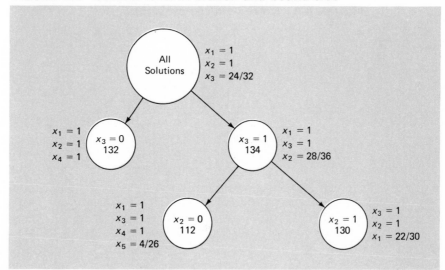

4. Consider a node to be fathomed if its upper bound is lower than a known feasible solution, the node contains no feasible solution, or the bounding process generated an integer solution whose value equals the upper bound of the node.

5. Stop only if all nodes have been fathomed; otherwise, go to step 2.

The general procedure for a minimization problem is identical except that lower bounds are used in place of upper bounds.

APPLICATIONS AND FORMULATION POSSIBILITIES

In addition to knapsack-type problems, integer programming has several other types of interesting applications; many of these will be covered in the problems at the end of the chapter. The nature of the 0–1 or integer variables enables us to model decision problems using integer programming that could not be formulated with noninteger or continuous variables.

fixed-charge **Fixed-Charge Problems**   *Fixed-charge* problems arise frequently in business applications where a fixed cost must be incurred to obtain a product or service. Consider, for example, the simple plant location problem shown in Figure 8.6. The graph resembles the standard transportation problem of Chapter 5, but there is one important difference; the plants, indicated by the dashed nodes, are not yet open. The problem is to decide which plants to open to minimize the combined costs of transportation

FIGURE 8.6   A fixed-charge problem

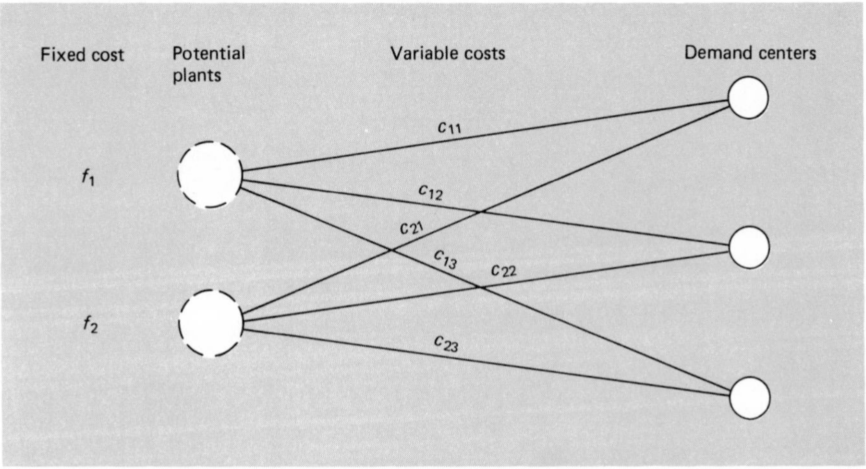

and the fixed costs required to operate and maintain the plant. It is assumed that each plant has enough capacity to supply all demand requirements. In order to formulate the problem, let

c_{ij} = unit transportation cost from plant i to demand center j
b_j = demand at demand center j
x_{ij} = amount shipped from plant i to demand center j
f_i = fixed cost of plant i
$$y_i = \begin{cases} 1 & \text{if plant } i \text{ is opened} \\ 0 & \text{otherwise} \end{cases}$$

We can formulate the simple plant location problem as a mixed-integer programming problem in which the x_{ij} variables are continuous and the y_i variables are 0–1 integer variables. The formulation is

$$\text{Minimize} \quad c_{11}x_{11} + c_{12}x_{12} + c_{13}x_{13} + c_{21}x_{21} + c_{22}x_{22} + c_{23}x_{23} \\ + f_1y_1 + f_2y_2$$

$$\text{subject to} \quad \left. \begin{array}{l} x_{11} + x_{21} = b_1 \\ x_{12} + x_{22} = b_2 \\ x_{13} + x_{23} = b_3 \end{array} \right\} \quad \text{demand constraints}$$

$$\left. \begin{array}{l} x_{11} + x_{12} + x_{13} \leq My_1 \\ x_{21} + x_{22} + x_{23} \leq My_2 \end{array} \right\} \quad \begin{array}{l} \text{constraints that force plant } i \\ \text{closed unless } y_i = 1 \end{array}$$

$$x_{ij} \geq 0 \quad \text{all } i \text{ and } j; \quad y_1, y_2 \quad 0 \text{ or } 1$$

In the last set of constraints, the M denotes an arbitrarily large number. These constraints do not allow plant i to be opened unless y_i equals 1, in which case the fixed cost of f_i is incurred in the objective function. When y_i equals 1, the M essentially allows the shipments out of plant i to be as large as necessary to satisfy all demand.

The presence of fixed costs destroys the linearity of the objective function. As shown in Figure 8.7, the fixed cost introduces a jump discontinuity in the total cost function and makes the problem much harder to solve than a linear problem.

Multiple-Choice Constraints   In addition to fixed charges, integer variables can be used to limit choices among competing alternatives. Suppose that in the simple plant location problem, we again let

$$y_i = \begin{cases} 1 & \text{if plant } i \text{ is opened} \\ 0 & \text{otherwise} \end{cases}$$

FIGURE 8.7 Cost function with fixed-cost component

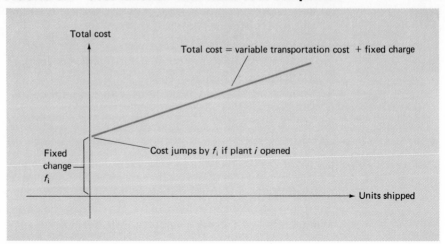

Suppose that we are considering five plant locations but have decided that only one plant will be opened. We can accomplish this by adding the following constraint to the simple plant location model:

$$y_1 + y_2 + y_3 + y_4 + y_5 = 1$$

Since the y_i are 0–1 variables, only one of the y_i can be 1; the others must be zero. Note that in linear programming, the variables can assume fractional values; thus the foregoing constraint forces multiple choices only if 0–1 variables are used.

K-**Out-of-***N*-**Alternatives Constraints**   Suppose that instead of selecting just one alternative, we are interested in selecting K out of N. For example, suppose that we want to open precisely three out of five possible plants. Extending the multiple-choice constraint idea, we have

$$y_1 + y_2 + y_3 + y_4 + y_5 = 3$$

Furthermore, we can model the opening of at most two plants by

$$y_1 + y_2 + y_3 + y_4 + y_5 \leq 2$$

and the opening of at least 2 plants with

$$y_1 + y_2 + y_3 + y_4 + y_5 \geq 2$$

These constraints all assume that the y_i are restricted to 0–1 variables.

If–Then Constraints   Sometimes it is necessary to tie together certain projects or alternatives. Dependency requirements can be met by requiring certain 0–1 variables to be dependent. For example, suppose in the example above that plant 2 can be opened only if plant 5 is opened. We can enforce this by

$$y_2 - y_5 \leq 0$$

If plants 2 and 5 are corequisite, that is, plant 2 is open when plant 5 is open, and vice versa, we must equate the two by

$$y_2 - y_5 = 0$$

Other formulation possibilities exist through the use of integer variables. We have presented some of the more useful formulation "tricks." The price that is paid for these formulation conveniences (relative to linear programming) is an increase in the difficulty of solving the problem. However, in many instances the use of integer variables is the only way to represent the problem as a mathematical model.

GOAL PROGRAMMING

Both linear and integer programming address problems that have a single goal represented by an objective function. This single goal usually involves profit maximization, cost minimization, or some other unidimensional objective. Many real-world decision problems involve multiple goals, many of which are incompatible or conflicting. For example, a company might wish to maximize profits, increase wages paid to workers, reduce energy consumption, reduce operating costs, and increase its inventories. Clearly, these goals are not achievable simultaneously.

goal
programming   *Goal programming* is a mathematical programming technique that has evolved in order to deal with multiple and sometimes incompatible objectives. It requires the *ordinal ranking* of goals. That is, it requires the
ordinal
ranking   decision maker to assign priorities to the goals of the decision problem. There can be several goals with the same priority; however, the solution algorithm sequentially satisfies the goals, starting with the highest priority goals. Obviously, if two goals are truly incompatible, both cannot be achieved to the fullest extent. Goal programming achieves as many higher-priority goals as possible and then attempts to "get as close as possible" to satisfying the remaining goals. Since not all goals are always
satisficing   achieved, this is sometimes called *satisficing,* or the achieving of a satisfactory solution.

Goal programming was originally developed as a linear programming extension. It has since been developed for integer and nonlinear models. In this chapter we limit our focus to linear goal programming models. In this case, goal programming is a straightforward generalization of linear programming.

A TWO-GOAL MODEL

One basic difference in goal programming compared to linear programming is that the goals are expressed as constraints of the model rather than directly in the objective function. In each constraint that represents *deviational* a goal, *deviational variables* are defined which measure the extent to *variables* which the goals are achieved. These deviational variables are equivalent to positive or negative slack variables in linear programming. In goal programming, however, they are placed in the objective function with priority rankings. These deviational variables represent positive or negative deviations from a goal; hence, these deviations are to be minimized.

To illustrate the goal programming formulation procedure, let us return to the familiar Faze Linear product mix problem of Chapters 2 to 5. Recall the LP formulation as

$$
\begin{array}{lll}
\text{Maximize} & 200x_1 + 500x_2 & \text{profit} \\
\text{subject to} & x_2 \leq 40 & \text{transistor availability} \\
& 1.2x_1 + 4x_2 \leq 240 & \text{assembly time} \\
& .5x_1 + 1x_2 \leq 81 & \text{inspection time} \\
& x_1, x_2 \geq 0 &
\end{array}
$$

where x_1 and x_2 represent the number of amplifiers and preamplifiers to produce, respectively. The optimal LP solution is to produce 28.5 preamps and 105 amps, for a total profit of $35,250.

Now let us assume that the Faze Linear management would like to achieve two goals:

Priority 1   achieve profit of $40,000
Priority 2   limit overtime of inspectors

Looking first at the highest-priority goal, introduce two deviational variables:

d_1^- = amount by which the target profit of $40,000 is underachieved
d_1^+ = amount by which the target profit of $40,000 is overachieved

We can now write the profit goal as a constraint:

$$200x_1 + 500x_2 + d_1^- - d_1^+ = 40,000$$

Notice that the \$40,000 profit goal need not be met exactly. If d_1^- has a positive solution value, we will fall short of 40,000, and if d_1^+ has a positive solution value, we will exceed 40,000.

Assuming that the 81 hours of inspection time is regular time (not overtime), we can formulate the second goal by defining deviational variables

d_2^- = amount by which inspection time is underutilized (i.e., short of 81 hours)

d_2^+ = amount by which inspection time is over utilized (i.e., more than 81 hours requires overtime)

We formulate the overtime goal as

$$.5x_1 + 1x_2 + d_2^- - d_2^+ = 81$$

Incorporating these goals as constraints in the LP formulation, we obtain the goal programming formulation:

$$
\begin{aligned}
\text{Minimize} \quad & P_1 d_1^- + P_2 d_2^+ \\
\text{subject to} \quad & \left. \begin{array}{l} x_2 \le 40 \quad \text{transistors} \\ 1.2x_1 + 4x_2 \le 240 \quad \text{assembly} \end{array} \right\} \text{resource constraints} \\
& \left. \begin{array}{l} 200x_1 + 500x_2 + d_1^- - d_1^+ = 40{,}000 \\ .5x_1 + 1x_2 + d_2^- - d_2^+ = 81 \end{array} \right\} \begin{array}{l} \text{goal} \\ \text{constraints} \end{array} \\
& x_1, x_2, d_1^-, d_1^+, d_2^-, d_2^+ \ge 0
\end{aligned}
$$

The P_1 and P_2 symbols in the objective function reflect the fact that d_1^- and d_2^+ represent priority 1 and 2 goals, respectively. Priorities of a higher rank are infinitely more important than those of a lower rank. Thus, the priority relationship is often expressed as

$$P_1 >>> P_2$$

where $>>>$ means "very much greater than."

The result of the ordinal priority rankings is that the profit goal will be achieved to the greatest extent possible before the overtime goal is considered. If satisfying any part of the overtime goal causes any reduction in the higher-ranking profit goal, the overtime goal will not be satisfied at all.

FIGURE 8.8

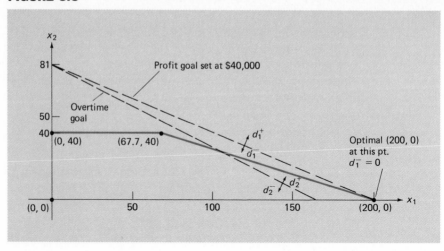

The graphical solution of the Faze Linear goal programming problem is shown in Figure 8.8. The solid lines define the fixed feasible region as bounded by the two resource constraints of the model. The two dashed lines represent the two goal constraints and are flexible, as they can be moved closer to or away from the feasible region. In satisfying the first priority goal of profit maximization, we want to minimize profit under-achievement by making variable d_1^- as small as possible by finding an extreme point that is on the profit constraint or on the d_1^+ side of the constraint. Examining the region we see that point (200,0) is on the $40,000 profit line and achieves a d_1^- value of 0. This solution of $x_1 = 200$, $x_2 = 0$ achieves the first priority goal to the fullest extent with a profit of $40,000.

Turning to the overtime goal, however, we find that minimizing overtime through the d_2^+ variable requires us to move toward the "southwest," away from point (200,0). Since lower-priority goals are never satisfied at the expense of higher-priority goals, no attempt is made to achieve the second goal and the point (200,0) is accepted as the optimum. Notice that Faze Linear is able to achieve an even higher profit than in the LP formulation, although it is at the expense of undesirable overtime. If the priorities were reversed and the overtime goal had priority 1, how would you argue the fact that the point (105,28.5) would become optimal?

THE SIMPLEX METHOD FOR GOAL PROGRAMMING

Larger goal programming models will obviously require a solution method that is solvable on a computer. The simplex method of linear programming is easily extended to the goal programming case. The only real modification involves the handling of multiple goals rather than a single goal. In a simplex tableau, this is accomplished by having a $c_j - z_j$ matrix rather than a single $c_j - z_j$ row. That is, there will be a $c_j - z_j$ row in the tableau for each goal having a different priority level.

Consider again the Faze Linear goal programming problem. Adding two slack variables to convert the problem to standard form, we have

Minimize $\quad P_1 d_1^- + P_2 d_2^+$

subject to
$$
\begin{aligned}
x_2 + s_1 &= 40 \\
1.2x_1 + 4x_2 + s_2 &= 240 \\
200x_1 + 500x_2 + d_1^- - d_1^+ &= 40{,}000 \\
.5x_1 + 1x_2 + d_2^- - d_2^+ &= 81 \\
x_j, s_j, d_i^+, d_i^- &\geq 0
\end{aligned}
$$

The initial tableau for the Faze Linear goal programming problem is shown in Tableau 8.1. There are several facts to notice in Tableau 8.1.

1. As usual, there are as many basic variables as there are constraints.

2. Those dummy variables (slack or deviational) with a $+1$ coefficient in the original constraints are basic in the initial tableau.

3. All c_j objective function coefficients are zero except for those deviational variables having a priority (P_i) ranking.

4. Since there are two levels of goal priorities, there are two $c_j - z_j$ rows; one for priority 1 (P_1) and one for priority 2 (P_2).

TABLEAU 8.1 Initial simplex tableau for goal programming problem

C_B	Basic variables	c_j x_1	0 x_2	0 s_1	0 s_2	P_1 d_1^-	0 d_1^+	0 d_2^-	P_2 d_2^+	Solution	Minimum ratio
0	s_1	0	①	1	0	0	0	0	0	40	$\frac{40}{1} = 40$
0	s_2	1.2	4	0	1	0	0	0	0	240	$\frac{240}{4} = 60$
P_1	d_1^-	200	500	0	0	1	-1	0	0	40,000	$\frac{40{,}000}{500} = 80$
0	d_2^-	.5	1	0	0	0	0	1	-1	81	$\frac{81}{1} = 81$
P_2	$c_j - z_j$	0	0	0	0	0	0	0	1	0	
P_1	$c_j - z_j$	-200	-500	0	0	0	1	0	0	40,000	

$\uparrow$

The $c_j - z_j$ for a given priority level is calculated precisely the same as in the linear programming case. Thus, for the $P_1 c_j - z_j$ row, we calculate z_1 in the column for x_1 by taking the product of the C_B column times the substitution coefficients in the x_1 column. This yields

$$z_1 = 0(0) + 0(1.2) + P_1(200) + 0(.5) = 200P_1$$

Since $c_1 = 0$, the final $c_1 - z_1$ calculation for the $P_1 c_j - z_j$ row is

$$c_1 - z_1 = 0 - 200 = -200$$

The remaining $c_j - z_j$ for the P_1 and P_2 rows are calculated similarly.

Since we are minimizing, we will look for negative entries in the $c_j - z_j$ row in order to improve the solution. Going first to the higher-priority P_1 row, we find that the most negative entry is a -500. Thus, we will bring x_2 into the solution to help satisfy the P_1 goal. Notice the last two numbers in the solution column in the P_1 and P_2 rows. These numbers, 0 and 40,000, represent the unattained portion of goals P_2 and P_1, respectively.

Having chosen the entering variable, we need to determine the variable leaving the basis. This is accomplished in exactly the same way as in the LP case, by calculating the minimum ratio. Here we find that variable s_1 leaves the solution.

The simplex procedure continues the pivoting process by bringing in variables having a negative $c_j - z_j$ in the highest-priority row. If there are no negative entries in the highest-priority row, we move to the next-highest-priority row and again search for negative entries. One difference, however, is that we must never bring in a variable x_j if it has a positive $c_j - z_j$ entry in a higher-priority $c_j - z_j$ row. That is, we must never improve a lower-priority goal at the expense of a higher-priority goal. The simplex method terminates with an optimal solution when all $c_j - z_j$ rows have nonnegative entries, or the satisfaction of a lower-priority goal can be accomplished only at the expense of a higher-priority goal.

After bringing x_2 into the solution, the simplex method continues through four iterations, achieving the optimal solution shown in Tableau 8.2. Notice that there are no negative entries in the $P_1 c_j - z_j$ row. There is, however, a $-.004$ in the second priority $P_2 c_j - z_j$ row. Nevertheless, we cannot bring d_1^- into the solution since d_1^- has a 1 in the $P_1 c_j - z_j$ row; this would negatively affect the attainment of the P_1 profit goal. Thus, no further improvements can be made and the solution is optimal. It is the same solution that we obtained in the graphical method with $x_1 = 200$, $x_2 = 0$. The last two numbers in the solution column indicate that the unattained portions of goals P_1 and P_2 are 0 and 19, respectively.

TABLEAU 8.2   Optimal simplex solution to goal programming problem

C_B	Basic variables	c_j 0 x_1	0 x_2	0 s_1	0 s_2	P_1 d_1^-	0 d_1^+	0 d_2^-	P_2 d_2^+	Solution
0	x_2	0	1	0	1	$-.006$	.006	0	0	0
0	x_1	1	0	0	-2.5	.02	$-.02$	0	0	200
P_2	d_2^+	0	0	0	$-.25$	.004	$-.004$	-1	1	19
0	s_1	0	0	1	-1	.006	$-.006$	0	0	40
P_2	$c_j - z_j$	0	0	0	.25	$-.004$	.004	1	0	19
P_1	$c_j - z_j$	0	0	0	0	1	0	0	0	0

A GOAL PROGRAMMING APPLICATION[2]

The Lord Corporation in Erie, Pennsylvania, established 10 goals in their research and development process:

1. No program may consume more than 10 percent of the resources.
2. Sales growth should exceed 15 percent per year.
3. Discounted cash flow rate of return should exceed 30 percent.
4. Projects have 5-year capital limits.
5. Projects promote constructive change in the industry.
6. Company develops leadership role.
7. Company develops new technology.
8. Advanced technology is interrelated.
9. Project provides diversification of product and market.
10. Current balance of allocations between units is to be maintained.

The first goal is insurance against a disastrous project; (2) to (4) are financial in nature; (5) to (9) relate to corporate purpose and image; and (10) prevents dislocations of competent technical personnel.

Faced with 25 potential R&D projects, the top management at Lord Corporation decided to use goal programming to assist in allocating funds

[2]Anthony A. Salvia and William R. Ludwig, "An Application of Goal Programming at Lord Corporation," *Interfaces,* 9 (August 1979), 129–133.

to the projects. A goal programming model was developed and four separate computer runs were made under a variety of assumptions. As a check, an integer programming model was also employed, but it proved to be not nearly so satisfactory as the goal programming approach. Fifteen projects were selected that were suggested by the majority of the goal programming runs. Three projects were also added by top management; two of these three were suggested by the integer programming solution.

Goal programming was of definite value to the Lord Corporation in the funding of R&D projects. It appeared to offer advantages over other math programming approaches in that a variety of variable types could be accommodated. It also helped management to assess the nature of the conflict between financial goals and goals relating to corporate purpose; it did this in a scientific manner—a departure from the often subjective or ad hoc top-management decision process.

DYNAMIC PROGRAMMING

The mathematical programming methods that we have discussed are concerned primarily with single-period or static decision problems. By contrast, dynamic programming is best suited for multiperiod or multistage decision problems in which the problem parameters change over time. Dynamic programming is also very flexible and is applicable to stochastic problems in which some parameters are probabilistic. Multistage or stochastic decision problems are common in business applications. Some of these applications include production and distribution problems, scheduling inventory control, resource allocation, replacement and maintenance problems, and various smoothing processes. Many of these types of problems are not amenable to analysis via other math programming approaches. Dynamic programming has evolved as a tool to

dynamic programming handle problems requiring a sequential decision process.

recursive optimization *Dynamic programming* would perhaps be better named serial or *recursive optimization*. It proceeds by breaking the problem into smaller subproblems called stages, and developing optimal policies or decisions for each stage. The stages are tied together through recursive relationships, so that when the last stage is calculated, the solution to the overall problem is determined. Dynamic programming, like branch and bound, does not exist in any standard form. It is a general mathematical approach that must be tailored for each different decision problem. It is impossible to present the theoretical aspects of dynamic programming in just this section of the chapter, and it is beyond the scope of this text. We will try to give an insight to the nature of the technique through two examples.

FIGURE 8.9 Reliability of lines in a telecommunication network

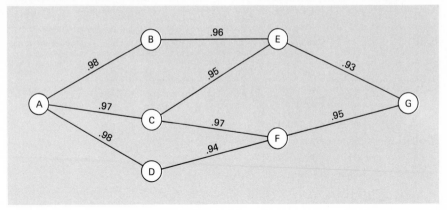

A RELIABILITY PROBLEM

Reliability is an important design factor in many business and engineering systems. Consider the telecommunication design problem as shown in Figure 8.9. The numbers on each arc of the network represent probabilities that the line will not have a failure or incur random noise during data transmission from one point to another. The objective is to determine the most reliable path of lines from node A to node G. The problem is much like the shortest route problem of Chapter 6 except that the probabilities must be multiplied rather than added to obtain the probability of a successful transmission from A to G. That is, the probability of a successful transmission from A to G along path A–B–E–G is .98 × .96 × .93 = .8749.

Dynamic programming can be applied to the reliability design problem by breaking the problem into subproblems or stages. Figure 8.10 illustrates how the problem naturally breaks into three stages. The dynamic programming approach proceeds sequentially from one stage to another. It begins at stage 1 and determines the most reliable path from each node to node G. It then moves to stage 2 and uses the information from stage 1 to determine the most reliable path from each node in stage 2 to node G. Finally, in stage 3 it uses the information from stage 2 to determine the optimal path from node A to node G. Working backward from stage to stage is the typical dynamic programming serial approach. It may seem like complete enumeration, but it is not, since at each stage it uses only the output or information from the immediately preceding stage.

Let us look more closely at the dynamic programming calculations by solving the reliability problem in detail. First we consider stage 1. If you are at node E or node F, you really have no choice but to go to node G.

FIGURE 8.10 Reliability problem broken into three stages

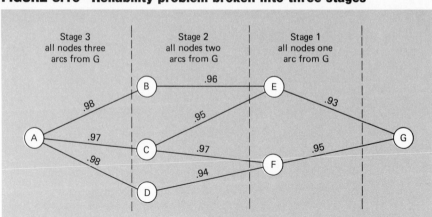

The reliabilities of the paths E–G and F–G are obtained directly from the graph in Figure 8.10 as .93 and .95, respectively. Thus, given that we are at node E or F, the optimal decision is clear.

Node	Optimal path from given node	Reliabiltiy factor
E	E–G	.93
F	F–G	.95

The optimal decisions for stage 2 are summarized below. These decisions depend on the optimal decisions from stage 1.

Node	Optimal path from given node	Reliability factor
B	B–E–G	.96 × .93 = .8928
C	C–F–G	.97 × .95 = .9215
D	D–F–G	.94 × .95 = .8930

For each node in stage 2, a decision must be made as to the successor node in stage 1. For nodes B and D we have no choice; therefore, let us focus on node C. From node C, we can choose to establish a line from C to either E or F. From the stage 1 calculations we know the optimal path and associated reliability from nodes E and F to the final destination. Thus, the optimal decision at node C is based on the best choice of reliability from C to E $\times$ reliability from E to G

or

reliability from C to F $\times$ reliability from F to G

We can write this as

$$\begin{aligned}
\text{Maximum reliability from C} &= \max(.95 \times .93, .97 \times .95) \\
&= .97 \times .95 \\
&= .9215
\end{aligned}$$

In stage 3 we have only node A. We use the optimal reliability decisions from stage 2 to calculate the optimal path from A to G.

Node	Optimal path from given node	Reliability factor
A	A–C–F–G	.97 $\times$ .922 = .8939

The calculations can be summarized as

$$\begin{array}{ccc}
\text{A to B} & \text{A to C} & \text{A to D}
\end{array}$$

$$\begin{aligned}
\text{Maximum reliability from A} &= \max(.98 \times .8928, .97 \times .922, .98 \times .893) \\
&= .97 \times .922 \\
&= .8939
\end{aligned}$$

Even though at stage 3 we only consider information from stage 2, the saving of the optimal decision at each stage provides the overall optimum to the problem once stage 3 is completed. Thus, in making the previous calculations from A to B, C, and D, respectively, we were implicitly evaluating the following complete paths:

Arc choice from node A	Complete path to node G	Reliability	
A–B	A–B–E–G	.8749	
A–C	A–C–F–G	.8939	← optimal choice
A–D	A–D–F–G	.8751	

The previous calculations may seem like complete enumeration and for very small examples such as this one, dynamic programming can approach complete enumeration. However, for larger problems, many computations are avoided by using dynamic programming and it is more efficient than complete enumeration.

FUNDAMENTAL CONCEPTS OF DYNAMIC PROGRAMMING

The foregoing example illustrates the basic ideas in dynamic programming, but it would be helpful to formalize the procedures. In particular, let us look at the terminology, underlying structure, and fundamental principles of dynamic programming. In every dynamic programming formulation, we have the following concepts.

stage 1. *Stage*—Each problem is broken into subproblems or stages. A stage corresponds to a point in time or a situation where a decision must be made.

state 2. *State*—States are associated with each stage and represent the various possible conditions of the system. Usually, state variables are used to describe the status of the system.

policy 3. *Policy*—A decision rule which, at any stage, determines the decision for each possible state. The effect of the policy decision at each stage is to transform the current stage into a state associated with the next stage.

optimal policy 4. *Optimal policy*—A policy that optimizes some criterion or objective. Usually, the optimal policy optimizes a return function which measures the quality of the possible decisions at each stage.

Additionally, we have the following fundamental *principle of dynamic programming:*

principle of optimality *Principle of Optimality*
An optimal policy has the property that whatever the initial state and initial decision are, the remaining decisions must constitute an optimal policy with regard to the state resulting from the first decision.

The relationships among stage, state, and policy is illustrated by the serial diagram in Figure 8.11.

We can further exemplify the meaning of stages, states, policy, and the principle of optimality by describing each of them in terms of the reliability example of Figure 8.10. The stages of the problem consisted of groups of nodes that had the common property of being a specific number of arcs away from the destination. Within each stage, a state simply consists of a particular node. For each possible state (node) we had to deter-

FIGURE 8.11 Relationships among stages, state, and policy

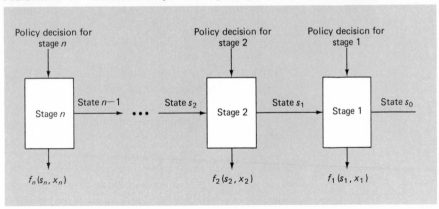

mine the optimal policy, which consisted of the choice of the best arc
return leading to the next stage. The criterion or *return function* consisted of a
function measure of reliability leading to the final node G. Given the current state,
the principle of optimality says that an optimal policy for the remaining
stages is independent of the policy adopted in previous stages. Knowledge
of the current state of the system conveys all the information for determining an optimal policy. Thus, at node C in Figure 8.10 we only need to know
the reliability measures at nodes E and F, not at preceding node A.

A PURCHASING-INVENTORY PROBLEM

In order to present a more formalized look at the dynamic programming
approach, let us consider a multiple-period purchasing and inventory
decision problem. A heating and air-conditioning distributor must make
quarterly purchasing decisions for a special type of compressor. Data
for the 3-month purchasing and storage problem is as follows:

Month	Demand	Cost per compressor at beginning of month	Storage cost for inventoried compressors
October	3	$150	$12
November	4	160	10
December	2	175	10

At the beginning of each month the company must purchase enough
compressors to satisfy demand. Excess purchases are carried over as
inventory for the next month. The company has zero units on hand October 1 and wants no inventory after December.

In order to present the dynamic programming formulation of this problem, let us use the following terms:

x_n = decision variable for stage n; the purchase quantity for month $n = 1, 2, 3$

s_n = state variable representing the amount of inventory on hand at the beginning of month n

d_n = demand in month n

$f_n(s_n, x_n)$ = return function, which measures the cost of decision x_n given state s_n

The problem breaks into natural stages, with each month representing a stage. We will let December represent stage 1, with November and October representing stages 2 and 3. In any month the cost will be comprised of purchasing plus storage costs. We need a return function that will account for the costs in the current time period as well as the preceding ones. If we let $p_n(s_n, x_n)$ = the cost of the purchasing and storage costs in stage n, then

$$p_n(s_n, x_n) = b_n x_n + c_n(s_n + x_n - d_n)$$

where b_n and c_n represent purchase and storage costs per unit in stage n. Note also that $s_n + x_n - d_n$ represents the amount by which beginning inventory plus purchases exceed current demand; hence $s_n + x_n - d_n$ equals inventory at the beginning of the succeeding month. Thus, the state transformation is described by

$$s_{i-1} = s_i + x_i - d_i$$

Finally, the overall return function in stage n, $f_n(s_n, x_n)$, is described by

$$f_n(s_n, x_n) = p_n(s_n, x_n) + f_{n-1}(s_n + x_n - d_n)$$

Notice the recursive nature of this function and how $f_n(s_n, x_n)$ depends on $f_{n-1}(s_n, x_n)$. By relating the impact of current-time-period decisions with succeeding-time-period decisions, we can arrive at an overall optimum.

In beginning the computation, let us examine how many possible states exist for December = stage 1. Since no inventory is desired at the end of the month and the December demand is only 2, we can have at most 2 units in inventory at the beginning of December; the least we can have is 0. Thus, state variable s_1 can be 0, 1, or 2. For each possible state we will need to compute total purchasing and inventory costs. This is conveniently done in the following table.

Stage 1.   Minimize $f_1(s_1, x_1) = 175x_1 + 10(x_1 + s_1 - d_1)$.

Possible states, s_1	$f_1(s_1, x_1)$ for:			Optimal solution	
	$x_1 = 0$	$x_1 = 1$	$x_1 = 2$	$f_1(s_1, x_1)$	x_1^*
0	—	—	350	350	2
1	—	175	—	175	1
2	0	—	—	0	0

The table shows the optimal decision given each possible inventory state. For example, if we enter December with $s_1 = 1$ units in inventory, the optimal decision is to purchase $x_1 = 1$ compressor. Since no storage is carried over, the return function $f_1(s_1, x_1)$ simplifies to $175x_1$.

In stage 2 there are seven possible states, since we can have as much as 6 units to cover the demand in November and December; we can also have a beginning inventory of 0.

Stage 2.   Minimize $f_2(s_2, x_2) = 160x_2 + 10(x_2 + s_2 - d_2) + f_1(x_2 + s_2 - d_2)$.

Possible states, s_2	$f_2(s_2, x_2)$ for:							Optimal solution	
	$x_2 = 0$	$x_2 = 1$	$x_2 = 2$	$x_2 = 3$	$x_2 = 4$	$x_2 = 5$	$x_2 = 6$	$f_2(s_2, x_2)$	x_2^*
0	—	—	—	—	990	985	980	980	6
1	—	—	—	830	825	820	—	820	5
2	—	—	670	665	660	—	—	660	4
3	—	510	505	500	—	—	—	500	3
4	350	345	340	—	—	—	—	340	2
5	185	180	—	—	—	—	—	180	1
6	20	—	—	—	—	—	—	20	0

In the table, the dashes indicate decision variable values that are too small to satisfy demand or too large and exceed stage 2 plus stage 1 demand. Performing a simple return function calculation for $s_2 = 2$ and $x_2 = 3$, we have

$$f_2(2, 3) = 160(3) + 10(3 + 2 - 4) + f_1(3 + 2 - 4)$$
$$= 480 + 10 + 175$$
$$= 665$$

Notice how the $f_1(1) = 175$ value is retrieved from the stage 1 calculations. This shows how we tie in optimal decisions from the previous stage;

it also shows that in computerized dynamic programming with discrete variables, the optimal decision for each stage must be stored in memory.

In stage 3 we have only one state variable value $s_3 = 0$, since we know that the beginning October inventory is zero. However, the purchase quantity can range from 3 to 9 units.

Stage 3.   Minimize $f_3(s_3, x_3) = 150x_3 + 12(x_3 + s_3 - d_3) + f_2(x_3 + s_3 - d_3)$.

Possible states, s_3	$f_3(s_3, x_3)$ for:							Optimal solution	
	$x_3 = 3$	$x_3 = 4$	$x_3 = 5$	$x_3 = 6$	$x_3 = 7$	$x_3 = 8$	$x_3 = 9$	$f_3(s_3, x_3)$	x_3^*
0	1430	1432	1434	1436	1438	1440	1442	1430	3

Given the optimal decision of $x_3 = 3$ for zero beginning inventory, we can determine the optimal decision in the previous two stages by a simple *state transformation*.

state transformation

$$s_2 = s_3 + x_3 - d_3 = 0 + 3 - 3 = 0$$

Thus, $x_2 = 6$ for $s_2 = 0$ (from the table of stage 2 calculations),

$$s_1 = s_2 + x_2 - d_2 = 0 + 6 - 4 = 2$$

and $x_1 = 0$ for $s_1 = 2$.

The optimal decision is to purchase 3, 6, and 0 compressors in October, November, and December, respectively; the minimum purchasing and inventory cost is $1,430.

ADVANTAGES AND DISADVANTAGES OF DYNAMIC PROGRAMMING

In our two example problems we have focused on problems having discrete variables. Dynamic programming is also applicable to continuous-variable decision problems. In fact, dynamic programming is one of the more powerful mathematical modeling techniques, in that it can be applied to such a wide range of problems. However, what it gains in breadth it sometimes sacrifices in efficiency. We turn now to the major advantages and disadvantages of the technique.

Advantages

1. For some problems in such areas as inventory management, control theory, or chemical engineering design, dynamic programming is the only technique that can solve the problems.

2. It is particularly well suited for multistage, multiperiod, or sequential decision processes.

3. Dynamic programming is very broad in scope and is applicable to linear or nonlinear problems, discrete or continuous variables, and deterministic or stochastic problems.

4. It is readily adapted to the computer and can provide some degree of sensitivity analysis.

Disadvantages

1. No general formulation of the dynamic programming problem exists and each problem must be modeled uniquely. This requires ingenuity, experience, and insight.

2. The *"curse of dimensionality"* requires that the number of state variables be kept relatively low to prevent excessive computational requirements.

3. In general, the dynamic programming approach is not particularly efficient when compared to other math programming algorithms, such as the simplex method.

SUMMARY

Many real-world problems can be modeled and solved as mathematical programming models that are not pure LP models. In this chapter, we have examined the three most widely used mathematical programming approaches (not including LP).

Integer programming extends LP by allowing the requirements of whole-number solutions. The types of integer models include pure, mixed, and 0–1. The branch-and-bound partial enumeration procedure is generally the most successful approach to achieving integer solutions. Using integer-valued variables permits the formulation of many discontinuous-type problems, such as the fixed-charge problem.

Goal programming extends linear programming by accommodating multiple objectives. These objectives must be ordinally ranked and are satisfied in order of priority. Often, a final solution satisfices rather than completely achieves all goals. Linear goal programming models can be solved by a modified version of the simplex method. Many applications exist for goal programming, particularly in the public sector.

Dynamic programming is especially appropriate for multistage or sequential decision problems. Unlike LP, integer, or goal programming, it can be more easily applied to probabilistic and nonlinear problems. However, it requires a unique formulation for each different type of decision problem and is not always efficient. In spite of its efficiency, dynamic programming is sometimes the only viable optimization approach to a real-world problem.

SOLVED PROBLEMS

PROBLEM STATEMENT

Consider the following 0–1 integer programming model:

$$\text{Maximize} \quad 35x_1 + 40x_2 + 42x_3$$
$$\text{subject to} \quad 7x_1 + 6x_2 + 13x_3 \leq 75$$
$$2x_1 - x_2 + x_3 \leq 30$$
$$x_1, x_2, x_3 \quad 0 \text{ or } 1$$

Reformulate the problem so that no more than two decision variables are nonzero and if $x_2 = 1$ then $x_3 = 1$, and vice versa.

SOLUTION

$$\text{Maximize} \quad 35x_1 + 40x_2 + 42x_3$$
$$\text{subject to} \quad 7x_1 + 6x_2 + 13x_3 \leq 75$$
$$2x_1 - x_2 + x_3 \leq 30$$
$$x_1 + x_2 + x_3 \leq 2$$
$$x_2 - x_3 = 0$$
$$x_1, x_2, x_3 \quad 0 \text{ or } 1$$

PROBLEM STATEMENT

Recall the Faze Linear LP model of the goal programming section of this chapter. Its LP formulation is relisted as follows:

$$\text{Maximize} \quad 200x_1 + 500x_2$$
$$\text{subject to} \quad x_2 \leq 40$$
$$1.2x_1 + 4x_2 \leq 240$$
$$.5x_1 + 1x_2 \leq 81$$
$$x_1, x_2 \geq 0$$

Reformulate the Faze Linear model as a goal programming model with the following goals:

Priority 1:   Produce at least 10 preamps and 150 amps.

Priority 2:   Maximize profit.

Priority 3:   Limit assembly overtime to 10 hours.

SOLUTION

$$\text{Minimize} \quad P_1(d_1^- + d_2^-) + P_2 d_3^- + P_3 d_4^+$$

$$\text{subject to} \qquad\quad x_2 \le 40 \left.\vphantom{\begin{matrix}1\\1\end{matrix}}\right\}$$
$$.5x_1 + 1x_2 \le 81 \quad\quad \text{resource constraints}$$
$$x_1 + d_1^- - d_1^+ = 150 \left.\vphantom{\begin{matrix}1\\1\end{matrix}}\right\}$$
$$x_2 + d_2^- - d_2^+ = 10 \quad \text{priority 1}$$
$$200x_1 + 500x_2 + d_3^- - d_3^+ = 999{,}999 \qquad \text{priority 2}$$
$$1.2x_1 + 4x_2 + d_4^- - d_4^+ = 250 \qquad \text{priority 3}$$
$$x_j, d_i \ge 0$$

In the priority 2 goal constraint, the 999,999 represents an unrealistically high profit. It is simply used as a target, that is, to get as close as possible to this profit.

PROBLEM STATEMENT

Consider the following three-item knapsack problem:

Item	Weight, w_i	Value, v_i	
1	5	5	capacity = 10
2	8	10	
3	3	6	

a. Identify the dynamic programming structure for this problem; that is, determine the stages, states, and specify the recursive relationship between stages through the return function.

b. Solve the problem.

SOLUTION

a. The stages are naturally defined by each item, since a decision must be made for each item. Thus, there are three stages. The critical factor at each stage is the amount of capacity remaining in the knapsack. Thus, let state variable s_i = weight capacity available at stage i. The general formulation of the return function is

$$f_i(s_i, x_i) = \max_{x_i \ 0 \text{ or } 1} \{v_i x_i + f_{i-1}(s_i - w_i x_i)\}$$

where x_i denotes the binary decision variable of whether to take item i or not, and v_i and w_i denote the value and weight of item i, respectively. Notice that $s_i - w_i x_i = s_{i-1}$ = the capacity available for the preceding stage.

At stage 1 the possible states of the system are 2, 7, or 10, depending on whether item 2, item 3, or no items have been loaded at the other two stages.

Stage 1:   Max $f_1(s_1, x_1) =$ Max $5x_1$
$$x_1 \ 0 \text{ or } 1$$

Possible states s_1	$f_1(s_1, x_1)$ for: $x_1 = 0$	$x_1 = 1$	Optimal solution $f_1(x_1)$	x_1^*
2	0	—	0	0
7	0	5	5	1
10	0	5	5	1

Stage 2:   Max $f_2(s_2, x_2) = \max \{10x_2 + f_1(s_2 - 8x_2)\}$
$$x_2 \ 0 \text{ or } 1$$

Possible states, s_2	$f_2(s_2, x_2)$ for: $x_2 = 0$	$x_2 = 1$	Optimal solution $f_2(x_2)$	x_2^*
7	5	—	5	0
10	5	10	10	1

Stage 3:   Max $f_3(s_3, x_3) = \max [6x_3 + f_2(s_3 - 3x_3)\}$
$$x_3 \ 0 \text{ or } 1$$

Possible states, s_3	$f_3(s_3, x_3)$ for: $x_3 = 0$	$x_3 = 1$	Optimal solution $f_3(x_3)$	x_3^*
10	10	11	11	1

Thus, the optimal solution is $x_1 = 1$, $x_2 = 0$, and $x_3 = 1$ for a value of 11.

REVIEW QUESTIONS

1. Explain how each of the following differ from LP.
   a. integer programming
   b. goal programming
   c. dynamic programming
2. How does branch and bound avoid complete enumeration?
3. Which of the math programming techniques of this chapter are applicable to stochastic problems?

4. List 3 types of formulation possibilities that can be modeled through integer programming.

5. What is meant by the ordinal ranking of goals in goal programming?

6. List two advantages and two disadvantages of dynamic programming.

7. In what way is the simplex method modified for the goal programming approach?

8. Contrast the state of the art in the solution capabilities of linear versus integer programming.

9. Explain the difficulties in using LP with rounding to obtain integer solutions.

10. Under what conditions is a node fathomed in the branch and bound process?

11. In selecting R & D projects, the Lord Corporation did not use just one computer run. What did they do?

PROBLEMS

8.1 *Research and Development Project Selection.* The Kleber Corporation is considering six R & D projects for the next fiscal year. They have allocated $250,000 for research and development projects. All projects must be completely funded or not funded at all. Given the expected rate of return for the six projects in the table, formulate a mathematical model to maximize return from the R & D projects.

Project	Rate of return	Cost
1	20%	$80,000
2	23	50,000
3	30	40,000
4	15	70,000
5	18	80,000
6	25	60,000

8.2 In problem 8.1 above, let $x_i = 1$ if project i is selected and 0 otherwise. Specify the appropriate constraints for each of the following conditions:

a. At most 5 projects are to be selected.

b. If project 1 is selected then project 5 is not selected.

c. Exactly four projects are to be selected.

d. If project 2 is selected then project 4 is also selected.

e. Either constraint (a) or (b) above applies, but not both.

8.3   Solve the following knapsack problem by branch and bound.

$$\text{Maximize} \quad 180x_1 + 80x_2 + 130x_3 + 110x_4$$
$$\text{subject to} \quad 7x_1 + 2x_2 + 6x_3 + 5x_4 \leq 15$$
$$x_1 \quad 0 \text{ or } 1$$

8.4   Solve the previous knapsack problem (8.3) by dynamic programming.

8.5   Specify whether each of the following models are pure integer, mixed integer, 0–1 integer, or linear.

    a. Maximize $\quad x_1 + x_2$
        subject to $\quad 3x_1 + 2x_2 \leq 20$
                    $4x_1 + x_2 \leq 50$
                    $x_i \ 0 \text{ or } 1$

    b. Minimize $\quad 3x_1 + 4x_2 + 6x_3$
        subject to $\quad x_1 + x_2 + x_3 \geq 3$
                    $2x_1 - x_2 + 3x_3 = 18$
                    $x_1 \text{ integer}$
                    $x_2, x_3 \geq 0$

    c. Minimize $\quad 4x_1 + 5x_2$
        subject to $\quad 2x_1 + 3x_2 \geq 40$
                    $6x_1 + 2x_2 \geq 30$
                    $x_1, x_2 \geq 0$

    d. Maximize $\quad 3x_1 + 7x_2$
        subject to $\quad x_1 + x_2 \leq 10$
                    $8x_1 + 9x_2 \leq 100$
                    $x_1, x_2 \text{ integer}$

8.6   *Personnel Recruiting.* Midwestern University must fill 30 faculty and 10 staff positions for next year. In order to control costs and better satisfy EEOC requirements. Midwestern has the following goals:

Priority 1: at least 30% of new hirings are to be minorities
              at least 20% of new hirings are to be women

Priority 2: stay within recruiting budget of $40,000

Priority 3: limit budget overrun to $10,000

Assume that it costs $1,100 to recruit a faculty member and $300 to recruit a staff member. Furthermore, it costs 20% more to recruit a minority or female faculty member. Formulate the above problem as a goal programming model.

8.7 Solve the following goal programming problem graphically.

$$\begin{aligned}
\text{Minimize} \quad & P_1(d_1^- + d_1^+) + P_2 d_2^- \\
\text{subject to} \quad & 2x_1 + 3x_2 && \geq 12 \\
& x_1 && \geq 3 \\
& x_1 + x_2 + d_1^- - d_1^+ && = 6 \\
& x_2 + d_2^- - d_2^+ && = 3 \\
& x_1, x_2\, d_1^-, d_1^+, d_2^-, d_2^+ \geq 0
\end{aligned}$$

8.8 Solve problem 8.7 by the modified simplex method.

8.9 *Purchase and Storage Cost Minimization.* Sound Waves Inc. plans to stock the new Tofler amplifier kit. The kit is aimed at the high end market and demand of 2, 5, and 3 units is anticipated for the next three months. The following table indicates the purchase and storage costs during each month.

Month	Cost per kit at beginning of month	Storage cost per kit per month
Nov.	$395	$20
Dec.	435	21
Jan.	450	22

No inventory is desired at the end of January. Use dynamic programming to determine the optimal purchasing and storage strategy to minimize costs, assuming no beginning inventory.

8.10 Given a knapsack problem with 5 items, what is the maximum number of nodes that could possibly comprise the branch and bound tree?

8.11 Consider the pure integer problem given.

$$\begin{aligned}
\text{Maximize} \quad & 3x_1 + 4x_2 \\
\text{subject to} \quad & x_1 && \leq 4 \\
& x_2 \leq 3 \\
& 3x_1 + 4x_2 \leq 22 \\
& x_1, x_2 \geq 0 \text{ and integer}
\end{aligned}$$

a. Graph the constraints and plot all feasible lattice points.

b. Ignore the integer restrictions, and solve the LP relaxation of the problem graphically.

    c. Specify an upper and lower bound on the value of the optimal integer solution.

    d. Determine the optimal integer solution.

8.12 *Production Planning.* The Crosby Co. has contracted to produce 500 fittings next week for one of its customers. Crosby has 3 machines in its machine shop that can produce the fitting, but at different variable and fixed costs. These costs and weekly production limits are shown in the table. The fixed cost is incurred only if the machine is set up to produce the fitting.

Machine	Per unit production cost	Fixed set up cost	Weekly production limit
1	$1.12	$60	300
2	1.40	55	250
3	1.23	50	270

Formulate an integer programming model to determine how to produce the 500 fittings at minimal cost.

8.13 *Investment Decision Problem.* Assume one of your friends has just inherited $100,000 after taxes. He has several ideas for the money, but is unable to do them all. He would like to invest in gold, with an expected return of 20% but a risk factor of .15. He would also like to invest in an uninsured money market C.D. yielding 11.5% with a risk factor of .10. His other ideas are to invest in an insured passbook account yielding 7% with risk factor .02 and to invest in a mutual fund yielding 9.5% with risk .07. Finally, he would like to loan you $25,000 to start your own business upon graduation. Since not all of these ideas are simultaneously possible, he has specified the following priorities:

P_1: total investments must absolutely not exceed $100,000

P_2: achieve an average yield of 10%

P_3: achieve an average risk of no more than .06

P_4: loan you $25,000

Formulate the investment decision problem as a goal programming model.

8.14 Recall the shortest route exercise of problem number 1 in chapter 6. Solve this problem by dynamic programming. *Hint:* the problem is much like the reliability problem at the beginning of this chapter except that the relationships are additive rather than multiplicative.

8.15 *Project Management.* A construction contractor has four construction projects underway and wants to minimize the time required to complete all projects. The following table reflects the estimated time required to complete the project for a specified number of foremen assigned to the project.

Project	Number of foremen assigned		
	1	2	3
A	5	3	2
B	7	5	3
C	9	8	7
D	11	8	8

Given that the contractor has only 6 foremen and he wishes to minimize the sum of the project completion times, (assuming each project is assigned at least one foreman):

a. Formulate the problem as a dynamic programming problem. Identify the stages, states, and return function.

b. Solve the problem.

8.16 Consider problem 8.15 with a different objective. Suppose the contractor wants to minimize the maximum time required to complete any one of the four projects rather than the sum of project times.

a. Formulate the mini-max problem as a dynamic programming problem.

b. Solve the problem.

8.17 *Advertising Strategy.* A major sporting goods manufacturer is bringing out a new line of graphite golf clubs, and wants to accomplish several goals in its new advertising campaign. The campaign will focus on ads in the leading golf magazine and television ads during coverage of P.G.A. tournaments. A magazine ad costs $12,000 and has a "reach" of 350,000 effective exposure units. A television ad costs $20,000 and achieves 1,400,000 effective exposure units. The company has allocated $500,000 for advertising the new line of clubs. Formulate a goal programming model to incorporate the following goals:

P_1: stay within advertising budget of $500,000

P_2: maximize the audience "reach," that is, the number of effective exposure units

P_3: run at least 10 television ads

P_4: run at least 8 magazine ads

8.18 Solve problem 8.17 by the graphical goal programming method.

8.19 *Cargo Loading.* An independent trucker makes a weekly trip from Los Angeles to New Orleans. In order to make his trip more profitable he has decided to be more selective in how he loads his truck. His truck has a volume capacity of 2,500 cubic feet and a weight capacity of 40,000 pounds. The following table lists the types of items and their weight, boxed volume, and profitability.

	Weight (lbs.)	Volume	Profit contribution
Electric ranges	180	20	$17
Washing machine	250	24	20
Refrigerator	380	54	25
Dishwasher	120	19	9
Television	100	18	13
Stereo speakers	90	15	10

a. Formulate the cargo loading problem as an integer programming problem, assuming profit maximization as the goal.

b. Formulate the cargo loading problem as a dynamic programming problem. Do not solve.

c. Comment on the relative desirability of solving the problem through integer or dynamic programming.

8.20 *Staff Shift Scheduling.* Northern Airlines is in the process of finalizing an on-line reservations system. To staff the system, telephone reservationsists will need to be available in the following quantities:

Period	Time	Reservationists needed
1	6 A.M.–8 A.M.	3
2	8 A.M.–10 A.M.	12
3	10 A.M.–12 noon	13
4	12 noon–2 P.M.	10
5	2 P.M.–4 P.M.	12
6	4 P.M.–6 P.M.	10
7	6 P.M.–8 P.M.	6
8	8 P.M.–10 P.M.	5
9	10 P.M.–12 midnight	4
10	12 midnight–2 A.M.	3

National plans to have six work shifts, of which two are split shifts. The shift times are as follows:

Shift	Times
1	6 A.M.–2 P.M.
2	8 A.M.–4 P.M.
3	10 A.M.–6 P.M.
4	6 P.M.–2 A.M.
5	10 A.M.–1 P.M. and 4 P.M.–8 P.M.
6	8 A.M.–11 A.M. and 5 P.M.–9 P.M.

The airlines wants to assign reservationists to shifts in order to meet demand. However, they want to hire the minimal number of people to meet demand. Formulate an integer programming model to determine the minimum number of reservationists required for each shift.

8.21   *System Reliability Design.* A subsystem for the automatic pilot function on an aircraft consists of four electronic components, each of which has a specified probability of failure. In order to reduce the probability of failure it is possible to install parallel backup components that will take over whenever its predecessor component fails. The following table gives the probability of failure of each component function for a given number of backup units.

Number of backup units	*Probability of failure of individual components*			
	Component 1	Component 2	Component 3	Component 4
0	.01	.015	.01	.02
1	.0001	.000225	.0001	.0004
2	.000001	.000003375	.000001	.000008

The probability that the total subsystem will function is the product of the probabilities that each individual component will function. The success probability is the complement of the failure probability. Thus, the probability of the subsystem functioning with no backup units is $.99 \times .985 \times .99 \times .98 = .946$.

The material and installation cost of the components is $30, $40, $35, and $45 for components 1, 2, 3, and 4, respectively. Given a budget of $350, use dynamic programming to determine the optimal number of backup units for each component in order to maximize the probability that the subsystem will function.

8.22   *Curve Fitting Via Goal Programming.* Several factors are used to predict graduate school performance. For MBAs, their GMAT test scores are often used together with other information. The development of predicting equations that regress one variable against another is usually done by the method of least squares. However, the least squares method develops a predicting equation that minimizes the sum of the squares of the residuals or differences between actual and predicted dependent variable values. Unfortunately extreme or outlying cases can bias the resulting equation to an undesirable extent. The use of goal programming can reduce the effect of "outliers" by minimizing the sum of the absolute value of residuals rather than the squared value.

Returning to the prediction of G.P.A. given GMAT test scores, we want an equation

$$\text{predicted GPA} = ax + b$$

where x = the student's GMAT score and a and b are to be determined.

Goal programming can be used by applying the equation

$$\text{predicted GPA}_i + r_i = \text{actual GPA}_i$$

where the residual r_i = actual GPA$_i$ − predicted GPA$_i$ for the i'th observation

For n observations, the goal programming objective function would be

$$\text{Minimize} \quad \sum_{i=1}^{n} (d_i^- + d_i^+)$$

where $r_i = d_i^- - d_i^+$

Listed below are 10 real GMAT scores and G.P.A.s for 10 randomly selected MBAs at a Southwestern University.

GMAT	G.P.A.
665	3.20
629	3.63
588	3.00
523	3.60
513	3.00
483	3.00
452	3.10
442	3.00
441	3.15
388	2.50

    a. Formulate a goal programming model that will predict G.P.A. given GMAT scores based on the sample given.

    b. If you have access to an LP computer package, solve the model on the computer to determine the predicting equation.

BIBLIOGRAPHY

Charnes, Abraham, and William W. Cooper, *Management Models and Industrial Applications of Linear Programming.* New York: John Wiley & Sons, Inc., 1961.

Denardo, E. V., *Dynamic Programming: Theory and Application.* Englewood Cliffs, N.J.: Prentice-Hall, Inc., 1975.

Dreyfus, S., and A. M. Law, *The Art and Theory of Dynamic Programming.* New York: Academic Press, 1977.

Garfinkel, R. S., and G. L. Nemhauser, *Integer Programming.* New York: John Wiley & Sons, Inc., 1972.

Hu, T. C., *Integer Programming and Network Flows.* Reading, Mass.: Addison-Wesley, 1969.

Ignizio, James P., *Goal Programming and Extensions.* Lexington, Mass.: D. C. Heath and Company, 1976.

Lee, Sang M., *Goal Programming for Decision Analysis.* Philadelphia: Auerbach Publishers, Inc., 1972.

Loomba, Narendra P., and Efrian Turban, *Applied Programming for Management.* New York: Holt, Rinehart and Winston, Inc., 1974.

Nemhauser, George L., *Introduction to Dynamic Programming.* New York: John Wiley & Sons, Inc., 1966.

Plane, Donald R., and Claude McMillan, Jr., *Discrete Optimization.* Englewood Cliffs, N.J.: Prentice-Hall, Inc., 1971.

Salkin, H. M., *Integer Programming.* Reading, Mass.: Addison-Wesley, 1975.

Taha, Hamdy A., *Integer Programming: Theory, Applications and Computations.* New York: Academic Press, 1975.

Zionts, Stanley, *Linear and Integer Programming,* Englewood Cliffs, N.J.: Prentice-Hall, Inc., 1974.

PART III

Stochastic Models

9

Probability Concepts
and Distributions

LAS VEGAS, NEVADA[1]

People win in gambling casinos all over the world from Las Vegas to Monte Carlo. One thing remains constant: over the long term, the house always wins. This means that you, the individual gambler, have little chance to be a constant winner. The reason for this state of affairs is that casino managers are better students of probability theory than are their customers.

Edward Thorp, in his book <u>Beat the Dealer</u>, shows that if one conscientiously applies the theory of probability to the game of black jack, that person can turn the tables on the gambling casinos.

Being a student of probability theory, Mr. Thorp has developed several strategies for winning the game of black jack, or twenty-one. Although he validated his strategies theoretically and even tested them on the computer, he decided to test his ideas in Nevada. One spring vacation Mr. Thorp left MIT, where he was on the faculty, and went to Nevada for a casino test of his system. Two large-scale New York gamblers had agreed to "bankroll" Mr. Thorp's test by investing $100,000. The casino test proved so successful that many casinos refused to let the MIT professor play. Other casinos tried to limit the effectiveness of his system by shuffling the deck more often and changing the house rules of the game. Some casinos just made it unpleasant for him to play, and others resorted to cheating in order to switch the odds back in their favor. In 30 man-hours of playing, Mr. Thorp had built $10,000 into $21,000. The maximum amount he was ever down was $1,300. Thorp states that "Our experiment was a success, and my system performed in practice just as the theory on which it is based predicted it would." He concludes his chapter on his trip to Nevada as follows:

My trip to Nevada gives an ironic twist to the words of a casino operator who was being interviewed on a national television program. When he was asked whether the customers in Nevada ever walked away winners, he

---

[1]Edward O. Thorp, *Beat the Dealer* (New York: Vintage Books), 1966.

said, "When a lamb goes to the slaughter, the lamb might kill the butcher. But we always bet on the butcher."

The day of the lamb had come.

INTRODUCTION

Earlier, you learned that there are three states in which decisions are made: certainty, in which all relevant information is known; stochastic, or risk, conditions, in which limited information (usually in terms of probabilities) is available; and total uncertainty, in which little or nothing is known. Decisions under certainty are, of course, the easiest to make. When information is certain, a systematic analysis of even large-scale decision problems can usually be made. However, most real-world decision problems are made under conditions that are neither completely certain nor completely uncertain. The decision maker usually has some information to work with but is uncertain to a degree about what will happen after the decision is made.

The use of probability theory can be of great help in making decisions under risk conditions. By organizing relevant information, assessing the likelihood of various alternatives, and systematically analyzing the problem, the decision maker can usually reach a more effective decision than by the seat-of-the-pants, or intuitive, approach. Overall goals or objectives can best be met when probabilistic information is considered in a systems context. For example, probability theory can be useful in helping a contractor decide whether or not to bid on a $100,000 contract that costs $5,000 in bidding expenses. Or, a production manager might use probability theory to decide how much inventory to stock in order to avoid large stock-outs and provide an adequate level of service to the customer.

Founded in mathematics, probability theory is rigorous and well defined. In this chapter, we shall develop only the aspects you will need for the material in the rest of this book. In effect, then, this is a brief and specialized review. If you have not studied probability theory before, you will find an elementary introduction to the subject here.

In simple terms, a probability is a measure of the likelihood that an event will occur. If we reach into a deck of cards, we can say that the likelihood of getting a card that is a club is $^{13}/_{52}$, or .25. The .25 is a quantification of the likelihood that we will draw a club. Thus, a probability is actually a measure of chance. Probability is the mathematical expression of uncertainty; modern probability has its foundations in mathematical measure theory.

objective probability   We shall be concerned with probabilities as they pertain to decision making. Probabilities of two types are used in decision making. *Objective probabilities* are those for which there is definitive historical information or rigorous analysis to support the assignment of probabilities. For instance, the .25 probability of drawing a club from a deck of cards is an objective probability. The probability of getting a head in tossing a fair coin is .50 and is an objective probability. Past experience has shown that this statement of likelihood is true, and it can easily be argued mathematically.

subjective probability   Frequently, a decision maker is confronted with a situation in which an exact objective probability is not available. For example, the exact probability of receiving a contract is not known, or the probability of next month's sales exceeding $50,000 is not known with certainty. A *subjective probability* is based on the personal experience of the decision maker. It may rely in part on previous records or outside information, but it represents the decision maker's degree of belief that a particular event will occur. The odds a bookie gives for major sports events are subjective probabilities, but they are based also on past records, outside information, and so on. A retail clothing buyer's sales estimates also qualify as subjective probabilities. The buyer must consider the desirability of various lines and then subjectively estimate potential sales. In deciding how much to order, the buyer may subjectively assess the probabilities that sales will be at or below different volumes.

Subjective probabilities are essentially educated guesses, and some people feel that subjective probabilities should not be included as input to formal analysis of a decision problem. These objectivists feel that subjective input should be considered only after a formal analysis is accomplished with the available objective information. Subjectivists, on the other hand, believe in using subjective estimates and probabilities in analyzing a decision problem. They argue that people who run businesses and others who make consequential decisions do so based on their experience, intuition, and hunches. Subjectivists feel that the decision process is more likely to be correct if subjective estimates and probabilities are used in a formal or systematic analysis.

BASIC CONCEPTS

event   In probability applications, we often want to determine the likelihood of a particular random phenomenon or occurrence. In probability theory, we call a specified outcome of a random phenomenon an *event*. If we perform a statistical experiment in coin tossing, we may ask what the probability is of the event *getting two heads in a row*. An inventory manager may want to determine the probability of the event *incurring a stock-out next month*.

simple event   Events may be classified as simple or compound. A *simple event* consists of a single possible outcome of a random phenomenon. For example, suppose we toss three coins and consider the event *getting three heads*, *compound* or *HHH*. This is a simple event. A *compound event,* on the other hand, *event* consists of two or more simple events. The event of getting two heads when we toss three coins is a compound event since it consists of the three simple events *HHT, THH,* and *HTH.*

In assessing probabilities for a particular problem, it is necessary to *sample* specify the universe of all possible outcomes. A simple event is called a *point* *sample point,* and the collection of all possible sample points is called the *sample* *sample space.* We denote the sample space by the letter S. Thus, in the ex-*space* ample of tossing three coins, the sample space S consists of all possible outcomes. In this case $S = \{HHH, HHT, HTH, THH, TTH, HTT, THT, TTT\}$. Assuming that the coins are fair, each of the sample points in S is equally likely to occur; thus, the probability of each sample point is $\frac{1}{8}$.

Let us consider another random experiment in which a single die is cast. The six-sided cube will show from one to six dots. If we let the simple events be defined by the number of dots showing, then $S = \{1, 2, 3, 4, 5, 6\}$. In Figure 9.1 we represent S with a Venn diagram. Consider the event E_1, which is defined as getting a one or a two. E_1 is the outlined area in Figure 9.1. Event E_1 is a compound event, and its probability is equal to the probability of the simple events of which it is composed. If we denote $P(E_1)$ as the probability of E_1, we have $P(E_1) = \frac{1}{6} + \frac{1}{6} = \frac{1}{3}$.

complemen- For every event E there exists a *complementary event* $\overline{E}$. The comple-*tary event* ment $\overline{E}$ consists of all the sample points in S that are not in E. Thus, in Figure 9.1, $\overline{E}_1 = \{3, 4, 5, 6\}$. Together, an event and its complement must comprise the entire sample space. By knowing the probability of each individual sample point, we can calculate the probability of each event in S. Thus, $P(\overline{E}_1) = \frac{1}{6} + \frac{1}{6} + \frac{1}{6} + \frac{1}{6} = \frac{2}{3}$. However, this counting process is not convenient for large or infinite sample spaces. Fortunately, basic probability laws can be used to help determine probabilities in more general situations.

FIGURE 9.1   The sample space S

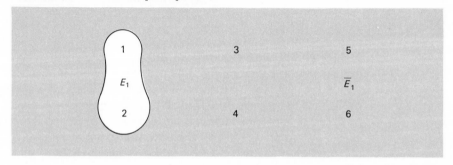

PROBABILITY AXIOMS

Certain properties of probability are fundamental to the understanding and application of probability theory. For example, the probability of any event being between 0 and 1 is a fundamental property. Let E_i represent any event in the sample space S; then we have the following three axioms.

Nonnegativity   The probability of any event in S is greater than or equal to 0 and less than or equal to 1.

$$0 \leq P(E_i) \leq 1 \qquad \text{for any } E_i \text{ in } S$$

Additivity   If two events E_i and E_j are both in S but have no sample points in common, the probability that at least one of these events occurs is the sum of $P(E_i)$ and $P(E_j)$.

$$P(E_i \text{ or } E_j) = P(E_i) + P(E_j)$$

Completeness of sample space   The probability of the entire sample space is 1.

$$P(S) = 1$$

mutually exclusive events   The additivity property of the second axiom refers to events that are mutually exclusive. *Mutually exclusive events* cannot occur at the same time and are characterized by not having any sample points in common. Figure 9.2 graphically illustrates two mutually exclusive events E_i and E_j. In Figure 9.1, E_1 and $\overline{E}_1$ are also mutually exclusive events. An event and its complement are always mutually exclusive. But an event and its complement are also collectively exhaustive. A group of events is *collectively*

collectively exhaustive events

FIGURE 9.2   Mutually exclusive events E_i and E_j

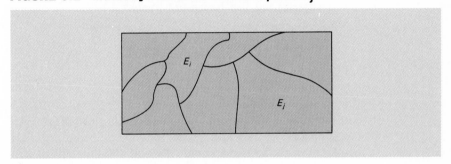

319

exhaustive if together they include all the sample points in the sample space. Thus, $E_1 = \{1, 2\}$ and $\overline{E}_1 = \{3, 4, 5, 6\}$ are collectively exhaustive in $S = \{1, 2, 3, 4, 5, 6\}$.

MARGINAL, CONDITIONAL, AND JOINT PROBABILITIES

So far, we have only considered the probabilities of events that are unaffected by the outcome of other events. Unconditional probabilities that do not depend on other events are sometimes called *marginal* probabilities. The term *marginal* applies since these probabilities (as we shall see) can be found in the margin of a probability table.

marginal probability

If we roll a die and ask what the probability of a five is, then we are asking for a marginal probability since it does not depend on other events or outside information. For a fair die, the probability of a five is $\frac{1}{6}$. But suppose we consider another event that constitutes additional information concerning the outcome of the die. Suppose you cannot see the die at first and someone tells you that it does not show a three. Now what is the probability of a five? The probability is now $\frac{1}{5}$ rather than $\frac{1}{6}$ since one of the six possibilities has been eliminated. This is an example of a *conditional probability*, a probability that depends on the outcome of another event.

conditional probability

Conditional probabilities are important in the business world, for there are many instances in which decisions under uncertainty depend on the outcome of other factors. For instance, we might want to know the probability of small car sales given new government fuel efficiency regulations, or we might want to estimate the chances of success for a new product given a nationwide advertising effort.

We denote conditional probability as $P(A|B)$, which is read, "the probability of A, given B." If we roll a die and let A equal the event of getting a five, and B the event a three or four does not show, then we have $P(A) = \frac{1}{6}$ but $P(A|B) = \frac{1}{4}$. If we let C equal the event that a four or five does not show, then $P(A|C) = 0$.

We determined the foregoing probabilities by logical reasoning, but there exists a formula for conditional probability:

$$P(A|B) = \frac{P(A \text{ and } B)}{P(B)} \qquad \text{provided that } P(B) > 0 \qquad [9.1]$$

We only consider conditional probabilities when $P(B) > 0$ anyway, because it makes little sense to consider the probability of A given B if B never occurs. By $P(A \text{ and } B)$, we mean the probability that both A and B occur. In order to understand this and the concept of conditional prob-

FIGURE 9.3 Venn diagram of conditional probability

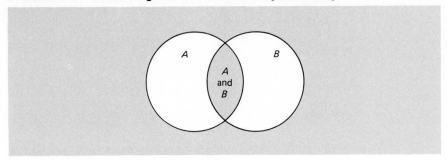

ability, consider the Venn diagram in Figure 9.3. Notice that the shaded area *A* and *B* is the intersection of event *A* and event *B*. We can intuitively explain formula 9.1 for conditional probability by assuming that the areas *A, B,* and *A* and *B* correspond to actual probabilities. Thus, if a sample point falls in *B*, the probability that it also falls in *A* is equal to the ratio of the area of *A* and *B* to the area of *B*. Thus we get $P(A|B) = [P(A \text{ and } B)]/[P(B)]$.

joint   The probability of two or more events occurring is called a *joint prob-*
probability *ability*. Thus $P(A \text{ and } B)$ is a joint probability.

EXAMPLE   Let us illustrate some of these conditional and joint probabilities with an example. For a graduate thesis, a student is attempting to determine the relationship between the success of OR/MS projects and the formalization of OR/MS procedures within the company. To gather information, 100 companies are surveyed about their OR/MS operations. The student finds that 70 of the companies report that their OR/MS projects are successful, and 50 report formalization of OR/MS procedures. Let us define four different events:

      A = company reports success
      B = company reports failure
      C = company has formalized OR/MS procedures
      D = company does not have formalized OR/MS procedures

Based on the 100-company sample, the student calculated the probabilities shown in Table 9.1. We shall use these data for insight into the nature of various probabilities by posing some pertinent questions, then showing you how to find the answers.

    Regardless of whether the company formalized procedures or not, what is the probability that the company had successful OR/MS applications? The required probability is $P(A)$, which is an unconditional or marginal probability found in the margin of Table 9.1. There you see that $P(A) = .70$.

TABLE 9.1 Probabilities revealed by 100-company survey

		Formalized	Not formalized	
	Event	C	D	Marginal probability
Success	A	.40	.30	.70
Failure	B	.10	.20	.30
Marginal probability		.50	.50	

If you were to pick one of the companies surveyed at random, what is the probability that it would report both formalized procedures and project success? This probability is a joint probability involving both events A and C. From the table we can see that the graduate student has calculated P(A and C) and found it to be .40.

What is the probability that a company surveyed had not formalized OR/MS procedures? This is another marginal probability, this time represented by P(D). We can read that P(D) = .50 from the bottom margin of the table.

What is the probability that a company reported OR/MS success given that it had formalized procedures? This question requires a conditional probability. Specifically, we seek P(A|C). From formula 9.1 we have P(A|C) = [P(A and C)]/[P(C)] = $^{.40}/_{.50}$ = .80.

What is the probability that a company reported OR/MS success given that it had not formalized procedures? Again we seek a conditional probability, P(A|D) = [P(A and D)]/[P(D)] = $^{.30}/_{.50}$ = .60.

Notice the probabilities of success of .80 and .60, respectively, given formalized and nonformalized procedures. If the foregoing survey were actual and had been carefully performed, these probabilities would lead you to some reasonable conclusions about formalized versus nonformalized OR/MS procedures. You could then make decisions that would significantly improve the probability of project success. And that is what this book is all about.

THE ADDITIVE AND MULTIPLICATIVE LAWS

additive law In addition to the axioms of probability, two other rules are helpful in calculating probabilities. The *additive law* pertains to the union of two events; we read P(A or B) as the probability that either A or B occurs. The additive law states that

$$P(A \text{ or } B) = P(A) + P(B) - P(A \text{ and } B) \qquad [9.2]$$

This formula makes sense intuitively if you look again at Figure 9.3. The sum $P(A) + P(B)$ includes $P(A$ and $B)$ twice. Thus $P(A$ or $B) = P(A) + P(B) - P(A$ and $B)$. In the special case where A and B are mutually exclusive events, the additive rule is equivalent to the additivity axiom, yielding $P(A$ or $B) = P(A) + P(B) - 0 = P(A) + (B)$.

multiplic-ative law   The *multiplicative law* pertains to the intersection of events; it can be derived directly from the conditional probability formula 9.1. In fact, the multiplicative law is merely another statement of the definition of conditional probability. The multiplicative law states that

$$P(A \text{ and } B) = P(A) \cdot P(B|A) \qquad [9.3]$$

The multiplicative and additive rules are useful in determining probabilities of compound events. Compound events, you will recall, consist of two or more simple events. Let us explore some examples.

EXAMPLE   The Bugle Company (newspaper publishers) conducted a survey to determine the readership of the various newspapers within the city. The company publishes both a morning and an evening paper. The survey indicated that 60 percent of subscribers to any newspaper read the morning *Bugle,* 30 percent read the evening *Bugle,* and 10 percent read both.

What is the probability that a subscriber in the city received either the morning or the evening paper from the Bugle Company? We define two events. Let

$$A = \text{a subscriber reads the morning } Bugle$$
$$B = \text{a subscriber reads the evening } Bugle$$

The desired probability is $P(A$ or $B)$. From the additive law, we have $P(A$ or $B) = P(A) + P(B) - P(A$ and $B)$. Since $P(A$ and $B)$ is given in the problem as .10, we have $P(A$ or $B) = .60 + .30 - .10 = .80$.

What is the probability that a subscriber receives neither a morning nor an evening paper from the Bugle Company? This probability is the complement of $(A$ or $B)$ that we found in the preceding question. Thus, the probability that a subscriber takes neither paper is $1 - P(A$ or $B) = 1 - .80 = .20$. Clearly, the Bugle Company has a lion's share of the market.

EXAMPLE   The Medalist Golf Ball Company sells its products in boxes of a dozen balls. Quality control consists of testing two balls taken randomly from each box. The box is rejected only if both balls tested prove to be defective. Suppose that a box actually has two defective balls. What is the probability that it will be rejected?

First, define the events:

$$A = \text{first ball is defective}$$
$$B = \text{second ball is defective}$$

Then, we want $P(A \text{ and } B)$. From the multiplicative law we have that $P(A \text{ and } B) = P(A) \cdot P(B|A)$. $P(A) = \frac{2}{12}$ since there are 2 defectives out of 12 balls. However, $P(B|A) = \frac{1}{11}$ since if A occurs there are only 11 balls in the box and only 1 is defective. Thus $P(A \text{ and } B) = (\frac{2}{12})(\frac{1}{11}) = \frac{2}{132}$ $= .0164$. The probability that the box would be rejected is quite small.

INDEPENDENT AND DEPENDENT EVENTS

We have already defined three relationships between events; we have discussed complementary, mutually exclusive, and collectively exhaustive events. The meaning of independent events is easy to perceive. Two events A and B are independent if the outcome of one has no affect on the probability of the outcome of the other. More formally, events A and B are *independent* if

$$P(A|B) = P(A) \text{ or } P(B|A) = P(B)$$

If these conditions do not hold, then the events are *dependent*.

Imagine flipping a coin in your left hand and another in your right hand. Does the outcome of one coin affect the outcome of the other? It does not. The probability of a head is $\frac{1}{2}$ for each hand regardless of the outcome in the other hand. In the golf balls example, however, we had a case of dependence. The probability of drawing a defective golf ball on the second draw did depend on the outcome of the first draw.

For independent events, the multiplicative law simplifies since $P(A|B) = P(A)$. Thus, for independent events, we have

$$P(A \text{ and } B) = P(A) \cdot P(B) \qquad [9.4]$$

Formula 9.4 extends to more than two events, as the following example illustrates.

EXAMPLE   Consider a coin tossing experiment in which we toss a fair coin five times.

If a head has appeared four times in a row, what is the probability of a head on the fifth trial? Since each trial is an independent event, the probability of a head on the fifth trial is still $\frac{1}{2}$.

What is the probability of tossing five straight heads? Each trial is an independent event, but in this case we are asking for the probability that all five events will happen. Thus, the multiplicative law yields the probability $(\frac{1}{2})$ $(\frac{1}{2})$ $(\frac{1}{2})$ $(\frac{1}{2})$ $(\frac{1}{2})$ = $\frac{1}{32}$.

EXAMPLE   Consider a playing card problem in which we have an ordinary deck of 52 cards composed of four suits of 13 cards each. Suppose we randomly draw 1 card and then another without replacing the first.
    What is the probability that both cards are clubs? Define the events:

$$A = \text{first card is a club}$$
$$B = \text{second card is a club}$$

Then, it is straightforward to find that $P(A \text{ and } B) = P(A) \cdot P(B|A) = \frac{13}{52}(\frac{12}{51}) = \frac{156}{2,652} = .059$. In this case, the second draw is dependent on the first.
    What is the probability of drawing two clubs if the first is replaced? Since the events are now independent we have $P(A \text{ and } B) = P(A)P(B) = \frac{13}{52}(\frac{13}{52}) = \frac{169}{2,704} = .063$.

BAYES' THEOREM

Bayes' law is often helpful in computing conditional probabilities. In fact, Bayes' law is so important to statistical and business decision theory that decision theory is often called Bayesian decision theory. Bayes' law or Bayes' Theorem, as it is sometimes called, is

$$P(A_i/B) = \frac{P(A_i)P(B/A_i)}{\sum\limits_{j=1}^{k} P(A_j)P(B/A_j)}$$

where A_j represent mutually exclusive events.
    To give you an intuitive justification for Baye's law, consider two events A and B. We know from the general law of multiplication that

$$P(A \cap B) = P(A/B)P(B)$$

If we divide both sides of the above equation by $P(B)$, we get:

$$P(A/B) = \frac{P(A \cap B)}{P(B)}$$

Now, since $P(A \cap B) = P(B/A)P(A)$, we have

$$P(A/B) = \frac{P(B/A)P(A)}{P(B)}$$

Since A and $\overline{A}$ are mutually exclusive and are the only events that jointly occur with B, we know

$$P(B) = P(A \cap B) + P(\overline{A} \cap B)$$
$$= P(B/A)P(A) + P(B/\overline{A})P(\overline{A})$$

Therefore,

$$P(A/B) = \frac{P(B/A)P(A)}{P(B/A)P(A) + P(B/\overline{A})P(\overline{A})}$$

The expression above can be generalized for more than two events jointly occuring with B to give Bayes' law, which is in the equation, page 325.

EXAMPLE   Consider the following problem. There are 100 opaque urns, each filled with 10 balls. There are two different kinds of urns. Type I holds five black balls and five white balls. Type II urn has eight black balls and two white balls. There are 70 Type I urns and 30 Type II urns. An urn is picked at random from the 100 urns and you are asked to guess whether it is Type I or Type II urn. If you are allowed to take one ball from the urn and it is black, what is the probability that the urn is Type I? What is the probability that the urn is Type II given drawing a black ball?

Let A be the event that the urn chosen is of Type I. Let C be the event that the urn chosen is of Type II. Let B be the event of choosing a black ball and W be the event of choosing a white ball. The probability of a Type I urn given a black ball is denoted by:

$$P(A/B)$$

and Baye's law says

$$P(A/B) = \frac{P(B/A)P(A)}{P(B/A)P(A) + P(B/C)P(C)}$$

Since there are five black and five white balls in Type I urns,

$$P(B/A) = .5$$

Since there are 700 Type I urns out of a total of 1000,

$$P(A) = .7$$

Similarly, $P(B/C) = .8$ and $P(C) = .3$
Therefore, the probability of a Type I urn given a draw of a black ball is

$$P(A/B) = \frac{(.5)(.7)}{(.5)(.7) + (.8)(.3)} = \frac{.35}{.59}$$
$$= .593$$

The probability of an urn of Type II given a black ball is

$$P(C/B) = \frac{P(B/C)P(C)}{P(B/C)P(C) + P(B/A)P(A)}$$
$$= \frac{(.8)(.3)}{.59} = \frac{.24}{.59}$$
$$= .407$$

In a similar fashion, we can calculate the probability of each type of urn given the draw of a white ball.

$$P(A/W) = \frac{P(W/A)P(A)}{P(W/A)P(A) + P(W/C)P(C)}$$
$$= \frac{(.5)(.7)}{(.5)(.7) + (.2)(.3)}$$
$$= \frac{.35}{.41} = .854$$
$$P(C/W) = \frac{P(W/C)P(C)}{P(W/C)P(C) + P(W/A)P(A)}$$
$$= \frac{(.2)(.3)}{.41} = \frac{.06}{.41}$$
$$= .146$$

PROBABILITY DISTRIBUTIONS

In this section, we shall define a random variable and examine the concepts of a probability distribution. In addition, we shall describe several discrete probability distributions and several continuous probability distributions.

You learned earlier that an event is a specified outcome of an experiment or a random phenomenon. An example is the toss of a coin. The outcomes associated with the experiment are the displays of a head or of a tail. Now, if a numerical value, such as 0 or 1, is attached to each of the two possible outcomes, then the elementary, or individual, outcomes of the experiment can be termed a random variable. More specifically, a *random variable* is a function whose numerical value depends on the outcome of some experiment. For example, the roll of one die can be thought of as an experiment with the outcomes being the spots on the face of the die. The random variable could then be defined as the number of spots on

random variable

TABLE 9.2   Random variables

Number of spots on face of the die	Possible value of the random variable	Possible value of the random variable
1	1	25
2	2	50
3	3	75
4	4	100
5	5	200
6	6	35

the face of the die or any other similar function, such as those described in Table 9.2. Remember, a random variable is a function that assigns a numerical value to an elementary outcome of an experiment.

probability distribution A *probability distribution* relates a probability to the values a random variable can take on. These values of the random variable represent an exhaustive and mutually exclusive set of values. Consequently, the probabilities of a probability distribution must add to 1.

DISCRETE PROBABILITY DISTRIBUTIONS

Discrete probability distributions are probability distributions in which the random variables are discrete. That is, the random variable takes on specific and discontinuous values. In other words, there are gaps between values that the random variable can take on. In a continuous probability distribution, on the other hand, the random variable can take on the value of any real number between the limits of the distribution. An example of a discrete probability distribution is a simple toss of a coin where a head is assigned the value of 0 and a tail is assigned the value of 1. Table 9.3 defines this probability distribution.

TABLE 9.3   Probability distribution of a coin toss

Random variable	Probability
0	.50
1	.50
	1.00

If the example is expanded to the toss of four coins and the random variable is defined as the number of heads, then the probability distribution in Table 9.4 is defined. You can verify the probability reflected in Table 9.4 by listing all the possible outcomes and adding those outcomes that yield a specific number of heads. There are 2^4, or 16, possible outcomes. The probability distribution in Table 9.4 is graphed in Figure 9.4.

TABLE 9.4   Discrete probability distribution

Random variable	Probability
0	$\frac{1}{16}$
1	$\frac{4}{16}$
2	$\frac{6}{16}$
3	$\frac{4}{16}$
4	$\frac{1}{16}$

cumulative probability distribution A *cumulative probability distribution* is a function of some random variable that defines the probability of the random variable's being less than or equal to a specific value of the random variable. In other words,

$$F(x) = P(X \le x) \qquad [9.5]$$

where X = random variable
  x = value of the random variable

In the discrete case,

$$F(x) = \sum_{x_i \le x} P(x_i) \qquad [9.6]$$

Given our previous example of four coin tosses, the cumulative probability function is shown in Table 9.5 and Figure 9.5.

FIGURE 9.4   Discrete probability distribution for number of heads in four tosses of a fair coin

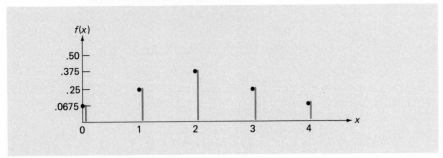

TABLE 9.5   Cumulative probability distribution for four coin tosses

x	Probability	Cumulative probability
0	$\frac{1}{16}$	$\frac{1}{16}$
1	$\frac{4}{16}$	$\frac{5}{16}$
2	$\frac{6}{16}$	$\frac{11}{16}$
3	$\frac{4}{16}$	$\frac{15}{16}$
4	$\frac{1}{16}$	1.0

Binomial distribution   One of the most common discrete probability distributions is the binomial distribution. In order for you to make sense of the binomial distribution, you must first understand what is meant by a Bernoulli trial. A *Bernoulli trial,* sometimes called a Bernoulli *process,* is a random phenomenon involving two mutually exclusive and exhaustive events. A flip of a coin is a Bernoulli trial. An acceptance or rejection of a shipment of parts is a Bernoulli trial. Typically, the two events are referred to as success and failure. The probability of a success is denoted by p and the probability of a failure is $1 - p$, which is denoted by q. Suppose that there are 100 balls in an urn, 5 gold and 95 silver. We draw 1 ball from the urn at random. If a gold ball is considered a successful draw and a silver ball is considered a failure, $p = .05$ and $q = .95$.

The random variable of a binomial distribution is the number of successes in n *independent* Bernoulli trials where the probability of a success remains constant. In the case of drawing balls from an urn, the ball must be placed back in the urn for independence to be maintained. Let us return to our example of tossing a coin four times. The random variable is the number of heads. What we have is four independent Bernoulli trials with a head defined as a success and a tail defined as a failure. In this case, p is equal to .50 and q is equal to .50. If the random variable is the

Bernoulli trial (margin note)

FIGURE 9.5   Cumulative probability distribution for four coin tosses

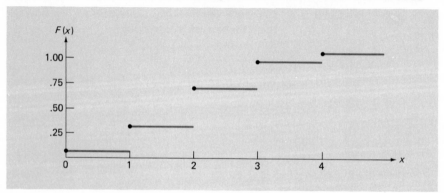

330

TABLE 9.6   **Binomial distribution with $p = .5$, $n = 4$**

x	P(x)
0	.0625
1	.2500
2	.3750
3	.2500
4	.0625

number of heads in four tosses, then that random variable is binomially distributed, as shown in Table 9.6.

In order to assess probabilities for binomial random variables with any number of Bernoulli trials and any probability of success, the following probability function can be used.

$$P(x) = (_nC_x)(p^x q^{n-x}) \qquad\qquad [9.7]$$

where   x = number of successes

      $_nC_x$ = number of combinations of n things taken x at a time

      p = probability of success

      q = probability of failure

$$_nC_x = n!/[x!(n-x)!]$$

where $n! = (n)(n-1)(n-2) \ldots (1)$

      $0! = 1$

To illustrate the use of this function, consider the following problem. A shipment of 20 light bulbs has just been received. Historically, 10 percent of the light bulbs received from the supplier have been defective. If each bulb is tested and a defective bulb is designated as a success, then the probability distribution of the number of defective bulbs in a random shipment of 20 is as shown in Table 9.7. As you can see from Table 9.7, the probability that there would be more than 9 defective bulbs is virtually zero.

Let us illustrate the use of the probability function to calculate one of these discrete probabilities.

$$
\begin{aligned}
P(x = 2) &= [20/2!(20-2)!](.1)^2(.9)^{18} \\
&= (20 \cdot 19/2)(.1)^2(.9)^{18} \\
&= (190)(.01)(.1502) \\
&\cong .2852
\end{aligned}
$$

As you can easily see, the computation of binomial probabilities can get very laborious, even using an electronic calculator. For this reason, bi-

TABLE 9.7 Binomial distribution with $p = .1$, $n = 20$

Number of defective bulbs	Probability
0	.1216
1	.2702
2	.2852
3	.1901
4	.0898
5	.0319
6	.0089
7	.0020
8	.0004
9	.0001
10	.0000
11	.0000
.	.
.	.
.	.
20	.0000

nomial tables are included as Appendix D. To illustrate the use of the binomial table, let us find one of the probabilities reflected in Table 9.7. The probability of having 3 or fewer defective bulbs can be found by looking in the table for $n = 20$, $p = .1$, and $c = 3$. From the table, then, $P(x \leq 3) = .8670$. Now, to find the probability that there are exactly 3 defective bulbs we must find the probability of having 2 or fewer defective bulbs and subtract that probability from the probability of having 3 or fewer. In other words,

$$P(x = 3) = P(x \leq 3) - P(x \leq 2)$$

From the table, $P(x \leq 2) = .6769$. Therefore, $P(x = 3) = .8670 - .6769 = .1901$. You should verify the values in Table 9.7 by using the binomial tables.

Poisson distribution   The other discrete probability distribution we shall discuss in this chapter is the Poisson distribution, derived by Siméon Poisson in 1837. We examine the Poisson distribution because of its significant application in queuing theory (the subject of Chapter 12). Let us define a random variable as the number of events that occur during a certain interval of time or space. The random variable could be the number of telephone calls in an hour, the number of arrivals at a toll gate in 15 minutes, or the number of customers to shop at a store in a day. If the following three conditions are present, the random variable is said to be Poisson distributed.

1. During some interval Δt, the probability of an occurrence of an event (such as an arrival) is constant, regardless of when Δt starts.

2. The occurrence of an event is independent of any other occurrence of the event.

3. If Δt is chosen such that the probability of the occurrence of an event within Δt is small, then the probability that the event will occur is approximately proportional to the width of the interval. For example, let $\Delta t = 1$ second. If $P(\text{occurrence in } \Delta t) = .005$, then $P(\text{occurrence in } 2\Delta t) = .01$.

If a random variable is distributed in a Poisson manner, the probability that the random variable will take on any value k is given in equation 9.8. This function is called a *probability mass function*.

probability mass function

$$P(X = k) = e^{-m}m^k/k! \qquad \text{for } m > 0; k = 0, 1, 2, \ldots \qquad [9.8]$$

where e = the base of natural logarithms, with a value approximately equal to 2.71828

m = mean number of events occurring in a given time interval

k = number of events

Consider the following example. An average of three cars per minute arrives at a toll gate according to a Poisson process. The probability distribution of the number of cars arriving at the toll gate per minute is contained in Table 9.8.

TABLE 9.8 Poisson distribution with $m = 3$

Arrivals to toll gate in 1 minute	Probability
0	.0498
1	.1494
2	.2240
3	.2240
4	.1680
5	.1008
6	.0504
7	.0216
8	.0081
9	.0027
10	.0008
11	.0002
12	.0001

To illustrate how these probabilities are calculated, let us find the probability of four cars arriving during 1 minute.

$$P(X = 4) = e^{-3}3^4/4!$$
$$= 3^4/[(2.71828^3)(4)(3)(2)(1)]$$
$$= 81/[(20.0837)(24)]$$
$$= .1680$$

Poisson tables are included at the end of the book so that you won't have to work probability calculations out for yourself. To illustrate how to use the Poisson table, Appendix E, let us find $P(x = 4)$ in the table. Since the table reflects cumulative probabilities, it is necessary to look up $P(x \leq 4)$ and the $P(x \leq 3)$ to calculate $P(x = 4)$. The probability that $x \leq 4$ is found by looking in the row $\mu = 3.0$ and the column $r_o = 4$. Therefore, $P(x \leq 4) = .815$. Similarly, $P(x \leq 3) = .647$. Since $P(x = 4) = P(x \leq 4) - P(x \leq 3)$, $P(x = 4) = .815 - .647 = .168$.

CONTINUOUS PROBABILITY DISTRIBUTIONS

Continuous probability distributions are analogous to discrete probability distributions. The only difference is in the nature of the random variable. If a random variable can take on all values of the real number system between two limits, then it is said to be *continuous*. For example, the number of customers arriving at a supermarket is a discrete random variable, but the time between customer arrivals is continuous because time can be measured on a continuous scale.

Continuous probability distributions can be hard to understand if you have not been exposed to the integral calculus because these probabilities can no longer be calculated by a simple counting procedure. With continuous random variables, it is not appropriate to define the probability of the random variable taking on some specific value. The probability that the random variable equals some value k is zero, or, in notation, $P(X = k) = 0$. It is only appropriate to ascertain the probability that the random variable will fall within some range of values. For example, the probability that a randomly selected 35-year-old man will weigh between 175 and 200 pounds can be calculated given certain assumptions about the probability distribution of the weight of 35-year-old men. The probability of a man weighing 175 pounds exactly, and not the most minute fraction more or less, is theoretically zero. A *probability density function* (pdf) describes a continuous probability distribution. On a graph, the pdf is represented by a curve. The total area under the curve defined by pdf is equal to 1.

probability density function (pdf)

This all becomes easier to understand if you look at Figure 9.6. The probability that the random variable x falls between 0 and 3 equals the

FIGURE 9.6 Probability density function (pdf)

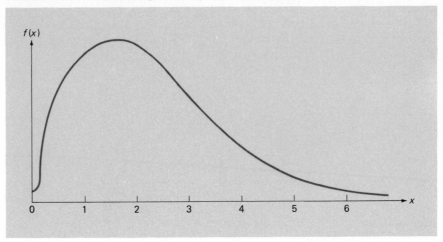

ratio of the area under the curve between 0 and 3 to the total area under the curve, which, by definition, must equal 1. By merely looking at the graph in Figure 9.6, you might estimate that the probability that x will fall between 0 and 3 is approximately .60. To calculate $P(0 < x < 3)$ exactly, the calculus must be used. Fortunately, the tables at the end of the book relieve you of the necessity of calculating probabilities directly. In actuality, the exact probability is found by taking the definite integral from 0 to 3 of $f(x)[\int_0^3 f(x)\,dx]$. In the following sections, we are going to examine the two continuous probability distributions most commonly used in management science.

Uniform distribution   The probability density function for the uniform distribution is the simplest of pdfs. If b is the upper limit that the random variable x can take on and a is the lower limit, then the pdf for the uniform distribution is

$$f(x) = \begin{cases} \dfrac{1}{b-a} & \text{for } a \leq x \leq b \\ 0 & \text{elsewhere} \end{cases} \qquad [9.9]$$

The graph of the pdf in equation 9.9 is shown in Figure 9.7.

The key to understanding the uniform distribution is this: You must realize that the probability of a uniformly distributed random variable's falling within a certain range is merely the ratio of the width of that interval to the entire width of the uniform distribution. For example, suppose that a random variable x is uniformly distributed between 2 and 10. The pdf for this distribution is $f(x) = 1/(10 - 2)$ for $2 \leq x \leq 10$, and zero elsewhere; so the $P(2 \leq x \leq 4)$ is merely $\frac{2}{8}$, or .25. Figure 9.8 shows graphi-

FIGURE 9.7 Uniform distribution

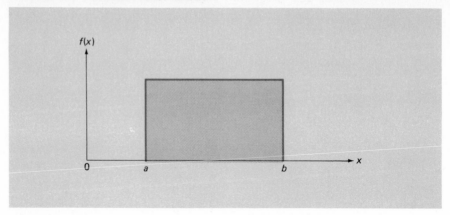

cally that the area under the curve from 2 to 4 is 25 percent of the area under the curve.

The cumulative probability distribution function is expressed as follows:

$$F(x) = \begin{cases} 0 & \text{for } x < a \\ \dfrac{x - a}{b - a} & \text{for } a \leq x \leq b \\ 1 & \text{for } x > b \end{cases}$$

where $F(x) = P(X \leq x)$
 X = random variable

FIGURE 9.8 Uniform distribution with $a = 2$, $b = 10$

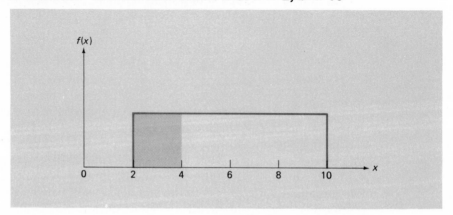

If we apply it to the preceding example, the probability that x will be ≤ 6 is $F(6) = (6 - 2)/(10 - 2) = \frac{4}{8} = .50$.

Normal distribution   Perhaps the most useful of the continuous probability distributions is the normal, also referred to as the *Gaussian*, distribution. Reasons for the normal distribution's utility include the following:

1. The normal can be used under certain conditions to approximate both the binomial distribution and the Poisson distribution.
2. Many random phenomena behave according to a normal distribution, including such examples as height of adult females, IQ scores, classroom performances of students, and so on.
3. Due to the central limit theorem, if x is a random variable with mean μ and variance σ^2, then the mean of random samples of size n is normally distributed with mean μ and variance σ^2/n, irrespective of the distribution of the random variable.

The pdf of the normal distribution is:

$$f(x) = \left(\frac{1}{\sigma\sqrt{2\pi}}\right)e^{-(x-\mu)^2/2\sigma^2} \qquad \text{for } -\infty < x < \infty \qquad [9.10]$$

where $\mu = $ mean
$\sigma = $ standard deviation

Because the foregoing function (equation 9.10) cannot be integrated directly, probabilities associated with the normal distribution are calculated by using a table of probabilities for a standard normal distribution with a mean of zero and a standard deviation of one. In order to use this table for a normal distribution with mean μ and variance σ^2, the following transformation is necessary:

$$Z = \frac{x - \mu}{\sigma} \qquad [9.11]$$

where $Z = $ a normally distributed random variable with mean 0 and standard deviation 1. Once Z is calculated, it is easy to look the probability up in the normal tables at the end of the book.

To illustrate the use of the normal tables, let us assume that a random variable is normally distributed with mean 10 and standard deviation 2. What is the probability that random variable x is less than 14? First, when we calculate Z we get $Z = (14 - 10)/2 = 2$. The normal distribution table in Appendix C gives the probability that the random variable Z is

FIGURE 9.9 Normal distribution with $\mu = 10$, $\sigma = 2$

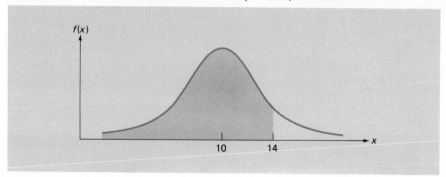

less than or equal to some specific value z_i, $P(Z \le z_i)$; in other words, the table gives the area under the standard normal curve from $-\infty$ to z_i.

To find $P(x \le 14)$, which is the shaded area in Figure 9.9, we merely look in the normal table for $P(Z \le 2)$, which is the shaded area in Figure 9.10, because $P(x \le 14) = P(Z \le 2)$.

The standard normal table gives the probability that the random variable Z will be less than or equal to some specific value. If it is necessary to find $P(a \le x \le b)$ or $P(x \ge b)$, you must use the symmetry properties of the normal distribution. For example, suppose you had $P(10 \le x \le 14)$ $= P(0 < Z < 2)$ (see Figure 9.11). We know that half the distribution lies to the left of $Z = 0$; therefore, $P(0 \le Z \le 2) = .97725 - .5 = .47725$. Similarly,

$$P(X > 14) = 1 - P(x < 14)$$
$$= 1 - .97725$$
$$= .02275$$

One final example: What is the probability that x will fall between 12 and 14? Looking at Figure 9.12, it is easy to see that $P(12 < x < 14) = P(x \le 14)$

FIGURE 9.10 Normal distribution with $\mu = 0$, $\sigma = 1$

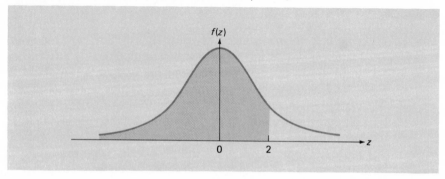

FIGURE 9.11   Normal distribution with $\mu = 0$, $\sigma = 1$

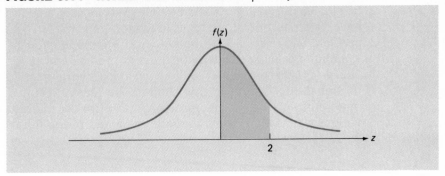

$- P(x \leq 12)$. Remember that

$$
\begin{aligned}
P(x \leq 14) &= P[Z \leq (14 - 10)/2] \\
&= P(Z \leq 2) \\
&= .97725
\end{aligned}
$$

$$
\begin{aligned}
P(x \leq 12) &= P[Z \leq (12 - 10)/2] \\
&= P(Z \leq 1) \\
&= .8413
\end{aligned}
$$

Therefore, $P(12 \leq x \leq 14) = .97725 - .8413 = .1359$.

FIGURE 9.12   Normal distribution with $\mu = 10$, $\sigma = 2$

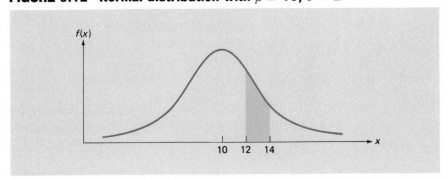

SUMMARY

The real world is a world in which events do not occur with absolute certainty. Demand for products and services are not known with certainty. The amount of oil to be recovered in a field is not known. Even internal costs and the availability of resources are often only estimated.

In short, we live in a stochastic world. Management science models can be classified as deterministic models or stochastic models. Thus far, we have discussed only those types of models in which the parameters of the problem were assumed to be known. In the remainder of this text, we examine stochastic models. In order to understand these probabilistic models, it is necessary for you to have at least a rudimentary background in probability theory. In this chapter, we have attempted to introduce those concepts which are most important for an understanding of the various stochastic models that are examined in the following chapters.

SOLVED PROBLEMS

PROBLEM STATEMENT

A country club has three kinds of memberships available, golf, tennis, and swimming. Of the 1,000 members, 300 have golf memberships, 400 have swimming memberships, and 300 have tennis memberships. One hundred golfers also have swimming and tennis memberships. If a member is selected at random, what is the probability that he or she will have

a. A tennis membership?

b. A tennis or golf membership?

c. A tennis or swimming membership?

d. A tennis and golf membership?

SOLUTION*

a. Let A be the event of a member having a tennis membership only and B be the event of a member having both a golf and a tennis membership. Since A and B are mutually exclusive,

$$P(\text{tennis membership}) = \frac{300}{1,000} + \frac{100}{1,000} = \frac{4}{10} = .4$$

b. Let A = tennis membership
B = golf membership

---

*The symbol $\cup$ means "or"; $\cap$ means "and."

Then

$$P(A \cup B) = P(A) + P(B) - P(A \cap B)$$
$$= .4 + .3 - .1$$
$$= .6$$

c. Let A = tennis membership
B = swimming membership

Since A and B are mutually exclusive,

$$P(A \cup B) = P(A) + P(B)$$
$$= .4 + .3$$
$$= .7$$

d. Let A = tennis membership
B = golf membership

Then

$$P(A \cap B) = P(A|B)P(B)$$
$$= \frac{1}{3} \cdot \frac{3}{10}$$
$$= .1$$

PROBLEM STATEMENT

Two ocean liners are crossing the Atlantic Ocean at the same time. From past history, ship A has a 75 percent chance of arriving on schedule and ship B a 95 percent chance of arriving on schedule.

a. What is the probability of both ships arriving on schedule?
b. What is the probability of either ship A or ship B arriving on schedule?
c. What is the probability of both ships being late?

SOLUTION

Let A = ship A arriving on schedule
B = ship B arriving on schedule

a. Since A and B are independent events,

$$P(A \cap B) = P(A) \cdot P(B)$$
$$= (.75)(.95)$$
$$= .7125$$

b. $P(A \cup B) = P(A) + P(B) - P(A \cap B)$
$$= .75 + .95 - .7125$$
$$= .9875$$

c. $P(\overline{A} \cap \overline{B}) = P(\overline{A}) \cdot P(\overline{B})$
$$= (.25)(.05)$$
$$= .0125$$

PROBLEM STATEMENT

A soccer team has a six-game season. At the beginning of the season the coach estimates the probability of winning any single game as .6, or slightly better than 50–50.

a. What is the probability of an undefeated season?
b. What is the probability of a winless season?
c. What is the probability of winning at least one game?
d. What is the probability of winning only one game?

SOLUTION

a. Let A_i = the event of winning game i. Then

$$P(\text{undefeated season}) = P(A_1) \cdot P(A_2) \ldots P(A_6)$$

Assuming independence,

$$P(\text{undefeated season}) = P(A_1) \cdot P(A_2) \ldots P(A_6)$$
$$= .6^6$$
$$= .0467$$

b. $P(\text{winless season}) = P(\overline{A}_1) \cdot P(\overline{A}_2) \ldots P(\overline{A}_6)$
$$= .4^6$$
$$= .004096$$

c. $P(\text{at least one game}) = 1 - P(\text{no games})$
$$= 1 - .004096$$
$$= .9959$$

d. P(winning only one game)

$= P(A_1)P(\overline{A}_2) \ldots P(\overline{A}_6)$

$\quad + P(\overline{A}_1 \cap A_2 \cap \overline{A}_3 \cap \overline{A}_4 \cap \overline{A}_5 \cap \overline{A}_6)$

$\quad + P(\overline{A}_1 \cap \overline{A}_2 \cap A_3 \cap \overline{A}_4 \cap \overline{A}_5 \cap \overline{A}_6)$

$\quad + P(\overline{A}_1 \cap \overline{A}_2 \cap \overline{A}_3 \cap A_4 \cap \overline{A}_5 \cap \overline{A}_6)$

$\quad + P(\overline{A}_1 \cap \overline{A}_2 \cap \overline{A}_3 \cap \overline{A}_4 \cap \overline{A}_5 \cap \overline{A}_6)$

$\quad + P(\overline{A}_1 \cap \overline{A}_2 \cap \overline{A}_3 \cap \overline{A}_4 \cap \overline{A}_5 \cap A_6)$

$= (6)(.6)(.4)^5$

$= .036864$

PROBLEM STATEMENT

A medical laboratory has taken blood samples from 10 adult males between the ages of 45 and 50. Nationwide, it has been found that 20 percent of men in this age group have dangerously high cholesterol in their blood. For our group, what is the probability of:

a. Two people having high cholesterol?

b. More than 8 having high cholesterol?

c. None of the men in the sample having a cholesterol problem?

SOLUTION

Since each blood test can be defined as an independent Bernoulli trial and a positive test classified as a success, the number of high cholesterol samples in 10 is a binomially distributed random variable:

$$n = 10$$

$$p = .2$$

a. $P(x = 2) = \dfrac{10!}{2!8!} \cdot 2^2 \cdot 8^8$

$\quad\quad\quad\quad = .3020$

b. $P(x > 8) = .0000$

c. $P(x = 0) = .1074$

PROBLEM STATEMENT

Arrivals at an ice cream store are distributed in a Poisson manner, at an average rate of 10 per hour. What is the probability that there will be

a. Exactly 4 arrivals?

b. Less than 5 arrivals?

c. More than 7 arrivals?

SOLUTION

a. $P(x = 4) = \dfrac{e^{-10} \cdot 10^4}{4!}$

$\qquad = .019$

b. $P(x < 5) = P(x \leq 4) = .029$ (table look-up)

c. $P(x > 7) = 1 - P(x \leq 7) = 1 - .220$

$\qquad = .780$

PROBLEM STATEMENT

A train consistently runs between 0 and 5 minutes late. Late time is uniformly distributed. What is the probability that the train will be

a. Less than 2 minutes late?

b. More than 3 minutes late?

c. Between 2 and 3 minutes late?

SOLUTION

a. $P(x < 2) = \dfrac{2 - 0}{5 - 0} = .4$

b. $P(x > 3) = \dfrac{5 - 3}{5 - 0} = .4$

c. $P(2 < x < 3) = \dfrac{3 - 2}{5 - 0} = .2$

PROBLEM STATEMENT

Scores on college entrance exams are normally distributed with a mean of 450 and a standard deviation of 50. What is the probability that a score selected at random is

a. Greater than 550?

b. Less than 400?

c. Between 400 and 500?

SOLUTION

a. $Z = \dfrac{550 - 450}{50} = 2$

$P(x > 550) = P(Z > 2) = .0228$

b. $Z = \dfrac{400 - 450}{50} = -1$

$P(x < 400) = P(Z < -1) = .1587$

c. $Z_{400} = \dfrac{400 - 450}{50} = -1$

$Z_{500} = \dfrac{500 - 450}{50} = 1$

$P(400 < x < 500) = P(-1 < Z < 1)$
$= .6826$

REVIEW QUESTIONS

1. Why is an understanding of probability important for making business decisions?

2. Explain the difference between objective and subjective probabilities. Give an example of each.

3. An event and its complement have no points in common. Are they independent or dependent? Explain.

4. What is conditional probability?

5. Distinguish between mutually exclusive events and independent events.

6. If a collection of events is mutually exclusive and collectively exhaustive, what is the sum of their probabilities?

7. Define and give an example of a random variable.

8. What is a probability distribution?

9. Distinguish between a discrete probability distribution and a continuous probability distribution.

10. Define and give an example of a cumulative probability distribution.

11. What is a Bernoulli trial? Give an example.

12. Why is the Poisson distribution important to management science?

PROBLEMS

9.1 Suppose that you flip a fair coin four times:

a. What is the probability that you will obtain the outcome *HTHT*?

b. What is the probability of getting four heads in a row?

c. What is the probability of getting a tail in the fourth trial given that the results the first three times were heads?

9.2 Consider an urn that has six black and four white balls:

a. Suppose that after each ball is drawn it is replaced. What is the probability of drawing a white ball?

b. What is the probability of drawing three white balls in a row?

c. Suppose now that the balls are not replaced after drawing. What is the probability of drawing a white on the second trial given that the first trial resulted in a black ball?

9.3 *Project Management.* A project manager is currently supervising four projects. The probabilities that each one will be completed on time are .70, .90, .80, and .60, respectively. Assuming that the project times are independent, what is the probability that all four projects will be completed on time?

9.4 *Sales Management.* A marketing executive is going on a short trip to attempt to close two important deals. His subjective probability is .7 that he will be successful with the first deal and .5 that he will be successful with the second deal. What is the probability that

a. He will successfully close both deals?

b. He will close one or the other?

c. He will close the first deal but be unsuccessful on the second?

9.5 *Retail Sales.* Daily demand for a particular TV model runs from 0 to 4, with the following respective probabilities: .1, .2, .35, .2, .15.

a. What is the probability of two or more TV sets being demanded?

b. What is the probability of fewer than two TV sets being demanded?

9.6 *Market Research.* A market survey conducted in four cities pertained to preference for brand A soap. The responses are shown by city in the table.

	Dallas	Atlanta	Chicago	New York
Yes	45	55	60	50
No	35	45	35	45
No opinion	5	5	5	5

a. What is the probability that a consumer selected at random preferred brand A?

b. What is the probability that a consumer preferred brand A and was from Chicago?

c. What is the probability that a consumer preferred brand A given that he was from Chicago?

d. Given that a consumer preferred brand A, what is the probability that she was from New York?

9.7 *Recreation.* Membership at a local tennis facility is divided on the issue of facility maintenance. Some members favor a low-cost, do-your-own-cleaning policy, whereas others prefer to pay to have the maintenance done. There are 1,000 members, 800 men and 200 women. During a recent referendum, 100 women voted to pay for maintenance and only 25 voted against. Five hundred men voted against paying and 100 men voted for paying.

a. If we choose a member at random and ask his/her opinion, what is the probability of that person favoring low-cost maintenance? High-cost maintenance?

b. If we randomly choose a man and a woman, what is the probability that they will both favor low-cost maintenance?

c. If we randomly choose two members regardless of sex, what is the probability of at least one of them favoring the high-cost solution to the maintenance problem?

9.8 *Manufacturing Quality Control.* An electronic firm purchases a particular transistor from three different sources. Source A supplies 30 percent, source B, 50 percent, and source C, 20 percent. Based on historical data, the probability of a defective transistor is as shown in the table.

Supplier	Probability of defective transistor
A	.02
B	.01
C	.03

a. What percent of transistors purchased will be defective?

b. If the transistor is found to be defective, what is the probability that it came from supplier B? Supplier C?

c. If the transistor is good, what is the probability that it came from supplier A?

9.9 *University Administration.* Eight out of ten professors at State University have a Ph.D., whereas only one out of ten have a Ph.D. at City College. If one professor is chosen from each institution at random, what is the probability that

a. Both hold a Ph.D?

b. State University's professor does not hold a Ph.D. and City College's professor does?

c. Both professors have earned doctorates?

d. Neither professor has a Ph.D?

9.10 *Retail Sales.* The owner of a ski shop has observed closely the buying habits of his female customers. Fifty percent of the women coming in the store buy ski outfits; 30 percent buy ski boots and skis.

a. What is the probability that a female customer will buy skis, boots, and clothes?

b. What is the probability that she won't buy anything?

c. What is the probability that she will buy either clothes or equipment?

9.11 *Aerospace Engineering.* The NASA space shuttle has two oxygen systems. If the probability of the primary system failing is .01 and the probability of the secondary system failing is .03.

a. What is the probability of both systems failing?

b. What is the probability that either the primary system or the secondary system is defective?

9.12 *University Administration.* The age of students in the freshman class at a certain university varies from 16 to 23. The ages of 2,000 incoming freshmen are distributed as shown in the table.

Age	Frequency
16	50
17	800
18	900
19	50
20	45
21	55
22	60
23	40

a. Using the relative frequency, plot the probability mass function and cumulative density function.

b. What is the probability of a randomly selected student being less than 20 years old?

    c. What is the probability that the student selected will be either 17 or 18?

9.13 *University Administration.* The College of Business at a large university has 15 scholarships to offer to potential business majors. In the past, about 75 percent of those students who were offered scholarships accepted them. Compute the following probabilities.

    a. The probability of fewer than 5 acceptances.

    b. The probability of between 5 and 10 acceptances.

    c. The probability of 100 percent acceptance.

9.14 *Forecasting Demand.* A production manager has studied past daily demand for widgets and has arrived at the following probability distribution for demand shown in the table. What is the probability of 2 or more units of demand during any day?

Demand	Probability
0	.10
1	.20
2	.30
3	.25
4	.15

9.15 *Auditing.* An accountant has to audit 20 accounts of a firm. Fifteen of these accounts are high-volume and 5 are low-volume. If the accountant randomly selects 4 accounts, what is the probability that none are low-volume accounts?

9.16 *Market Research.* A market survey conducted in four cities pertained to preference for Flagrant soap. The responses are shown by city in the table.

	Los Angeles	Chicago	Boston	Miami
Yes	47	50	63	45
No	33	50	30	48
No opinion	10	8	7	7

    a. What is the probability that a consumer selected at random preferred Flagrant?

    b. What is the probability that a consumer preferred Flagrant and was from Chicago?

    c. What is the probability that a consumer preferred Flagrant given that he was from Chicago?

d. Given that a consumer preferred Flagrant, what is the probability that she was from Miami?

9.17 *Insurance Sales.* An insurance broker estimates that there is a 30 percent chance of a sale upon initial contact with a client. However, on a call-back there is a 60 percent chance of a sale. If the broker is limited to one call-back per prospective customer, what is the probability that any prospect will buy?

9.18 *Accounting.* Suppose that the failure rate for candidates initially sitting for the C.P.A. exam is 70 percent. If four candidates sit for the exam for the first time, what is the probability that three will pass?

9.19 *Construction.* Sturdy Construction has submitted a bid for project. If Sturdy's leading competitor submits a bid, then the management at Sturdy feels its chance of getting the contract is .50. However, if the leading competitor does not submit a bid, Sturdy's chances increase to .80. If there is a .90 chance that the leading competitor will submit a bid, what are Sturdy's chances of receiving the contract?

9.20 *Medical Research.* A new procedure has been developed to test for the presence of a rare disease. The procedure is accurate 95 percent of the time in diagnosing a patient who has the disease. The procedure is accurate 90 percent of the time in diagnosing a patient who does not have the disease. Given a positive test result, what is the actual probability that the patient has the disease? Assume that roughly 20 percent of those who take the test have the disease.

9.21 *University Administration.* An M.B.A. class has 35 students, whose ages are distributed as shown in the table.

Age	Number of students
21	15
22	5
23	5
24	4
25	3
28	2
40	1

a. Define the probability distribution of the age of the student.

b. Define the cumulative probability distribution of the age of the student.

c. If a student is picked out of the class at random, what is the probability that the student will be less than 24 years old?

d. What is the probability that a student randomly chosen will be 22 or 23 years old?

9.22 *Sales.* A door-to-door salesman has a 10 percent chance of making a sale at any one house.

   a. If he makes 10 calls during 1 day, what is the probability of making 2 sales?

   b. If he makes 15 calls during 1 day, what is the probability of making 2 sales?

   c. If he makes 10 calls, what is the probability of making more than 3 sales?

   d. If he makes 12 calls during the day, define the probability distribution of the number of sales during the day.

9.23 *University Administration.* A prestigious university accepts approximately 25 percent of applicants applying for admission to its Ph. D. program in English. The program is quite small and this year had only 25 applicants.

   a. What is the probability that the first-year Ph.D. class in English will exceed 10 students?

   b. What is the probability of fewer than 2 students being admitted to the program?

9.24 *Quality Control.* Upon receiving a shipment of valves, a company inspects a random sample of 15 valves. Historically, 10 percent of the inspected valves have been defective. If management has decided that the entire shipment should be rejected if 2 or more bad valves are found in the sample, what is the probability that the shipment will be accepted?

9.25 *Demand Forecasting.* Demand at a TV store for the 25-inch color TV set has been about 2 sets per week.

   a. What is the probability that 10 sets will be sold in the next 4 weeks?

   b. What is the probability that fewer than 10 sets will be sold in the next 4 weeks?

   c. What is the probability that between 7 and 14 sets will be sold in the next 4 weeks?

9.26 *Professional Football.* A professional football team has a firm policy of drafting defensive linemen that have certain attributes. One attribute is height. If a college prospect is less than 6 feet 3 inches tall, the policy states that he cannot be drafted. The height of college defensive linemen is normally distributed, with a mean of 6 feet 5 inches and a standard deviation of 3 inches.

   a. What proportion of defensive linemen will be rejected due to height?

b. What is the probability that a college defensive lineman will be between 6 feet 2 inches and 6 feet 9 inches tall?

9.27 *Dairy Industry.* A local dairy has a machine that fills gallon cartons of milk automatically. State regulations allow a tolerance of ±1 ounce for a gallon of milk. The amount the machine automatically puts in the carton is normally distributed, with a mean of 128 ounces and a standard deviation of .5 ounce.

a. What percentage of the gallon cartons are in violation of state regulations?

b. What is the probability that a carton chosen at random will contain less than 126 ounces?

c. What is the probability that a carton chosen at random will contain between 126 and 130 ounces?

9.28 *Education.* Assume that IQ scores are normally distributed, with a mean of 100 and a standard deviation of 10.

a. What is the minimum score that would put a person in the top 10 percent?

b. What is the probability of a person's scoring between 90 and 110?

c. If people scoring over 140 are classified as geniuses, what percent of the population is in this category?

9.29 *Computer Operations.* If we assume that computer run time is normally distributed with a mean of 30 seconds and a standard deviation of 10 seconds, what is the probability

a. That the job will run longer than 1 minute?

b. That the job will take less than 5 seconds?

9.30 *Computer Operations.* If we assume that computer run time is uniformally distributed with parameters $a = 0$ seconds and $b = 60$ seconds, what is the probability that

a. The job will run longer than $\frac{1}{2}$ minute?

b. The job will run between 20 and 40 seconds?

9.31 *Manufacturing.* Jobs arrive at a machine center in a Poisson fashion at an average rate of 5 per day. Show the probability distribution for the number of arrivals in 1 day.

9.32 *Quality Control.* Metal tennis rackets are tested by X-raying the welds. Historically, 5 percent of the rackets tested have been rejected due to faulty welds. A sample of 10 rackets is drawn. What is the probability that

a. No rackets will fail the X-ray test?

b. Fewer than 2 rackets will fail?

c. Exactly 1 racket out of 10 will be found defective?

9.33 *Professional Football.* A professional football team chooses its running backs based on several criteria, one of which is speed in the 40-yard dash. The head coach has ruled out any back slower than 4.6 in the 40-yard dash. It has been determined that the mean speed of major college running backs is 4.5 and the standard deviation is .2 second. What is the percentage of running backs that do not meet the head coach's criterion?

9.34 *Water Department Forecast.* The mean water demand for a certain town is 60,000 gallons and the standard deviation is 8,000 gallons. Demand has been found to be normally distributed.

a. What demand level will be exceeded 75 percent of the time?

b. What is the probability that demand will exceed 75 gallons?

9.35 *Inventory Control.* The food concession at a local soccer stadium has the capacity to sell 10,000 hot dogs. Hot-dog demand is estimated by a normal distribution with a mean of 7,000 and a standard deviation of 2,500. What is the probability of a sellout of hot dogs?

9.36 *University Administration.* Students arrive at a professor's office at an average rate of 5 per hour. In a Poisson manner, what is the probability that

a. No student will arrive?

b. Exactly 5 students will arrive?

c. More than 8 students will arrive?

BIBLIOGRAPHY

Breiman, Leo, *Probability.* Reading, Mass.: Addison-Wesley Publishing Co., Inc., 1968.

Burr, Irving W., *Applied Statistical Methods.* New York: Academic Press, Inc., 1974.

Chao, L. L., *Statistics: Methods and Analyses.* New York: McGraw-Hill Book Company, 1969.

Feller, William, *An Introduction to Probability Theory and Its Applications,* vol. I, 2nd ed., 1957; vol. II, 3rd ed., 1968. New York: John Wiley & Sons, Inc.

Mendenhall, William, and James E. Reinmuth, *Statistics for Management and Economics.* North Scituate, Mass.: Duxbury Press, 1971.

Richmond, Samuel B., *Statistical Analysis,* 2nd ed. New York: The Ronald Press Company, 1964.

Stockton, John R., and Charles T. Clark, *Introduction to Business and Economic Statistics,* 5th ed. Cincinnati, Ohio: South-Western Publishing Company, 1975.

10
Decision Theory

CUTLER-HAMMER
INCORPORATED[1]

Cutler-Hammer is an electrical corporation with annual sales exceeding $400 million. In the mid-1970s, the president of the AIL Division of Cutler-Hammer was confronted with an important and difficult decision. An independent inventor has given him the opportunity to invest in a new, patented flight-safety product. The potential product was related to one of the company's major areas of business and consequently, the company had the engineering and production capabilities to refine, produce, and market the product. The decision was fairly straightforward; AIL could pay $50,000 to purchase a 6-month option on the patent. Rather than make a "seat-of-the-pants" decision, the president of AIL decided to form a task team for the purpose of using a more scientific or rational approach to the problem. Because of the nature of the problem, a decision theory approach seemed to be the logical choice. After some analysis, three events occurring after the initial decision were identified to have an important impact. Within 6 months of purchasing the option, AIL would have to decide whether or not to enter into a licensing agreement with the inventor/patent holder. Presumably this decision would depend heavily upon the market studies to be undertaken during the 6 months. If AIL decided to enter into the licensing agreement, it would cost the company an additional $300,000 for a front-end royalty payment and $500,000 for a marketing and development effort. This development effort would take 2½ years. If AIL were successful in getting a defense contract for the device, manufacturing facilities would have to be set up. These facilities would cost $250,000 and require a year to complete. To complicate the problem more, because of the nature of Department of Defense funding, a follow-on contract 5 years after the initial decision to purchase the patent option could

[1]Jacob W. Ulvila, Rex V. Brown, and Karle S. Packard, "A Case in On-Line Decision Analysis for Product Planning," Decision Sciences, 8 (July 1977), 598–615.

be secured by AIL or a competitor. If a competitor won the bid for the second defense contract, AIL would receive royalties from the successful bidder. The problem is further complicated by trying to assess probabilities for different events, as well as accurately estimating costs and payoffs.

The task team successfully modeled the problems; estimated costs, payoffs, and probabilities; and presented their findings to top management. "In the final stages of the decision-making process, the analysis served as a vehicle to focus discussion on the critical issues surrounding the decision and to minimize the consideration of irrelevant issues. In the end, the decision to wait [not to purchase the patent] was reached easily and unanimously, without reservation on the part of any of the participants."

Even though it is premature to determine if the decision was a good decision, top management expressed confidence in the decision theory approach and agreed to use the approach more extensively in the future.

INTRODUCTION

Earlier, we said that management science is a rational methodology for making management decisions. Decision theory fits the same generic definition; but, actually, decision theory constitutes a particular branch of management science. Most complex executive decisions are decisions that must be made in an environment of uncertainty. For example, capital expansion decisions must be made even though such important factors as product demand, cost of materials, and cost of labor are not known with certainty. Often, the manager must choose between several different courses of action in an attempt to optimize his decision process. Decision theory helps the decision maker to address the problem of making complex choices under uncertain conditions. It must be noted that decision theory does not generate alternative courses of action; it merely provides a rational way of choosing among several alternative strategies.

For example, a marketing vice-president of a cosmetic firm may need to make the decision to introduce or not to introduce a particular new product. What does this decision depend on? The potential payoff or profit generated from the new product would have to be considered. This payoff would depend on a number of factors, such as demand for the product, the actions of competitors, price, and promotional strategy. Obviously, the "simple" product development problem is much more complicated than it appears on the surface. It is further complicated by the uncertain nature of factors such as levels of demand and actions of competitors. Some risk or uncertainty might be reduced by spending money on market research. (Whether to do so involves another potentially difficult decision.) Decision theory can be very helpful in confronting a multifaceted decision such as this.

Decision theory can be used for a wide range of problems. These problems generally involve discrete choices and probabilistic events that have a bearing on the desirability of the various actions the decision maker can take. The following applications indicate the flexibility of decision theory.

1. *Natural resources development* Should an oil or gas well be drilled? What set of seismic experiments should be run? What is the expected payoff of the investment in exploration?

2. *Agricultural applications* What crops should be planted? Should excess acreage be planted? What actions should be taken to fight pests?

3. *Financial applications* What is the proper investment portfolio? What capital investments should be made this year?

4. *Marketing applications* Which new product should be introduced? What is the best distribution channel to use? What is the best inventory strategy?

5. *Production applications* Which of several different types of machine should be purchased? What maintenance schedules should be used?

6. *Personal decisions* What college should you go to? What should you major in? Should you go to graduate school or to work? If to work, which job offer should you accept? Should you get married?

To illustrate the general approach of decision theory, let us look at the following example.

EXAMPLE Imagine yourself as the president of a small manufacturing firm. One of your bright young engineers has developed a new household gadget for roasting hot dogs and has obtained a U.S. patent on the device. Since she developed the hot-dog roaster on her own time, she is offering to sell the patent rights for $50,000, or $25,000 plus a 2 percent royalty on total revenue. From your experience, you surmise that demand for the roaster will be one of three levels. One, the roaster will find no acceptance by the consuming public, in which case your total investment in the patent will be lost, as will the $100,000 needed to develop and promote the product. The second demand level possible is one of 20,000 units. The selling price of the roaster is expected to be $20, and the variable cost (not including patent cost and developmental cost) is estimated to be approximately $12.00. The third level of demand is estimated to be 100,000 units. Now that you have the parameters of the problem, what is the correct decision? If you do not have a decision off the top of your head, let us try to analyze the problem systematically using a decision theory approach. First, we must identify the alternative decisions we could make. There are three conceivable decisions. Let

d_1 = buy patent rights outright for $50,000
d_2 = buy patent rights for $25,000 and agree to pay a 2 percent royalty
d_3 = refuse to get involved in the hot-dog-roaster product

Second, we must define the various events or states of nature that affect the quality of the decision. In this problem, the states of nature correspond to the different levels of demand. Let

s_1 = no demand for the hot-dog roaster
s_2 = demand of 20,000 units
s_3 = demand of 100,000 units

Since our decision is a financial one, it is necessary to compute the payoffs given the different decisions we can make and the different states of nature. It is convenient to depict these payoffs in tabular form, called a payoff table or payoff matrix. The payoff table for the hot-dog roaster is depicted in Table 10.1. The dollar values in the table represent the net profit to the firm for each combination of decision and state of nature. For example, if you decide to buy the patent outright (d_1) and the demand is for 20,000 units (s_2), the payoff or profit would be $10,000. These payoffs are computed using the following formula: payoff = revenue − patent cost − royalty − variable cost − developmental cost.

To illustrate, let us calculate the payoff for paying $25,000 for the patent plus 2 percent royalty if the demand is for 100,000 units (d_2/s_3).

TABLE 10.1 Payoff table for hot-dog roaster

Alternative decision	State of nature		
	s_1	s_2	s_3
d_1	−$150,000	$10,000	$650,000
d_2	−125,000	27,000	635,000
d_3	0	0	0

$$\text{payoff} = [(\$20.00)(100,000)] - \$25,000 - [(\$20.00)(100,000)(.02)]$$

revenue — patent cost — royalty

$$- [(\$12.00)(100,000)] - \$100,000$$

variable cost — development cost

$$= 2,000,000 - 25,000 - 40,000 - 1,200,000 - 100,000$$
$$= \$635,000$$

Given the payoff matrix in Table 10.1, you should be able to make a more rational decision concerning the hot-dog roaster simply because you have organized the pertinent information in a rational way. The rest of this chapter discusses methodology helpful in determining the best decision given various criteria for decision making. As you have probably already guessed, much of the utility of decision theory and other management science techniques is that it forces a systematic and rational structuring of the pertinent information for making a given decision.

CRITERIA FOR DECISION MAKING WHEN STATE-OF-NATURE PROBABILITIES ARE UNKNOWN

Often, a decision maker is faced with making a decision in which he or she can identify the possible alternative decisions, can define the various states of nature, and can reasonably calculate the relevant payoffs, but is unable to ascertain or subjectively estimate the probabilities of the various states of nature. If the probabilities of the states of nature are unknown, there are various criteria that can be used to rationally make a decision. Let us examine several criteria briefly and apply each to the hot-dog-roaster problem.

THE MAXIMIN CRITERION

The maximin criterion simply maximizes the minimum payoffs given the various decisions that are possible. It is a simple two-step process once the payoff table has been formulated. The first step is to identify the minimum payoff for each decision. The second step is to pick the largest minimum payoff. Let us illustrate by applying the maximin criterion to the hot-dog-roaster problem. Table 10.2 shows the payoff table with minimum payoffs for each decision circled. Since d_3 has the maximum minimum payoff of the three decision alternatives, the maximin criterion

TABLE 10.2 Payoff table for hot-dog roaster

Alternative decision	State of Nature		
	s_1	s_2	s_3
d_1	$\$ -150{,}000$	$\$10{,}000$	$\$650{,}000$
d_2	$-125{,}000$	$27{,}000$	$635{,}000$
d_3	0	0	0

maximin decision →

would dictate that you should not buy the patent rights for the roaster. Obviously, the maximin rule is a very conservative one that takes a pessimistic view of the various states of nature.

THE MAXIMAX CRITERION

The maximax criterion maximizes the maximum payoffs for the different decisions. We start by identifying the maximum payoffs for each alternative decision. Then the maximax decision is that decision which yields the largest maximum payoff. As shown in Table 10.3, the maximax decision for the hot-dog-roaster problem is to buy the patent rights outright for $50,000 ($d_1$).

TABLE 10.3 Hot-dog-roaster payoff table

Alternative decision	State of nature		
	s_1	s_2	s_3
d_1	$\$ -150{,}000$	$\$10{,}000$	$\$650{,}000$
d_2	$-125{,}000$	$27{,}000$	$635{,}000$
d_3	0	0	0

(maximax decision)

It should be obvious that the maximax rule is an extremely optimistic criterion for choosing alternative decisions.

THE MINIMAX REGRET CRITERION

The minimax regret criterion involves the construction of an opportunity loss or regret matrix prior to applying the minimax rule. To construct an opportunity loss table, we must transform each element in the payoff table to an opportunity loss. The magnitude of the opportunity loss for a given element is the loss incurred by not selecting the optimal alterna-

TABLE 10.4 Opportunity loss table

Alternative decision	State of nature		
	s_1	s_2	s_3
d_1	$150,000	$17,000	0
d_2	125,000	0	$ 15,000
d_3	0	27,000	650,000

tive decision given a state of nature. To convert a payoff table to an opportunity loss table is a two-step iterative process. The first step is to find the largest element in the first column. This element represents the best decision given a particular state of nature. The second step is to subtract each element in the column from the largest element to compute the opportunity loss. This two-step process is repeated for each state of nature (each column in the payoff table). The opportunity loss table for the hot-dog-roaster problem is given in Table 10.4.

Now that we have constructed the opportunity loss table, it is possible to apply the minimax regret criterion to determine the appropriate decision. The minimax regret rule says to identify the maximum regret (opportunity loss) for each decision and then choose that decision with the smallest maximum regret. Table 10.5 reflects the minimax regret decision for the hot-dog-roaster problem.

It should be clear that once you have organized a given decision problem into a payoff table, the decision you make is going to depend on the criterion you use for decision making. We have examined three criteria, and when applied to the hot-dog-roaster problem, each decision rule indicated that a different decision should be made. Other decision criteria exist and you could possibly devise your own rules. Which rule is best depends on the decision parameters, the decision environment, and the attitude of the decision maker. In the rest of the chapter, we introduce

TABLE 10.5 Regret table

Alternative decision	State of nature		
	s_1	s_2	s_3
d_1	$150,000	$17,000	0
minimax→ regret decision d_2	125,000	0	$ 15,000
d_3	0	27,000	650,000

probabilities to the decision process which will facilitate the decision-making process by giving the decision maker more information upon which to base decisions.

CRITERIA FOR DECISION MAKING WHEN STATE-OF-NATURE PROBABILITIES ARE KNOWN

It is a rare decision when the decision maker has no estimate of the relative likelihood of the various states of nature. If the probabilities of the states of nature can be estimated, we can calculate expected values of various decisions. Let us illustrate this concept with the following problem.

A BASIC DECISION PROBLEM

There are 100 opaque urns, each filled with 10 balls. There are two different kinds of urn. Type I urn holds 5 black balls and 5 white balls. Type II urn has 8 black balls and 2 white balls. There are 70 type I urns and 30 type II urns. An urn is picked at random from the 100 urns, and you are asked to guess whether it is type I or type II. If you guess that it is a type I urn and it is, you win $500; if it is a type II urn, you lose $200. If you guess that it is an urn of type II and it is, you win $1,000; but if it is a type I urn, you lose $150. Remember that the urn in front of you, the decision maker, is either a type I or type II urn. In other words, there are two states of nature, s_1 and s_2, corresponding to the urns of type I and type II. You have three alternatives: You can guess either type I or type II or refuse to take the gamble. Which action would you take? What could you expect to gain or lose from your decision? These are the kinds of questions decision theory can answer.

The facts of this decision problem are summarized in Table 10.6. If you know the expected value of each of the three alternative actions, you can simply choose the alternative with the highest expected value. The *expected monetary value* (EMV) of d_1 (the first alternative, namely, guessing that the urn is type I), is simply

expected monetary value (EMV)

$$EMV = \sum_{i=1}^{2} p(s_i)x_i$$

where $p(s_i)$ = probability that the true state of nature is s_i
x_i = payoff for the alternative action, given s_i is the true state of nature

TABLE 10.6 Payoff table for the urn problem

Alternative decision	State of Nature		EMV
	s_1	s_2	
d_1	$500	−$200	$290
d_2	−150	1,000	195
d_3	0	0	0
Probability of state of nature	.7	.3	

Hence,

$$\text{EMV}[d_1] = (.7)(500) + (.3)(-200)$$
$$= 350 - 60$$
$$= \$290$$

$$\text{EMV}[d_2] = (.7)(-150) + (.3)(1,000)$$
$$= -105 + 300$$
$$= \$195$$

$$\text{EMV}[d_3] = (.7)(0) + (.3)(0)$$
$$= 0$$

Therefore, if your objective is to maximize the expected monetary value of the urn decision problem, you would guess that the urn in front of you is type I. You can feel confident that if you were allowed to take this gamble a large number of times, on the average you could expect to gain $290. However, if you are allowed only one chance to guess, you stand a good chance of losing $200.

DECISION TREES

decision tree A *decision tree* presents another way to visualize the typical decision theory problem. Figure 10.1, for example, shows an unevaluated decision tree for the urn problem. There are four didactic, or instructive, parts to a decision tree: decision nodes (shown as squares in the illustrations); chance nodes (shown as circles); alternative branches (straight lines that state alternatives); and probabilistic branches (straight lines that state probabilities).

FIGURE 10.1   Decision tree for the basic urn problem

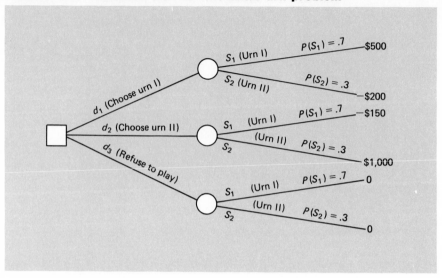

A *decision node* represents the choice between alternatives. From it come *alternative branches* that show, or name, the choices. These branches lead to *chance nodes,* which represent factors in the decision situation over which the decision maker has no control. From these chance nodes come *probabilistic branches* that state the actual or estimated numerical likelihood of various chances. Since the events, or states of nature, are mutually exclusive and exhaustive, the probabilities associated with each event must add to 1.

decision node
alternative branch
chance node
probabilistic branch

Can you see that a decision tree is an analog of a particular kind of problem? A decision must be made among several alternatives. One or more alternatives is associated with chance factors. These chances, however, can be assessed probabilistically. On the basis of evaluation at several stages, therefore, the decision maker can regard the alternatives rationally and choose the one most compatible with ultimate goals.

HOW TO EVALUATE DECISION TREES

In order to evaluate a decision tree, it is necessary to evaluate each chance node and each decision node. These two types of nodes are evaluated differently. Chance nodes are evaluated using the expected value, and the value of a decision node is the expected value of the most desirable alternative action. Nodes 2, 3, and 4 in the decision tree in Figure 10.2 are chance nodes, and consequently their values are equal to the expected values calculated earlier. Node 1 is a decision node where the decision maker is asked to choose among d_1, d_2, and d_3. Since the highest EMV

FIGURE 10.2 Evaluated decision tree for the urn problem

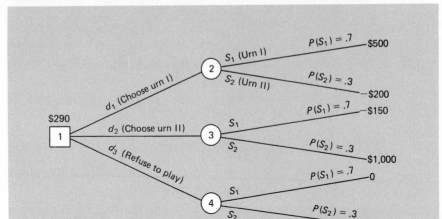

of the alternative actions is $290, the value of node 1 is $290. Given that the decision maker wishes to maximize EMV, d_1 is the appropriate choice, rather than d_2 or d_3.

In the urn problem, the probabilities associated with the two states of nature were known because the total number of each type of urn was known and the urn was chosen randomly (each urn had an equal chance of being chosen). In real problems, these probabilities are rarely known with certainty, and usually the decision maker is forced to estimate the various probabilities subjectively. The quality of the decision, therefore, can depend greatly upon reliable subjective probabilities.

EXAMPLE Fred Fudd is graduating from high school this year and must decide first what college to attend and then what course of study to pursue. Because of parental pressure, Fred must go to college, but he is free to select which college to attend. He has narrowed his choice to two very dissimilar schools. He has been accepted at State University and his home town college, Wood. In addition to choosing between schools, Fred must decide whether to major in engineering or business. Because of the nature of the two schools, Fred has a different probability of success (that is, of graduating) depending on which college he attends and which field he majors in.

1. If he goes to State University and chooses business, his probability of graduating is .60.

2. If he chooses State University and chooses engineering, his probability of success is .70.

3. If he goes to Wood and chooses business, his probability of success is .90.

4. If he goes to Wood and chooses engineering, his probability of success is .95.

5. A State University graduate in business averages $25,000 per year for the first 5 years of full-time employment.

6. A State University graduate in engineering averages $20,000 per year for the first 5 years of full-time employment.

7. A Wood graduate in business averages $14,000 per year for the first 5 years of full-time employment.

8. A Wood graduate in engineering averages $15,000 per year for the first 5 years of full-time employment.

9. If Fred doesn't graduate, he will average $8,000 per year for the first 5 years of full-time employment.

In approaching Fred's problem, let us assume that his sole criterion for making a decision is to maximize average expected income over the first 5 years of his career. Having made that assumption, it is fairly easy to solve Fred's problem using decision theory. What decisions must Fred make? First, he must decide which university to attend; then, he must decide what to major in. So he has two decisions to make. What are the states of nature associated with the alternatives? No matter what school or discipline Fred chooses, he will either graduate or flunk out. Let

s_1 = graduate from State University Business School
s_2 = fail to graduate from State University Business School
s_3 = graduate from State University Engineering School
s_4 = fail to graduate from State University Engineering School
s_5 = graduate from Wood Business School
s_6 = fail to graduate from Wood Business School
s_7 = graduate from Wood Engineering School
s_8 = fail to graduate from Wood Engineering School
d_1 = choose to go to State University
d_2 = choose to go to Wood College
d_3 = choose to major in business
d_4 = choose to major in engineering

Figure 10.3 shows the decision tree presenting Fred's problem. In order to show more clearly how to evaluate a decision tree, let us evaluate each node in Figure 10.3 individually. Nodes 4 to 7 are chance nodes and are, therefore, evaluated by finding the expected value. Nodes 1 to 3 are decision nodes whose value is the expected value of the most desirable alternative action.

FIGURE 10.3 Decision tree for the college problem

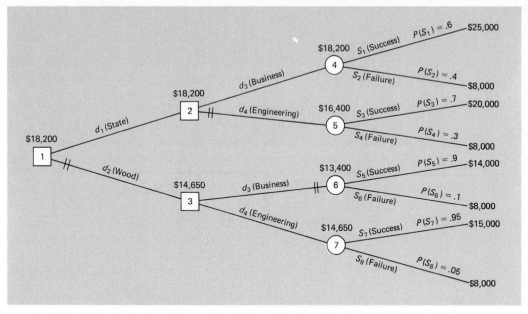

Node 7 $N_7 = (.95)(15,000) + (.05)(8,000)$
         $= \$14,650$

Node 6 $N_6 = (.9)(+14,000) + (.1)(8,000)$
         $= \$13,400$

Node 5 $N_5 = (.7)(20,000) + (.3)(8,000)$
         $= \$16,400$

Node 4 $N_4 = (.6)(25,000) + (.4)(8,000)$
         $= \$18,200$

Node 3   Since $N_7 > N_6$, $N_3 = N_7$ and action d_4 is preferable to d_3,
         $N_3 = \$14,650$

Node 2   Since $N_4 > N_5$, $N_2 = N_4$ and action d_3 is preferable to d_4,
         $N_2 = \$18,200$

Node 1   Since $N_2 > N_3$, $N_1 = N_2$ and action d_1 is preferable to d_2,
         $N_1 = \$18,200$

You should verify each number on the decision tree and work through
the process of arriving at the decision. Go over it until you are sure you
understand this example thoroughly.

THE DECISION PROBLEM
WITH AN OPPORTUNITY
TO OBTAIN ADDITIONAL INFORMATION

So far, we have considered the most basic, and least complex, decision theory problem. Actually, however, real-world problems are seldom so simple. Now, we will complicate the basic decision problem so that you will see how more realistic problems can be solved.

Often, the decision maker has an opportunity to gather or purchase additional information that may have a bearing on the decision process. Most decision problems in the real world include the option of obtaining additional information. For example, as the urn-chooser in our first problem, it would certainly be beneficial if you had the opportunity to sample a ball from the urn in front of you in order to better guess the real state of nature. The question is, how does the additional information change the basic decision problem? The answer is that the *probabilities* of the various states of nature are actually changed. If the probabilities are changed, then obviously the EMVs of the various actions are also changed. What might have been the optimal decision before the additional information was obtained might now be least desirable.

Let us change the original urn problem by allowing you, as the decision maker, to draw one ball out of the urn. Let us further assume that the cost of drawing the ball from the urn is $50. You now have two decisions to make: first, you must decide whether or not to buy the information; and second, you must guess which type of urn has been placed in front of you. If you elect to pay for the opportunity to sample from the urn, either of two outcomes is possible: You will select a white ball or a black ball. Based on this limited information, you must decide on the type of urn.

A decision tree helps to clarify the decision process when additional information is obtainable. Notice that the lower part of the decision tree in Figure 10.4 has not changed from the original problem. However, if you choose to pay $50 to sample a ball from the urn, the decision tree becomes considerable larger; that is, the changing situation is reflected by new branches. To evaluate the top of the decision tree, we must assess new probabilities, such as the probability of S_1 given that a white ball is chosen from the urn [$P(S_1|W)$]. There are basically two types of chance node in the Figure 10.4 decision tree. Chance determines what color ball is drawn, and chance determines which kind of urn is on the table. Therefore, it is necessary to assess the following probabilities:

$P(S_1|W)$ = probability of urn type I given that a white ball is drawn
$P(S_1|B)$ = probability of urn type I given that a black ball is drawn

FIGURE 10.4 Urn decision tree when sampling is possible

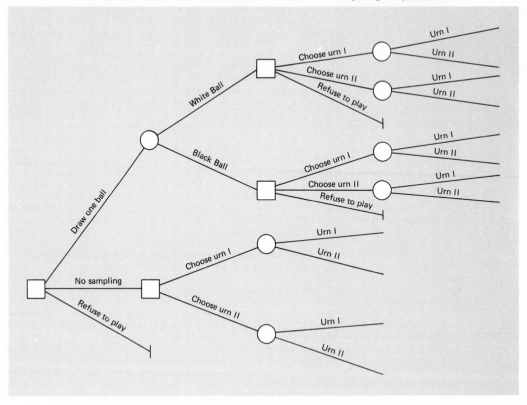

$P(S_2|W)$ = probability of urn of type II given that a white ball is drawn
$P(S_2|B)$ = probability of urn of type II given that a black ball is drawn
$P(W)$ = probability of drawing a white ball
$P(B)$ = probability of drawing a black ball

REVISING PRIOR PROBABILITIES

Bayes'
theorem

In order to determine the foregoing probabilities, it is necessary to use Bayes' theorem. Bayes' theorem allows us to revise the probabilities of the states of nature given new information. Bayes' theorem states:

$$P(A_i/B) = \frac{P(A_i)P(B/A_i)}{\displaystyle\sum_{i=1}^{k} P(A_i)P(B/A_i)} \qquad [10.1]$$

If we apply Bayes' theorem to our example, we have

$$P(S_1/W) = \frac{P(W/S_1)P(S_1)}{P(W/S_1)P(S_1) + P(W/S_2)P(S_2)} \qquad [10.2]$$

We know how many balls of each color are in both types of urn and the distribution of types of urn. We know all the probabilities on the right side of equation 10.2. Therefore, it is a simple matter of arithmetic to calculate $P(S_1/W)$:

$$P(S_1/W) = [(.5)(.7)]/[(.5)(.7) + (.2)(.3)]$$
$$= .35/.41$$
$$= .854$$

Similarly,

$$P(S_2/W) = [P(W/S_2)P(S_2)]/[P(W/S_2)P(S_2) + P(W/S_1) \cdot P(S_1)]$$
$$= [(.2)(.3)]/[(.2)(.3) + (.5)(.7)]$$
$$= .06/.41$$
$$= .146$$

$$P(S_1/B) = [P(B/S_1)P(S_1)]/[P(B/S_1) \cdot P(S_1) + P(B/S_2)P(S_2)]$$
$$= [(.5)(.7)]/[(.5)(.7) + (.8)(.3)]$$
$$= .35/.59$$
$$= .593$$

$$P(S_2/B) = [P(B/S_2)P(S_2)]/[P(B/S_1)P(S_1) + P(B/S_2) \cdot P(S_2)]$$
$$= [(.8)(.3)]/.59$$
$$= .24/.59$$
$$= .407$$

a posteriori probabilities These conditional probabilities are called *a posteriori probabilities* because they cannot be established exclusive of some other property of the problem. In this example, we cannot determine the a posteriori probabilities until after the sampling is completed. Since S_1 and S_2 are mutually exclusive and exhaustive, $P(W \text{ and } S_1) + P(W \text{ and } S_2) = P(W)$; and since $P(W \text{ and } S_1) = P(W/S_1)P(S_1)$, then

$$P(W) = P(W/S_1)P(S_1) + P(W/S_2)P(S_2)$$
$$= (.5)(.7) + (.2)(.3)$$
$$= .41$$

Similarly,

$$P(B) = P(B/S_1)P(S_1) + P(B/S_2)P(S_2)$$
$$= (.5)(.7) + (.8)(.3)$$
$$= .59$$

Obviously, since the ball that is drawn in the sample must be either a white or a black ball, $P(W) + P(B)$ must equal 1. Remember: the probabilities at any chance node must add to 1. Now that we have calculated the necessary probabilities, it is a fairly mechanical procedure to evaluate the tree. Notice in Figure 10.5 that the cost of the additional information is subtracted from each applicable payoff at the ends of the decision tree. The same adjustment can be achieved if we leave the payoffs the same and charge a tariff of \$50 at branch d_1.

Let us evaluate the decision tree in Figure 10.5 node by node:

Node 14 $N_{14} = (.593)(-50) + (.407)(-50)$
$$= -\$50$$

Node 13 $N_{13} = (.593)(-200) + (.407)(950)$
$$= -118.60 + 386.65$$
$$= \$268.05$$

Node 12 $N_{12} = (.593)(450) + (.407)(-250)$
$$= 266.85 - 101.75$$
$$= \$165.10$$

Node 11 $N_{11} = (.854)(-50) + (.146)(-50)$
$$= -\$50$$

Node 10 $N_{10} = (.854)(-200) + (.146)(950)$
$$= 170.80 + 138.70$$
$$= -\$32.10$$

Node 9 $N_9 = (.854)(450) + (.140)(-250)$
$$= 384.30 - 36.50$$
$$= \$347.80$$

Node 8 $N_8 = (.7)(-150) + (.3)(1,000)$
$$= -105 + 300$$
$$= \$195$$

Node 7 $N_7 = (.7)(500) + (.3)(-200)$
$$= 350 - 60$$
$$= \$290$$

Node 6   Since $N_{13} > N_{12} > N_{14}$, d_5 is the most attractive alternative and $N_6 = \$268.05$

FIGURE 10.5 Expanded urn decision tree when sampling is possible

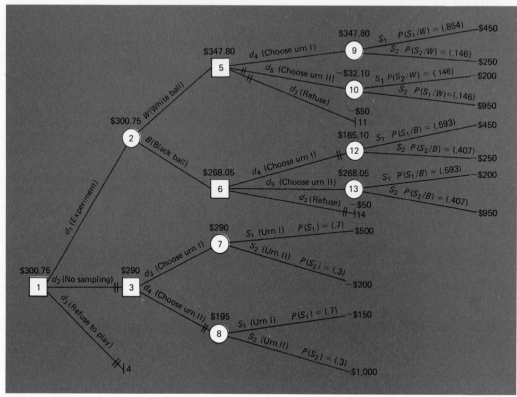

Node 5 Since $N_9 > N_{10} > N_{11}$, d_4 is the best alternative and $N_5 = $ $347.80

Node 4 $N_4 = (.7)(0) + (.3)(0)$
$= 0$

Node 3 Since $N_7 > N_8$, d_3 is the best alternative and $N_3 = \$290$

Node 2 $N_2 = (.41)(347.80) + (.59)(268.05)$
$= 142.60 + 158.15$

Node 1 Since $N_2 > N_3 > N_4$, it seems wise to experiment and $N_1 = $ $300.75

optimal, or Bayesian, strategy According to our evaluation of this decision tree, the *optimal strategy* (sometimes referred to as the *Bayesian strategy*) would be to sample one ball and if it is white, guess that the urn is type I. If the sampled ball is black, then you should guess that the urn is type II. The expected monetary value of the urn decision is $300.75.

THE VALUE OF INFORMATION

In order to make the decision whether or not to buy additional information, it is often helpful to ascertain the expected value of sample information (EVSI) and the expected value of perfect information (EVPI). Clearly, most information is imperfect; hence, the upper bound on the amount you would be willing to pay for information is the expected value of perfect information. The *expected value of sample information* is merely the EMV with the information minus the EMV without any information. Therefore, in our urn example, the EVSI = $350.75 − $290, or $60.75.

expected value of sample information (EVSI)

The value of perfect information is a legitimate issue when you are deciding whether or nor to buy information. Clearly, if the expected value of a market research project is $10,000, it would be foolish to pay $15,000 for the study. The *expected value of perfect information* can be calculated by subtracting the EMV without information from the EMV with perfect information.

expected value of perfect information (EVPI)

Let us take the urn example (see Figure 10.6). The EMV without information is $290. The EMV with perfect information is

$$\sum_{i=1}^{N} P(S_i)P_i$$

where $P(S_i)$ = probability that S_i is the true state of nature
P_i = optimal payoff if S_i is the true state of nature
N = number of states of nature

Therefore,

EMV with perfect information = $(.7)(500) + (.3)(1,000)$
= 350 + 300
= $650

Consequently,

EVPI = 650 − 290
= $360

If you are one who makes decisions by maximizing EMV (an *EMVer*), then you would pay up to $360 for perfect knowledge of the type of urn that is sitting on the table.

FIGURE 10.6 Urn decision tree when perfect information is not available

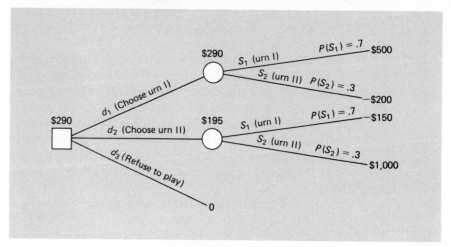

EXAMPLE   A contractor has been invited to bid on a construction job. The value of the contract depends on the length of time it takes to complete the project. If the project is finished on time, there is profit of $50,000. If the contractor is late finishing the project, he will lose $10,000. Weather is the sole determinant of whether the project will be late. If the weather is good, the project will be completed on time; if it is bad, the project will not be completed on schedule. Based on his past experience the contractor's subjective probability of good weather is 20 percent. The contractor, however, has the opportunity to buy a long-range forecast from an independent weather-forecasting company. The weather-forecasting company has a fairly good track record for these long-range forecasts. Its files indicate that 70 percent of the time it successfully predicted good weather, and 80 percent of the time it was able to predict bad weather. In other words,

$$P(I_1/S_1) = .7 \qquad P(I_1/S_2) = .20$$
$$P(I_2/S_1) = .3 \qquad P(I_2/S_2) = .80$$

where I_1 = prediction of good weather
  I_2 = prediction of bad weather
  S_1 = good weather
  S_2 = bad weather

The cost of the weather-forecasting service is $5,000.

In developing the decision tree for the contractor's problem, it is helpful to identify what decisions the contractor must make and in what sequence those decisions must be made. First, he must make the decision

374

FIGURE 10.7 Contract bid decision tree

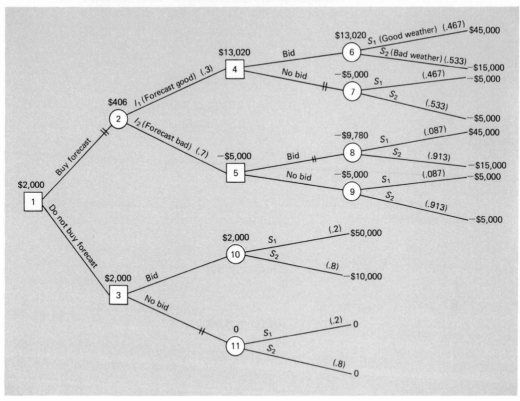

whether to buy the weather forecast information. If the decision is made to buy the information, the contractor must make the bid decision based on the forecast. The decision tree in Figure 10.7 is fairly straightforward.

To evaluate the decision tree in Figure 10.7, it is necessary to calculate the a posteriori probabilities.

$$P(S_1/I_1) = [P(I_1/S_1)P(S_1)]/[P(I_1|S_1)P(S_1) + P(I_1/S_2)P(S_2)]$$
$$= [(.7)(.2)]/[(.7)(.2) + (.2)(.8)]$$
$$= .14/(.14 + .16)$$
$$= .14/.30$$
$$= .467$$

$$P(S_2/I_1) = [(.2)(.8)]/.30$$
$$= .16/.30$$
$$= .533$$

$$P(S_1/I_2) = [(.3)(.2)]/[(.3)(.2) + (.8)(.8)]$$
$$= .06/.70$$
$$= .087$$

$$P(S_2/I_2) = [(.8)(.8)]/.7$$
$$= .64/.70$$
$$= .913$$

$$P(I_1) = P(I_1/S_1)P(S_1) + P(I_1/S_2)P(S_2)$$
$$= (.7)(.2) + (.2)(.8)$$
$$= .30$$
$$P(I_2) = .70$$

Once the probabilities have been calculated, the tree is evaluated by assessing the value of each chance node and each decision node.

Node 11 $N_{11} = (0)(.2) + (0)(.8)$
$$= 0$$

Node 10 $N_{10} = (.2)(50,000) + (.8)(-10,000)$
$$= 10,000 - 8,000$$
$$= \$2,000$$

Node 9 $N_9 = (.087)(-5,000) + (.913)(-5,000)$
$$= -\$5,000$$

Node 8 $N_8 = (.087)(45,000) + (.913)(-15,000)$
$$= 3,915 - 13,695$$
$$= -\$9,780$$

Node 7 $N_7 = (.467)(-5,000) + (.533)(-5,000)$
$$= -\$5,000$$

Node 6 $N_6 = (.467)(45,000) + (.533)(-15,000)$
$$= 21,015 - 7,995$$
$$= \$13,020$$

Node 5   Since $N_9 > N_8$, the value of node 5 is $-\$5,000$

Node 4   Since $N_6 > N_7$, the value of node 4 is $13,020

Node 3   Since $N_{10} > N_{11}$, the value of node 3 is $2,000

Node 2 $N_2 = (.3)(13,020) + (.7)(-5,000)$
$$= \$406$$

Node 1   Since $N_2 < N_3$, the value of node 1 is $2,000

Therefore, the Bayesian, or optimal, strategy is to bid on the project without buying the forecast.

The expected value of sample information is EMV with information minus EMV without. Therefore, EVSI is $406 + $5,000 − $2,000 = $3,406. Since we subtracted $5,000 from payoffs in the upper part of the decision tree, it is necessary to add back this $5,000 when computing the EVSI.

The EVPI is calculated in the following manner: EMV with perfect information is (.2)($50,000) + (.8)(0) = $10,000. The EMV without perfect information is $2,000. Therefore, the EVPI is $10,000 − $2,000 = $8,000. Consequently, the upper bound on the value of a weather forecast is $8,000.

DECISION PROBLEM FOR NON-EMVers

Decision makers can be classified in three categories:

1. Risk takers
2. EMVers
3. Risk averters

A risk taker might choose a gamble that has a negative EMV. People who gamble in Nevada know that the expected value of their gamble is negative, but because they enjoy the excitement or the thrill of winning they are willing to play against the odds. A risk taker might take the gamble pictured in Figure 10.8 even though the EMV is −$20.

People who take action strictly on the basis of the EMV of the decision probably constitute the smallest category of decision maker. Later in this section, we shall discuss methodology to deal with decisions under uncertainty for the non-EMVer.

The last category of decision maker is that of risk avoiders, or risk averters. Most people fit into this category when they are confronted with decisions that entail significant monetary payoffs. Would you pay $250 to be allowed to gamble on the flip of a coin that has a payoff of $1,000 if you win and −$500 if you lose? If not, what would you pay for the chance

FIGURE 10.8 Negative EMV gamble

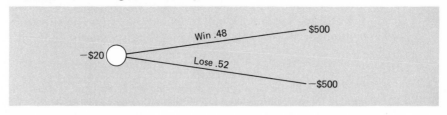

FIGURE 10.9 Simple coin flip gamble

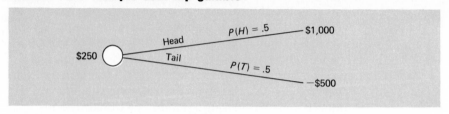

pictured in Figure 10.9? If you would not pay $250 or more for the gamble, you are a risk avoider. If you would pay more than $250 for the chance to play the coin flip gamble, you are a risk taker.

If you have decided you would pay up to $250 for the Figure 10.9 gamble, what about the gamble pictured in Figure 10.10? An EMVer would be willing to pay up to $899 to take this gamble. Would you? Would you take the gamble for nothing? By now, you probably realize that at least for some ranges of monetary payoffs, many people are not EMVers.

Let us reconsider the urn problem without any experimental options. One way to proceed is to determine the value of each chance node subjectively instead of computing the expected value. This value is known *certainty* as the *certainty equivalent* of a gamble. In other words, ask yourself the *equivalent* question, What is the gamble at node 2 in Figure 10.11 worth? If, after some deliberation, you determine that you would pay $100 for the gamble, assign a value of $100 to node 2. Similarly, suppose you decide the certainty equivalent of the node 3 gamble is $25; then you would choose urn I. If you had an extreme aversion to risk, you might not assign positive values to nodes 2 and 3. That is, someone might have to pay you to take either of these gambles.

It becomes less feasible to assign a certainty equivalent to each chance node in a decision process as the number and complexity of the chance nodes increase. In other words, what if the chance node has more than two or three states of nature and its probabilities are difficult to assess subjectively? For example, what would your certainty equivalent be for the gamble pictured in Figure 10.12?

Fortunately, there is a procedure for dealing with the psychology of the nonEMVer. The basic idea is to measure the decision maker's attitude toward risk and then to substitute payoffs modified by the decision maker's risk attitude for the original monetary payoffs. The substitute payoffs can be thought of as specially designed lottery tickets[2] that entitle the owner

---

[2]Raiffa, Howard, *Decision Analysis: Introductory Lectures on Choices Under Uncertainty* (Reading, Mass.: Addison-Wesley Publishing Co., Inc., 1968), p. 57.

FIGURE 10.10   Simple gamble

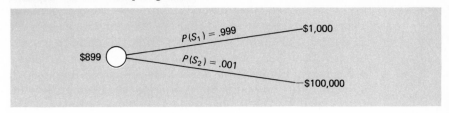

FIGURE 10.11   Urn decision tree

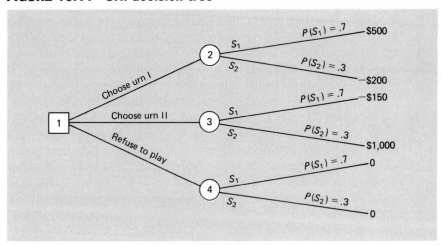

FIGURE 10.12   Complex gamble

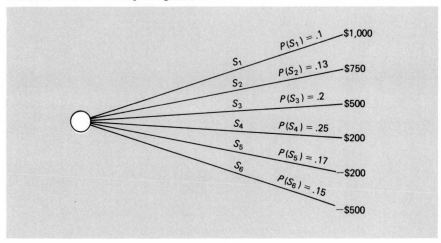

to a p chance at winning W and a $1 - p$ chance at winning L. (Usually, L is a negative dollar amount.) The only requirements are that W be clearly preferable to L and that the decision maker be a rational person. If W and L are monetary values, then the monetary value of a lottery ticket with $p = 1$ is W, and a lottery ticket with $p = 0$ has a dollar value of L. Since attitudes toward risk differ among individuals, these are probably the only two points that a group of decision makers can agree upon. If W and L are sufficiently wide apart to encompass all the payoffs of a decision problem, then intermediate points relating relevant dollar values to lottery tickets can be determined.

Let us return to the urn problem to illustrate how to adjust for non-EMVers. Figure 10.13 shows the original decision tree. In the urn problem thus depicted, W can be set equal to $1,000 and L to $-$200. We can then measure the decision maker's attitude toward risk by asking a series of questions such as the following: What would you pay for a 50–50 chance at winning $1,000 or losing $200? What would you pay for a 75 percent chance at winning $1,000 and a 25 percent chance at losing $200? What would you pay for a 25 percent chance at winning $1,000 and a 75 percent chance at losing $200? If someone would have to pay you to take a specific lottery ticket, how much would they have to pay you? (Remember, lottery tickets represent various gamble parameters.)

Let us assume that a decision maker has answered a series of these kinds of questions and the answers are summarized in Table 10.7. These values can be plotted and a smooth, concave curve fitted to them. (We have done so in Figure 10.14.) This curve represents the locus of points

FIGURE 10.13   Decision tree for the basic urn problem

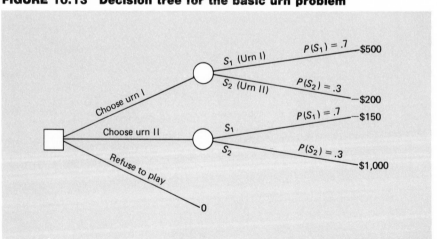

TABLE 10.7 Lottery ticket dollar equivalence

p	Certainty equivalent
0.00	$-200
.25	-50
.50	50
.75	200
1.00	1,000

where a particular decision maker professes indifference between the choices of taking a precisely defined gamble and a certain amount of money. You will note that the illustration contrasts the non-EMVer's indifference curve with an EMVer's.

Once the indifference curve has been drawn, it is easy to use the decision theory developed thus far in this chapter to solve decision problems in terms of the individual decision maker's attitude toward risk. The simple procedure is based upon one very reasonable principle: If a gamble is modified by substituting a different payoff and if the decision maker is indifferent between the original payoff and the new payoff, then that same decision maker should be indifferent between the original gamble and the modified gamble if all else remains unchanged.

Therefore, if a decision maker is indifferent between x dollars and a lottery ticket with a specific value for p, it is reasonable to substitute the lottery ticket for the monetary payoff. If lottery tickets with different

FIGURE 10.14 **Non-EMVer's indifference curve contrasted with EMVer's**

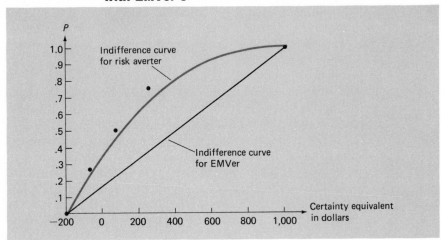

values of p are substituted for each monetary payoff, and the decision tree is evaluated in terms of expected p values, then the strategy that optimizes expected p values is the optimal strategy for that decision maker's particular attitude toward risk. Obviously, this optimal strategy may differ from the optimal strategy of an EMVer or even of another risk averter. To further understand the use of decision theory for a non-EMVer, consider the next example.

EXAMPLE   An editor of a large publishing company has just received a prospectus and four chapters of a manuscript. After reviewing the material, the editor's intuition is that the proposed book has a 40 percent chance to be successful and a 60 percent chance to fail. If it is successful, the publishing company can expect to make a profit of $100,000 over a period of 5 years. If the book is a failure, the company will lose $50,000. If the editor decides to publish the book, there is only a 50–50 chance of convincing the authors to sign a contract with the editor's publishing company. The manuscript can be sent off for review by outside experts for a cost of $1,000. In the past, this review process has successfully predicted the success or failure of a book 80 percent of the time; that is, P(predicted success and the book was successful) $= .80$ and P(predicted failure and the book failed) $= .80$. An EMVer's decision tree for this problem is depicted in Figure 10.15.

If the editor were an EMVer, the manuscript should be sent out for review and the project signed if the reviews are positive or abandoned if the reviews are negative. This particular editor, however, has an aversion to risk and wonders whether the strategy of an EMVer is consistent with this attitude toward risk. Using $99,000 as W and $-$51,000 as L, the editor has decided after considerable deliberation that the indifference parameters are established by p chance at winning $100,000 and $1 - p$ chance at losing $51,000 (the publishing company's money) and the dollar amounts shown in Table 10.8.

Figure 10.16 fits an indifference curve to the points in Table 10.8. With the function graphed in Figure 10.16, it is now possible to substitute (from the indifference curve) lottery tickets with specific p values for monetary payoffs in the editor's original decision tree (Figure 10.15). Once the substitution is made, it is simply a mechanical procedure to evaluate the tree in terms of p values and thus find the optimal strategy for the editor's individual attitude toward risk. This is done in Figure 10.17.

As you can see by comparing Figure 10.15 and 10.17, an EMVer would not act differently from an individual with an attitude toward risk similar to the editor's as graphed in Figure 10.16. Why?

FIGURE 10.15 Editor's decision tree

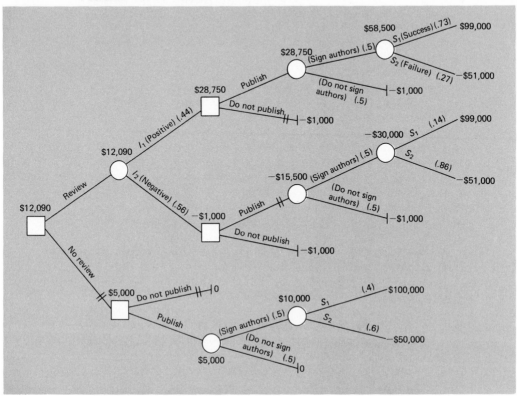

TABLE 10.8 Indifference table

p	Certainty equivalent
0.00	\$ −51,000
.10	−45,000
.25	−35,000
.50	−10,000
.75	15,000
.90	55,000
1.00	100,000

383

FIGURE 10.16   Editor's indifference curve

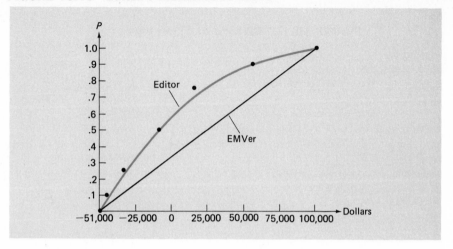

FIGURE 10.17   Editor's decision tree with *p* values as payoffs

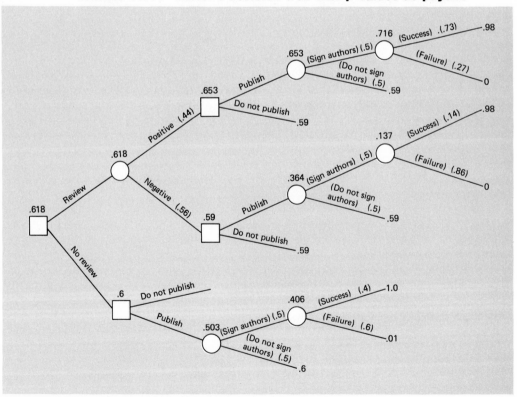

384

SUMMARY

A great many decision problems exist in which a decision must be made among several alternative actions. The consequences of those alternatives devolve from the existence of one or more states of nature, each of which has some probability of being the true state of nature. Critics of decision theory contend, however, that because probability estimates are subjective in nature, the theory is of little practical value. The fact that subjective probabilities are imperfect should make you cautious in your use of decision theory, but it should not prevent you from using it. A decision maker should, however, be aware of the sensitivity of a basic decision made under decision theory to plausible changes in the probabilities. These can be considered by perturbing the various probabilities and re-evaluating the decision tree.

SOLVED PROBLEMS

PROBLEM STATEMENT

The president of a large oil company must decide how to invest the company's $10 million of excess profits. He could invest the entire sum in solar energy research, or he could use the money to research better ways of processing coal so that it will burn more cleanly. His only other option is to put half of this R&D money into solar research and half into coal research. The president estimates 1,000 percent return on investment if the solar research is successful and a 500 percent return on investment if the coal research is successful.

a. Construct a payoff table for the president's R&D investment problem.

b. Based on the maximin criterion, what decision should the president make?

c. Based on the maximax criterion, what decision should the president make?

d. Based on the minimax regret criterion, what decision should the president make?

Let

s_1 = neither coal nor solar research is successful
s_2 = solar research is successful and coal research is not
s_3 = coal research is successful and solar research is not
s_4 = both coal and solar research are successful

d_1 = invest in solar R&D only
d_2 = invest in coal R&D only
d_3 = invest 50 percent in coal and 50 percent in solar R&D

SOLUTION

a.   TABLE 10.9   Payoff table for the R&D problem

	State of nature (all payoffs are in millions)			
Alternative decisions	s_1	s_2	s_3	s_4
d_1	−$10	$100	−$10	$100
d_2	−10	−10	50	50
d_3	−10	45	20	75

b.   Since the maximin loss for each of the three decisions is the same ($10 million), the maximin criterion indicates that the president could choose any of the three options he has identified.

c.   The maximax criterion dictates the choice of d_1 (solar research only) because it has a potential return of $100 million.

d.   The opportunity loss table for this problem is reflected in Table 10.10.

TABLE 10.10   Opportunity loss table for the R&D problem

	State of nature (millions)			
Alternative decision	s_1	s_2	s_3	s_4
d_1	0	0	$60	0
d_2	0	$110	0	$50
d_3	0	55	30	25

The minimax regret criterion would choose d_3 (invest in both types of research).

PROBLEM STATEMENT

Given the previous R&D decision problem, the president estimates that the probability of the solar research being successful is .25 and the probability of successful research on coal is .50. If the president is an EMVer, what is his optimal strategy?

SOLUTION

The decision tree is shown below.

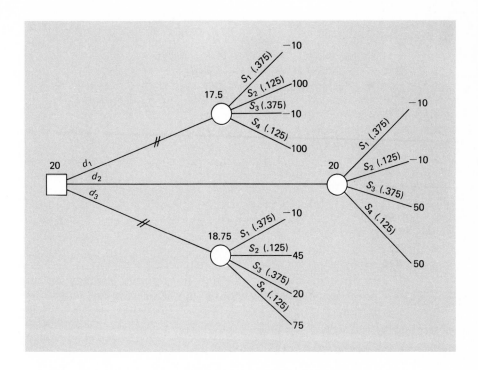

The calculation of the probabilities of the states of nature might require some explanation. If we let

$$A = \text{event that solar research is successful}$$
$$B = \text{event that coal research is successful}$$

We can then describe the states of nature as composite events of A and B, and their complements are shown below.

$S_1 = \overline{A \cup B}$ = neither solar nor coal research is successful

$S_2 = A \cap \overline{B}$ = solar research is successful and coal research is unsuccessful

$S_3 = B \cap \overline{A}$ = coal research is successful and solar research is not

$S_4 = A \cap B$ = both solar and coal research are successful

$$P(S_1) = P(\overline{A \cup B}) = 1 - (A \cup B)$$
$$= 1 - P(A) + P(B) - P(A \cap B)$$
$$= 1 - .25 + .50 - .125$$
$$= .375$$

$$P(S_2) = P(A \cap \overline{B})$$
$$= P(A) \cdot P(\overline{B})$$
$$= (.25)(.5)$$
$$= .125$$

$$P(S_3) = P(B \cap \overline{A})$$
$$= P(B) \cdot P(\overline{A})$$
$$= (.5)(.75)$$
$$= .375$$

$$P(S_4) = P(A \cap B)$$
$$= P(A) \cdot P(B)$$
$$= (.25)(.5)$$
$$= .125$$

As the decision tree indicates, the optimal strategy for an EMVer is to invest in coal research only (d_2). This strategy yields an EMV of $20 million.

PROBLEM STATEMENT

The Ace Trucking Co. of Chicago has a request to haul two shipments, one to St. Louis and one to Pittsburgh. Because of scheduling problems, Ace cannot accept both assignments. The St. Louis customer has guaranteed a return shipment, but the Pittsburgh customer indicates that the probability of a return shipment is 50–50. The value of the St. Louis contract is $2,500. The value of the Pittsburgh contract is $2,000 without return shipment and $4,000 with return.

The Ace Trucking Co. can phone a Pittsburgh dispatcher and can ask whether shipping activity is busy or slow. If the report is busy, the chances of obtaining a return shipment are increased. If I_1 is a busy report, I_2 is a slow report, S_1 is getting a return shipment, and S_2 is failure to get a return shipment, the prior conditional probabilities are given below:

$$P(I_1/S_1) = .8 \qquad P(I_2/S_1) = .2$$
$$P(I_1/S_2) = .3 \qquad P(I_2/S_2) = .7$$

a. Construct the decision tree for this problem.

b. Assume that you are an EMVer; what is the optimal strategy?

c. What is the EMV?

d. What is the EVSI?

SOLUTION

a.

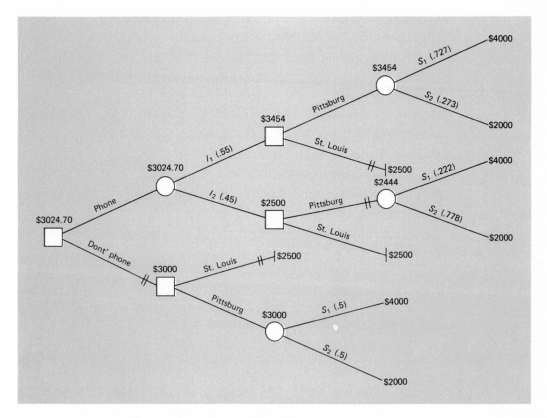

b. The optimal strategy is to phone, and if the dispatcher indicates that shipping activity is active in Pittsburgh (I_1), accept the Pittsburgh assignment. If the dispatcher says that business is slow, take the St. Louis shipment.

c. $3,024.70

d. EVSI = $3,024.70 − $3,000.00 = $24.70

REVIEW QUESTIONS

1. Define *decision theory*.

2. Distinguish among the maximin, maximax, and minimax regret criteria for decision making.

3. When is decision theory most helpful?

4. Does decision theory generate answers to problems? Explain.

5. Describe several decisions that you often make where decision theory could be applied.

6. Distinguish between subjective probabilities and objective probabilities.

7. What does EMV stand for? How is EMV calculated?

8. In your own words, how is a decision tree evaluated?

9. What does EVSI stand for? How is EVSI calculated?

10. Why is it sometimes important to know the expected value of perfect information?

11. In your own words, how is EVPI calculated?

12. What does Bayes' theorem contribute to decision theory?

13. State Bayes' theorem algebraically.

14. Distinguish between EMVers and risk averters.

15. What are the major criticisms of decision theory?

PROBLEMS

10.1   Given the following payoff table, what is the recommended decision under each of the following criteria?

a. Maximin

b. Maximax

c. Minimax regret

Payoff table

Alternative decision	State of nature			
	s_1	s_2	s_3	s_4
d_1	$500	$ 400	$450	$300
d_2	425	400	350	375
d_3	200	450	300	250
d_4	−100	1,000	200	100

10.2   *Stock Market Investment.* You are trying to determine what stock to invest in. The wisdom of your decision depends on the state of the stock market in one year. There are three possible states of nature: the market could go down, stay about the same, or it could go up. You have narrowed your investment choices to four stocks. The payoffs for the various combinations of investment choices and market conditions are shown in the table.

Payoff table

Alternative decision— invest in:	State of nature		
	Market is up	Market is unchanged	Market is down
Stock A	$ 20,000	$5,000	$ −15,000
Stock B	10,000	8,000	6,000
Stock C	100,000	0	−50,000
Stock D	15,000	5,000	−10,000

What are the correct investment choices given the following decision making criteria?

a.   Maximin

b.   Maximax

c.   Minimax regret

10.3   *Stock Market Investment.* If the probabilities of the various stock market conditions in Problem 10.2 were each $\frac{1}{3}$, what would the optimal strategy of an EMVer be?

a.   Draw and label the decision tree.

b.   Evaluate the decision tree.

c.   What is the EMV of the optimal decision?

10.4   *Construction Industry.* The Ace Construction Company has been asked to make a sealed bid on building 40 lighted tennis courts for State University. It costs $10,000 to build each court, and just to bid costs $5,000. The company is considering five bids; and, based on previous experience, each bid has a different subjective probability of being the winning bid. The bids and probabilities are summarized in the table.

Bid number	Amount of bid	Probability of winning
1	Cost + 5%	.90
2	Cost + 10%	.75
3	Cost + 15%	.60
4	Cost + 20%	.40
5	Cost + 25%	.10

a. Draw the decision tree for this problem.

b. Assuming that Ace Construction Company wants to maximize the EMV, what bid should it submit to State University?

10.5 *Personal Decision Making.* You have a trip to make next week, and you are trying to decide whether to make the trip by air, automobile, or train. The weather is the primary determinant of your enjoyment of the trip. The weather bureau has forecast an 80 percent chance of good weather next week. Your trip enjoyment in case of good and bad weather are measured in utiles in the table.

Weather	Airplane	Auto	Train
Good	100	65	50
Bad	0	20	50

a. Draw the decision tree for this problem, labeling all branches, states of nature, payoffs, and probabilities.

b. If you wished to maximize expected utiles, which mode of transportation would you choose?

10.6 *Retail Sales.* You are the owner of a local sporting goods shop, and you have an opportunity to buy leather soccer balls at a special price if you buy the balls sometime before July 31. You must, however, buy in even dozens. If you buy early, you can buy the balls for $10 each. If you buy during the soccer season, the balls will cost $12 each. If you overstock and must sell the balls after the soccer season, you feel you will have to sell them for $8 each. The balls retail for $18 and the level of demand shown in the table is predicted. Notice that sales are also in even dozens.

Demand (dozen)	Probability
2	.25
3	.30
4	.30
5	.15

a. Draw the decision tree, labeling properly.

b. Evaluate the tree.

c. How many soccer balls would an EMVer order early?

10.7 *Personal Decision Making.* Your are an engineering student and are trying to decide whether, upon graduation, to go to work as an engineer or spend another year in school getting an M.B.A. Since you are an EMVer, all you really care about is your expected income. Presently, the market for engineers is depressed, and the probability of getting an engineering job is only .50. Your subjective probability of getting a job requiring an M.B.A. in 1 year is .70. However, you can do some research into expected strength of the market for M.B.A.s. You feel that this research will be correct with a probability of .70. The states of nature are that you will be able to get a job utilizing your education or you will not; that is, $P(I_1/S_1) = .7$. The average M.B.A. earns $14,000 per year to start, and the average engineering student makes $12,000 at the start. If you can't get a job utilizing your education, you can always drive a taxi for $9,000 per year. Use 5-year earnings to determine the optimal strategy.

a. Draw the decision tree and label it.

b. What is the optimal strategy of an EMVer?

c. What is the optimal EMV?

d. What is the expected value of sample information?

10.8 *Gambling Decisions.* You are a betting person and wish to bet on the State University varsity/alumni game. You have no information on the odds for either team's winning. The only information you have is that the varsity has won 12 and the alumni have won 8. Ties are broken by sudden death playoffs. You have an opportunity to do some research into the strengths and weaknesses of the two teams; the outcome of this research will indicate a winner. The only bet you can make is an even $100.

I_1 = research indicates varsity will win
I_2 = research indicates the alumni will win
S_1 = varsity will win
S_2 = alumni will win

$P(I_1/S_1) = .70$

$P(I_2/S_1) = .30$

$P(I_1/S_2) = .40$

$P(I_2/S_2) = .60$

a. Draw the decision tree.

b. Indicate the optimal strategy for an EMVer.

c. Interpret the decision tree in your own words.

d. Would your decision strategy be the same as an EMVer's strategy? Explain.

10.9 *Drilling Decision.* An oil company is trying to decide on its bidding policy for the purchase of some offshore drilling rights. Based on the history of other areas of similar characteristics, the management of the oil company thinks that there are three possible levels of oil in the offshore area in question, with the probabilities reflected in the table.

State of nature	Payoff	Probability
1	Not enough recoverable oil to cover drilling and production costs (i.e., total loss of $25 million)	.40
2	Total oil production of 50 million barrels	.50
3	Total oil production of 100 million barrels	.10

Drilling costs and production costs are estimated at $100 million for the life of the area. The current market price of oil is $31 per barrel. The problem is that management does not know whether to bid or how much to bid for the oil rights. Its policy is that management should select one of the three bidding strategies and bid $22, $23, or $24 per expected barrel of oil based on its supposition of what the competition will bid. Management's subjective probabilities on this aspect of the problem of getting the drilling rights are summarized in the following table.

Bid ($)	Probability of outbidding the competition
22	.10
23	.30
24	.60

a. Draw the decision tree and label it properly.

b. Evaluate the decision tree from the point of view of an EMVer.

c. What is the optimal strategy, and what is the EMV of the oil company's drilling rights problem?

10.10 *Product Development.* A small firm has developed a new machine to manufacture printed circuit boards. The machine is a considerable improvement over machines currently on the market. If management decides to manufacture this new machine, it is almost certain that the larger firms in the industry will copy the design and take the majority of the market through price competition. Therefore, management feels that the decision of whether or not to manufacture depends solely on expected profit in the first year of production. The costs of setting up the production lines and marketing the new machine are estimated to be $250,000. The variable cost of the machine is about $10,000 per machine, and the firm plans to sell the machine for $15,000. To simplify the problem, let us assume that the market demand will be either 50 or 75 machines. Assume that demand and production are evenly distributed throughout the year. Management believes that these two levels of demand are equally likely. Market research can be done at a cost of $10,000. In the past, this market research has successfully predicted demand level 75 percent of the time; that is, P(research indicates demand will be for 50 machines and the demand is for 50 machines) = .75.

a. Draw and label the decision tree.

b. Evaluate the decision tree.

c. What is the optimal strategy of an EMVer?

d. Interpret the decision tree.

e. What is the expected value of sample information?

f. What is the expected value of perfect information?

10.11 *Oil Drilling.* An oil company must decide whether or not to drill an oil well in a particular area. The decision maker believes that the area could be dry, reasonably good, or a bonanza, with the respective probabilities of .40, .40, and .20. If the well is dry, no revenue is generated. If the well is reasonably good, the expected revenue is $75,000. If the well is a bonanza, the expected revenue is $200,000. In any case, the cost of drilling the well is $40,000. At a cost of $15,000, the company can take a series of seismic soundings that usually help determine the underlying geological structure at the site. These experiments will disclose whether there is no structure, open structure, or closed structure. Let us denote these experimental outcomes as I_1, I_2, and I_3, respectively. Let

$$S_1 = \text{dry hole}$$
$$S_2 = \text{reasonably good potential}$$
$$S_3 = \text{bonanza}$$

Past experience has indicated the following conditional probabilities:

$$P(I_1/S_1) = .60 \qquad P(I_1/S_2) = .40 \qquad P(I_1/S_3) = .10$$
$$P(I_2/S_1) = .30 \qquad P(I_2/S_2) = .40 \qquad P(I_2/S_3) = .40$$
$$P(I_3/S_1) = .10 \qquad P(I_3/S_2) = .20 \qquad P(I_3/S_3) = .50$$

a. Draw and label the decision tree for this problem.
b. Evaluate the decision tree.
c. What is the optimal strategy for an EMVer?
d. What is the EMV of the optimal strategy?
e. What is the EVSI?
f. What is the EVPI?

10.12 *Capital Investment.* XYZ Manufacturing Company has made a bid to supply a major piece of industrial equipment to another company. If XYZ Company gets the contract, a capital investment of $300,000 would be justified to enable XYZ Company to economically build the equipment. The problem is that the lead time on the capital investment is too long, and consequently a decision concerning capital expenditure must be made now. If XYZ Company gets the contract and buys the capital equipment, it will net $600,000 on the deal. If XYZ Company does not get the contract, the entire capital investment is lost. If the company gets the contract and uses existing facilities (that is, there is no capital investment), it will lose $100,000 on the contract. Marketing has estimated that XYZ Company has a 50–50 chance of winning the contract.

a. Draw and evaluate the decision tree and label it properly.

b. What should XYZ Company do?

c. What is the EMV of the decision?

10.13 *Capital Investment.* The XYZ Company in Problem 10.12 could spend $25,000 to obtain information concerning the probability of getting the contract. In the past, this type of information proved accurate about 80 percent of the time.

a. Draw and evaluate the decision tree for this new problem.

b. What is the Bayesian strategy?

c. What is the EVSI?

10.14 *Personal.* You are presently taking a course on a pass/fail basis and want to decide whether or not to drop the course. If you drop before the first test, all your tuition will be refunded. If you drop after the first test, no tuition will be refunded. At present, you believe you have a 75 percent chance of passing the course. The following are your subjective estimates of the prior conditional probabilities.

$$P(I_1/S_1) = .9 \qquad P(I_1/S_2) = .3$$
$$P(I_2/S_1) = .1 \qquad P(I_2/S_2) = .7$$

where S_1 = passing the course
  S_2 = failing the course
  I_1 = passing the test (first test)
  I_2 = failing the test (first test)

The payoffs are in utiles and are the following:

pass = 100 utiles
fail = 0 utiles
drop before test = 50 utiles
drop after test = 25 utiles

a. Draw the decision tree.

b. Evaluate the decision tree.

c. What is the Bayesian strategy?

10.15 Design a series of questions and try to find a friend's indifference curve for various levels of dollar investment.

10.16 Assume that you are the president of Ace Construction Company in Problem 10.4. What would your optimal strategy be, given your personal attitude toward risk?

10.17 Measure your personal attitude toward the risk involved in Problem 10.11. Substitute p values for monetary payoffs, and then find your optimal strategy. Discuss and interpret your answer.

BIBLIOGRAPHY

Conrath, D. W. "From Statistical Decision Theory to Practice: Some Problems with the Transition," *Management Science*, 19 (April 1973), 873–883.

Dunford, R. R. "Decisions, Decisions." *Industrial Research*, 16 (July 1974), 27–30.

Eilon, S. "What Is a Decision?" *Management Science*, 16 (December 1969), B172–B189.

Flinn, R. A., and E. Turban. "Decision Tree Analysis for Industrial Research," *Research Management*, 13 (January 1970), 27–34.

Hammond, J. S., III. "Better Decision with Preference Theory," *Harvard Business Review* (November–December 1967), 123–141.

Ives, D. "Decision Theory and the Practicing Manager," *Business Horizons*, 16 (June 1973), 38–40.

Lindgren, B. W. *Elements of Decision Theory*. New York: Macmillan Publishing Co., Inc., 1971.

Longbottom, D. A. "The Application of Decision Analysis to a New Product Planning Decision." *Management Decision*, 24 (March 1973), 9–17.

Meador, C. L., and D. N. Ness. "Decision Support Systems: An Application to Corporate Planning." *Sloan Management Review*, 15 (Winter 1974), 51–68.

Newman, J. W. *Management Applications of Decision Theory.* New York: Harper & Row, Publishers, Inc., 1971.

Pratt, J. W., Howard Raiffa, and R. Schlaifer. *Introduction to Statistical Decision Theory.* New York: McGraw-Hill Book Company, 1965.

Radford, K. J. *Managerial Decision Making.* Reston, Va.: Reston Publishing Company, Inc., 1975.

Raiffa, Howard. *Decision Analysis: Introductory Lectures on Choices Under Uncertainty.* Reading, Mass.: Addison-Wesley Publishing Co., Inc., 1968.

Schlaifer, R., *Analysis of Decisions Under Uncertainty.* New York: McGraw-Hill Book Company, 1969.

Simon, H. A. *The New Science of Management Decisions.* New York: Harper & Row, Publishers, Inc., 1960.

Sullivan, W. G., and W. W. Claycombe. "The Use of Decision Trees in Planning Plant Expansion." *Advanced Management Journal,* 40 (Winter 1975), 29–39.

Winkler, R. L., *Introduction to Bayesian Inference and Decision.* New York: Holt, Rinehart and Winston, Inc., 1972.

11
Forecasting

THE EXECUTIVE BRANCH OF THE FEDERAL GOVERNMENT

Imagine yourself in a meeting in the Oval Office of the White House. The general subject of the meeting is the U.S. economy and the president has assembled the Council of Economic Advisors. The presidential elections are a year away and the president is very concerned about the prospect of an untimely recession. He has several questions. First, are we headed for a recession in the next 6 months to a year? Second, if there is a good probability of a recession, how severe will it be? Finally, what can be done to avert the expected recession? To answer these questions, the various economic advisors are fortunate to have some very sophisticated econometric forecasting models at their disposal. Using these models and their collective judgment, they can provide fairly accurate answers to the president's questions. The first two questions involve a straight forecast of the future. For example, the various forecasting models utilized would predict real GNP, the unemployment rate, the rate of inflation, and many other variables that describe the state of the economy. The president's last question, regarding what to do about an impending recession, is not as easily answered. Each economist may have a different fiscal or monetary solution. One economist may advocate a tax rebate and another a corporate investment tax credit. Increased federal spending may be another advisor's solution. In short, there may be at least as many proposed solutions to the impending recession as there are economic advisors. A rational way to resolve the differences and to choose a reasonable strategy is to use an econometric model to test the various strategies and combinations of strategies proposed. Given the model forecasts using different strategies and the combined advice of the Council of Economic Advisors, the president can make a good decision concerning the appropriate fiscal action to recommend to Congress.

INTRODUCTION

Regardless of whether an organization's role in society is to provide medical care, police protection, safe streets, consumer goods, or consumer services, it needs accurate and timely forecasts. Hospitals need to predict the demand for resources such as X-ray facilities, surgical rooms, special nursing stations, and so on. Computer organizations must predict demand so that the appropriate hardware and software can be acquired. Farmers need weather forecasts for making planting and harvesting decisions. Automobile manufacturers need demand forecasts to develop the master schedules that are a necessary input to materials requirements planning and aggregate scheduling. In short, many planning decisions of the operations manager are based on various forecasts, and it is becoming increasingly important for the competitive firm to perform the forecasting function accurately and efficiently.

To emphasize this point, let us demonstrate the effect of a 10 percent error in the demand forecast for automobiles. Let us assume that demand for September is estimated at 100,000 automobiles. Based on this forecast, manpower planning, production schedules, inventory policies, and many other important planning decisions are made. Now assume that sales for September are 90,000 units rather than the 100,000 projected. If we oversimplify the consequences of the forecasting error by using the cost of holding additional inventory to measure the cost of that error, we can compute it in the following manner:

cost of forecast error
$$= \text{(cost of auto) (number of excess autos produced)(cost of capital)}$$

For illustrative purposes, let the per-unit cost of the automobile be \$5,000 and the cost of capital be 12 percent per year, or 1 percent per month. Then the cost of the forecast error for September is

$$(\$5,000)(10,000)(.01) = \$500,000$$

It ought to be obvious from this oversimplified example that accurate demand forecasts are not only important to the typical organization but are possibly the difference between surviving and not surviving in a competitive marketplace.

Regardless of whether the subject of the forecast is sales, cash flow, GNP, or the weather, forecasts can be categorized by their time horizon. *short-range* As depicted in Figure 11.1, *short-range forecasts* (up to 1 year, but typi- *forecasts* cally a quarter) help the management make current operational decisions *medium-range* such as production scheduling and short-term financing. *Medium-range forecasts* (1 to 3 years) aid in making planning decisions that have a lon-

FIGURE 11.1 Forecasting time horizon

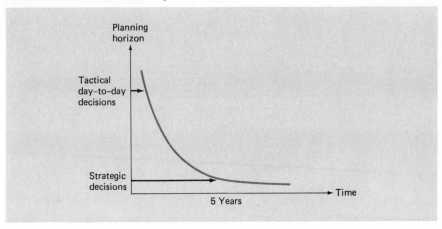

ger lead time. For example, a computer installation may use a 3-year forecast of demand in order to make decisions concerning hardware acqui-

long-range sitions necessary to satisfy that demand. *Long-range forecasts* (3 or more years) are used to make decisions that affect the organization further in the future. A utility company must make long-range forecasts concerning both its demand and the availability and cost of various fuels, in order to make decisions concerning new plant and equipment.

Forecasting techniques can be grouped into one of three categories:
qualitative qualitative techniques, time-series analysis, and causal methods. *Qualita-*
techniques *tive techniques* use qualitative data such as the aggregate opinion of the
time-series sales force to forecast the future. *Time-series analysis* relies entirely on
analysis historical data, focusing on seasonal and cyclical variations and trend
causal extrapolations. *Causal methods* attempt to define relationships between
methods independent and dependent variables in a system of related equations. Each of these three general categories can be further subdivided into individual forecasting techniques. See Figure 11.2 for a breakdown of commonly used forecasting methods. Obviously, the decision of which technique to use is dependent on the parameters of the individual forecasting problem. In this chapter, however, we attempt to indicate the comparative advantages, costs, and logical applications of the various techniques.

When selecting a forecasting technique, a decision maker must keep two types of costs in mind; cost of inaccuracy and cost of the forecast itself. The objective should be to minimize the total costs. In other words, it makes little sense to spend a large amount for a forecast of little significance to the organization. A "gut-feeling" forecast from the sales manager might be adequate. Alternatively, an important decision that is very sensitive to future conditions may warrant the expenditure of thousands of dollars to improve the forecast by only a small amount.

FIGURE 11.2 Breakdown of common forecasting techniques

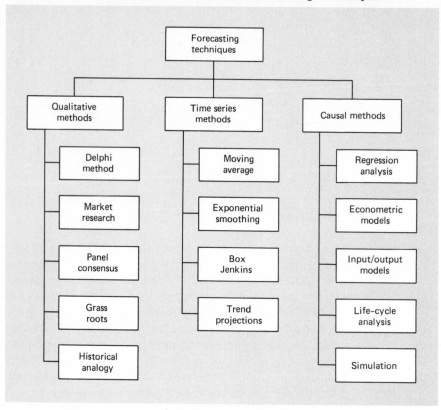

The selection of a forecasting technique depends on a multitude of factors. Many techniques require a substantial amount of historical data. If adequate and relevant historical data do not exist or are prohibitively expensive to accumulate, then many techniques can be automatically ruled out. Another factor to be considered is the planning horizon. Some techniques are more suited to short-term forecasts and some to long-term forecasts. The time available to make the forecast is an important consideration. If a manager needs a forecast for a current decision, he may not be able to wait 6 months to get it. Forecasting techniques vary as to cost and accuracy, and therefore it is important to identify the accuracy needed in the forecast and a reasonable cost for a given level of accuracy. Figure 11.3 gives some logical structure for deciding which forecasting technique is appropriate.

The first question to be asked concerns the availability of historical data. All quantitative forecasting techniques depend upon the existence of adequate and accurate historical data. Therefore, if adequate data do not exist, causal methods and time-series analysis techniques are not feasible alternatives. However, even if adequate data do not exist, if the forecast is important, there are qualitative techniques that can be employed that generally yield better results than a "gut-feeling" or "seat-of-the-pants" forecast. The more sophisticated qualitative techniques, however, usually take several months to implement, and therefore, if the decision maker cannot wait several months, a "gut-feeling" forecast is the forecaster's only alternative.

If adequate historical data do exist and the forecast is an important one, a wide variety of forecasting techniques are available. These methods range from quick-and-dirty time-series techniques to very sophisticated econometric models containing hundreds of equations and hundreds of variables. The cruder and simpler methods require very little time and involve little cost. The more commonly used time-series techniques are described later in this chapter. Some causal methods can require months and even years of development and thousands of dollars. The automobile

FIGURE 11.3   Forecast technique decision

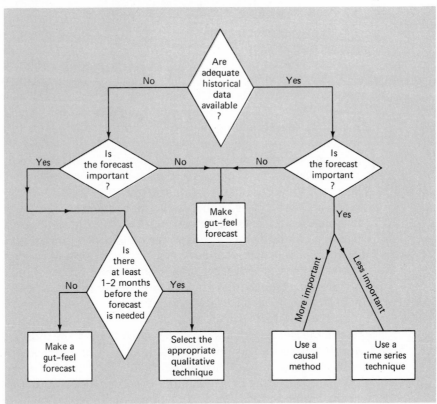

demand forecast mentioned earlier in this chapter would be a likely candidate for a causal forecasting method such as multiple regression or econometric modeling.

QUALITATIVE TECHNIQUES

Often, data necessary to generate a forecast using either time-series analysis or some type of causal model are not available, and the manager is forced to use some kind of qualitative technique that substitutes human judgment for historical data. This situation frequently arises with the introduction of new products or services. The qualitative forecasting methods discussed in this chapter can be and often are formalized, technical procedures designed to incorporate human judgment in the forecasting process.

In this chapter, we describe five commonly used qualitative techniques:

1. The Delphi method
2. Market research
3. Panel consensus
4. Grass-roots forecasting
5. Historical analogy

Delphi method   The *Delphi method* establishes a panel of experts. This panel is interrogated, using a series of questionnaires in which the answers to each questionnaire are used as input to designing the next. In this way, information is shared among the experts without the disadvantage of having individual experts influencing each other; in other words, the bandwagon effect of majority opinion is eliminated. As indicated in Table 11.1, the Delphi method is effective regardless of the forecast's planning horizon. The cost, however, can be rather high.

market research   *Market research* is probably the most sophisticated of the qualitative techniques and also the most quantitative. "Market research" encompasses an entire family of techniques that are helpful in revealing predictions about the size, structure, and configuration of markets for various goods and services. Market researchers obtain information about markets of interest through the use of mail questionnaires, telephone surveys, panels, and personal interviews. The data obtained are then subjected to various statistical tests so that hypotheses about the market can be tested. Market research techniques are generally the most expensive form of qualitative forecasting, take the longest to implement, and if properly applied are often the most accurate.

panel consensus   *Panel consensus* is a technique based on the assumption that several heads are better than one. With this technique, a panel of experts is as-

TABLE 11.1   Qualitative Forecasting Methods

	Delphi method	Market research	Panel consensus	Grass roots	Historical analogy
Accuracy					
Short-term	Fair to very good	Excellent	Poor to fair	Fair	Poor
Medium-term	Fair to very good	Good	Poor to fair	Poor to fair	Good to fair
Long-term	Fair to very good	Fair to good	Poor	Poor	Good to fair
Cost	$2,000 +	$5,000 +	$1,000 +	$1,000 +	$1,000 +
Time required	2 months +	3 months +	2 weeks +	2 months +	1 month +

Source: Adapted from J. S. Chambers, S. K. Mullich, and D. D. Smith, "How to Choose the Right Forecasting Technique," *Harvard Business Review* (July–August 1971).

sembled for the purpose of jointly developing a forecast. Free communication is encouraged, and the job is finished when a consensus opinion is arrived at. Obviously, the relative merit of this approach depends heavily on the configuration of the panel of experts, but it is generally considered inferior to most other qualitative methods with respect to accuracy. It can, however, be accomplished in a relatively short amount of time at a modest cost.

grass-roots forecasting   *Grass-roots forecasting* refers to asking the people closest to the problem to make individual forecasts for their territory. These individual forecasts are then aggregated to form the overall forecast. Sales forecasts are frequently accomplished in this way. This type of approach depends on the quality of the individual forecasts coming from the field. If done conscientiously, grass-roots forecasting can be very effective. The major argument against it is the opportunity cost. It is often argued that the sales force should spend its time selling and minimize its administrative duties. In addition, if salespeople are working on a commission basis, it is very likely that they will put little thought into a sales forecast.

The final qualitative forecasting tool to be discussed is the *historical analogy* approach. Like other qualitative methods, this approach is used when specific data are scarce. For example, if a firm is introducing a new product that has strong similarities to an established product, it may use sales data relevant to the established product to predict the relative success or failure of the new product for which no data exist. This technique, while having a modest cost, is dependent on the availability of several years of data on the model product or service. Historical analogy forecasts seem to perform better for medium- and long-range planning horizons than for short-range.

TIME-SERIES ANALYSIS

A time series is a set of raw data arranged chronologically; monthly sales is a good example. Time-series analysis is used when several years of data exist and when trends are both clear and relatively stable. Because time-series analysis is totally dependent upon historical data, its implicit assumption is that the past is a good guide to the future. Consequently, time-series analysis performs better in the short-term than in the long-term forecast. In addition, time-series analysis cannot predict turning points in trend. For example, typical seasonally adjusted sales for a textbook like this one over a 4-year period might behave as shown in Figure 11.4. If our historical data were limited to 1978 and 1979 sales data, we might project sales to be 8,000 copies by 1981 when in fact sales dropped to 1,000. A turning point in sales was caused by the existence of the used-book market, and mere time-series analysis does an extremely poor job of predicting turning points in trend. If the data exist, however, most time-series analysis techniques are extremely inexpensive, and projections can be produced on a computer in a matter of seconds.

A time series is composed of four basic elements: *a trend component, a seasonal component, a cyclical component,* and *an erratic or random component.* Trend refers to long-term growth or decay. A seasonal fluctuation in the forecasted variable recurs regularly at periodic intervals. Many products experience seasonal fluctuations with respect to demand. Cyclical fluctuations about trend are explainable fluctuations but differ from seasonal fluctuations in that their length of time and amplitude are not constant. Finally, if a forecaster could precisely measure trend, seasonability, and the cyclical factor, there would still be an unexplained variation between the forecast and reality. This unexplained variation is usually referred to as the erratic or random component in a time series.

In this chapter, we describe three common types of time-series forecasting techniques:

1. Moving average
2. Exponential smoothing
3. Trend projection

SIMPLE MOVING AVERAGE

The simple-moving-average forecasting method simply eliminates the effects of seasonal, cyclical, and erratic fluctuations by averaging the historical data points. Therefore, if seasonality, trend, and cyclical factors are not critical in the variable being forecast, the moving-average method is of some value. The effect of the simple-moving-average technique can be seen in Figure 11.5.

FIGURE 11.4 Sales time series

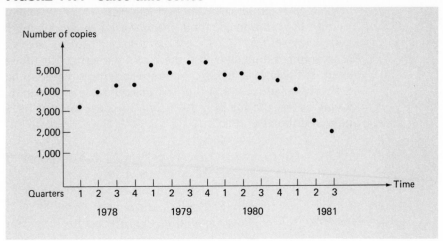

To compute a simple moving average, simply choose the number of points in the time-series data to include in the average. Then, as each time period evolves, add the new time-period data and subtract the oldest time-period data, and calculate a new average.

Mathematically, then,

$$F_t = \frac{\sum_{i=1}^{N} S_{t-i}}{N} \qquad [11.1]$$

FIGURE 11.5 Sales forecast using simple moving average

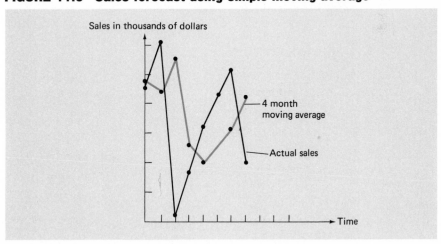

where F_t = forecast for time period t
S_{t-i} = actual sales for period $t - i$
N = number of time periods used in the averaging process

For example, let us calculate the moving average for the sales data contained in Table 11.2, using a 4-month moving average. Since our data go back only to January 1979, our first possible sales forecast using a 4-month moving average is for May 1979. The forecast for May 1979 can be computed as follows:

$$F_5 = \frac{S_1 + S_2 + S_3 + S_4}{4}$$
$$= \$238,250$$

Once May sales data are available, the forecast for June can be computed:

TABLE 11.2 Sales data for time-series analysis

Year	Month	Sales	Simple 4-month moving-average forecast
1979	January	$250,000	
	February	210,000	
	March	223,000	
	April	270,000	
	May	245,000	$238,250
	June	261,000	237,000
	July	212,000	249,750
	August	226,000	247,000
	September	241,000	236,000
	October	252,000	235,000
	November	261,000	232,750
	December	229,000	245,000
1980	January	247,000	245,750
	February	255,000	247,250
	March	271,000	248,000
	April	261,000	250,500
	May	258,000	258,500
	June	265,000	261,250
	July	250,000	263,750
	August	275,000	258,500
	September	245,000	262,000
	October	260,000	258,750
	November	255,000	257,500
	December	263,000	258,750

FIGURE 11.6 **Sales forecast using simple moving average**

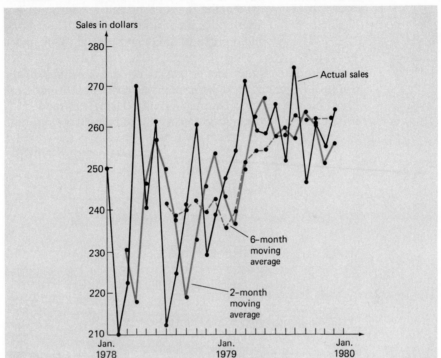

$$F_6 = \frac{S_2 + S_3 + S_4 + S_5}{4}$$
$$= \$237,000$$

It is obvious from Figure 11.6 that the longer the period over which the averaging takes place, the smoother the forecast function.

WEIGHTED MOVING AVERAGE

Often, it is desirable to vary the weights given to historical data in order to forecast future demand or sales. Past history may show that a significantly better forecast is computed when the more recent data are given heavier weight. Mathematically, the weighted moving average is computed as follows:

$$F_t = \frac{\sum\limits_{i=1}^{N} W_{t-i} S_{t-i}}{\sum\limits_{i=1}^{N} W_{t-i}} \qquad [11.2]$$

where F_t = forecast for time period t
      S_{t-i} = actual sales for time period $t - i$
      N = number of time periods used in the averaging process
      W_{t-i} = weight given to the $t - i$th period in the averaging process

For example, assume that a weight of 50 is assigned to the most recent month, a weight of 25 to the next most recent month, and weights of 15 and 10 to the next 2 months, respectively. Using the data in Table 11.2, the 4-month weighted moving average for May 1979 is computed as follows:

$$F_5 = \frac{(50)(270) + (25)(223) + (15)(210) + (10)(250)}{100}$$

$$= \$247,250$$

The data shown in Table 11.3 are plotted in Figure 11.7.

TABLE 11.3   Four-month weighted moving average

Year	Month	Actual sales	4-Month weighted moving average
1979	January	$250,000	
	February	210,000	
	March	223,000	
	April	270,000	
	May	245,000	$247,250
	June	261,000	244,450
	July	212,000	254,550
	August	226,000	235,000
	September	241,000	229,650
	October	252,000	234,900
	November	261,000	241,350
	December	229,000	252,250
1980	January	247,000	241,650
	February	255,000	245,100
	March	271,000	249,700
	April	261,000	259,200
	May	258,000	261,200
	June	265,000	260,400
	July	250,000	263,250
	August	275,000	256,050
	September	245,000	265,550
	October	260,000	255,250
	November	255,000	257,500
	December	263,000	256,750

FIGURE 11.7   Simple moving average versus weighted moving average

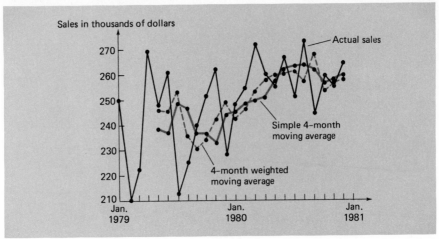

The major advantage of the moving-average technique is its simplicity, low cost, and little time necessary to implement. In general, however, the moving-average technique does a poor job for long-range and medium-range forecasts. For "quick-and-dirty" short-term forecasts that do not require a great deal of accuracy, a moving-average forecast may be a workable alternative to other forecasting methods.

EXPONENTIAL SMOOTHING

Exponential smoothing refers to a family of forecasting models that are very similar to the weighted moving average. The simplest exponential smoothing model is of the following form:

$$F_t = F_{t-1} + \alpha(A_{t-1} - F_{t-1})$$ [11.3]

where F_t = forecast for time period t
   A_{t-1} = actual value of variable being forecast in period $t - 1$
   α = smoothing constant

The value of α, which can range from 0 to 1, determines the degree of smoothing that takes place and how responsive the model is to fluctuation in the forecast variable. The setting of α is not a scientific process and is usually done by trial and error. Let us assume an α of .15 and a January 1980 forecast of 250 units. The actual January demand turned out to be 260 units. The forecast for February could be computed as follows:

TABLE 11.4   Effects of various smoothing constants

	Actual demand	Forecast: $\alpha = .05$	Forecast: $\alpha = .25$	Forecast: $\alpha = .4$
January	250	250	250	250
February	210	250.500	252.500	254.000
March	223	248.475	241.875	236.400
April	270	247.201	237.156	231.040
May	245	248.341	245.367	246.624
June	261	248.174	245.275	245.974
July	212	248.815	249.207	251.985
August	226	246.975	239.905	235.991
September	241	245.926	236.429	231.994
October	252	245.680	237.572	235.597
November	261	245.996	241.179	242.158
December	229	246.746	246.134	249.695

$$F_t = 250 + (.15)(260 - 250)$$
$$= 250 + 1.5$$
$$= 251.5 \text{ units}$$

Given the forecasts in Table 11.4, let us compare the effect of different smoothing constants by looking at Figure 11.8.

Other exponential smoothing models exist that compensate for the various components of a times series such as the seasonal or trend component. To illustrate more complex exponential smoothing models, let us con-

FIGURE 11.8   Effect of various smoothing constants

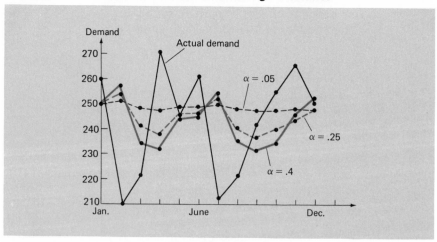

FIGURE 11.9 Trend lag

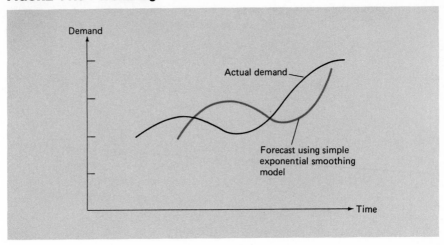

sider a model that has an adjustment for trend built into it. If trend exists in either a positive or a negative form, there will be a lag using the simple exponential smoothing model just described (see Figure 11.9). The basic idea behind the trend-adjusted model is to calculate a simple, exponentially smoothed forecast as described above and adjust the forecast for a trend lag.

Mathematically, the trend -adjusted model can be described as follows:

$$F'_t = F_t + \frac{1 - \beta}{\beta} T_t \qquad [11.4]$$

where F'_t = trend-adjusted forecast for time period t
F_t = simple exponential smoothing forecast for time period t
β = trend smoothing factor
T_t = exponentially smoothed trend for time period t

T_t is computed using the formula

$$T_t = T_{t-1} + \beta(t_t - T_{t-1}) \qquad [11.5]$$

where $t_t = F_t - F_{t-1}$.

To compute a trend-adjusted forecast is a four-step process:

1. Compute a simple forecast for time period t (F_t).
2. Compute t_t by finding the difference between F_t and F_{t-1}.

415

$$t_t = F_t - F_{t-1}$$

3. Calculate the exponentially smoothed trend.

$$T_t = T_{t-1} + \beta(t_t - T_{t-1})$$

4. Finally, calculate a trend-adjusted forecast by using the formula

$$F'_t = F_t + \frac{1 - \beta}{\beta} T_t$$

Let us illustrate how to compute a trend-adjusted, exponentially smoothed forecast using the demand data in Table 11.5 and smoothing constants α and β, equal to .3 and .25, respectively. Let the initial forecast be 11.5. The trend-adjusted forecast for period 2 is computed as follows:
The first step is to compute F_2:

$$\begin{aligned} F_2 &= F_1 + \alpha(A_1 - F_1) \\ &= 11.5 + .3(12 - 11.5) \\ &= 11.65 \end{aligned}$$

The next step is to calculate t_2:

$$\begin{aligned} t_2 &= F_2 - F_1 \\ &= 11.65 - 11.50 \\ &= .15 \end{aligned}$$

T_2 can now be calculated, assuming the initial trend adjustment is 0:

$$\begin{aligned} T_2 &= T_1 + \beta(t_2 - T_1) \\ &= 0 + .25(.15) \\ &= .0375 \end{aligned}$$

Finally, the trend-adjusted forecast for time period 2 can be computed:

$$\begin{aligned} F_2 &= F_2 + \frac{1 - .25}{.25} T_2 \\ &= 11.65 + 3(.0375) \\ &= 11.7625 \end{aligned}$$

Doing the same calculations for the remaining time periods for the time-series data shown in Table 11.5 results in the trend-adjusted forecasts reflected in Table 11.6. Figure 11.10 graphically contrasts the unadjusted and adjusted forecasts for the time series in Table 11.6.

TABLE 11.5 Time-series data in which trend is present

Period	Demand
1	12
1	12
2	17
3	19
4	16
5	22
6	24
7	30
8	29
9	33
10	34
11	37
12	38

Generally, exponential smoothing is considered superior to the moving-average methods previously discussed. Its cost is equivalent and its accuracy especially in the short term is usually better. Owing to their relatively small computational cost and computer storage requirement, exponential smoothing models are probably the most widely used of the time-series techniques. For longer-term forecasts, however, exponential smoothing is considered a poor technique.

TABLE 11.6 Trend-adjusted forecasts

Time period	Actual demand	F_t	t_t	T_t	F'_t
1	12	11.5000	0	0	11.5000
2	17	11.6500	.15000	.037500	11.7625
3	19	13.2550	1.60500	.429375	14.5431
4	16	14.9785	1.72350	.752906	17.2372
5	22	15.2849	3.06450	.641292	17.2088
6	24	17.2995	2.01451	.984598	20.2533
7	30	19.3096	2.01016	1.24099	23.0326
8	29	22.5167	3.20711	1.73252	27.7143
9	33	24.4617	1.94498	1.78563	29.8186
10	34	27.0232	2.56149	1.97960	32.9620
11	37	29.1162	2.09304	2.00796	35.1401
12	38	31.4814	2.36513	2.09725	37.7731

FIGURE 11.10 Time-series forecast with and without trend adjustment

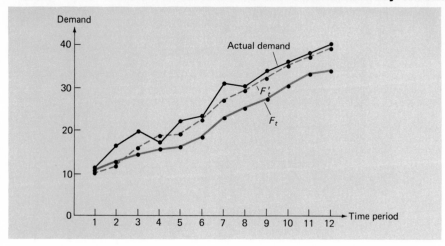

TREND PROJECTION

Trend projection using a technique called least squares is a special case of a category of causal forecasting methods called regression analysis. The basic idea in trend projection using least squares is to fit a function to a set of time-series data in which the independent variable is time and the dependent variable is the variable to be forecasted such as demand. This function can be linear or nonlinear and the basic idea and methodology are the same. In this chapter, however, we consider only linear trend projection.

Consider the scatter diagram in Figure 11.11. It is easy to imagine a straight line running through the data such that the sum of the differences between the data points and the trend line is minimized. If the equation of the trend line is a function of time, then it is a simple matter to "plug" a future time period into the function and calculate a forecast.

FIGURE 11.11 Scatter diagram

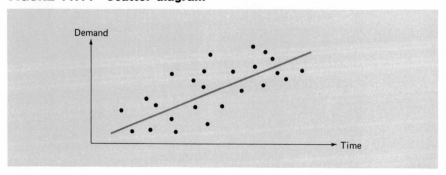

Recall that the general equation for a straight line is

$$y = mx + b \qquad\qquad [11.6]$$

where y = dependent variable
 b = y intercept
 m = slope of the line
 x = independent variable

See Figure 11.12 for a graphical interpretation of a straight line.

Now, if we define x as time and y as demand, and b (the y intercept) and m (slope of the line) are known, demand can be computed by merely letting x assume a value. For example, assume that the linear function is

$$y = 150x + 5{,}000$$

If 1981 is the tenth time period in the time series, the demand forecast for 1980 can be forecast, substituting 10 into the equation:

$$y = 150(10) + 5{,}000$$
$$= 6{,}500 \text{ units}$$

Now let us turn to the method of deriving the "best fit" linear equation for a set of time-series data. It is possible to find a line that provides a good fit of the data by merely "eyeballing" the scatter diagram and superimposing a line on it. Then, relying on the accuracy of the graph, a y intercept (b) can be read, and the slope of the line can be calculated as $\Delta y / \Delta x$.

FIGURE 11.12 Graph of linear equation

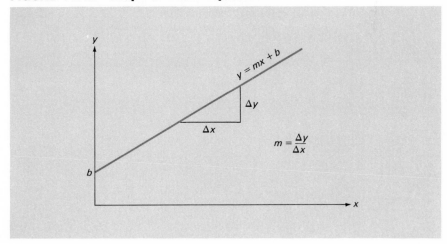

A more accurate way to find the linear equation that best fits the data is to solve the following equations simultaneously for b and m.

$$\sum_{i=1}^{n} y_i = nb + m \sum_{i=1}^{n} x_i \qquad [11.7]$$

$$\sum_{i=1}^{n} x_i y_i = b \sum_{i=1}^{n} x_i + m \sum_{i=1}^{n} x_i^2 \qquad [11.8]$$

where y_i = dependent variable for the ith time period
n = number of historical time periods
x_i = independent variable for the ith time period

normal equation Equations 11.7 and 11.8 are called *normal equations* and are derived using the differential calculus. To illustrate how the simple linear regression equation is found, let us use the data in Table 11.7.

dependent/ independent variable The *dependent variable* (y) is demand, whereas the time period is the *independent variable*. Looking at normal equations 11.7 and 11.8, it is clear that several sums are required. These values are computed in Table 11.8.

Substituting the appropriate sums into the two normal equations, we have the following two equations with two unknowns, b and m:

$$31,100 = 12b + 78m \qquad [11.9]$$

$$236,300 = 78b + 650m \qquad [11.10]$$

If we multiply both sides of equation 11.9 by 6.5 and subtract it from equation 11.10, the b terms will fall out:

TABLE 11.7   Historical demand data

Time period	Demand (units)
1	1,200
2	1,700
3	1,900
4	1,600
5	2,200
6	2,400
7	3,000
8	2,900
9	3,300
10	3,400
11	3,700
12	3,800

TABLE 11.8 Least-squares calculations

x_i	y_i	x_iy_i	x_i^2
1	1,200	1,200	1
2	1,700	3,400	4
3	1,900	5,700	9
4	1,600	6,400	16
5	2,200	11,000	25
6	2,400	14,400	36
7	3,000	21,000	49
8	2,900	23,200	64
9	3,300	29,700	81
10	3,400	34,000	100
11	3,700	40,700	121
12	3,800	45,600	144
78	31,100	236,300	650

$$236,300 = 78b + 650m$$
$$-\,202,150 = -78b - 507m$$
$$\overline{34,150 = 143m}$$

$$m = 238.811$$

Solving for b by substituting m into equation 11.9, we find

$$31,100 = 12b + 78(238.811)$$

$$b = 1,039.4$$

Therefore, the "best fit" linear forecasting equation is

$$y = 238.811x + 1,039.4 \qquad\qquad [11.11]$$

trend Once this equation has been derived, *trend extrapolation* is simply a
extrapolation mechanical procedure. If a prediction for the fourteenth time period is
desired, simply set x equal to 14 and solve for y using equation 11.11. The
forecast for time period 14 is therefore

$$y_{14} = 238.811(14) + 1,039.4$$
$$= 4,382.754$$

standard error If we compute a *standard error of estimate* to determine how well the
of estimate regression line fits the data, it is possible that more information about a
forecast can be obtained (see Figure 11.13). The standard error can be

421

FIGURE 11.13 Least-squares differences

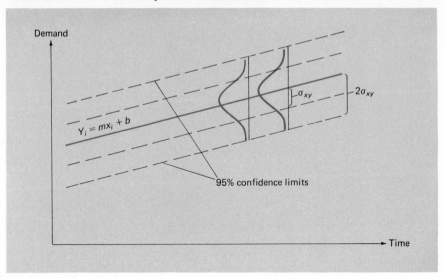

defined mathematically as

$$s_{yx} = \sqrt{\frac{\displaystyle\sum_{i=1}^{n} (y_i - Y_i)^2}{n - 2}}$$

where y_i = dependent variable for time period i
 (in our example, demand)
 Y_i = value for the dependent variable obtained
 from the regression equation
 n = number of historical time periods

To compute the standard error of estimate, we merely do the computation necessary to complete Table 11.9, using the data in Table 11.7 and the regression equation 11.11.

If we assume that demand is normally distributed around the regression line as depicted in Figure 11.13 and want 95.5 percent of the demand values to fall within our prediction interval, the prediction interval can be calculated as follows:

$$\text{prediction interval for } Y_i = Y_i \pm 2s_{yx}$$

where Y_i = regression equation value
 s_{yx} = standard error of estimate

TABLE 11.9 Standard error computation

x_i	y_i	Y_i	$y_i - Y_i$	$(y_i - Y_i)^2$
1	1,200	1,278.21	−78.211	6,116.96
2	1,700	1,517.02	182.978	33,480.90
3	1,900	1,755.83	144.167	20,784.10
4	1,600	1,994.64	−394.644	15,574.40
5	2,200	2,233.45	−33.455	1,119.24
6	2,400	2,472.27	−72.266	5,222.37
7	3,000	2,711.08	288.923	83,476.50
8	2,900	2,949.89	−49.888	2,488.81
9	3,300	3,188.70	111.301	12,387.90
10	3,400	3,427.51	−27.510	756.80
11	3,700	3,666.32	33.679	1,134.28
12	3,800	3,905.13	−105.132	11,052.70
				333,765.00

$$s_{yx} = \sqrt{\frac{333,765}{10}}$$
$$= 182.692$$

In our example:

$$\text{prediction interval for } Y_{14} = 4,382.754 \pm 2(182.692)$$
$$= 4,382.754 \pm 365.384$$

or

$$4,017.37 \leq Y_{14} \leq 4,748.14$$

Remember that we calculated Y_i and s_{yx} using historical data, and to say we are 95.5 percent confident that demand for time period 14 will fall between 4,017 and 4,748 units is to assume that the future is going to behave like the past. Also, a sample size of 12 is too small to assume normality, and a student's t distribution should be used when the sample size is small.

Simple linear regression using time period as the independent variable generally outperforms both moving average and exponential smoothing techniques with regard to forecast accuracy. Usually, very good short-term forecasts can be derived using trend projections, and often, good long-term forecasts can be based on least squares trend projections. If the historical data are available, the cost of the forecast is minimal and the time lapse required to derive the forecast is often less than one day.

In general, time-series methods such as those discussed in this section provide fairly accurate and very inexpensive short-term forecasts. It is therefore very common for one or more of these techniques to be integrated into computerized multiproduct inventory systems such as IBM's IMPACT system. In automated multiproduct inventory systems in which forecasts are automatically generated using a time-series technique such as exponential smoothing, it is necessary to consistently monitor the forecasting process to report to management when the forecast and actual demand for a time period differ significantly. This discrepancy may be due to keypunch errors, extraordinary market conditions, or the unsatisfactory performance of the forecasting technique. Whatever the reason, management must be alerted through some type of exception reporting that there is a need to investigate a product's forecast versus its demand and take the appropriate corrective action.

CAUSAL METHODS

When a particular forecast is of vital importance to an organization and adequate historical data exist, it is often advisable to develop a causal forecasting model in which the variable to be forecast is a function of several or many causal variables. Sales may be a function of price, advertising budget, competitors' actions, quality control budget, disposable personal income, or other independent variables. If the relationship between these independent variables can be adequately defined mathematically, superior forecasts can result. Causal models are the most sophisticated type of forecasting model and generally require more data, more time, and substantially more money than the time series approaches discussed earlier.

There are two predominant causal forecasting methods:

1. Multiple regression models
2. Econometric models

MULTIPLE REGRESSION MODELS

Multiple regression analysis is a simple extension of simple linear regression. The difference is that instead of one independent variable in the regression equation, there are several or many independent variables. The general form of a multiple regression equation is

$$Y = \sum_{i=1}^{n} a_i x_i + b$$

where a_i = coefficient of independent variable x_i
b = constant

x_i = independent variable
Y = forecast variable
n = number of independent variables

The method for deriving a multiple regression equation is analogous to the simple linear case and will not be described in this text. Instead, let us look at the following example.

A typewriter manufacturing firm wishes to forecast demand for 2 years' maintenance contracts for its most popular typewriter. It is felt that demand is a function of the advertising budget, the premium for a 1-year contract, the premium for a 2-year contract, and trend. Historical data for the last 10 years are available; they are shown in Table 11.10. These data were used to derive the following regression equation:

$$Y = .05085x_1 + 4.01746x_2 - 7.26361x_3 + 433.175784x_4 + 5,226.50$$

where Y = demand for two-year maintenance contracts
x_1 = annual advertising budget
x_2 = premium for 1-year contract
x_3 = premium for 2-year contract
x_4 = time period, using 1970 as time period 1

In order to calculate a forecast for 1981, values for x_1, x_2, x_3, and x_4 must be set. If the advertising budget for 1981 is set at \$90,000, the premium

TABLE 11.10   Maintenance contracts sales data

Year	Number of 2-year contracts sold	Annual advertising budget	Premium for 1-year contract	Premium for 2-year contract
1970	5,000	$50,000	$250	$550
1971	6,000	50,000	250	500
1972	6,500	55,000	250	550
1973	7,000	55,000	300	600
1974	6,000	45,000	300	650
1975	7,500	60,000	350	650
1976	8,000	60,000	300	650
1977	9,000	70,000	300	600
1978	10,000	75,000	325	550
1979	10,500	75,000	325	550
1980	12,000	80,000	325	500

for a 1-year contract at \$325, and the premium for a 2-year contract at \$550, then forecast demand can be calculated as

$$
\begin{aligned}
D = &(.05085)(90,000) + (4.01746)(325) - (7.26361)(550) + (433.17578)(12) \\
&+ 5,226.50 \\
= &12,311.80 \text{ contracts}
\end{aligned}
$$

Generally, multiple regression is less expensive but unfortunately frequently less accurate than econometric models. In other words, multiple regression is not as "quick-and-dirty" a method of forecasting as are the time-series techniques discussed earlier, but it is quicker and dirtier than econometric models.

ECONOMETRIC MODELS

An econometric model is a system of interdependent equations that describe some real phenomenon. For example, consider the following three-equation, eight-variable macroeconomic model:

$$
\begin{aligned}
C_t &= x_1 I_t + x_3 Y_t + x_4 C_{t-1} + x_5 R_t + U_1 \\
I_t &= \beta_1 + \beta_2 Y_t + \beta_3 R_t + U_2 \\
Y_t &= C_t + I_t + G_t
\end{aligned}
$$

where C_t = aggregate consumption in time period t
$\quad I_t$ = gross investment in time period t
$\quad Y_t$ = gross national product in time period t
$\quad G_t$ = government spending in time period t
$\quad R_t$ = short-term interest rate
$\quad U_t$ = error terms
$\quad x_i$ = parameter estimates for first equation
$\quad \beta_i$ = parameter estimates for second equation

These equations are solved simultaneously to find the values for unknown variables C_t, I_t, and Y_t.

Econometric models are used extensively in economic forecasting, and some of the models are very complex, with hundreds of variables and hundreds of simultaneous equations. These models often provide superior forecasts but are very costly and time-consuming to build and to maintain. The Wharton School econometric model, for example, has over 200 equations and 80 exogenous variables and cost thousands of dollars to develop and more thousands to maintain.

SUMMARY

Surveys have shown that forecasting techniques are the most widely used of all quantitative techniques in business.[1] This is not surprising when one looks at the importance of a good forecast to the health of an organization in the business or public sector. Almost all managerial decisions are based on forecasted information. In a business firm, financial decisions, marketing decisions, production decisions, and personnel decisions are all based on the firm's outlook of the future. Policy decisions of governments and nonprofit organizations are equally dependent on quality forecasts.

In this chapter, we have described the major forecasting methods and indicated areas of applicability. We divided forecasting methods into three categories: qualitative methods, time-series analysis techniques, and causal methods. In general, qualitative techniques are used when quantitative historical data are not available. Time-series-analysis techniques are used when the importance of the forecast is not great enough to justify the use of more expensive causal methods. Time-series techniques have found wide usage in automated multiproduct inventory systems. Causal methods are used when their extra cost and time of implementation can be justified by the importance to the organization of the forecast accuracy.

SOLVED PROBLEMS

PROBLEM STATEMENT

For the demand data in Table 11.11, calculate the four-quarter moving average for the fourth quarter of 1980 and the first quarter of 1981.

SOLUTION

$$\text{forecast for the 4th quarter of 1980} = \frac{50{,}000 + 65{,}000 + 75{,}000 + 80{,}000}{4}$$

$$= 67{,}500 \text{ units}$$

---

[1]George Thomas and Jo-Anne Da Costa, "A Sample Survey of Corporate Operations Research," *Interfaces,* 9 (August 1979).

TABLE 11.11 Calculator demand

Time period	TI-53 calculator demand (units)
1st quarter 1977	1,000
2nd quarter 1977	2,500
3rd quarter 1977	3,000
4th quarter 1977	4,000
1st quarter 1978	10,000
2nd quarter 1978	12,000
3rd quarter 1978	15,000
4th quarter 1978	14,000
1st quarter 1979	20,000
2nd quarter 1979	25,000
3rd quarter 1979	40,000
4th quarter 1979	50,000
1st quarter 1980	65,000
2nd quarter 1980	75,000
3rd quarter 1980	80,000
4th quarter 1980	100,000

$$\text{forecast for the 1st quarter of 1981} = \frac{65,000 + 75,000 + 80,000 + 100,000}{4}$$

$$= 80,000 \text{ units}$$

PROBLEM STATEMENT

Using a weighted five-quarter moving average with the weights as shown below, calculate the forecast for the first quarter of 1981 for Table 11.11 data.

	Period	Weight
Oldest data	1	.05
	2	.10
	3	.15
	4	.25
Most recent data	5	.45

SOLUTION

The forecast for the first quarter of 1981 is computed as follows:

$$F = \frac{(.05)(50{,}000 + (.1)(65{,}000) + (.15)(75{,}000) + (.25)(80{,}000) + (.45)(100{,}000)}{1.00}$$

$$= 85{,}250 \text{ units}$$

PROBLEM STATEMENT

Using a simple exponential smoothing model, calculate the forecast for the first quarter of 1981, given that the forecast for the last quarter of 1980 was 80,250 units. Use $\alpha = .15$.

SOLUTION

The exponentially smoothed forecast for the first quarter of 1981 is computed as follows:

$$F_t = F_{t-1} + \alpha(A_{t-1} - F_{t-1})$$
$$= 80{,}250 + .15(100{,}000 - 80{,}250)$$
$$= 83{,}212.5 \text{ units}$$

PROBLEM STATEMENT

Using a trend-adjusted exponential smoothing model, calculate the forecast for the first quarter of 1981. Use a smoothing factor of .15 for the simple model forecast and a smoothing factor of .1 for the trend-smoothing factor.

SOLUTION

The first step is to calculate the simple exponential smoothing forecast for the first quarter of 1981. This was accomplished in the preceding example:

$$F_t = 80{,}250 + .15(100{,}000 - 80{,}250)$$
$$= 83{,}212.5 \text{ units}$$

The next step is to calculate t_t:

$$t_t = F_t - F_{t-1}$$

$$t_t = 83{,}212.5 - 80{,}250$$
$$= 2{,}962.5$$

Now we must calculate T_t, assuming that the initial trend adjustment is 0.

$$T_t = T_{t-1} + \beta(t_t - T_{t-1})$$
$$= 0 + .1(2{,}962.5)$$
$$= 296.25$$

Finally, the trend-adjusted forecast for the first quarter of 1981 can be computed as follows:

$$F'_t = F_t + \frac{1 - \beta}{\beta}T_t$$

$$= 83{,}212.5 + \left(\frac{1 - .1}{.1}\right)296.25$$
$$= 83{,}212.5 + 2{,}666.25$$
$$= 85{,}878.75 \text{ units}$$

PROBLEM STATEMENT

Using the least-squares method, find the regression line for the data in Table 11.11 and calculate the forecast for the first quarter of 1981.

SOLUTION

In order to derive the regression equation, it is necessary to solve the following two normal equations simultaneously:

$$\sum_{i=1}^{n} y_i = nb + m \sum_{i=1}^{n} x_i$$

$$\sum_{i=1}^{n} x_i y_i = b \sum_{i=1}^{n} x_i + m \sum_{i=1}^{n} x_i^2$$

In order to solve the two equations simultaneously, the four sums in the two equations must first be found. This is done in Table 11.12.

Substituting these sums into the two normal equations, we get

$$516{,}500 = 16b + 136m$$

$$6{,}535{,}000 = 136b + 1{,}496m$$

To find what factor to multiply the first equation by to add it to the second to eliminate the b terms, we divide 136 by 16, getting 8.5. Therefore, if we multiply the first equation by -8.5 and add it to the second equation, we get

TABLE 11.12

x_i	y_i	$x_i y_i$	y_i^2
1	1,000	1,000	1
2	2,500	5,000	4
3	3,000	9,000	9
4	4,000	16,000	16
5	10,000	50,000	25
6	12,000	72,000	36
7	15,000	105,000	49
8	14,000	112,000	64
9	20,000	180,000	81
10	25,000	250,000	100
11	40,000	440,000	121
12	50,000	600,000	144
13	65,000	845,000	169
14	75,000	1,050,000	196
15	80,000	1,200,000	225
16	100,000	1,600,000	256
136	516,500	6,535,000	1,496

$$6,535,000 = 136b + 1,496m$$
$$\underline{-4,390,250 = -136b - 1,156m}$$
$$2,144,750 = 340m$$

Therefore,

$$m = \frac{2,144,750}{340}$$
$$= 6,308.0882$$

Once we have the value of one unknown, we can substitute it into either normal equation to find the other unknown. Hence,

$$6,535,000 = 136b + (1,496)(6,308.0882)$$
$$6,535,000 = 136b + 9,436,900$$
$$136b = -2,901,900$$
$$b = -21,337.5$$

We can now write the regression equation:

$$Y = 6,308.0882x - 21,337.5$$

To calculate first quarter 1981 demand, we merely plug in the x value corresponding to the first quarter 1981, which is 17.

$$\text{demand for 1st quarter 1981} = Y = (6{,}308.0882)(17) - 2{,}133.75$$
$$= 85{,}900 \text{ units}$$

PROBLEM STATEMENT

Management of the calculator manufacturing firm feels that in addition to time period, the demand for calculators is also a function of price. After price data for the 16 time periods were fed into a multiple regression software package on the company computer, the following regression equation was produced:

$$Y = 8121x_1 - 1{,}045x_2 - 5{,}525$$

where x_1 = time period
x_2 = price
Y = demand

What is the forecast for the first quarter of 1981 if the price of the TI-53 calculator is \$14.95?

SOLUTION

Forecasting demand for first quarter 1981 is a mechanical procedure of plugging the multiple regression equation with values of the independent variables:

$$Y = 8{,}121(17) - 1{,}045(14.95) - 5{,}525$$
$$= 116{,}909.25 \text{ units}$$

REVIEW QUESTIONS

1. Define the three basic time horizons for forecasts.
2. List the three categories of forecasting techniques described in this chapter.
3. When are qualitative forecasting techniques most useful?
4. What is the major advantage of time-series analysis?
5. How do causal methods differ from time-series analysis?
6. What is the major disadvantage of time-series analysis?

7. Which category of forecasting technique performs best for long-term forecasts?

8. List four factors to consider in selecting the proper forecasting techniques.

9. List five commonly used qualitative forecasting techniques.

10. Define the Delphi method.

11. Which of the qualitative forecasting techniques discussed in this chapter is the most sophisticated and the most expensive?

12. Which qualitative forecasting technique is generally considered to yield the most accurate forecasts?

13. How does panel consensus differ from a "grass-roots" approach?

14. Using a historical analogy approach depends on what?

15. What is a time series?

16. What are the four major components of a time series?

17. To what planning horizon is time-series analysis best suited?

18. Distinguish between moving average, exponential smoothing, and trend projection.

19. What is the effect of changing the smoothing constant?

20. Why is simple exponential smoothing inadequate when trend exists in time-series data?

21. Write the equation of a straight line and define each parameter and variable.

22. Why is it desirable to calculate the standard error of estimate?

23. Distinguish between simple linear regression and multiple regression.

PROBLEMS

11.1   Calculate the 4-year simple moving average for 1981, using the time-series data in Table 11.13.

11.2   For the data in Table 11.13, calculate a 6-year weighted moving average for 1981, using the following weights: .1, .1, .1, .2, .2, and .3 from the oldest to the most recent year.

11.3   Using an α of .25, calculate the 1981 forecast using the simple exponential smoothing model. Use the data in Table 11.13 and assume a 1980 forecast of $500,000.

11.4   Using trial-and-error techniques, determine the best α .10 or .25 for the data in Table 11.13. Assume a 1962 forecast of 250,000.

TABLE 11.13   Time-series data

Year	Sales
1962	$250,000
1963	262,000
1964	300,000
1965	351,000
1966	364,000
1967	365,000
1968	377,000
1969	402,000
1970	393,000
1971	400,000
1972	425,000
1973	415,000
1974	430,000
1975	440,000
1976	455,000
1977	457,000
1978	481,000
1979	492,000
1980	505,000

11.5   Again using Table 11.13 data, calculate the 1981 forecast using the trend-adjusted exponential smoothing model. Assume $\alpha = .15$, $\beta = .20$, and a 1980 forecast of $500,000.

11.6   For Problem 11.5 find an α and β that you think do a good job of forecasting sales by writing and running a computer search program.

11.7   Draw a scatter diagram for the time-series data of Table 11.13.

11.8   Using the method of least squares, find the regression equation for the time-series data in Table 11.13. Use the regression equation to forecast sales for 1982.

11.9   Find the interval estimate for the regression equation derived in problem 11.8 corresponding to a 95.5% confidence level. Assume normality.

11.10   Given the data in Table 11.14, compare a 6-month moving-average forecast and a 3-month moving average forecast for the 12 months of 1980.

11.11   Choose weights for a 6-month moving average that do a better job of forecasting demand than the simple 6-month moving average calculated in Problem 11.10.

11.12   Which is the better smoothing constant for the 1980 data in Table 11.14, $\alpha = .05$ or $\alpha = .25$? Justify your answer.

11.13 By a limited search procedure, define a good trend-adjusted exponential smoothing model for the 1980 time-series data in Table 11.14.

11.14 Write a computer program that will accomplish the search required by Problem 11.13.

11.15 Draw a scatter diagram of the time-series data of Table 11.14 on graph paper and "eyeball" a regression line. Read the slope and intercept off the graph to construct the regression equation.

11.16 Find the simple linear regression equation for the Table 11.14 data using the least-squares method.

11.17 How do the January 1981 demand forecasts differ using the "eyeballed" equation and the least-squares equation derived in Problem 11.16?

11.18 Given a confidence level of 90%, what is the prediction interval for demand for February 1981?

11.19 The number of pediatric admissions for 1 month can be forecasted using the following regression equation:

TABLE 11.14   Time-series data for Part No. 215-22000

Year	Month	Demand
1979	January	25,450
	February	25,000
	March	25,150
	April	24,950
	May	24,500
	June	24,600
	July	24,250
	August	23,000
	September	23,100
	October	22,900
	November	22,000
	December	19,500
1980	January	19,750
	February	18,950
	March	19,150
	April	18,740
	May	18,500
	June	18,250
	July	17,475
	August	17,500
	September	17,650
	October	17,250
	November	17,100
	December	16,550

$$Y = 5.1 + 5.72x_1 + .002x_2 + 4.16x_3$$

where Y = number of pediatric admissions for 1 month
x_1 = number of pediatricians on the hospital staff
x_2 = city population of people under 20
x_3 = number of obstetricians on the hospital staff

If the hospital has seven pediatricians and nine obstetricians and the under-20 population is 14,000, what is the monthly forecast for pediatrics admissions?

11.20 *Sales Forecast.* The ACME Corporation has experienced steady growth in annual sales in its 19-year history. The firm has traditionally used a 4-year moving average to predict sales for the coming year. The new vice-president of marketing feels that a simple 4-year moving average is too "simple minded" and results in extremely poor sales forecasts. Because these inaccuracies affect many important managerial decisions, the vice-president of marketing has asked you to determine the best time-series technique for estimating sales by comparing

a. The 4-year moving average.

b. A weighted 6-year moving average using the following weights: .1, .1, .1, .2, .2, .3 from the oldest to the most recent year.

c. A simple exponential smoothing model using an α of .25. Assume a 1962 forecast of $247,000.

Acme Corporation Annual Sales

1962	$247,000
1963	251,000
1964	257,000
1965	259,000
1966	271,000
1967	275,000
1968	295,000
1969	289,000
1970	287,000
1971	305,000
1972	328,000
1973	345,000
1974	370,000
1975	387,000
1976	404,000
1977	405,000
1978	419,000
1979	417,000

    d. A trend-adjusted exponential smoothing model using an $\alpha = .15$ and $\beta = .20$.

    e. A least-squares regression equation.

11.21 *Market Price Forecast.* The price of IBM Corporation has varied over the past year. The price at the end of each month is reflected in the table.

Month	Price per share	Month	Price per share
1	$55\frac{1}{8}$	7	$68\frac{3}{4}$
2	$57\frac{1}{4}$	8	$69\frac{1}{8}$
3	$57\frac{1}{2}$	9	$72\frac{1}{8}$
4	$59\frac{3}{8}$	10	$72\frac{3}{8}$
5	65	11	$72\frac{1}{8}$
6	$63\frac{1}{4}$	12	$75\frac{1}{5}$

    a. Draw a scatter diagram for these data.

    b. Forecast the next month's price per share using simple linear regression.

    c. Forecast next month's price per share using a trend adjusted exponential smoothing model with $\alpha = .2$ and $\beta = .3$. Assume $F_{12} = \$74.00$ per share and $T_{12} = 0$.

11.22 *Business Failures.* The small computer service bureau business is a very volatile and risk-ridden sector of the economy. In a large southwestern city the number of service bureaus going out of business in the last 3 years has been extremely high. The number of failures for each quarter of the previous 3 years is reflected in the table.

	1978		1979		1980
Quarter	Number of Failures	Quarter	Number of Failures	Quarter	Number of Failures
1	27	1	30	1	35
2	29	2	35	2	42
3	40	3	49	3	57
4	35	4	40	4	47

    a. What is your forecast for each quarter of 1981 using only the time-series data given and a trend adjusted exponential smoothing model with an $\alpha = .25$ and a $\beta = .15$.

    b. If the data were available, what other factors do you think would have an effect on service bureau bankruptcies?

11.23   *Gasoline Prices.* The price of gasoline in the United States has increased dramatically over the last 3 years. Using exponential smoothing only and the price data in the table, predict gasoline prices for January of 1981. Assume a January 1978 forecast of .50 and an $\alpha = .4$ and $\beta = .2$.

	Number of violent crimes		
Month	1978	1979	1980
January	12	19	35
February	11	22	32
March	14	21	37
April	13	25	38
May	13	23	41
June	15	25	40
July	16	24	45
August	15	27	38
September	18	26	47
October	17	18	49
November	18	23	48
December	20	30	55

11.24   *Crime.* Crime in the streets has been increasing in the last 3 years at a dramatic rate, and the mayor and the city council are trying to decide on what action to take to alleviate the situation. The police chief contends that if something isn't done soon, the number of violent crimes reported in a month will reach epidemic proportions. Using simple linear regression, predict the number of violent crimes that will be committed for January, June, and December of 1981.

	Demand (units)	
Month	1978	1979
January	12,150	10,002
February	12,043	10,041
March	12,220	9,679
April	11,980	9,683
May	11,570	9,555
June	11,245	9,145
July	11,247	8,512
August	11,050	8,672
September	10,550	8,444
October	10,600	8,554
November	10,243	8,312
December	10,076	8,001

11.25 *Unemployment.* The unemployment rate in the United States for the years 1977, 1978, and 1979 has fluctuated as shown in the table. Which, if any, time-series techniques would you apply to the data to predict unemployment levels for 1980? How would you improve your forecast?

	Unemployment rates in the United States		
Quarter	1977	1978	1979
1st	7.46	6.2	5.73
2nd	7.1	6.0	5.73
3rd	6.9	5.96	6.10
4th	6.63	5.83	6.21

11.26 *University Enrollment.* Enrollment in the College of Business Administration at State University has been increasing in the last few years. The dean of the college is preparing a 5-year plan in which he is asking the university's central administration for significant increases in human and financial resources. These requested resources are based on the dean's forecast of future enrollments in the College of Business. Given semester enrollment for the last 5 years, what is your best estimate of full-time equivalent (FTE) enrollment at the end of the next 5 years? Use simple linear regression. What is wrong with using a simple time-series forecast to predict enrollment at the end of 1985?

	Full-time equivalent enrollment	
Year	Semester 1	Semester 2
1976	1,077	998
1977	1,117	1,103
1978	1,353	1,297
1979	1,471	1,419
1980	1,503	1,475

11.27 For the sales data in Table 11.13, find an α and β that you think do a good job of forecasting sales by writing and running a computer search program. Does this trend-adjusted model outperform the least-squares regression equation found in Problem 11.8?

11.28 *Demand.* ZUKON manufacturing company held a patent on their number 1 selling product until 2 years ago. Since that time, demand has been decreasing. Monthly demand for the last 2 years is reflected in the table.

	Gasoline Prices		
Month	1978	1979	1980
January	$.55	$ .88	$1.21
February	.55	.89	1.25
March	.56	.89	1.25
April	.56	.89	1.25
May	.56	.93	1.26
June	.56	.95	1.28
July	.58	.95	1.30
August	.58	.95	1.30
September	.58	.95	1.30
October	.57	.98	1.35
November	.58	.99	1.35
December	.58	1.00	1.35

a. Use the least-squares method to develop a simple linear regression equation.

b. Draw a scatter diagram and visually fit a straight line to the data.

c. Using the regression equation in part a, forecast demand for April 1981.

d. What is your forecast for the total demand for 1981?

11.29 For the time-series data in Problem 11.28, define a good trend-adjusted exponential smoothing model. Is your model a more accurate forecasting model than the least-squares model developed in Problem 11.28?

11.30 For the time-series data in Problem 11.28, define a good weighted-moving-average model. Is this model superior to either the exponential smoothing model of Problem 11.29 or the least-squares model of Problem 11.28?

BIBLIOGRAPHY

Adam, Everett E., and Ronald J. Ebert, *Production and Operations Management.* Englewood Cliffs, N.J.: Prentice-Hall, Inc., 1978.

Bright, James R., ed., *Technological Forecasting for Industry and Government Methods and Applications.* Englewood Cliffs, N.J.: Prentice-Hall, Inc., 1968.

Brown, Robert G., *Smoothing, Forecasting, and Prediction of Descrete Time Series.* Englewood Cliffs, N.J.: Prentice-Hall, Inc., 1962.

Chambers, J., S. K. Mullich, and D. D. Smith, "How to Choose the Right Forecasting Technique," *Harvard Business Review* (July–August 1971).

Chase, Richard B., and Nicholas J. Aquilano, *Production and Operations Management*. Homewood, Ill.: Richard D. Irwin, Inc., 1977.

Chow, Wen M., "Adaptive Control of the Exponential Smoothing Constant," *Journal of Industrial Engineering*, 16 (September–October 1965), 314–317.

Clark, Charles T., and Lawrence, L. Schkade, *Statistical Methods for Business and Economics*. Cincinnati, Ohio: South-Western Publishing Company, 1977.

Hoel, Paul G., and Raymond J. Jessen, *Basic Statistics for Business and Economics*. New York: John Wiley & Sons, Inc., 1977.

Monks, Joseph G., *Operations Management: Theory and Problems*. New York: McGraw-Hill Book Company, 1977.

Parker, G. C., and Edelberto L. Segura, "How to Get a Better Forecast," *Harvard Business Review*, 49 (March–April 1971), 99–109.

Shore, Barry, *Operations Management*. New York: McGraw-Hill Book Company, 1977.

12
Queuing Models

THE XEROX CORPORATION[1]

"Run off a Xerox copy ..." is evidence of the dominant role the Xerox Corporation plays in the office copier and duplicator marketplace. A major reason for this dominance has been attributed to the service that Xerox provides to its customers. In a recent application of queuing theory, Xerox has implemented a new service strategy for the 9200 duplicator which provides better customer service at less cost to Xerox.

Until the announcement of the Model 9200 duplicating system, Xerox copying machines were "convenience" machines, which dictated a certain level of service. Because the Model 9200 is directed at the offset printing market, it was designed as a revenue-generating system. Downtime changed from being an inconvenience to the customer to a genuine loss of revenue. Because of the increased impact of an inoperable machine, Xerox found it necessary to reorganize their service organization. Prior to the Model 9200 introduction, the national service department of Xerox was organized according to one-person territories. Because of the change brought about by the Model 9200 introduction, the one-person territory strategy was uneconomical and had to be discarded. It was decided that miniteams of technical representatives should replace the one-person territory strategy. The critical question was: How many technical representatives should comprise one team? Using analytical queuing models such as those described in this chapter, Xerox found that three-person miniteams yield the best balance between customer response times and tech rep utilization. By using queuing analysis, Xerox was able to reduce service cost for the Model 9200 duplicating system by almost 50 percent and at the same time improve customer service so that response times for customer-initiated service calls could be specified to prospective customers.

---

[1]W. H. Bleuel, "Management Science's Impact on Service Strategy," *Interfaces*, 6, Part 2 (November 1975), 1–12.

INTRODUCTION

queuing system Queue is another name for a waiting line, and a *queuing system* is simply a system that involves a waiting line. *Queuing theory* is a branch of management science that enables the analyst to describe the behavior of queuing systems.

queuing theory

It is clear that each of us comes in contact with many queuing systems every day. If you have ever taken a trip by airplane, you have been a member of many queues by the time the trip is over. First, you waited to obtain the services of a ticket agent. Then, the agent joined a queue to find out if the flight you wanted was full. After buying your ticket, you had to wait in line to check in at the gate where the flight was boarding. Next, you waited to board; and once on board, your plane became a member of the queue of planes waiting to use the runway for takeoff. Eventually, the plane was circling the destination airport, waiting to land. Once on the ground, the plane may have had to wait for an unloading gate; and then, you had to wait to deplane. Finally, there was the wait for luggage and possibly, a taxi.

The point is that the occasions for applying queuing theory are numerous and varied. When people who design systems that contain queues use queuing theory or digital simulation to estimate expected waiting calling units times, queue lengths, and so on, members of the queue, (or *calling units*) spend less time waiting in line.

For a sample list of queuing applications, see Table 12.1.

TABLE 12.1 Queuing applications

System	Calling units	Servers
Toll road	Automobiles, trucks, etc.	Toll booth
Machine shop	Jobs	Machine centers
Machine shop	Machines	Repairmen
Doctor's office	Patients	Nurse, doctor, lab, etc.
Computer system	Jobs, programs, messages	Computer
Class registration	Students	Student advisers
Ski resort	Skiers	Ski lifts
Harbor	Ships	Tugs, port facilities
Criminal court	Cases	Trial
Restaurant	Customers, orders	Tables, waiters, kitchen
Telephone	Callers	Switching equipment
Auto body shop	Wrecked automobiles	Body repair area, painting area
Professor's office	Students	Professor

The queuing analysis we undertake in this chapter is different in nature from some of the optimization techniques, such as linear programming, that you have already studied. Queuing theory does not address optimization problems directly. Rather, it uses elements of statistics and mathematics for the construction of models that describe the important descriptive statistics of a queuing system. This statistical description of the operation of the queuing system then becomes part of the data upon which optimization decisions are based. The queuing system descriptive statistics include such factors as the expected waiting time of the calling units, the expected length of the line, and the percentage of idle time for *service* the *service facility* (the source of goods or services for which the calling *facility* units wait).

When queuing theory is applied, management's objective is usually to minimize two kinds of costs: those associated with providing service and those associated with waiting time. After queuing theory has generated its statistical interpretation of the queuing system, the analyst assesses the various costs of providing service versus the costs of customer waiting in order to design the system that best meets the objectives of the organization.

THE QUEUING SYSTEM

As you can see in Figure 12.1, there are four parts of any queuing system—the calling population, the queue, the service facility, and the served calling units. Three of these entities have certain properties and characteristics that must be considered before appropriate modeling schemes can be formulated. We shall describe the calling population, the queue, and the service facility in some detail. In general, served calling units merely leave, or exit, the system.

FIGURE 12.1 Queuing system

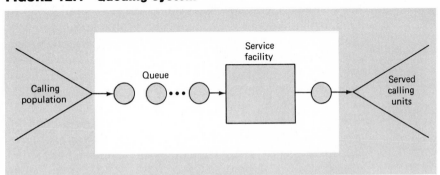

FIGURE 12.2 Calling population characteristics

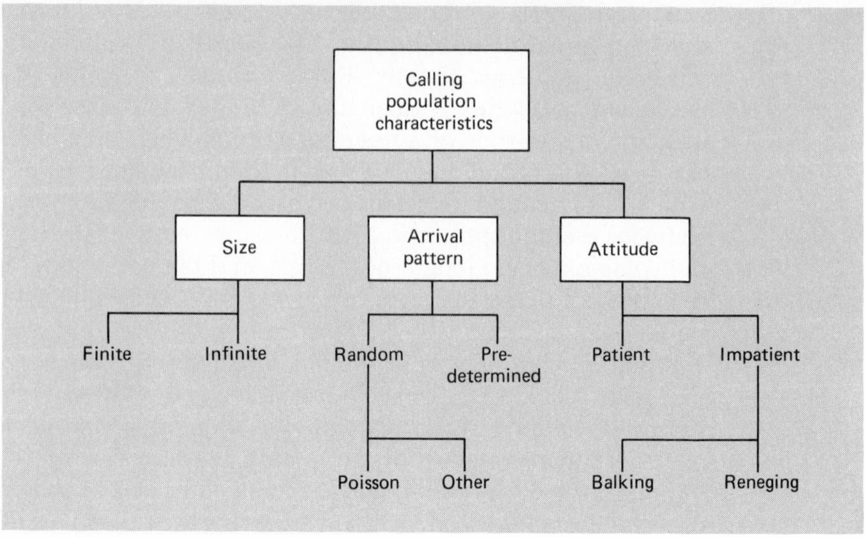

CHARACTERISTICS OF THE CALLING POPULATION

As shown in Figure 12.2, the calling population, often referred to as the *input source,* has three characteristics that are important to consider when deciding on what type of queuing model to apply:

1. The size of the calling population
2. The pattern of arrivals at the queuing system
3. The attitude of the calling units

Size of the calling population   This factor has a dramatic effect on the choice of queuing models. (Compare the number of alternatives associated with infinite versus finite calling populations in Figure 12.3.) Queuing systems in which the calling population can be considered *infinite* in size are generally more likely to be amenable to analytical modeling. Examples of infinite calling populations in queuing systems are cars on a toll road and patients at the emergency room of a hospital. It is much more difficult to derive queuing models that can be applied to systems in which the calling populations are very limited. Examples of *finite,* or *limited-source, queuing systems* include three in-house computers that must be serviced by a custom engineer if they break down and students who may take advantage of a professor's office hours for help in a specific course.

     The key to determining whether you can assume an infinite calling population is whether the probability of an arrival is significantly changed

infinite calling population

finite calling population

when a member or members of the population are receiving service and thus cannot arrive to the system. If there are only three calling units in a calling population and one is receiving service, the probability of another arrival is significantly reduced because the size of the calling population is cut by 33.3 percent. In general, a calling population greater than 200 in size is treated as infinite in queuing applications.

random
arrivals

Pattern of arrivals   Calling units arrive at the queuing system either according to some predetermined schedule or in a *random* fashion. If arrivals are scheduled, such as patients at a dentist's office, analytical queuing models are usually inappropriate. If arrivals are random, it is necessary to determine the probability distribution of the time between arrivals. It has been shown mathematically that if the probability density function of the interarrival times is exponential, calling units arrive according to a so-called *Poisson process*. Poisson arrivals are very common

Poisson
process

FIGURE 12.3   A representative sample of elementary queuing models

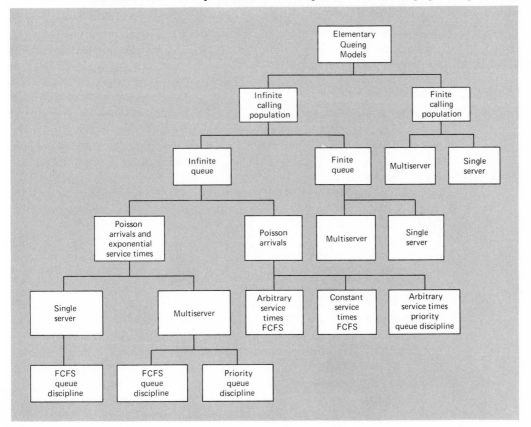

in queuing systems. They generally exist in situations where the number of arrivals during a certain time interval is independent of the number of arrivals that have occurred in previous time intervals. This basic property states that the conditional probability of any future event depends only on the present state of the system and is independent of previous states of the system. The *Poisson probability density function* gives the probability of *n* arrivals in time period *t*. The mathematical form of the Poisson probability function is

Poisson probability density function

$$P_n(t) = \frac{e^{-\lambda t}(\lambda t)^n}{n!} \qquad n = 0, 1, 2, \ldots$$

where n = number of arrivals
t = size of the time interval
λ = mean arrival rate per unit of time

Although many queuing systems have random arrivals that behave according to a Poisson process, it is possible for the interarrival times to be distributed in a nonexponential fashion. Therefore, it is necessary to determine the distribution and parameters of the interarrival time statistically before deciding on how to approach any queuing problem. How to determine the probability distribution of a random variable such as interarrival time is discussed in Chapter 13.

Attitude of the calling units   The final characteristic of the calling population that must be considered is the attitude of the calling unit. Calling units can be classified as being patient or impatient. A patient customer or calling unit is one that will enter the queuing system and stay regardless of the state of the system. An impatient calling unit may balk (refuse to enter the system) or renege (leave the system before receiving service). Generally, most analytical queuing models assume a very patient calling unit.

THE PROPERTY OF QUEUE LENGTH

This characteristic of queues is related in a sense to calling population size and, sometimes, to calling population attitude. In applying models, the queue is characterized by its maximum length, which can be *limited* or *unlimited*. Limitation is usually attributable either to customer attitude or to the space available for the queue. There are few choices for queuing systems that have finite queues. Generally, if you can assume that calling units join the queue regardless of its length, the probability of applying an analytical queuing model is greatly increased.

FIGURE 12.4 Characteristics of the service facility

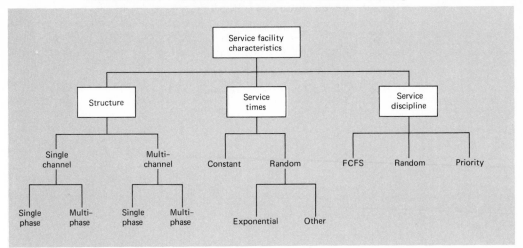

CHARACTERISTICS OF THE SERVICE FACILITY

As depicted in Figure 12.4, the three basic properties of the service facility are

1. The structure of the queuing system
2. The distribution of service times
3. The service discipline

Queuing system structure   Service facilities can be described as single-channel or multichannel. A *single-channel* system is a system with only one server. A *multichannel* system, on the other hand, has more than one server performing the same service. A drive-in bank facility is a single-channel system when there is only one teller on duty and a multichannel system when more than one teller is working.

single-channel

multichannel

In addition to multichannel versus single-channel, the service facility can be classified as single or multiphase. A *single-phase* system is one in which the calling unit receives service from only one type of server. A pay telephone, for example, is a single-phase queuing system. A *multiphase* system exists when the calling unit must obtain the services of several different types of server. Imagine a freighter pulling into the harbor to unload its cargo: First, that freighter must obtain the services of a tugboat; then, it must obtain a berth; then be unloaded; and after having been unloaded, the tug's services are needed again for the freighter's return to the open water. (Obviously, queuing systems can represent any combination of phases and channels.) An example of a multiphase, multi-

single phase

multiphase

449

FIGURE 12.5 A representative sample of elementary queuing system characteristics

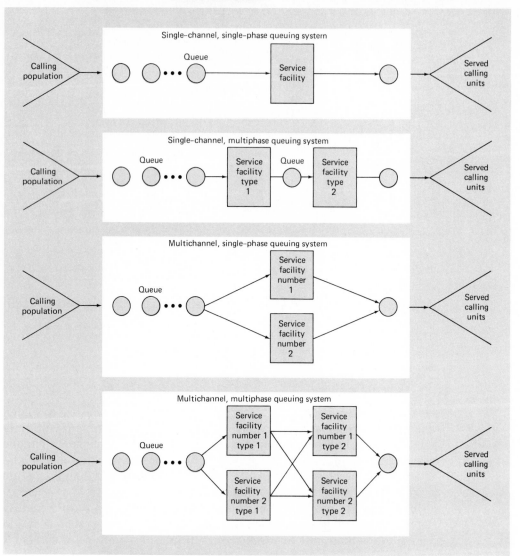

channel system is a harbor that has more than one tug and more than one berth. Figure 12.5 depicts schematics of several different queuing structures.

The great majority of queuing models are single-phase models. It is possible, nonetheless, to view a multiphase system as separate, single-phase systems in which the output from one server becomes the input for another server.

constant **Distribution of service times**   Service times can be *constant* or random
random in nature. If service time is a *random* variable, it is necessary for the
analyst to determine how that random variable is distributed. In many
cases, service times are exponentially distributed; when this is the case,
the probability of finding an applicable model is increased.

exponential   As you can see in Figure 12.6, if service times are *exponentially distributed,* the probability of relatively long service times is small. For example, the length of telephone calls has been shown to be exponentially
distributed.

The important point is that you should not make assumptions concerning either the service times of the various servers in the system or, equally
important, about the arrival pattern of calling units without using the appropriate nonparametric statistical tests.

Service discipline   This characteristic is the decision rule that determines which calling unit in the queuing system receives service. A service
discipline, (or *queue discipline,* as it is sometimes called), can be classified
in one of three ways:

1. First come, first served (FCFS)

2. Priority

3. Random

Most queuing systems that involve people operate with FCFS service
discipline, even though it has been shown to be somewhat inefficient,
simply because people usually do not tolerate other systems. Priority
disciplines can be divided into two categories—preemptive priority
preemptive and nonpreemptive priority. *Preemptive priority* disciplines allow calling
priority units that arrive at the queuing system to replace units already receiving
service. For example, consider an emergency room of a hospital when

FIGURE 12.6   Graph of $f(t) = \mu e^{-\mu t}$(exponential distribution)

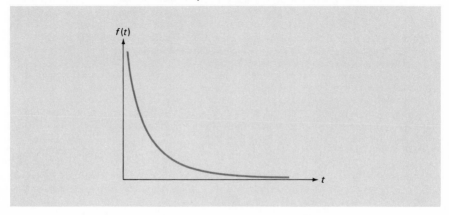

only one doctor is on duty. Obviously, if that doctor is treating a patient whose condition is not critical at the time a critically ill patient arrives, the patient who was being served is preempted because a calling unit has arrived to the system with a higher priority.

non-preemptive priority   *Nonpreemptive priority* simply causes the units in the queue to be arranged so that, when a service facility becomes available, the calling unit with the highest priority receives service first. There is no displacement of units in service. Computer systems frequently use priority scheduling.

random selection   It is also possible for a queuing system to have no formal queue discipline, in which case the server selects calling units at random. *Random selection* often exists at the candy and popcorn counter in a movie theater.

DESCRIPTIVE STATISTICS OF A QUEUING SYSTEM

Now that we have described certain properties of its major components, the calling population, the queue, and the service facility, you should have a good notion of the nature of the queuing system itself. Before we go on to the specific subject of queuing models, you should be aware that almost all such mathematical models reveal information about the operating characteristics of a queuing system in a *steady state*. As depicted in Figure 12.7, steady-state conditions exist when a system's behavior is not a function of time. Typically, a queuing system goes through a stage, called the transient stage, in which queuing statistics do not reflect the long-term expected values. This stage often occurs at a system's "start." For example, when a grocery store opens its doors in the morning, no customers are present in the system; therefore, there is a period of time

steady state

FIGURE 12.7   Transient versus steady-state conditioning

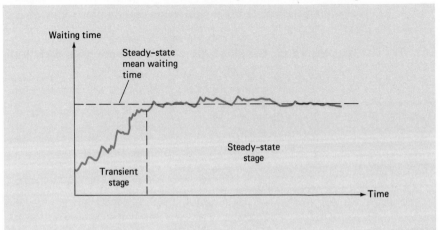

when a statistic such as the expected time spent waiting in line would be understated. Following the transient stage is the steady-state stage, in which system behavior is not affected by time.

ELEMENTARY QUEUING MODELS

In this section, we get down to defining some of the queuing models you first saw in Figure 12.3, and to showing the functions that describe various queuing statistics. Because the mathematics necessary to derive most queuing models is beyond the scope of this text, we have omitted model derivations. The emphasis, instead, is on identifying the assumptions of each model and on explaining how these models are used.

NOTATION AND DEFINITIONS

In order to help you understand the specific queuing statistics that are available from most queuing models, we must first define certain queuing terms and introduce a limited amount of notation. You should become familiar with the following list of notations and definitions before you read further in this chapter.

L_q = expected or mean length of the queue (number of calling units in the queue)

L_s = expected number of calling units in the system (number in the queue plus number being served)

W_q = expected or mean time spent waiting in line

W_s = expected or mean time spent in the system (including waiting time and service time)

λ = mean arrival rate (number of calling units per unit of time)

μ = mean service rate (number of calling units served per unit of time)

$1/\mu$ = mean service time for a calling unit

s = number of parallel (equivalent) service facilities in the system

$P(n)$ = probability of having n units in the system

ρ = server utilization factor (that is, the proportion of time the server can be expected to be busy)

MODELS THAT HAVE AN INFINITE CALLING POPULATION

All queuing models can be classified as either infinite source models or finite source models. Infinite source models are much more numerous and varied than models with finite calling populations. All models described in this text assume that μ is independent of the number of calling units in the system. Moreover, all queuing statistics given are steady-state statistics.

The basic single-server model   The assumptions of this model are:

1. Poisson arrival process
2. Exponential service times
3. Single server
4. FCFS service discipline
5. Infinite source
6. Infinite queue

The steady-state queuing statistics for the basic single-server model are given by the following formulas:

$$P(0) = 1 - (\lambda/\mu)$$
$$P(n) = P(0)(\lambda/\mu)^n$$
$$\rho = \lambda/\mu$$
$$L_s = \lambda/(\mu - \lambda)$$
$$L_q = \lambda^2/[\mu(\mu - \lambda)]$$
$$W_s = 1/(\mu - \lambda)$$
$$W_q = \lambda/[\mu(\mu - \lambda)]$$

EXAMPLE   To illustrate these results, consider the following application. A particular toll road has one attendant at an exit lane. Cars arrive at that toll gate in a Poisson fashion at a rate of 120 cars per hour, and it takes the attendant, on the average, 15 seconds to service a car. Service times are exponentially distributed. Assumptions of an infinite calling population and an infinite queue are reasonable. What are the basic queuing statistics for this very simple system?

First, it is necessary to determine the units of time for λ and μ. Obviously, λ and μ must be expressed in the same time units. Let's choose minutes. Therefore, $\lambda = 2$ cars per minute and $\mu = 4$ cars per minute. Thus, we have

$$P(0) = 1 - (\lambda/\mu) = 1 - (2/4)$$
$$= .5 \quad \text{(probability of an empty system)}$$
$$\rho = \lambda/\mu = 2/4 = .5 \quad \text{(proportion of time the server is busy)}$$
$$L_s = \lambda/(\mu - \lambda) = 2/(4 - 2)$$
$$= 1 \quad \text{(expected number of cars in the system)}$$
$$L_q = \lambda^2/[\mu(\mu - \lambda)] = 2^2/[4(4 - 2)] = 4/8$$
$$= .5 \quad \text{(expected number of cars waiting in the queue)}$$

$W_s = 1/(\mu - \lambda) = 1/(4 - 2) = .5$ minute

$\quad = 30$ seconds   (expected total time in the system for each customer)

$W_q = \lambda/[\mu(\mu - \lambda)] = 2/[4(4 - 2)] = 2/8 = .25$ minutes

$\quad = 15$ seconds   (expected waiting time for each customer)

Given these steady-state queuing statistics, it appears unnecessary to employ two attendants at the tollgate. In other words, a half-minute wait is probably not unreasonable; and therefore, the cost of another attendant could not be justified.

Multiserver model with Poisson arrivals and exponential service times
The assumptions of this model are identical to those of the basic single-server model described previously except that the number of servers is assumed to be greater than one. There is an additional assumption: All servers have the same rate of service.

$$P(0) = \cfrac{1}{\displaystyle\sum_{n=0}^{s-1} \frac{(\lambda/\mu)^n}{n!} + \frac{(\lambda/\mu)^s}{s!}\left(1 - \frac{\lambda}{s\mu}\right)^{-1}}$$

$$P(n) = \frac{(\lambda/\mu)^n}{n!}P(0) \qquad \text{for } 0 \le n \le s$$

$$\quad = \frac{(\lambda/\mu)^n}{s!s^{n-s}}P(0) \qquad \text{for } n \ge s$$

$\rho = \lambda/s\mu$ (assuming each server has the same mean service rate of μ units per time period)

$$L_q = \frac{P(0)(\lambda/\mu)^s\,\rho}{s!(1 - \rho)^2}$$

$$W_q = L_q/\lambda$$
$$W_s = W_q + (1/\mu)$$
$$L_s = L_q + (\lambda/\mu)$$

For computational convenience, a table of $P(0)$ can be found in Appendix H at the end of the book.

EXAMPLE   Consider the toll road example again, but let us assume that the arrival rate has increased to 600 cars per hour and that three attendants are on duty rather than one.

$$\lambda = 10 \text{ cars per minute}$$
$$\mu = 4 \text{ cars per minute}$$
$$s = 3$$

$$P(0) = \cfrac{1}{\displaystyle\sum_{n=0}^{2} \frac{(10/4)^n}{n!} + \frac{(10/4)^3}{3!} \cdot \left(\frac{1}{1 - (10/12)}\right)}$$

$$= \cfrac{1}{1 + \dfrac{10}{4} + \dfrac{25/4}{2} + \dfrac{1{,}000/64}{6} \cdot \dfrac{12}{2}}$$

$$= 64/1{,}424 = .045$$

$$L_q = \frac{.045(10/4)^3(10/12)}{3![1 - (10/12)]^2}$$

$$= 3.5 \text{ cars}$$
$$W_q = 3.5/10 = .35 \text{ minute per car}$$
$$WS = .35 + .25 = .60 \text{ minute per car}$$
$$LS = 3.5 + (10/4) = 6.01 \text{ cars}$$

Given these queuing statistics, three attendants would constitute a very tolerable service facility from a driver's point of view. However, for a more complete analysis, queuing statistics for two attendants should be computed to see if the degradation in service with fewer attendants is worth the decrease in cost. Obviously, since the value of driver waiting time is very vague, a value judgment must be made. The utility of the queuing model is that the value judgment you make after using it is more informed and generally should result in a better decision.

Single-server model with arbitrary service times   If the analyst has determined that arrivals to the system are Poisson-distributed but cannot accept the hypothesis that service times are exponentially distributed, it is quite possible that a valid model does exist. Specifically, the assumptions of this model are:

1. Poisson arrival process
2. Infinite calling population
3. Infinite queue
4. FCFS queue discipline
5. Single server
6. The distribution of service time is unknown, but it has a mean, $1/\mu$, and a variance, σ^2. These parameters are known.

The steady-state results are

$$L_q = (\lambda^2\sigma^2 + \rho^2)/[2(1 - \rho)]$$

$$\rho = \lambda/\mu$$
$$L_s = \rho + L_q$$
$$W_q = L_q/\lambda$$
$$W_s = W_q + (1/\mu)$$
$$P(0) = 1 - \rho$$

It is interesting to note that as σ^2 increases L_q, L_s, W_q, and W_s all increase. This means that the performance of the queuing system is not solely dependent on mean service time but on the variance in service time as well. Consequently, a server with a higher mean service time may still be the more productive if it is also the more consistent.

When service times are constant, as might be the case in a process such as a car wash, the foregoing model can be applied. The only difference is that the variance σ^2 is equal to zero. Therefore, $L_q = \rho^2/[2(1 - \rho)]$. The other relationships remain unchanged.

EXAMPLE   A savings and loan association is opening a branch in a nearby suburb. This branch is expected to need one savings counselor, but management wants to have descriptive queuing statistics to confirm an intuition that only one savings counselor is actually necessary. Plans are to transfer one savings counselor from the main office. Data concerning this particular counselor's time spent with a customer have been collected, but goodness-of-fit tests indicate that these service times are not exponentially distributed. It is further estimated that the mean service time is 15 minutes and variance is 10 minutes. Customers are expected to arrive in a Poisson manner at a rate of two per hour.

$$\lambda = 2 \text{ customers per hour}$$
$$\mu = 4 \text{ customers per hour}$$
$$\sigma^2 = 1/6 \text{ hour}$$
$$L_q = \frac{4(1/6) + (1/2)^2}{2[1 - (1/2)]}$$
$$= \frac{11/12}{1} = 11/12 = .92 \text{ customer}$$
$$\rho = 2/4 = 1/2$$
$$L_s = 1/2 + 11/12 = 17/12 = 1.42 \text{ customers}$$
$$W_q = \frac{11/12}{2} = 11/24 \text{ hour} = 27.5 \text{ minutes}$$
$$W_s = 11/24 + 6/24 = 17/24 \text{ hour} = 42.5 \text{ minutes}$$
$$P(0) = 1 - 1/2 = 1/2$$

The foregoing queuing statistics suggest that either the savings and loan customers are going to have to be very patient or the firm will lose savings customers if it carries out its plan to have only one savings counselor.

EXAMPLE The manager of a small, coin-operated car wash is thinking about adding a vacuum to the business so that customers can vacuum the inside of their automobiles. Service time for the vacuum is constant at 5 minutes, and arrivals are Poisson at a rate of 10 per hour. For this example, assume an infinite queue and calling population. Before investing in the vacuum, the manager wishes to know what to expect with respect to customers waiting for the vacuum.

$$\lambda = 10 \text{ customers per hour}$$
$$1/\mu = 1/12 \text{ hour per customer}$$
$$\sigma^2 = 0$$
$$\mu = 12 \text{ customers per hour}$$
$$\rho = 5/6 = .833$$
$$L_q = \frac{(5/6)^2}{2(1/6)} = 2.08 \text{ customers}$$
$$L_s = 5/6 + 25/12 = 2.92 \text{ customers}$$
$$W_q = \frac{25/12}{10} = .208 \text{ hour} = 12 \text{ minutes}$$
$$W_s = 12 + 5 = 17 \text{ minutes}$$

With these results, the manager might want to seriously consider two vacuums since the probability of a customer's joining the queue when there are two or more cars waiting is low.

Single-server model with arbitrary service times and a priority queue discipline Only limited results exist for queuing models that do not have an FCFS queue discipline. The model described in this section uses a nonpreemptive priority queue discipline and makes no assumption about the service time distribution. The explicit assumptions of this model are the following:

1. Poisson arrival process.
2. Infinite calling population.
3. Infinite queue.
4. The queue discipline divides calling units into classes, and service is FCFS within each priority class.
5. Single server.
6. The service time distribution for each priority class is unknown, but the mean service time and variance are known for each priority class.

The steady-state queuing statistics are given by the following expressions:

$$W_q^k = \frac{\sum\limits_{i=1}^{m} \lambda_i[(1/\mu_i)^2 + \sigma_i^2]}{2(1 - S_{k-1})(1 - S_k)}$$

where W_q^k = the expected waiting time for a calling unit in priority class k

λ_i = arrival rate of priority class i

μ_i = service rate of priority class i

σ_i^2 = variance in service time of priority class i

$S_k = \sum\limits_{i=1}^{k} \rho_i < 1, k = 1, 2, \dots m$

$S_0 = 0$

m = number of priority classes

$\rho_k = \lambda_k/\mu_k$

$L_q^k = \lambda_k W_q^k$

$W_s^k = W_q^k + (1/\mu_k)$

$L_s^k = L_q^k + \rho_k$

$W_q = \sum\limits_{k=1}^{m} \frac{\lambda_k}{\lambda} W_q^k \qquad$ where $\lambda = \sum\limits_{k=1}^{m} \lambda_k$

= expected waiting time for any customer

$W_s = \sum\limits_{k=1}^{m} \frac{\lambda_k}{\lambda} W_s^k$

= expected time spent in the system for any customer

EXAMPLE   Jobs to be run on a computer system are of two types and hence two different priorities. Only one job can run at one time. Both types of job arrive according to a Poisson process, but service time distributions are normal, with means of 5 minutes and 15 minutes. Variances for the two priority classes are 5 minutes and 2.5 minutes, respectively. Type I jobs arrive at a rate of three per hour and type II jobs arrive at a rate of two per hour. What are the steady-state queuing statistics?

$\rho_1 = 3/12 = .25$

$\rho_2 = 2/4 = .50$

$S_1 = .25$

$S_2 = .25 + .50 = .75$

$\lambda_1 = 3$ jobs per hour

$\lambda_2 = 2$ jobs per hour

$\mu_1 = 12$ jobs per hour

$\mu_2 = 4$ jobs per hour

$\sigma_1^2 = 1/12$ hour

$$\sigma_2^2 = 1/24 \text{ hour}$$

$$W_q^1 = \frac{3[(1/12)^2 + (1/12)] + 2[(1/4)^2 + (1/24)]}{2(1-0)[1-(3/12)]}$$

$$= .47916/1.5 \text{ hour} = .31944 \text{ hour} = 19.17 \text{ minutes}$$

$$W_q^2 = \frac{3[(1/12)^2 + (1/12)] + 2[(3/12)^2 + (1/24)]}{2[1-(3/12)][1-(3/12+2/4)]}$$

$$= \frac{(39/144) + (30/144)}{(18/12)(3/12)} = 23/18 \text{ hours} = 1.278 \text{ hours}$$

$$= 76.6 \text{ minutes}$$

$$L_q^1 = 3(.31944) = .96 \text{ job}$$
$$L_q^2 = 2(1.278) = 2.56 \text{ jobs}$$
$$W_s^1 = 19.17 + 5 = 24.17 \text{ minutes}$$
$$W_s^2 = 76.6 + 15 = 91.6 \text{ minutes}$$
$$L_s^1 = .96 + .25 = 1.21 \text{ jobs}$$
$$L_s^2 = 2.56 + .5 = 3.06 \text{ jobs}$$
$$W_q = (3/5)(19.17) + (2/5)(76.6) = 42.14 \text{ minutes}$$
$$W_s = .6(24.17) + .4(91.6) = 51.14 \text{ minutes}$$

This model might be used to evaluate the desirability of a priority queue discipline as opposed to a FCFS queue discipline. How might you accomplish such a comparison?

Single-server model with a finite queue   Often, queue length constitutes a constraint on the queuing system. If queue length is limited either by customer attitude or the physical facilities, it is not desirable to use any of the models previously described. The model we present in this section has assumptions identical to the first basic single-server model we developed in this chapter *except that* the restriction of an infinite queue length can be dropped. The steady-state results that have been derived are as follows:

$$P(0) = \frac{1 - (\lambda/\mu)}{1 - (\lambda/\mu)^{M+1}}$$

where M = maximum number of calling units in the system and the maximum queue length is $M - 1$

$$P(n) = P(0)(\lambda/\mu)^n \qquad \text{for } n = 0, 1, \dots M$$

$$L_s = \frac{\lambda/\mu}{1 - (\lambda/\mu)} - \frac{(M+1)(\lambda/\mu)^{M+1}}{1 - (\lambda/\mu)^{M+1}}$$

$$L_q = L_s + P(0) - 1$$

$$W_q = \frac{L_q}{\lambda[1 - P(M)]}$$

$$W_s = W_q + 1/\mu$$

The foregoing results require that $\lambda < \mu$.

EXAMPLE A basic programming course includes a lab at which a student "consultant" is on duty to help students debug their programs. It can be assumed that no student will get in line for help if there are more than three other students waiting. Students arrive at the lab according to a Poisson process at an average rate of four per hour. Service times are exponential, and the mean service time is 10 minutes. Because the class is large, an infinite calling population can be assumed. What are the steady-state queuing statistics?

$$M = 4$$
$$\lambda = 4$$
$$\mu = 6$$
$$P(0) = \frac{1 - (2/3)}{1 - (2/3)^5} = .384$$
$$P(4) = .384(4/6)^4$$

= probability of a full system so that a student refuses to join the queue

= .076

$$L_s = \frac{2/3}{1 - (2/3)} - \frac{5(2/3)^5}{1 - (2/3)^5}$$
$$= 2 - .757 = 1.243 \text{ students}$$
$$L_q = 1.243 + .384 - 1 = .627 \text{ student}$$
$$W_q = .627/[4(1 - .076)] = .17 \text{ hour, or } 10.2 \text{ minutes}$$
$$W_s = .17 + 1/6 = .336 \text{ hour, or } 20.2 \text{ minutes}$$

Given these queuing statistics, it is probable that university administrators are quite satisfied with the lab system because there is only a 7.6 percent chance of a student's not being serviced, and those that choose to wait, wait only 10.2 minutes, on the average.

There is a multiserver extension of this model, which is beyond the scope of this text.

Models that have a finite calling population   In some queuing systems, the size of the calling population is so small that to assume it to be infinite would seriously degrade the usefulness of a queuing model. Some results that have been derived for a limited source model are presented in this section. The model described next assumes a Poisson arrival process and exponentially distributed service times. It can be applied to a multiserver queuing system or a single-server system whose queue discipline is FCFS.

The steady-state descriptive statistics are

$$P(0) = \cfrac{1}{\left[\displaystyle\sum_{n=0}^{s-1} \frac{N!}{(N-n)!n!}\left(\frac{\lambda}{\mu}\right)^n + \sum_{n=s}^{N} \frac{N!}{(N-n)!s!s^{n-s}}\left(\frac{\lambda}{\mu}\right)^n\right]}$$

where N = number of calling units in the calling population
λ = mean arrival rate for *each* individual unit

$$P(n) = \begin{cases} P(0)\dfrac{N!}{(N-n)!n!}\left(\dfrac{\lambda}{\mu}\right)^n & \text{for } 0 \le n \le s \\[2ex] P(0)\dfrac{N!}{(N-n)!s!s^{n-s}}\left(\dfrac{\lambda}{\mu}\right)^n & \text{for } s \le n \le N \\[2ex] 0 & \text{for } n > N \end{cases}$$

$$L_s = \sum_{n=1}^{N} nP(n)$$
$$W_s = L_s/\lambda_e \quad \text{where } \lambda_e = \lambda(N - L_s)$$
$$W_q = W_s - (1/\mu)$$
$$L_q = \lambda_e W_q$$

EXAMPLE   In a certain computer facility, three central processing units (CPUs) are serviced by two customer engineers. Each CPU breaks down in a Poisson manner on the average of every 4 hours. Repair times are exponentially distributed, with a mean of 3 hours. Determine the steady-state queuing statistics.

$$\lambda = .25 \text{ per hour}$$
$$\mu = .33 \text{ per hour}$$
$$P(0) = 1\bigg/ \left[\frac{3!}{(3-0)!0!}\cdot\left(\frac{25}{33}\right)^0 + \frac{3!}{(3-1)!1!}\cdot\left(\frac{25}{33}\right)^1 \right.$$
$$\left. + \frac{3!}{(3-2)!2!2^0}\cdot\left(\frac{25}{33}\right)^2 + \frac{3!}{(3-3)!2!2^1}\cdot\left(\frac{25}{33}\right)^3\right]$$
$$= .177095$$

$$P(1) = .177095 \cdot \left(\frac{3!}{2!1!}\right)\left(\frac{25}{33}\right)^1 = .402489$$

$$P(2) = .177095 \cdot \left(\frac{3!}{1!2!}\right)\left(\frac{25}{33}\right)^2 = .304916$$

$$P(3) = .177095 \cdot \left(\frac{3!}{0!2!2^1}\right)\left(\frac{25}{33}\right)^3 = .115498$$

$$L_s = .402489 + 2(.304916) + 3(.115498) = 1.36 \text{ CPUs}$$
$$\lambda_e = .25(3 - 1.36) = .41$$
$$W_s = 1.36/.41 = 3.31707 \text{ hours}$$

$W_q = 3.31707 - 3.0 = .31707$ hour, or 18.7 minutes
$L_q = .41(.31707) = .13$ CPU

An economic analysis of this queuing system would be possible, since the cost of waiting could conceivably be computed, as could the cost of additional repairmen. Consequently, the queuing model could be used to make a very rational decision regarding the optimal number of repairmen.

For a concise summary of the models presented in this chapter, see Table 12.2.

APPLICATION OF QUEUING THEORY

So far in this chapter, we have described the structure and characteristics of queuing systems and have defined several representative queuing models. By now, it is obvious to you that before a queuing model can be applied, the actual queuing system must be carefully analyzed.

Such an analysis of the queuing system should include the identification and verification of the system characteristics we described earlier in this chapter. Once the system has been analyzed, the analyst must identify the decision variables. In simple queuing systems these variables are usually the number of servers and, often, the type of server. The queue discipline often constitutes another controllable variable. Having identified decision variables, each of which is generally discrete in nature, the analyst must determine the criteria for a good set of decision variables. These criteria are usually economic in nature. The cost of the queuing system must be weighed against the waiting time of the calling units.

Two approaches to the problem of applying queuing theory to making decisions are common. One approach is to explicitly define the cost of one calling unit waiting one unit of time and then minimize an objective function such as

$$Z = C_q + C_w$$

where C_q = cost of the queuing system
C_w = cost of waiting

As shown in Figure 12.8, the cost of operating the queuing system and the cost of waiting are in direct opposition to each other. As the cost of the system increases, the waiting time is typically decreased. If the cost functions depicted in Figure 12.8 can be explicitly defined, then finding the best solution to the queuing problem is fairly easy.

If you are trying to decide on how many teller windows to have open

TABLE 12.2 Summary of basic queuing models

Model name	Model assumptions	P(0)
Basic single server	(1) Poisson arrivals (2) Exponential service times (3) Single server (4) FCFS (5) Infinite source (6) Infinite queue	$1 - (\lambda/\mu)$
Basic multi-server	(1) Poisson arrivals (2) Exponential service times (3) Multiserver (4) FCFS (5) Infinite source (6) Infinite queue	$\dfrac{1}{\displaystyle\sum_{n=0}^{s-1}\dfrac{(\lambda/\mu)^n}{n!} + \dfrac{(\lambda/\mu)^s}{s!}\left(1 - \dfrac{\lambda}{s\mu}\right)^{-1}}$
Single server with arbitrary service times	(1) Poisson arrivals (2) Service time distribution unknown (3) Infinite source (4) Infinite queue (5) FCFS (6) Single server	$1 - \rho$
Single server with priority queue discipline	(1) Poisson arrivals (2) Infinite source (3) Infinite queue (4) FCFS within priority class (5) Single server (6) Unknown service distribution with known mean and variance	
Single server, finite queue	(1) Poisson arrivals (2) Exponential service times (3) Single server (4) FCFS (5) Infinite source (6) Finite queue	$\dfrac{1 - (\lambda/\mu)}{1 - (\lambda/\mu)^{M+1}}$
Limited source	(1) Poisson arrivals (2) Exponential service times (3) Single or multiserver (4) FCFS (5) Limited input source (6) Infinite queue	$\dfrac{1}{\left[\displaystyle\sum_{n=0}^{s-1}\dfrac{N!}{(N-n)!n!}\left(\dfrac{\lambda}{\mu}\right)^n + \sum_{n=s}^{N}\dfrac{N!}{(N-n)!s!s^{n-s}}\left(\dfrac{\lambda}{\mu}\right)^n\right]}$

in a bank or how many checkout counters to have open in a supermarket, the loss of goodwill caused by long lines and long waits is difficult to measure. If, however, you are trying to decide on the number of repairmen to have available to fix your productive machinery, these costs can be reasonably estimated.

The second approach to applying queuing theory is to seek to minimize a cost function subject to a set of constraints about the line length and expected waiting times. Although this approach is not as clear-cut or

$P(n)$		L_q	L_s	W_q	W_s
$P(0)(\lambda/\mu)^n$		$\lambda^2/[\mu(\mu-\lambda)]$	$\lambda/(\mu-\lambda)$	$\lambda/[\mu(\mu-\lambda)]$	$1/(\mu-\lambda)$
$\dfrac{(\lambda/\mu)^n}{n!}P(0)$ $\dfrac{(\lambda/\mu)^n}{s!s^{n-s}}P(0)$	for $0 \le n \le s$ for $n \ge s$	$\dfrac{P(0)(\lambda/\mu)^s\rho}{s!(1-\rho)^2}$	$L_q + (\lambda/\mu)$	L_q/λ	$W_q + (1/\mu)$
		$\dfrac{(\lambda^2\sigma^2 + \rho^2)}{[2(1-\rho)]}$	$\rho + L_q$	L_q/λ	$W_q + (1/\mu)$
		$L_q^k = \lambda_k W_q^k$	$L_s^k = L_q^k + \rho_k$	$\sum_{k=1}^m \dfrac{\lambda_k}{\lambda} W_q^k$ where $W_q^k = \dfrac{\sum_{i=1}^m \lambda_i[(1/\mu_i)^2 + \sigma_i^2]}{2(1-S_{k-1})(1-S_k)}$	$\sum_{k=1}^m \dfrac{\lambda_k}{\lambda} W_s^k$ where $W_s^k = W_q^k + (1/\mu_k)$
$P(0)(\lambda/\mu)^n$ for $n = 0, 1, \ldots M$		$L_s + P(0) - 1$	$\dfrac{\lambda/\mu}{1-(\lambda/\mu)} -$ $\dfrac{(M+1)(\lambda/\mu)^{M+1}}{1-(\lambda/\mu)^{M+1}}$	$\dfrac{L_q}{\lambda[1-P(M)]}$	$W_q + 1/\mu$
$P(0)\dfrac{N!}{(N-n)!n!}\left(\dfrac{\lambda}{\mu}\right)^n$ $P(0)\dfrac{N!}{(N-n)!s!s^{n-s}}\left(\dfrac{\lambda}{\mu}\right)^n$ 0	for $0 \le n \le s$ for $s \le n \le N$ for $n \ge M$	$\lambda_e W_q$	$\sum_{n=1}^N nP(n)$	$W_s - (1/\mu)$	L_s/λ_e

objective as explicitly estimating the cost of waiting, it is often more acceptable to management.

Once the queuing system has been analyzed and the criteria for decision making have been defined, the analyst must then decide on the solution methodology. Either an analytical queuing model, such as one of the models presented in this chapter, can be applied or a computer simulation model can be written. The advantages of using an analytical model as opposed to a simulation model are computational efficiency and the

FIGURE 12.8 Queuing system costs

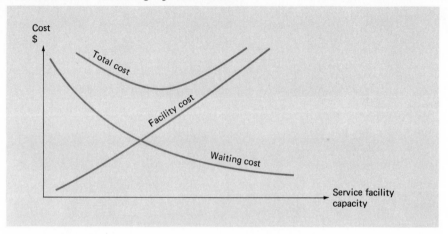

absence of sampling error. Although queuing theory has advanced considerably in recent years and many models have been derived, real-world queuing systems often do not have a mathematical counterpart. Rather than force a real queuing system to fit a mathematical model by simplifying the assumptions about system properties, computer simulation should be used. This relatively new tool is discussed in detail in the next chapter. In addition to having the flexibility to model any queuing system, simulation is not restricted to a few steady-state operating characteristics. For example, the frequency distribution of waiting times can be determined, not just the mean or expected value of waiting time.

Regardless of whether an analytical or simulation model is used to evaluate the different sets of decision variables, you should realize that determining the "best" set of decision variables is a trial-and-error process. Queuing theory is not an optimization technique; it is a descriptive tool.

SUMMARY

Queuing systems exist everywhere in the real world and queuing theory can play an important role in the design of systems involving waiting lines and the scheduling of many services. The importance of *properly* applying analytical queuing models cannot be overstated. In order to avoid misapplication, system properties must be carefully analyzed before an appropriate model can be selected.

We have examined only a small fraction of the queuing models that have been derived, but you should realize that there is a large probability that an analytical queuing model that fits the real-world system you are interested in may not exist and may be impossible to derive mathematically. If such is the case, simulation is often used to analyze queuing systems that are too complex to be described using an analytical queuing model.

When analyzing queuing systems it is important to understand that queuing theory, like computer simulation, is a descriptive tool that yields expected operating characteristics of the queuing system under differing configurations. Decision variables such as queue discipline, number of servers, speed of the server, and so on, must be supplied to the model and are not output from the model. Typically, the output from queuing models becomes an input to a judgmental decision concerning the configuration of the queuing system.

SOLVED PROBLEMS

PROBLEM STATEMENT

The city council of a small town has decided to build a tennis court in the central park. Players are expected to arrive on the average of 10 sets of players per 12-hour day. Playing time is exponentially distributed with a mean of 1 hour. Arrivals are Poisson. What are the expected queuing statistics assuming the basic single-server model?

SOLUTION

If we let hours be the time unit

$$\lambda = {}^{10}\!/_{12} \text{ arrival per hour}$$
$$\mu = 1 \text{ departure per hour}$$

The probability of no one using the tennis court is

$$P(0) = 1 - \frac{\lambda}{\mu} = 2/12 = .1667$$

The expected utilization of the tennis court is

$$\rho = \frac{\lambda}{\mu} = 10/12 = .8333$$

The number of groups expected to be waiting for a court is

$$L_q = \frac{\lambda^2}{\mu(\mu - \lambda)} = \frac{(10/12)^2}{1(1 - 10/12)} = 4.167 \text{ groups}$$

The number of groups expected to be waiting and playing tennis is

$$L_s = \frac{\lambda}{\mu - \lambda} = 5 \text{ groups}$$

The expected waiting time is

$$W_q = \frac{\lambda}{\mu(\mu - \lambda)} = 5 \text{ hours}$$

The expected time waiting and playing is

$$W_s = \frac{1}{\mu - \lambda} = 6 \text{ hours}$$

PROBLEM STATEMENT

Given the steady-state queuing statistics found in the previous example, the city council wants to investigate the effect of building 2 tennis courts rather than 1.

SOLUTION

$$\lambda = \frac{10}{12} \qquad \mu = 1 \qquad s = 2$$

The probability of empty tennis courts is

$$P(0) = \frac{1}{\displaystyle\sum_{n=0}^{s-1} \frac{(\lambda/\mu)^n}{n!} + \frac{(\lambda/\mu)^s}{s!}\left(1 - \frac{\lambda}{s\mu}\right)^{-1}}$$

$$= \frac{1}{\displaystyle\frac{(10/12)^0}{0!} + \frac{(10/12)^1}{1!} + \frac{(10/12)^2}{2!}\left(1 - \frac{10/12}{2}\right)^{-1}}$$

$$= \frac{1}{1.83 + .59523}$$

$$= \frac{1}{2.425} = .4123$$

The average utilization of the tennis courts is

$$\rho = \frac{\lambda}{s\mu} = \frac{10/12}{2} = .4167$$

The number of groups expected to be waiting for a court is

$$L_q = \frac{P(0)(\lambda/\mu)^s \rho}{s!(1 - \rho)^2}$$

$$= \frac{(.4123)(10/12)^2(.4167)}{2!(1 - .4167)^2}$$

$$= \frac{.1193}{.6805}$$

$$= .1753 \text{ group}$$

The number of groups expected to be waiting and playing is

$$L_s = L_q + \frac{\lambda}{\mu}$$

$$= .1753 + 10/12$$

$$= 1.009 \text{ groups}$$

The expected waiting time is

$$W_q = \frac{L_q}{\lambda}$$

$$= \frac{.1753}{10/12}$$

$$= .21 \text{ hour or } 12.6 \text{ minutes}$$

The average time spent playing and waiting is

$$W_s = W_q + \frac{1}{\mu}$$

$$= 12.6 \text{ minutes} + 60 \text{ minutes}$$

$$= 72.6 \text{ minutes}$$

PROBLEM STATEMENT

If the assumption about exponential service times is dropped from the single-tennis-court problem and the variance is 30 minutes, what would the queuing statistics be? Remember: $\lambda = .8333$ group per hour and $\mu = 1$ group per hour.

SOLUTION

The expected length of the queue is

$$
\begin{aligned}
L_q &= \frac{\lambda^2\sigma^2 + \rho^2}{2(1 - \rho)} \\
&= \frac{(.8333^2)(\frac{1}{2})^2 + .8333^2}{2(1 - .8333)} \\
&= 2.6 \text{ groups waiting}
\end{aligned}
$$

The expected utilization of the tennis courts is

$$
\begin{aligned}
\rho &= \frac{\lambda}{\mu} \\
&= \frac{10/12}{1} = .8333
\end{aligned}
$$

The average number of groups playing and waiting is

$$
\begin{aligned}
L_s &= \rho + L_q \\
&= .8333 + 2.6 \\
&= 3.4333 \text{ groups}
\end{aligned}
$$

The average waiting time is

$$
\begin{aligned}
W_q &= \frac{L_q}{\lambda} \\
&= 2.6/.8333 \\
&= 3.12 \text{ hours}
\end{aligned}
$$

The average time spent waiting and playing is

$$
\begin{aligned}
W_s &= W_q + \frac{1}{\mu} \\
&= 3.12 + 1 \\
&= 4.12 \text{ hours}
\end{aligned}
$$

Finally, the probability of the court not being used is

$$P(0) = 1 - \rho$$
$$= 1 - .8333$$
$$= .1667$$

PROBLEM STATEMENT

Because of budgetary restrictions, city managers feel that only 1 tennis court can be built at the present time. Someone has suggested limiting play to 1 hour for each group in order to reduce waiting time and lines. How would this suggestion change the queuing statistics?

SOLUTION

By prescribing 1 hour of playing time, the problem reduces to a single-server model with constant service times. The expected queuing statistics are as follows:

The expected utilization of the court remains

$$\rho = \frac{\lambda}{\mu} = .8333$$

The average number of groups waiting to play is

$$L_q = \frac{\rho^2}{2(1 - \rho)}$$
$$= \frac{.8333^2}{2(1 - .8333)}$$
$$= 2.08 \text{ groups}$$

The average number of groups playing and waiting is

$$L_s = \rho + L_q$$
$$= .8333 + 2.08$$
$$= 2.9133 \text{ groups}$$

The average waiting time is

$$W_q = \frac{L_q}{\lambda}$$
$$= 2.08/.8333$$
$$= 2.496 \text{ hours}$$

The average time spent playing and waiting is

$$W_s = W_q + \frac{1}{\mu}$$
$$= 2.496 + 1$$
$$= 3.496 \text{ hours}$$

Therefore, it looks as though some improvement can be made by restricting play to 1 hour.

PROBLEM STATEMENT

One member of the city council has challenged the validity of the assumption of an infinite queue. He contends that people will not wait on the court if 2 groups are already waiting. What effect does the omission of the infinite queue have on the queuing statistics?

SOLUTION

The maximum number of calling units in the system is 3. The probability of the tennis courts being idle is

$$P(0) = \frac{1 - \lambda/\mu}{1 - (\lambda/\mu)^{M+1}}$$
$$= \frac{1 - .8333}{1 - (.8333)^4}$$
$$= .3219$$

The probability of the court being used but no line is

$$P(1) = P(0)\left(\frac{\lambda}{\mu}\right)^1$$
$$= (.3219)(.8333)$$
$$= .2682$$

The probability of 1 group waiting is

$$P(2) = (.3219)(.8333)^2$$
$$= .2235$$

The probability of 2 groups waiting or probability of a group arriving and not staying is

$$P(3) = (.3219)(.8333)^3$$
$$= .1863$$

The expected number of groups playing and waiting is

$$L_s = \frac{\lambda/\mu}{(1 - \lambda/\mu)} - \frac{(M + 1)(\lambda/\mu)^{M+1}}{1 - (\lambda/\mu)^{M+1}}$$
$$= \frac{.8333}{1 - .8333} - \frac{(3 + 1)(.8333)^4}{1 - (.8333)^4}$$
$$= 4.9988 - 3.7246$$
$$= 1.2742 \text{ groups}$$

The expected number of groups waiting is

$$L_q = L_s + P(0) - 1$$
$$= 1.2742 + .3219 - 1$$
$$= .5961$$

The expected time spent waiting is

$$W_q = \frac{L_q}{\lambda[1 - P(M)]}$$
$$= \frac{.5961}{.8333(1 - .1863)}$$
$$= .8791 \text{ hours}$$

The expected time spent waiting and playing is

$$W_s = W_q + \frac{1}{\mu}$$
$$= .8791 + 1$$
$$= 1.8791 \text{ hours}$$

REVIEW QUESTIONS

1. Define what is meant by the term "queuing theory."
2. How does queuing theory differ from linear programming?
3. What are the two major costs involved in any queuing system?
4. What are the basic elements of a queuing system?

5. What characteristics of the calling population must be analyzed when applying a queuing model to a real queuing system?

6. What three basic properties of the service facility must be analyzed when applying queuing models?

7. What is meant by "steady-state queuing statistics"?

8. Explain two basic approaches used in applying queuing theory to decision making.

9. How would you classify the structure of a hospital's emergency room?

10. What is meant by "queue discipline"?

11. What is meant by "customers arrive according to a Poisson process?"

12. Distinguish between preemptive and nonpreemptive priority queue disciplines.

13. What is meant by the statement that queuing theory is *not* an optimization technique?

14. List three reasons you might choose to use digital simulation rather than queuing theory.

PROBLEMS

12.1   Analyze the following queuing systems by describing their various system properties:

a. Barber shop

b. Bank

c. Machine repairman

d. Traffic light

e. Grocery store checkout counter

f. Tugs in a harbor

g. Airport runway

h. Computer system

i. Hospital emergency room

j. Gas station

k. Car wash

l. Tool crib

m. Laundromat

12.2   *Retail.* A large department store is preparing for the Christmas season. Last year, the store had two Santas for the children to talk to. Lines were long, and the store is trying to decide how many Santas to employ this year. Describe this problem as a queuing problem. Be sure to identify all pertinent characteristics. Include a representative schematic of the system.

12.3   *Manufacturing.* Consider a tool crib in a large factory. At the present time, one worker operates the tool crib, but the vice-president of production has noticed rather long lines of workers waiting for tools. Factory employees arrive to the tool crib at a rate of 25 per hour. Service times are exponential, with a mean of 2 minutes. The arrival process is Poisson. Analyze the desirability of adding a second tool crib clerk.

12.4   *State Government.* The Toll Road Authority wants to know how many toll booths to design into its Main Road exit. Naturally, an objective is to minimize cost, but there is also a stipulation that the expected line length during peak hours should not exceed 5 cars. From data taken from other toll road exits, it has been determined that interarrival times and service times are exponentially distributed. The peak arrival rate is expected to be 10 cars per minute. The average service time is 15 seconds. How many toll booths should be designed into the system?

12.5   *Amusement Park.* At Disneyland, plans are being made to install a new ride. Management would like to get a feel for the length of lines and the expected waiting times for this ride so that a decision can be made whether to have one or two such installations. People arrive in a Poisson manner, but the time the ride takes is constant. Estimates are that people will arrive at a rate of one every 2 minutes. The ride takes 1.75 minutes. Analyze the queuing system.

12.6   *Barber Shop.* Consider a one-chair barbershop. At the present location, a barber has, on the average, 10 customers per day. The average haircut takes 20 minutes. Cutting time has been shown to be exponentially distributed. It has been this barber's experience that customers do not wait for a haircut if two people are already waiting. A move to a new location is possible. The new location would probably increase the number of customers per day to 15. Analyze the present system and the proposed system by computing the queuing statistics for each system. Make a recommendation concerning the proposed move.

12.7   *University.* A certain professor holds office hours 2 hours each day. Three types of people need to see this professor: female students, other faculty, and male students. Many students complain that the queue discipline is not FCFS but a priority discipline with the priority scheme as follows: (1) female students, (2) other faculty members, and (3) male students. The conference time has been analyzed using historical data and has been found to be normal, with a mean of 5 minutes and a standard deviation of 2 minutes. People arrive at the professor's office in a Poisson manner (that is, no appointments are allowed during office hours). The arrival rate for female students is three per hour. The arrival rates for faculty members and male students are two and four per hour, respectively. What would be the effect on the queuing statistics if the professor changed to a FCFS queue discipline? Assume an infinite queue and calling population.

12.8 *Supermarket.* The local supermarket has the policy that checks are cashed by the store manager only. Customers wishing to cash checks arrive in a Poisson manner at an average rate of 45 customers per hour. The manager takes, on the average, 1 minute to cash a check. This service time has been shown to be exponentially distributed. Accomplish the following:

    a. Compute the percentage of time that the manager spends cashing checks.

    b. Compute the average time a customer is expected to wait.

    c. Compute the number of customers waiting to get checks cashed.

    d. Compute the probability of the manager attending to some other function assuming that check cashing is the manager's first priority.

    e. Explain to the manager how you would analyze the effect of adding the assistant manager to the check-cashing function.

12.9 *Legal Practice.* Two lawyers are in partnership. Each lawyer has a secretary. Jobs arrive to each secretary in a Poisson manner at a rate of three per hour, on the average. It takes either secretary an average of 15 minutes to accomplish each individual job. This service time is exponentially distributed.

    a. Assuming that each secretary does only the work of one lawyer, what is the expected waiting time for each job?

    b. What would be the effect of pooling the secretaries?

12.10 *Aerospace Manufacturing.* A certain aerospace company has five identical, numerically controlled milling machines. Each machine fails on the average of three times per week, and it takes a technician on the average 2.5 hours to fix the machine. Historical data indicate a Poisson arrival process and exponential service times. Because of serious scheduling consequences, management does not want a machine down for more than 3 hours. For this reason, it has been decided that expected waiting time should not exceed $\frac{1}{2}$ hour. Assume that the plant operates the equipment only during the prime shift.

a. What are the expected times a machine will have to wait with one technician on duty? With two technicians on duty?

b. What is your recommendation to management?

c. What options do you think management has in addition to the number of technicians?

12.11 *Airline Industry.* A large domestic airline employs one reservation clerk in a local office during the day. The reservation clerk has suggested that another clerk be hired so that customers calling for reservations will not have to wait an inordinate amount of time. Management has decided that on the average, a customer should not have to wait more than 2 minutes. In order to study the desirability of adding another reservation clerk, a study was done to determine the distribution of arrival times and service times. Calls arrived in a Poisson manner on the average of 30 per hour. The time it took to make a reservation was exponentially distributed with a mean of 1.5 minutes. Given the company's policy of an average waiting time of less than 2 minutes, what should the manager of the local office do with regard to hiring additional reservations clerks?

12.12 *Hospital Administration.* An administrator at a small hospital is contemplating a relocation of the hospital's X-ray facility. Currently, the X-ray department is located such that only two patients can be waiting for the X-ray machine at one time. This has resulted in emergency patients being sent back to emergency and other in-patients being sent back to their rooms. The potential new location would double the amount of waiting space available. Arrivals to X-ray occur in a Poisson manner at a rate of 6 per hour. On the average, it takes about 8 minutes to service an X-ray request. These service times have been shown to be exponential. Analyze the administrator's decision problem using queuing theory.

12.13 *Port Administration.* Ships arrive at a harbor in a Poisson fashion at a rate of 5 per 8-hour day. It takes the one tug servicing the harbor on the average of 1 hour per ship. Tugging has been shown to be normally distributed with a variance of 16 minutes. Compute the steady-state queuing statistics for the harbor tug operation.

12.14 *Hospital Administration.* A free one-doctor outpatient clinic of a hospital takes patients without appointments from 1:00 to 5:00 in the afternoon. Patients arrive according to a Poisson process at a rate of 5 per hour. Service times are exponential with a mean of 10 minutes. Patients are taken on a first come, first served basis. Apply the appropriate queuing model and calculate pertinent queuing statistics. What assumptions did you make about the outpatient clinic?

12.15 Can two doctors be justified in your judgment for the outpatient clinic described in Problem 12.14?

12.16 *Service Station.* A one-pump service station has room for only 2 cars waiting. Cars arrive to the station in Poisson manner at a rate of 10 cars per hour. It takes on the average 4 minutes to service a customer. These times are thought to be exponential. What are the expected queuing statistics for the service station? What, specifically, are the assumptions of your queuing model?

12.17 *Flying Club.* A flying club is contemplating the construction of its own private airport. Plans are to build one landing strip. Demand for the landing strip is estimated by club members to be 7 planes per hour. Landing times are known to be normally distributed with a mean of 5 minutes and a standard deviation of 2 minutes. If arrivals are assumed to be Poisson, what are the expected queuing statistics?

12.18 *Department Store.* The manager of a large department store has noticed long customer lines in the catalog sales department. At present the department has 2 clerks. The manager has asked you to do a study and recommend changes in the system to decrease customer waiting time and the length of the lines. You have collected arrival and service-time data and have found that arrivals are Poisson-distributed and that service times are exponentially distributed. Customers arrive at an average rate of 20 per hour and the average catalog sale takes 5 minutes. Analyze the problem and make your recommendation to the store manager.

BIBLIOGRAPHY

Cox, David R., and Walter L. Smith, *Queues.* Agincourt, Ont.: Methuen Publications, 1961.

Hillier, Fredrick S., and Gerald J. Lieberman, *Introduction to Operations Research,* 3rd ed. San Francisco: Holden-Day Inc., 1980.

Morse, Philip M., *Queues, Inventories and Maintenance.* New York: John Wiley & Sons, Inc., 1958.

Saaty, Thomas L., *Elements of Queuing Theory.* New York: McGraw-Hill Book Company, 1961.

Taha, Hamdy A., *Operations Research: An Introduction,* 2nd ed. New York: Macmillan Publishing Co., Inc., 1976.

Trueman, Richard E., *An Introduction to Quantitative Methods for Decision Making.* New York: Holt, Rinehart and Winston, Inc., 1974.

13
Discrete Digital Simulation

UNITED AIRLINES[1]

Good advertising slogans, such as "Fly the Friendly Skies of United," have helped United Airlines become America's largest domestic airline. Having a management team progressive enough to aggressively use management science tools such as discrete digital simulation has also played a critical role.

Because "Congestion at the major airports results in over 25,000 hours of delay per month, inconvenience to the traveling public, and increases the direct operating costs by more than $10 million per month for the domestic airline industry," a management science team consisting of representatives from the Federal Aviation Administration, O'Hare Airport, and the major airlines operating out of O'Hare was organized. The goal of the O'Hare Delay Task Force was to find ways of relieving the congestion at O'Hare Airport and thus reduce costly delays. With the use of the O'Hare simulation model, various decision strategies were evaluated and analyzed. Because of the complex nature of the problem, no other management science tool was appropriate for attacking the airport congestion problem and, consequently, the only alternative to using simulation would have been to implement various strategies at O'Hare and measure their relative effectiveness on the real system.

On the basis of the study, three strategies appeared to have the greatest short-term payoff:

1. Selecting the best runway configurations for the existing wind and weather conditions.

2. Installing equipment to determine the minimum safe separation of airplanes.

3. Improving the systems for controlling the traffic demand during peak periods.

The results of the study were dramatic. The average inbound holding delays at O'Hare have been reduced by 2 to 3 minutes. A conservative estimate of

---

[1]Herbert B. Hubbard, "Terminal Airspace/Airport Congestion Delays," *Interfaces*, 8 (February 1978), 1–14.

United Airlines' annual savings at O'Hare Airport alone is in excess of $1.2 million. In addition to the dollars that can be saved using a simulation approach to the airport congestion problem, the domestic airline industry can conserve up to 5 million barrels of jet fuel annually by minimizing traffic delays due to airport congestion.

INTRODUCTION

Simulation was used in the United Airlines application as a method of last resort, because no other tool in the management scientist's bag could have been applied successfully to the airport congestion problem. Because simulation is often the technique of last resort, and because of its flexibility, it is also the most widely used management science technique. Turban found that simulation was used in approximately 25 percent of the projects involving management science methodology.[2] Cook and Russell reported that only 11 percent of the *Fortune 500* companies surveyed did not use discrete digital simulation to aid their decision-making process.[3] In this chapter, we describe discrete digital simulation, which is often referred to as *Monte Carlo simulation*. In general, simulation is a descriptive, rather than an optimization technique that involves developing a model of some real phenomenon and then performing experiments on that model. This broad definition applies to types of simulation other than discrete digital simulation. A spacecraft simulator, a wind tunnel, a model airplane, and an analog simulation of some continuous process are all examples of simulations that differ fundamentally from the discrete digital simulation used in management science. To be more specific, discrete digital simulation is a numerical technique that involves modeling a stochastic system on a digital computer with the intention of predicting the system's behavior.

Monte Carlo simulation

A simulation model serves the management scientist in much the same way as a laboratory serves the physical scientist. By making changes in the various parameters of a simulation model, the management scientist can observe the results of the simulation and infer how different configurations of the real system would behave under various circumstances.

---

[2]E. Turban, "A Sample Survey of Operations Research Activities at the Corporate Level," *Operations Research,* (May–June 1972), 708–721.
[3]T. M. Cook and R. A Russell, "A Survey of OR/MS Activities in the 1970's," *Proceedings of the 1976 National AIDS Conference,* 122–124.

REASONS FOR USING SIMULATION

The many reasons why a manager uses simulation to solve a problem can be clustered into two major categories.

Experimentation with the real system may be impractical or impossible. A hospital administrator may have difficulty justifying experimenting with the real coronary care unit to determine the optimal number of beds and the best medical team configuration, whereas experimentation on a surrogate system, a computer simulation model, would be totally acceptable.

The real system may be too complex to permit mathematical representation or model solution. Often, if experimentation with the real system is impractical, an alternative would be to develop a mathematical model of the system or problem in question. As was the case with O'Hare Airport, the real system is often too complex to model or solve mathematically, and simulation is used as the tool of last resort.

SIMULATION APPLICATIONS

The literature contains a wealth of diverse applications of discrete digital simulation. The list below represents a small sample of successful applications.

Health Care Applications   Simulation has been used to predict the effect of various physician mixes on the utilization of hospital resources, plan the configuration of emergency rooms, coronary care units, and other hospital facilities. Staffing of nursing stations, primary care teams, and scheduling operations and admissions are all problems that have been attacked using computer simulation. Even the optimal location of ambulances has been examined using simulation.

Urban Applications   Cities have used simulation to solve some of their most pressing problems. Problems such as police dispatching and beat design, the planning and design of transit systems, evaluating operating alternatives at airports, planning for snow emergencies, garbage collection, the location of emergency vehicles, long-range financial planning, and many more urban problems have been solved using computer simulation.

Industrial Applications   Manufacturing organizations have used simulation to schedule their productive process, make inventory policy decisions, design productive systems, determine machine maintenance schedules, design distribution systems, and even to test the effects of increased production on the operation of an overhead crane.

TABLE 13.1 Real-world applications of simulation

Air traffic control queuing
Aircraft maintenance scheduling
Airport design
Ambulance location and dispatching
Assembly line scheduling
Bank teller scheduling
Bus (city) scheduling
Circuit design
Clerical processing system design
Communication system design
  Computer time sharing
  Telephone traffic routing
  Message system
  Mobile communications
Computer memory-fabrication
  test-facility design
Consumer behavior prediction
  Brand selection
  Promotion decisions
  Advertising allocation
  Court system resource allocation
Distribution system design
  Warehouse location
  Mail (post office)
  Soft drink bottling
  Bank courier
  Intrahospital material flow
Enterprise models
  Steel production
  Hospital
  Shipping line
  Railroad operations
  School district
Equipment scheduling
  Aircraft
Facility layout
  Pharmaceutical center
Financial forecasting
  Insurance
  Schools
  Computer leasing
Insurance manpower hiring decisions
Grain terminal operation
Harbor design
Industry models
  Textiles
  Petroleum (financial aspects)

Information system design
Intergroup communication (sociological
  studies)
Inventory reorder rule design
  Aerospace
  Manufacturing
  Military logistics
  Hospitals
Job shop scheduling
  Aircraft parts
  Metals forming
  Work-in-process control
Shipyard
Library operations design
Maintenance scheduling
  Airlines
  Glass furnaces
  Steel furnaces
  Computer field service
National manpower adjustment system
Natural resource (mine) scheduling
  Iron ore
  Strip mining
Parking facility design
Numerically controlled production
  facility design
Personnel scheduling
  Inspection department
  Spacecraft trips
Petrochemical process design
  Solvent recovery
Policy response system design
Political voting predicting
Rail freight car dispatching
Railroad traffic scheduling
Steel mill scheduling
Taxi dispatching
Traffic light timing
Truck dispatching and loading
University financial and operational
  forecasting
Urban traffic system design
Water resources development

Source: James R. Emshoff and Roger L. Sisson, *Design and Use of Computer Simulation Models* (New York: Macmillan, 1972), p. 264. Copyright © 1953 by Macmillan Publishing Co., Inc.

Financial Applications   The rapid growth in the use of simulation as a financial planning tool is evidenced by the more than 25 financial modeling software packages currently available commercially. All kinds of pro forma statements are produced using financial simulation packages. Portfolio selection models are common, as are capital budgeting models.

Military Applications   Large-scale military battles as well as individual weapon systems have been simulated to aid in the design both of weapon systems and of strategic and tactical operations.

Agricultural Applications   Simulation has been used to make decisions concerning equipment on a sugar plantation, to predict the effects of various policy alternatives on the Venezuelan cattle industry, and to aid in the design of regional grain collection, handling, and distribution in Canada.

Table 13.1 is a sample listing of real-world applications of simulation.

MANUAL SIMULATION

In order to give you some understanding of the technique of computer simulation, let us analyze a very simple problem. Two new ship docking facilities are being finished this year and a decision of how many tugs will be necessary to service ships wishing to dock must be made. Using data from similar ports and a great deal of subjective judgment, the time between ship arrivals is distributed as shown in Table 13.2. Time spent at the dock was estimated in similar manner. That probability distribution is reflected in Table 13.3. Tugging time is fairly constant at 1 hour per tug, and ships are taken on a first come, first served basis, with ships being tugged to sea having priority over those being tugged to port. The flow of a ship through the port facility is shown in Figure 13.1. Notice that a tug is needed initially to tow the ship to the berth and it is then released while the ship is unloaded. Once the ship is ready to leave the berth, a tug is needed to tow the ship into the open water.

TABLE 13.2   Ship interarrival time distribution

Time between ship arrivals (hr)	Probability
1	.30
2	.25
3	.15
4	.15
5	.05
6	.05
7	.05
	1.00

TABLE 13.3 Unloading time distribution

Unloading time (hrs)	Probability
1	.05
2	.15
3	.20
4	.25
5	.30
6	.05
	1.00

FIGURE 13.1 **Ship flow through port facility**

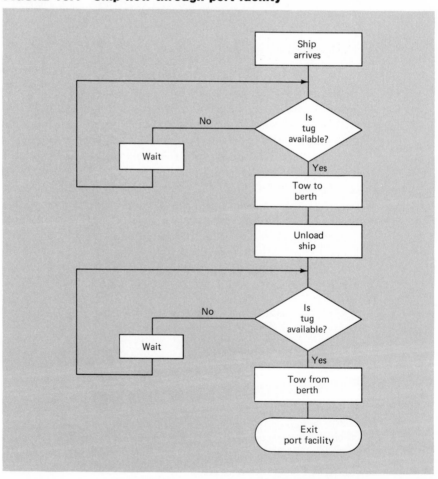

The first step in developing the simulation is to develop a way of generating the two stochastic variables in the system: ship arrival times and unloading times. This is done using numbers from a uniform distribution whose parameters are 0 and 1. Remember that a uniform probability distribution is one in which the random variable is defined over a range from a to b. If the parameters of the uniform distribution are 0 and 1, then $P(x \le .25)$, for example, is equal to 0.25, and $P(.25 \le x \le .75) = .5$. Figure 13.2 depicts the uniform distribution in graphic form.

The process of generating stochastic variables is basic to computer simulation; it is accomplished by defining a function that relates a uniformly distributed random variable to a random variable distributed *Process* in another manner. Remember that once this function, known as a *process generator* *generator*, has been developed, it is easy to sample from a uniform distribution and transform that uniformly distributed random variate into an arrival time or an unloading time. For the sake of simplicity, both stochastic variables are treated as discrete variables. In a real simulation of the harbor problem, these variables would be continuous in nature. The function describing arrival times and unloading times can be found by defining the cumulative probability distributions of the two variables and relating that distribution to a uniform random variable between 0 and 1. Because a number chosen from a uniform distribution with parameters 0 and 1 will fall in the 0 to .3 range 30 percent of the time, 30 percent of the ships generated according to the function described in Table 13.4 will arrive 1 hour after the preceding ship. Similarly, 15 percent of the arrivals will come just 4 hours after the preceding ship.

The generation of unloading times is accomplished in a similar manner. If a random number is chosen between 0 and .05, the generated unloading time is 1 hour. If the random number is between .4 and .65, the generated

FIGURE 13.2 Uniform distribution

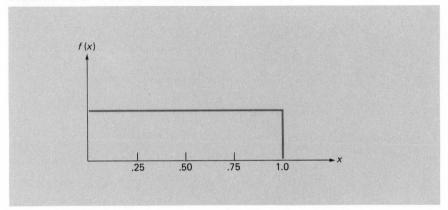

TABLE 13.4   Ship interarrival time generating function

Uniform random variable	Time between arrivals (hrs)
0–.30	1
.30–.55	2
.55–.70	3
.70–.85	4
.85–.90	5
.90–.95	6
.95–1.0	7

unloading time is 4 hours. See Table 13.5 for the unloading-time generating function.

You must remember, however, that we are describing a random process, and it would take a large number of ship arrivals for these percentages to be considered very accurate. In other words, if only 50 arrivals were generated, it would not be unreasonable for 12 or 13 ships to take 3 hours to unload, even though the expected number of ships taking 3 hours to unload is 10 (.2 times 50).

Having defined the system and the process generators, we are now ready to simulate the harbor operation. First, we must decide on what experiments we are interested in running. For illustration, let us run two experiments, one with one tug and the other with two tugs. The critical output variable from the simulator is the average time spent by a ship waiting on a tug. Let us simulate 48 hours and assume an around-the-clock operation. Let us also assume that the random numbers needed to generate ship arrivals are chosen from the random numbers in Table 13.6, starting in the upper left-hand corner. Random numbers to generate unloading times are chosen from the same table, starting in the upper right-hand corner. In a computer simulation, these random numbers would be generated by a random-number-generating function, not chosen from a table.

Looking at Table 13.7, because the random number .445282 falls between .3 and .55, the first ship is simulated to arrive 2 hours into the sim-

TABLE 13.5   Unloading-time generating function

Uniform random variable	Unloading time (hrs)
0–.05	1
.05–.20	2
.20–.40	3
.40–.65	4
.65–.95	5
.95–1.0	6

TABLE 13.6 Random-number table

.445282	.353333	.112460	.494758	.956412	.285648	.106182
.066257	.441906	.055118	.353555	.625270	.569627	.790333
.615352	.579120	.936548	.407208	.014319	.421038	.397360
.594821	.992685	.602720	.682154	.668440	.871255	.211575
.428152	.664736	.135047	.827656	.750516	.054190	.570499
.935282	.477204	.445679	.379244	.264349	.172899	.658255
.393437	.436322	.077000	.535109	.517650	.289920	.080668
.874724	.522334	.261491	.867939	.854214	.313831	.195065
.345906	.319852	.805962	.957102	.488950	.319787	.518168
.230927	.722047	.253941	.025220	.865850	.968126	.016103
.383484	.155976	.484498	.503207	.658759	.423696	.613343
.866792	.680668	.282878	.571261	.881661	.148613	.956734
.402887	.806714	.214300	.025378	.223563	.112981	.665817
.978072	.876081	.453834	.838279	.945164	.126478	.252390
.376035	.984704	.523906	.281099	.971441	.298754	.049552
.608526	.205187	.754386	.679630	.288311	.613193	.084362
.987430	.165323	.105069	.142509	.909431	.174001	.859131
.588776	.800478	.503880	.818984	.378979	.903020	.007307
.916667	.434235	.355410	.224342	.147361	.865086	.864270
.399848	.620655	.125302	.165914	.867769	.713384	.470383
.401840	.177596	.449017	.095737	.533275	.338016	.228617
.329558	.919797	.552755	.038363	.255378	.187000	.823605
.258627	.139314	.508244	.795636	.199622	.037007	.425445
.219602	.488609	.955238	.333945	.406528	.433665	.943236
.756436	.049489	.489014	.488679	.530948	.787576	.946926
.593372	.037899	.887044	.981170	.903624	.591212	.414656
.167034	.270299	.118483	.278210	.602910	.113570	.255230
.509250	.758433	.967347	.978183	.162974	.174195	.578402
.902657	.210320	.138008	.935174	.368968	.797242	.462741
.601267	.442931	.246182	.490711	.728634	.955403	.174712
.449643	.125448	.705902	.106384	.285185	.753657	.955278
.948750	.094997	.031238	.332454	.713580	.289390	.314123
.280228	.854264	.603533	.932821	.165132	.595403	.086226
.158733	.176363	.629582	.190230	.475139	.138766	.556342
.089161	.527890	.364889	.438324	.345949	.130772	.671094
.849617	.057854	.700570	.682735	.791279	.603053	.496812
.553393	.849053	.113780	.041200	.223180	.968275	.801036
.091737	.341098	.220956	.255856	.546529	.976471	.940064
.852144	.652287	.244428	.595987	.376065	.892506	.970457
.790186	.007002	.930339	.519015	.741036	.775080	.981155
.911208	.636852	.620241	.989783	.356524	.231102	.177894
.987448	.323640	.054813	.416119	.003391	.275281	.621161
.249438	.906181	.192145	.997242	.254147	.549703	.010896
.118046	.610211	.598851	.101210	.217602	.394718	.409892
.906891	.752321	.351903	.340528	.876046	.191524	.264726
.864643	.805323	.050154	.053020	.866732	.723211	.538683
.723195	.491027	.437407	.205195	.294510	.920305	.871236
.944672	.826904	.459380	.314145	.750449	.675389	.298291
.711250	.582876	.096009	.330172	.116949	.730150	.328360
.398807	.437603	.036349	.279671	.350884	.588266	.371640

TABLE 13.7 Harbor simulation—one-tug configuration (all time in hours)

Ship number	Random number	Arrival time	Time when tug was engaged (to berth)	Arrival time at berth	Random number	Time unloading is finished	Time when tug was engaged (from berth)	Time tug was released	Time spent waiting
1	.445282	2	2	3	.106182	5	5	6	0
2	.066257	3	3	4	.790333	9	9	10	0
3	.615352	6	6	7	.397360	10	10	11	0
4	.594821	9	11	12	.211575	15	15	16	2
5	.428152	11	12	13	.570499	17	17	18	1
6	.935282	17	18	19	.658255	24	24	25	1
7	.393437	19	19	20	.080668	22	22	23	0
8	.874724	24	25	26	.195065	28	28	29	1
9	.345906	26	26	27	.518168	31	31	32	0
10	.230927	27	27	28	.016103	29	29	30	0
11	.383484	29	30	31	.613343	35	35	36	1
12	.866792	34	34	35	.956734	41	41	42	0
13	.402887	36	36	37	.665817	42	42	43	0
14	.978072	43	43	44	.252390	47	47	48	0
15	.376035	45	45	46	.049552	47	48	49	1
16	.608526	48	49	50	.084362	52	52	53	1

TABLE 13.8 Harbor simulation—two-tug configuration (all time in hours)

Ship number	Random number	Arrival time	Time when tug was engaged (to berth)	Arrival time at berth	Random number	Time unloading is finished	Time when tug was engaged (from berth)	Time tug was released	Time spent waiting
1	.445282	2	2	3	.106182	5	5	6	0
2	.066257	3	3	4	.790333	9	9	10	0
3	.615352	6	6	7	.397360	10	10	11	0
4	.594821	9	9	10	.211575	13	13	14	0
5	.428152	11	11	12	.570499	16	16	17	0
6	.935282	17	17	18	.658255	23	23	24	0
7	.393437	19	19	20	.080668	22	22	23	0
8	.874724	24	24	25	.195065	27	27	28	0
9	.345906	26	26	27	.518168	31	31	32	0
10	.230927	27	27	28	.016103	29	29	30	0
11	.383484	29	29	30	.613343	34	34	36	0
12	.866792	34	34	35	.956734	41	41	42	0
13	.402887	36	36	37	.665817	42	42	43	0
14	.978072	43	43	44	.252390	47	47	48	0
15	.376035	45	45	46	.049552	47	47	48	0
16	.608526	48	48	49	.084362	51	51	52	0

ulated time period. The next ship arrives only 1 hour later, because its random number, .066257, falls between 0 and .3. Since a tug is available at 2 hours into the simulation, it is assigned immediately to the first ship, and 1 hour later the ship is ready for unloading. Unloading time for ship 1 is generated at 2 hours because .106182 is between .05 and .20. The one tug is assigned to ship 2 immediately after servicing ship 1 but is idle for an hour waiting for ship 1 to be unloaded. To make sure you understand how the simulation is working, you should verify the numbers in Tables 13.7 and 13.8.

Upon examination of Tables 13.7 and 13.8, it is apparent that if the object were to minimize ship waiting time, two tugs should be employed, since the average wait time is reduced from .5 hours (hours spent waiting/number of ships) to 0 hours. If, however, the objective is to minimize the cost of waiting plus the cost of operating the port, then costs of waiting and the cost of operating a tug would have to be determined.

Figure 13.3 is a listing of a GPSS computer program that simulates the harbor problem. The experiments described in Tables 13.7 and 13.8 were run on the computer for a simulated time of 4,800 hours instead of 48 hours. It took a medium-size third-generation computer less than 5 CPU seconds to simulate 4,800 hours of harbor operation. The GPSS program took less than 1 hour to write and debug. During that simulated time, 1,745 ships arrived to the port facility. The results of the two experiments are summarized in Table 13.9.

Although the correlation between the manual and computer simulations is quite close for the two-tug configuration, the computer simulation of the

FIGURE 13.3   GPSS simulation model—harbor problem

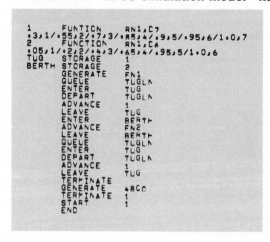

```
1          FUNTICN     RN1,C7
.3,1/.55,2/.7,3/.85,4/.9,5/.95,6/1.0,7
2          FUNCTION    RN1,C6
.05,1/.2,2/.4,3/.65,4/.95,5/1.0,6
TUG        STORAGE     1
BERTH      STORAGE     2
           GENERATE    FN1
           QUEUE       TUGLN
           ENTER       TUG
           DEPART      TUGLN
           ADVANCE     1
           LEAVE       TUG
           ENTER       BERTH
           ADVANCE     FN2
           LEAVE       BERTH
           QUEUE       TUGLN
           ENTER       TUG
           DEPART      TUGLN
           ADVANCE     1
           LEAVE       TUG
           TERMINATE
           GENERATE    4800
           TERMINATE   1
           START       1
           END
```

TABLE 13.9 Harbor simulation results

Configuration	Total number of ships generated	Average tug utilization	Average berth utilization	Average time spent waiting on a tug (hr)
1-tug	1745	.727	.676	1.172
2-tug	1745	.363	.671	.03

one-tug configuration gives an average waiting time of more than twice that given by the manual simulation. It should be clear that the reason we include an example of a manual simulation in this chapter is to give you a more in-depth understanding of what computer simulation is—not to suggest that real problems are solved using manual simulation.

STEPS IN A SIMULATION STUDY

The harbor situation introduced you to simulation as an idea and a technique. In the rest of this chapter, we reinforce this intuitive understanding by describing the various stages or tasks in a simulation study. Figure 13.4 depicts the steps or phases of a simulation study.

PROBLEM FORMULATION

It's difficult to arrive at the right answer if you are working on the wrong problem. Therefore, the first step is to formulate the problem properly. Often, the manager has only a vague idea of what the problem is. It is the job of the management scientist to translate this vague idea into an explicit, written statement of the objectives of the study. The explicit original statement of the problem should not be considered sacrosanct, however, for this reason: As the simulation study progresses, the management scientist becomes more knowledgeable about the system being simulated and about the objectives of the organization. Consequently, it is sometimes necessary to modify the objectives as the nature of the problem becomes clearer. Usually, the statement of objectives takes the form of questions to be answered, hypotheses to be tested, and effects to be estimated. Obviously, it is also necessary to identify the criteria to be used to evaluate these questions.

FIGURE 13.4 Phases in simulation study

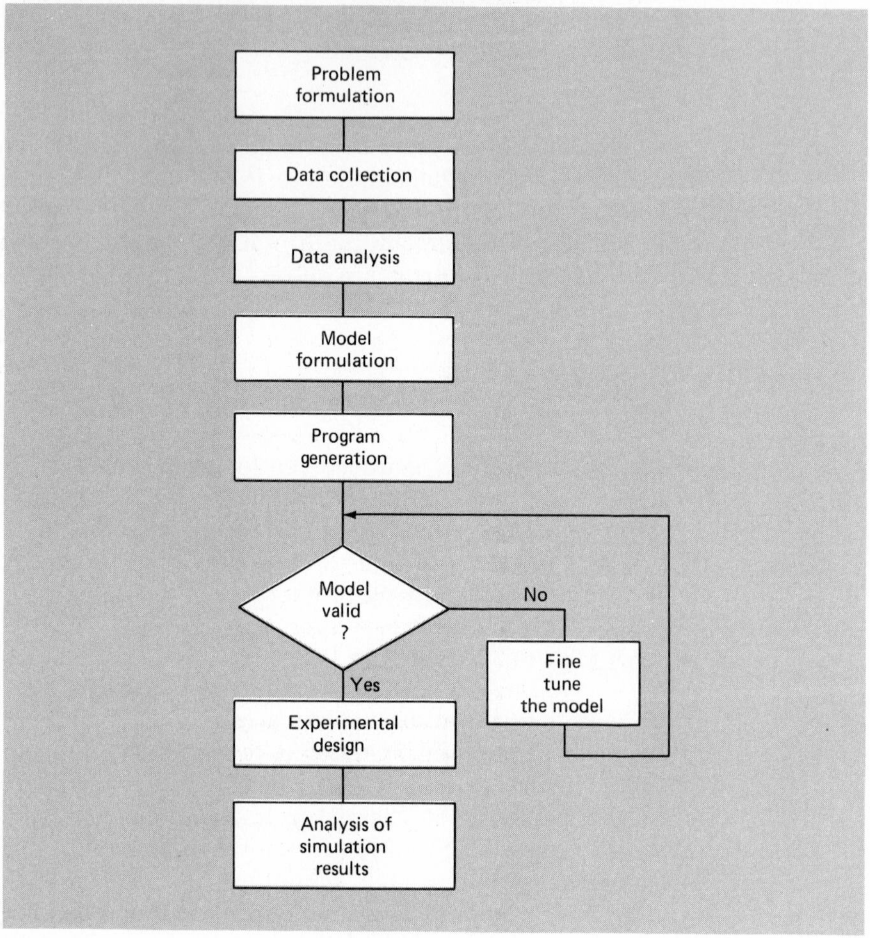

DATA COLLECTION

The second task, and possibly the most time-consuming step in a simulation study, is the job of collecting data. Quantitative data are necessary for several reasons. First, data are required to describe the system being simulated. If you do not understand the real system thoroughly, it is not very likely that you will simulate the system properly. Second, data must be gathered as the foundation for generating the various stochastic variables in the system. For example, in a simple queuing system, real data concerning arrivals and service times must be gathered and analyzed to determine the proper probability distributions and their parameters. Finally, data are necessary to test and validate the model. In order to use a simulation model to make decisions, the decision maker must be confident that the real-world phenomenon has been adequately and accurately represented. Often, the best way to accomplish this validation is to compare simulator output with historical data.

DATA ANALYSIS

Once the data have been collected, they must be analyzed and the proper generating functions must be developed. In the harbor example, the stochastic variables—ship arrival times and unloading times—were generated using cumulative probability distributions. These were estimated subjectively using limited data. Actually, subjective probability distributions are somewhat atypical; probability distributions based on empirical data usually yield more reliable simulation results and thus are preferable.

Two basic tasks must be accomplished in order to generate random variables. First, the raw data of a stochastic variable must be analyzed to determine how that random variable is distributed. Then, a function must be derived to generate the stochastic variable using a uniformly distributed random number between 0 and 1. The following procedure is typically used to determine how a random variable is distributed:

1. The data are grouped into a frequency distribution.
2. This frequency distribution is depicted graphically either as a histogram or a frequency polygon.
3. From the shape of the histogram, a probability distribution is hypothesized.
4. Probability distribution parameters are estimated using sample statistics.
5. The hypothesis is tested using one of several statistical tests such as the *chi-square* or *Kolmogorov–Smirnov test*.

chi-square and Kolmogorov-Smirnov tests

495

6. If the hypothesis is rejected, distribution parameters can be *perturbed,* or changed slightly, and the new hypothesis tested.

7. If no known probability distribution can be found to fit the sampled data, the management scientist is often forced to use the cumulative probability distribution of the sample data.

Let us illustrate these steps by a simple example. The following service times at a gas station were collected during one day: 3.4, 5.4, 4.2, 5.5, 7.9, 0.6, 9.5, 0.0, 9.5, 5.1, 6.7, 1.6, 6.2, 0.5, 1.9, 9.6, 7.9, 6.9, 4.2, 2.7, 5.5, 4.8, 1.8, 9.0, 3.5, 3.9, 6.5, 0.5, 8.8, 3.6, 8.9, 2.4, 0.4, 4.7, 0.8. The frequency distribution for these raw data is reflected in Table 13.10 and a graphical representation is shown in Figure 13.5.

From the shape of the histogram in Figure 13.5, let us hypothesize that the random variable (gas station service times) is uniformly distributed with parameters 0 and 10. Therefore,

H_0 : Sample is drawn from a uniformly distributed population with $a = 0$ and $b = 10$

$H\alpha$: Population is not uniformly distributed with $a = 0$ and $b = 10$

To test this null hypothesis, either a standard chi-square test or the Kolmogorov–Smirnov, a generally more powerful test, can be used. The latter entails the following steps:

1. Formulate the null hypothesis and the alternative hypothesis.

2. Establish the theoretical probability for each class by taking the definite integral of the hypothesized probability density function.

3. Calculate the relative frequency for each class by dividing the number of observations in a class by the sample size.

4. Compute the cumulative probability distribution of the sample data by successively adding the relative frequencies of each class. (This is also called the *observed cumulative distribution,* or *OCD.*)

5. Establish the cumulative probability distribution of the theoretical distribution that has been hypothesized by successively adding the

TABLE 13.10   Frequency distribution

Class	Frequency of observations
0–2	9
2–4	6
4–6	8
6–8	6
8–10	6

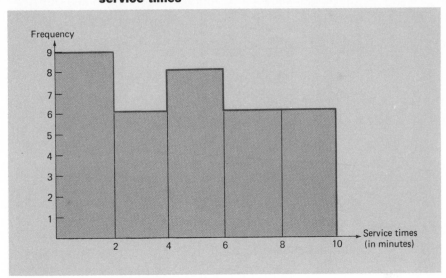

FIGURE 13.5 Histogram of frequency distribution of gas station service times

theoretical probabilities of each class. (This is also called the *theoretical cumulative distribution,* or *TCD.*)

6. Compute the absolute difference between the observed cumulative distribution and the theoretical cumulative distribution for each class in the frequency distribution by subtracting the TCD from the OCD. This operation gives you the *absolute difference.*

7. Compare the absolute difference for each class interval with the critical value found in a standard Kolmogorov–Smirnov table. If the critical value exceeds every absolute difference then the null hypothesis cannot be rejected.

The results of submitting the gas station data to this procedure are shown in Table 13.11. Because the critical Kolmogorov–Smirnov value with a level of significance of .05 is equal to .23, the null hypothesis cannot be rejected. (Verify these values in the Kolmogorov–Smirnov table in Appendix G.)

The next step in analyzing the data is to develop the functions necessary to generate a nonuniformly distributed random variable from a uniform random number between 0 and 1. If the random variable is discrete, it is easy to use the cumulative probability distribution, as we did in the manual simulation of the harbor.

For example, let x be the number of arrivals at an emergency room in 1 hour. Let us assume that this random variable, x, is distributed in a

TABLE 13.11 Kolmogorov–Smirnov test applied to gas station data

Class	Theoretical probability	Relative frequency	Theoretical cumulative distribution	Observed cumulative distribution	Absolute difference
0–2	.2	.257	.2	.257	.057
2–4	.2	.171	.4	.428	.029
4–6	.2	.229	.6	.657	.057
6–8	.2	.171	.8	.828	.029
8–10	.2	.171	1.0	.999*	.001
	1.0	.999*			

*Failure to sum to 1.0 is due to truncation error.

Poisson manner with a mean of 1. This probability distribution is shown in Table 13.12. It is then a simple matter to generate a uniform random number between 0 and 1 and use this random number to determine the value of x. For example, if the random number is .63278, x takes on the value of 1. If the random number is less than .3679, no arrivals occurred during that hour. The generating function is as shown in Table 13.13.

To derive a generating function for continuous random variables, you must use the integral calculus, but the basic idea is the same. The object is to define the stochastic variable in terms of a uniformly distributed random number. For example, the process generator for a random variable distributed according to a negative exponential distribution is

$$x = -\frac{1}{\lambda}\ln(r)$$

where x = exponentially distributed random variable
r = uniform random number between 0 and 1

TABLE 13.12 Poisson distribution with mean = 1

Number of arrivals	Probability	Cumulative probability
0	.3679	.3679
1	.3679	.7358
2	.1839	.9197
3	.0613	.9810
4	.0153	.9963
5	.0031	.9994
6	.0005	.9999
7	.0001	1.0000

TABLE 13.13 Poisson generating function

Random number	x
0–.3679	0
.3679–.7358	1
.7358–.9197	2
.9197–.9810	3
.9810–.9963	4
.9963–.9994	5
.9994–.9999	6
.9999–1.000	7

MODEL FORMULATION

A simulation model is an abstraction—usually mathematical—of some real phenomenon or system. Model building is a very difficult step in the simulation process, because the model builder must strike a balance between model realism and the cost of developing that model. If a crucial variable or function relationship is omitted, the model does not accurately predict the behavior of the real system. If the model is too close to the real-world system, it can easily be too expensive to collect data for or to program and execute. The goal of the model builder is to build a model that adequately describes the real system at a minimum cost of human and computer resources. You can imagine that model building is an art rather than a science.

PROGRAM GENERATION

Most management science studies require the use of the computer, but for simulation the management scientist has no alternative. The computer is an absolute necessity. The computer language you use is, therefore, a matter of some consequence.

Computer programming languages can actually be thought of in a hierarchy. The assembler languages of the various computer manufacturers are at the lowest level, but they are almost never used in simulation studies. For one thing, they are machine-dependent, which means that an assembler language program will not run on a machine other than the model for which it was created. An IBM 370 assembler language program, for example, cannot run on a Honeywell computer. Also, it is excessively complex to write a simulation program in assembler language. A simple, single-channel queuing simulator might take as many as 5,000 assembler language instructions.

Compiler languages, the next level of programming languages, are used for simulation. FORTRAN, BASIC, PL/1, and ALGOL are the most popular of these for simulation. Compiler languages are machine-independent, and because they are more sophisticated than assembler languages, a programmer has far less detail to be concerned with; so the programming effort is reduced.

Special-purpose simulation languages, such as SIMSCRIPT, GPSS, DYNAMO, and GASP, simplify programming even more. This advantage is graphically demonstrated in Figures 13.6 and 13.3. The manual simulation we performed in the harbor problem is coded in FORTRAN in Figure 13.6 and in GPSS in Figure 13.3.

In view of these illustrations, you can readily see why the management scientist should use a special-purpose simulation language to write a simulation program. The reason for the obvious reduction in programming effort with a simulation language such as GPSS is that each GPSS statement or block can be thought of as a FORTRAN subroutine (a small program in itself); and such things as the simulation clock and next-event logic are preprogrammed into the GPSS software. An additional benefit is that the probability of creating a valid program is increased.

Why, then, are most simulators written in compiler languages such as FORTRAN and BASIC? One reason is that special-purpose simulation languages such as GPSS and SIMSCRIPT are not so widely available as the compiler languages. All but the very smallest computers have FORTRAN, COBOL, or BASIC compilers in their software packages. Often, a simulation language such as GPSS is not used because the management scientist conducting the simulation study may not know a special-purpose language and may be unwilling to invest the time needed to learn one. Clearly, an organization that uses management science techniques to aid in its decision process should consider acquiring a simulation processor such as GPSS or SIMSCRIPT, and then train its staff in the use of the simulation language.

MODEL VALIDATION

Perhaps the most difficult step in a simulation study is validating the simulation model. It is foolish to use simulation results in the decision-making process unless you are quite confident that the simulation model represents the real-world situation accurately. Absolute validation is probably unattainable, but it is possible to gain confidence in a simulation model by making certain verifications.

Program testing   One aspect of a simulation that must be validated is whether the programmer has instructed the computer properly. It is possible that a simulation model is valid as designed but invalid as implemented on the computer. Standard program-testing techniques should be employed to insure congruence between simulator design and simu-

FIGURE 13.6 FORTRAN source listing for harbor problem

```fortran
C     FORTRAN BY   SHARON WILSON    11-1-73
      DIMENSION X(15),Y(15),A(16),B(16),EVENT(15,20),ITEMP(20)
      DIMENSION C(15),D(15),E(20),F(20),IT(20)
    1 READ(5,10,END=1000)NUMBER,ISET,ITIME,IFREQ,N
   10 FORMAT(1015)
      WRITE(6,11)NUMBER,ITIME,IFREQ,N
   11 FORMAT('1',////,'  * * * * THIS PROGRAM WILL CALCULATE',I5,' SIMUL
     1ATIONS STARTING AT',I5,' HOURS',/,3X,'WITH ONE ARRIVAL EVERY',I5,
     2' MINUTES AND',I5,' TOTAL NUMBER OF ARRIVALS.',////)
      READ(5,20)(X(I),I=1,15)
   20 FORMAT(15F5.0)
      DO 21 I=1,15
      IF(X(I).EQ.0.0)GO TO 22
   21 CONTINUE
   22 LX=I-1
      WRITE(6,23)(X(I),I=1,LX)
   23 FORMAT('0 PROBABILITIES FOR INCOMING EVENTS',/,15F8.4)
      IF(ISET.EQ.0)GO TO 40
C
      READ(5,20)(Y(I),I=1,15)
      DO 31 I=1,15
      IF(Y(I).EQ.0.0)GO TO 32
   31 CONTINUE
   32 LY=I-1
      WRITE(6,33)(Y(I),I=1,LY)
   33 FORMAT('0 PROBABILITIES FOR OUT GOING EVENTS',/,15F8.4)
   40 CONTINUE
      SUM=0.0
      DO 41 I=1,LX
   41 SUM=SUM+X(I)
   50 IF(ISET.EQ.0)GO TO 55
      SUM=0.0
      DO 51 I=1,LY
   51 SUM=SUM+Y(I)
   55 IX=9
      LXX=LX
      LYY=LY
      LX=LX+1
      LY=LY+1
      TIME = ITIME
      READ(5,20)(C(I),I=1,LXX)
      WRITE(6,24)(C(I),I=1,LXX)
   24 FORMAT('0 EARLY TIME ARRIVALS',/,15F8.1)
      IF(ISET.EQ.0) GO TO 54
      READ(5,20)(D(I),I=1,LYY)
      WRITE(6,25)(D(I),I=1,LYY)
   25 FORMAT('0 DURATION TIME',/,15F8.1)
   54 CONTINUE
      A(1)=0.0
      DO 57 I=1,LX
   57 A(I+1)=A(I)+X(I)
      IF(ISET.EQ.0)GO TO 60
      B(1)=0.0
      DO 56 I=1,LY
   56 B(I+1)=B(I)+Y(I)
   60 DO 500 IJ=1,NUMBER
      WRITE(6,61)IJ
   61 FORMAT('1',29X,'* * * * * * * * * * * * * * * * * * *',/,' ',
     129X,'* * S I M U L A T I O N ',I5,' * * *',/,' ',29X,
     2'* * * * * * * * * * * * * * * * * * *',////)
      CALL MOVE(0,EVENT,0,1200)
      DO 70 J=1,N
      CALL RANDNO(IX,IY,RAND)
      RAND=ABS(RAND)
      IX=IY
      IF       (RAND.LT.0.0.OR.RAND.GT.1.0)RAND=0.0
      DO 71 I=1,LX
      IF(A(I).LE.RAND.AND.RAND.LE.A(I+1))GO TO 73
   71 CONTINUE
      GO TO 70
   73 EVENT(I,J)=1.
   70 CONTINUE
      IF(ISET.EQ.0)GO TO 100
      DO 80 J=1,N
      CALL RANDNO(IX,IY,RAND)
      RAND=ABS(RAND)
      IX=IY
      IF(RAND.LT.0.0.OR.RAND.GT.1.0)RAND=0.0
      DO 81 I=1,LY
      IF(B(I).LE.RAND.AND.RAND.LE.B(I+1))GO TO 83
   81 CONTINUE
      GO TO 80
   83 EVENT(I,J)=EVENT(I,J)+2.
   80 CONTINUE
  100 CONTINUE
      DO 110 I=1,N
  110 E(I)=IFREQ*(I-1)
      WRITE(6,150)
  150 FORMAT(12X,'PROBABILITY',14X,'ARRIVAL NUMBER',/,11X,74('-'))
      DO 175 I=1,LXX
      K=1
      DO 160 J=1,N
      IF(EVENT(I,J).EQ.1.0.OR.EVENT(I,J).EQ.3.0)GO TO 159
      GO TO 160
  159 ITEMP(K)=J
      K=K+1
  160 CONTINUE
      K=K-1
      IF(K.EQ.0) GO TO 170
      WRITE(6,165)I,A(I),A(I+1),(ITEMP(KK),KK=1,K)

  165 FORMAT(' EVENT ',I2,2X,':',F5.3,'-',F5.3,':',20(I2,'/'))
      GO TO 175
  170 WRITE(6,165)I,A(I),A(I+1)
  175 CONTINUE
      WRITE(6,180)
  180 FORMAT(11X,74('-'))
      IF(ISET.EQ.0)  GO TO 300
      WRITE(6,250)
  250 FORMAT(////,12X,'PROBABILITY',14X,'DEPARTURE NUMBER',/,11X,74('-'))
      DO 275 I=1,LYY
      K=1
      DO 260 J=1,N
      IF(EVENT(I,J).EQ.2.0.OR.EVENT(I,J).EQ.3.0) GO TO 259
      GO TO 260
  259 ITEMP(K)=J
      K=K+1
  260 CONTINUE
      K=K-1
      IF(K.EQ.0) GO TO 270
      WRITE(6,165)I,B(I),B(I+1),(ITEMP(KK),KK=1,K)
      GO TO 275
  270 WRITE(6,165)I,B(I),B(I+1)
  275 CONTINUE
      WRITE(6,180)
  300 CONTINUE
      WRITE(6,600)
  600 FORMAT(//,24X,'*************',/,24X,'***SCHEDULE***',/,24X,
     1'*************')
      WRITE(6,601)
  601 FORMAT('0',12X,'   ARRIVAL        ARRIVAL      DEPARTURE',/,14X,
     1'   NUMBER         TIME           TIME    ',/,12X,
     2'                 IN HOURS       IN HOURS',/,12X,40('-'))
      DO 650 J=1,N
      DO 640 I=1,LXX
      IF(EVENT(I,J).EQ.1.0.OR.EVENT(I,J).EQ.3.0) GO TO 639
      GO TO 640
  639 IT(J)=J
      E(J)=E(J)-C(I)
  640 CONTINUE
  650 CONTINUE
      CALL ORDER(N,E,IT)
      IF(ISET.EQ.0) GO TO 775
      DO 750 J=1,N
      DO 740 I=1,LYY
      IF(EVENT(I,J).EQ.2.0.OR.EVENT(I,J).EQ.3.0) GO  TO 739
      GO TO 740
  739 F(J)=D(I)
  740 CONTINUE
  750 CONTINUE
  775 CONTINUE
      INDEX=IT(1)
      IF(ISET.EQ.0) GO TO 780
      TEMPO=((E(1)+F(INDEX))/60.)+TIME
  780 TEMP1=(E(1)/60.)+TIME
      IF(ISET.EQ.0) WRITE(6,800) INDEX,TEMP1
      WRITE(6,800)INDEX,TEMP1,TEMPO
  800 FORMAT(12X,I7,6X,2(F10.3,3X))
      DO 900 ICHEAT=2,N
      INDEX=IT(ICHEAT-1)
      IF(ISET.EQ.0) F(INDEX)=0.
      IF(E(ICHEAT).GE.(E(ICHEAT-1)+F(INDEX)))GO TO 875
      FUDGE=E(ICHEAT-1)+F(INDEX)-E(ICHEAT)
      E(ICHEAT)=E(ICHEAT)+FUDGE
      INDEX=IT(ICHEAT)
      IF(ISET.EQ.0) GO TO 850
      TEMPO=((E(ICHEAT)+F(INDEX))/60.)+TIME
  850 TEMP1=(E(ICHEAT)/60.)+TIME
      IF(ISET.EQ.0) WRITE(6,800) INDEX,TEMP1
      WRITE(6,800)INDEX,TEMP1,TEMPO
      GO TO 900
  875 INDEX=IT(ICHEAT)
      IF(ISET.EQ.0) GO TO 880
      TEMPO=((E(ICHEAT)+F(INDEX))/60.)+TIME
  880 TEMP1=(E(ICHEAT)/60.)+TIME
      IF(ISET.EQ.0) WRITE(6,800) INDEX,TEMP1
      WRITE(6,800)INDEX,TEMP1,TEMPO
  900 CONTINUE
  500 CONTINUE
      GO TO 1
 1000 CONTINUE
      CALL END
      STOP
      END
      SUBROUTINE ORDER(LX,X,IT)
      DIMENSION X(2),IT(2)
      K=0
      DO 20 J=1,LX
      K=K+1
      INDEX=K
      DO 10 K=K,LX
   10 IF(X(INDEX).GT.X(K))INDEX=I
      XMIN=X(INDEX)
      IMIN=IT(INDEX)
      X(INDEX)=X(J)
      IT(INDEX)=IT(J)
      IT(J)=IMIN
   20 X(J)=XMIN
      RETURN
      END
      SUBROUTINE RANDNO(IX,IY,YFL)
      IY=IX*65539
      IF(IY)5,6,6
```

501

lator program. These techniques include manual calculations, program traces, and so on. It is necessary to verify the absence of programming errors when you are validating a simulation, but this step alone is not sufficient. The program can be perfect and the simulation model may still be totally invalid.

Variable generation test   Earlier in this chapter we applied nonparametric goodness-of-fit tests to hypotheses concerning the distributions of the various stochastic variables. These same tests should be applied to the output from the various generating functions to insure that the real-world variables and simulated variables are distributed in the same manner. For example, if the interarrival time in a real queuing system is normally distributed with a mean of 5 minutes and a standard deviation of 2 minutes, then the random variable of interarrival times being generated in the simulation program should also be normally distributed with $\mu = 5$ and $\sigma = 2$.

Subjective validation   The design as well as the output of the simulation model ought to be reviewed by the people who are most familiar with the real system. This subjective validation should properly be done by people not directly involved in the simulation study.

Historical validation   If the simulator is designed to simulate an existing system, it is often possible to simulate the system as it is presently configured and then compare actual historical data to simulation output. For example, if the real system is a harbor operation, vital statistics such as the average wait time of a vessel and the average time a vessel spends in the harbor should be compared to the distribution of various output variables. The absence of significant differences between simulated results and historical results may tend to validate the simulator; but it does not guarantee that the simulator will accurately predict the behavior of the real system under different conditions.

Confidence in the validity of a simulation model is crucial to the successful use of simulation. For this reason, the management scientist should leave no stone unturned when performing the validation step of a simulation study.

EXPERIMENTAL DESIGN

Once a simulation model has been implemented and validated, it can be used for its original purpose, experimentation. Simulation, you will recall, is a means of providing information necessary for decision making when a real-world system cannot be sufficiently manipulated. A simulation model synthetically gathers the information necessary to describe the system under study. The object is to gather the information necessary for decision making—at the lowest possible cost. Usually, real-world experiments are more costly than simulation experiments, and thus the management scientist can experiment with a greater number of alternatives when using a simulation model. For example, if the system under study is a harbor and the decision variables are the number of tugs, the number of berths, and the queue discipline, by means of simulation the management scientist can experiment with many combinations of decision variables to determine the optimal harbor configuration. If, however, experiments were made on the real system, far fewer alternatives could be evaluated.

The questions of the length of simulation runs, initialization periods, sample sizes, and optimization procedures are beyond the scope of this text. Many of the answers are contained in the traditional literature concerning experimental design.

ANALYSIS OF SIMULATION RESULTS

If the simulation model is valid and the simulation experiments have been designed properly, analysis of simulation output is fairly straightforward. It is the function of the management scientist to interpret simulation results and make the appropriate inferences necessary for rational decision making. Often, certain statistical techniques, such as analysis of variance, can be helpful in analyzing simulation results.

WHEN TO SIMULATE

Once the problem has been formulated, the management scientist must decide whether or not to attempt to solve the problem using discrete digital simulation. This decision process is depicted in Figure 13.7.

FIGURE 13.7   When to simulate

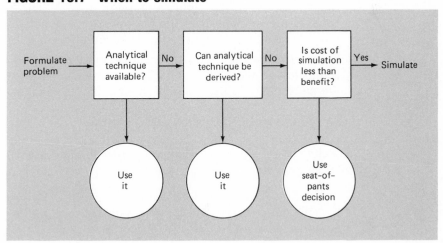

As we said earlier in this chapter, the problem should be formulated explicitly in terms of hypotheses to be tested and questions to be answered. After the problem has been formulated, a solution technique other than simulation is often judged to be more appropriate. The important point is that choosing a solution methodology must succeed, not precede, the problem formulation phase of any management science study. If an analytical technique or model is available or can be adapted to the problem, it should probably be used. If an analytical technique such as classical inventory theory or queuing theory cannot be applied, then the management scientist must make the decision between simulating and making an intuitive, seat-of-the-pants decision. This judgment, in turn, depends on the nature of the individual decision. In other words, is the decision important enough to justify the estimated cost of developing, validating, and experimenting with a simulation model?

ADVANTAGES OF SIMULATION

In deciding whether or not to simulate, the management scientist must weigh the advantages of the technique.

1. The greatest advantage is that simulation allows the management scientist to model complex and dynamic phenomena that otherwise could not be dealt with in a scientific way.
2. Simulation permits experimentation that might be impossible or infeasible otherwise. "What if" questions can be asked using simulation.
3. By simulating the system, the management scientist gains valuable insight into the system and into the relative importance of the different variables.
4. Simulation allows for the compression of real time. To predict the behavior of a system over the period of a year may take only a few seconds or minutes using computer simulation.
5. To comprehend the basic concept of simulation does not require a sophisticated mathematical background and, consequently, managers are more likely to use simulation as a decision-making tool.

DISADVANTAGES OF SIMULATION

Naturally, there are some significant disadvantages to using discrete digital simulation to solve management decision-making problems.

1. Simulation is not an optimization technique. Typically, different system configurations are experimented with to find a good, but *not* guaranteed best, solution.

2. Simulation is an expensive way to solve a problem. In addition to the cost of building and validating a simulation model, experimentation using computer simulation can be quite costly.

3. Because of the nature of simulation, sampling error exists in all output from simulation models. Of course, this sampling error can be reduced by increasing the sample size or by lengthening the computer run time.

4. A real disadvantage is that simulation is often misused because many people who are qualified to write a simulation program are not qualified to perform a total simulation study. In other words, many programmers do not possess the necessary statistical background.

5. Probably the most serious shortcoming of simulation is that it is a tool of solution evaluation and thus does not generate problem solutions. Therefore, the decision maker has to develop proposed solutions; then, simulation can be used to test the relative desirability of those solutions.

THE FUTURE OF SIMULATION

At the beginning of this chapter, we said that simulation was the most commonly used management science technique. There are four major reasons why discrete digital simulation will continue to expand into almost every imaginable area of application.

1. Simulation is probably the most powerful of management science techniques. Many different kinds of problems can be solved using simulation.

2. The cost of computing has been decreasing and will continue to do so at a very rapid rate.

3. Simulation languages will continue to evolve and, indeed, to be invented, thus making it less expensive and less time-consuming to solve problems by means of this technique.

4. Finally, as more managers are made aware of the power of simulation as a tool for the decision-making process, the more popular simulation will become.

SUMMARY

Discrete digital simulation is probably the most potent, most flexible, and consequently, one of the most commonly used tools in the tool kit of the management scientist. Simulation's major contribution is that it allows the decision maker to predict the behavior of a complex system under various circumstances and configurations.

The application of simulation to solving management problems is on a steep growth trend. Simulation is being applied to a rapidly increasing variety of problems mainly because of its ability to model complex and dynamic systems that could otherwise not be modeled. Another reason for the recent explosion in simulation applications is that the major disadvantages of simulation, cost and the unavailability of data necessary to build and validate the model, are being mitigated by the rapid advances that have been made and are being made in computer hardware and software technology.

SOLVED PROBLEM

PROBLEM STATEMENT

A car wash chain is planning to build another car wash facility and is trying to decide how many stalls to build. Past experience has shown that the time between arriving customers is exponentially distributed. The mean of the distribution depends on the traffic count per hour going by the facility. Based on city traffic engineering data, the mean time between arrivals is estimated to be 10 minutes. The time required to wash a car is 10 minutes and constant. Also, it has been established that people generally do not get in line if there are more than 2 cars waiting. If management wants to build a facility such that there is a low probability of losing customers due to the length of the line but at the same time does not want to overbuild, how many stalls should be built? Simulate for 8 hours, or 480 minutes.

SOLUTION

The process generator for the exponential distribution is

$$x = -\frac{1}{\lambda} \ln(r)$$

In order to calculate the time between arrivals, merely substitute the random number into the function shown above. For example,

$$r = .494$$
$$x = -10 \ln(.494)$$
$$= (-10)(-.7052)$$
$$= 7.052 \quad \text{rounded to 7 minutes}$$

		1 Stall			
Random no.	Time of arrival	Time in	Time out	No. in line	Lost customer?
.494	7	7	17	0	No
.353	17	17	27	0	No
.407	26	27	37	0	No
.682	30	37	47	0	No
.827	32	47	57	1	No
.379	42	57	67	1	No
.535	48	67	77	1	No
.867	49	—	—	2	Yes
.957	49	—	—	2	Yes
.025	86	86	96	0	No
.503	93	96	106	0	No
.571	99	106	116	0	No
.025	136	136	146	0	No
.838	138	146	156	0	No
.281	151	156	166	0	No
.679	155	166	176	1	No
.142	175	176	186	0	No
.818	177	186	196	0	No
.224	192	196	206	0	No
.165	210	210	220	0	No
.095	234	234	244	0	No
.038	267	267	277	0	No
.795	269	277	287	0	No
.333	280	287	297	0	No
.488	287	297	307	0	No
.911	288	307	317	0	No
.278	301	317	327	1	No
.978	301	—	—	2	Yes
.935	302	—	—	2	Yes
.490	309	327	337	1	No
.106	331	337	347	0	No
.332	342	347	357	0	No
.932	343	357	367	1	No
.190	360	367	377	0	No
.438	368	377	387	0	No
.682	372	387	397	1	No
.041	404	404	414	0	No
.255	418	418	428	0	No
.595	423	428	438	0	No
.519	430	438	448	0	No
.989	430	448	458	1	No
.416	439	458	468	1	No
.997	439	—	—	2	Yes
.101	462	468	478	0	No
.340	473	478	488	0	No
.053	502	—	—		

		2 Stalls				
Random no.	Time of arrival	Stall no.	Time in	Time out	No. in line	Lost customer?
.494	7	1	7	17	0	No
.353	17	1	17	27	0	No
.407	26	2	26	36	0	No
.682	30	1	30	40	0	No
.827	32	2	36	46	0	No
.379	42	1	42	52	0	No
.535	48	2	48	58	0	No
.867	49	1	52	62	0	No
.957	49	2	58	68	0	No
.025	86	1	86	96	0	No
.503	93	2	93	103	0	No
.571	99	1	99	109	0	No
.025	136	1	136	146	0	No
.838	138	2	138	148	0	No
.281	151	1	151	161	0	No
.679	155	2	155	165	0	No
.142	175	1	175	185	0	No
.818	177	2	177	187	0	No
.224	192	1	192	202	0	No
.165	210	1	210	220	0	No
.095	234	1	234	244	0	No
.038	267	1	267	277	0	No
.795	269	2	269	279	0	No
.333	280	1	280	290	0	No
.488	287	2	287	297	0	No
.911	288	1	290	300	0	No
.278	301	1	301	311	0	No
.978	301	2	301	311	0	No
.935	302	1	311	321	0	No
.490	309	2	311	321	1	No
.106	331	1	331	341	0	No
.332	342	1	342	352	0	No
.932	343	2	343	353	0	No
.190	360	1	360	370	0	No
.438	368	2	368	378	0	No
.682	372	1	372	382	0	No
.041	404	1	404	414	0	No
.255	418	1	418	428	0	No
.595	423	2	423	433	0	No
.519	430	1	430	440	0	No
.989	430	2	433	443	0	No
.416	439	1	440	450	0	No
.997	439	2	443	453	0	No
.101	462	1	463	473	0	No
.340	473	1	474	484	0	No
.053	502					

The time until the next arrival is 7 + x, where

$$x = -10 \ln (.353)$$
$$= (-10)(-1.04)$$
$$= 10 \text{ minutes} \quad \text{rounded}$$

Therefore, the second customer arrives at 17 minutes into the simulation. The rest of the solution tables merely keep track of the system as simulated time progresses.

   If management were to use the simulation to make a decision concerning the number of stalls, the profit lost from customers not stopping would have to be weighed against the cost of the second stall. Another important statistic might be the average time a customer spent waiting. Obviously, the prudent management scientist would run the simulation for more than 8 hours, so that the sampling error inherent in simulation studies could be significantly reduced.

REVIEW QUESTIONS

1. Define "discrete digital simulation."
2. How does simulation differ from LP?
3. Discuss two major reasons for using simulation for solving decision problems.
4. Why is a computer necessary when simulating a real system?
5. What are the major phases in a simulation study?
6. What is a Kolmogorov–Smirnov test used for?
7. What is a process generator?
8. What are uniform random numbers used for in simulation?
9. Why aren't assembler languages used to code simulation models?
10. Why is FORTRAN the most popular language used for simulation?
11. Why should a management scientist use a special-purpose simulation language?
12. List two advantages GPSS has over FORTRAN as a simulation language.
13. Why is validation an important step in any simulation study?
14. How does historical validation differ from subjective validation?
15. List three advantages of using simulation.
16. List three disadvantages of using simulation.
17. Why is the application of simulation likely to increase significantly in the near future?

PROBLEMS

13.1 *Milk Company.* The Page Milk Company has a large, gallon-bottling machine that occasionally breaks down due to bearing failure. The machine has two bearings of this type. In order to replace one of the bearings, the machine must be shut down. This machine shutdown costs the company approximately $30 per hour. The bearings are relatively inexpensive, at $5 per bearing. At the present, a bearing is replaced only when it fails. The time between bearing failures is distributed as shown in the first table. The time it takes to replace a bearing is fairly deterministic at 1 hour. An

Hours between bearing failures	Probability
20	.05
40	.07
60	.13
70	.35
80	.30
90	.07
100	.03

employee has suggested that, since it is as easy to replace both bearings as one, the company should try a new policy of replacing both bearings when either one fails. Limited experience with similar bearings has yielded the following probability distribution of bearing failures when both bearings are replaced:

Hours between bearing failures	Probability
40	.05
75	.10
100	.15
125	.25
150	.20
180	.15
200	.10

Use manual or computer simulation to solve this policy problem. If you simulate manually, simulate for the period of 1 month. Assume a 24-hour work day and a 7-day work week.

13.2 *Port Administration.* The following times have been collected at the local harbor. How are these two random variables distributed?

Docking times (min)				Unloading times (min)			
8.59	9.62	9.29	11.34	47.78	17.55	23.82	5.58
13.84	12.89	13.52	12.02	11.93	4.40	18.06	11.16
13.59	13.99	14.87	11.03	48.10	53.61	45.82	12.32
9.29	8.79	13.13	13.86	54.90	43.57	29.43	7.61
12.79	11.03	10.00	13.41	56.65	3.25	36.63	11.24
9.89	13.32	11.62	13.98	23.00	38.50	27.78	58.47
14.14	9.44	13.58	9.57	25.65	15.94	9.77	12.15
13.08	13.89	12.29	8.69	29.76	103.05	7.92	9.88
10.86	13.86	16.66	13.38	27.62	3.00	66.32	34.73
11.39	12.62	14.23	10.73	88.40	59.47	8.79	26.62
12.71	12.03	11.67	8.73	9.40	11.36	21.46	13.29
10.70	9.63	9.56	12.47	2.75	4.21	45.32	57.50
9.20	10.12	13.71	12.78	3.28	89.12	2.38	67.63
11.49	11.24	10.66	11.18	53.67	21.62	17.70	35.54
14.90	15.95	11.76	11.22	1.97	23.51	128.14	3.48
10.09	13.06	11.43	12.27	65.01	30.41	70.32	15.82
12.62	10.21	11.96	13.53	40.49	80.90	23.95	19.19
10.92	9.21	12.56	12.57	19.32	59.24	5.36	4.76
12.70	9.77	12.86	10.17	6.03	44.61	.97	29.71
7.77	12.88	10.75	13.54	51.45	67.02	37.99	17.87
12.26	13.14	12.63	11.91	9.86	14.91	.64	1.08
10.01	14.44	9.98	10.54	10.73	11.32	32.70	5.68
16.45	13.03	10.36	11.03	9.97	13.42	47.02	37.98
15.85	13.26	8.75	12.09	136.41	12.20	44.65	42.04
9.68	13.99	13.28	11.53	14.89	42.75	22.21	1.85

13.3 *Barber Shop.* The Checkmate Barbershop presently has only one barber. Business is quite good, and the proprietor is trying to decide whether to hire an additional barber. Customers arrive to the barbershop in a Poisson manner at a rate of 3 per hour (interarrival times are distributed exponentially, with a mean of 20 minutes). The time it takes to give a haircut is exponentially distributed, with a mean of 15 minutes. The barber has noticed that when 2 customers are waiting for a haircut, a new customer generally will not join the queue. Haircuts cost $4, and a new barber would cost the shop $100 per week plus $1 for each haircut. Use simulation to help in the decision of whether or not to hire the additional barber.

13.4 *Doctor Schedule.* Dr. Williams has the appointment schedule reflected in the following table. Based on his past experiences, Dr. Williams' estimate of arrival times are:

10% chance of a patient arriving 15 minutes early

20% chance of a patient arriving 5 minutes early

45% chance of a patient arriving on time

15% chance of a patient arriving 10 minutes late

5% chance of a patient arriving 20 minutes late

5% chance of a patient failing to arrive

Dr. Williams' appointment schedule

Appointment time	Patient	Expected appointment duration (min)
9:00	Dupont	30
9:15	Austin	20
9:45	Stratman	20
10:00	Rief	30
10:30	Hoffer	20
11:00	Stoltz	30
11:30	Gilbert	20
11:45	Collins	30

The duration of each patient's appointment is a stochastic variable that, from past experience, is estimated to be distributed as follows:

10% chance that it will take 80% of the expected time

15% chance that it will take 90% of the expected time

40% chance that it will take 100% of the expected time

25% chance that it will take 110% of the expected time

5% chance that it will take 120% of the expected time

5% chance that it will take 130% of the expected time

Dr. Williams is due in surgery at 1:30 P.M. and must leave the office by 12:15 in order to make it. Dr. Williams would like to know the probability of not canceling any appointments and being on time for surgery. Assume that Dr. Williams gets to the office at 9:00 and sees patients on a first come, first served basis. Use manual or computer simulation to answer Dr. Williams' question. If you simulate manually, simulate five mornings.

13.5 *Inventory Control.* A ski shop carries a particularly popular pair of skis that sells for $150 and wishes to know how many pairs to order and when to order. Demand is not known with certainty (see the first table). The lead time is 7 days. The cost of the skis, which depends on the quantity ordered, is reflected in the second table. It costs $25 to place an order and a stock-out is assumed to cost $25 per unit. The cost of carrying inventory is 20 percent of the value of inventory per year (.055 percent per day).

Historical frequency of demand

Demand per day	Number of observations
0	20
1	26
2	41
3	50
4	38
5	13
6	8
7	3
8	1
	200

Price schedule

Order	Price per pair of skis
Less than 25	$100
25 or more	95
50 or more	90
100 or more	80

a. Simulate the following two inventory policies for 1 month (assume a 30-day month and a beginning inventory of 15 pairs, with no skis on order).

   1. Order 15 pairs when inventory reaches 10 pairs.

   2. Order 25 pairs when inventory reaches 20 pairs.

b. Which of the two policies is better? Explain.

c. What other experiments should be run?

13.6 *Laundromat.* The owner of a large laundromat is considering the opening of a second store. The location she has in mind can accommodate 20 washers and 10 dryers. At peak times she has found arrivals to be Poisson-distributed at a mean rate of 6 customers per hour. The number of washers used by 1 customer is random and distributed according to the table. Dryers can accommodate 2 loads of washing. Both washers and dryers take 30 minutes. The owner has found that in order to make a profit, the washers must be operated at 40% capacity during peak hours. Simulate manually for 2 hours. Should the new laundromat be installed at the proposed location? Assume that there are 5 customers waiting when the doors are opened for business.

Number of washers	Relative frequency
1	.20
2	.35
3	.20
4	.15
5	.05
6	.03
7	.01
8	.01
	1.00

13.7   *Automobile Parts Department.* Consider a parts department in an auto dealership. At the present time, one clerk operates the parts department, but the owner-manager of the dealership has noticed rather long lines of mechanics waiting for parts. Mechanics arrive to the parts counter at a rate of 10 per hour in a Poisson manner. Service times are exponential, with a mean of 5 minutes. By simulating 25 arrivals, analyze the desirability of adding a second parts clerk.

13.8   *Manufacturing Machine Shop.* A machine shop has two machine centers. Jobs arrive at the shop according to the following distribution shown below.

Number of jobs per 8-hour day	Relative frequency
0	.40
1	.20
2	.20
3	.10
4	.05
5	.05
	1.00

A given job can take one of the following four possible paths through the machine shop, with the indicated relative frequencies.

machine center 1 only—25%

machine center 2 only—10%

machine center 1, then machine center 2—50%

machine center 2, then machine center 1—15%

Time required for jobs at each machine center behave according to the following probability distributions.

Machine center 1

Time (hr)	Relative frequency
1	.10
2	.10
3	.15
4	.20
5	.10
6	.10
7	.08
8	.07
9	.07
10	.03
10	1.00

Machine center 2

Time (hr)	Relative frequency
1	.10
2	.15
3	.20
4	.20
5	.15
6	.10
7	.03
8	.03
9	.02
10	.02
10	1.00

Simulate the machine shop for ten 8-hour days using the following machine loading rules.

1. First come, first served.

2. Priority based on the amount of processing time left for the job. For example, if 2 jobs are waiting for machine center 2 and one has 5 hours of processing left and the other has 7 hours left, the job with 5 hours left would have priority.

13.9 *Medical Insurance.* The AAA Health Insurance Company is concerned with its cash outflows on a weekly basis. AAA is being considered for a large group policy. If AAA wins the contract and insures the group, the daily frequency of claims is estimated as follows:

Number of claims	Relative frequency
0	.05
1	.06
2	.08
3	.10
4	.33
5	.14
6	.11
7	.07
8	.04
9	.02
	1.00

The probability distribution of the cost of each claim has been estimated using historical data. The probability distribution is as follows:

Cost per claim	Probability
$800	.30
900	.24
1,000	.22
1,100	.18
1,200	.06
	1.00

a. Manually simulate 7 days to estimate weekly cash outflow.

b. Write a program that will output a frequency distribution of monthly cash outflows.

13.10 *Newsstand.* A newsstand proprietor is trying to decide how many copies of a weekly news magazine to stock. The magazines sell for $1 and he purchases them for $.60. If he has old magazines at the end of the week, they must be discarded and the proprietor loses his total purchase cost. The demand distribution for the papers is reflected shown in the table.

Number of magazines	Probability
50	.10
55	.15
60	.20
65	.30
70	.15
75	.10
	1.00

Use simulation to determine the number of magazines to be purchased for sale at the newsstand.

13.11 *Agriculture.* Although other factors affect the yield per acre, the amount of rain is the most significant factor in the growing of corn on an Iowa farm. The per-acre yield can be estimated by the following regression equation:

$$y = 35x + 50$$

where y = yield per acre
x = monthly rainfall (inches)

The monthly rainfall for the growing season is distributed as reflected in the table. Estimate the mean of yield per acre by simulating 10 growing seasons.

Average monthly rainfall	Probability
1.0	.08
1.5	.10
2.0	.15
2.5	.21
3.0	.20
3.5	.12
4.0	.08
4.5	.03
5.0	.02
6.0	.01
	1.00

13.12 *Project Scheduling.* Consider the project information shown in the table.

Task	Immediate predecessor	Expected time (weeks)
A	—	5
B	A	4
C	A	3
D	B	4
E	C	5
F	D	2
G	E	3

a. Simulate the completion of this project 10 times to estimate the probability distribution of project completion times. Assume an exponential distribution for each task time.

b. Write a simple program to perform the simulation and simulate the project completion 1000 times.

BIBLIOGRAPHY

Blum, A. M., "Digital Simulation of Urban Traffic," *IBM Systems Journal,* 3 (1964).

Bryant, J. W., "A Simulation of Retailer Behavior," *Operations Research Quarterly,* 26 (April 1975), 133–149.

Cohen, Kalman J., and E. J. Elton, "Inter-Temporal Portfolio Analysis Based on Simulation," *Management Science,* 14 (September 1967), 5–18.

Cook, Thomas M., and Bradley S. Alprin, "Snow and Ice Removal in an Urban Environment," *Management Science,* 23 (November 1976), 227–235.

————, and Lawrence J. Gitman, "Cash Budgeting—A Simulation Approach," *Journal of the Midwest Financial Association* (1973), 87–94.

DeMaire, J. Douglas, "The Overhead Crane," *Industrial Engineering,* 6 (March 1974), 12–17.

Eden, Colin L., "Rules for Scheduling Semi-Automatic Machines with Deterministic Cycle Times," *International Journal of Production Research,* 13 (January 1975), 41–55.

Eilon, Samuel, and Stephen Mathewson, "A Simulation Study for the Design of an Air Terminal Building," *IEEE Transactions on Systems, Man and Cybernetics,* SMC-3, (July 1973), 308–317.

Fetter, R. B., and J. D. Thompson, "The Simulation of Hospital Systems," *Operations Research* (September–October 1965), 689–711.

Gordon, Geoffrey, *The Application of GPSS V to Discrete System Simulation.* Englewood Cliffs, N.J.: Prentice-Hall, Inc., 1975.

Hannan, Edward, "Planning an Emergency Department Holding Unit," *Economic Planning Science,* 9 (October 1975), 179–188.

Hershauer, James C., and Ronald G. Egert, "Search and Simulation Selection of a Job-Shop Sequencing Rule," *Management Science,* 21 (March 1975), 833–843.

Hertz, D. B., "Risk Analysis in Capital Budgeting," *Harvard Business Review,* 42 (January–February 1964), 95–106.

Jurecka, W., and H. Stauble, "A Deterministic Simulation of the Concrete Construction of a Dam," *Operations Research,* 19 (December 1975), B195–B207.

Kwak, N. K., P. J. Kuzdrall, and Homer H. Schmitz, "The GPSS Simulation of Scheduling Policies for Surgical Patients," *Management Science,* 22 (May 1976), 982–989.

Lasdon, Gail S., "Planning the Delivery of Outpatient Services Using Simulation," *IEEE Transactions on Systems, Man, and Cybernetics,* SMC-3, (September 1973), 508–513.

Levene, S. M., and J. G. Watson, "An Assessment of the Application of On-Line Computers to Control of an Underground Railway—A Simulation Study," *Transportation Research*, 8 (April 1974), 123–135.

Miller, Peter J., and James S. Burgess, Jr., "Simulating a Municipal Problem," *Journal of Industrial Engineering*, 7 (June 1975), 10–14.

Miller, S. F., "Systems-Simulation in a Practical Policy-Making Setting: The Venezuelan Cattle Industry," *American Journal of Agricultural Economics*, 55 (August 1973), 920–932.

Nanda, R., "Simulating Passenger Arrivals at Airports," *Industrial Engineering*, 4 (March 1972), 12–19.

Naylor, Thomas H., et al., *Computer Simulation Techniques*. New York: John Wiley & Sons, Inc., 1966.

New, C. C., "Matching Batch Sizes to Machine Shop Capabilities: An Example in Production Scheduling," *Operations Research Quarterly*, 23 (December 1972), 561–572.

Nolan, Richard L., "Productivity Estimates of the Strategic Airlift System by the Use of Simulation," *Naval Research Logistics Quarterly*, 19 (December 1972), 737–752.

Petersen, Clifford C., "Simulation of an Inventory System," *Industrial Engineering*, 5 (June 1973), 35–44.

Schriber, Thomas J., *Simulation Using GPSS*. New York: John Wiley & Sons, Inc., 1974.

Shannon, Robert E., *Systems Simulation: The Art and Science*. Englewood Cliffs, N.J.: Prentice-Hall, Inc., 1975.

Sissouras, A. A., and B. Moores, "The 'Optimum' Number of Beds in a Coronary Care Unit," *OMEGA, International Journal of Management Science*, 4 (1976), 59–65.

Sorenson, Eric E., and J. F. Gilheany, "A Simulation Model for Harvest Operations Under Stochastic Conditions," *Management Science*, 16 (April 1970), 549–565.

Uyeno, Dean H., "Health Manpower Systems: An Application of Simulation to the Design of Primary Care Teams," *Management Science*, 20 (February 1974), 981–989.

Wells, Gary R., "A Sensitivity Analysis of Simulated River Basin Planning for Capital Budgeting Decisions," *Computers and Operations Research*, 2 (April 1975), 49–54.

14
Inventory Systems

THE UNITED STATES AIR FORCE[1]

The 1979 military budget for the United States was approximately $126 billion. This budget represented about 32 percent of the 1979 federal budget and approximately 5 percent of the gross national product. If each agency, department, and organization within the federal government that manages inventories could effect cost savings similar to those reported by the Air Force Logistical Command, a significant tax cut could be passed by Congress with no degradation in governmental services.

The Air Force Logistics Command (AFLC) manages an inventory for 250,000 expendable (nonreparable) weapon system spare parts. Annual procurement for these spare parts totals approximately $350 to $400 million. For the last 25 years AFLC has been using basic EOQ techniques such as those described in this chapter to effect significant cost savings. Recently, however, these basic techniques were studied and revised. Consequently, additional cost savings resulted.

The AFLC study illustrates the interrelated nature of the many techniques of management science. The study team was broken into four groups as follows:

1. Group 1 was responsible for building a valid simulation model of the AFLC inventory system so that alternative policies could be evaluated.

2. Group 2 was assigned to study the cost data relevant to holding inventory.

3. Group 3 was responsible for investigating ways of improving the forecasting of demand.

4. Group 4 was to investigate the feasibility of the use of price discount inventory models and was also responsible for the analysis of ordering cost.

---

[1]Larry M. Austin, "Project EOQ: A Success Story in Implementing Academic Research," *Interfaces*, 7 (August 1977), 1–11.

The results of the study were dramatic. By simply changing the forecasting methodology from a simple moving average to a simple exponential smoothing model, demand forecast accuracy was improved by a factor of 3. Obsolescence cost represents more than half of the AFLC holding-cost parameter. Obsolescence cost before the study was considered constant for all inventory items. By investigating obsolescence cost, the project net annual savings was projected to total $7.8 million. This annual savings increased significantly when price discounts are allowed in the system. By using a price discount model similar to the price discount model discussed in this chapter, more millions of dollars were saved. The computer simulation model projected net annual savings of $21.5 million dollars if the average price discount were 3 percent and $68.2 million if the average discount were a more realistic 8 percent. The simulation model was instrumental in getting AFLC to implement the recommendations of the study groups. Real savings experienced after implementation are proving the utility of the management science techniques used.

INTRODUCTION

An inventory is a stock of goods that is held for the purpose of future production or sales. Raw materials, work in progress, and finished goods can all be classified as inventory items, and the decisions about them are similar. Obviously, such decisions often have a critical effect on the health of the firm. Organizations carry inventories for a number of the following reasons.

Smooth production   Often, the demand for an item fluctuates widely due to a number of factors such as seasonality and production schedules. For example, 50 percent of all the toys manufactured in 1 year may be sold in the 3 weeks before Christmas. If toy manufacturers were to try to produce 50 percent of a year's output in 3 weeks, they would need a tremendous influx of labor as well as huge manufacturing facilities. Instead, firms find it more economical to produce goods over a longer, slower schedule and store them as inventory. Thus, they keep the labor force fairly stable, and expenditures for capital equipment are lower.

Product availability   Most retail goods and many industrial goods are carried in inventory to ensure prompt delivery to customers. Not only does a good inventory provide a competitive edge, it often means the difference between success and failure. If a firm gains a reputation for constantly being out of stock, it may lose a significant number of customers.

Advantages of producing or buying in large quantities   Most production runs involve machine setup time and production time. If setup time is significant, real savings can be achieved by producing in large lots. In addition, many firms offer quantity discounts for buying in large quantities.

Hedge against long or uncertain lead times   The time between order-

lead time ing and receiving goods is known as *lead time*. Firms do not want to stop manufacturing or selling goods during lead time; so it is necessary to carry inventory.

Inventory models, such as the ones to be discussed in this chapter, seek to minimize the total cost of the inventory system. These costs fall into three basic categories: ordering costs, carrying costs, and shortage costs.

ordering costs   *Ordering costs* are the costs involved in ordering and receiving inventory. These costs typically consist largely of salaries in the purchasing and accounting departments and wages in the receiving area; they also include purchase and transportation charges. If a firm produces its own inventory instead of purchasing from an outside source, production setup costs are analogous to ordering costs. Ordering costs are usually expressed by a dollar amount per order.

carrying,   *Carrying costs,* also referred to as *holding costs,* are the costs that hold-
or holding, ing inventory entails. Components of carrying costs are both direct and
costs indirect, including:

1.   Interest on the money invested in inventory

2.   Storage or warehousing costs, including rent, electricity, wages, insurance, security, data processing, and so on

3.   Obsolescence (If the good is held too long in inventory, its value may decrease substantially)

Carrying costs are typically calculated as a percentage of inventory value or a dollar value per unit of inventory.

shortage, or   The third category of inventory costs is *shortage,* or *stock-out, costs.*
stock-out, If demand for an off-the-shelf good exists and a firm does not have the
costs good in inventory, there is an inevitable loss of customer good will as well as loss of the profit from the sale. The dollar value of this loss of good will is, at best, difficult to measure. If you had to assess it, relevant questions would include: Will the firm lose the sale? Will the firm lose the customer? What are the probabilities of these losses? What is the dollar value of that particular customer?

If the inventory is being carried for internal use (that is, production), a stock-out can have very serious effects. A stock-out can shut down an assembly line, and to shut down a typical automobile assembly line, for example, can cost as much as $20,000 per minute. The shortage cost is typically expressed as dollar cost per unit of inventory per unit of time.

Gene Woolsey, writing for *Interfaces*, emphasizes the importance of controlling inventories:

> **The second stop on the required tour is the production line of machinists making part X. We proceed as follows. First look for a 5 by 5 by 3 foot bin of gears or parts that looks like it has been there awhile. Pick up a gear and ask, casually, "How much is this worth?" You then ask, "How many of these are in the bin?" followed by, "How long has this bin been here?" and, "What's your cost of money for this company?" I recall one case in a nameless South American country where the unit cost times the number of parts times the time it had been there times the interest rate resulted in a cost per day figure that would insure a comfortable retirement for the plant manager on the bank of the Rio de la Plata at one of the better resorts to be found there. The plant manager suddenly realized that what he was holding was not just a chunk of high-test steel, but was real money. He then pointed out that he now understood the value of the inventory but could I suggest a way to drive the point home to upper management? I suggested that he go to the accounting department and borrow enough money to be equal to the bin's value for as long as it had been sitting there, and pile it on the top of the bin. I further suggested that he do that for every bin on the production line. We rapidly figured out that by the time we had the money piled up on the bin, you would not even be able to see the bin. My opinion was that if the upper managers were given a tour of the line with the money piled up, they would never forget it.[2]**

There are two basic functions that must be performed in order to effectively control an organization's inventory. First, management must have a system for accounting or keeping track of inventory. This system can be either a periodic series of physical numerations or a continuous inventory system in which quantities in inventory are calculated each time units are added to or drawn from inventory. A continuous inventory accounting system can be either manual or computer-based. The second function that must be performed for effective inventory control is the decision-making function. Decisions must be made regarding how much to order and when to order. To make intelligent inventory decisions, accurate information about demand and the inventory status for each item must be available to the decision maker.

Demand for inventory items can be classified as dependent or independent. *Dependent demand* is demand for those items in inventory that is determined ultimately by the demand for an end item or final product for which the inventory items are components. An example would be the demand for engine pistons; if the demand for each type of automobile is forecasted, the demand for engine pistons can be calculated directly based

---

[2]Gene Woolsey, "On Doing Good Things and Dumb Things in Production and Inventory Control," *Interfaces*, 5 (May 1975), 66–67.

on the number of pistons required for each automobile. The demand for automobiles is an example of *independent demand*. Although dependent-demand items are very common to the manufacturing sector of the economy, the service sector is concerned almost exclusively with independent-demand items.

During the last 10 years a methodology for coping with the problems of dependent demand items, materials requirements planning (MRP), has experienced extremely rapid growth in its application. Because of the importance of this relatively new technology, we devote a section later in this chapter to a discussion of MRP.

Fortunately, a large number of optimization models have been developed for independent-demand inventories, to aid the decision maker in making good inventory decisions. Therefore, the organization that effectively and efficiently controls inventory has an effective inventory information system and makes use of appropriate mathematical models in making inventory decisions.

Obviously, using a computer-based inventory information system and sophisticated operations research techniques to control the paper-clip inventory might be absurd. For this reason, many organizations choose to classify inventory items into three basic categories, usually according to annual dollar volume. The logic of this classification scheme (*ABC classification*) is to spend money and time controlling only important inventory items, in the realization that the cost of closely controlling relatively unimportant inventory items cannot be justified. To give you a feeling for how this classification is effected, let us assume that a firm has only 12 individual inventory items. These items and their annual dollar volume are shown in Table 14.1.

TABLE 14.1 Annual dollar-volume usage

Item no.	Annual demand	Per-unit cost	Total annual value
22213	100	$10,000	$1,000,000
22157	2,000	500	1,000,000
22545	200	1,500	300,000
22432	400	500	200,000
22511	150	700	105,000
22457	240	100	24,000
22111	300	50	15,000
22331	10	100	1,000
22471	10	100	1,000
22512	25	25	625
25531	30	20	600
22122	50	10	500
			$2,647,725

TABLE 14.2 ABC analysis

Category	Total annual volume	Percent of total
A	$2,000,000	75.5
B	629,000	23.8
C	18,725	.7
	$2,647,725	100.0

The ABC classification typically seeks to put approximately 15 percent of the items in category A, 35 percent in category B, and 50 percent in category C. There is nothing sacred about these percentages, but these are often used. Since in our example we have 12 items, 2 would make up 16.6 percent and 4 would be 33.3 percent. Therefore, you might put items 22213 and 22157 in category A, and 22545, 22432, 22511, and 22457 in category B, with the remaining items in category C. Table 14.2 shows that if we closely controlled only 2 items, we would be controlling 75.5 percent of the annual inventory dollar volume.

It is possible, of course, that an item that is placed in category C because of its low annual dollar volume may be of a critical nature and therefore deserves greater control. A simple solution is to arbitrarily place that item in category A.

INVENTORY ACCOUNTING SYSTEMS

physical inventory system

Inventory accounting systems can be classified as physical or continuous. A *physical inventory system* is a system in which management periodically reviews inventory levels of the various items in order to make inventory decisions. A common example of this type system might be in the small grocery store. Each day, various delivery people stop at the store to replenish inventory. For example, the milkman may come daily, take a physical inventory, and decide what he needs to leave in the dairy case. Each week it may be necessary to order canned goods and other relatively nonperishable items. In order to do this, the manager must look at each item and make a decision on whether to order the item and how much to order.

continuous inventory systems

Continuous inventory systems are typically more sophisticated than periodic ordering systems. They keep track of the inventory level of each item on a continuous basis. In other words, as items are added to or drawn from inventory, these events are recorded and the new inventory level is computed.

Continuous inventory accounting systems can range from the extremely simple manual system to very sophisticated computer-based systems. An example of a manual but continuous inventory system might be the local blood bank. For each type of blood, there might be a card on which is recorded the number of units in inventory. As units are demanded or added to inventory, a clerk merely makes the appropriate notation on the card. Hence, there is a permanent record of the inventory status of each blood type at all times.

batch-processing inventory

Computerized inventory accounting systems can be classified as batch-processing systems or real-time systems. A *batch-processing inventory system* is a system in which inventory transactions (additions to and withdrawals from inventory) are collected periodically, batched together, and processed to update the current inventory master file. In the simplified example, graphically represented in Figure 14.1, an inventory control clerk creates a transaction document each time an item is drawn from inventory and each time an order is received. Periodically, these documents are "batched" together and sent to data processing, where the information is transcribed into machine-readable form. These data are then processed against the current inventory master file to create an updated master file. Output from this processing would include a list of items that need to be ordered, a list of the status of all inventory items, purchase orders, a value-of-inventory report, suggested order quantities, and so on.

FIGURE 14.1   Simplified example of batch inventory accounting system

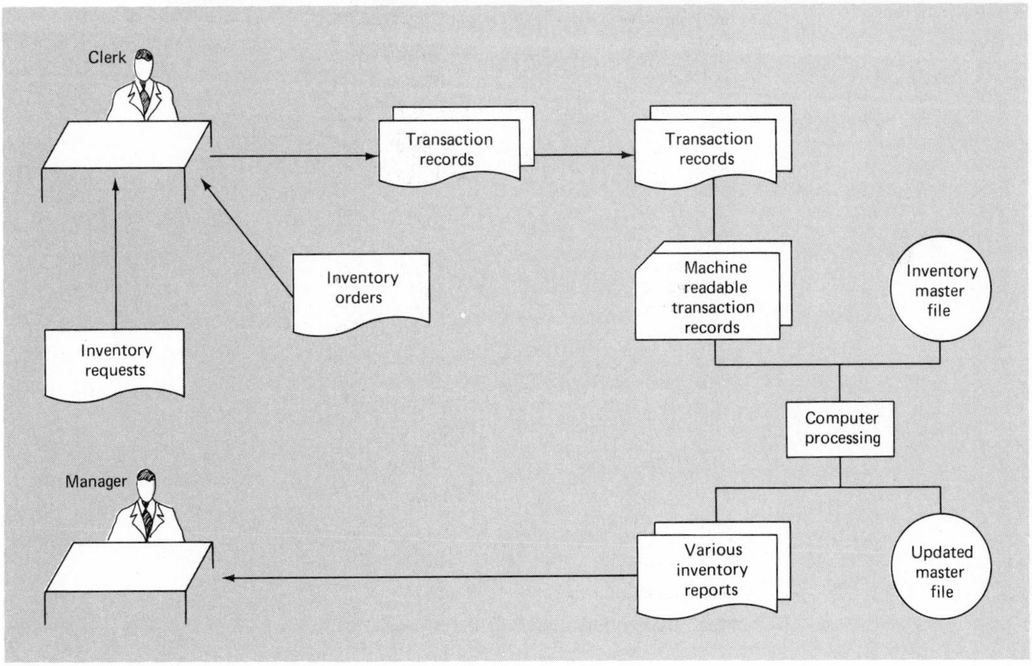

FIGURE 14.2 Simplified real-time inventory accounting system

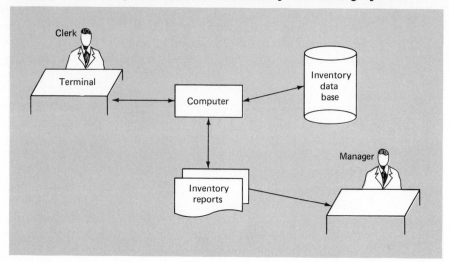

Therefore, in a batch-processing environment, the inventory master file is only as current as the date of the last update.

real-time systems *Real-time systems* keep the inventory master file continuously up to date. When a unit is drawn out of or added to inventory, that event is recorded immediately and the master file reflects the change immediately. Figure 14.2 graphically depicts this process. Typically, real-time systems are significantly more costly than batch systems, but as the cost of computing continues to decrease, the number of real-time inventory systems will inevitably increase.

Regardless of the mode of processing, a computer-based inventory system can vary according to the amount of inventory decision making that is delegated to the system. Some systems provide only information and all ordering decisions are made by people, whereas with some systems, the computer calculates reorder points and order quantities, and even writes the purchase order or shop order. These are two extremes, and many systems fall somewhere in between. Jack Bishop, Jr., reports a system he designed that calculated order quantities based on the information system and the appropriate inventory models.[3] He emphasizes, however, that the key to the success of the system was that order quantities were not dictated by computer-based system but rather were just suggestions to operating personnel. His experience was that a system characterized by this kind of human-computer partnership has a far better

---

[3]Jack L. Bishop, Jr., "Experience with a Successful System for Forecasting and Inventory Control," *Operations Research,* 22, No. 6, 1224–1231.

chance of success. Initially, people were overriding computer-generated order quantities 80 percent of the time. A year later, only 10 percent of the inventory decisions made by the computer were manually overridden.

MODELS FOR INVENTORY DECISION MAKING

As mentioned earlier in this chapter, there are two basic functions necessary to effectively control inventory. In this section, we deal with a scientific approach to performing one of those functions: inventory decision making for independent-demand items.

The objective of any inventory model is to minimize total inventory cost. Minimizing just one of the three components of inventory cost is easy, and of little value. For example, to minimize carrying cost, a firm can simply stop carrying any inventory. This action, however, can be expected to create unreasonable stockout or order costs. The actual process for minimizing total inventory costs entails two basic decisions: how much and when to order. Understandably, these are the two decision variables that inventory models use in optimizing an inventory system.

In this section, we discuss the five essential steps in analyzing inventory problems: determining inventory properties, formulating and developing the appropriate inventory model, solving or manipulating the model, performing sensitivity analysis on the model, and incorporating the model in the inventory control system.

DETERMINING SYSTEM PROPERTIES

Inventory system properties can be classified in four categories: demand properties, replenishment properties, cost properties, and constraints. In order to prevent the misapplication of an inventory model, it is extremely important for you to identify and consider each property of an inventory system properly.

Demand properties   These characteristics include the size of demand, *size of* the rate of demand, and the pattern of demand. The *size of demand* can *demand* be constant or variable depending on the nature of the good. A constant demand merely means that, for each time period, the quantity of goods demanded is constant. The size of demand for a good can be deterministic or stochastic. Given a production schedule, for example, it may be a simple calculation to determine demand for a particular period of time. However, the demand of many inventory items cannot be predicted with any degree of certainty; hence, the problem is a stochastic or probabilistic problem rather than a deterministic one.

rate of demand   The *rate* of demand is the size of demand over a particular unit of time. For example, Worldwide Widgets has a total demand for the year of 600 widgets, and its records verify that the monthly demand rate is $^{600}/_{12}$, or 50 units per month. Clearly, demand rate can be variable or constant, deterministic or stochastic.

demand pattern   The *pattern* of demand refers to the manner in which units are drawn from inventory. Some items may be drawn from inventory at the beginning of the time period, others at the end, still others at a uniform rate during the period. Many variations of demand pattern are possible, and it is important to try and identify the demand pattern of the inventory item in question. Figure 14.3 shows some common demand patterns.

Replenishment properties   When you analyze replenishment properties, it is necessary to define the *scheduling period*. The scheduling period is the length of time between decisions concerning replenishments. This time period can be prescribed or variable. For example, the local supermarket orders fresh lettuce twice a week (prescribed), whereas canned kidney beans are ordered when the inventory reaches a certain reorder point (variable). Variable scheduling periods require a continuous accounting for inventory. In most medium and large firms, an inventory accounting system is, or should be, totally computerized.

lead time   *Lead time,* you will recall, is the time between ordering a replenishment of inventory and actually receiving the goods into inventory. Lead time can be either a deterministic constant or variable, or a stochastic variable. If lead time is known with a high degree of certainty, its existence is easily treated in inventory modeling. On the other hand, if lead

FIGURE 14.3   Demand patterns

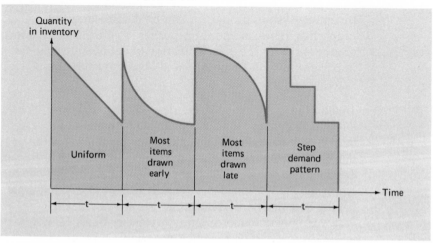

time is stochastic with a large variance, the difficulty in finding an appropriate inventory model is greatly increased.

replenishment, or lot, size   Like demand, the *size of replenishment* can also be stochastic. In other words, the quantity ordered may not be the same as the quantity received. Replenishment size is often called *lot size.*

replenishment period   The *replenishment period* is the time during which units of a particular order are added to inventory. In a purchasing situation, the replenishment period may be insignificant; but in a production environment, units are added to inventory over a period of time (that is, as they are produced). If a significant replenishment period exists, then units are added to inventory according to some *replenishment pattern.* Replenishment patterns are similar to demand patterns except the flow of goods is going in the opposite direction.

replenishment pattern

order level   Often, instead of specifying the lot size, an inventory policy specifies an *order level.* An order level is the quantity that will be in inventory after replenishment.

Cost properties   Earlier in this chapter, we said that inventory systems were systems comprised of three types of cost: ordering cost, holding cost, and shortage cost. These parameters of an inventory model are rarely known with certainty. Consequently, the management scientist usually must determine the sensitivity of the optimal solution to small and reasonable changes in these parameters.

System constraints   In addition to determining system properties, before you can decide on solution methodology you must analyze system constraints. For example, if the inventory storage area holds only 100 units, an optimal order quantity of 1,000 units is irrelevant. Similarly, if working capital is severely limited and the optimal inventory policy calls for carrying a huge inventory, the optimal policy may not be feasible. Typical inventory system constraints are listed below:

1. *Space* The amount of storage space may put limits on the order quantity.
2. *Scheduling period* If the scheduling period is prescribed, many inventory models cannot be used.
3. *Shortage* Management may make a decision that stock-outs cannot be allowed. On the other hand, shortages may be allowed and may or may not result in lost sales.

dependent demand   4. *Dependent demand* In most inventory models, demand is considered independent of the demand of the preceding period. When independent demand is not characteristic of a particular inventory system, it is generally more difficult to optimize the system.

5. *Continuous nature of inventory units* Most analytical models used for optimizing inventory systems depend on the calculus for their derivation. Consequently, if inventory units are not, or cannot be considered, continuous in nature, a majority of the analytical optimization models cannot theoretically be applied. Usually however, when large quantities are involved, the assumption of continuousness is not damaging.

Determining system properties is crucial to analyzing inventory systems. If we expect to find or develop an appropriate model of the inventory system in question, we must analyze the system properties and characteristics in depth.

FORMULATING THE MODEL

The second step in analyzing inventory systems is to discover or derive the appropriate inventory model to solve the particular inventory problem. Basically, there are two types of inventory models: deterministic models and stochastic models. The parameters of deterministic inventory models are assumed to be known with certainty. For example, demand is assumed to be perfectly predictable. Stochastic inventory models contain uncontrollable variables, such as demand or lead time, that are probabilistic in nature. Generally, stochastic inventory models are mathematically more difficult to derive and solve. As the number of stochastic variables increases, it becomes increasingly difficult to derive an analytical optimization model. In addition, if a stochastic variable is not distributed according to a known probability density function, the likelihood of finding or deriving an analytical inventory model is drastically reduced. When an analytical model cannot be developed to model a particular inventory system adequately, simulation can usually be used to determine a good inventory policy. The decision of whether to simulate an inventory system hinges on the cost/benefit of the simulation.

SOLVING THE MODEL

The third step in the analysis of inventory systems is to solve the analytical model or run the simulation model. This is typically the easiest part of the process if the first two steps have been performed properly. Because the solution of analytical inventory models is not an iterative process, a computer is not considered an absolute necessity. If a computer is used, very few computer resources (memory, time) are necessary to solve analytical inventory models.

An analytical model is preferable to a simulation model for two reasons. First, the cost in computer resources is considerably less. Second, an analytical model yields an optimal solution, whereas a simulation model can only search for a good solution. In short, analytical inventory models cost *much* less than simulation models to find the *best* answer. This is not to say, however, that a real system should be modeled using an analytical model whose assumptions do not adequately fit the real system properties. This is a common error in practice, and it is for this reason that we state explicitly the assumptions of each model we present in this chapter.

PERFORMING SENSITIVITY ANALYSIS

Some models yield order quantities that are extremely sensitive. In other words, slight changes in the order quantity cause significant changes in the total cost of the inventory system. In addition, it is usually helpful to the decision maker to know the relative sensitivity of such inventory variables as demand, lead time, and replenishment quantity. Unlike LP, inventory models cannot easily determine the sensitivity of the system's various parameters and decision variables. Instead, the parameter or variable in question is perturbed, and the effect of the change is observed.

INTEGRATING THE MODEL INTO THE INVENTORY CONTROL SYSTEM

Once a model has been found and tested that makes good inventory decisions, it must be integrated into the inventory control system. For example, let us assume that model A calculates an order quantity for a particular item that minimizes cost. If that model is programmed into the software of the inventory system, then anytime that item reaches its reorder point, an order quantity can be calculated and suggested to management.

ANALYTICAL MODELS FOR INDEPENDENT DEMAND ITEMS

In this chapter, we are going to consider several deterministic analytical models and one stochastic model. These models represent only a small sampling of the inventory models that have been developed and used since the first one was introduced in 1915.

BASIC ECONOMIC ORDER QUANTITY MODEL (EOQ)

Before examining it, we must identify the assumptions of the basic EOQ model so that you will know under what conditions to apply it. If the following assumptions cannot be accepted, thereby indicating that the real-world inventory system may not be adequately represented by the basic EOQ model, it is inappropriate to use this particular model.

1. *Deterministic demand* It must be possible to predict demand with a high degree of confidence.

2. *Constant rate of demand* Not only is it necessary to know the total demand, but units must be drawn from inventory at a uniform rate. For example, if 365 units are used each year, these items must be drawn 1 per day during the year to strictly satisfy this assumption.

3. *No shortages* Inventory replenishments are made whenever the inventory level reaches zero. Shortages are not allowed to occur. This assumption implies that, of the three costs involved in an inventory system, stock-out cost does not exist in the basic EOQ model.

4. *Constant replenishment size* The replenishment size, denoted by q, is the only decision variable in the basic EOQ model. The other decision variable—when to reorder—is fixed because demand is at a constant rate and replenishments occur when the inventory level reaches zero.

5. *Zero lead time* It is assumed that no appreciable time elapses between placing an order and receiving that order. This assumption can be easily dealt with as we explain later in conjunction with Figure 14.9.

6. *Infinite replenishment rate* Replenishment rate is defined as the rate at which units are added to inventory. An infinite replenishment rate implies that inventory replenishment occurs at one time. In other words, it takes zero time to receive an order. This assumption is reasonable for most purchased goods but is often unreasonable for manufactured goods. Typically, manufactured goods are put into inventory at some finite rate.

7. *Constant inventory costs* Both costs in the basic EOQ model are constant. Ordering cost is expressed as dollars per order and holding cost is expressed as dollars per unit per time period.

These assumptions for the basic EOQ model determine the graph in Figure 14.4.

Inventory systems in which the decision variable is the order quantity have the objective function in equation 14.1.

Minimize $C(q) = A(q) + B(q) + D(q)$ [14.1]

where $C(q)$ = total cost function
$A(q)$ = function of q that defines the holding cost
$B(q)$ = function of q that represents the shortage cost
$D(q)$ = function of q that defines the ordering cost

FIGURE 14.4 Graphic representation of the basic EOQ model

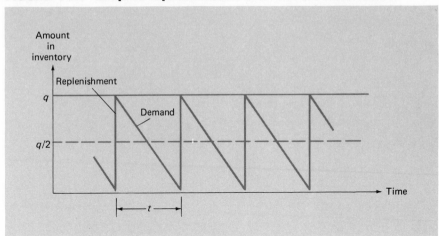

In order to determine the optimal value of q, it is necessary to develop the functions $A(q)$, $B(q)$, and $D(q)$ for the basic EOQ model:

$$A(q) = C_1(q/2)$$

where C_1 = holding cost per unit of inventory.

A look at Figure 14.4 will reveal to you that $q/2$ represents the average number of units in inventory. In other words, half the time there are more than $q/2$ units in inventory, and half the time the amount in inventory is less than $q/2$ units. Therefore, if we multiply a per-unit holding cost by the average number of units in inventory, that product is the holding cost. Since no shortages are allowed in the basic EOQ model due to the zero lead time and zero reorder point assumptions, $B(q)$ is not present in the total cost function. Ordering cost can be thought of as the cost of placing an order multiplied by the number of orders placed in a particular time period. More specifically,

$$D(q) = C_3(r/q)$$

where C_3 = cost of processing one order
   r = total demand for a given period of time
   r/q = number of orders

Given the preceding defined functions, the total cost function can be written as shown in equation 14.2.

FIGURE 14.5 Inventory cost basic EOQ model

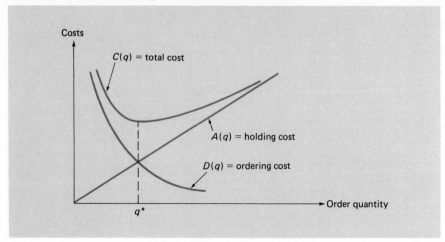

$$C(q) = A(q) + D(q) \qquad\qquad [14.2]$$
$$C(q) = C_1(q/2) + C_3(r/q)$$

Remember, the question is to determine the value of q that minimizes the objective function $C(q)$. Figure 14.5 graphs the three functions $A(q)$, $C(q)$, and $D(q)$. From Figure 14.5, it is apparent that the minimum of $C(q)$ occurs at the same level of q where functions $A(q)$ and $D(q)$ intersect. It is possible, therefore, to set $A(q)$ equal to $D(q)$ and solve for q to find q^*, the optimal value of q. It must be noted that this relationship is not universally true.

$$A(q) = D(q) \qquad\qquad [14.3]$$
$$C_1(q/2) = C_3(r/q)$$
$$C_1(q^2/2) = C_3 r$$
$$q^2/2 = C_3 r/C_1$$
$$q^2 = 2C_3 r/C_1$$
$$q^* = \sqrt{2C_3 r/C_1}$$

The majority of inventory models are derived using the differential calculus. The basic methodology involves deriving a cost function. This function is differentiated with respect to the decision variable. The derivative is set equal to zero and the function is solved for the optimal value of the decision variable. This methodology is illustrated in the appendix at the end of this chapter.

EXAMPLE Now, let us look at an example of how to use the basic EOQ model. The XYZ Company uses 10,000 valves per year. Each valve costs $1. The Materials Department estimates that it costs $25 to order a shipment of valves and the Accounting Department estimates the holding cost is 12.5 percent. All the assumptions of the basic EOQ model are valid.

$$C_1 = \$.125 \text{ per valve per year } [(.125)(1.00)]$$
$$C_3 = \$25 \text{ per order}$$
$$r = 10{,}000 \text{ valves}$$
$$q^* = \sqrt{2C_3r/C_1}$$
$$= \sqrt{2(25)10{,}000/.125}$$
$$= \sqrt{4{,}000{,}000}$$
$$= 2{,}000 \text{ valves}$$

If the XYZ Company buys 2,000 valves every time inventory reaches zero, the total annual cost of this policy is

$$C(q^*) = .125(2{,}000/2) + 25(10{,}000/2{,}000)$$
$$= 125 + 125$$
$$= \$250$$

Once q^* is calculated, it is a simple matter to calculate the optimal number of orders per year and the time between each order.

$$N^* = \text{optimal number of orders}$$
$$= r/q^*$$
$$= 10{,}000/2{,}000$$
$$= 5$$
$$t^* = \text{optimal time between orders (optimal reorder schedule)}$$
$$= \text{planning period}/N^*$$
$$= 365/5 = 73 \text{ days}$$

SENSITIVITY OF THE BASIC EOQ MODEL

As indicated in Figure 14.5, the shape of the total cost curve, $C(q)$, is relatively flat. Consequently, $C(q)$ is not very sensitive to small changes in q. To illustrate this fact, let us assume that the XYZ Company orders 1,000 valves in each order instead of the optimal 2,000 valves.

$$C(1{,}000) = .125(1{,}000/2) + 25(10{,}000/1{,}000)$$
$$= 62.50 + 250$$
$$= \$312.50$$

Hence, a change of 50 percent in q resulted in only a 25 percent increase in the total inventory cost. (See Table 14.3 for a more complete sensitivity analysis.) This means that if total demand, r, is incorrectly estimated, thus causing a suboptimal q to be calculated, the consequences are not as critical as they would be if the shape of the total cost curve were more peaked.

TABLE 14.3 Sensitivity analysis of order quantity

Order quantity	Order cost	Carrying cost	Total cost
100	$2,500.00	$6.25	$2,506.25
500	500.00	31.25	531.25
750	333.33	46.88	380.21
1,000	250.00	62.50	312.50
1,250	200.00	78.13	278.13
1,500	166.65	93.75	260.40
1,750	142.85	109.38	252.23
2,000	125.00	125.00	250.00
2,250	111.10	140.63	251.73
2,500	100.00	156.25	256.25
3,000	83.33	187.50	270.83
4,000	62.50	250.00	312.50
10,000	25.00	625.00	650.00

BASIC EOQ SYSTEM
WITH FINITE REPLENISHMENT RATE

Often, it is unrealistic to assume an infinite replenishment rate. If a firm is purchasing off-the-shelf items for its inventory, typically, when an order is delivered the entire replenishment quantity is delivered at one time; hence, an infinite replenishment rate. If, however, a company is producing for inventory, units are added to inventory over a finite period of time. Therefore, the inventory system has a finite replenishment rate. If it can be assumed that this replenishment rate is uniform and all other assumptions of the basic EOQ model hold, the appropriate model is the basic EOQ system with a finite replenishment rate. The graphic representation of the model is given in Figure 14.6.

The total cost function of the inventory system depicted in Figure 14.6 is

$$C(q) = \frac{C_1 q(1 - r/p)}{2} + \frac{C_3 r}{q} \qquad [14.4]$$

Following a procedure similar to the one set forth in the appendix at the end of the chapter, the expression for the optimal order quantity shown in equation 14.5 can be derived.

$$q^* = \frac{\sqrt{2rC_3/C_1}}{\sqrt{1 - r/p}} \qquad [14.5]$$

538

FIGURE 14.6 Basic EOQ system with uniform replenishment rate

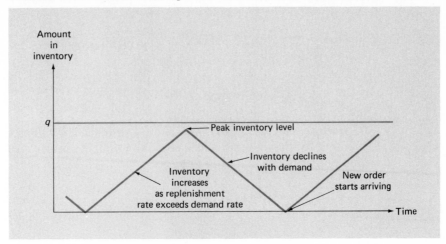

where r = total demand for a given period of time
C_3 = setup cost per setup
C_1 = carrying cost per unit
p = uniform replenishment rate expressed in units per time period

The minimum total inventory cost is given by the following function:

$$C^* = \sqrt{2rC_1C_3} \sqrt{1 - r/p} \qquad\qquad [14.6]$$

where C^* = the minimum inventory cost.

EXAMPLE Let us change our previous example just slightly so that the replenishment rate changes from infinite to a uniform 500 valves per day. To restate, the XYZ Company uses 10,000 valves per year. Each valve costs $1. The Production Engineering Department estimates setup costs at $25, and the Accounting Department estimates that the holding cost is 12.5 percent of the value of inventory.

$$r = 10{,}000 \text{ valves}$$
$$C_3 = \$25 \text{ per order}$$
$$C_1 = \$.125 \text{ per valve per year}$$
$$p = 125{,}000 \text{ valves per year}^\dagger$$

---

†It was necessary to convert the per-day production of valves to per-year production of valves because the time units must be compatible; that is, r was expressed in units per year. Assumes 5-day week and 50-week year.

$$q^* = \sqrt{\frac{2rC_3/C_1}{1-(r/p)}}$$
$$= \sqrt{\frac{2(10,000)25/.125}{1-(10,000/125,000)}}$$
$$= \sqrt{4,000,000/.92}$$
$$= \sqrt{4,350,000}$$
$$= 2,086$$

Therefore, the XYZ Company should order 2,086 valves every time inventory for the valves reaches zero. The total inventory cost of this ordering policy is calculated as follows:

$$C^* = \sqrt{2rC_1C_3}\ \sqrt{1-(r/p)}$$
$$= \sqrt{2(10,000).125(25)}\ \sqrt{1-(10,000)/125,000}$$
$$= \sqrt{62,500}\ \sqrt{.92}$$
$$\cong \$239.75$$

Therefore, if the XYZ Company orders 2,086 valves approximately 5 times a year, inventory cost related to this particular valve is minimized at about $240 per year.

BASIC ORDER LEVEL SYSTEM

The basic order level system is very similar to the basic EOQ system previously described. In fact, all properties are the same except that shortages are allowed and back-ordered and the scheduling period is prescribed. This type of system is very common in the real world when an organization places orders for certain inventory items on a regularly scheduled basis, such as once a month. An advantage of a prescribed scheduling period is that it does *not* necessitate continuous monitoring of inventory levels.

The basic order level system has the following properties:

1. Demand is deterministic.
2. The rate of demand is constant; that is, it is a linear demand function.
3. The scheduling period is prescribed.
4. The lead time is zero.
5. The replenishment rate is infinite.
6. Shortages are made up; that is, there are no lost sales.

7. The decision variable is the order level, S; that is, the decision variable is the amount of inventory after replenishment.

8. Holding cost is constant and is expressed as dollars per unit per time period.

9. Shortage cost is constant and expressed as dollars per unit per time period.

The basic order level system is depicted in Figure 14.7.

Since the scheduling period is prescribed, the only controllable inventory costs are the carrying and shortage costs. Since order level is the decision variable in this inventory model, the total cost function is a function of order level, S. It can be shown geometrically, using similar triangles, that the total cost function is

$$C(S) = C_1 S^2/2q_p + C_2(q_p - S)^2/2q_p \qquad [14.7]$$

where C_1 = carrying cost per unit
   S = order level
   q_p = prescribed lot size (rate of demand multiplied by the prescribed time period)
   C_2 = shortage cost per unit

Minimizing this total cost function, the optimal order level is

$$S^* = q_p C_2/(C_1 + C_2)$$

FIGURE 14.7 Basic order level system

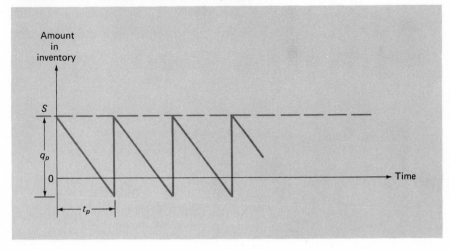

EXAMPLE   A local television store reviews its stock of 25-inch color television sets every month, then orders for the next month. Last year, it sold 120 25-inch color sets (q_p = 10 sets per month), and sales were spread evenly throughout the year. Predictions are that this year's sales will be approximately the same. Lead time is effectively zero, and shortages are made up. The holding cost is $80 per set per year, and shortage cost has been determined to be $10 per set per month. The optimal order level, therefore, is

$$S^* = 10(120)/(80 + 120)$$
$$= 6 \text{ sets}$$

To find the minimum cost of this solution, merely substitute S^* into the cost function:

$$C(6) = 80[6^2/(2 \cdot 10)] + 120(10 - 6)^2/20$$
$$= \$240$$

In summary, the inventory policy of the local television store is to order 10 25-inch color TV sets whenever backorders reach 4. This policy costs $240 per year in inventory cost; any other policy would cost the TV store more. The graph of this inventory policy is shown in Figure 14.8.

FIGURE 14.8 Order level system with stock-outs

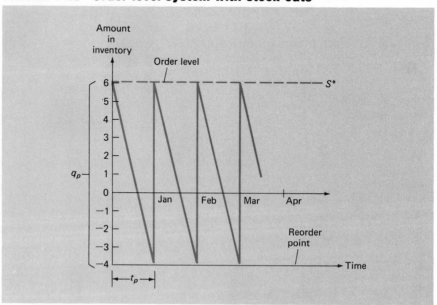

BASIC EOQ MODEL
WITH DISCRETE PRICE BREAKS

As the Air Force Logistics Command found, it is often advantageous to procure inventory items in large quantities in order to get quantity discounts. A supplier often sells a product at a price that fluctuates with the quantity purchased. Usually, the price-break scheme is discrete in nature. For example, the per-unit cost of an item might be $25 for quantities of 50 or less; $22 for quantities of less than 100 but more than 50; and $20 per unit for more than 100 units. As reflected in Table 14.4, buying in large quantities has several advantages and disadvantages.

Buying large quantities has advantages other than merely lowering the per-unit cost of the particular inventory item. Obviously, because fewer orders are placed, ordering costs are reduced when an organization takes advantage of quantity discounts and buys in larger quantities. Transportation costs, also, are usually lower for a few large shipments rather than many small shipments. If demand is stochastic and lead time is not zero, buying in larger quantities results in fewer stock-outs.

As you have probably realized, buying in large quantities has some very important disadvantages, too. The most obvious is that, because the average amount in inventory is increased with large orders, the carrying cost of the inventory item is increased. In addition to increased carrying cost, more capital is required to buy larger quantities. For firms with limited capital, this can be a critical drawback, and sometimes it prevents taking advantage of quantity discounts. If the inventory item is perishable or has an otherwise limited life, buying in larger quantities may also be disadvantageous to a firm. High-fashion, ready-to-wear clothing is an example of such an inventory item. Even if a manufacturer is willing to give a quantity discount that would ordinarily minimize the retailer's total

TABLE 14.4 Quantity buying advantages and disadvantages

Advantages	Disadvantages
1. Lower unit cost	1. Higher holding cost
2. Lower ordering cost	2. Higher capital requirements
3. Fewer stock-outs	3. Increased risk of deterioration
4. Preferential treatment by suppliers	and obsolescence
5. Lower transportation cost	4. Older stock on hand
6. Increase uniformity in goods (coming from the same shipment)	
7. Security (against such factors as strikes and price increases)	

inventory cost, it may be wiser to buy the smaller quantity due to the potential obsolescence of the article.

The model we describe in this section is a simple, discrete price-break model. The assumptions concerning demand and replenishment properties are the same as the basic EOQ model except that in this model there exists the condition of discrete prices based on the quantity ordered. Since the cost of goods purchased is no longer constant but is a function of the price, the objective function is composed of ordering cost, carrying cost, and the cost of goods. More specifically,

$$C(q_i) = fq_ib_i/2 + (C_3r/q_i) + rb_i \qquad [14.8]$$

where f = carrying cost fraction
  q_i = order quantity for price break i
  b_i = unit cost for price break i
  C_3 = ordering cost per order
  r = total demand

If you look carefully at the objective function in equation 14.8, you can see that it closely resembles the total cost function of the basic EOQ model. In fact, the first two terms are identical if you realize that the carrying cost (C_1) in dollars per unit per time period is simply the cost fraction (f) multiplied by the unit cost (b_i). The only difference is the existence of more than one price level and the addition of the cost of goods.

As depicted in Figure 14.9, the total cost function for the price-break model is not continuous. Therefore, it is not possible to use the calculus

FIGURE 14.9   Discontinuous cost function

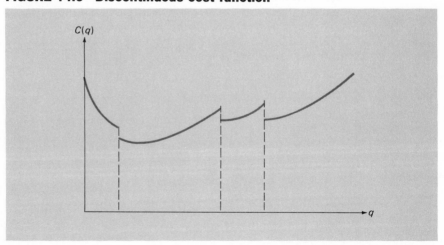

FIGURE 14.10 Discrete price-break algorithm

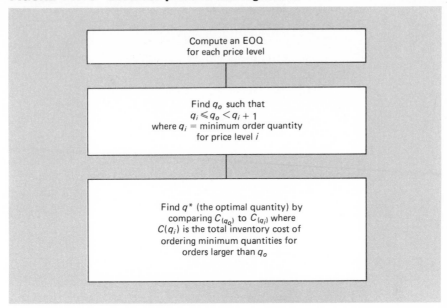

to derive a simple formula to compute the optimal order quantity. Instead, we need an algorithm. The algorithm for the discrete price break model is presented in flow-chart form in Figure 14.10. The first step in the algorithm is to compute the EOQ for each price level, starting at the price level that has the lowest cost per unit, until an EOQ fits in the relevant range of its price level. In other words, let q_o be the largest EOQ for which $q_i \leq q_o < q_{i+1}$, where q_i = minimum order quantity for price level i. The next step is to compare the total cost of q_o with the total cost of all minimum quantities for orders larger than q_o. In other words, compare $C(q_o)$ to $C(q_j)$ for $j > i$, where q_j = the minimum order quantity for price level j and i = the price level for q_o.

EXAMPLE A manufacturing company has planned its production schedule for the coming year based on forecast demand, back orders, and plant capacity. Instead of making a particular hydraulic pump that goes into the final product, the company has decided to buy the pump. There are two such pumps in the end product, and the production schedule calls for producing 10,000 units of the end product. Therefore, 20,000 pumps will be needed next year. Ordering costs are estimated at $50 per order, and the carrying cost fraction for the firm is .20. A request for bids has

TABLE 14.5 Victor Pumps Inc., price schedule

Quantity ordered	Unit price
1–1,999	$15.00
2,000–4,999	13.50
5,000–7,999	12.50
8,000–19,999	12.00
20,000 and over	11.50

yielded only one supplier, Victor Pumps Inc., who is approved by the Engineering Department; hence, the Purchasing Department has only one basic decision. That decision concerns the quantity to be ordered. Victor Pumps Inc., has submitted the price schedule shown in Table 14.5 together with its technical proposal.

$$EOQ_5 = \sqrt{\frac{2(20,000)50}{.2(11.50)}} \qquad b_5 = 11.50$$
$$\cong 933$$

$$EOQ_4 = \sqrt{\frac{2(20,000)50}{.2(12)}} \qquad b_4 = 12.00$$
$$\cong 913$$

$$EOQ_3 = \sqrt{\frac{2(20,000)50}{.2(12.50)}} \qquad b_3 = 12.50$$
$$\cong 894$$

$$EOQ_2 = \sqrt{\frac{2(20,000)50}{.2(13.50)}} \qquad b_2 = 13.50$$
$$\cong 861$$

$$EOQ_1 = \sqrt{\frac{2(20,000)50}{.2(15)}} \qquad b_1 = 15.00$$
$$\cong 816$$

The largest EOQ that falls in the relevant range of order quantities is $q_0 = 816$, falling between 1 and 1,999. What remains to be done is to compare the total cost of $q_0 = 816$ to order quantities equal to the minimum levels of the different price breaks. This is done by substituting the various order quantities into equation 14.8.

$$C(816) = \frac{.2(816)15}{2} + 50\left(\frac{20,000}{816}\right) + 20,000(15)$$
$$= \$302,449.45$$

$$C(2{,}000) = \frac{.2(2{,}000)13.50}{2} + 50\left(\frac{20{,}000}{2{,}000}\right) + 20{,}000(13.50)$$

$$= \$273{,}200$$

$$C(5{,}000) = \frac{.2(5{,}000)12.50}{2} + 50\left(\frac{20{,}000}{5{,}000}\right) + 20{,}000(12.50)$$

$$= \$256{,}450$$

$$C(8{,}000) = \frac{.2(8{,}000)12}{2} + 50\left(\frac{20{,}000}{8{,}000}\right) + 20{,}000(12)$$

$$= \$249{,}725$$

$$C(20{,}000) = \frac{.2(20{,}000)11.50}{2} + 50\left(\frac{20{,}000}{20{,}000}\right) + 20{,}000(11.50)$$

$$= \$253{,}050$$

According to the foregoing analysis, the manufacturing company should order 8,000 pumps in order to minimize total inventory cost for the pump. In addition to the assumptions described for this simple price-break model, it must be noted that buying in quantities of 8,000 is going to require significantly more capital investment in inventory and, consequently, may not be the wisest choice if money is tight for the firm.

A STOCHASTIC DEMAND MODEL

Until now, we have assumed that all demand parameters of an inventory system are known with certainty. In addition, we have assumed that lead time is zero. If we loosen only this latter assumption, very little has to change except that we must order prior to running out of inventory to prevent stock-outs. (Figure 14.11 illustrates the basic EOQ system with nonzero lead time.) In this situation, let us say, for example, that demand is 10 units per day and lead time is known to be 5 days; then the reorder point, s, is equal to 50 units. Therefore, whenever inventory reaches 50 units, an order for q units should be processed.

If we loosen the assumption of known or certain demand, then the problem of when to order becomes more complicated. As you can see in Figure 14.12, there is now the danger of stock-outs.

If an inventory system has all the properties of the basic EOQ system except that lead time is not zero and demand is not deterministic and constant, we can proceed in the following manner. The problem is still how much, and when, to order. If we assume that a reasonable estimate of the optimal order quantity can be calculated using the basic EOQ formula, then the problem reduces to merely determining the reorder point. In most real situations, using the EOQ formula when demand is not known

FIGURE 14.11 Basic EOQ with nonzero lead time, deterministic demand

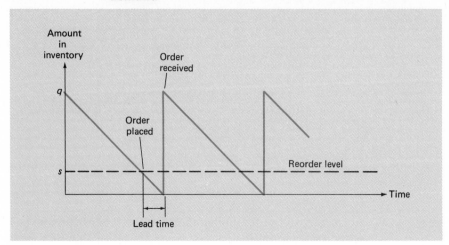

with certainty has little effect on total inventory costs because of the relative insensitivity of total costs to moderate changes in the order quantity.

Since the order quantity is given, ordering costs should not be affected by changes in the reorder point. The inventory costs affected by changes in the reorder point are the carrying costs and the stock-out costs. The problem, however, is that when stock-out costs are lowered by increasing the safety stock, carrying costs are increased because the average value of inventory is increased.

FIGURE 14.12 Stochastic demand

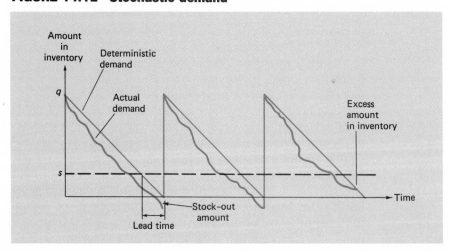

To illustrate how to determine the reorder point, let us consider the following problem. A sporting goods store wants to determine the proper reorder point for a T-3000 Wilson tennis racket. Annual demand is for 1,000 rackets sold at a rate of approximately 4 per day. It takes 5 days between the day the order is placed and the receipt of the shipment from Wilson. The question is, at what point does the sporting goods store order T-3000 tennis rackets? In order to answer the question, it is necessary to have some idea of the probability distribution of the number of rackets demanded in any 5-day period. This information is summarized in Table 14.6. In order to determine a good reorder point, it is possible to look at six reorder points and calculate the expected cost of each, then simply choose the reorder level with the smallest total cost. In order to determine this total cost, it is necessary to ascertain a per-unit stock-out cost. Let us assume this stock-out cost is $10 per racket, carrying cost is $5 per racket per year and ordering cost is $25 per order.

$$q^0 = \sqrt{[2(1,000)(25)]/5}$$
$$= \sqrt{10,000}$$
$$= 100$$

If the sporting goods company reorders when inventory hits 10 rackets, there is a high probability (90%) of having a shortage before the shipment is received. The shortage cost associated with this policy can be calculated in the following way:

$$C_2 = \left[\sum_{i=1}^{n} x_i P(x_i) c_2 \right] \left(\frac{r}{q} \right) \qquad [14.9]$$

TABLE 14.6   Frequency distribution of 5-day demand for T-3000 tennis rackets

Demand for 5-day periods	Frequency of specified demand	Relative frequency	Cumulative relative frequency
10	5	.10	.10
15	15	.30	.40
20	20	.40	.80
25	5	.10	.90
30	4	.08	.98
35	1	.02	1.00
	50	1.00	

where C_2 = shortage cost for year
      x_i = number short during lead time
    $P(x_i)$ = probability of being short x_i units
      c_2 = per-unit shortage costs
       r = total annual demand
      q = order quantity
      n = number of reorder points to be examined

Given that the reorder point is 10

$$C_2 = [0(.1)10 + 5(.3)10 + 10(.4)10 + 15(.1)10$$
$$+ 20(.08)10 + 25(.02)10](1{,}000/100)$$
$$= \$910.00$$

Stock-out costs for other reorder points are shown in Table 14.7.

The incremental carrying costs for the various reorder points under consideration are represented by

$$\Delta C_1 = \sum_{i=1}^{n} y_i P(y_i) c_1 \qquad [14.10]$$

where y_i = number of units in inventory at the time of replenishment
   ΔC_1 = incremental carrying cost
   $P(y_i)$ = probability of y_1 units in inventory at the time of replenishment
      c_1 = per-unit carrying cost
      n = number of demand levels

Given a reorder point of 10,

$$\Delta C_1 = 0(.1)5 + 0(.3)5 + 0(.4)5 + 0(.1)5 + 0(.08)5 + 0(.02)5$$
$$= 0$$

TABLE 14.7   Stock-out costs

Reorder point	Stock-out costs
10	$910
15	460
20	160
25	60
30	10
35	0

TABLE 14.8 Cost of reorder point policies

Reorder point	Expected stock-out costs	Expected incremental carrying costs	Total costs, $C_2 + \Delta C_1$
10	$910.00	0	$910.00
15	460.00	$2.50	462.50
20	160.00	12.50	172.50
25	60.00	32.50	92.50
30	10.00	55.00	65.00
35	0	79.50	79.50

For a reorder point of 25,

$$\Delta C_1 = 15(.1)5 + 10(.3)5 + 5(.4)5 + 0(.1)5 + 0(.08)5 + 0(.02)5$$
$$= 32.50$$

Table 14.8 reflects total incremental costs per year based on reorder point. Since the total incremental cost of the various reorder point policies is minimized when the reorder point is 30, the optimal inventory policy for the sporting goods company is to order 100 tennis rackets 10 times a year whenever the inventory level reaches 30 rackets.

SIMULATION APPROACH

Although there are many more inventory models than the few we have discussed in this chapter, it is very common for a real inventory system not to have an analytical counterpart. In other words, a model may not exist or be derivable mathematically that adequately describes a real inventory system. This is especially true when several properties are stochastic in nature. For example, many systems with stochastic demand, stochastic lead time, and nonconstant cost parameters have no mathematical model that can be solved analytically. As in the case of complex queuing systems, simulation can usually be applied when inventory systems become too complex to be optimized analytically. The trouble with simulation as a means for solving inventory system problems is that simulation is a descriptive technique, not an optimization technique. Simulation can answer questions regarding the desirability of various inventory policies; but it cannot, by itself, assign values to the various decision variables.

EXAMPLE   You can gain specific insight into how simulation is used to answer inventory questions by working through a simple inventory simulation. A ski shop carries a particularly popular pair of skis that sells for $120 and wishes to know how much, and when, to order. Because demand is not known with certainty (see Table 14.9) and lead time is not known with certainty (see Table 14.10) simulation appears to be a proper approach to the problem. The cost of the skis, which depends on the quantity ordered, is reflected in Table 14.11. Ordering cost is estimated at $25 per order, and the carrying cost fraction is .2. Stock-out cost is assumed to be $25 per unit.

TABLE 14.9   Historical frequency of demand

Demand per day	Number of observations	Relative frequency
0	19	.095
1	27	.135
2	42	.210
3	49	.245
4	34	.170
5	17	.085
6	9	.045
7	2	.010
8	1	.005
	200	1.000

TABLE 14.10   Historical frequency of lead time

Lead time (days)	Number of observations	Relative frequency
4	11	.22
5	7	.14
6	3	.06
7	21	.42
8	5	.10
9	2	.04
10	1	.02
	50	1.00

TABLE 14.11   Price schedule

Order	Price per pair of skis
Less than 25	$100
25 or more	95
50 or more	90
100 or more	90

In order to utilize simulation to solve this inventory problem, we must develop functions that can be used to generate the two stochastic variables in the problem, namely, demand and lead time. Let us assume that no known probability distribution can be fitted to the two sets of historical data and that we are forced to use these empirical distributions. Hence, the generating functions we need can be found merely by using the cumulative frequency distribution of the two stochastic variables. (See Tables 14.12 and 14.13 for these distributions.) You can refer back to Chapter 13 if necessary, for an explanation of how the two generating functions were derived.

Once we have the generating functions, the next step is to experiment with a particular inventory policy. For example, let us compare two inventory policies:

1. Order 25 pairs of skis when inventory reaches 10 pairs of skis.

2. Order 25 pairs of skis when inventory reaches 15 pairs of skis.

TABLE 14.12   Demand generating function

Random-number range	Demand per day
0–.095	0
.095–.230	1
.230–.440	2
.440–.685	3
.685–.855	4
.855–.940	5
.940–.985	6
.985–.995	7
.995–1.00	8

TABLE 14.13   Lead-time generating function

Random-number range	Lead time (days)
0–.22	4
.22–.36	5
.36–.42	6
.42–.84	7
.84–.94	8
.94–.98	9
.98–1.0	10

For illustrative purposes, we first simulate 1 month manually. Then, using a computer, we simulate a number of different policies to determine a good inventory policy. Tables 14.14 and 14.15 reflect the results of the manual simulation for both inventory policies we established. Look at the carrying cost and the stock-out costs for the two policies simulated in Tables 14.14 and 14.15. (Ordering costs and the cost of goods are constant for the two policies.) You can see that, by increasing the reorder level five units, the stock-out cost is decreased by $150 with only a $1.50 increase in the month's carrying cost.

Obviously, other inventory policies need to be examined and the number of days simulated must be significantly increased before we can have much faith in the results of the simulation experiments. To give you some idea of what it costs to "solve" the ski inventory problem using computer simulation, we wrote and ran a simulation program to determine the effects of various inventory policies. The program, reflected in Figure 14.13, was written in GPSS, a special-purpose simulation language. It took approximately 2 hours to write and debug. One experiment simulating 4 years took .1214 minute to run on a Xerox Sigma 6 computer. In all, 15 experiments were run at a total computer cost of approximately $9. As you can see in Table 14.16, the best inventory policy concerning skis is to order 100 pairs whenever inventory level reaches 25 pairs.

MATERIAL REQUIREMENTS PLANNING— A METHOD FOR DEPENDENT-DEMAND ITEMS

Thus far in this chapter, we have examined a sampling of classical analytical inventory methods. These methods are useful for managing distribution inventories or items subject to independent demand. Demand for a given inventory item is independent when it is unrelated to demand for other items. Thus, end products and items stocked to meet customer demand are subject to independent demand. Since independent demand is not known exactly, it must be forecasted, and statistical order-point or EOQ methods are appropriate.

materials requirements planning (MRP) Now let us examine the *materials requirements planning* (MRP) approach to dependent-demand items. An item has *dependent demand* whenever its demand depends on the demand for another item or product. For example, the demand for automobile engines or transmissions depends directly on the demand for the final product, automobiles. The MRP approach is particularly appropriate for manufacturing operations in which the demand for subassemblies, component parts, and raw materials is dependent upon an end product. These dependent-demand items have a demand pattern that is not smooth over time, but lumpy. Demand

TABLE 14.14 Simulation: reorder point = 10, order quantity = 25

Day number	Random number	Demand	Amount ordered (pairs)	Random number	Lead time (days)	Amount received (pairs)	Ending inventory	Carrying cost	Stock-out cost	Cost of goods	Order cost	Total cost
1	.134	1	25	.344	5		14	$1.06				$1.06
2	.909	5					9	.69		$2,375	$25	2,400.69
3	.204	1					8	.61				.61
4	.906	5					3	.23				.23
5	.387	2					1	.08				.08
6	.045	0					1	.08				.08
7	.894	5				25	0	0.00	$100			100.00
8	.172	1					24	1.82				1.82
9	.380	2					22	1.67				1.67
10	.390	2					20	1.52				1.52
11	.513	3					17	1.29				1.29
12	.563	3					14	1.06				1.06
13	.670	3					11	.84				.84
14	.428	2	25	.633	7		9	.68				.68
15	.589	3					6	.46				.46
16	.040	0					6	.46				.46
17	.738	4					2	.15				.15
18	.460	3					0	0.00	25			25.00
19	.007	0					0	0.00				0.00
20	.775	4					0	0.00	100			100.00
21	.421	2				25	23	1.78		2,375	25	2,401.78
22	.072	0					23	1.78				1.78
							Total	$16.26	$225	$4,750	$50	$5,041.26

TABLE 14.15 Simulation: reorder point = 15, order size = 25

Day	Random number	Demand	Amount ordered (pairs)	Random number	Lead time (days)	Amount received (pairs)	Ending inventory	Carrying cost	Stock-out cost	Cost of goods	Order cost	Total cost
1	.134	1	25	.344	5		14	$1.06		$2,375	$25	$2,401.06
2	.909	5					9	.69				.69
3	.204	1					8	.61				.61
4	.906	5					3	.23				.23
5	.387	2					1	.08				.08
6	.045	0					1	.08				.08
7	.894	5				25	20	1.52				1.52
8	.172	1					19	1.44				1.44
9	.380	2					17	1.29				1.29
10	.390	2	25	.633	7		15	1.14		2,375	25	2,401.14
11	.513	3					12	.91				.91
12	.563	3					9	.68				.68
13	.670	3					6	.46				.46
14	.428	2					4	.30				.30
15	.589	3					1	.08				.08
16	.040	0					1	.08				.08
17	.738	4					0	0	$75			75.00
18	.460	3				25	22	1.67				1.67
19	.007	0					22	1.67				1.67
20	.775	4					18	1.37				1.37
21	.421	2					16	1.22				1.22
22	.072	0					16	1.22				1.22
							Total	$17.80	$75	$4,750	$50	$4,892.80

FIGURE 14.13 GPSS program

```
        REALLOCATE BLO,50,XAC,50,FAC,1,STO,1,QUE,1
        REALLOCATE LOG,5,TAB,1,FUN,3,VAR,30,BVR,1,FSV,15
        REALLOCATE HSV,10,BVR,1,FMS,1,HMS,1,CHA,5,COM,5000
        SIMULATE
* X1 = CARRYING COST
* X2 = STOCKOUT COST
* X3 = COST OF GOODS
* X4 = ORDER COST
* X5 = TOTAL COST
* X6 = ENDING INVENTORY
* X7 = REORDER POINT
*X8 = ORDER QUANTITY
* X9 = COST PER UNIT
        INITIAL     X6,30
        INITIAL     X9,8000
        INITIAL     X7,10
        INITIAL     X8,100
1       VARIABLE    X9*X6*2/2500   CARRYING COST
2       VARIABLE    X6*(-2500)   STOCKOUT COST
3       VARIABLE    X9*X8    COST OF GOODS
4       VARIABLE    X1+X2+X3+X4   TOTAL COST
1       FUNCTION    RN2,D9    DEMAND FUNCTION
.095,0/.23,1/.44,2/.685,3/.855,4/.94,5/.985,6/.995,7/1,8
2       FUNCTION    RN3,D7    LEAD TIME FUNCTION
.22,4/.36,5/.42,6/.84,7/.94,8/.98,9/1,10
        GENERATE    1,0,,1000    GENERATE 1 DAY
        SAVEVALUE   6-,FN1    ADJUST ENDING INVENTORY
        TEST GE     X6,0,NEG   CHECK FOR STOCKOUT
        TEST GE     X6,X7,ORDER    CHECK FOR REORDER LEVEL
        SAVEVALUE   1+,V1    ACCUMULATE CARRYING COST
        TERMINATE   1
NEG     SAVEVALUE   2+,V2    ACCUMULATE STOCKOUT COST
        SAVEVALUE   6,0   ZERO ENDING INVENTORY
TEM     TERMINATE   1   END THE DAY
ORDER   GATE LR     1,TEM    HAS ORDER BEEN MADE??
        LOGIC S     1    SET THE ORDER SWITCH
        SAVEVALUE   4+,2500   ACCUMULATE ORDERING COST
        SAVEVALUE   3+,V3   ACCUMULATE COST OF GOODS
        SAVEVALUE   1+,V1    ACCUMULATE CARRYING COST
        PRIORITY    10    SET PRIORITY OF AN INCOMING ORDER
        ADVANCE     FN2    LEAD TIME
        SAVEVALUE   6+,X8    INCREMENT ENDING INVENTORY
        LOGIC R     1    RESET ORDER SWITCH
        TERMINATE   1
        GENERATE    1001    GENERATE TIMER TRANSACTION
        SAVEVALUE   5,V4    ACCUMULATE TOTAL COST
        TERMINATE   1
        START       1001
```

TABLE 14.16 Simulation results: total adjusted inventory costs (including cost of goods)

Order quantity	Reorder level				
	10	15	20	25	30
25	$283,258	$276,738	$271,863	$269,611	$269,055
50	$263,589	$259,330	$256,271	$255,367	$254,937
100	$232,559	$229,395	$228,529	$227,777	$227,828

that is lumpy occurs in discrete batches at different points in time. This type of pattern is very unlike the steady-demand-rate assumption of the basic EOQ models. Thus, MRP was developed to better cope with the lumpy demand patterns of dependent-demand items.

THE DEVELOPMENT OF MRP

MRP has the distinction of being hailed by many as the new way of life in production and inventory management. It is a methodology that has been developed "on the firing line" in industry rather than by academicians and theoreticians. It has been in use by some companies for many years, and is now finding its way into academic courses. MRP has been successful largely because it addresses some of the basic time-phasing problems that confront the inventory manager. It is concerned with an all-important problem; getting the right materials to the right place at the right time.

MRP has grown out of a certain disenchantment of practitioners with classical inventory methods for dependent-demand items. Some practitioners felt a need for better data processing and timing rather than better statistical or mathematical methods. MRP has experienced a very rapid growth and level of acceptance since 1970. Its adoption rate among practitioners is growing faster than that of any other inventory control method. This growth is partly attributed to the "MRP crusade" carried out by the *APICS* APICS (*American Production and Inventory Control Society*). APICS is a 12,000-member professional society for the advancement of the practice of production and inventory management. The APICS effort to promote the utility of MRP was spearheaded by such professionals as Joseph Orlicky of IBM, Oliver Wight, George Plossl, and Walter Goddard. The list of firms using MRP has grown rapidly from 150 in 1971 to 700 by 1975, and over 1,000 in 1976; all indications are that the list will continue to grow.

THE NATURE OF MRP

MRP is a technique for determining when to order dependent-demand items and how to replan and reschedule orders to adjust for changes in demand estimates from the master production schedule. The MRP system consists of inventory records, bills of material, and usually computer programs that translate the master production schedule into time-phased net requirements and planned coverage of these requirements for each component item needed. Because of the large amounts of data that usually need to be manipulated, MRP systems are computerized; they are, in a sense, a data-processing approach to dependent-demand inventory control. Successful MRP systems are taking the systems approach to inventory; they coordinate not only inventory, but purchasing, manufacturing, scheduling, and planning.

MRP avoids the "averaging process" of statistical inventory methods in managing inventory and calculates a specific quantity of what parts to order and when. Thus, an essential feature of MRP is the *calculation* of exact inventory needs rather than a statistical estimation. The calculation *bill of* is based on a planned production quantity of an end item and the *bill of* *materials* *materials* (BOM) for that item, which specifies a list of all subassemblies and parts required to produce the end item. The MRP systems interact with production scheduling to correctly time the release orders for all required items.

The purpose of an MRP system is more than to maintain inventory levels by ordering the right quantities of items at the right time. A properly functioning MRP system aids in priority and capacity planning. It helps to establish valid order priority by revising due dates that have been invalidated. An MRP system is an integral part of the priority planning system. It provides valuable information for both purchasing and production operations. However, it cannot cause due dates for purchasing or operations to be met. Thus, MRP must be supplemented by a priority control system in the factory. The control system provides the means to enforce adherence to plans.

PREREQUISITES AND ASSUMPTIONS OF MRP

MRP is primarily intended for manufacturing operations and has been used in such general applications as assembly operations, general machine shops, and fabrication assembly operations. It can be applied to any operation provided that certain assumptions or prerequisites are satisfied. The following conditions are the primary prerequisites for using MRP:

1. The existence of a realistic master production schedule that can be stated in bill-of-material terms.

2. An accurate bill of material for each product that not only lists all components of the product, but also reflects how the product is actually made in steps.

3. Having each inventory item identified with a unique code or part number.

4. Data-file integrity pertaining to inventory status data and bill-of-material data. The system will not function properly without accurate input data.

5. Known lead times on all inventory items.

BENEFITS AND COSTS OF MRP

The benefits and costs of using an MRP system will vary with individual companies, and efficiency increases will depend on how well the company was doing with its previous inventory system. However, successful adopters of MRP have noted the following potential benefits:

1. Lower inventories. The ability to plan ahead and the flexibility to reschedule rather than maintain large safety stocks allows significant reduction in inventory levels; reductions of up to 50 percent are not unusual.

2. Improved customer service. The percentage of late orders and stockouts is reduced, sometimes up to 75 percent.

3. Reduced overtime and idle time—the result of smoother and better planned production.

4. Reduced sales price and improved response to market demands.

5. Ability to modify the master schedule and respond to unanticipated changes in demand.

6. Ability to aid in capacity and priority planning. MRP not only aids the expediting of "hot orders," but also helps in deexpediting orders that must be delayed.

7. Reduced subcontracting the purchasing costs.

The largest cost or disadvantage of any MRP system is the computing cost to support the function. However, with increasing inventory and production costs, along with decreasing computation costs, an MRP system is getting easier to justify. An MRP system will also require personnel with MRP expertise and computer programmers to interact with the system, although the actual MRP system software is usually purchased from major computer manufacturers. Additional costs include system maintenance costs and the trials and tribulations of a system changeover.

But once functioning smoothly, the MRP system offers really significant advantages to weigh against the costs. The actual benefits depend upon how bad the performance of the current system really is. For example, one company that had some serious inventory problems installed an MRP system and achieved a 12 percent reduction in finished inventories, a work-in-process inventory reduction of 30 percent, and a 35 percent increase in the number of on-time deliveries.[4]

---

[4]Jeffrey G. Miller and Linda G. Sprague, "Behind the Growth in Materials Requirements Planning," *Harvard Business Review* (September–October 1975), 83–91.

ILLUSTRATION OF LUMPY DEMAND

Having briefly discussed the nature of MRP and its potential benefits, let us look at an example of dependent or lumpy demand (requirements) to demonstrate the superiority of MRP in handling this type of inventory problem. Let us assume we are to produce a final product A whose demand is uniform at the rate of 4 units per week. From Figure 14.14 which illustrates the product structure tree for product A, we can see that it takes 1 unit of component B and 2 units of component C to make 1 unit of A. Also, each B requires 3 Ds, and each C requires 1 D. Even though demand for product A is uniform, the production of A occurs in lot sizes of 20 units every 5 weeks. This is shown in Figure 14.15.

Given that 20 units of A take 1 week to produce and that parts B, C, and D have lead times (for internal production or external ordering) of 2, 4, and 1 week respectively, when should we release orders so that 20 units of A can be ready for distribution at the end of week 6? We are faced with the basic problem of time phasing and getting the right parts to the right place at the right time.

In order to have 20 units of product A ready at the end of week 6 (we are concentrating only on these 20 units in week 6), we can see from the product structure in Figure 14.14 that we will need 20 units of B and $2 \times 20 = 40$ units of C at the beginning of week 6. Given the lead times of B and C, we should place orders for 20 units of B at the beginning of week 4 and 40 units of C at the beginning of week 2. This in turn would require 60 units of D to be ordered (for the assembly of B) at the beginning of week 3 and 40 units of D to be ordered at the beginning of week 1. These order release dates are summarized in Figure 14.16. Looking at the gross requirements for part D in that figure, we see that the requirements follow a "lumpy pattern" of 0 40 0 60 0 0. In spite of the fact that

FIGURE 14.14 Product structure for A

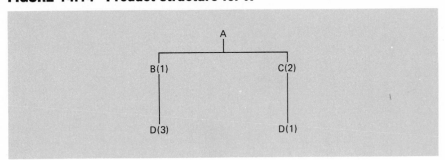

FIGURE 14.15 Master production schedule for product A

	Week 1	Week 2	Week 3	Week 4	Week 5	Week 6
Demand for Product A	4	4	4	4	4	4
Production	20					20

the demand for the end product A is uniform at 4 per week, the resulting dependent demand for part D is quite lumpy.

Figure 14.17 illustrates the large amount of error that can result in trying to statistically forecast demand when in fact you can calculate it after end-item production quantities have been established. The forecast in Figure 14.17 is based on exponential smoothing, where: forecast = previous period forecast $+ \alpha$(previous demand $-$ previous forecast), where $\alpha =$ the smoothing constant. For example, using an α of .2, and assuming a previous period forecast of 10 units and demand of 0 units, we obtain:

FIGURE 14.16 Lumpy demand

ITEM B Leadtime 2 weeks	week					
	1	2	3	4	5	6
Gross requirements						20
Planned order releases				20		

ITEM C Leadtime 4 weeks						
	1	2	3	4	5	6
Gross requirements						40
Planned order releases		40				

ITEM D Leadtime 1 week						
	1	2	3	4	5	6
Gross requirements		40		60		
Planned order releases	40		60			

forecast in period 1 = 10 + .2(0 − 10) = 8
forecast in period 2 = 8 + .2(0 − 8) = 6.4
forecast in period 3 = 6.4 + .2(40 − 6.4) = 14.12
forecast in period 4 = 14.12 + .2(0 − 14.12) = 11.3
forecast in period 5 = 11.3 + .2(60 − 11.3) = 21.0
forecast in period 6 = 21.0 + .2(0 − 21.0) = 15.8

It is clear from the figure that dependent-demand quantities should be calculated once firmed production quantities have been determined from the master production schedule.

PRINCIPLES OF MRP

The example above dealing with lumply demand illustrates the basic process in MRP—working backward from the scheduled completion dates of end products to determine the dates when the various component parts and materials are to be ordered, and the quantities to be ordered. Of course, the example was a simple one, but the basic process is the same for large-scale real-world manufacturing operations.

The calculations of dependent-demand quantities and order dates are performed by the MRP computer program. The computer program is but one aspect of the overall MRP system, whose structure Figure 14.18 de-

FIGURE 14.17   MRP calculated demand versus statistically forecasted demand

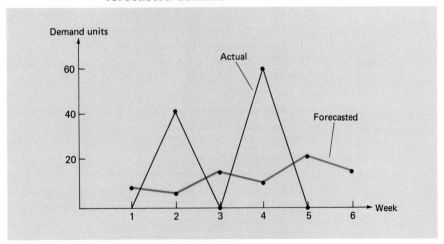

picts. Chronologically, the MRP system begins with the aggregate production plans, which are refined into a master production schedule. Forecasts of independent-demand items such as end products serve as input to aggregate plans and the master schedule. The master schedule is broken into firm and tentative plans. Firm production schedules are needed for short-range time frames covering up to a month or two; tentative production plans may range from a month up to a year. Tentative plans are sometimes revised according to market reactions, new forecasts, and capacity output reports of the MRP computer program.

The MRP computer program has three major sources of input—the master production schedule, the inventory records file, and the product structure or bill-of-materials file. Using these three inputs, the MRP computer program schedules order releases and production dates for the entire manufacturing operation. The MRP computer program must schedule not only orders for regular customer demand, but also random orders or orders external to the planned master schedule. These external orders can include service and repair parts, interplant orders, and items specially selected for experimentation or testing.

Given random demand, the MRP computer program schedules orders by combining information from the master schedule, the bill-of-materials file, and the inventory record file. The master schedule specifies production quantities and due dates, the inventory record file states the number of units on hand and an order for each item, and the bill-of-materials file lists all the items needed to produce a given end product. The logic processor within the MRP computer program then "explodes" the net requirements for the production of the end product and schedules order releases, taking into account any lead times of items.

As can be seen in Figure 14.18, there are three important output reports from the MRP computer program. Order release reports are the principal output, and they represent planned orders in the current period. They form the basis for new shop orders, new purchase requisitions, and due dates for production scheduling. The order reschedule reports call for changes in due dates for open orders. These reports are major input for priority planning and rescheduling, and they also provide expediting information. The planned order reports tentatively schedule orders for release in future periods. These provide information in forecasting inventory and future workcenter loads. This visibility into the future is very helpful in capacity planning and the development of realistic master schedules. Other, secondary reports not shown in Figure 14.18 can include performance reports for forecasted usages and costs, and exception reports, which signal errors such as late orders, nonexistent parts numbers, or a due date of an open order outside the planning horizon.

FIGURE 14.18 Structure of MRP system

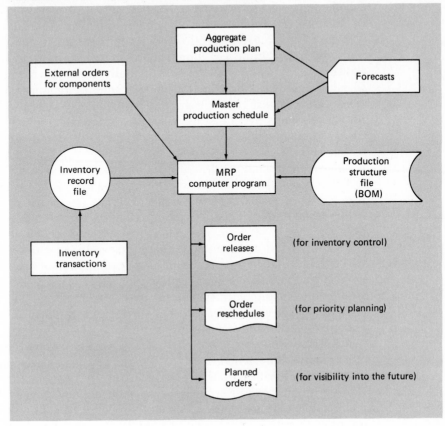

Our purpose here has not been to give you an in-depth understanding of MRP and how it works. Rather, we hope you have gained some insight into the nature of MRP, some of its advantages, and where it can be successfully applied. Joseph Orlicky's book and other MRP references listed at the end of the chapter are recommended to the student seeking more material on MRP.

SUMMARY

In order to implement truly effective inventory management, an organization must have an integrated management information system for the purpose of inventory control. In most organizations, inventory control is nothing more than an inventory accounting system. In other words, whether the system is computer-based or not, it merely keeps track of inventory items and alerts management when inventory levels get low. Typically, the system has little capacity for decision making about when, and how much, to order. Some progressive organizations, however, are developing or using systems that actually integrate inventory models like the ones we described in this chapter into their management information systems. These more progressive systems may be real-time or batch-oriented systems. What distinguishes the management information system from the inventory accounting system is the decision-making capability of the MIS.

Management science's primary challenge in relation to inventory theory is the successful application of existing theory. More theory is always useful, but unless organizations can be persuaded to apply the inventory theory thus far developed, the marginal utility of new theory is questionable.

To apply existing inventory theory successfully, you must beware of two pitfalls. First, you must avoid the misapplication of various inventory models by carefully examining the properties of an existing inventory system and making sure system properties adequately match model assumptions. Too many firms do not distinguish between dependent and independent demand items in their inventory. Consequently, models are being misapplied with very costly consequences. Second, to implement a decision-making management information system, many human factors must be dealt with carefully. People naturally resist change, especially when it threatens their security or self-image. Many times, it is more effective, for example, to have the management information system suggest an order quantity rather than automatically print the purchase or production order. A major reason why management science has not progressed faster in most organizations is a failure to take into consideration the human factors connected with organizational change. Unless the people in an organization are in favor of a change, that change, regardless of its individual merits, will not succeed.

DERIVATION
OF THE BASIC EOQ MODEL APPENDIX

From equation 14.2,

$$C(q) = (C_1 q/2) + C_3 r/q$$

To optimize, take the first derivative with respect to q, set it equal to zero, and solve for q. Thus

$$\frac{dC(q)}{dq} = \frac{C_1}{2} - \frac{C_3 r}{q^2}$$

$$\frac{C_1}{2} - \frac{C_3 r}{q^2} = 0$$

Solve for q:

$$\frac{C_1}{2} = \frac{C_3 r}{q^2}$$

$$q^2 = \frac{2C_3 r}{C_1}$$

$$q^0 = \sqrt{2C_3 r / C_1}$$

To determine whether q^0 is a maximum or a minimum, take the second derivative: If it is greater than zero, q^0 is a minimum; if $d^2C(q)/dq^2$ is less than zero, q^0 is a maximum. Thus,

$$\frac{d^2C(q)}{dq^2} = \frac{2qC_3 r}{q^4} = \frac{2C_3 r}{q^3}$$

Since C_3, r, and q are all greater than zero, the second derivative is greater than zero. Therefore, q^0 is a minimum.

SOLVED PROBLEMS

PROBLEM STATEMENT

A local TV distributor has found from experience that demand for a certain model TV is fairly constant at a rate of 50 sets per month. Lead time is effectively zero and no shortages are to be allowed. If the sets cost $300, the carrying-cost fraction is 20 percent per year, and ordering cost is estimated to be $50, how many sets should be ordered, and how many orders must be processed per year?

SOLUTION

Using the basic EOQ model, the optimal order quantity is

$$q^* = \sqrt{\frac{2C_3 r}{C_1}}$$

where $C_3 = \$50$ per order
$\quad r = (12)(50) = 600$ sets per year
$\quad C_1 = (.2)(300) = \$60$ per set per year

$$q^* = \sqrt{\frac{(2)(50)(600)}{60}}$$
$$= 31.62 \text{ sets per order}$$

Owing to the relative insensitivity of q^*, we can round q^* up or down with little effect. Let $q^* = 32$ sets per order. This means that the number of orders processed per year is

$$N = 600/32 = 18.75 \text{ orders}$$

PROBLEM STATEMENT

A basket factory has decided to try to apply an inventory model to its most popular item. Demand is fairly deterministic at a rate of 5,000 baskets per month. Lead time is zero and no shortages are allowed by management. The factory can produce the baskets at a rate of 15,000 per month. Carrying costs are \$.20 per basket per year, and setup costs are \$100. What is the optimal lot size?

SOLUTION

Using the finite replenishment-rate model, we obtain

$$q^* = \frac{\sqrt{2rC_3/C_1}}{\sqrt{1 - r/p}}$$

where $\quad r = $ annual demand $= (5,000$ baskets per month$)(12) = 60,000$ baskets
$\quad C_3 = $ setup cost $= \$100$

C_1 = per-basket carrying cost per year = \$.20
p = replenishment rate—15,000 baskets/month = 180,000 baskets per year

$$q^* = \frac{\sqrt{(2)(60,000)(100)/.2}}{\sqrt{1 - (60,000/180,000)}}$$

$$\cong 9487 \text{ baskets}$$

The minimum cost of implementing an order quantity of 9487 is

$$C^* = \sqrt{2rC_1C_3} \sqrt{1 - r/p}$$
$$= \$1264.94$$

PROBLEM STATEMENT

A glass company has patented an extra-strength glass and currently sells it in 25-square-foot sheets. Because the product is patented, being out of stock does not result in a lost sale. A stock-out, however, is bad for customer good will, and management has assigned a stock-out cost of \$50 per sheet per month. The sheets cost \$1,000 to make, but because of the unusual process, orders can be filled in less than one day. Demand for the glass has averaged 150 sheets per month. Annual holding costs for the company are assumed to be 15 percent of the value of inventory. Lot sizes are 150 sheets (owing to production scheduling, the hi-test glass can be produced only once monthly). The pertinent question is, What is the optimal order level?

SOLUTION

$$S^* = \frac{q_pC_2}{C_1 + C_2}$$

where q_p = 150 sheets
C_2 = (50)(12) = \$600
C_1 = (1,000)(.15) = \$150

$$S^* = \frac{(150)(600)}{150 + 600}$$
$$= 120$$

In other words, back orders would reach 30 sheets of glass before inventory was replenished.

The cost of the solution is

$$
\begin{aligned}
C^* &= \frac{C_1 S^2}{2q_p} + \frac{C_2(q_p - S)^2}{2q_p} \\
&= \frac{(150)(120)^2}{2(150)} + \frac{600(150 - 120)^2}{2(150)} \\
&= \$9,000
\end{aligned}
$$

REVIEW QUESTIONS

1. List four reasons for carrying inventory.
2. Why is it critical to manage an organization's inventory effectively?
3. What are the two major functions that must be performed in order to effectively control an organization's inventory?
4. In your own words, explain the rationale behind ABC analysis.
5. Classify inventory accounting systems into two categories.
6. Distinguish between real-time inventory control systems and batch-processing systems.
7. Why is it likely that the number of real-time inventory systems will increase in the future?
8. What is the object of inventory models?
9. What are the two major decision variables in inventory models?
10. Describe the three components of inventory cost.
11. Briefly explain the five basic steps in analyzing an inventory system.
12. Why is the determination of system properties so important?
13. What is meant by demand patterns?
14. Define "lead time."
15. Distinguish between stochastic demand and deterministic demand.
16. Define "replenishment period."
17. Distinguish between order level and reorder level.
18. Why is it sometimes necessary to simulate an inventory system?
19. Why is sensitivity analysis an important step in analyzing inventory systems?
20. List the assumptions of the basic EOQ model.
21. Distinguish between finite and infinite replenishment rate.

22. What is the major difference between the basic EOQ model and the basic order level model?

23. Why is simulation often used for inventory problems?

24. What are two major disadvantages of using a simulation approach to inventory problems?

25. What distinguishes a management information system from an inventory accounting system?

26. Why haven't inventory models been more widely applied?

27. List four advantages and two disadvantages of buying in large quantities.

28. What is the difference between dependent and independent demand?

29. Explain how errors can arise in applying statistical order point procedures to lumpy demand.

30. Where did MRP originate?

31. What are the three main inputs to any MRP computer program?

32. What kind of information is held in the BOM file? The inventory records file?

PROBLEMS

14.1   Given the following information, perform an ABC analysis on the data. Discuss your results.

Item No.	Annual demand	Cost per unit
157	100	$25
222	50	30
315	1,000	50
719	250	15
244	300	20
367	400	25
219	2,000	20
234	345	20
577	500	25
619	750	10
621	1,000	35
322	900	5
357	432	10
192	150	15
334	225	30

14.2   *Blood Bank.* You are asked by the manager of a blood bank to study its inventory problem and make recommendations for optimizing costs. The manager has been taking some night courses; she has been taught the following formula and wonders if it might be applied to the problem:

$$q^* = \sqrt{2C_3 r / c_1}$$

Specifically, do the following:

a.   Indicate to the manager what an inventory model is meant to do.

b.   Discuss properties of this inventory problem.

c.   Recommend use of the aforementioned formula or state specific reasons why it should not be used.

14.3   *Drill Rig Manufacturer.* A drill-rig company has a contract with Saudi Arabia to produce 60 drill rigs during the next year. The plan is to produce these rigs at a rate of 5 per month. A valve used in the drill rig is purchased off the shelf from a nearby supplier; no lead time is required. Each drill rig requires 4 valves. The valves cost $100 each. Holding cost for the valves is $10 per year per valve. In addition, it costs $75 to order these valves and receive them from the vendor.

a.   What is the optimal order quantity?

b.   What is the optimal number of orders per year?

c.   How frequent should the orders be?

d.   What is the total inventory cost of ordering the optimal order quantity?

e.   Perform a limited amount of sensitivity analysis on the order quantity.

14.4   *Auto Manufacturer.* An automobile manufacturer plans to produce 30,000 cars in the next month. All cars planned for production use the same headlamps; therefore, demand for the headlights for the next month is known to be 60,000. The purchasing agent wants to know how many headlamps to buy at one time. Historically, headlamps have been received on the same day they were ordered. It costs $35 to order headlamps, and the carrying-cost fraction used by the auto company is 15% per year. The lamps cost $.87 each.

a.   What is the optimal order quantity?

b.   What is the optimal number of orders per year?

c.   What is the frequency of orders? Assume 22 working days.

d. What is the total inventory cost of ordering the optimal order quantity?

e. Show the inventory cost for q's of 10,000, 20,000, 25,000, 30,000, and 40,000 units.

14.5 *Drill-Rig Manufacturer.*

a. Referring to Problem 14.3, what should the drill-rig company do if lead time is 1 month rather than zero? In other words, what should the inventory policy be?

b. Does the existence of lead time change the total inventory cost of the valves? If so, what is the total cost of the new inventory policy?

14.6 *Drill-Rig Manufacturer.* Management has decided to make the valves in Problem 14.3 rather than buy them from an outside vendor. The demand is for 240 valves for the next year, or 20 valves per month. To make the valves costs the company $90 each, and setup time amounts of $100 per set up. Holding cost remains at $10 per valve. Since these valves are not being bought off the shelf, replenishment of inventory is not simultaneous. In fact, the production department says it can produce 200 valves per month given present human and capital resources.

a. What is the optimal order quantity?

b. What is the optimal number of setups per year?

c. What is the optimal time between orders? Assume 250 working days.

d. What is the total inventory cost of the optimal order policy?

14.7 *Auto Manufacturer.* The automobile manufacturer in Problem 14.4 has decided to make the headlamps. It has been determined that 150,000 headlamps per month can be produced; but owing to various resource constraints, management has decided to buy half the necessary quantity of headlamps and make the other half. It costs the company $.75 to make each headlamp, and setup costs are $50 per setup. Refer to Problem 14.4 for the parameters of the purchasing decision.

a. What is the optimal order quantity to be purchased from the outside supplier?

b. What is the EOQ for in-house production?

c. What is the total inventory cost for the headlamps?

d. What is the optimal number of purchase orders per month?

e. What is the optimal number of production runs per month?

14.8   *Mail Order Supply.* A mail-order stereo firm reviews its stock of amplifiers each month and orders for the next month. Its most popular amp last year was the SEA-700. Last year, 600 amps were sold; these sales were spread evenly throughout the year. Predictions are that this year's sales will be approximately the same. Lead time from the manufacturer is effectively zero, and no sales are lost owing to shortages; instead, the amps are merely delivered one month later. A recent market survey revealed that 60 percent of the customers surveyed would not buy amps again from this firm if they were made to wait an extra month. Profit on an SEA-700 amp is $50. Management, therefore, has estimated stock-out cost to be .6 (profit on two future sales), or $60, or $720 per amp per year. Holding cost per amp is $75 per year.

a.   What is the optimal order level?

b.   What is the minimum inventory cost for the SEA-700 amp?

c.   What is the order-level sensitivity?

14.9   *Bicycle Manufacturer.* A deluxe bicycle store sells a particular model men's bike for $200. The bike costs the store $150, including selling cost. The wholesale cost of the bike is $125. Demand for the bike is stochastic; past demand is reflected in the table. Total demand for 1 year is forecast to be 52 units. Stock-out cost is assumed to be the profit lost, or $50. Lead time is 1 month. Ordering costs are $50 per order. Carrying cost is 20 percent per year of the inventory value.

a.   What is the best inventory policy for the bicycle in this problem?

b.   What are the expected stock-out and incremental carrying costs of the selected inventory policy?

Monthly demand	Frequency
0	1
1	3
2	6
3	7
4	8
5	11
6	7
7	5
8	2
	50

14.10 Given the policy you recommended in Problem 14.9, simulate manually 1 year's activity. Interpret your simulation results. Assume a beginning inventory of 10 units.

14.11 *Charter Airline.* A small charter airline company wants to know how much aviation fuel to buy. Demand for flight fuel has been somewhat constant at 50,000 gallons per month. Fuel costs are $.75 per gallon, and the company's annual carrying-cost fraction is .10. If it costs $100 to get a delivery with no lead time required:

  a. What is the optimal order quantity?

  b. What assumption did you make in answering part a?

  c. If storage capacity for the fuel were limited to 10,000 gallons, how would you analyze the problem?

14.12 *Hospital.* Demand for pacemakers has been running at a rate of 10 per month. The cost of a pacemaker to the hospital is $1,000. It costs $50 to place an order, and the hospital's annual carrying cost is 12 percent of inventory value.

  a. What information would you need to determine the optimal order quantity?

  b. Assuming the basic EOQ model, what are q^* and the minimum inventory cost?

  c. If lead time were 7 days, what is the proper reorder point, assuming a constant rate of demand?

14.13 *Hospital.* If lead time for the pacemakers in Problem 14.12 is 1 day and daily demand is distributed according to the following table, what is the reorder point if stock-outs are not allowed?

Daily demand	Probability
0	.30
1	.40
2	.15
3	.10
4	.05
	1.00

14.14 *Sawmill.* A sawmill has been operating at peak capacity for several years. To keep the mill running takes 2,000 trees per day. The supplier of raw material (trees) can deliver only 10,000 trees per day. Trees cost an average of $100. Ordering costs are extremely high at \$5,000 per order. The annual carrying-out cost fraction is 12 percent. Assume a 365-day operation of the mill.

a. What is the optimal order quantity?

b. What is the total inventory cost?

c. What assumption about system properties did you make in calculating the optimal order quantity?

14.15 *Aerospace.* An aerospace company has a contract with the U.S. Navy to produce 120 airplanes during the next year. The plan is to produce these airplanes at a rate of 10 per month. An actuating cylinder used to move the wing flap is purchased off the shelf from a nearby supplier; no lead time is required. Since there are 2 wings, 2 cylinders are needed per airplane. The actuating cylinders cost \$200. Holding cost for the cylinders is \$20 per year per cylinder. In addition, it costs \$75 to order these cylinders and receive them from the vendor.

a. What is the optimal quantity?

b. What is the optimal number of orders per year?

c. What is the optimal time between orders?

d. What is the total inventory cost of ordering the optimal order quantity?

e. Perform a limited amount of sensitivity analysis on the order quantity.

14.16 *Aerospace.* Referring to Problem 14.15.

a. What should the aerospace company do if lead time is 1 month rather than zero? In other words, what should the inventory policy be?

b. Does the existence of lead time change the total inventory cost of the actuating cylinders? If so, what is the total cost of the new inventory policy?

14.17 *Mail-Order Supply.* A mail-order, auto supply firm reviews its stock of tires each month and orders for the next month. Its most popular tire last year was the XR-100 radial. Last year, 1,600 sets were sold, these sales were spread evenly throughout the year. Predictions are that this year's sales will be approximately the same. Lead time from the manufacturer is effectively zero, and no sales are lost due to shortages. Instead, the tires are merely delivered 1 month later. A recent market survey revealed that 50 percent of the customers surveyed would not buy tires again from this firm if they were made to wait an extra month. Profit on a set of tires is $70. Management, therefore, has estimated stock-out cost to be .5 (profit on two future sales), or $70, or $840 per set per year. Holding cost per set of tires is $75 per year.

a. What is the optimal order level?

b. What is the minimum inventory cost for the XR-100 radial tire?

c. What is the order level sensitivity?

14.18 *Automobile Dealer.* An automobile dealer has the exclusive rights to market a foreign car. For this reason, no sales are lost if he is out of stock when a customer wants to buy. Demand for the car has been running at 20 units per month. The dealer orders one time per month and receives the order within a day or two. The dealer's subjective estimate of the cost of the loss of customer good will is $100 per month. The dealer cost on the cars is $4,000 and his carrying cost fraction is approximately 15 percent per year.

a. What is the optimal order level?

b. What is the minimum inventory cost for the foreign car?

c. What is the sensitivity of the order level?

14.19 *Hospital.* A large hospital's nursery uses disposable diapers for its newborn babies at a rate of 60 cases per day. Ordering costs have been estimated at $50 per order. The hospital's Accounting Department has assigned an annual carrying cost fraction of .15 to the nursery supplies. All the assumptions of the basic EOQ model, such as zero lead time, are applicable. The purchasing agent for the hospital has an opportunity to take advantage of one of several quantity discounts. The pricing schedule is listed in the table.

Quantity ordered (cases)	Unit price
0–1,999	$2.50
2,000–4,999	2.45
5,000–9,999	2.40
10,000 and over	2.35

a. What is the optimal order quantity?

b. What is the minimum inventory cost?

14.20 *Restaurant.* A large restaurant sells 600 16-ounce strip steaks each week. It costs the restaurant $25 to order steaks from a local meat packer, and since the meat packer is close there is effectively no lead time involved. The restaurant's accountant has estimated the annual carrying cost fraction to be .2. The local meat packer has submitted the price schedule listed in the table. Assume that the restaurant has ample freezing capacity.

a.   What is the optimal order quantity?

b.   What is the minimum total cost?

c.   How much initial investment capital would it require to implement the optimal inventory policy?

d.   What policy would you recommend to the restaurant manager?

Quantity ordered	Price per pound
Less than 500	$2.00
500–999	1.90
1,000–1,999	1.85
2,000–3,999	1.80
4,000–6,999	1.75
7,000–9,999	1.73
10,000 and over	1.70

14.21   *Retail Chain Store.* A large retail chain store sells a vacuum cleaner for $150. The cost of the vacuum cleaner, including selling cost, is $120. Cost of goods is $100. Demand for this vacuum cleaner model is stochastic; past demand is reflected in the table. Total demand for 1 year is forecast to be 260 units. Stock-out cost is assumed to be the profit lost, or $30. Lead time is 7 days. Ordering costs are $40 per order. Carrying cost is 23 percent of the inventory value.

Weekly demand	Frequency
0	2
1	7
2	10
3	7
4	12
5	20
6	14
7	10
8	9
9	7
10	2
	100

    a. What is the best inventory policy for the model LX-1002 vacuum cleaner?

    b. What do the expected stock-out and incremental carrying costs of the selected inventory policy total?

14.22 *Retail Chain Store.* Given the policy you recommended in Problem 14.22, simulate manually 1 month's activity. Interpret your simulation results.

14.23 Compute the net requirements for items A, B, and C if we want to produce 40 units of X.

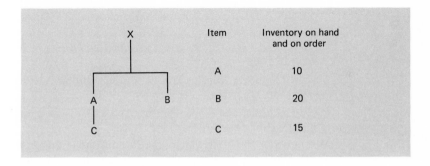

Item	Inventory on hand and on order
A	10
B	20
C	15

14.24 Calculate the gross and net requirements for the following BOM and quantities. Assume that you want to produce 50 end items.

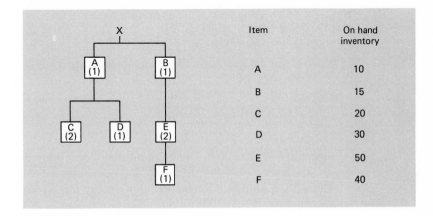

Item	On hand inventory
A	10
B	15
C	20
D	30
E	50
F	40

BIBLIOGRAPHY

American Production and Inventory Control Society, *APICS Special Report: Materials Requirement Planning by Computer.* Washington, D.C.: American Production and Inventory Control Society, 1971.

Berry, W. L., "Lot Sizing Procedures for Requirements Planning Systems: A Framework for Analysis," *Production and Inventory Management* (2nd Quarter 1972), 19–34.

Bishop, Jack L., Jr., "Experience with a Successful System for Forecasting and Inventory Control," *Operations Research, 22,* No. 6, 1224–1231.

Buffa, Elwood S., *Operations Management: The Management of Productive Systems.* New York: Wiley–Hamilton, 1976.

———, *Production-Inventory Systems: Planning and Control.* Homewood, Ill.: Richard D. Irwin, Inc., 1968.

Chase, Richard B., and Nicholas J. Aquilano, *Production and Operations Management: A Life Cycle Approach.* Homewood, Ill.: Richard D. Irwin, Inc., 1977.

Davis, Edward W., "A Look at the Use of Production-Inventory Techniques: Past and Present," *Production and Inventory Management,* 16 (December 1975), 1–19.

Everdell, Romeyn, "Master Production Scheduling," *APICS Training Aid.* Washington, D.C.: APICS, 1974.

Hadley, George, and T. M. Whitin, *Analysis of Inventory Systems.* Englewood Cliffs, N.J.: Prentice-Hall, Inc., 1963.

International Business Machines Corporation, *Communications Oriented Production Information and Control System,* Publications G320–1974 through G320–1981.

Lee, W. B., and C. P. McLaughlin, "Corporate Simulation Models for Aggregate Materials Management," *Production and Inventory Management* (1st Quarter 1974), 55–67.

Miller, Jeffrey G., and Linda G. Sprague, "Behind the Growth in Materials Requirements Planning," *Harvard Business Review,* Vol. 53, No. 5 (September–October 1975), 83–91.

Naddor, Eliezer, *Inventory Systems.* New York: John Wiley & Sons, Inc., 1966.

Orlicky, Joseph, *Materials Requirements Planning.* New York: McGraw-Hill Book Company, 1975.

Plossl, G. W., and O. W. Wight, "Materials Requirement Planning by Computer," Washington, D.C.: APICS, 1971.

———, *Production and Inventory Control.* Englewood Cliffs, N.J.: Prentice-Hall, Inc., 1967.

Schmidt, J. W., and R. E. Taylor, *Simulation and Analysis of Industrial Systems.* Homewood, Ill.: Richard D. Irwin, Inc., 1970.

Thurston, Phillip H., "Requirements Planning for Inventory Control," *Harvard Business Review* (May–June 1972), 67–71.

Wagner, Harvey M., *Principles of Operations Research*, 2nd ed. Englewood Cliffs, N.J.: Prentice-Hall, Inc., 1975.

Wight, Oliver W., *Production and Inventory Management in the Computer Age*. Boston: Cahners Books, 1974.

Woolsey, Gene, "On Doing Good Things and Dumb Things in Production and Inventory Control," *Interfaces*, 5 (May 1975), 66–67.

15
Markov
Processes

NAPA STATE HOSPITAL[1]

At Napa State Hospital, California's second largest hospital for the mentally ill, a progressive resocialization program was initiated for the express purpose of deinstitutionalizing geriatric patients from the mental wards of the hospital. A Markov chain model was used to provide appropriate quantitative measures for predicting the long-term success or failure of the program.

In order to predict the expected cost of patient care until death and other relevant measures of program effectiveness, five patient "states" were identified. Each state represented a condition or environment in which a geriatric patient may find himself. These states were:

The Geriatric Resocialization Program (GRP)

A Hospital Ward

Home From the Hospital Ward

Home From GRP

Death

One-month transition probabilities (probabilities of moving from one state to another) were developed as was the monthly cost of being in any of the five states. These data together with the theory of Markov chains made it possible to predict the amount of time each patient can expect to remain in any one state and the total expected cost of treating a patient until death given the present state of the patient.

A Markov chain model was used to predict the total cost effectiveness of the GRP program. The Markovian model predicted an expected per patient savings of $25,100 until death. Without GRP, the states' cost of caring for Napa State Hospital's geriatric patients until death would have cost 30 percent

---

[1]Jack Meredith, "A Markovian Analysis of a Geriatric Ward," *Management Science,* 19, no. 6 (February 1973), 604–12.

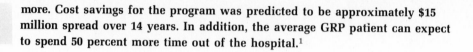

more. Cost savings for the program was predicted to be approximately \$15 million spread over 14 years. In addition, the average GRP patient can expect to spend 50 percent more time out of the hospital.[1]

INTRODUCTION

Markov process models are useful when studying the evolution of stochastic systems over repeated trials or time periods. For example, queuing systems are stochastic systems in which Markov analysis has aided management scientists in deriving models that describe queuing system operating characteristics. In addition, stochastic processes such as consumer brand switching can be directly analyzed using Markov analysis. If the market is the stochastic system, often relative market shares for some future time periods can be predicted using Markov models. Like queuing theory and simulation, Markov process models are descriptive rather than normative in nature. Both major outputs from a Markov model involve probabilities. The probability of finding the system in any particular state
steady-state at any given time period is one output and the long-run or *steady-state*
probabilities *probabilities* of the system being in each various state is the other major output.

For example, consider a bank customer's checking account. If we describe the account using just two states, a positive balance and overdrawn, then a Markov model could be used to determine the probability of being in either state (overdrawn or a positive balance) after a given number of days. In addition, a Markov model could tell bank management what the steady-state probabilities of being in either state are.

Markov process models can be used for a wide number of applications. These applications include consumer brand switching, the aging of accounts receivable, inventory control, consumer response to advertising, and the maintenance of capital equipment. In this chapter, we restrict our discussion of Markov processes to those processes that have a finite number of states and to those in which the probabilities of moving from one state to another remain constant.

ASSUMPTIONS AND DEFINITIONS

In order to define some key terms and identify the various assumptions of Markov process models, let us use the following stochastic system. The system is the quality of air in a large industrial city. Each day the air in the city is analyzed and a pollution index is calculated. Given certain ranges of the pollution index, the Air Quality Board issues a statement classifying the city's air as either good, unhealthful, or hazardous. These classifications by the Air Quality Board are referred to as states of the system. The day-to-day change in the air quality classification is a stochastic (probabilistic) process. Because the air quality on any given day depends only on the air quality of the previous day, the stochastic process *Markov* is classified as a *Markov process*. The *Markov property* or memoryless *process* property means that the probability of moving from one state to another depends only on the present state of the system and is not in any way dependent upon the previous history of the system. Transition probabilities measure the probability of the system moving from one state or condition to another. The transition matrix in Table 15.1 reflects the probabilities of the system moving from one state to another state in one time period. Each probability in the transition matrix is a conditional probability. For example, P(good air tomorrow/good air today) = .75 and P(unhealthful air tomorrow/good air today) = .20. More generally, $P_{ij} = P$(state j/state i). If these probabilities remain constant over time, the process is called a homogeneous Markov chain.

To summarize, a *homogeneous Markov chain* is a stochastic process that has the following three properties:

1. The process has a finite number of discrete states.
2. The state of the process in any given period depends only on its state in the preceding period and the transition probabilities.
3. The transition probabilities remain constant over time.

PROBABILITY CHANGES
OVER TWO OR MORE TRANSITIONS

transition The *transition matrix* is useful for describing single-period conditional *matrix* probabilities. Often it is desirable, however, to ascertain the probabilities of the various states of a system after two or more time periods or transitions. In our example, it might be useful to know the probability of hazardous air next weekend so that people and organizations could more

TABLE 15.1 Transition matrix

Today's air quality	Tomorrow's air quality		
	Good	Unhealthful	Hazardous
Good	.75	.20	.05
Unhealthful	.25	.65	.10
Hazardous	.05	.75	.20

FIGURE 15.1 Probability tree

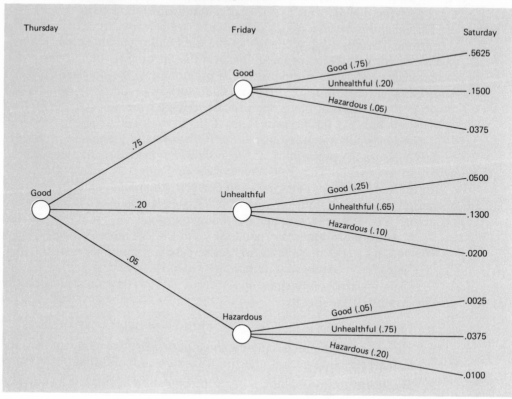

intelligently plan their weekend activities. Let us suppose that today is Thursday and the air quality is good. We would like to know the probability of Saturday's air being hazardous. To compute the probability of Saturday's air quality given that Thursday's air quality was classified as good, we can construct a probability tree, as shown in Figure 15.1.

The probability of each path through the probability tree represents a joint probability that can be calculated as the product of the probabilities on each branch. Thus, the probability of the air quality being good on Friday and Saturday given that Thursday's air quality is good is $.75^2$, or .5625. The joint probabilities of each path are calculated and reflected in Figure 15.1. To compute the probability of hazardous air quality on Saturday we can add the probabilities of those paths that end in hazardous air quality. Therefore, P(Saturday's air will be hazardous/Thursday's air is good) = .0375 + .0200 + .0100 = .0675. The P(Saturday's air will be good/Thursday's air is good) = .5625 + .0500 + .0025 = .615. The P(Saturday's air will be unhealthful/Thursday's air is good) = .1500 + .1300 + .0375 = .3175.

It should be obvious that to compute probabilities of being in various states in future time periods can be very tedious using probability trees, especially when there are a large number of states and more than just a few transitions or time periods. In order to compute the probabilities of each state of air quality on Saturday given each state of the system on Thursday, a fairly large probability tree is required. See Figure 15.2 for the appropriate probability tree. Fortunately, matrix multiplication affords a computationally more efficient procedure for computing transition matrices for two or more time periods. A brief review of matrix algebra is

FIGURE 15.2   2-Step probability tree

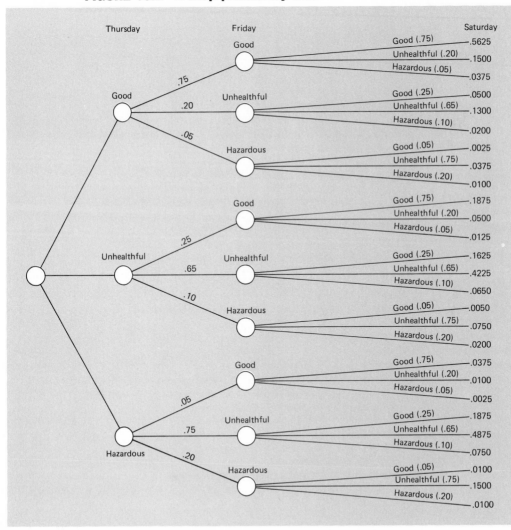

included as Appendix A to this chapter for those students needing a review. In order to compute the probabilities of being in any particular state after n transitions or time periods, we merely multiply the transition matrix by itself n times. If we let $\mathbf{P}$ represent the transition matrix and $\mathbf{P}^n$ represent the n-step transition matrix, then

$$\mathbf{P}^n = \mathbf{P}_i \cdot \mathbf{P}_{i+1} \cdots \mathbf{P}_n$$

where all $\mathbf{P}_i = \mathbf{P}$.

To illustrate how to compute and to how interpret the n-step transition matrix, let us return to our air pollution example. The one-step transition matrix given in Table 15.1 is repeated here for convenience:

		Tomorrow's air quality	
Today's air quality	Good	Unhealthful	Hazardous
Good	.75	.20	.05
Unhealthful	.25	.65	.10
Hazardous	.05	.75	.20

Therefore,

$$\mathbf{P} = \begin{bmatrix} .75 & .20 & .05 \\ .25 & .65 & .10 \\ .05 & .75 & .20 \end{bmatrix}$$

To answer our question concerning the probability of hazardous air quality on Saturday given that Thursday's air quality is good, we do not need to compute the entire two-step transition matrix. Nevertheless, let us compute $\mathbf{P}^2$ and interpret the probabilities of the two-step transition matrix.

$$\mathbf{P}^2 = \mathbf{P} \cdot \mathbf{P} = \begin{bmatrix} .75 & .20 & .05 \\ .25 & .65 & .10 \\ .05 & .75 & .20 \end{bmatrix} \begin{bmatrix} .75 & .20 & .05 \\ .25 & .65 & .10 \\ .05 & .75 & .20 \end{bmatrix}$$

$$= \begin{bmatrix} (.75)(.75) + (.2)(.25) + (.05)(.05) & (.75)(.20) + (.2)(.65) + (.05)(.75) & (.75)(.05) + (.2)(.1) + (.05)(.2) \\ (.25)(.75) + (.65)(.25) + (.1)(.05) & (.25)(.2) + (.65)(.65) + (.1)(.75) & (.25)(.05) + (.65)(.1) + (.1)(.2) \\ (.05)(.75) + (.25)(.75) + (.2)(.05) & (.05)(.2) + (.75)(.65) + (.2)(.75) & (.05)(.05) + (.75)(.1) + (.2)(.2) \end{bmatrix}$$

$$= \begin{bmatrix} .6150 & .3175 & .0675 \\ .3550 & .5475 & .0975 \\ .2350 & .6475 & .1175 \end{bmatrix}$$

TABLE 15.2 Two-step transition matrix

Thursday's air quality	Saturday's air quality		
	Good	Unhealthful	Hazardous
Good	.6150	.3175	.0675
Unhealthful	.3550	.5475	.0975
Hazardous	.2350	.6475	.1175

If you do not remember how to multiply matrices, you can refer to Appendix A at the end of this chapter. The two-step transition matrix is given in Table 15.2. Interpreting Table 15.2, we can say that if Thursday's air quality is good, the probability of good air on Saturday is .6150 and the probability of hazardous air quality on Saturday is .0675. If you refer back to the probability tree in Figure 15.1, you will notice that these are the same probabilities if you add the appropriate path probabilities. The probability of unhealthful air quality on Saturday given that Thursday's air quality is hazardous is .6475. In other words, the probability of being in state 2 after two time periods given that the system is presently in state 3 is .6475.

To compute Sunday air quality probabilities Thursday, we merely multiply the transition matrix by itself one more time to find the three-step transition matrix.

$$
\begin{aligned}
\mathbf{P}^3 &= \text{Sunday's transition matrix} \\
&= \mathbf{P} \cdot \mathbf{P} \cdot \mathbf{P} \\
&= \mathbf{P}^2 \cdot \mathbf{P}
\end{aligned}
$$

Since we have already computed the two-step transition matrix, it is a simple process to calculate the three-step transition matrix.

$$
\mathbf{P}^3 = \begin{bmatrix} .6150 & .3175 & .0675 \\ .3550 & .5475 & .0975 \\ .2350 & .6475 & .1175 \end{bmatrix} \begin{bmatrix} .75 & .20 & .05 \\ .25 & .65 & .10 \\ .05 & .75 & .20 \end{bmatrix}
$$

$$
= \begin{bmatrix} .544 & .380 & .076 \\ .408 & .500 & .092 \\ .344 & .556 & .100 \end{bmatrix}
$$

Sunday's air quality probabilities are reflected in Table 15.3.

TABLE 15.3 Three-step transition matrix

	Sunday's air quality		
Thursday's air quality	Good	Unhealthful	Hazardous
Good	.544	.380	.076
Unhealthful	.408	.500	.092
Hazardous	.344	.556	.100

STEADY-STATE CONDITIONS (EQUILIBRIUM)

In the majority of Markov chains, the process stabilizes in the long run. A stabilized system is said to be in steady state or in equilibrium. This *equilibrium condition* occurs when additional transitions do not affect the probabilities of finding the process in the various states. Not all Markov chains reach equilibrium but it can be shown that *a Markov chain will reach a steady-state n-step transition matrix as n approaches infinity if, for some n-step transition matrix, all probabilities in the matrix have nonzero values.*

Let us return to the air pollution problem to illustrate the transition matrix in steady state. Since the one-step transition matrix has no zero elements, we know that the process does stabilize and reaches a steady-state n-step transition matrix. One way of finding the steady-state n-step transition matrix is by multiplying the one-step transition matrix by itself a number of times and when the n-step matrix is equal to the $(n-1)$-step transition matrix, steady-state has been achieved. As shown below, the air quality process reaches steady state in the 12th period or transition.

$$\mathbf{P}^1 = \begin{bmatrix} .75 & .20 & .05 \\ .25 & .65 & .10 \\ .05 & .75 & .20 \end{bmatrix}$$

$$\mathbf{P}^2 = \begin{bmatrix} .615 & .318 & .067 \\ .355 & .548 & .097 \\ .235 & .648 & .117 \end{bmatrix}$$

$$\mathbf{P}^3 = \begin{bmatrix} .544 & .380 & .076 \\ .408 & .500 & .092 \\ .344 & .556 & .100 \end{bmatrix}$$

$$\mathbf{P}^4 = \begin{bmatrix} .506 & .413 & .081 \\ .436 & .476 & .088 \\ .402 & .505 & .093 \end{bmatrix}$$

.

.

.

$$\mathbf{P}^{11} = \begin{bmatrix} .466 & .448 & .085 \\ .466 & .449 & .085 \\ .465 & .449 & .085 \end{bmatrix}$$

$$\mathbf{P}^{12} = \begin{bmatrix} .466 & .449 & .085 \\ .466 & .449 & .085 \\ .466 & .449 & .085 \end{bmatrix}$$

$$\mathbf{P}^{13} = \begin{bmatrix} .466 & .449 & .085 \\ .466 & .449 & .085 \\ .466 & .449 & .085 \end{bmatrix}$$

.

.

.

$$\mathbf{P}^{100} = \begin{bmatrix} .466 & .449 & .085 \\ .466 & .449 & .085 \\ .466 & .449 & .085 \end{bmatrix}$$

The steady-state transition matrix shows that the probability of being in a given state is not dependent on where the process starts. For example, as shown in Table 15.4, the probability of unhealthful air is .449 regardless of what the air quality was several weeks or more ago. This means that 44.9 percent of the time the city can expect unhealthful air.

TABLE 15.4   Steady-state probabilities

	Air quality		
Air quality	Good	Unhealthful	Hazardous
Good	.466	.449	.085
Unhealthful	.466	.449	.085
Hazardous	.466	.449	.085

Fortunately, there is an alternative to the brute-force method of determining the steady-state transition matrix. The probabilities of being in any given state are called state probabilities. If the Markov chain is a three-state process, as in our air quality example, the state probabilities can be represented as a vector such as $[\pi_1 \quad \pi_2 \quad \pi_3]$. The state probabilities for the next transition can be computed by multiplying the current period's state probabilities times the transition matrix. In other words, if $[\pi_1(1), \pi_2(1), \pi_3(1)]$ is the vector of state probabilities after one transition and $[\pi_1(2), \pi_2(2), \pi_3(2)]$ is the vector of state probabilities after two transitions, then

$$\pi_2 = \pi_1 \mathbf{P}$$

where $\pi_1 = [\pi_1(1) \quad \pi_2(1) \quad \pi_3(1)]$
$\pi_2 = [\pi_1(2) \quad \pi_2(2) \quad \pi_3(2)]$
$\mathbf{P} = $ the transition matrix

To illustrate, let us compute the state probabilities of the air quality problem after two transitions given an initial starting condition of good air quality. Therefore,

$$\pi_0 = [1 \quad 0 \quad 0]$$

$$\pi_1 = \pi_0 \mathbf{P}$$

$$\pi_1 = [1 \quad 0 \quad 0] \begin{bmatrix} .75 & .20 & .05 \\ .25 & .65 & .10 \\ .05 & .75 & .20 \end{bmatrix}$$

$$= [.75 \quad .20 \quad .05]$$

$$\pi_2 = \pi_1 \mathbf{P}$$

$$\pi_2 = [.75 \quad .20 \quad .05] \begin{bmatrix} .75 & .20 & .05 \\ .25 & .65 & .10 \\ .05 & .75 & .20 \end{bmatrix}$$

$$= [.615 \quad .318 \quad .067]$$

As we have seen, as the Markov process approaches steady-state the difference in the state probabilities decrease. Consequently, if n is sufficiently large, the subscripts in the following matrix equation can be omitted:

$$\pi_{n+1} = \pi_n \mathbf{P}$$

and we have $\pi = \pi\mathbf{P}$. This result can be used in finding the steady-state transition matrix.

Again, let us illustrate using our air quality example.

$$\pi = [\pi_1 \quad \pi_2 \quad \pi_3]$$

$$\mathbf{P} = \begin{bmatrix} .75 & .20 & .05 \\ .25 & .65 & .10 \\ .05 & .75 & .20 \end{bmatrix}$$

Since

$$[\pi_1 \quad \pi_2 \quad \pi_3] = [\pi_1 \quad \pi_2 \quad \pi_3] \begin{bmatrix} .75 & .20 & .05 \\ .25 & .65 & .10 \\ .05 & .75 & .20 \end{bmatrix}$$

then

$$\pi_1 = .75\pi_1 + .25\pi_2 + .05\pi_3$$

$$\pi_2 = .20\pi_1 + .65\pi_2 + .75\pi_3$$

$$\pi_3 = .05\pi_1 + .10\pi_2 + .20\pi_3$$

Given the foregoing set of three equations and three unknowns, you might be tempted to solve directly for π_1, π_2, and π_3. Unfortunately, because of the redundancy of one of the equations, solving directly does not result in a unique solution. It is possible, however, to use the fact that the state probabilities must add to one as a replacement for the redundancy in the previous three equations. Therefore, the method for finding the steady-state probabilities is to arbitrarily choose two of the three equations together with the equation $\pi_1 + \pi_2 + \pi_3 = 1$ and solve three equations and three unknowns. For example,

$$\pi_1 = .75\pi_1 + .25\pi_2 + .05\pi_3$$

$$\pi_2 = .20\pi_1 + .65\pi_2 + .75\pi_3$$

$$1 = \pi_1 + \pi_2 + \pi_3$$

A good way of solving a system of linear equations is to use Gaussian elimination. For a review see Appendix B at the end of this chapter. Using Gaussian elimination, we get:

Step 1: Manipulate the equations so that only constants appear on the right side:

$$-.25\pi_1 + .25\pi_2 + .05\pi_3 = 0$$
$$.20\pi_1 - .35\pi_2 + .75\pi_3 = 0$$
$$\pi_1 + \pi_2 + \pi_3 = 1$$

Step 2: Eliminate π_1 from all but the first equation:

$$\pi_1 - 1\pi_2 - .2\pi_3 = 0$$
$$- 15\pi_2 + 79\pi_3 = 0$$
$$2\pi_2 + 1.2\pi_3 = 1$$

Step 3: Eliminate π_2 from all but the second equation:

$$\pi_1 \qquad - 5.4667\pi_3 = 0$$
$$\pi_2 - 79/15\pi_3 = 0$$
$$11.7333\pi_3 = 1$$

Step 4: Eliminate π_3 from all but the third equation:

$$\pi_1 \qquad\qquad = .466$$
$$\pi_2 \qquad = .449$$
$$\pi_3 = .085$$

A quick glance at Table 15.4 will verify our steady-state probabilities.

APPLICATIONS OF MARKOV CHAINS

BRAND SWITCHING

A large eastern city in the United States has three daily newspapers. The publishing editor of the *Tribune* would like to find answers to the following types of questions concerning daily subscriptions:

1. What will be the market shares for the three newspapers at some future time?
2. Will the competitive market stabilize?
3. If the market shares will reach equilibrium, what are the steady-state market shares for each paper?
4. What is the effect of certain promotional efforts in terms of the loss or gain of market share?

The manager in charge of daily subscriptions could probably tell the publishing editor the number of subscriptions lost in a given month and the number of subscriptions gained in a single month. This information, unfortunately, does not answer the publishing editor's questions. To answer those questions, more detailed information is needed concerning the

TABLE 15.5 Sample newspaper survey

| | May | | | |
April	Tribune	News	Times	Total subscribers in April
Tribune	450	35	15	500
News	50	320	30	400
Times	20	20	60	100
Total subscribers in May	520	375	105	1000

newspaper switching habits of the market. To gather the necessary information, 1,000 newspaper subscribers were canvassed to determine their propensity to switch papers. This information is summarized in Table 15.5.

The results of the survey indicate that the *Tribune* gains subscribers mainly at the expense of the *News*. If we use the survey results to construct a transition matrix, the relative frequencies of the newspaper switching can be used as surrogate transition probabilities. The transition matrix containing these surrogate probabilities is shown in Table 15.6.

To answer the publishing editor's first question depends on how many months into the future the editor wants to look. If he wants to estimate market shares in June, he can use the following result:

$$\pi_n = \pi_{n-1}\mathbf{P}$$

where π_n is equal to June market shares and π_{n-1} is equal to May's market shares. To determine June's market share, we multiply:

$$\pi_{\text{June}} = \left[\frac{520}{1,000} \quad \frac{375}{1,000} \quad \frac{105}{1,000} \right] \begin{bmatrix} .900 & .070 & .030 \\ .125 & .800 & .075 \\ .200 & .200 & .600 \end{bmatrix}$$

$$= [.536 \quad .357 \quad .107]$$

TABLE 15.6 Transition matrix brand switching

	Tribune	News	Times
Tribune	450/500 = .900	35/500 = .070	15/500 = .030
News	50/400 = .125	320/400 = .800	30/400 = .075
Times	20/100 = .200	20/100 = .200	60/100 = .600

Interpreting π_{June}, we can say that if market conditions do not change, the different market shares for June can be estimated by π_{June}. That is, the *Tribune* can expect to capture 53.6 percent of the market. The *News* can expect to capture approximately 35.7 percent and the *Times* would have 10.7 percent. To look further into the future, there are two methods that could be utilized. First, we could use an iterative process that would use the result that

$$\pi_n = \pi_{n-1}\mathbf{P}$$

For example, to find the probable market shares for July, we could use June's market share vector and the original transition matrix. These calculations are:

$$\pi_{\text{July}} = \pi_{\text{June}}\mathbf{P}$$

$$= [.536 \quad .357 \quad .107] \begin{bmatrix} .900 & .070 & .030 \\ .125 & .800 & .075 \\ .200 & .200 & .600 \end{bmatrix}$$

$$= [.548 \quad .345 \quad .107]$$

An alternative way of computing the probable market shares for some period in the future can be used. It can be shown that

$$\pi_n = \pi_1 \mathbf{P}^{n-1}$$

where π_n = vector of market shares in time period n
     π_1 = vector of market shares at the present time
      $\mathbf{P}$ = transition matrix

For example, let us compute the probable market shares for July given the market shares in May.

$$\pi_{\text{July}} = \pi_3$$
$$= \pi_1 \mathbf{P}^{3-1}$$
$$= \pi_1 \mathbf{P}^2$$

$$= [.520 \quad .375 \quad .105] \begin{bmatrix} .900 & .070 & .030 \\ .125 & .800 & .075 \\ .200 & .200 & .600 \end{bmatrix}^2$$

$$= [.548 \quad .345 \quad .107]$$

To compute the probable market shares for December, we would have

$$\pi_{\text{Dec}} = \pi_8$$
$$= \pi_1 P^7$$

$$= [.520 \quad .375 \quad .105] \begin{bmatrix} .900 & .070 & .030 \\ .125 & .800 & .075 \\ .200 & .200 & .600 \end{bmatrix}^7$$

$$= [.520 \quad .375 \quad .105] \begin{bmatrix} .649 & .261 & .090 \\ .493 & .389 & .118 \\ .538 & .340 & .122 \end{bmatrix}$$

$$= [.579 \quad .317 \quad .104]$$

The publishing editor could use this vector of state probabilities to estimate subscription sales in December if he could estimate the total market for daily newspaper subscriptions. He could also use the market shares vector to determine the effect of a promotional effort on the part of the *Tribune* or the effect of certain actions by competing newspapers. The market shares vector for December represent the expected market shares given no change in the process. In other words, if the three newspapers made no overt moves to affect the daily subscription market, the *Tribune* can expect to capture 57.9 percent of the total market. If December sales indicate that the *Tribune* has captured 70 percent of the market, then something has happened to favorably affect the *Tribune*'s marketing success. In this way *Tribune* management can better judge the success or failure of various decisions that are made that affect the daily subscription market.

Another question the publishing editor had concerned the question of whether or not the market will stabilize and what the steady-state market shares would be. Because the one-step transition matrix has no zero elements, we know that if external forces on the market are nonexistent, the process will eventually reach equilibrium. To find the steady-state market shares, we must develop three equations and solve for the individual market shares. Remember that at steady state, $\pi = \pi P$, or

$$[\pi_1 \quad \pi_2 \quad \pi_3] = [\pi_1 \quad \pi_2 \quad \pi_3] \begin{bmatrix} P_{11} & P_{12} & P_{13} \\ P_{21} & P_{22} & P_{23} \\ P_{31} & P_{32} & P_{33} \end{bmatrix}$$

For our newspaper problem,

$$[\pi_1 \quad \pi_2 \quad \pi_3] = [.9\pi_1 + .125\pi_2 + .20\pi_3, .07\pi_1 + .8\pi_2 + .2\pi_3, \\ .03\pi_1 + .075\pi_2 + .6\pi_3]$$

Therefore,

$$\pi_1 = .9\pi_1 + .125\pi_2 + .20\pi_3$$
$$\pi_2 = .07\pi_1 + .8\pi_2 + .2\pi_3$$
$$\pi_3 = .03\pi_1 + .075\pi_2 + .6\pi_3$$

Also,

$$\pi_1 + \pi_2 + \pi_3 = 1$$

Taking any two of the first three equations and the equation stating that the individual proportions of the market must add to 1, we have three equations and three unknowns. To illustrate let us use the first two equations together with the last equation and solve for π_1, π_2 and π_3.

$$.1\pi_1 - .125\pi_2 - .2\pi_3 = 0$$
$$-.07\pi_1 + .2\pi_2 - .2\pi_3 = 0$$
$$\pi_1 + \pi_2 + \pi_3 = 1$$

If we solve these three equations simultaneously, we find that

$$\pi_1 = .4901$$
$$\pi_2 = .3730$$
$$\pi_3 = .1369$$

These results mean that if the newspaper market is allowed to reach steady state, the *Tribune* would hold approximately 49 percent and the *News* slightly more than 37 percent, with the *Times* capturing the remaining market share.

CAR RENTAL

A small car rental company rents cars from any of three regional airports and is trying to decide where to build its maintenance facility. From industry data, the probabilities of where a car is returned given that it is checked out at one of the airports are reflected in the one-step transition matrix given in Table 15.7.

To answer the question of which airport to locate the maintenance facility, management would like to know the steady-state probabilities of an automobile being at each of the three airports. These probabilities could be multiplied by the size of the fleet to get the expected number of cars at each airport.

To find the steady-state probabilities, we must solve the following three equations and three unknowns.

TABLE 15.7 Car rental one-step transition matrix

To / From	Airport A	Airport B	Airport C
Airport A	.80	.10	.10
Airport B	.20	.70	.10
Airport C	.30	.05	.65

$$\pi_1 = .8\pi_1 + .2\pi_2 + .3\pi_3$$
$$\pi_2 = .1\pi_1 + .70\pi_2 + .05\pi_3$$
$$\pi_1 + \pi_2 + \pi_3 = 1$$

Using the augmented matrix as discussed in Appendix B, we can solve for the steady-state probabilities as follows:

$$\begin{bmatrix} -.2 & 0.2 & 0.30 & | & 0 \\ 0.1 & -.3 & 0.05 & | & 0 \\ 1.0 & 1.0 & 1.00 & | & 1 \end{bmatrix}$$

$$\downarrow$$

$$\begin{bmatrix} 1 & -1.0 & -1.5 & | & 0 \\ 0 & -.2 & 0.2 & | & 0 \\ 0 & 2.0 & 2.5 & | & 1 \end{bmatrix}$$

$$\downarrow$$

$$\begin{bmatrix} 1 & 0 & -2.5 & | & 0 \\ 0 & 1 & -1.0 & | & 0 \\ 0 & 0 & 4.5 & | & 1 \end{bmatrix}$$

$$\downarrow$$

$$\begin{bmatrix} 1 & 0 & 0 & | & .556 \\ 0 & 1 & 0 & | & .222 \\ 0 & 0 & 1 & | & .222 \end{bmatrix}$$

Therefore,

$$\pi_1 = .556$$
$$\pi_2 = .222$$
$$\pi_3 = .222$$

If management wanted to place the maintenance facility where the majority of cars would be, Airport A would be the logical choice. If the fleet size were 1,000 cars, we would expect to find approximately 556 cars at Airport A once equilibrium has been achieved.

SUMMARY

In this chapter, we have continued our study of stochastic models. Markovian models such as the ones described in this chapter are descriptive in the sense that they are used to describe the state of a system at some time period in the future. Markov models do not provide direct answers to decision problems but rather can be used to aid in the decision-making process. The direct application of Markov processes to real-world decision problems has not been as common as some of the other techniques of management science, such as linear programming or simulation. However, the utility of Markov processes is not limited to direct application to real-world problems. Markov processes form the foundation for many of the queuing models and inventory models that have been developed for direct real-world application. If it were not for Markov processes, many of the normative and more useful descriptive models often used in management science would not have been derived.

SOLVED PROBLEM

PROBLEM STATEMENT

A large department store has 700 accounts that are past due. These accounts are classified 0–30 days overdue, 30–60 days, or 60–90 days overdue. Presently, the store has 400 accounts in the 0–30-day category, 200 accounts in the 30–60-day category, and 100 accounts in the 60–90-day category. Accounts are written off as being uncollectable after 90 days. From past experience, the accounts receivable manager knows that the payment process behaves like a Markov chain. He has estimated the 1-month transition matrix as shown below. He wishes to estimate the number that will have to be written off as bad debts.

One-month transition matrix

	0–30 days	30–60 days	60–90 days	Paid	Uncollectable
0–30 days overdue	0	.7	0	.3	0
30–60 days overdue	0	0	.8	.2	0
60–90 days overdue	0	0	0	.5	.5
Paid	0	0	0	1	0
Uncollectable	0	0	0	0	1

SOLUTION

To find the number of accounts that are expected to be uncollectable and paid, it is necessary first to compute the 3-month transition matrix.

$$
\mathbf{P}^3 = \begin{bmatrix} 0 & .7 & 0 & .3 & 0 \\ 0 & 0 & .8 & .2 & 0 \\ 0 & 0 & 0 & .5 & .5 \\ 0 & 0 & 0 & 1 & 0 \\ 0 & 0 & 0 & 0 & 1 \end{bmatrix}^3
$$

$$
= \begin{bmatrix} 0 & 0 & 0 & .72 & .28 \\ 0 & 0 & 0 & .60 & .40 \\ 0 & 0 & 0 & .50 & .50 \\ 0 & 0 & 0 & 1 & 0 \\ 0 & 0 & 0 & 0 & 1 \end{bmatrix}
$$

The three-step transition matrix gives us the probabilities of an account being either collected or written off as a bad debt. For example, the probability of a 0–30-day overdue account being paid is .72, and the probability of a 30–60 day overdue account being paid is .60. Therefore, to predict the total number of accounts currently delinquent that will be paid, we can multiply:

$$(.72)(400) + (.60)(200) + (.50)(100) = 458 \text{ accounts}$$

The expected number of delinquent accounts that will eventually be written off as bad debts is 242 accounts.

REVIEW QUESTIONS

1. How do Markov models differ from linear programming models?
2. What are the two major outputs from a Markov chain model?
3. Define what is meant by the Markov property.
4. What do the elements in a one-step transition matrix measure?
5. What are the necessary three properties of a homogeneous Markov chain?
6. Define equilibrium as it relates to a Markov process.
7. How can it be ascertained whether a Markov chain will reach equilibrium?
8. List three common applications of Markov processes.

PROBLEMS

15.1 *Market Share.* The marketing vice-president of a leading German automobile manufacturer would like to estimate the equilibrium share of the U.S. market for his firm. He has broken the market into three categories and has estimated the one-step transition matrix shown.

U.S automobile market

	Domestic models	Other export models	Our models
Domestic models	.80	.10	.10
Other export models	.10	.70	.20
Our models	.05	.10	.85

Given no change in the market, what are the steady-state shares of the U.S. automobile market?

15.2 *Hospital Administration.* Heart patients at a local hospital can be found in one of two places: the coronary care unit or at a regular nursing station. Of all heart patients, 83 percent leave the hospital alive and the other 17 percent die while at the hospital. If we assume that the number of alive heart patients remains constant and that the 1-day transition probabilities are as shown, what are the steady-state probabilities for an individual heart patient?

One-day transition probabilities—heart patients

	CCU	Hospital rehabilitation	Discharged or deceased
CCU	.700	.200	.100
Hospital rehabilitation	.050	.800	.150
Discharged or deceased	.015	.005	.980

15.3 *Hospital Administration.* If all the new heart patients in Problem 15.2 went to a competing hospital and there was a 25 percent chance for a patient to leave the competing hospital each day.

a. How would you change the one-day transition matrix?

b. What would the steady-state probabilities be?

15.4 *Accounts Receivable.* A large oil company has a computer-based customer billing system. Accounts are classified as being paid on time, being delinquent, or being written off as a bad debt. The company has 750,000 accounts. A program was written to display a breakdown on the transition among the three account receivable categories. The output from that program is summarized in the table. Assuming that no new credit customers are added; (a) what percentage of customers will be in each category on August 1? (b) at the end of the year?

			From		
June 1	Paid	Delinquent	Bad debt	July 1
Paid	150,000	142,500	10,000	0	152,500
Delinquent	375,000	7,500	350,000	0	357,500
Bad debt	225,000	0	15,000	225,000	240,000

15.5 *Computer Maintenance.* Although great strides have been made in computer hardware technology, computers still suffer from a certain amount of downtime. Assume that the basic properties of a Markov chain apply to the hardware downtime. Further assume that the transition period is 1 hour and the one-step transition matrix is as shown.

From \ To	Up	Down
Up	.95	.05
Down	.60	.40

  a. If the computer is up (running) presently, what is the probability that it will be up after 3 hours of operation?

  b. What are the steady-state probabilities for the hardware being up or down?

15.6 *Computer Maintenance.* Refer to Problem 15.5. The management of the computer center is contemplating replacement of the current computer with a newer, more reliable computer whose one-step transition matrix is shown.

From \ To	Up	Down
Up	.97	.03
Down	.60	.40

If the cost of system downtime is estimated at $600 per hour, what is the monthly breakeven cost for the new hardware? Assume the computer is in use 720 hours per month.

15.7 *Computer Maintenance.* Computer Company A claims its computer is more maintainable than the firm's present computer or the proposed computer in Problem 15.6. In other words, because of modularity in construction it takes less time to fix Computer Company A's computer. The transition matrix is as shown. Which replacement computer would save the computer center the most money assuming that they are equivalently priced?

To From	Up	Down
Up	.95	.05
Down	.90	.10

15.8 *Pollution Control.* Pollution is a major problem in modern industrialized cities. There are five levels of pollution that Air Quality Control Division of the City Council Health Department classify. These pollution levels are good, moderate, unhealthful, very unhealthful, and hazardous. If we assume that the air quality is a Markov process with the following one-step transition matrix, what is the probability of being in each of the various states Saturday given that the air quality is moderate on Thursday? What are the steady-state probabilities for the various levels of air pollution?

One-step transition matrix for air quality

	Good	Moderate	Unhealthful	Very unhealthful	Hazardous
Good	.80	.10	.02	.05	.03
Moderate	.60	.30	.05	.04	.01
Unhealthful	.50	.30	.15	.04	.01
Very unhealthful	.40	.40	.10	.05	.05
Hazardous	.10	.40	.35	.05	.10

15.9 *Blood Inventory.* A wartime field hospital has just received 2,000 pints of type O blood. Blood can be stored in the field for only 3 days before it must be thrown away. There is a 30 percent chance that a pint of blood will be used in a given day.

a. Formulate the appropriate transition matrix.

b. Assuming no new blood shipments, what proportion of 2,000 pints will be used and what proportion will be thrown away?

15.10 *Market Share.* The country's major manufacturer of computers, BIM, presently has captured 62 percent of the total market. The company's management fears antitrust action if the market share grows to 70 percent. Based on historical data, the operations research group has formulated the transition matrix shown. Given that the remaining 38 percent is divided evenly between BIM's major competitor and all other competition, will BIM face an antitrust action, and if so, when?

One-year transition matrix

	BIM	Major competitor	Other competitors
BIM	.90	.07	.03
Major competitor	.30	.60	.10
Other competitors	.40	.20	.40

15.11 *Market Share.* Refer to Problem 15.10. If BIM changes its marketing strategy to reduce the probability of capturing business from its major competitor by 50 percent, would this action avert an antitrust suit? Explain your answer. Assume that the probability of the major competitor holding on to a customer is increased by .15.

15.12 *Computer Maintenance.* The state of computer systems can be described as three-state Markov process. The three states are

1. Up and running

2. Down due to a hardware failure

3. Down due to a failure in system software

Given the recent history of ABC Corporation's computer center, the 1-hour transition matrix is estimated as shown. What are the steady-state probabilities?

	Up	Down due to hardware	Down due to software
Up	.96	.03	.01
Down due to hardware	.90	.10	0
Down due to software	.90	0	.10

15.13 *Software Savings.* The computer vendor in Problem 15.12 is promising significant improvement in the next release of the operating system. Specifically, the 1-hour transition matrix will change as shown. Given that the computer system is leased for $100,000 per month and runs 24 hours per day (720 hours per month), what is the potential cost savings for the new release of the operating system?

	Up	Down due to hardware	Down due to software
Up	.96	.03	.01
Down due to hardware	.90	.10	0
Down due to software	.90	0	.10

15.14 *Personnel Administration.* The ACME Manufacturing Company employs 500 machine operators. These operators are classified as apprentice, machinist, and master machinist. Company policy dictates that all new operators are hired at the apprentice level. Currently, there are 200 apprentices, 250 machinists, and 50 master machinists. ACME's union contract specifies that 15 percent of all operators in each class are to be promoted each year. It is estimated that 15 percent of the apprentices leave the company each year and 10 percent of the machinists leave and 5 percent of the master machinists leave. Assume that due to economic conditions, for each employee lost, the company does not rehire.

  a. Construct the one-step transition matrix.

  b. In 3 years, what will be ACME's operator mix?

  c. If the process is allowed to reach equilibrium, what proportion of operators will be in the various classifications?

15.15 *Personnel Administration.* ACME Manufacturing Company is considering a new fringe-benefit package that will reduce the number of machinists leaving the company. Rough estimates of the impact of the proposed fringe-benefit package is that about 50 percent of those leaving the company in all labor categories would elect to stay.

  a. How does that affect the one-step transition matrix?

  b. Given the adoption of the new fringe-benefit package, what will ACME's operator mix be in 3 years?

  c. Given the fringe-benefit package, how many operators will be in each labor classification at equilibrium?

15.16 *Youth Soccer.* Youth soccer has come to a large southwestern city. The competition for practice fields and playing fields between the various sports is becoming critical. To analyze the problem, the Parks and Recreation Department has taken data from other cities that can be used in defining the one-step transition matrix shown.

One-season transition matrix

	Soccer	Football	Baseball
Soccer	.90	.07	.03
Football	.60	.35	.05
Baseball	.50	.30	.20

Presently, the proportion of children playing the various sports is

20%	soccer
50%	football
30%	baseball

For planning purposes, the Parks and Recreation Department wants to know the proportions of children in each of the three sports for the next five seasons. In addition, the steady-state proportions should be calculated to help the Parks and Recreation Department in their long-range planning.

APPENDIX A: MATRIX ALGEBRA

INTRODUCTION

matrix A *matrix* is a rectangular arrangement of numbers of the following form:

$$\begin{bmatrix} a_{11} & a_{12} & a_{13} & \cdots & a_{1n} \\ a_{21} & a_{22} & & \cdots & a_{2n} \\ a_{31} & & & \cdots & a_{3n} \\ \cdot & & & & \cdot \\ \cdot & & & & \cdot \\ \cdot & & & & \cdot \\ a_{m1} & a_{m2} & a_{m3} & \cdots & a_{mn} \end{bmatrix}$$

A matrix consists of m rows and n columns. An individual element is identified by its row-and-column subscript. Thus, a_{34} is found by looking in the third row and fourth column. The first subscript is always the row subscript and the second subscript is always the column subscript.

Often, it is convenient or necessary to represent a series of numbers in a matrix that has just one column or one row. A matrix consisting of *column vector* only one column is also called a *column vector,* and a matrix consisting *row vector* of only one row is also called a *row vector.* Vectors may be written with only one subscript and are of the following form:

$$[a_1 \quad a_2 \quad \cdots \quad a_n]$$

or

$$\begin{bmatrix} a_1 \\ a_2 \\ \cdot \\ \cdot \\ \cdot \\ a_n \end{bmatrix}$$

There are several alternative matrix notations. The brackets enclosing a matrix are often replaced with

$$(\quad) \qquad \text{or} \qquad \| \quad \|$$

Therefore, the following represent the same matrix:

$$\begin{bmatrix} 2 & 5 & 7 \\ 9 & 14 & 21 \\ 31 & 32 & 45 \end{bmatrix} \qquad \begin{pmatrix} 2 & 5 & 7 \\ 9 & 14 & 21 \\ 31 & 32 & 45 \end{pmatrix} \qquad \begin{Vmatrix} 2 & 5 & 7 \\ 9 & 14 & 21 \\ 31 & 32 & 45 \end{Vmatrix}$$

With the emergence of the computer and operations research, the importance of vectors and matrices has increased significantly. As any computer programmer knows, computing without the use of vectors and matrices would be virtually impossible because of the necessity of naming memory locations. In computer jargon, a vector is called a single or one-dimensional array and a matrix with more than one row and more than one column is called a double or two-dimensional array. A single 100 row $\times$ 100 column matrix can be used to store 10,000 numbers in 10,000 different memory locations in the computer. It is then a simple matter to access any of the 10,000 memory locations simply by specifying the name of the matrix or array and the row and column subscript.

Before discussing the basic operations of matrix algebra and examining how matrices can be utilized in solving simultaneous linear equations, *order* it is necessary to define some terms. The *order* of a matrix, often called the dimensions of a matrix, simply describes the size of the matrix. The order of a matrix within m rows and n columns is simply $m \times n$ (read m by n). For example, if

$$\mathbf{A} = \begin{bmatrix} 5 & 7 & 2 & 1 \\ 3 & 2 & 4 & 1 \end{bmatrix}$$

then the order of $\mathbf{A}$ is 2×4. The number of elements in the matrix can be found by multiplying the number of rows by the number of columns. *square* A matrix that has an equal number of rows and columns is called a *square* *matrix* *matrix*. Two matrices are equal if they are of the same order and corresponding elements are equal.

In this section, we describe the basic operations of matrix algebra. We begin by defining the operations of addition, multiplication, and transposition of vectors. Then we expand these operations to matrices.

VECTOR ALGEBRA

Two vectors can be added if they are both row vectors or both column vectors and they are of the same order. If two vectors $\mathbf{A}$ and $\mathbf{B}$ are of the same order, then

$$\mathbf{A} + \mathbf{B} = \mathbf{C}$$

where $\mathbf{C}$ is a vector of the same order and each element of $\mathbf{C}$ is the sum of the corresponding elements of $\mathbf{A}$ and $\mathbf{B}$. In other words, if

$$\mathbf{A} = \begin{bmatrix} a_1 \\ a_2 \\ \cdot \\ \cdot \\ \cdot \\ a_n \end{bmatrix} \quad \text{and} \quad \mathbf{B} = \begin{bmatrix} b_1 \\ b_2 \\ \cdot \\ \cdot \\ \cdot \\ b_n \end{bmatrix}$$

then

$$\mathbf{C} = \begin{bmatrix} a_1 + b_1 \\ a_2 + b_2 \\ \cdot \\ \cdot \\ a_n + b_n \end{bmatrix}$$

Let us illustrate vector addition using the following examples.

EXAMPLE

$$A = \begin{bmatrix} 1 \\ 5 \\ 7 \\ 9 \\ 10 \\ 11 \end{bmatrix} \qquad B = \begin{bmatrix} 10 \\ 12 \\ 9 \\ 8 \\ 7 \\ 5 \end{bmatrix}$$

Since vectors A and B have the same order, 6×1,

$$A + B = \begin{bmatrix} 11 \\ 17 \\ 16 \\ 17 \\ 17 \\ 16 \end{bmatrix}$$

EXAMPLE

$$A = [14 \quad 25 \quad 17 \quad 22] \qquad B = [14 \quad 25 \quad 10 \quad 14]$$

$$A + B = [28 \quad 50 \quad 27 \quad 36]$$

EXAMPLE

$$A = [14 \quad 25 \quad 17 \quad 22]$$

$$B = \begin{bmatrix} 15 \\ 22 \\ 14 \\ 31 \end{bmatrix}$$

$A + B$ is undefined because the order of A is 1×4 and the order of B is 4×1. It might be noted that the commutative law of addition holds for vector addition. That is, if A and B are vectors of the same order,

$$A + B = B + A$$

It should also be clear that the associative law of addition holds for vectors also. In other words, if A, B, and C are vectors of the same order, then $(A + B) + C = A + (B + C)$. Hence, writing $A + B + C$ is unambiguous because regardless of whether we compute $(A + B) + C$ or $A +$

vector addition (**B** + **C**), we end up with the same result. Consequently, *vector addition* can be generalized to include the summation of any number of vectors of the same order. This is accomplished by merely adding corresponding elements.

EXAMPLE

$$\mathbf{A} = [1 \quad 5 \quad 7 \quad 9 \quad 10] \qquad \mathbf{B} = [2 \quad 5 \quad 9 \quad 7 \quad 10]$$
$$\mathbf{C} = [4 \quad 5 \quad 6 \quad 10 \quad 2]$$

$$\mathbf{A} + \mathbf{B} + \mathbf{C} = [7 \quad 15 \quad 22 \quad 26 \quad 22]$$

If we want to multiply a vector by a constant (*scalar*), we simply multiply each element in the vector by the scalar. This type of multiplication is *scalar multiplication* called *scalar multiplication*. Let us illustrate the value of scalar multiplication using the following example.

vector multiplication   *Vector multiplication* of a $1 \times n$ row vector followed by an $n \times 1$ column vector is accomplished by multiplying corresponding elements of the row and column vector and adding the products. The result of vector multiplication is always a number. If

$$\mathbf{A} = [a_1 \; a_2 \cdots a_n]$$

and

$$\mathbf{B} = \begin{bmatrix} b_1 \\ b_2 \\ \cdot \\ \cdot \\ \cdot \\ b_n \end{bmatrix}$$

then

$$\mathbf{AB} = \sum_{i=1}^{n} a_i b_i$$

Let us illustrate vector multiplication using the following examples.

EXAMPLE

$$\mathbf{A} = [2 \quad 4 \quad 6 \quad 8]$$

$$\mathbf{B} = \begin{bmatrix} 1 \\ 2 \\ 2 \\ 1 \end{bmatrix}$$

$$AB = (2 \cdot 1 + 4 \cdot 2 + 6 \cdot 2 + 8 \cdot 1)$$
$$= 30$$

EXAMPLE   Next month's forecasted demand for Acme Manufacturing Company's 6 major products is represented by the following vector

product 1 demand

$$A = [100 \quad 500 \quad 300 \quad 200 \quad 150 \quad 250]$$

The current price list is represented by vector **B**:

product 1 price

$$B = \begin{bmatrix} \$23.50 \\ 15.95 \\ 29.95 \\ 37.50 \\ 23.95 \\ 19.95 \end{bmatrix}$$

For cash budgeting purposes, management wants to know what the company's next month revenue would be if production could satisfy forecast demand.

To compute total revenue it is necessary to multiply **A** and **B**.

$$AB = \$35{,}390.00$$
$$= \text{total revenue generated by meeting next month's demand}$$

MATRIX ALGEBRA

matrix Often, it is desirable to add two matrices. *Matrix addition* is a generaliza-
addition tion of vector addition. Addition of two matrices is defined only if the matrices are of the same order. Therefore, a 5 × 4 matrix cannot be added to anything but another 5 × 4 matrix. If two matrices have the same dimensions, the sum of two matrices is a matrix whose elements are the sum of the corresponding elements of the two matrices. In other words, let

$$A = \begin{bmatrix} a_{11} & \cdots & a_{1n} \\ \vdots & & \vdots \\ a_{m1} & \cdots & a_{mn} \end{bmatrix}$$

$$\mathbf{B} = \begin{bmatrix} b_{11} & \cdots & b_{1n} \\ \vdots & \vdots & \vdots \\ b_{m1} & \cdots & b_{mn} \end{bmatrix}$$

$$\mathbf{A} + \mathbf{B} = \begin{bmatrix} a_{11} + b_{11} & \cdots & a_{1n} + b_{1n} \\ \vdots & \vdots & \vdots \\ a_{m1} + b_{m1} & \cdots & a_{mn} + b_{mn} \end{bmatrix}$$

Let us illustrate with the following examples.

EXAMPLE

$$\mathbf{A} = \begin{bmatrix} 1 & 5 & 7 \\ 9 & 10 & 12 \\ 2 & 4 & 7 \end{bmatrix}$$

$$\mathbf{B} = \begin{bmatrix} 2 & 5 & 9 \\ 7 & 2 & 1 \\ 4 & 3 & 1 \end{bmatrix}$$

$$\mathbf{A} + \mathbf{B} = \begin{bmatrix} 1+2 & 5+5 & 7+9 \\ 9+7 & 10+2 & 12+1 \\ 2+4 & 4+3 & 7+1 \end{bmatrix} = \begin{bmatrix} 3 & 10 & 16 \\ 16 & 12 & 13 \\ 6 & 7 & 8 \end{bmatrix}$$

Understanding how matrix addition is defined should make it clear that matrices obey the same commutative and associative laws as vectors. In other words, if $\mathbf{A}$, $\mathbf{B}$ and $\mathbf{C}$ are matrices of the same order:

$$\mathbf{A} + \mathbf{B} = \mathbf{B} + \mathbf{A} \qquad \text{commutative law of matrix addition}$$

$$\mathbf{A} + (\mathbf{B} + \mathbf{C}) = (\mathbf{A} + \mathbf{B}) + \mathbf{C} \qquad \text{associative law of matrix addition}$$

Finally, if $\mathbf{O}_{m \times n}$ represents the matrix of order $m \times n$ having all elements equal to 0, $\mathbf{O}_{m \times n}$ is the *zero matrix* for the set of matrices of order $m \times n$, since $\mathbf{O}_{m \times n} + \mathbf{A} + \mathbf{O}_{m \times n} = \mathbf{A}$ for any $m \times n$ matrix, $\mathbf{A}$.

SCALAR MULTIPLICATION

Scalar multiplication of matrices is totally analogous to scalar multiplication of a vector. To multiply a matrix by a constant, we simply multiply each element of the matrix by the constant. In other words, let

$$A = \begin{bmatrix} a_{11} & \cdots & a_{1n} \\ \vdots & & \vdots \\ a_{m1} & \cdots & a_{mn} \end{bmatrix}$$

and c be a scalar:

$$cA = \begin{bmatrix} ca_{11} & \cdots & ca_{1n} \\ \vdots & & \vdots \\ ca_{m1} & \cdots & ca_{mn} \end{bmatrix}$$

Let us illustrate scalar multiplication of a matrix using the following examples.

EXAMPLE   Let

$$A = \begin{bmatrix} 1 & 5 & 7 \\ 9 & 2 & 4 \\ 3 & 1 & 5 \end{bmatrix}$$

$$5A = \begin{bmatrix} 5 & 25 & 35 \\ 45 & 10 & 20 \\ 15 & 5 & 25 \end{bmatrix}$$

EXAMPLE   If a chain store firm has five stores that market five products that they want to put on sale for 20 percent off, and the prices of the products are represented in the following matrix, create a new sale price matrix. This can be done using scalar multiplication, using .80 as the scaler.

Current price matrix

		Product				
	Store	1	2	3	4	5
	1	$205.00	$345.00	$255.00	$351.00	$511.00
	2	195.00	349.00	249.00	370.00	509.00
A =	3	200.00	340.00	235.00	369.00	505.00
	4	190.00	357.00	240.00	315.00	499.00
	5	210.00	361.00	237.00	362.00	519.00

New price matrix

Store	Product 1	2	3	4	5
1	$164.00	$276.00	$204.00	$280.80	$408.80
2	156.00	279.20	199.20	296.00	407.20
3	160.00	272.00	188.00	295.20	404.00
4	152.00	285.60	192.00	252.00	399.20
5	168.00	288.80	189.60	289.60	415.20

$.8\mathbf{A} =$ (shown to the left of the table)

Therefore, element a_{ij} in the new price matrix represents the sale price of product j at store i.

MATRIX MULTIPLICATION

As indicated in Figure 15.3, *multiplication of two matrices is defined only when the number of columns of the first matrix is equal to the number of rows of the second matrix*. In other words. if $\mathbf{A}$ is an $a \times b$ matrix and $\mathbf{B}$ is a $c \times d$ matrix, $\mathbf{AB}$ is defined if and only if $b = c$. $\mathbf{AB}$ is an $a \times d$ matrix, whose entry in the ith row and the jth column is obtained by adding the products formed by multiplying, in order, each entry in the ith row of $\mathbf{A}$ by the corresponding entry in the jth column of $\mathbf{B}$.

Let us illustrate matrix multiplication using the following examples.

EXAMPLE   Let

$$\mathbf{A} = \begin{bmatrix} 2 & 1 & 7 \\ 3 & -1 & 5 \end{bmatrix}$$

$$\mathbf{B} = \begin{bmatrix} 1 & 0 & 5 \\ -1 & -5 & 3 \\ 4 & 2 & 1 \end{bmatrix}$$

FIGURE 15.3   Matrix multiplication

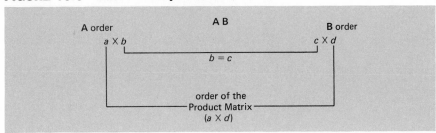

615

$$\mathbf{AB} = \begin{bmatrix} 2 & 1 & 7 \\ 3 & -1 & 5 \end{bmatrix} \begin{bmatrix} 1 & 0 & 5 \\ -1 & -5 & 3 \\ 4 & 2 & 1 \end{bmatrix}$$

Since **A** is 2 × 3 and **B** is 3 × 3, **AB** is defined and will result in a matrix that is 2 × 3.

$$\mathbf{AB} = \begin{bmatrix} (2)(1) + (1)(-1) + (7)(4) & (2)(0) + (1)(-5) + (7)(2) & (2)(5) + (1)(3) + (7)(1) \\ (3)(1) + (-1)(-1) + (5)(4) & (3)(0) + (-1)(-5) + (5)(2) & (3)(5) + (-1)(3) + (5)(1) \end{bmatrix}$$

$$= \begin{bmatrix} 29 & 9 & 20 \\ 24 & 15 & 17 \end{bmatrix}$$

EXAMPLE   Multiply the vector **A** by the matrix **B**.

$$\mathbf{A} = \begin{bmatrix} 5 & 1 & 2 & 5 \end{bmatrix}$$

$$\mathbf{B} = \begin{bmatrix} 5 & -2 & -4 \\ 2 & 2 & 2 \\ 2 & 0 & 1 \\ 4 & 7 & 1 \end{bmatrix}$$

Since the order of **A** is 1 × 4 and the order of **B** is 4 × 3, **AB** is defined and the product is a matrix whose order is 1 × 3.

$$\mathbf{AB} = \begin{bmatrix} 51 & 27 & -11 \end{bmatrix}$$

EXAMPLE   A company manufactures three basic products and uses three types of labor. If the amount of each type of labor for each product is represented by matrix **A** below and the company has five orders for product 1, 10 orders for product 2, and 12 orders for product 3, how many hours of labor will be necessary for each product?

Matrix A

Labor type	Product 1	2	3
1	20	15	19
2	30	35	22
3	40	70	41

If we let the number of orders be represented by the vector **B**, then

BA = number of labor hours required for each product

B = [5   10   12]

$$\mathbf{BA} = [5 \quad 10 \quad 12] \cdot \begin{bmatrix} 20 & 15 & 19 \\ 30 & 35 & 22 \\ 40 & 70 & 41 \end{bmatrix}$$

$$= [(5)(20) + (10)(30) + (12)(40) \quad (5)(15) + (10)(35) + (12)(70)$$
$$\qquad (5)(19) + (10)(22) + (12)(41)]$$

$$= [880 \quad 1{,}265 \quad 807]$$

Interpreting our result, it would take 880 labor hours for product 1, 1,265 labor hours for product 2, and 807 hours for product 3.

It should be clear from the definition of matrix multiplication that the multiplication of two matrices is not commutative. Indeed, it may be the case that **AB** is defined and **BA** is not. For example, suppose that **A** is a 2 × 3 matrix and **B** is a 3 × 4 matrix. **BA** is not defined, although **AB** is. Even if the orders of **A** and **B** are such that both **AB** and **BA** are both defined, it still is not necessarily the case that **AB** = **BA**. For example, let

$$\mathbf{A} = \begin{bmatrix} 2 & 4 \\ 7 & 1 \\ 3 & 2 \end{bmatrix}$$

and

$$\mathbf{B} = \begin{bmatrix} 3 & 3 & 4 \\ 2 & 1 & 3 \end{bmatrix}$$

Then

$$\mathbf{AB} = \begin{bmatrix} 14 & 10 & 20 \\ 23 & 22 & 31 \\ 13 & 11 & 18 \end{bmatrix}$$

$$\mathbf{BA} = \begin{bmatrix} 39 & 23 \\ 20 & 15 \end{bmatrix}$$

Obviously, **AB** ≠ **BA**.

Matrix multiplication does, however, satisfy the associative property, and matrix multiplication is distributive over addition. In other words, if all sums and products are defined,

A(BC) = **(AB)C**	associative property
A(B + C) = **AB** + **AC**	left-hand distributive property
(A + B)C = **AC** + **BC**	right-hand distributive property

APPENDIX B:
SOLVING SIMULTANEOUS LINEAR EQUATIONS WITH GAUSSIAN ELIMINATION

Solving simultaneous linear equations is often important in the world of business. The following example illustrates the utility of being able to simultaneously solve a system of n linear equations with n unknowns.

EXAMPLE   Let us assume that the amount of corn that buyers are willing to buy is defined by the function

$$d = 50,000 - 7500p \qquad 1.00 < p < 5.00$$

where d = demand (bushels)
$\quad\quad p$ = price (dollars per bushel)

Furthermore, the amount farmers are willing to supply is s:

$$s = -15,000 + 11,000p \qquad 1.00 < p < 5.00$$

where s = supply (bushels)
$\quad\quad p$ = price (dollars per bushel)

Often, it is desirable to know the point at which supply is equal to demand. Economists call this point the equilibrium point. Figure 15.4 graphs the supply and demand functions.

If we wish to find the equilibrium point (where $d = s$), we can equate d and s to another variable y and we have two simultaneous equations with two unknowns, $y = 50,000 - 7,500p$ and $y = -15,000 + 11,000p$. To find the value of the two unknowns (y and p) that simultaneously satisfy the foregoing equations, we could read the values for p and y off the graph or we could solve the two simultaneous equations. Obviously, when we have more than two equations and two unknowns, graphical procedures become impractical or impossible and an algebraic procedure is required. One of the most useful business applications of matrices is solving simultaneous linear equations.

There are several haphazard approaches to solving a system of linear equations which do not always yield a solution or find all solutions. The procedures described in this section for solving a system of simultaneous linear equations are superior because they are guaranteed to indicate when there is no solution, to find the solution when there is only one, and to find all multiple solutions when multiple solutions exist. Our plan is to describe Gaussian elimination without using matrices, then augment the approach by using matrices.

FIGURE 15.4 Equilibrium point

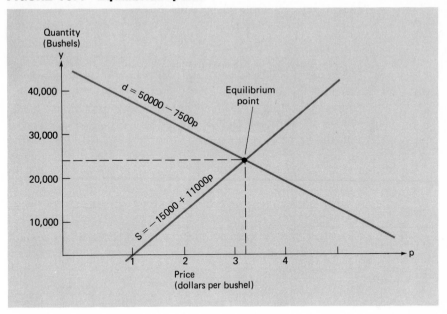

Consider the following set of linear equations:

$$2x_1 + 4x_2 + 2x_3 = 2$$
$$3x_1 + x_2 - x_3 = 5$$
$$x_1 - 3x_2 + 2x_3 = 4$$

The idea behind Gaussian elimination is to eliminate all variables from the ith equation except the ith variable by adding multiples of the equations. This procedure is analogous to pivoting in the simplex logarithm. Let us demonstrate by using the foregoing set of equations.

Our first step is to eliminate x_1 from all but the first equation. To make the arithmetic easier, let us first divide the first equation by 2 to get a coefficient of 1 for x_1.

$$x_1 + 2x_2 + x_3 = 1 \qquad \text{equation 1}$$

Now, to eliminate x_1 in the second equation, we multiply equation 1 by -3 and add it to the second equation. Remember, equals added to equals result in equals.

$$
\begin{array}{r}
3x_1 + x_2 - x_3 = 5 \\
-3x_1 - 6x_2 - 3x_3 = -3 \\
\hline
-5x_2 - 4x_3 = 2 \qquad \text{equation 2}
\end{array}
$$

Next, we want to eliminate x_1 from the third equation. This can be accomplished by subtracting equation 1.

$$\begin{array}{r} x_1 - 3x_2 + 2x_3 = 4 \\ - x_1 - 2x_2 - x_3 = -1 \\ \hline - 5x_2 + x_3 = 3 \qquad \text{equation 3} \end{array}$$

After eliminating x_1 from all but the first equation, we have an equivalent system of equations, that is, a system of equations with precisely the same solution set:

$$\begin{array}{r} x_1 + 2x_2 + x_3 = 1 \\ - 5x_2 - 4x_3 = 2 \\ - 5x_2 + x_3 = 3 \end{array}$$

Repeating the process with x_2, we first divide the second equation by a -5, getting

$$x_2 + \tfrac{4}{5}x_3 = -\tfrac{2}{5} \qquad \text{equation 2}$$

Now, if we multiply the equation above by -2 and add the resultant equation to the first equation, we get

$$\begin{array}{r} x_1 + 2x_2 + \phantom{\tfrac{8}{5}}x_3 = 1 \\ - 2x_2 - \tfrac{8}{5}x_3 = \tfrac{4}{5} \\ \hline x_1 - \tfrac{3}{5}x_3 = \tfrac{9}{5} \qquad \text{equation 1} \end{array}$$

Next, we multiply the second equation by 5 and add it to equation 3 as follows:

$$\begin{array}{r} - 5x_2 + x_3 = 3 \\ 5x_2 + 4x_3 = -2 \\ \hline 5x_3 = 1 \qquad \text{equation 3} \end{array}$$

Hence, our new set of equations is

$$\begin{array}{r} x_1 - \tfrac{3}{5}x_3 = \tfrac{9}{5} \\ x_2 + \tfrac{4}{5}x_3 = -\tfrac{2}{5} \\ 5x_3 = 1 \end{array}$$

If we eliminate x_3 from the first two equations, we will have a solution. The first step is to divide the third equation by 5:

$$x_3 = \tfrac{1}{5} \qquad \text{equation 3}$$

Using this equation to eliminate x_3 in the first equation, we have

$$
\begin{array}{r}
x_1 - \tfrac{3}{5}x_3 = \tfrac{9}{5} \\
\tfrac{3}{5}x_3 = \tfrac{3}{25} \\
\hline
x_1 = \tfrac{48}{25} \qquad \text{equation 1}
\end{array}
$$

Repeating the procedure for the second equation, we have

$$
\begin{array}{r}
x_2 + \tfrac{4}{5}x_3 = -\tfrac{2}{5} \\
- \tfrac{4}{5}x_3 = -\tfrac{4}{25} \\
\hline
x_2 = -\tfrac{14}{25} \qquad \text{equation 2}
\end{array}
$$

The answer to the simultaneous equations are

$$
\begin{aligned}
x_1 &= \tfrac{48}{25} \\
x_2 &= -\tfrac{14}{25} \\
x_3 &= \tfrac{1}{5}
\end{aligned}
$$

After every iteration, the previous set of equations has been replaced by an equivalent set of equations. The foregoing method of solving simultaneous linear equations may seem exceptionally tedious, and it is. The procedure is somewhat simplified by representing the equations in matrix form and by performing elementary row operations on the matrix.

If we represent simultaneous linear equations with a matrix of coefficients, augment that matrix by adding a column that corresponds to the right-hand sides of the equations, and then, through elementary row operations, transform the original matrix of coefficients into an identity matrix, then the right-hand sides represent the solution. Let us return to our example to illustrate the utility of the matrix in Gaussian elimination. For convenience, the equations are repeated below.

$$
\begin{aligned}
2x_1 + 4x_2 + 2x_3 &= 2 \\
3x_1 + x_2 - x_3 &= 5 \\
x_1 - 3x_2 + 2x_3 &= 4
\end{aligned}
$$

The matrix of coefficients then is

$$
\begin{bmatrix}
2 & 4 & 2 \\
3 & 1 & -1 \\
1 & -3 & 2
\end{bmatrix}
$$

Now, if we augment the coefficient matrix by adding the right-hand-side column, we have

$$\begin{bmatrix} 2 & 4 & 2 & | & 2 \\ 3 & 1 & -1 & | & 5 \\ 1 & -3 & 2 & | & 4 \end{bmatrix}$$

Each row in the *augmented matrix* represents an equation. The matrix that yields the solution is

$$\begin{bmatrix} 1 & 0 & 0 & | & a \\ 0 & 1 & 0 & | & b \\ 0 & 0 & 1 & | & c \end{bmatrix}$$

where $x_1 = a$, $x_2 = b$, and $x_3 = c$.

Finding a, b, and c is a matter of combining the following *elementary row operations* in such a way as to yield the foregoing solution matrix.

1. Any two rows in the augmented matrix can be interchanged.
2. Any row can be multiplied by a nonzero real number.
3. Any row can be replaced by adding to it a multiple of another row.

Any combination of the three row operations above can be accomplished without affecting the solution set of the original system of equations. Gaussian elimination merely replaces a given system of equations with an equivalent system of equations using the elementary row operations above. Let us return to our problem and solve the system of equations using the augmented matrix and elementary row operations.

$$\begin{bmatrix} 2 & 4 & 2 & | & 2 \\ 3 & 1 & -1 & | & 5 \\ 1 & -3 & 2 & | & 4 \end{bmatrix}$$

Step 1. Multiply row 1 by $\frac{1}{2}$.

$$\begin{bmatrix} 1 & 2 & 1 & | & 1 \\ 3 & 1 & -1 & | & 5 \\ 1 & -3 & 2 & | & 4 \end{bmatrix}$$

Step 2: Multiply row 1 by -3 and add to row 2.

$$\begin{bmatrix} 1 & 2 & 1 & | & 1 \\ 0 & -5 & -4 & | & 2 \\ 1 & -3 & 2 & | & 4 \end{bmatrix}$$

Step 3: Multiply row 1 by -1 and add to row 3.

$$\begin{bmatrix} 1 & 2 & 1 & | & 1 \\ 0 & -5 & -4 & | & 2 \\ 0 & -5 & 1 & | & 3 \end{bmatrix}$$

Step 4: Multiply row 2 by $-\frac{1}{5}$.

$$\begin{bmatrix} 1 & 2 & 1 & | & 1 \\ 0 & 1 & \frac{4}{5} & | & -\frac{2}{5} \\ 0 & -5 & 1 & | & 3 \end{bmatrix}$$

Step 5: Multiply row 2 by -2 and add to row 1.

$$\begin{bmatrix} 1 & 0 & -\frac{3}{5} & | & \frac{9}{5} \\ 0 & 1 & \frac{4}{5} & | & -\frac{2}{5} \\ 0 & -5 & 1 & | & 3 \end{bmatrix}$$

Step 6: Add 5 times row 2 to row 3.

$$\begin{bmatrix} 1 & 0 & -\frac{3}{5} & | & \frac{9}{5} \\ 0 & 1 & \frac{4}{5} & | & -\frac{2}{5} \\ 0 & 0 & 5 & | & 1 \end{bmatrix}$$

Step 7: Multiply row 3 by $\frac{1}{5}$.

$$\begin{bmatrix} 1 & 0 & -\frac{3}{5} & | & \frac{9}{5} \\ 0 & 1 & \frac{4}{5} & | & -\frac{2}{5} \\ 0 & 0 & 1 & | & \frac{1}{5} \end{bmatrix}$$

Step 8: Add $\frac{3}{5}$ times row 3 to row 1.

$$\begin{bmatrix} 1 & 0 & 0 & | & \frac{48}{25} \\ 0 & 1 & \frac{4}{5} & | & -\frac{2}{5} \\ 0 & 0 & 1 & | & \frac{1}{5} \end{bmatrix}$$

Step 9: Multiply row 3 by $-\frac{4}{5}$ and add to row 2.

$$\begin{bmatrix} 1 & 0 & 0 & \Big| & {}^{48}\!/_{25} \\ 0 & 1 & 0 & \Big| & -{}^{14}\!/_{25} \\ 0 & 0 & 1 & \Big| & {}^{1}\!/_{5} \end{bmatrix}$$

Since the matrix yielded by step 9 is of the form we are looking for, the solution can be read directly.

$$\begin{aligned} x_1 &= {}^{48}\!/_{25} \\ x_2 &= -{}^{14}\!/_{25} \\ x_3 &= {}^{1}\!/_{5} \end{aligned}$$

The augmented matrix can be interpreted as

$$\begin{aligned} 1x_1 + 0x_2 + 0x_3 &= {}^{48}\!/_{25} \\ 0x_1 + 1x_2 + 0x_3 &= -{}^{14}\!/_{25} \\ 0x_1 + 0x_2 + 1x_3 &= {}^{1}\!/_{5} \end{aligned}$$

Let us summarize the steps in solving a system of simultaneous linear equations using the augmented matrix and elementary row operations.

1. Begin with the first row and multiply the row by the multiplicative inverse of the coefficient of the first variable.
2. Then use the row to eliminate the first variable from all other rows using elementary row operations.
3. Go to the next row and repeat the process for the next variable.
4. Continue the process until only the identity matrix of coefficients is left.
5. Once the identity matrix has been formed, the solution can be read directly from the column farthest to the right.

BIBLIOGRAPHY

Hadley, G., and M. C. Kemp, *Finite Mathematics in Business and Economics.* New York: North-Holland/American Elsevier Publishing Co., 1972.

Haeussler, Ernest F., and Richard S. Paul, *Introductory Mathematical Analysis.* Reston, Virginia: Reston Publishing Company, 1976.

Hillier, Frederick S., and Gerald J. Lieberman, *Introduction to Operations Research* 3e. San Francisco: Holden-Day, Inc., 1980.

Kemeny, John G., et al., *Finite Mathematics with Business Applications.* Englewood Cliffs, N.J.: Prentice-Hall, Inc., 1972.

Wagner, Harvey M., *Principles of Operations Research.* Englewood Cliffs, N.J.: Prentice-Hall, Inc., 1975.

PART IV
Conclusion

16

MIS and Decision Support Systems

THE LIBERTY NATIONAL BANK[1]

In the early 1970s the banking industry found itself in a different type of financial position. The Liberty National Bank was no exception and had to change the ways in which it acquired funds. A significant entry into "manageable liabilities" increased the bank's leverage and reduced liquidity, making it more vulnerable to rises and falls in interest rates. As a result of these changes and a rapidly changing economy, the banking industry's managerial techniques were strained almost to the breaking point.

The Liberty Bank posed the question of how to improve their managerial techniques. Their decision was to provide a better marriage between management and automation through a management information system. Their so-called MRS system is a combination of information, planning, and communication systems, with the emphasis on reporting just what information management needs for decision making—no more and no less.

At the heart of the MRS system is a time-sharing model developed by Olson Research Associates; it maintains a 2-year moving data base. The system analyzes the data and projects past performance for balance sheet positions, yields, cost factors, and other operating ratios. Statistical projections are plotted so that management can interact with the data. These projections and management's judgment about key elements of the business enter a simulation model which develops pro forma financial reports. Corporate decisions can thus be fine-tuned by asking "what if" questions such as: "What will be the effect of lower interest rates?" or "What about the new capital or investment policy changes?"

A key issue at Liberty Bank (as at other banks) is to what extent they should trade off liquidity for earning power. At Liberty it was decided to use

[1]James W. Bruce, Jr., "Management Reporting System: A New Marriage Between Management and Financial Data Through Management Science," *Interfaces,* 6 (November 1975), 54–63.

the MRS system and linear programming to resolve this critical issue on a continuing basis. The LP model reflected the concepts of how the bank should be run; it included capital and risk constraints as well as policy restrictions. The output of the LP model suggested guidelines for resource (capital) allocations.

A unique feature of the system was that the output was presented in computer-generated graphics that top management could understand and relate to without being a management scientist. The decision support system was very successful and added a new dimension to critical decision making at Liberty.

Just how successful was the MRS system? The Chief Executive Officer (CEO) at Liberty credits the system with $.25 per share of the operating earnings for 1973 and $.65 per share of 1974's earnings. The bank also widened their interest margin from $14.1 million in 1972 to $15.3 million in 1974—during very difficult economic times. The people at Liberty say that they could not have accomplished this without the MRS system. They are proud of the fact that many banks across the nation are adopting their basic approach.

INTRODUCTION

In the first fifteen chapters we surveyed the majority of the salient techniques and topics that comprise the discipline of operations research/management science. These tools have covered the range of decision-making problems from deterministic problems to problems under risk and uncertainty. These tools can be very powerful and useful decision-making aids when applied to the proper decision-making circumstances. However, the usefulness of each method is usually limited to a specific set of circumstances; these scientific-based methods do not apply to all types of managerial decision-making problems. In particular, they do not seem to be as helpful in everyday decision problems, where timely, accurate information and insightful human judgment are the primary requirements.

MIS   To help cope with a broader range of decision-type problems, the field of *management information systems (MIS)* has evolved. As we shall see, this new discipline has partially evolved from and with management science. In the remainder of this chapter we shall examine the concepts of data and information. From there we will look at management information systems, what they are, and what they do. Finally, we will look at the MIS and OR/MS interface and the emerging new area of decision support systems.

DATA AND INFORMATION

data Data and information, although closely related, are technically different. *Data* are the raw material for information and consist of groups of symbols which represent quantities, actions, objects, and so on. In quantitative analysis applications, data are almost always comprised of numbers that represent such things as costs, profits, and resource usage and availability. As such, data are the necessary input to decision-making models.

information Quantitative models themselves often generate data as output. Usually, however, the output of models is information or actual decisions to problems. *Information* is data that have been processed into a form that is meaningful and useful in a decision-making context. It is a function of information systems to provide and analyze information, not just data.

Raw data originate from several sources. Often data are available from past records or transactions. It is also obtainable from direct observation, model output, or even forecasts of the future. Once accumulated, data are generally stored on computer cards, magnetic tape, disks, or computer memory. If raw data are not available, it may take months or even a few years to collect enough data to support a well-founded quantitative analysis. This is one reason data remain a critical element of the OR/MS process.

Data are often refined or preprocessed before they are usable as input to a model or a decision process. The refining or structuring of data usually involves putting the data in a special form summarizing it, or calculating statistics based on it, such as yearly sales, average wait time, and so on.

MANAGEMENT INFORMATION SYSTEMS (MIS)

Accurate and timely information is vital in order for an organization to make sound, well-informed decisions. Devices called information systems have evolved to provide information and support the managerial decision-making process. A *management information system* (MIS) has been defined as an integrated, human/machine system for providing information to support operations, management, and decision-making functions in an organization.[2]

management
information
system Early information systems were primarily data-processing-oriented, with emphasis on recording, processing, and storing data. These tasks are still integral functions of information systems, but current responsibilities extend to improving information flow and communication between departments and aiding decision making at all levels of management. The

---

[2]Gordon B. Davis, *Management Information Systems: Conceptual Foundations, Structure and Development* (New York: McGraw-Hill Book Company, 1974), p. 5.

three levels of management are generally referred to as top management, middle management, and operating (or lower) management. Top-management responsibilities are strategic in nature and involve long-range planning and development of organizational policies. Middle-management decisions are tactical and affect intermediate-range plans and include such responsibilities as resource allocation, budget management, and personnel management. Operating management is concerned with the day-to-day operations and such activities as scheduling operations, processing transactions, and inventory management. Figure 16.1 illustrates the three levels of management to which management information systems are applicable.

Each level of management requires a means of keeping abreast of the various activities which are taking place within the various levels of the organization. Information systems aid in the planning and coordination of activities throughout the organization. Integrative decision making is also required among the functional areas of production, marketing, finance, and accounting. Each of the functional areas must be aware of the needs of the other areas and demands it makes on the entire organization. Viewing the organization as a system, we can see how information systems can aid in a systems approach to decision making. Figure 16.2 shows that information flow is a vital link to integrated decision making which is required to achieve the goals of the organization as a whole.

COMPUTER-BASED INFORMATION SYSTEMS

In theory it is not necessary for an information system to be computerized to be useful, but the volume of data and transactions that need to be processed require a high-speed computer in all but the simplest systems.

FIGURE 16.1   The three levels of managerial decision making

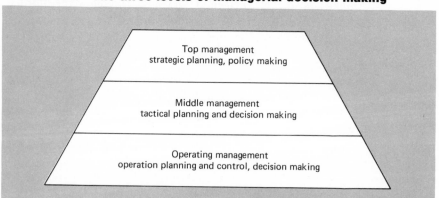

FIGURE 16.2 Information as a link in integrated decision making

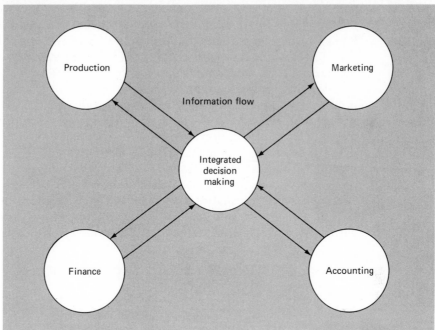

Thus, we will assume that we are discussing computer-based information systems in the remainder of the chapter.

Physically, a management information system consists of the following components:

1. Computer hardware
2. Computer software
3. Data base
4. Operating personnel

hardware The *computer hardware* consists not only of the central processing unit (CPU) but all peripheral equipment, such as tape drive, memory, disk drives, printers, and so on, including the computer terminals that the *software* decision maker might use to interact with the system. The *software* is comprised of general computer operating systems software and all programs used to process data, generate reports, and manage the data base. *data* The *data base* is an integrated collection of stored files that contain data *base* useful in the operation of the organization. An MIS often contains several different data bases that support different types of functions. The data bases are so critical to the function of most organizations that a special software tool called a data base management system is often employed to manage the development and utilization of the data bases. The last and perhaps most important part of the information system is comprised of the operating personnel. Information has meaning only in the context of human intelligence. However, human ability to recognize, comprehend, and utilize data or information is limited and, consequently, is a constraining factor in the development of information systems.

Given the physical system, an MIS is to support the decision-making process. Just as models and heuristics serve various purposes in the decision-making process, so do information systems. The general range of tasks that an information system performs includes transaction processing, data file definition and maintenance, report generation, inquiry processing, and limited decision making. Each of these types of activities are performed in varying degrees by different types of information systems. Although each information system at different organizations is unique, they all fall into one of three types of systems. These systems are categorized according to the level of decision making to which they contribute.

TRANSACTION PROCESSING (CLERICAL) SYSTEMS

A transaction is an event that affects a business organization. Examples include sales, purchases, and inventory withdrawals or replenishments. Systems that process transactions are primarily record-keeping procedures and a computerized form of data processing. In this most elementary state the computer processing system is not really a true MIS, but all management information systems involve some *transaction processing*. A great majority of the computer-based processing systems are of the transaction-processing variety. Many of the advances in computer processing systems have been at this level. Examples include:

1. Computerized payroll systems
2. Dividend calculation systems
3. Accounts payable systems
4. Customer billing systems

Transaction processing systems are not decision-oriented, but two types of reports can be generated that do provide some information. Control reports can provide information on errors that were detected during the transaction processing. Monitoring reports provide information that allows various activities to be observed or summarized. Examples include payroll summaries and basic accounting performance reports. These reports do not aid directly in the decision-making process; true information systems are characterized by providing information for specific decision problems.

INFORMATION SYSTEMS

Unlike a transaction processing system, a true information system contains information and not just data. It contains the kind of information that is pertinent for a specific decision-making problem. An effective information system will provide the required information in a meaningful form and at the right time.

An information system differs from a mundane data processing system by having its own data base, information retrieval capabilities, report generating software, and possibly some planning or decision models. The extent to which an information system is successful is measured by the degree that it supports the management and decision-making functions of the organization.

Information retrieval

The typical information system performs two basic functions. These functions are information retrieval and preparation of reports. *Information retrieval* refers to the accessing of specific data or information stored in the data base. This information may be used to answer a specific inquiry but is usually retrieved to prepare a specific report. A list of the typical types of reports is shown in Table 16.1.

The output of these types of reports support such decision situations as:

Inventory reordering and status reporting

Quality control

Budget analyses

Sales analyses

Depreciation decisions

Projected income statements

TABLE 16.1   MIS-generated reports

Type of report	Purpose
Special retrieval requests	To answer a specific question or provide information for a specific problem.
Regular report	To support the operating and control functions on a regularly scheduled basis.
Exception report	To signal an out-of-control or unusual situation.
Special report	To support a specific one-time decision problem. Prepared only on request.

More advanced information systems include more than the ability to provide information. These decision-oriented systems have some capability to help evaluate possible strategies and to determine potential consequences of various decisions or courses of action. This capability most often involves the use of some type of decision model to generate alternatives. The approach is a simulation-based mechanism which allows the decision maker to evaluate "what if" questions. Examples of these types of questions include:

What if prices of our products are raised?

What if we develop a new product line?

What if we close the eastern warehouse?

What if we modify our corporate debt structure?

Generally, the MIS is to help determine the effects if certain conditions occur or certain decisions are made. This capability is a further extension of the sensitivity analysis that we studied in Chapter 4 and the simulation models that we studied in Chapter 13. All these approaches are related in that they help management evaluate and select courses of action.

This special analysis capability of an MIS usually involves some kind of data analysis procedure. Most common among these are statistical computer routines that do forecasting or regression and correlation analysis. Other routines may include net-present-value calculations, inventory EOQ models, and even mathematical programming models such as linear programming. The output of these models enables the MIS to move from a report-generating level to an evaluative and prescriptive level. It is through the use of these models that MIS and OR/MS "team up" to tackle managerial decision problems.

on line inquiry processing When the special analysis of answering what if questions is performed on *line* with a computer terminal, this is called *inquiry processing*. Inquiry processing offers the advantage of being able to refine information needs while actually using the system. This approach enables the decision maker to deal with decision problems on a real-time basis. Until recently, this type of MIS was considered the state of the art in information system development. We now turn to an emerging new type of system that promises to further redefine the state of the art in the support of managerial decision making.

DECISION SUPPORT SYSTEMS (DSS)

We have discussed the evolution of information systems from transaction processing systems to information systems that generate reports and other information which support managerial decision making. Some more advanced systems even employ decision models to support the decision process. As information systems become more sophisticated, they will increasingly rely upon appropriate decision models. No longer will the models be used in an ad hoc, nonintegrated basis. They will need to become part of an integrated system composed of decision models, decision maker, and data base.

decision support system   This new breed of information system has been labeled a *decision support system (DSS).* It is an exciting new concept which promises to extend the range of decision problems that OR/MS and MIS can support. In particular, it promises to help decision makers deal with *unstructured problems* which are often encountered in real-world decision making. Just as early MIS helped to extend OR/MS applications by providing accurate timely data, DSS extends OR/MS by dealing with problems that do not have enough structure to be "solved completely" by any particular OR/MS model or MIS report.

Most problems encountered by real-world decision makers require some degree of human judgment or input; very few real decision problems can be completely solved by the straightforward application of a decision model. It is the incorporation of the human judgmental process that further distinguishes decision support systems from other information systems. There is definitely some overlap among MIS, OR/MS, and DSS—especially since DSS is an integration of MIS and OR/MS. However, these disciplines are differentiated in terms of their relative emphasis and relevance to managers. In a recent book, Keen and Morton further delineate the differences among the three approaches.[3] They explain the differences in emphasis and impact as follows:

1. Management information systems:
    a. The main impact has been on structured tasks where standard operating procedures, decision rules, and information flows can be reliably predefined.
    b. The main payoff has been in improving efficiency by reducing costs, turnaround time, and so on, and by replacing clerical personnel.
    c. The relevance for managers' decision making has mainly been indirect, for example, by providing reports and access to data.
2. Operations research/management science:

---

[3]Peter G. W. Keen and Michael S. Scott Morton, *Decision Support Systems: An Organizational Perspective* (Reading, Mass.: Addison-Wesley Publishing Co., Inc., 1978).

a. The impact has mostly been on structured problems (rather than tasks) where the objective, data, and constraints can be prespecified.

b. The payoff has been in generating better solutions for given types of problems.

c. The relevance for managers has been the provision of detailed recommendations and new methodologies for handling complex problems

3. Decision support systems (these are claims as much as accomplishments):

a. The impact is on decisions in which there is sufficient structure for computer and analytic aids to be of value but where managers' judgment is essential.

b. The payoff is in extending the range and capability of managers' decision processes to help them improve their effectiveness.

c. The relevance for managers is the creation of a supportive tool, under their own control, which does not attempt to automate the decision process, predefine objectives, or impose solutions.

One of the key differences in decision support systems is that the decision maker's insights and judgments are used at all stages of problem solving—from problem formulation, to data selection, to model building and selection, to solution evaluation.

CHARACTERISTICS OF DSS

Several decision support systems have been developed and reported in the literature to date (for instance, the Liberty Bank example); however, these systems are not all alike and are the forerunners of even more sophisticated systems. With decision support systems just coming out of the embryonic stage let us take a look at what some leading authors and researchers have to say concerning the structure and mission of DSS.

Sprague and Watson have studied early decision support systems and have observed certain characteristics which are prevalent and indicative of developing trends.[4] The following characteristics were found:

---

[4]Ralph H. Sprague, J. R. Watson, and Hugh J. Watson, "A Decision Support System for Banks," OMEGA, The International Journal of Management Science, 4, No. 6 (1976), 657–671.

1. The DSS is designed specifically to *support decision making*. Attention to information flows, report structure, and data-base design is specifically related to this primary objective.

2. The DSS is interactive to allow the manager or his or her representative *fast access* to models and data. The interactive capability is not necessarily to provide immediate access to minutes-old data, but, rather, to give access to data and models at a speed that matches the thought processes of the manager.

3. The DSS is *flexible* enough to satisfy the decision-making requirements of many types of managers—those in different functional areas, at various managerial levels, and with different management styles.

4. The DSS is an *integrated* set of data and models which allows the models to work together, and thus avoid suboptimization whenever possible.

5. The DSS is *dynamic* enough to keep itself up to date without major or frequent *ad hoc* revisions.

6. The DSS is *sophisticated,* utilizing modern information processing and management science techniques whenever appropriate.

STRUCTURAL FRAMEWORK FOR DSS

Figure 16.3 presents the conceptual framework of a decision support system as conceived by Sprague and Watson. Note that there are three major subsystems, consisting of the data base, decision models, and the decision maker. The data base consists of data both from sources internal and external to the organization. The dynamic nature of decision making requires the data to be updated frequently. The *decision models subsystem* contains models that support all three levels (top, middle, lower) of management. These different levels of models require communication linkages to achieve a systems approach and avoid suboptimization. Note the existence of model building blocks that are not complete models. These are model-building aids (probably in subroutine form) that can be put together by the decision maker to form a complete model for a problem. Examples of building-block routines are multiple regression analysis, linear programming, net-present-value calculations, and so on.

The decision maker is the hub of the decision support system. He must have the capability to interact with all components of the system. To facilitate this interaction, a *"command language"* is needed to direct the

FIGURE 16.3 Conceptual structure of a decision support system

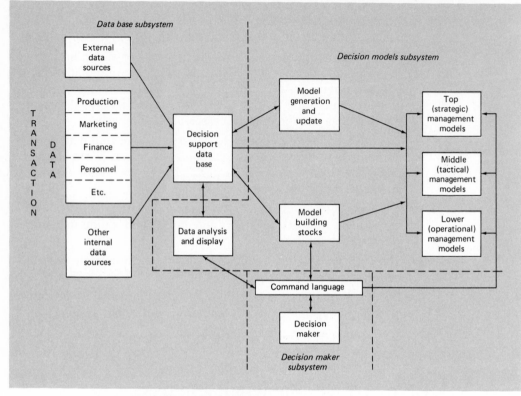

Source: Ralph Sprague and Hugh Watson, "A Decision Support System for Banks,"
Omega, 4 (1976), 657–676.

activities in the system. This language needs to give the decision maker a
wide range of capabilities so that he or she can retrieve and display data
or output, select models, and evaluate solutions.

DESIGN CRITERIA FOR DSS

Given the general structure of a decision support system, what are the
important design criteria? Carlson[5] has specified four design criteria for
decision support systems. These criteria are:

1.   Representations—the use of CRT terminals to generate reports, charts,
     graphs, and so on.

---

[5]Eric Carlson, ed., "Proceedings of a Conference on Decision Support Systems," *Data Base*,
8 (Winter 1977).

2.   Support of intelligence, design, and choice activities—comparison of current status with goals and objectives, exception reporting, and preliminary calculations.

3.   Memory aids—English-like data base management systems, which allow flexible interactive access to data.

4.   Decision-maker control—human/machine interaction capability, on-line and real-time without the intermediary of programmers.

BEYOND OPTIMIZATION—WHERE WILL IT LEAD?

Given the technology of DSS, how will it extend the decision maker's capabilities? To answer this, let us look at Vazsonyi's categorization of the four phases of the OR/MS process.[6]

1.   Exploration—initial structuring of the decision situation

2.   Modeling and optimization

3.   Interpretation of postmodeling—translation of model results are translated into plain English and communicated to the decision maker

4.   Implementation

Vazsonyi claims that traditional OR/MS has made great progress in (2) but not (1), (3), and (4). On the other hand, "DSS provides the capability *real-time* to store, retrieve, present, and manipulate data in an on-line, *real-time* fashion. It provides the capability of man/machine dialogs. In addition it can provide on-line, real-time structuring of a situation and building a model. This means that OR/MS can get out of the straight-jacket of canned programs and predetermined data bases and become flexible and quickly react to meet changing requirements. In summary, DSS can provide the technology to support the process of (a) exploring/structuring; (b) interpreting, and (c) implementing.

Vazsonyi concludes by predicting that the benefits of DSS technology will be as follows:

1.   Decreased cost and time required to perform the various phases of decision making

2.   Increased applicability and efficiency of the process of structuring managerial situations

3.   Improvement in the process of collaboration between manager, OR/MS analyst, and information systems analyst

---

[6]Andrew Vazsonyi, *Decision Support Systems: The New Technology of Decision Making? Interfaces*, 9 (November 1978), 72–77.

At this point we cannot measure the impact that DSS technology will have on decision making and the utilization of OR/MS techniques and models. We can certainly surmise that it will have positive effect. And we can definitely conclude that DSS will take us one step closer to the embodiment of a true systems approach in the decision-making process.

SUMMARY

Managerial decision making requires a wide range of different types of support. OR/MS models and techniques have had great impact on solving structured problems with clear goals and available data. The application of these techniques has resulted in new methodologies and more effective solutions to complex problems. Management information systems have had success in aiding less complex and more standard types of decision problems. The main benefit to management has been rapid access to data, informative reports, and reduction of clerical personnel. A wide variety of MIS exists, ranging from transaction processing systems to information systems that go beyond report generation and include some decision models for evaluative purposes.

The current evolution in MIS is toward decision support systems. These integrated types of information systems incorporate OR/MS methods when appropriate to help solve the less structured types of decision problems. DSS extend the range and capability of manager's decision processes to improve their effectiveness. DSS can provide the technology to support the processes of exploring/structuring, interpreting, and implementing. The decision maker is an integral part of the DSS and in control of the defining, modeling, and evaluating processes. In this format the decision maker is more inclined to utilize a scientific-based approach to decision making. DSS will undoubtedly facilitate a true systems approach to decision making.

REVIEW QUESTIONS

1. What is an MIS?
2. What is the difference between data and information?
3. Comment on the MIS and OR/MS interface.
4. Characterize differences among MIS, OR/MS, and DSS.
5. How do true information systems differ from transaction processing systems?
6. To what extent must managers be able to program a computer in order to use MIS?

7. Are different types of decision models required to support the three different levels of management?

8. How does DSS bring us closer to the systems approach?

9. List an example of a transaction processing system, an MIS, and a DSS.

10. List four common output reports of an MIS.

11. List the characteristics of a DSS.

12. What are the three main subsystems of a DSS?

13. List four design criteria for a DSS.

14. What are some potential benefits of DSS?

BIBLIOGRAPHY

Ackoff, Russell L., "Management Misinformation Systems," *Management Science,* 14 (December 1967), B147–B156.

Bruce, James W., Jr., "Management Reporting System: A New Marriage Between Management and Financial Data through Management Science," *Interfaces,* 6 (November 1975), 54–63.

Carlson, Eric, ed., "Proceedings of a Conference on Decision Support Systems," *Data Base,* 8 (Winter 1977).

Davis, Gordon B., *Management Information Systems: Conceptual Foundations, Structure and Development.* New York: McGraw-Hill Book Company, 1974, p. 5.

————, and Gordon C. Everest, *Readings in Management Information Systems.* New York: McGraw-Hill Book Company, 1976.

Dock, Thomas, Vincent Lushsinger, and William Cornette, *MIS—A Managerial Perspective.* Chicago: SRA, 1977.

Keen, Peter G. W., and Michael S. Scott Morton, *Decision Support Systems: An Organizational Perspective.* Reading, Mass.: Addison-Wesley Publishing Co., Inc., 1978.

Senn, James A., *Information Systems in Management.* Belmont, Calif.: Wadsworth Publishing Co., Inc., 1978.

Sprague, Ralph H., Jr., and Hugh J. Watson, "A Decision Support System for Banks," *OMEGA, The International Journal of Management Science,* 4, No. 6 (1976), 657–671.

Vazsonyi, Andrew, "Decision Support Systems: The New Technology of Decision Making?" *Interfaces,* 9 (November 1978), 72–77.

17

Management Science: Present and Future

INTRODUCTION

Much progress has been made in management science during the past 30 years. The growth in technical literature has been explosive. Many new procedures have been developed, and many existing techniques have been refined, extended, and improved. Perhaps the most important accomplishments are the successful applications that have been achieved by both government and industry. In spite of these advances, the field is not without its present problems and future challenges. In this final chapter, we shall examine present conditions and current trends as well as some differing points of view about new directions for management science.

One fruitful way to gain insight into the present and future of management science is to examine the discipline in relation to its prior developmental phases. John F. Magee, president of Arthur D. Little, Inc., has described management science as having progressed through three overlapping phases.[1]

The primitive stage   This stage occurred from World War II through the 1950s. The emphasis during this time was on solving practical operational problems. The problems generally were well defined and small enough to be handled by the relatively unsophisticated computers of the day. Research activity focused on the development of quantitative techniques in order to get optimal solutions to clearly defined problems. The professionals in the field—far fewer than today—were drawn mostly from related disciplines such as mathematics, physics, and chemistry. Academic interest in OR/MS was limited; only three universities offered formal programs in the discipline.

---

[1]John F. Magee, "Progress in the Management Sciences," *TIMS Interfaces,* 3 (February 1973), 35–41.

The academic phase   The academic phase occurred during the 1960s. It was characterized by the tremendous growth of academic interest in OR/MS. In 1962, only 6 institutions offered programs of study; by 1968, 37 did.

As a consequence of the expanding educational programs, people who had some exposure to OR/MS began to appear at the management level. These people naturally caused OR/MS to be accepted more widely, used more often, and applied more innovatively than ever before. Nonetheless, an emphasis on the development of quantitative techniques prevailed; new techniques were generated and others refined. The simultaneous development of computer hardware and software also expanded the range of operational problems that could be solved successfully. Computer manufacturers developed "canned" programs (commercial software packages) for the application of various standard techniques. Computer-based management information systems were designed during this period. The systematic approach to information utilization characteristic of management information systems also helped to supply the data necessary for OR/MS procedures. One of the more important results of the actual use of OR/MS during the sixties was that professionals gained a more realistic understanding of the strengths and limitations of management science.

Research during the sixties, however, was often academic, rather than practical, in nature. It tended to be directed at development and elaboration of technique, apparently without concern or interest for management issues. Practitioners sometimes did not understand the more esoteric developments and thought they were irrelevant to actual decision making. Emphasis was placed on developing techniques instead of on obtaining good data, understanding the behavior and values of organizations, and identifying options.

The maturing phase   Some signs of the maturing phase of the 1970s were evident as early as the 1950s. The maturing phase is characterized by a better balance between theory and observation, greater attention to qualitative aspects of problem solving, and increased interest in investigating processes as well as solutions. During the maturing phase, management scientists have become more reflective about the goals and accomplishments of their discipline. The Institute of Management Sciences' (TIMS) credo states a concern for identifying, extending and unifying scientific knowledge pertaining to management. In the maturing phase, more attention has been given to real management problems. Magee's summary of the characteristics of the maturing phase is, in itself, a statement of the most worthy objectives of management science today:

1. "More realistic understanding by both managers and management scientists of what the management sciences can and cannot accomplish."

2. "More attention paid to getting the facts, describing what is going on and why, compared with development of abstract sophisticated techniques."

3. "Less attention to finding 'optimum' answers, more to developing processes and evolving successively better answers, adapted to evolving circumstances."

4. "Better integration of behavioral, functional, and quantitative analysis, fuller appreciation of the importance of values as well as arithmetic, a clearer understanding of the importance of assumptions as well as of logic."[2]

A LOOK AT MANAGEMENT SCIENCE IN ORGANIZATIONS

Since the 1950s, several researchers have tried to determine the status of OR/MS usage in industry and government. These investigations seek to establish whether and how OR/MS use is growing, which techniques are used, what kinds of personnel are employed, and what usage trends are evident.

A particularly thorough investigation into the growth and development of OR/MS activities in industry and government has been carried out by a team of researchers at Northwestern University. Over a 13-year period, Radnor and associates have conducted several surveys that include the United States and 20 foreign countries. In 1968 an investigation of 66 large U.S. corporations (all but nine among *Fortune's* top 500 companies) suggested several trends and factors related to the integration and utilization of OR/MS activities in U.S. business organizations. Some of the more significant trends were:

1. "A shift in the types of OR/MS personnel away from the mathematics-science professionals toward the more generally trained and management-oriented organizationals."

2. "A movement of core OR/MS groups out of research and engineering locations toward finance-accounting and later top management or planning positions, together with an increasing degree of organizational diffusion of OR/MS skills and endeavors, and a growing interdependence between OR/MS and computer activities."

---

[2]Magee, "Progress in the Management Sciences," pp. 35–41.

3. "A shift in work portfolios, initially away from major large-scale projects, toward a mixed portfolio containing short-run, limited projects, as well as large programs."

4. "A generally increasing, but not yet stabilized, level of integration into the organization of OR/MS activities, together with a low but increasing degree of management understanding and support."[3]

A follow-up study[4] through December 1970 extended the results of the 1968 investigation. The 1970 study was more extensive and included 108 large U.S. corporations. In general, most of the trends identified in the 1968 study were found to have continued through 1970. In brief, the study made the following observations:

1. The field of OR/MS is exhibiting signs of maturity; it is in a "success phase" in its developmental history.

2. There exists a definite trend toward the diffusion of OR/MS capabilities within the firm.

3. The actual process of performing an OR/MS analysis has become increasingly formalized—and increasingly routine.

4. The level of management acceptance shows a strong upward trend.

5. The data-processing or management information system function is increasingly viewed as a distinct entity, and OR/MS tends to be located or associated with the management information system function within the firm.

Based on the Radnor investigations, it appears that OR/MS functions are still in a state of change; stable or static conditions are not indicated. Thus, OR/MS activities are probably in a transitional state within the organization; but, for the most part, they seem to be undergoing steady improvement in terms of acceptance, significance, and the utilization of their outputs. These trends, identified by Radnor et al. in the late 1960s and early 1970s, have been confirmed in the late 1970s by a study conducted by Thomas and DaCosta.[5]

---

[3]M. Radnor, H. Rubenstein, and A. Bean, "Integration and Utilization of Management Science Activities in Organizations," *Operational Research Quarterly,* 19 (1968), 117–141.

[4]M. Radnor and R. Neal, "The Progress of Management-Science Activities in Large U.S. Industrial Corporations," *Operations Research,* 21 (1973), 427–450.

[5]G. Thomas and J. A. DaCosta, "A Sample Survey of Corporate Operations Research," *Interfaces,* 9 (August 1979), 102–111.

AREAS OF APPLICATION

Questionnaire surveys conducted over the past two decades can, with qualifications, give important insight into the ways corporations use OR/MS. Surveys made in the late 1950s and mid-1960s were followed up by the authors with a comparative survey in 1974 and by Thomas and DaCosta in 1977. The four surveys were conducted in a similar manner: They all examined OR/MS activities in large-scale U.S. corporations. Table 17.1 shows approximately how applications have changed during the periods of each survey. Keep in mind that the comparative estimates are rough, and each is subject to sampling error. In order to view the results of the surveys as objectively as possible, you must remember that such samples are incomplete and can involve biased responses. Given these qualifications, there is strong evidence from Table 17.1 that applica-

TABLE 17.1 Areas of application of OR/MS techniques

Area of application	Percent of companies reporting activity			
	1958	1964	1974	1977
Forecasting	57	73	89	88
Production scheduling	47	90	69	70
Inventory control	45	90	68	70
Transportation	26	54	60	51
Capital budgeting	11	39	58	56
Plant location	15	32	55	42
Optimum capacity studies	na	na	45	40
Advertising and sales research	20	27	39	35
Equipment replacement	15	27	31	33
Product development	na	na	31	na
Accounting procedures	16	17	27	27
Quality control	33	51	26	40
Loading and sequencing	na	na	25	na
Plant layout	na	na	18	na
Maintenance and repair	16	32	16	28
Routing	na	na	11	na
Personnel selection	na	na	11	na
Tax assessment analysis	na	na	8	na
Weapon systems analysis	na	na	8	na
Packaging	13	7	7	9
Paperwork scheduling	na	na	6	na

tions involving forecasting, transportation, capital budgeting, and plant location have grown significantly since 1958.

In the two most recent surveys, more than half the companies responding indicated applications in forecasting, production scheduling, inventory control, transportation, and capital budgeting. Most of the listed applications show increasing use over the course of the four surveys. (In fact, OR/MS activity in general has a healthy long-term growth pattern.) In 1958 and 1964, the percentage of companies reporting OR/MS activity was 68 and 75, respectively. In 1974, 80 percent of the respondents reported OR/MS activity.

EDUCATIONAL BACKGROUND OF OR/MS PERSONNEL

The educational backgrounds of an OR/MS staff are typically quite diversified. Table 17.2 compares the backgrounds of the OR/MS personnel in each of the 1958, 1964, 1974 and 1977 surveys. One noteworthy trend is the increase in personnel who actually have a degree in OR/MS. There is also a very significant increase in personnel who have a degree in business administration. The M.B.A. degree appears to be desirable for practitioners of OR/MS in industry. The Radnor and Neal study showed that the "most desired" person had a quantitative or engineering undergraduate degree, some form of computer experience, and an M.B.A. This trend reflects the emphasis in the practice of OR/MS on understanding how a business functions and on solving real-world problems.

TABLE 17.2 The educational background of OR/MS personnel

Major field	B.A. (%)	M.A. (%)	Ph.D. (%)	All degrees			
				1958	1964	1974	1977
OR/MS	7.0	18.0	33.3	na	na	14.0	14.6
Industrial engineering	16.1	10.2	10.8	7	14	13.0	7.3
Mathematics and statistics	21.3	18.5	23.7	27	30	20.0	21.2
Mechanical engineering	10.1	4.9	1.1	12	13	7.1	na
Business administration	17.1	32.8	3.2	6	8	23.2	20.6
Economics	9.4	4.4	15.1	4	7	7.6	4.3
Aeronautical engineering	3.3	2.6	2.2	10	6	2.8	na
Chemistry	1.8	.7	3.2	8	6	1.4	na
Physics	3.7	2.7	1.1	na	na	3.0	na
Electrical engineering	4.7	2.7	4.3	7	2	3.8	na
Other	5.4	2.7	2.2	19	14	3.9	32.0
Totals	100.0	100.0	100.0	100	100	100.0	100.0

TABLE 17.3 Educational level of OR/MS staff

Educational level	1977	1969	1964	1958
Bachelor's degree	22%	27%	48%	61%
Master's degree	65%	53%	41%	28%
Ph.D. degree	13%	20%	11%	11%

As shown in Table 17.3, the decrease in the percentage of OR/MS staff with a bachelor's degree continues. The trend in Ph.D.-level OR/MS staff, however, has reversed. Thomas and DaCosta hypothesize that the decline in the percentage of Ph.D.s hired is closely linked to both the maturity of the OR/MS field and the decentralization of OR/MS in organizations.

IMPLEMENTATION OF MANAGEMENT SCIENCE

From the start, *implementation* has been management science's most rewarding aspect—and its most troublesome. It is one thing to build models and propose solutions, and it is quite another to implement a solution or proposed change successfully in the real world. Implementation always requires some kind of change within the organization, whether of attitude, behavior, or activity. Successful implementations must overcome Murphy's law, which states that if there is any way for something to go wrong, it will, and at the most inopportune moment! Some of the most serious implementation problems involve inaccurate data or behavioral difficulties arising from management attitudes and lack of communication.

Despite continual problems, progress has been made in implementing management science in business and government organizations. In the fifties and sixties, management scientists had to justify their existence and thus spent much time trying to "sell" the discipline. Earlier, management was skeptical that there were real monetary benefits to be gained by using management science. Today, a larger percentage of top management realizes the potential contributions that management science can make. Management scientists are seldom required to justify their existence these days, but they often have to cost-justify the various projects they consider.

Several of the surveys we have discussed examined the nature of implementation problems. The Radnor and Neal study found that almost all the 105 companies surveyed had some implementation problems. However, only 13 were identified as having very serious implementation problems. Their long-term studies seem to suggest that implementation problems were less severe in 1970 than in the sixties.

In the 1974 survey, we found that 65 percent of the companies that use OR/MS reported no major implementation difficulties. (Incidentally, one of the respondents said that anyone who answered no to the question about having implementation problems was either a liar, an idiot, or could walk on water.) When asked to comment on the nature of their implementation difficulties, many respondents cited problems that typically exist between OR/MS personnel and an organization's management. The most frequently encountered problems were: poor communication between staff and user; lack of top-level management support or commitment; lack of quality data; lack of objectivity in management attitudes; and failure (often of awareness or education) on management's part to utilize the results of an OR/MS project successfully. Other problems reported by the respondents included the difficulty in selling OR/MS projects to management, interorganization politics, and project failures.

In a more recent survey, Watson and Marett polled 300 nonacademic members of TIMS/ORSA.[6] The response of 112 returns represented a wide diversity of organizations and should be fairly representative of OR/MS implementation problems in general. Watson and Marett found that most of the implementation problems could be classified into 10 categories. These 10 classes of problems are shown in Table 17.4.

In spite of these implementation problems, occasional project failures, and in rare instances an OR staff disbandment, OR/MS is more readily accepted by top management than ever before. Radnor and Neal found several reasons for management's increased interest in OR/MS:

1. The size and complexity of the business situation is ever increasing.
2. There is a growing need for faster response times.
3. Organizations want to utilize more fully the potential of their computer facilities.
4. It is important to have complete and rapid exchange of information about new techniques, particularly with relation to what competitors are doing.
5. It is imperative to answer on an equivalent basis the more sophisticated questions top management is being asked about its operations by customers, regulating agencies, and stockholders.

TOWARD MORE SUCCESSFUL IMPLEMENTATION

Management scientists have progressed toward better implementation, but there is still room for improvement. In this section, we examine certain factors relating to the success or failure of implementation. In another

---

[6]H. Watson and P. Marett, "A Survey of Management Science Implementation Problems," *Interfaces,* 9 (August 1979), 124–128.

TABLE 17.4 Survey results from practicing management scientists

Implementation problem	Percentage of respondents
1. Selling management science methods to management	35
2. Neither top nor middle management have the educational background to appreciate management science methods	34
3. Lack of good clean data	32
4. There is never time to analyze a real problem using a sophisticated approach	23
5. Lack of understanding by those that need to use the results	22
6. Hard to define problems for applications	19
7. The payoff from using unsophisticated methods is sufficient	16
8. Shortage of personnel	12
9. Poor reputation of management scientists as problem solvers	11
10. Individuals feel threatened by management scientists and their methods	10

study on implementation in industry and government,[7] Radnor et al. name three categories that relate to the nature of implementation problems. These categories involve the nature of the client/researcher relation, the level and kind of support from top management, and the organizational and external environment in which the research activity is pursued. Most implementation problems fall into the first two categories.

Arguments have been set forth blaming either management, the management scientist, or both for implementation problems. Often, line managers have been away from school for many years and are not familiar with current advances. This lack of familiarity often breeds their reluctance to use a tool they do not understand. In some cases, new procedures can pose a threat to job security or decision-making power. Some managers may appreciate the benefits of OR/MS but hesitate to get directly involved because they feel they lack the technical competence or understanding. Communication problems may exist between the manager and the management scientist. Management scientists have been criticized not so much for their technical approach but for their failure to take into con-

---

[7]M. Radnor, A. Rubenstein, and D. Tansik, "Implementation in Operations Research and R & D in Government and Business Organization," *Operations Research,* 18 (November–December 1970), 967–991.

sideration the human and organizational factors that are affected when solutions are implemented. Failure to consider political factors or the personalities of managers has sometimes led to the rejection of OR/MS projects. Management scientists have also been criticized for not having the patience nor the diplomatic skill to get their output used. Too often, it is said, they feel that their approach is scientifically sound and thus should not have to be explained, interpreted, or justified.

PARTICIPATION OF MANAGEMENT

Positive steps, however, help to promote more successful implementation. Perhaps the most important of these is to effect the direct participation of management in an OR/MS project. Many OR/MS projects cut across different departments or organizational structures; consequently, they must have the support and guidance of top management. Top management is in the best position to decide whether proposed projects contribute adequately to the overall goals of the organization. The support of top management is also required to establish the credibility of a project for line managers and other operating personnel.

Operating management must also be directly involved in an OR/MS project. Lack of support at this level can lead to project failure early or late. These managers should participate in the project's formulation, administration, and evaluation. Their firsthand, comprehensive understanding of operations, limitations, and constraints is necessary input to any OR model. Moreover, operating management's confidence (or lack of it) in the project carries down to the people who are directly affected by proposed changes and who thus affect the ultimate success of the project.

It is management's responsibility to make organizational objectives clearly known. These must be translated into operational goals that serve as guidelines for project undertakings and criteria for measuring success. Organizational policies regarding external factors as well as operations must be specified. Mathematical models are useless unless they reflect the constraints pertaining to operational restrictions. OR/MS projects must take into account management's attitudes and policies in such areas as social responsibility, government regulations, pollution control standards, public relations, and employment levels. These policies clearly must be considered by any mathematical model or OR/MS project that is truly meant to benefit the organization.

In the aforementioned study on implementation, Radnor et al. offer several suggestions for implementing an OR/MS project. These suggestions cannot guarantee success, but they certainly enhance the likelihood.

1. Make sure that there is a clear and recognized need for the results at the time the project is undertaken.

2. Involve the ultimate user of the results early in the process, and maintain communication with this person throughout the project.

3. Focus the direction or strategy of the project in an individual or small group that can review progress and, if necessary, make changes.

4. Gain enthusiastic support from top management.

5. Allow and encourage researchers to follow projects into applications and make careers there, if they so desire.

In their paper on implementation problems, Watson and Marett offer the following suggestions:

1. Since management frequently requires a "quick and dirty" analysis, it would help if management scientists would attempt to better understand what information is needed and how much time and money should be expended on the analysis effort.

2. Initial OR/MS efforts should begin with small tentative models with intensive involvement by the end user, and evolving more comprehensive models only when clearly justified. This is basically an expression of the "think big but start small philosophy."

3. Since management scientists may often not fully understand management's information requirements, and managers may not understand the resource requirements of certain types of analyses, further education through executive development programs is recommended. It might even be helpful to create training programs attended by both managers and management scientists.

Successful implementation clearly involves a meeting of the minds, with input and cooperation from both management and OR/MS staff. Without sincere commitments from both sides, potentially successful projects will either fail or fall short of expectations.

A LOOK AT THE FUTURE

Up to now, we have looked at management science's evolution over a period of forty-odd years. Comments about the future can only be speculative; however, if we extrapolate certain trends, we can make some forecasts.

Organizations, both private and governmental, will exist in a world that is more complex and subject to even more rapid change than today's. The term *future shock* will be ever more appropriate. The world will have more people; and at least over the short term, these people will be competing for dwindling supplies of the natural resources used at present.

Standards of living will, in general, continue to move in their present directions. Underdeveloped countries will have increasing impact on international politics. Technology will grow at an ever-increasing rate and will have many positive benefits if properly managed. The new frontiers will be space and the earth's oceans. Proportionately greater effort will be directed at solving pressing social problems. World issues such as energy, food supply, transportation, environmental control, pollution, urban development, and war will be among the most pressing problems.

Organizations will have to survive in this world of increased complexity. Institutions will become more organized and specialized. Government will play a larger role in business and society in general. People will be more demanding of their leaders and organizations. There is a strong move now toward accountability for both business and government leaders. Decision makers will need to rely further on rational means for justifying various courses of action. Consequently, OR/MS will be more widely practiced in institutions of all kinds.

That there will be a need for management science to aid in managerial decision making in this future environment is obvious. However, more and better procedures are necessary for future progress. Continual development and refinement of quantitative techniques is required if we are to tackle ever more complex problems. Such progress is typical of advancements in the past and can be expected to continue to do so. Advances have greatly increased the size of problems that can be solved by LP and other mathematical programming approaches. Future developments will be tied to computer hardware and software advances as well as to mathematical breakthroughs. Such advances will no doubt cause certain seldom used techniques such as nonlinear, dynamic, and integer programming to be utilized more often.

Advances will also be made in multicriteria decision making. In this elementary text we have focused primarily on single-objective function criteria. In many applications, however, more than one goal may be sought. For this reason, goal programming and multiple-objective decision-making methodology will be further developed, refined, and applied. This is particularly true for social and public sector problems which often have multiple objectives.

Management science must also progress in the area of increasingly difficult stochastic problems. Most developments in management science have dealt with problems that have the nice, accessible properties of certainty and well-defined objectives and constraints. Decision makers in the future will often face shorter time frames and, in some cases, increased uncertainty. In order to contribute more to actual management problems, management science will have to deal with problems that are complex, fuzzy, and loosely structured. Some signs of progress in this area have already begun to appear. Research on *fuzzy sets* and *fuzzy mathematics* is presently being applied to cognitive and decision processes.

Progress in management science is directly related to technological progress in computer hardware and software development. Second and third generation computers greatly advanced problem solving when they were introduced, and a fourth generation of computers already exists. No one knows what technological advancements subsequent computers will be capable of. Every significant computer development increases the classes of problems that can actually be solved.

Currently, the revolution in mini and microcomputers promises to bring high-speed computer equipment to small businesses as well as to individuals. The long-term effect of the proliferation of computer technology should have a significant impact on OR/MS usage. Whereas mostly large companies utilize OR/MS currently, minicomputers can bring the capability of modern quantitative analysis to small companies. Procedures such as forecasting, inventory control, and even small-scale LP models are possible on minicomputers. It will be interesting to observe the future impact of minicomputers on the decision-making process.

Time-sharing computer facilities and management information systems have brought dramatic changes in decision making. Time-sharing facilities make it possible to monitor business transactions continuously, just as they make it simple to retrieve information for real-time decision making. Time sharing also facilitates the use of management science models in decision situations that require fast response times. More decision makers of the future will have access to computer time-sharing terminals. Successful decision making requires accurate, timely information. Management information systems are designed to provide this required information. The interfacing of management science and management information systems can make significant contributions to the art and science of decision making. You may recall that one of the impediments to implementing OR/MS is the lack of timely or quality data. The evolving interface between OR/MS and MIS through decision support systems should not only provide needed data, but the capability to respond to the less structured problems often faced by management.

CHALLENGES AND CHANGES

As you can see, the future is full of challenges for the field of management science. In this section, we shall consider the views of three experienced management scientists about which new directions to take.

It is customary for each new president of The Institute of Management Sciences to make a formal statement about the past and future courses of the organization. In his message from the president, Donald Rice challenges management scientists to develop analytical methods for problems in the public sector. As Rice points out, these intractable societal problems are not amenable to straightforward, single objective analysis:

> The objectives of many programs in the public sector—education, welfare, and housing, to name a few—are much more difficult to identify and to specify in terms that make it possible for the application to traditional analytical methods to help the decision maker.
>
> Indeed, most such problems are marked by multiple and, worse yet, sometimes conflicting objectives. The nature of the constraints, as reflected in energy or other resource limitations, environmental factors, human preferences, and others, all add to the complexities involved in trying to model many public sector problems. Approaches different from those used in the past must be taken to increase theory and understanding, as well as relevant data, to deal with such problems.
>
> Social program experiments are one recent analytical development that can help to generate relevant data for analysis and provide an opportunity to gain greater insight into these complex problem areas. But much work is needed on the theory and practice of experimentation under the conditions encountered in social problem areas.[8]

More radical changes are proposed by Milan Zeleny for the future landscape of management science. Zeleny feels that management science has made great strides in improving man's capabilities for solving well-defined, well-structured problems of a quantitative nature. But, if the discipline "has been successful where it has improved or replaced man's analytical faculties in dealing with problems, it has been less successful in trying to approach new complex problems and has not even tried to enhance man's intuitive faculties."[9] Zeleny calls for the marriage of both analytical and intuitive aspects in the managerial decision process because "most problems are neither purely analytical nor purely intuitive; rather they combine both components in an intricate interaction."[10]

Zeleny also implies that the transition to a new management science will require a different attitude or mentality. He says, "Linear and nonlinear programming, queueing theory, inventory theory, critical path, dynamic programming, etc., all have been around right from the beginning. Nothing really new has been added to these seminal ideas and concepts ... we need to be effective more than efficient ... we need new

---

[8]Donald B. Rice, "Message from the President," *OR/MS Today*, 3 (September 1975), 5.
[9]Milan Zeleny, "Notes, Ideas and Techniques: New Vistas of Management Science," *Computers and Operations Research*, 2 (1975), 121.
[10]Ibid., p. 123.

ideas."[11] Zeleny feels that the biggest challenge for management science is the development of new ideas that will enhance the intuitive powers of managers. Among these will be:

1. Psychological models of the human decision-making process
2. Interactive programming
3. Management science linguistics
4. Fuzzy mathematics
5. Multiple criteria decision making
6. Qualitative management science
7. Intergroup and intragroup decision making
8. Organic systems analysis

Harvey Wagner is a past president of TIMS and an experienced consultant. Wagner feels that the fundamental breakthrough for management science so far has been the "repeated demonstration that formal model building, energized by computer systems, is able to improve pivotal managerial decisions."[12] However, many challenges remain. Even though many industrial applications of OR/MS have taken place, it is still a frustratingly difficult task to carry out these applications. Wagner calls for improvement in the mechanical aspects of applying OR/MS. He also claims that operations researchers and management scientists must develop better ways to diagnose the benefits that management can expect from OR/MS efforts.

Wagner also cites some progress within the discipline on large-scale programming problems, but surprisingly little progress has been made with daily operational problems. Problems of the latter kind are being tackled by systems analysts not using OR techniques. In Wagner's opinion, "a reexamination by operations researchers of the real nature of daily operating problems is vitally needed."[13]

Since quality data is such a limiting factor in OR/MS applications, Wagner suggests that more effort be directed toward a science of data collection and measurement. Such a science would consider how to obtain accurate information from managers, accountants and engineers, as well as study procedures for estimating unknown parameters.

In order to tackle the challenges of the future, contributions are needed by talented people of many different types. Wagner concludes by offering

---

[11]Ibid., p. 122.
[12]Harvey M. Wagner, "The ABC's of OR," *Operations Research,* 19 (October 1971), 1262.
[13]Ibid., p. 1266.

challenges to practitioners, theoreticians, and educators in OR/MS. The high-priority tasks for *practitioners* are to:

1. "Improve the mechanics of applying operations research so as to reduce the resource costs for developing, analyzing, and implementing OR models."
2. "Devise diagnostic techniques to predict accurately the economic benefits that will accrue from a proposed OR application."
3. "Expand the purview of OR into new areas of management, including formulating a corporation's growth strategy, structuring organizational responsibilities, bridging cultural gaps within a company, improving a company's profit performance, designing management information systems, and delineating the enterprise's public responsibilities."

The challenges open to management science *theoreticians* are to:

1. "Develop insightful models that sidestep the axiom of managerial rationality."
2. "Propose analytic concepts that enable managers to deal with the future as reality."
3. "Build practical models for treating day-to-day operating problems."
4. "Find new ways to exploit the full power of computers."
5. "Explore approaches to model building that encompass principles of behavioral science."

The challenges for *educators* are that they:

1. "Assess the appropriate mix between professional and technical training to best prepare students for having a practical influence on managerial decision making."
2. "Examine the relative merits of the various approaches to OR higher education that have been in vogue for over a decade."[14]

SUMMARY

Management science procedures have proved their usefulness for solving problems of many kinds. With the use of computers, management scientists have been able to deal with complicated decision problems that human intelligence alone cannot resolve. The discipline has enabled management to improve the efficiency of operations and various decision

---

[14]Ibid., p. 1281.

processes significantly. This, in turn, has freed management to apply its creativity to policy and other, less well-structured problems.

Management science is a dynamic field that is evolving over time. It shows trends toward the expansion and application of its techniques and procedures into problems in the social sciences, the public sector, and the environment, many of which are problems of worldwide concern. OR/MS is becoming a tool not only for industrial management but for decision makers in general.

In order to help meet the demands of the future, progress is badly needed in such areas as implementation, data collection and estimation, and the interfacing of behavioral and analytical procedures. Future progress in management science will not only require effort at theoretical levels but also necessitate a concerted attempt to understand and deal with the kinds of problems real-world decision makers face.

These decision problems are mind-boggling in scope and complexity. Future decision makers must become familiar with management science and learn how to synthesize the objective information provided by OR/MS with their own insight and intuition. For the decision maker of the future, a working knowledge of management science will be a necessity. What is perceived as progressive practice today will be standard procedure tomorrow.

REVIEW QUESTIONS

1. What are the three phases through which OR/MS has evolved?
2. What are the characteristics of the maturing phase?
3. To what types of problems has OR/MS been mostly successfully applied?
4. To what types of problems would management like to have better OR/MS procedures applied?
5. What gaps exist between management science theory and the practice of management science?
6. What are some of the emerging trends in management science?
7. Discuss the relationship between management science and management information systems.
8. List some of the main problems that must be overcome to achieve a successful OR/MS implementation.
9. How does management science benefit all levels of management?
10. What kinds of contributions will be required of theoreticians, practitioners, and educators in order to meet the decision-making challenges of the future?

11. Briefly discuss the role that minicomputers might play in the future of OR/MS.

12. Why is multiple-criteria decision-making methodology of particular importance in the public sector?

13. Interpret the "think big but start small" philosophy of implementation.

BIBLIOGRAPHY

Grayson, C. Jackson, Jr., "Management Science and Business Practice," *Harvard Business Review*, 51 (July–August 1973), 41–48.

Harvey, A., "Factors Making for Implementation Success and Failure," *Management Science*, 16 (February 1970), B312–B321.

Heany, Donald F., "Is TIMS Talking to Itself?" *Management Science*, 12, 4 (December 1965), B146–B155.

Hertz, D. B., "The Unity of Sciences and Management," *Management Science*, 11, 6 (April 1965), B89–B97.

Miller, David W., and Martin K. Starr, *Executive Decisions and Operations Research*, 2nd ed. Englewood Cliffs, N.J.: Prentice-Hall, Inc., 1969.

Radnor, M., A. H. Rubenstein, and A. S. Bean, "Integration and Utilization of Management Sciences Activities in Organizations," *Operational Research Quarterly*, 19 (June 1968), 117–141.

———, A. H. Rubenstein, and D. A. Tansik, "Implementation in Operations Research, and R & D in Government and Business Organizations," *Operations Research*, 18 (November–December 1970), 967–991.

Schumacher, C. C., and B. E. Smith, "A Sample Survey of Industrial Operations Research Activities II," *Operations Research*, 13 (November–December 1965), 1023–1027.

Thierauf, Robert J., and Robert C. Klekamp, *Decision Making Through Operations Research*, 2nd ed. New York: John Wiley & Sons, Inc., 1975.

Thomas, George, and Jo-Ann DaCosta, "A Sample Survey of Corporate Operations Research," *Interfaces*, 9 (August 1979), 102–111.

Turban, E., "A Sample Survey of Operations Research Activities at the Corporate Level," *Operations Research*, 20 (May–June 1972), 708–721.

Wagner, Harvey M., "The ABC's of OR," *Operations Research*, 19 (October 1971), 1259–1281.

———, *Principles of Management Science*, 2nd ed. Englewood Cliffs, N.J.: Prentice-Hall, Inc., 1975.

Watson, Hugh J., and Patricia Gill Marett, "A Survey of Management Science Implementation Problems," *Interfaces*, 9, 4 (August 1979), 129–133.

Zeleny, Milan, "Notes, Ideas and Techniques: New Vistas of Management Science," *Computers and Operations Research*, 2 (September 1975), 121–125.

PART V
Appendices

Appendix A
Glossary

additive law axiom pertaining to the union of two events.

algorithm a systematic procedure used to derive a solution to a problem.

all integer programming model a linear mathematical model in which all the decisions variables are restricted to be integer values.

alternative optima occurs whenever an LP problem has more than one optimal solution. The condition can be observed whenever a nonbasic variable has a zero $c_j - z_j$ value in the optimal simplex tableau.

analog model a physical model that substitutes one property for another; thus, it does not look like the object or phenomenon that it represents.

arc capacity the maximum allowable flow on an arc in a network.

artificial variable dummy variable added to an $=$ or $\geq$ constraint in order to get a starting feasible solution. At optimality all artificial variables must have a zero value or the LP problem has no solution.

basic feasible solution a basic solution that also satisfies all constraints of an LP problem; geometrically, it corresponds to an extreme point of the feasible region.

basic solution a solution to a linear programming problem with n variables and m constraints in which $n - m$ of the variables are set equal to zero and the m equations are solved in terms of the remaining m variables.

basis In an LP problem with m constraints and n variables, the basis consists of those m variables which are not set automatically to zero and are used to determine the solution to the problem.

batch-processing system a data-processing system in which transactions are accumulated and master files are updated periodically.

Bayes theorem a mathematical theorem used to revise the probability of an event given new information.

Bayesian strategy   the optimal decision strategy with respect to expected value.

Bernoulli trial   a random phenomenon involving two mutually exclusive and exhaustive events.

beta distribution   a continuous probability distribution often used in stochastic PERT analysis.

bill of materials (BOM)   a list that specifies all component items that a product comprises.

binomial distribution   a discrete probability distribution.

branch and bound   a partial enumeration procedure for integer or other combinatorial problems in which the set of feasible solutions is partitioned into smaller and smaller subsets until the optimal solution is found.

calling population (also called input source)   consists of all customers or calling units that can arrive to a queuing system. When the calling population is finite, it is referred to as a finite calling population or limited-source calling population. An infinite calling population refers to a calling population containing an infinite number of calling units.

carrying cost (also called holding cost)   one of three components of inventory costs. Carrying costs are those costs incurred for holding inventory.

chi-square test   a nonparametric goodness-of-fit test used to test the hypothesis that a random variable is distributed in a specified manner.

cell   cell (i, j) in a transportation tableau is associated with the route from origin i to destination j.

certainty   conditions under which all parameters of a decision problem are known exactly.

$c_j - z_j$ row   a row in the simplex tableau that gives the opportunity cost of bringing each variable into the basis. This row is used to check for optimality.

collectively exhaustive events   a group of events that together include all the sample points in the sample space.

column vector   a matrix consisting of only one column.

complementary event   consists of all points in the sample space not included in the event.

compound event   consists of more than one simple event.

computer hardware   the physical equipment comprising a computer system such as CPU, card reader, disks, memory, and so on.

computer simulation   a numerical technique that involves modeling a stochastic system on a digital computer with the intention of predicting the system's behavior.

computer software   the computer programs and procedures used to process data and enable the computer to function.

conditional probability   probabilities that depend on the outcome of another event.

constraints   mathematical expressions that state resource limitations or other physical restrictions in a particular decision model.

continuous inventory system   a system of accounting for inventory that updates inventory levels whenever there is an inventory replenishment or decrement.

crashing   the process of reducing the time necessary to complete a project by adding resources.

critical activities   activities in a PERT network that are on the critical path and consequently have zero slack time.

critical path   the longest path through a PERT network. The critical path is composed of activities with zero slack time.

critical-path method   a project scheduling and control method similar to PERT.

cumulative probability distribution   a function of some random variable that defines the probability of the random variable being less than or equal to a specific value.

data base   an integrated and organized collection of stored files and data useful in the operation of an organization.

decision support system (DSS)   a type of information system which involves the decision maker himself, a data base, and possibly some decision models to aid in the decision process. DSS are most helpful in dealing with problems that lack enough structure to be approached solely by straightforward OR/MS techniques.

decision tree   a network representation of a decision problem containing decision nodes and chance nodes.

decision variables   variables whose values (when determined) will solve a given mathematical model or problem.

degeneracy   a condition in which one or more basic variables assume a zero value in the simplex solution to an LP problem.

delphi method   a qualitative forecasting technique that utilizes a panel of experts and a series of questionnaires to develop a forecast.

dependent demand   demand whose magnitude depends on the demand for another item or product.

destination   a customer or demand location in a transportation problem.

deterministic PERT   a project-scheduling technique in which the activity times are assumed to be known with certainty.

deterministic problem   problem in which all the data and relevant parameters are known with certainty.

dual problem   a counterpart LP problem associated with the primal formulation. Unique relationships exist between the primal and dual, such as the fact that the solution to one yields the solution to the other.

dummy destination   a destination added to make demand equal to supply in a transportation problem. The fictitious demand is equal to the excess of supply over demand.

dummy source   an origin added to a transportation problem whenever demand exceeds supply. It is assigned a fictitious supply so that supply and demand are equal.

dynamic programming   a serial optimization method that decomposes a problem into smaller interrelated problems in order to find the overall optimum solution.

equilibrium condition   occurs when additional transitions do not affect the probabilities of finding a Markov process in the various states.

event   in PERT analysis, the completion of an activity or task.

expected critical path   the path in a stochastic PERT network that would be the critical path if the length of each activity were the expected time.

expected value of perfect information   measures the economic value of perfect information.

expected value of sample information   measures the economic value of new information.

extreme point   a vertex of the convex region defined by the constraints of a mathematical model.

feasible   in mathematical programming, feasible means within the region defined by the constraints or physical limitations.

Gantt chart   a simple bar chart depicting the starting time and completion time for various project tasks.

Gaussian elimination   an algebraic procedure for solving a set of simultaneous linear equations.

goal programming   a mathematical programming technique that solves optimization problems having multiple and sometimes incompatible goals.

grass-roots forecasting   a qualitative forecasting technique in which individual forecasts are generated at the end of the distribution channel and are aggregated to generate the total forecast.

gross requirements   the quantity of an item that will have to be disbursed to support the production of a parent item.

heuristic   a method or rule of thumb that determines good but not necessarily optimal solutions to a problem.

historical analogy   a qualitative forecasting technique that forecasts demand based upon past experience with a similar product or service.

holding costs   (see carrying costs)

homogeneous Markov chain   a specific type of stochastic process.

Hungarian method   an algorithm used to determine an optimal solution to an assignment problem.

iconic model   physical replica or representation of the object it represents.

independent demand   demand that is not dependent on the demand for an end item.

independent events   events whose probability of occurrence is not affected by the occurrence of another event.

infeasibility   a condition which exists when an LP problem has no feasible solution, that is, there are no points which satisfy all constraints.

input source   (see Calling population)

integer programming a type of mathematical programming in which the decision variables are restricted to whole number values.

inventory a stock of goods that is held for the purpose of future production or sales.

iterative technique is a solution process that repeats certain phases of the solution process until a solution is found.

joint probability the probability of two or more events occurring.

Kolmogorov-Smirnov test a nonparametric goodness-of-fit test.

lead time the time between the release of an order and the time the goods start being added to inventory.

least-squares method a method for deriving a function that best fits a set of data.

linear programming a mathematical technique that can be used to maximize (minimize) a linear objective function subject to certain linear constraints.

lower bound a value which is less than or equal to the value of any solution to a problem.

management information system (MIS) an integrated human/machine system for providing information to support operations, management, and decision-making in an organization.

management science the discipline devoted to studying and developing scientific procedures to help in the process of managerial decision making (see operations research).

marginal probability probabilities that do not depend on other events.

market research a family of qualitative forecasting techniques that is helpful in revealing predictions about the size, structure, and configuration of markets for various goods and services.

Markov process a stochastic process where the probability of moving from one state to another depends only on the present state of the system.

materials requirements planning (MRP) a system of logically related records, procedures, and decision rules that translate the master schedule into time-phased net requirements and planned coverage of these requirements for all component items needed.

mathematical model mathematical symbols and equations used to represent a given situation.

mathematical programming the art of developing mathematical models to solve various types of decision problems.

matrix a rectangular arrangement of numbers.

matrix addition the algebraic operation of adding two matrices of the same dimensions.

matrix multiplication the algebraic operation of multiplying two matrices.

maximal flow the maximum amount of flow that can enter into or out of a network system per unit of time.

maximax criterion the decision criterion that maximizes the maximum payoffs of various decisions.

maximin criterion   the decision criterion that maximizes the minimum payoffs of various decisions.

minimax regret criterion   a decision criterion that minimizes the maximum opportunity losses of various decisions.

minimum spanning tree   a tree of minimal total arc length that spans or connects all nodes in a network.

mixed integer programming model   a linear mathematical model in which some but not all variables are required to have integer values.

model   representation or an abstraction of an object or phenomenon.

model relaxation   the dropping of certain restrictions in a model. For example, a linear relaxation of an integer model is implemented when the integer restrictions are dropped.

modified distribution method (MODI)   a streamlined simplex algorithm used to find the optimal solution to a transportation problem.

Monte Carlo simulation   a simulation using a sampling technique that consists of the generation of random variates from a specified probability distribution.

most likely time   a PERT activity time estimate management believes to be the most likely.

multiple choice constraint   a constraint requiring the sum of 0–1 variables to equal 1; any solution thus selects one alternative out of several.

multiplicative law   axiom pertaining yo the intersection of two events.

mutually exclusive events   events which cannot occur at the same time.

net requirements   the quantity of additional component items to procure in order to support the production of a parent item. Net requirements = Gross requirements − Scheduled receipts − Inventory on hand.

network   a graphical representation of a problem or situation consisting of a collection of nodes connected by links (lines).

0–1 integer programming model   a linear mathematical model in which the decision variable values are restricted to 0 or 1.

objective function   an equation or mathematical expression that is used to measure the effectiveness of proposed solutions to a problem.

objective function ranging   the process of determining how much each objective function coefficient c_j can be increased and decreased before the basis would change.

objective probability   a probability measure for which there is definitive historical information or rigorous analysis.

on-line   being under direct control of the computer at that point in time. Thus, users who interact directly with the computer via a remote terminal are on-line as opposed to submitting job for batch processing.

operations research   the discipline devoted to studying and developing scientific procedures to help in the process of making decisions (see Management science).

optimistic time a PERT activity time estimate based on the assumption the activity will progress ideally.

order costs the costs incurred when processing an order for inventory.

order level the inventory level after replenishment.

origin a source or supply location in a transportation problem.

panel consensus a qualitative forecasting technique that involves assembling a panel of experts for the purpose of jointly developing a forecast.

parameters the input data constants whose values govern the solution to a model.

path a sequential series of activities in a PERT network.

payoff table a matrix of payoffs for a decision problem.

PERT (see program evaluation and review technique).

PERT chart a network diagram of a project.

PERT/Cost a methodology for planning, scheduling, and controlling the cost of a project.

pessimistic time a PERT activity time estimate based on the assumption that the most unfavorable conditions will occur.

physical inventory system an inventory accounting system in which management periodically reviews levels of the various items in inventory in order to make inventory decisions.

pivoting the process of updating the simplex tableau in the simplex method.

pivot element in the simplex method, the element of the simplex tableau that is in both the pivot row and pivot column.

Poisson probability density function a discrete probability function that yields the probability of n events occurring in a given time interval.

Poisson process usually refers to a random arrival process where the number of arrivals in a time period is distributed according to a Poisson probability distribution.

Posteriori probabilities the revised conditional probabilities of the various states of nature after applying Bayes theorem.

primal problem the original formulation of a linear programming problem.

principle of optimality in dynamic programming, an optimal policy has the property that whatever the inital state and initial decision are, the remaining decisions must constitute an optimal policy with regard to the state resulting from the first decision.

probability density function the function that describes a continuous probability distribution.

probability distribution a function that relates a probability to the values a random variable can take on.

probability mass function a function describing a discrete probability distribution.

process generator a function that transforms a uniformly distributed random number into a nonuniform random variate.

program evaluation and review technique (PERT)   a technique for scheduling and controlling large projects.

project scheduling   the scheduling of major tasks that require a significant amount of time to accomplish.

queue discipline (also called service discipline)   the decision rule that determines which calling unit in the queuing system receives service.

queuing system   any system that has a waiting line as an element of the system.

queuing theory   a branch of operations research that through mathematical models describes the behavior of queuing systems.

random variable   a function whose numerical value depends on the outcome of some random event.

real-time system   a computer-based system that is on-line to the computer. This enables instantaneous response to inquiries and often instantaneous update of a data base.

regression analysis   a forecasting technique yielding a forecasting equation that predicts the dependent variable as a function of one or more independent variables.

reorder level   the inventory level at the time of placing the order.

replenishment period   the time it takes to replenish inventory once replenishment has begun.

return function   the value or measure of effectiveness of a specific decision at stage n given state S_n in a dynamic programming problem.

right hand side ranging   the process of determining how much each r.h.s. coefficient in the primal LP model can be increased and decreased before the current basis becomes infeasible.

row-minimum method   a heuristic used to find an initial feasible solution to a transportation problem.

row vector   a matrix consisting of only one row.

sample point   see simple event.

sample space   collection of all possible sample points.

satisficing   the process of getting as close as possible to the achievement of a goal, possibly without reaching the goal completely.

scalar   a constant

scalar multiplication   the multiplication of each matrix element by a scalar.

sensitivity analysis   the analysis of how an optimal solution and the value of its objective function are affected by changes in the various inputs or components of the decision model.

service discipline   (see queue discipline)

service facility   a server in a queuing system.

shadow price   the marginal value of a resource associated with a linear programming constraint at optimality.

shortage costs (also called stockout costs)   inventory costs associated with being out of stock.

shortest route   shortest path between two nodes in a network.

simple event   consists of a single possible outcome of a random phenomenon.

simplex method   an algebraic procedure for iteratively solving LP models. It begins with a feasible extreme point and moves from one adjacent extreme point to another making successive improvements until the optimal solution is determined (if it exists).

simplex tableau   a tabular form used to perform hand calculations to carry out the simplex method. It contains all equation coefficients plus other information needed to check solution quality.

sink   a destination node in a network that has a demand.

slack time   in PERT analysis, the amount of time an activity can be delayed without delaying the entire project.

source   an origin node in a network that has a positive supply.

steady state   a queuing system is in a steady-state condition when its behavior is not a function of time.

stochastic PERT   a project-scheduling technique in which the activity times are of a probabilistic nature.

stage   a subproblem in a dynamic programming formulation that corresponds to a situation where a decision must be made.

standard form of an LP model   the form in which all constraints have been converted to equations.

state variable   a variable whose value describes the status of the system at any stage in a dynamic programming problem.

stochastic problem   problem in which the data and parameters are not known with certainty, but a probability distribution is known.

subjective probability   a probability which is based on someone's experience.

systems approach   a modern integrated approach to decision making in which all relevant factors (including intra-organizational and environmental or external factors) are considered in the decision process. The objective is to achieve the goals of the organization as a whole.

time phasing   the process of timing inventory needs to arrive at the point in time when they are needed.

transaction processing system   a computer based system that primarily handles simple data processing and clerical activities such as sales, purchases, and inventory changes.

transition matrix   a matrix describing single-period conditional probabilities.

transition probability   the transition probability p_{ij} is the probability of moving from state i to state j in one transition period.

transportation tableau   a table used to facilitate the solution to a transportation problem. Its rows correspond to origins, its columns to destinations, and its cells to costs.

transshipment point   a node in a network that has entering and exiting arcs and zero supply or demand.

unbounded solution   a solution to an LP problem in which the value of some variable can be made arbitrarily large without violating any of the constraints.

uncertain problem   problem in which the data or parameters are uncertain or unknown.

uniform distribution   a continuous probability distribution.

upper bound   a value which is greater than or equal to the value to any solution to a problem.

Vogel's approximation method (VAM)   a heuristic used to find an initial feasible solution to a transportation problem.

work package   the smallest element in the work-breakdown structure.

APPENDIX B
Cases

CASE 1 COASTAL STATES
CHEMICALS AND FERTILIZERS*

In December, 1975, Bill Stock, General Manager for the Louisiana Division of Coastal States Chemicals and Fertilizers, received a letter from Fred McNair of Cajan Pipeline Company which notified Coastal States that priorities had been established for the allocation of natural gas. The letter stated that Cajan Pipeline, the primary supplier of natural gas to Coastal States, might be instructed to curtail natural gas supplies to its industrial and commercial customers by as much as 40 percent during the ensuing winter months. Moreover, Cajan Pipeline had the approval of the Federal Power Commission (FPC) to curtail such supplies.

Possible curtailment was attributed to the priorities established for the use of natural gas:

First Priority: Residential and commercial heating

Second Priority: Commercial and industrial users whereby natural gas is used as a source of raw material

Third Priority: Commercial and industrial users whereby natural gas is used as boiler fuel

---

*From *Cases in Production and Operation Management* by Iverstine and Kinard, Charles E. Merrill Publishing Company, Columbus, Ohio, © 1977.

673

Almost all of Coastal States' use of natural gas was in the "second" and "third" priorities. Hence, its plants were certainly subject to brown-outs, or natural gas curtailments. The occurrence and severity of the brown-outs depended on a number of complex factors. First of all, Cajan Pipeline was part of an interstate transmission network which delivered natural gas to residential and commercial buildings on the Atlantic Coast and in northeastern regions of the United States. Hence, the severity of the forth-coming winter in these regions would have a direct impact on the use of natural gas.

Secondly, the demand for natural gas was soaring because it was the cleanest and most efficient fuel. There were almost no environmental problems in burning natural gas. Moreover, maintenance problems due to fuel-fouling in fireboxes and boilers were negligible with natural gas systems. Also, burners were much easier to operate with natural gas as compared to the use of oil or the stoking operation when coal was used as fuel. Finally, the supply of natural gas was dwindling. The traditionally depressed price of natural gas had discouraged new exploration for gas wells; hence, shortages appeared imminent.

Stock and his staff at Coastal States had been aware of the possibility of shortages of natural gas and had been investigating ways of converting to fuel oil or coal as a substitute for natural gas. Their plans, however, were still in the developmental stages. Coastal States required an imme-diate contingency plan to minimize the effect of a natural gas curtailment on its multiplant operations. The obvious question was, what operations should be curtailed, and to what extent to minimize the adverse effect upon profits? Coastal States had the approval from the FPC and Cajan Pipeline to specify which of its plants would bear the burden of the cur-tailment if such cutbacks were necessary. McNair, of Cajan Pipeline, replied, "It's your 'pie': we don't care how you divide it if we make it smaller."

THE MODEL

Six plants of Coastal States Louisiana Division were to share in the "pie". They were all located in the massive Baton Rouge-Geismar-Gramercy industrial complex along the Mississippi River between Baton Rouge and New Orleans. Products produced at those plants which required signifi-cant amounts of natural gas were phosphoric acid, urea, ammonium phos-phate, ammonium nitrate, chlorine, caustic soda, vinyl chloride monomer, and hydrofluoric acid.

Stock called a meeting of members of his technical staff to discuss a contingency plan for allocation of natural gas among the products if a curtailment developed. The objective was to minimize the impact on

TABLE 1 Contribution to profit and overhead

Product	Dollars/ton
Phosphoric acid	60
Urea	80
Ammonium phosphate	90
Ammonium nitrate	100
Chlorine	50
Caustic soda	50
Vinyl chloride monomer	65
Hydrofluoric acid	70

TABLE 2 Operating data

Product	Capacity (tons/day)	Production rate (percent of capacity)	Natural gas consumption (1000 cu ft/ton)
Phosphoric acid	400	80	5.5
Urea	250	80	7.0
Ammonium phosphate	300	90	8.0
Ammonium nitrate	300	100	10.0
Chlorine	800	60	15.0
Caustic soda	1000	60	16.0
Vinyl chloride monomer	500	60	12.0
Hydrofluoric acid	400	80	11.0

profits. After detailed discussion, the meeting was adjourned. Two weeks later, the meeting reconvened. At this session, the above data were presented (Tables 1 and 2).

Coastal States' contract with Cajan Pipeline specified a maximum natural gas consumption of 36,000 cu ft $\times 10^3$ per day for all of the six member plants. With these data, the technical staff proceeded to develop a model that would specify changes in production rates in response to a natural gas curtailment. (Curtailments are based on contracted consumption and not current consumption.)

CASE DISCUSSION QUESTIONS

1. Develop a contingency model and specify the production rates for each product for (a) a 20 percent natural gas curtailment and (b) a 40 percent natural gas curtailment.

2. Explain which of the products in Table 2 should require the most emphasis with regard to energy conservation.

3. What problems do you foresee if production rates are not reduced in a planned and orderly manner?

4. What impact will the natural gas shortage have on company profits?

CASE 2 AMERICAN BRANDS, INC.*

Brad Holgate's early interest in soaps began when he discovered that he could make small amounts of it with his chemistry set. After graduating from college, Brad could not find a suitable job and decided it was time to go back to making soaps. Brad's uncle, Mr. Wilfred, who was running a drugstore in his hometown, agreed to put on his store shelves any soap that Brad might manufacture, provided he was satisfied with the quality and only after informal trials had been carried out.

Soap manufacture in small quantities does not require an elaborate setup—a few vats, ladles, a hearth, and the ability to judge when the soap is just right. Brad started with an initial investment of $350 to buy the necessary equipment and chemicals. After a few spoiled batches, Brad came out with a quality of bath soap satisfactory to him and he distributed these as free samples. The response was quite gratifying. The next batch was again distributed as free samples and the comments confirmed the results of the first trial. Two weeks later, in July 1964, "Bradbar" soap made its appearance at the corner drugstore. As Brad was his favorite nephew, Mr. Wilfred made special efforts to induce trial by his customers, particularly by those whose business he was confident of not losing even if the soap proved unsatisfactory. Things moved slowly for the first three weeks and Brad's soap looked like any other "also ran," when suddenly, in the next three days, not only the same customers started coming back for a repeat purchase but also their friends to whom it had been recommended. The shelves were swept clean within the week and Brad had to make a rush repeat order. Business began to grow until five years later Mr. Bradley Holgate, President, Holgate & Co. was selling bath soaps in five different brand names. Holgate and Company could now boast of twenty-three employees including one salesman and one salesman-cum-accountant. A large number of drug stores in Northeastern Delaware now carried Holgate products. However, Brad found the going tougher than ever be-

---

*This case was reprinted by permission of Holden Day from *Management Science Cases and Applications,* by Aggarwal and Khera, 1972.

fore. Though he firmly believed in, as he called it, the intrinsic worth of his product, he felt that the growth of his company was limited. He realized that he needed better organization and a stronger financial base. He would also be entering into a market where much larger and established companies were operating. Sandy, an old school friend and a successful businessman, was visiting him on a summer evening and, on listening to Brad's problems, he hinted that it might be worthwhile to investigate possible relations with some other company that might be in a similar situation. He knew of just such a company in the sourthern part of the state and offered to discuss the matter with them. In spite of Brad's earlier misgivings, Holgate and Lashley merged in 1968 to form American Brands, Inc., with a 65-35 partnership between Brad and Mr. Lashley. Mr. Lashley was getting on in years and was content with being the minority partner.

From 1969 onwards the sales of American Brands grew rapidly and so did their problems. (See Table 1). Although they had become larger, with gross sales at $8.2 million, and had a full-time Marketing Manager, Production Supervisor, and Controller, they were finding it difficult to meet the seasonal demands for their bath soaps. (See Figure 1). The consumption of bath soaps became particularly heavy during the summer months and rose considerably above winter month requirements. This heavy imbalance placed a severe strain on the production facilities in the one month preceding summer and caused production to slack off abruptly with the onset of winter. The problem was further complicated by the fact that American Brands has been marketing two product lines, regular and luxury. While the regular line had four product items, the luxury line had three. The projected demand for 1979 for the two product lines is given in Table 2.

Anthony Seagram, the Production Supervisor, frequently complained about losses incurred from the switching in production between the luxury and the regular lines of soap because of the seemingly capricious demands made by the Marketing Manager, Jack Daniels. No sooner did Anthony settle down to the production of one line, when Jack would come out with a change of priorities. Not only did this result in frequent stockouts of raw materials (as proper inventory planning was not possible) but it also caused a loss in production capacity. Each time the product line had to be changed from regular to luxury, some additional equipment had to be put in place, temperature control devices installed, and molds changed. It

TABLE 1 American Brands, Inc., gross sales*

1969	1970	1971	1972	1973	1974	1975
1.6	2.7	3.5	4.9	6.1	7.2	8.2

*Millions of dollars.

FIGURE 1 American Brands, Inc., organization chart

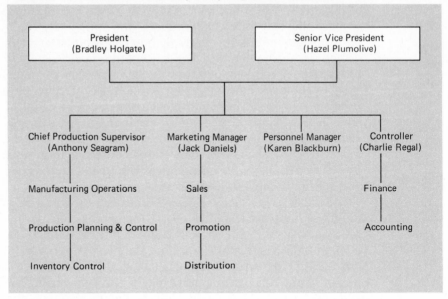

was Anthony's estimate that the changeover from regular to luxury meant a loss of two hours forty-five minutes and the change from luxury to regular caused a one hour loss. Additional time lost in trial runs when the product line was changed was, on the average, one hour for the luxury line, and one-half hour for the regular line. Frequent trial runs also resulted in a rise in the percentage of waste. Jack put the blame on Anthony and his production department who "were never able to produce enough and on time." He felt he had no control over demand and simply conveyed what the market demanded. He felt it was up to Anthony to figure out the ways and means to produce it. As it was, he complained, sales could easily be pushed up by at least 7% if only Anthony could produce orders on time, particularly those for the luxury items. Jack felt that the sales of luxury soaps could be increased by at least 5%, starting immediately. Not only did he feel that opportunities were being missed but also that sales were getting hurt by another 5% due to the ill will generated by delayed shipments. Charlie Regal, the Controller, was opposed to the idea of increasing production without an accurate estimate of expected sales. He regarded Jack's attitude as being unrealistic and wanted some additional long-term orders before he would okay any proposals for increased production. He contended that if Jack could forecast the demand better, loss in capacity could be reduced. Anthony tended to agree and said that he could produce, given proper batch runs, up to 180,000 cases per month,

TABLE 2 American Brands, Inc., 1979 sales forecasts*

Month	Regular	Luxury	Total
January	40	24	64
February	61	27	88
March	64	61	125
April	83	109	192
May	88	126	214
June	106	137	243
July	124	165	289
August	135	161	296
September	97	147	244
October	84	114	198
November	76	62	138
December	51	46	97
Total	1,009	1,179	2,188

*Sales given in thousands of cases.

and with overtime he could produce another 30,000 cases. Charlie, however, would not agree to overtime as this meant an additional cost per hour of $1.20. This increased cost would push up the costs per case by 80¢ for regular and $1.00 for luxury items. With storage charges at 10¢ per case per month, and the deterioration that might take place while in storage he felt the total cost may have become too high. Anthony, however, pointed out that bath soaps have a reasonably long shelf life (though the humidity in the warehouse would have to be increased slightly at a negligible cost) and consequently no deterioration was likely to occur. Jack was also opposed to overtime, as he feared that the increased manufacturing costs would necessitate higher prices which would, in turn, make his task even more difficult. If any overtime had to be resorted to, he did not want it during production of luxury items. It was his belief that any increase in its price in the present market would make it practically unsaleable. Anthony pointed out that it would not be possible for him to change to regular line production at the end of each day just so luxury soap would not be produced during overtime. The luxury brands would have to take their share of the overtime premium. However, he would try to avoid it as best as he could. Anthony, on the other hand, believed that the luxury line should be dropped altogether as the per case productivity for the regular line was 10% higher. Jack felt that it would be suicidal to drop the luxury items as it would have repercussions on the sales of the regular product also. Many of the stores would find it more convenient to drop both if one was discontinued and their main competitor in the region was looking for just such an opportunity. It was therefore decided not to drop the luxury line.

American's profits had increased by only 3% in 1978 whereas sales for the same year had increased by 14%. Anthony Seagram had to develop a production schedule that would indicate the number of cases of the regular and the luxury lines that should be produced each month during 1979. The objective was to have available enough soap of each grade to meet each month's forecasted demand while minimizing capacity loss, overtime production, and storage charges.

CASE DISCUSSION QUESTIONS

1. Develop a model that will enable American Brands, Inc., to determine an optimal production schedule.
2. Solve the model and specify the number of cases of the regular and the luxury lines that should be produced each month during 1979.

CASE 3 I. C. ENGINES, INC.*

I. C. Engines was incorporated in Delaware on June 30, 1924 as the successor to the Business of Steadfast, a Wisconsin manufacturer of internal combustion engines. The company is now a leading producer of high-speed diesel engines used to power trucks, busses, shovels, industrial locomotives, logging equipment, farm and mining machinery, electric generator sets, construction equipment, and various other off-highway machines. The manufacture of service parts is an important phase of the business; and the company also rebuilds its own engines and repair parts for resale. Engines are sold through a network of distributors in the United States, Canada, and abroad.

I. C. Engines, Inc., operates 68 plants and related facilities in 29 states, Canada, Mexico, Australia, and Western Europe. In addition, it has two industrial parts and warehouse facilities, and 160 other facilities, including repair and service shops, light manufacturing plants, and small warehouses throughout the United States and several foreign countries. During 1977, the company employed 23,800 individuals and had sales of $1,022,759,000. 63% of sales were accounted for by diesel engines, parts, and related products, while foreign sales contributed 37%. The sales volumes of the company for the past ten years are presented in Table 1.

---

*This case was reprinted by permission of Holden Day from *Management Cases and Applications,* by Aggarwal and Khera, 1972.

TABLE 1 I. C. Engines, Inc., annual sales ($000)

Year	Sales	Year	Sales
1974	$987,508	1969	$729,214
1973	862,103	1968	663,858
1972	707,299	1967	306,747
1971	636,741	1966	240,089
1970	665,637	1965	203,165

In January 1976, the company introduced a new model of a revolutionary, lightweight diesel engine designed for use in small-scale irrigation and power generation. The engine, Model SL350, was lighter and more fuel efficient than any other diesel engine of its kind in the world. Consequently, distributors in several countries had placed relatively large orders for this model. The brisk sales of the engines in three developing countries were also assisted by the low-cost loans of hard currency provided these countries by the United States Agency for International Development.

During the first few months of 1979, the SL350s seemed to be performing up to expectations even though one of the test engines at the company's Racine, Wisconsin plant had revealed certain weaknesses in the aluminum-tungston camshaft. By late April, several of the engines in the field had developed camshaft problems and Mr. Karl Benz, Chief Design Engineer at the Racine plant, was given the responsibility of correcting the problem.

Since Mr. Benz had already been working with the test engines, it took him and his team only six weeks to redesign the shaft to eliminate the weak spots in the original design. Once the new camshaft was exhaustively tested, Mr. Benz presented his new design to Don Biddle, Marketing Vice President, and Jim Bardi, Distribution Manager for overseas sales. He recommended that even though the expected failure rate for the old camshaft was expected to be only 6–7%, it would be advisable to replace the part in all the SL350 engines sold to date. Mr. Biddle agreed because future business in several foreign countries was at stake along with I. C. Engine's reputation for product quality. It was decided to start production of the new camshaft immediately and to finish the shipment of the new parts to service centers in all five of the company's zones within a five-week period. Mr. Bardi indicated that a total of 5,500 engines had been shipped to the five zones. After a lengthy discussion of the priorities concerning each zone, the following shipping schedule was agreed upon. (See Table 2).

Because of the complex nature of the shipment, only one order could be sent out in any one week. Consequently, even if all 9,000 units could be manufactured in one week, it would not be possible to ship more than one order during any given week. The North American zone therefore could

TABLE 2

Zone	Shipping Date	Units
South Asia	Week 1	2,000
Pacific	Week 2	1,000
North Africa	Week 3	1,000
South America	Week 4	3,000
North America	Week 5	2,000
Total		9,000

not receive its total needs for 2,000 camshafts before the fifth week even if they were manufactured during the first week. Mr. Benz indicated that once the production run began, the average variable cost of producing each new camshaft would be $35.00, if they were produced in runs of 1,000; otherwise the cost would be prohibitive because there would be a $1,500 start-up cost associated with each new production run. Thus, if all 9,000 units were produced during the first week's run, there would be a single start-up cost of $1,500. On the other hand, if each week's requirement was produced during that week, there would be a total start-up cost of $7,500.00. However, the total variable cost of production would be the same in either case (TVC = 9,000(35) = $315,000).

At this point Mr. Bardi, the Distribution Manager, indicated that even though it would be cheaper to produce all 9,000 units in a single run during the first week, he had a critical shortage of storage space. He estimated that it would cost him 70¢ to store a camshaft for one week. Thus, if all shafts were produced in a single run during the first week, then in addition to the $1,500 weekly start-up cost, the company would incur a storage charge for one week of $4,900 for 7,000 units not shipped during week 1, plus $4,200 for 6,000 camshafts not shipped during week 2, plus $3,500 storage for 5,000 units not shipped during week 3, and $1,400 storage charges for 2,000 camshafts not shipped during week 4. Thus, if all 9,000 camshafts were produced during week 1, the company would incur total storage fees of $14,000.

It was decided that Mr. Benz would calculate the appropriate production schedules to implement the program at a minimum cost to I. C. Engines, Inc.

CASE DISCUSSION QUESTIONS

1. Develop a model to determine the optimal production schedule for I. C. Engines, Inc.

2. Solve the model to determine specific production quantities in each of the 5 weeks.

CASE 4 EDGARTOWN FISHERIES*

On a rainy day in March 1969, Lars Dyson, M.B.A. '48, businessman and adventurer, president of Edgartown Fisheries, faces a difficult and perplexing decision problem.

Edgartown Fisheries is in the shark-fishing business and operates one fishing boat especially equipped for sharking in the North and Middle Atlantic. The Company was formed in order to exploit a technique which had previously been little used for shark fishing, a technique called "longline" fishing, in which arrays of long, baited lines are suspended from buoys. Dyson has now had a few years' experience using this technique, and he and his crew feel that they have acquired a substantial skill in catching shark this way. Nevertheless, he feels anxious about Edgartown Fisheries' future, largely because of uncertainties about the size of the catch and the price which the fish will command.

On this particular rainy day, Dyson has just received a letter from an Italian shark importer who offers to make a one-season contract with Edgartown Fisheries for 300,000 pounds of shark at 55 cents a pound, delivered in Italy. The shark is to be delivered by October 10, 1969, but Edgartown Fisheries may, under the terms of the proposed contract, divide the 300,000 pounds into partial shipments in any way it desires. Dyson has to decide whether or not to accept the contract within the next few days, and he has assembled the following information to help him with his decision.

SHARK PRODUCTION AND MARKET

The Atlantic sharking season runs from April 1 through October 31. However Edgartown Fisheries ordinarily obtains only about 120 days of active fishing, the other 90 days being spent either in port or traveling to and from the fishing grounds. (The travel and port time is somewhat affected by various factors, particularly the weather.) There are two distinct types of season. In a good season, Edgartown Fisheries can catch about 600,000 pounds of shark; in a bad season, about 480,000 pounds. The variation in the size of the catch from day to day is small enough to be ignored, so that Dyson is willing to think of his catch as being a constant 5,000 pounds per fishing day if the season is good or 4,000 pounds per fishing day if the season is bad. Thus it is possible to determine, after the first few weeks of the season have passed, whether the season will be good or bad. Unfortunately, it is impossible to tell ahead of the start of the season what kind of a season it will be.

*Copyright © 1975 by the President and Fellows of Harvard College. Reproduced by permission. This case was prepared by Richard F. Meyer.

TABLE 1   Anticipated price per pound of shark landed in New Bedford

Pacific catch	Atlantic catch	
	Large	Small
Large	30¢	35¢
Small	40¢	45¢

Shark is caught not only in the Atlantic but also in the Pacific, primarily by the Japanese. The price for Atlantic shark, therefore, depends not only on whether the Atlantic catch is large or small, but also on the size of the catch in the Pacific. Table 1 shows the price per pound which Dyson expects for shark landed in New Bedford (his home port) under each of the four conditions that may occur. For example, if Dyson encounters a large catch (5,000 pounds per day) and the Pacific catch turns out small, Dyson expects to receive 40 cents per pound landed in New Bedford.

As with the Atlantic catch, it is impossible to tell before the start of the season whether the Pacific catch will be large or small. However, after the first few weeks of the season have passed, the size of the Pacific catch to date provides a reliable indication of the rest of the season. Dyson's wife can obtain this information and radio it to him.

As he looks forward to the season, the four possible conditions that may occur all seem equally likely to Dyson, so he assigns them the probabilities given in Table 2.

SHIPPING TO ITALY

Dyson can store shark already caught in a cold-storage warehouse for as long as one season at essentially no cost. He is therefore not constrained to ship the fish to Italy as soon as they are caught. He can ship fish from New Bedford to Italy at a cost of 19 cents per pound by a standard freighter service offering weekly departures. Any one freighter will take all or any part of the 300,000-pound order.

TABLE 2   Probabilities of various catch sizes

Pacific catch	Atlantic catch	
	Large	Small
Large	.25	.25
Small	.25	.25

Alternatively, Dyson could ship the 300,000 pounds by sending his own vessel to Italy. His boat can carry only 150,000 pounds of shark packed in ice, so that two trips of his own boat would be required to deliver the entire shipment of 300,000 pounds. In each round trip to Italy, his boat would lose the equivalent of about 20 fishing days. (Note that the 300,000 pounds must be delivered before the end of the season.) In comparing the cost of operating his boat for fishing with the cost of operating his boat for transporting fish to Italy, Dyson finds that the additional fuel required to transport the fish just about balances the cost of the bait that would have been used in the corresponding time spent fishing. Use of the boat to transport the fish will actually reduce the cost of tackle, since no tackle will be used in a transport operation whereas tackle is regularly lost while fishing.

COSTS AND ASSETS

On April 1, 1969, at the start of the season, Dyson will have assets which, besides his boat and some office equipment, include $20,000 cash and 40 miles of ready-to-use tackle. Excluding tackle, his total costs for the entire fishing season (interest payment on boat mortgage, crew's wages, office rent, etc., and fuel and bait) will be about $160,000. Regarding tackle, in his normal fishing operations Dyson carries 20 miles of tackle on board his boat; the other 20 miles he has are stock he carries for replacement purposes. Loss of tackle turns out to depend directly not on the number of days of fishing, but rather on the number of pounds of shark caught. Based on past experience, Dyson knows that he will have to replace about one mile of tackle for every 50,000 pounds of shark caught. The cost of ready-to-use tackle (including hooks, buoys, radar reflectors, etc.) from Dyson's regular supplier is $1,000 per mile. However, 30 miles of Dyson's present tackle were purchased used from the estate of another shark fisherman in New Bedford at a cost of $22,500. This is the only instance that Dyson has ever encountered of used tackle being for sale, and he considers future availability of used tackle to be a virtual impossibility.

CASE DISCUSSION QUESTIONS

1. What basic decisions does Mr. Dyson have to make?
2. Construct and evaluate the decision tree for Mr. Dyson's problem.
3. Assuming Mr. Dyson is an EMVer, what is his optimal strategy?
4. How much money can Mr. Dyson expect to make during the coming season?

CASE 5 PIERCE AND PIERCE PUBLIC WAREHOUSE*

Jerry and John Pierce are making plans for their new public warehouse in Memphis, Tennessee. Presently, the Pierce brothers own and operate a public warehouse in Tulsa, Oklahoma. Their father, Sinclair Pierce, built it in 1948 and financed it by an inheritance received in 1946. Prior to the inheritance, Sinclair Pierce managed a supply depot for one of the major oil-drilling companies in Tulsa. The idea for a public warehouse originated because the drilling company received numerous requests from area industrial firms to store equipment and supplies in its large, well-secured depot warehouses. The oil-drilling company issued storage permits as a favor to area firms, but permits were always temporary and were quickly rescinded if the storage space was required by the drilling company. Hence, Sinclair Pierce had a "readymade" market for his warehouse in 1948.

Pierce's sons, Jerry and John, took over the management of the warehouse in 1967 when Sinclair retired after a minor heart attack. Jerry directs the operations of the warehouse, and John is primarily responsible for customer relations. Although each owns 50 percent of the company, their father appointed the elder son, Jerry, to the position of president and as the ultimate decision maker in the company's operations. Under this arrangement, the warehouse has enjoyed a great deal of success. The Tulsa warehouse was expanded by 50 percent in 1970. Clients are both private firms and public organizations, including the Tulsa County School Board and the City of Tulsa Streets and Parks Commission.

Because of the success of the Tulsa warehouse, the Pierce brothers have decided to build another facility in Memphis. The site was selected because Memphis is located at the intersection of Interstate Highways 55 and 40 and is located on the Mississippi River. Also, Memphis is one of the main hubs of the Illinois Central Railroad. Hence, in 1973, land was purchased to build the new facility on a spur of the ICRR in southeast Memphis.

A major factor in planning the new warehouse is the determination of the number of docking platforms to service the incoming and outgoing trucks. The Pierce brothers do not own any trucks, so the warehouse schedule is to be almost totally dependent upon the arrival of customer trucks and common carriers for receipt and shipment of equipment and supplies. (The warehouse will also receive and ship materials by rail,

---

*From *Cases in Production and Operation Management* by Iverstine and Kinard, Charles E. Merrill Publishing Company, Columbus, Ohio, © 1977.

but this activity can be accurately scheduled by working closely with the Illinois Central Railroad yard in Memphis.)

The frequency of arrival of customer trucks and common carriers, together with the time required to service these trucks, will determine the number of docking platforms and the number of docking crews that will be required. The number of docking platforms will determine the warehouse configuration and roadway design. The number of docking crews will dictate staffing requirements and the number of forklift trucks. (Typically, a forklift truck is used by each docking crew, and one or more are used for general warehouse operations.)

From market forecasts in the Memphis area and data from the Tulsa warehouse, four trucks per hour are expected to arrive for loading or unloading during the planned warehouse hours of 7:00 A.M. to 5:00 P.M. (Monday through Friday). The time required for servicing the trucks is expected to average 50 minutes, with a standard deviation of 15 minutes. With this information, the Pierce brothers believe that they can make docking and servicing plans.

CASE DISCUSSION QUESTIONS

1. How many docking platforms and servicing crews would you recommend for the new warehouse?

2. What nonquantitative factors would you include in this analysis?

3. What additional information would be helpful? How might you obtain this information?

CASE 6 BLANCHARD IMPORTING AND DISTRIBUTING CO., INC.*

Upon completing his first year at the Harvard Business School, Hank Hatch accepted summer employment with Blanchard Importing and Distributing Co., Inc., a Boston firm which dealt in the processing and wholesaling of alcoholic beverages. Early in June 1972, Hank had met with Toby Tyler, the general manager of the company, who was a recent graduate of

---

*This case was prepared by Alan H. Drinan under the supervision of Paul W. Marshall. Copyright © 1972 by the President Fellows of Harvard College. Reproduced by permission.

the Harvard Business School. Toby had described the initial tasks which he wished Hank to perform, as follows:

> Hank, during your first few days at Blanchard, I'd like you to become familiar with the general scope of operations of the firm. As you investigate our various product lines, I think you will find that the most rapidly expanding demand for alcoholic beverages is in the wine market. At the present time we estimate that we can earn a before-tax return of 20% on any money we put into wine merchandising. However, to date, Carmen Petrillo, our Wine Division manager, and Dave Rubin, the Sales Department manager, have been unable to exploit this trend due to lack of funds needed to hire experienced wine salesmen and build up an adequate inventory of wines. Here is a recent balance sheet [see Table 1] which shows that we have just about reached the limit of our borrowing capability. It appears that a reduction in inventory level is the only substantial source of funds available to us. That's where you come in.
>
> After you've become acquainted with our operations, I'd like you to spend some time analyzing the inventory situation and recommend ways in which we can economize in that area. Initially, you can look into the method we

TABLE 1   Blanchard Importing and Distributing Co., Inc., balance sheet as of January 31, 1972 (in thousands)

Assets		Equity	
Current Assets:		Current Liabilities:	
Cash	34	Payroll Withheld	1
A/R (net)	483	Unsecured Notes Payable	809
Inventory*	1,050	Accounts Payable	173
Prepaid Expenses	32	Federal Distilled Spirits Taxes Payable	337
Total Current Assets	1,589	Accrued Taxes	40
		Accrued Expenses	11
Fixed Assets:		Total Current Liabilities	1,371
Plant and equipment, net of depreciation	287	Long-Term Debt	64
		Total Liabilities	1,435
Registered trademarks	8	Stockholders' Equity:	
Total Fixed Assets	295	Capital Stock	100
		Retained Earnings	349
Total Assets	1,884	Total Equity	1,884

*Inventory was subdivided into the following categories:

Finished case goods (uncontrolled stock)	311
Finished case goods (controlled stock)	362
Customs bond (raw bulk and uncontrolled finished case goods stock)	171
IRS bond (raw bulk)	175
Miscellaneous (bottles, cartons, labels, flavors, etc.)	31

use in scheduling production runs of those beverages which we bottle ourselves. The current scheduling system, which was initiated in October 1969, calls for bottling of an Economic Order Quantity (EOQ) of an item when the stock level of that item falls below a fixed Re-order Point (ROP). This Re-order Point trigger level is equal to 3 1/2 weeks' worth of the average weekly demand throughout the year ending October 31, 1969. I suspect that many of the EOQ and ROP quantities calculated in 1969 should be recalculated based on changes in annual demand over the past 2 1/2 years. As a first assignment you can update the EOQ and ROP figures. While you're at it, keep thinking about ways in which we can reduce expenses and cut back on unnecessarily high stock levels—any cash which can be made available for wine merchandising will be greatly appreciated by Carmen and Dave.

BACKGROUND

Product Lines   During the first week of June, Hank learned that Blanchard was a full-line alcoholic beverage house which distributed both imported and domestic goods including wine, beer, distilled spirits, cordials, and pre-mixed cocktails. Blanchard purchased pre-bottled goods (called "uncontrolled stock") for resale to retail outlets at wholesale prices. Uncontrolled stock accounted for 45% of the firm's annual sales. The remaining 55% of Blanchard's revenue was attributed to sale of "controlled stock," those items which Blanchard bottled and sold under its own brands and private labels.

In June 1972, controlled stock consisted of 158 products which Blanchard processed in its own bottling facility. These 158 items were differentiated by bottle size, type and proof of beverage, and brand label. Blanchard produced 25 items in half-gallons, 63 in quarts, 42 in fifths, 12 in pints, and 16 in half-pints.

History of the Firm   The Blanchard name was originally established as a chain of retail liquor stores, the first of which was opened in 1938 by John D. Corey. In 1957, Mr. Corey became interested in the wholesaling of alcoholic beverages and began distributing case goods to retail outlets. In order to devote his full efforts to this new venture, he transferred ownership of the chain of Blanchard retail outlets to other members of the Corey family. In 1964, the present warehouse and office facility was completed, and in 1966, equipment was installed to permit the conversion of raw bulk spirits to bottled goods for sale under the firm's own brands and private labels. When Mr. Corey died in 1968, his son, John D. Corey, Jr., assumed responsibilities as president and treasurer of the company. As of June 1972, the firm's annual revenue was $4 million, of which $3 million represented sales to the seven Blanchard retail stores owned by other members of the Corey family.

Warehouse Layout Figure 1 depicts the layout of the recently completed Blanchard warehouse. Most of the warehouse space was set aside for stocks of bottled case goods. These areas included a large margin for future growth, and actual finished-goods inventories had never occupied more than 50% of the reserved space.

In addition to the areas set aside for storage of finished case goods, space was occupied by two U.S. bonded warehouses and the rectification and bottling equipment used for processing controlled stock. The government required that all products imported to the United States by Blanchard, including both prebottled goods and raw bulk spirits, enter the Blanchard facility by way of the Customs Bonded Warehouse. In addition, all the raw bulk spirits which Blanchard purchased for processing in its bottling operation were required to pass through the IRS Bonded Warehouse prior to rectification. The flow of goods into and out of the two bonded warehouses was closely monitored by federal officials to ensure that the required tax and customs duty obligations were met by the company.

FIGURE 1 Blanchard Importing and Distributing Co., Inc., warehouse layout

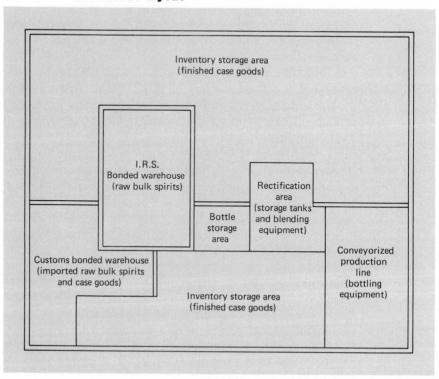

CONVERSION OF RAW BULK SPIRITS INTO BOTTLED CASE GOODS

In preparation for his first assignment, Hank made a thorough study of the method used by Blanchard to process controlled stock. Hank learned that two salaried employees, Bob Young and Eliot Wallace, were in charge of this operation. Bob Young, a skilled machinery operator, had worked for Blanchard since 1969, and Eliot Wallace, a chemistry expert with a degree in food technology, had worked for Blanchard for seven years. The combined annual wage of these two employees was $23,000. Bob and Eliot explained that the conversion process followed three steps: withdrawal of raw spirits from bulk storage, rectification of the spirits, and bottling of the finished product.

Withdrawal from Bulk Storage   Raw bulk was purchased by the barrel and stored either in the Customs Warehouse or the IRS Warehouse, depending on whether the spirits were imported or domestic. When a bottling run called for use of a particular type of raw bulk, Bob and Eliot withdrew the spirits from one of the two bonded warehouses and pumped it into mixing tanks for rectification; imports were withdrawn from the Customs Warehouse via the IRS Warehouse, incurring both a customs duty and federal distilled spirits tax liability, while domestic spirits incurred only the federal distilled spirits tax liability upon withdrawal from IRS Warehouse storage.

Rectification   Rectification of withdrawn bulk consisted of diluting the spirits with distilled water to attain the desired "proof," mixing several different types of spirits to form combinations such as blended whiskey, and adding nonalcoholic ingredients to yield cocktails such as screwdrivers and whiskey sours. Eliot Wallace was responsible for performing chemical tests on each rectified beverage to verify that the appropriate ratio of ingredients had been established before releasing the beverage to the bottling line.

Bottling   The bottling operation utilized a fully automated conveyorized line of equipment, including machines which filled each bottle, screwed on a cap, attached a brand label, and affixed the government seal which protected the consuming public against unauthorized opening of a container following bottling. Since 1966, the demand for controlled stock items had required operation of the bottling line less than one out of every three available working days. Thus, the capacity of the bottling line equipment was more than adequate to support the current level of sales. Bob Young was responsible for maintenance and repair of this equipment and verified the setup of each machine prior to initiating a bottling run.

Bob Young and Eliot Wallace worked together in completing all preparations for a bottling run, including the withdrawal and rectification of spirits and the setup of the bottling equipment for each size and label combination. When preparations were complete, Bob and Eliot were joined by five part-time workers drawn from the local area who were each paid $2.50 per hour. While Bob and Eliot supervised overall operation of the bottling line, these five laborers packed filled bottles into cartons, labeled and stamped each carton with appropriate information, and stacked the cartons on pallets for transfer to the controlled stock case goods storage area. The five temporary laborers were paid soon after completion of the bottling run.

Tax and Customs Duty Considerations   It was the practice at Blanchard to delay withdrawal of bulk spirits from storage in the two bonded warehouses until just before the start of a bottling run to avoid incurring tax and custom duty liabilities earlier than necessary. Consequently, the length of time between withdrawal of bulk spirits from storage and transfer of the bottled product to finished case goods storage never exceeded one week.

In addition to the federal distilled spirits tax and customs duty charge, two other taxes were levied against alcoholic beverages: a federal rectification tax was incurred during blending of certain items, depending on the mixing process, and a state tax was incurred upon sale of the finished product by Blanchard. Federal and state regulations required the company to pay the customs duty charge, federal rectification tax, and state tax within a few days after these liabilities were incurred; however, payment of the federal distilled spirits tax was not required until one month after sale.

FORMAL EOQ/ROP SCHEDULING SYSTEM

Before making corrections to the EOQ and ROP figures for each of the 158 items bottled by Blanchard, Hank located the documents showing how the formal scheduling system was developed in 1969. These records, which are reproduced in Table 2 indicate the general method used to determine EOQ and ROP quantities for each Blanchard product. During his review of the system, Hank made the following observations about the inputs to the EOQ calculations:

TABLE 2 Blanchard Importing and Distributing Co., Inc., EOQ and ROP calculation method

$$EOQ = \sqrt{\frac{2RS}{CK}} \qquad ROP = \frac{3.5}{52} \times R$$

where:

Annual demand, R:
Demand for an item for year ending October 31, 1969, in cases of bottles.

Setup cost, S:
Setup cost per bottle run of an item.

S = blending setup cost + size changeover cost + label changeover cost + order processing cost.

Blending setup cost = actual cost of labor for blending during rectification and is different for each item.

Size changeover cost = average cost of labor to reset all machines for a change in bottle size and is a constant $8.85 for all 158 items.

Label changeover cost = average cost of labor to reset labeling machine for a change in labels and is a constant $11.78 for all 158 items.

Order processing cost = average cost of administrative labor to process an order for a bottling run and is a constant $51.43 for all 158 items.

Unit cost, C:
Cost per case of bottles of an item after bottling and packaging.

C = materials cost + bottling labor + fixed overhead allocation + variable overhead + customs duty + federal distilled spirits tax + federal rectification tax.

Materials cost = cost of raw bulk, bottles, caps, and labels.

Bottling labor = cost of part-time bottling line labor per case of bottles produced and is a constant $0.10 per case for all 158 items.

Fixed overhead allocation = total company fixed overhead for the year divided by the number of cases sold per year and is a constant $1.31 per case for all 158 items.

Variable overhead = total direct expense (other than material and direct labor costs) resulting from production of one case of an item and is a constant $.50 per case for all 158 items.

Customs duty = charge on imported spirits and varies with the alcoholic content of the beverage.

Federal distilled spirits tax = IRS tax on all spirits sold in the United States and varies with the alcoholic content of the beverage.

Federal rectification tax = IRS tax on certain mixed beverages and varies with the alcoholic content of the item.

Carrying cost percentage, K:
Percent of average inventory value which represents annual cost of carrying inventory of an item.

K = cost of capital + other carrying costs.

Cost of capital = 9% for all items.

Other carrying costs, including estimated costs of obsolescence, shrinkage, insurance, and year-end inventory tax = 2.5% for all items.

693

Setup Costs, S   Blending setup cost was based on the annual salaries of Bob Young and Eliot Wallace and the length of time required for these men to withdraw the appropriate spirits from bulk storage and complete rectification for a given item.

Size changeover cost equaled the cost of resetting all machinery for a change in bottle size divided by the average number of different items of a given size processed between size changeovers.[1] The cost of resetting all machines for a change in bottle size was based on the annual salaries of Bob and Eliot and the fact that it took these two men one full day to complete all the machinery adjustments required for a size changeover.

Label changeover cost was based on the average length of time that the bottling line was shut down to change from one label to another label of a given bottle size. This idle time was assumed to be 30 minutes, which included 20 minutes to reset the labeling machine and 10 minutes to restore the labeling machine to continuous error-free operation following the change in labels. Since the part-time bottling laborers remained idle during the label changeover, the cost of this 30 minutes of downtime was based on both the hourly wage rate of these five workers and the annual salaries of Bob and Eliot.

Order-processing cost equaled the yearly cost of two office workers, who earned a combined annual salary of $18,000, divided by the total number of separate item-bottling runs per year. These two clerks worked full time processing the customs duty forms, federal tax forms, state tax forms, and other paperwork required to support the bottling operation.

Unit Cost, C   Blanchard used a standard form titled "Cost and Price Data" to determine the wholesale price per case of each item. This price was based on a "full unit cost" figure, which included all direct expenses incurred in producing and selling an item plus an allocation of the total fixed expenses of the company. Since the state tax liability was not incurred until sale of the finished product, the "unit cost" used in the EOQ formula was determined by deducting the state tax from the "full unit cost" figure shown on the Cost and Price Data form.

Carrying Cost Percentage, K   The only substantial component of the inventory carrying cost was the cost of capital. Equity was not considered a source of funds, since all common stock was privately held by John D. Corey, Jr., who wished to maintain full control of the company. As a re-

---

[1]In a typical year, Blanchard operated the bottling line for 77 days during the year. The bottling equipment was adjusted approximately 35 times during the year for a change in bottle size; however, an average of 10 different items of a given bottle size were processed between size changeovers, resulting in about 350 separate item-bottling runs during the year.

sult, the cost of capital was assumed to be 9%, the prevailing interest rate for debt available to Blanchard. Components of the carrying cost percentage other than cost of capital were small and amounted to only 2.5%.

ACTUAL SCHEDULING SYSTEM IN USE

Hank decided to make his first corrections to EOQ and ROP figures for the items to be produced during an upcoming bottling run. He learned that Bob and Eliot planned to bottle the following items during the last week in June:

Number of cases to be bottled	Item	Number of cases on hand as of June 20, 1972
1,000	Blanchard's 80 proof vodka (quarts)	144
600	Blanchard's 80 proof gin (quarts)	55
60	MacCoy & MacCoy 86 proof scotch (quarts)	54
120	Triple 7 86 proof blended whiskey (quarts)	301
50	Blanchard's 80 proof Ron Cores rum (quarts)	45

Hank then located the cost and price data and the original EOQ and ROP Calculation Sheets for these five items and summarized the data in tabular form (see Tables 3 and 4). Hank compared the annual demand for the year ending October 31, 1969 (see Table 1) with the monthly sales summary report for the fiscal year ending January 31, 1972 (see Table 5) and noted significant shifts in demand between the years ending October 1969 and January 1972, especially for the MacCoy & MacCoy Scotch and Ron Cores Rum products.

On June 21, Hank finished recalculating the EOQ and ROP figures and decided to find out how the schedule for the upcoming bottling run had actually been determined. He found Bob and Eliot in the blending area, where they were withdrawing corn spirits from the IRS Warehouse prior to rectification of Triple 7 Blended Whiskey, and questioned them about the schedule:

HANK: How did you decide on these particular items for next week's run, Bob?

BOB: Well, every week the computerized inventory control system issues us a card for each item that has dropped below the 3½-week ROP stock level. As of yesterday, we had several half-gallon and quart items which have dropped below their ROP levels, including the vodka and gin quart products scheduled for bottling next week.

	Blan-chard's 80 proof vodka	Blan-chard's 80 proof gin	MacCoy & MacCoy 86 proof scotch	Triple 7 86 proof blended whiskey	Blan-chard's 80 proof Ron Cores rum
Wholesale price	$43.99	$43.99	$57.39	$49.87	$47.39
Materials—beverage	.93	1.08	4.46	2.52	2.74
Materials—packaging	1.27	1.27	1.27	1.27	1.27
Direct labor	.10	.10	.10	.10	.10
State tax	10.08	10.08	10.08	10.08	10.08
Federal distilled spirits tax	25.20	25.20	27.09	27.09	25.20
Federal rectification tax				.76	
Customs duty			1.55		
Variable overhead	.50	.50	.50	.50	.50
Fixed overhead allocation	1.31	1.31	1.31	1.31	1.31
Full unit cost	$39.39	$39.54	$46.36	$43.63	$41.20
Profit before income tax	$4.60	$4.45	$11.03	$6.24	$6.19

HANK: Why don't you bottle both the half-gallon and quart items next week?

BOB: It takes Eliot and me just about one full day to make all the adjustments to the bottling equipment required for a size change. Consequently, we limit each bottling run to a single size and process several combinations of beverages and labels in that size during the run. Since quarts are our most popular size, we plan to bottle only quarts next week. We'll try to make a run of half-gallons in three weeks. Hopefully, the 3½-week advance notice will keep us from stocking out of any half-gallon items.

HANK: What about the rum, whiskey, and Scotch quart products: How did they get added to the schedule?

ELIOT: After we decided to bottle quarts based on the low gin and vodka inventories, we checked the stock level for each of the remaining 61 quart items. We're going to try to make a run of quarts every four weeks for the next two months. So the June 20 stock level of any quart item which we *don't* schedule for bottling next week has to last at least six weeks until the following run is completed at the end of

TABLE 4 Blanchard Importing and Distributing Co., Inc., summary of EOQ and ROP calculation sheet data

	Blending setup cost	All other setup costs	Total setup cost (S)	Annual demand (R)	Carrying cost (%) (K)	Unit cost (C)*	EOQ $\sqrt{\dfrac{2RS}{CK}}$	ROP $\left[\dfrac{3.5}{52} \times R\right]$
Blanchard's 80 proof vodka	$1.15	$72.06	$73.21	2,455	11.5%	$29.31	327	165
Blanchard's 80 proof gin	1.08	72.06	73.14	1,421	11.5%	29.46	248	96
MacCoy & MacCoy 86 proof scotch	3.24	72.06	75.30	800	11.5%	36.28	170	54
Triple 7 86 proof blended whiskey	2.62	72.06	74.68	3,096	11.5%	33.55	346	208
Blanchard's 80 proof Ron Cores rum	2.33	72.06	74.39	449	11.5%	31.12	137	30

*Unit cost (C) = Full unit cost (see Table 3) minus state tax (Table 3).

July. The stocks of MacCoy Scotch, Triple 7 Whiskey, and Ron Cores Rum were all below the six-week level when we checked yesterday, so we added them to the list.

HANK: How, do you minimize the length of time that the line is idle when you shift from one item to another?

ELIOT: We process the lighter beverages first, so that we can switch from one item to the next with only a few bottles of distilled water in between to rinse the bottling machine. As a result, the bottling machine is ready after about only eight minutes of rinsing. We have sixteen tanks for storing rectified beverages prior to bottling which have a combined volume equivalent to 10,000 cases of half-gallons, quarts, pints, or half-pints. This is more than enough storage capacity for all items scheduled for a single bottling run. Since Bob and I finish rectification of all beverages during the week before a scheduled bottling run, each item is always ready when the schedule calls for bottling to begin. No adjustment for bottle shape is necessary, since we only run one size at a time and each size has a standard shape. That leaves label changeover as the controlling item; right, Bob?

BOB: Yes, every time we shift from one item to the next, I have to adjust the labeling machine and load in a stack of labels for the new item. This takes about 20 minutes, and during that time, the five part-time workers are idle. Once in a while the labels for two items in a row are the same shape, which permits me to make the change in about three minutes. At any rate, Eliot usually finishes purging the bottling machine and completes the shift to the new blending storage tank well before I have the labeling machine ready to resume bottling.

HANK: Once you have decided on the items you intend to bottle and the order in which you intend to bottle them, how did you determine the number of cases of each item to process? Did you use the EOQ figure that was calculated in 1969 when the scheduling system was originally developed?

BOB: Not exactly, Hank. Since we'll probably be bottling quarts every four weeks for a while, we tried to predict what the demand for each item will be between runs; then we took into account the inventory on hand and scheduled production of enough cases to last until the next scheduled bottling run for quarts.

HANK: How did you go about predicting what the demand for each item will be?

BOB: We used the data from the monthly sales summary [see Table 5] to see what the demand was last month. Then we adjusted this May 1972 sales figure by adding a safety factor to offset any difference between sales in May and July.

TABLE 5   Blanchard Importing and Distributing Co., Inc., monthly sales summary data (in cases of quart bottles) (February 1971–May 1972)

		Feb.	Mar.	Apr.	May	June	July	Aug.	Sept.	Oct.	Nov.	Dec.	Jan.	Year total
Blanchard's 80 proof vodka	(1971)	128	136	233	219	284	343	368	230	162	246	252	114	2,715
	(1972)	210	303	275	463									
Blanchard's 80 proof gin	(1971)	51	52	74	157	150	257	179	83	72	89	181	42	1,387
	(1972)	166	142	133	213									
MacCoy & MacCoy 86 proof scotch	(1971)	79	82	151	66	127	96	85	61	67	103	131	39	1,087
	(1972)	82	68	66	38									
Triple 7 86 proof blended whiskey	(1971)	163	180	198	183	217	207	186	171	205	266	257	654	2,887
	(1972)	177	163	162	256									
Blanchard's 80 proof Ron Cores rum	(1971)	10	34	44	26	33	35	51	16	15	26	43	22	355
	(1972)	11	28	61	55									

HANK: Then the planned production volume for each of the five items scheduled for bottling next week represents your predicted demand for July, with an adjustment made for the current inventory on hand?

BOB: Yes, except for the gin and vodka. We're finding it difficult to accurately predict demand for these two items because sales are up substantially from last year. So we've decided to bottle enough gin and vodka to last us *two* months, through the end of August. If our predicted sales volumes for gin and vodka are correct, we can omit production of these products during the July bottling run of quarts and save the cost of blending and label changeover for these two items. However, if demand continues to spiral and exceeds our prediction, we can add these items to the July schedule and avoid a stockout.

CONCLUSION

The day after Hank's discussion with Bob Young and Eliot Wallace, Toby Tyler asked Hank to report what he had accomplished on his first assignment and to recommend appropriate action based on his findings. Hank realized that the scheduling system in use bore little resemblance to the formal EOQ/ROP system developed in 1969. In preparation for his meeting with Toby, Hank decided to evaluate the disadvantages of both the original scheduling system and the improvised system developed by Bob and Eliot. Based on this analysis, Hank felt that he could determine if improvements could be made which would warrant adoption of one of the two systems on a permanent basis.

CASE DISCUSSION QUESTIONS

1. What is wrong with applying the Basic EOQ Model to the inventory problem at Blanchard?
2. Why isn't the EOQ Model currently being used for making replenishment decisions?
3. What are the shortcomings of the present system for determining replenishment quantities and production scheduling?
4. How would you approach the problem?

CASE 7 FORECASTING THE DEMAND FOR PLASTIC WET PANTS AT TINY TOGGS COMPANY*

The third stockout of sheet plastic in the past five months, and the sixth in 14 months, had just occurred. Mr. Dave Chatham, tri-owner and sole operating manager of Tiny Toggs Company, was turning over in his mind the inventory control policy he had practiced the past 14 months.

Until now my primary concern has been to keep a minimum amount of working capital tied up in inventory. Perhaps this latest stockout is enough to convince me that this policy, at least in the long run, is 'penny wise and pound foolish.' Stockouts cost money too. Maybe it's about time I gave a little thought to planning my inventory, both raw materials and finished goods. Before this third stockout, anyone would have had a hard time convincing me that I could or should slow down long enough to plan ahead. I had always felt that taking the time to plan was a luxury I couldn't afford. The costly experience of all these stockouts has taught me that I can't afford not to take time to plan. I guess I had better give a little thought to forecasting the demand for sheet plastic, the material from which my most profitable item (plastic wet pants) is made.

HISTORY OF THE COMPANY

With the assistance of a Small Business Administration (SBA) loan, Tiny Toggs Company was founded 14 months ago by Dave Chatham and his two younger brothers, Pat and Mac. The company produces infant wear and related items. The company initially had 15 items in its product line but it has produced as many as 50 different items over the past 14 months. The product line presently includes such infant wear as plastic wet pants and infant-related items such as terry cloth-covered pillows and nursery calendars made from terry cloth. The Chatham brothers are presently dropping many of the items from the product line because production capacity is limited and because many of the items were originally produced only as a means of "building up" business. The plastic wet pants have been particularly successful in the market. The brothers are there-

---

*This case was prepared by Professor Bill D. Fortune of Texas A&M University and Professor Brian Belt of the University of Missouri-Kansas City as a basis for classroom discussion and not to illustrate either effective or ineffective handling of an administrative situation. The case was presented at a Southern Case Research Association workshop.

fore dropping many of the other items in the product line to concentrate on this item. To date, despite the six costly stockouts of sheet plastic, the company has made a significant profit each of the 14 months. The brothers expect profits to increase with the reduction of the product line because of the subsequent reduction in the production costs associated with a broad line (e.g., set up costs, lost efficiency of the workers changing from the production of one item to another, inventory costs, better utilization of the industrial sewing machines used to produce the infant wear and other items, etc.).

The three brothers had extensive experience in the manufacture of infant-related items before founding their own company. Dave and Mac, for instance, worked in their father's company, Tidy Ties Corporation, a manufacturer of various infant products. Pat also worked in his father's company and later owned his own company, which manufactured infant night lights and lamps, before joining his two brothers. Dave handles the production of the "baby things" while Pat and Mac handle the marketing of them. The largest markets for the company's products are in California and New York. Thus, Pat lives in Los Angeles and Mac lives in New York City where they call on their existing customers to take orders and call on prospective customers. The largest customers of the company consist of infant wear specialty stores and department stores.

The company employs 22 people, all of whom work an 8-hour, 5-day week. Fifteen of these people operate the industrial sewing machines used to produce various items in the product line: one pattern cutter cuts all the different materials used in making the plastic wet pants and other articles; three people work in the shipping room packing filled orders and marking their destination: two people keep the sewing machine operators supplied with materials; and, one person serves as secretary and receptionist for the company. Although Dave has recognized the need of an assistant for managing the operations of the company, he has had no success in finding a person with the desired qualifications.

The company's production facilities are located in a three story building that used to be a hotel. The Chatham brothers purchased the hotel and personally redesigned its interior to suit their needs. Space is limited in the building which, in addition to keeping a minimum amount of working capital tied up in inventory, accounts for the need to keep raw materials and finished goods inventories at the lowest practical levels.

PROCESS STEPS FOR MAKING PLASTIC WET PANTS

The manufacturing process for making plastic wet pants consists of four steps: cut pattern into two triangular shaped pieces, sew the pieces together on an industrial sewing machine, trim the excess plastic from around the waist and leg openings, and sew a colored border (blue, pink, or yellow made of net material) around the waist and leg opening. The plastic pants are made in three sizes (small, medium, and large) which all require the same process steps. Dave estimated that an average of 5000 pounds of sheet plastic is used during peak demand periods (or months) for plastic pants. "The problem," he said, "is to determine when these peak monthly demand periods will occur."

NATURE OF THE PLASTIC WET PANTS INDUSTRY

Tiny Toggs Company is only one of about three companies with the production capacity capable of supplying the large quantities of plastic wet pants demanded by the purchasers of this item. It is characteristic of the purchasers of plastic wet pants to purchase all their requirements from a single source, if possible, in order to reduce ordering costs. The industry is very price competitive. The purchasers of plastic wet pants desire a quick delivery of their orders. Dave estimated that failure to fill an order within 1–2 weeks after it is received is "really pushing your luck." While the quality of the pants is important, quality control is not a problem.

NATURE OF THE SHEET PLASTIC INDUSTRY

Sheet plastic is available in 125 pound rolls. Each roll is approximately 2 feet in diameter and 54 inches long. The plastic now sells for 67 cents a pound but the price increases about 5 cents every 6 months. The delivery time presently averages 2–3 weeks but has been as long as 8–9 weeks. The variation in the delivery time of the sheet plastic does not follow any discernible pattern. Although there is more than one supplier of sheet plastic, the difference in their prices and delivery times do not favor any one supplier.

INVENTORY AND PRODUCTION CONTROL OF PLASTIC WET PANTS

Sheet plastic is the primary material or component item from which plastic wet pants is made; therefore, the demand for sheet plastic is dependent on sales of the wet pants. Because of the dependent demand of sheet plastic and because plastic wet pants has been the best selling and most profitable item in the company's product mix, Dave is most concerned with planning and controlling the inventory and production of this item. Sales have generally increased over the 14-month history of the company but have fluctuated from month to month (see Table 1).

TABLE 1 Monthly sales of plastic wet pants (in dozens)

Month	Sales
September	1514
October	2321
November	1258
December	3010
January	3278
February	4762
March	4972
April	4051
May	4683
June	2378
July	2646
August	2854
September	3963
October	2860

In the past, Dave has used what he refers to as the "eyeball-method" of controlling the inventory of sheet plastic. When asked to explain this method of inventory control, he replied, "My goal has been to keep inventory as low as possible. However, whenever it looked as if inventory was getting too low, more was ordered." Further explanation of the "eyeball-method" by Dave revealed that the method was in no way similar to a min-max or two-bin inventory system. Also, Dave makes no reference to past sales before purchasing additional plastic. Thus, systematically determined order points and order quantities are not used to determine how much plastic to order or when to order it.

It was only after the latest stockout that Dave began to compile and to tabulate the monthly sales of plastic wet pants. Prior to this time, sales figures were available only by a difficult and time consuming search of the sales invoices. Still, at this time, however, the sales data have not been broken down by pant size or by customer. Because of this, Dave could only estimate that the monthly sales figures presented in Table 1 represent an approximately equal number of small, medium, and large pant sizes, that approximately 35 percent of the sales were made to three customers, and that the remainder of the sales were made to approximately 15 customers.

The company does all of its manufacturing of plastic wet pants to customers' orders. That is, the company does not start producing the pants until first a firm order is received from Pat or Mac in the field, specifying the number of pants, the size(s), the color(s) of the borders, and the suggested delivery date. According to Dave, "We usually have orders up to our capacity so we're continuously producing plastic pants."

Dave described the production rate of plastic pants as "full out." He had no idea how long it took to produce a single pair of pants. With the present product mix, he roughly estimated that 5000 dozen pants is the maximum he can produce in a month. He again roughly estimated that he could almost double the production of pants if he stopped producing the items mentioned earlier, resulting from "freeing up" the industrial sewing machines.

The first step in order processing is to calculate the amount of sheet plastic required. The plastic requirements for each size of pants are multiplied by the number of pants of each size that has been ordered by the customer. This provides the total sheet plastic requirements, assuming no process losses. This figure is increased by about 2 percent for each order to provide for losses in the manufacturing process. Once the amount of plastic is determined for an order, then Dave checks, by using the above-mentioned eyeball-method, to see if enough sheet plastic is on hand to satisfy the order. If not enough, he orders more sheet plastic. The slight differences in the pant sizes (small, medium, and large) do not significantly affect the amount of sheet plastic required to satisfy an order. Consequently, when ordering sheet plastic, Dave always orders enough to produce all large size pants. This procedure insures enough plastic to produce any proportion of sizes and generally allows for manufacturing process losses.

The basic production scheduling rule is first come, first served. Because there has been no attempt to forecast the demand for sheet plastic, Dave has no planned production schedule.

STOCKOUT COSTS

Dave stated that he had not explicitly considered all of the costs associated with a stockout but he said that he believed they would be "quite high." He found that the local supply of experienced industrial sewing machine operators was in short supply. The stockouts only complicated this problem, for Dave estimated that 3 percent of the operators he had to "lay off" (or furlough) each time a stockout occurred did not return to work when a new supply of plastic was received. He also estimated that it cost him $1,800.00 to train each replacement for those laid off operators who did not return to work. The production efficiency of those operators who return to work is lowered because they tend to lose their rhythm when they do not operate their machines each work day.

Dave is not aware of the company losing any of its present customers because of the stockouts. But, he does know that the company has lost at least seven potential longstanding customers who called another supplier when Dave could not fill their orders during the stockout.

CASE DISCUSSION QUESTIONS

1. Suggest and defend a model appropriate for forecasting the demand for plastic wet pants in the short run and the long run.

   You may find the following comments by James L. Riggs (author of *Production Systems: Planning, Analysis, and Control,* New York: John Wiley and Sons, Inc., 1976, p. 93) helpful in directing the discussion of this question:

   > **Cost versus benefits is always a critical issue to management, and forecasting is no exception, although the dollar values are less certain than in most other management decisions. First, a manager has to estimate losses that might accrue from inaccurate forecasts; this is essentially a forecast of the forecasting results—uncertainty compounded. Then the manager must evaluate forecasting methods in terms of practicality and cost. A balance is sought between making the best use of data to meet real needs and applying costly techniques that promise potentially greater accuracy but may require more information and competence than is available.**

   Riggs (pp. 92–93) states that the selection of a forecasting method, or model, may depend on any or all of the factors listed below:

   a. Availability and accuracy of historical data

   b. Degree of accuracy expected from the prediction

   c. Cost of developing the forecast

   d. Length of the prediction period

   e. Time available to make the analysis

   f. Complexity of factors affecting future operations

2. Use the simple exponential smoothing model to forecast the demand for plastic wet pants in November. What value of the smoothing constant did you use for forecasting the demand? Why?

3. Use the straight-line trend model to forecast the demand for plastic wet pants for each of the next two months.

CASE 8 McCULLOUGH-HYDE HOSPITAL*

The McCullough-Hyde Hospital serves the needs of the residential community of Oxford, Ohio and the surrounding area with an approximate total population of 30,000. The hospital also meets the needs of Miami University with a student enrollment of approximately 15,000.

In 1976 the hospital acquired a new administrator and a corresponding desire to make some improvements in hospital operation. One project that is of current interest to hospital administration is the consideration of a possible restructuring of the hospital admissions procedure.

For the purpose of processing admissions, the hospital could categorize its patients as follows:

1. Emergency Patient
   a. Acute
      There is a possibility of the loss of life or limb, or there is extreme pain. Immediate treatment is obviously required.
   b. Regular
      There is no threat of the loss of life or limb if the patient is not treated immediately, but patient discomfort suggests that treatment is currently required.
2. Inpatient
      An overnight stay at the hospital is expected for this patient.
3. Outpatient
      This would include patients coming in for X-rays, lab work, minor surgery, physical therapy, or nuclear medicine.

At the present time the admissions procedure at the hospital does not have a common location in the building for all patient categories. In particular, the inpatient admitting location is separated from the combined emergency and outpatient admitting location. This is of concern to hospital administration because they believe that the separation of admission locations leads to more complex paper flows and attendant inefficiencies.

Inpatient admitting is located on the first floor of the hospital among various business offices, and it seems to be somewhat difficult to find. The

---

*Copyright © 1977 by Miami University. Reproduced by permission.

office is relatively small and not particularly pleasant. It was pointed out by a hospital administrator that a patient confined to a wheelchair is unable to fit the wheelchair into the office.

The inpatient admitting office is staffed by one person from 8 A.M. to 4 P.M. seven days a week and additionally from 4 P.M. to 8 P.M. on Monday through Friday only. The majority of scheduled inpatients arrive before 4 P.M. (See the arrival pattern for the periods indicated in Tables 1–6.) Any patient arriving after 8 P.M. is admitted by the switchboard operator or other workers on the evening shift in the business office.

The duties of the inpatient admitting office worker include filling out admission forms, scheduling admittances, making room assignments, and constructing patients' hospital bracelets. Much of the inpatient processing work can be performed before a patient arrives; such as, the partial typing of the admission form, constructing the hospital bracelet, etc. (See Table 7 for a copy of the inpatient admission form.) The worker on the 4 P.M. to 8 P.M. shift is a part-time worker and when not admitting patients performs typing and filing duties.

Outpatient and emergency admitting share a common location in the basement of the hospital. This area is easily accessible through a door from the hospital parking lot which is located in the rear of the building. The doorway is clearly marked and the area is easily found by those using the parking lot. The admissions area is spacious.

The combined outpatient and emergency admitting duties are performed by one person on each of two shifts, i.e., 8 to 4 and 4 to 12 during the seven day week. Those patients arriving between midnight and 8 A.M. (i.e., emergency patients) are admitted by the night nurse. During the 8 to 4 shift there is an additional person who shares the admitting office and works on hospital billing.

The bulk of the duties of the admitting personnel for outpatients and emergency patients consists of typing the admission forms and logging them as they occur. When not occupied with the admitting function, the clerks work on Blue Cross billings and sort hospital charges.

Emergency patients proceed from the admission area to a treatment area. Acute emergencies are treated immediately. Regular emergencies not requiring immediate treatment wait in an area adjacent to the admitting desk until a physician is available.

After outpatients have their admissions form filled out, they proceed to the outpatient receiving desk and waiting room which is located a short distance down a hall from the admitting area (see Figure 1). Here the patients wait to receive treatment. This area is clearly marked, spacious, and attractive. The receiving desk is staffed by a secretary from 8 A.M. to 4 P.M. six days a week. After 4 P.M. or on Sunday one of the technical staff directs the patients to the appropriate treatment room.

TABLE 1 Average arrivals per hour; emergency (regular); (March 14, 1976–May 13, 1976)

Hour ending	Weekdays*	Weekends**
1 AM	.327	.576
2	.311	.412
3	.218	.206
4	.156	.206
5	.124	.224
6	.109	.124
7	.218	.188
8	.327	.494
9	.264	.371
10	.684	.576
11	.467	.782
12	.498	.782
1 PM	.544	1.441
2	.467	1.482
3	.513	1.400
4	.622	1.812
5	.778	.947
6	1.338	1.523
7	1.353	1.441
8	.949	1.359
9	.933	1.029
10	.949	.576
11	.716	.988
12	.467	.453

*Average over 45 weekdays
**Average over 17 weekends

TABLE 2 Average arrivals per hour; emergency (acute); (March 14, 1976–May 13, 1976)

Hour ending	Weekdays*	Weekends**
1 AM	.140	.247
2	.133	.176
3	.093	.088
4	.067	.088
5	.053	.070
6	.046	.053
7	.093	.106
8	.014	.212
9	.113	.159
10	.293	.247
11	.200	.335
12	.213	.335
1 PM	.233	.618
2	.200	.635
3	.220	.600
4	.267	.776
5	.333	.406
6	.573	.653
7	.580	.618
8	.407	.582
9	.400	.441
10	.407	.247
11	.307	.424
12	.200	.194

*Average over 45 weekdays
**Average over 17 weekends

TABLE 3 Average arrivals per hour; emergency (regular); (July 15, 1976–August 14, 1976)

Hour ending	Weekdays*	Weekends**
1 AM	.133	.28
2	.100	.21
3	.100	.49
4	.100	.14
5	.067	.07
6	.167	.07
7	.067	.00
8	.333	.21
9	.600	.70
10	.667	.77
11	.733	.91
12	.567	.84
1 PM	.900	1.19
2	.700	1.12
3	.600	1.26
4	.733	1.12
5	.767	1.26
6	1.067	1.19
7	1.200	1.12
8	.967	1.19
9	.900	1.61
10	1.100	.77
11	.833	.77
12	.200	.49

*Average over 21 weekdays
**Average over 10 weekends

TABLE 4 Average arrivals per hour; emergency (acute); (July 15, 1976–August 14, 1976)

Hour ending	Weekdays*	Weekends**
1 AM	.057	.12
2	.043	.09
3	.043	.21
4	.043	.06
5	.029	.03
6	.071	.03
7	.029	.00
8	.112	.09
9	.257	.3
10	.286	.33
11	.314	.39
12	.243	.36
1 PM	.386	.51
2	.300	.48
3	.257	.54
4	.314	.48
5	.329	.54
6	.457	.51
7	.514	.48
8	.414	.51
9	.386	.69
10	.471	.33
11	.357	.33
12	.086	.21

*Average over 21 weekdays
**Average over 10 weekends

TABLE 5 Average arrivals per hour; inpatient; (March 1976)

Hour ending	Weekdays*	Saturday**	Sunday***
1 AM	.174	.250	0
2	.348	.500	.250
3	.087	.250	.750
4	.130	.250	.250
5	.261	0	0
6	.130	0	0
7	.043	.250	.250
8	.174	0	.250
9	.348	.250	0
10	.478	1.500	.500
11	.826	1.250	0
12	.739	.750	0
1 PM	1.478	.500	1.750
2	1.565	.250	2.000
3	1.043	0	1.250
4	.522	.250	.500
5	.826	0	.250
6	.696	.500	1.000
7	.522	0	0
8	.435	.250	.500
9	.348	.250	.750
10	.391	0	.250
11	.261	.250	1.000
12	.304	0	0

*Average over 23 weekdays
**Average over 4 Saturdays
***Average over 4 Sundays

In the past, there has been some confusion in the outpatient receiving area in that some patients entering through the back door go directly to the area to wait for treatment and do not have their admission forms processed. These patients are quite disappointed, when, after waiting for treatment for some time, they discover that they must return to the outpatient-emergency admitting area to be admitted before they can receive treatment.

Hospital administration was currently considering the relocation of inpatient admitting and wondered what impacts various possible new locations might have on the admitting function and overall hospital efficiency. There were a number of alternative locations for inpatient admitting that seemed reasonable. A few of the possibilities are as foll ws:

TABLE 6 Average arrivals per hour; outpatient; (February 8, 1976–February 25, 1976)

Hour ending	Weekdays*	Saturday**	Sunday***
1 AM	0	0	0
2	0	0	0
3	0	0	0
4	0	0	0
5	0	0	0
6	0	0	0
7	.538	0	0
8	4.000	0	.667
9	2.385	1	0
10	2.230	3	.333
11	2.846	1.5	.667
12	1.385	1	0
1 PM	1.538	0	0
2	2.462	0	0
3	2.538	0	.333
4	3.154	0	.333
5	1.538	0	0
6	1.231	0	0
7	1.923	0	0
8	.231	0	0
9	.154	0	0
10	.154	0	0
11	0	0	0
12	0	0	0

*Average over 13 weekdays
**Average over 2 Saturdays
***Average over 3 Sundays

1. Combine inpatient, outpatient, and emergency admissions at the present location of outpatient and emergency admissions in the hospital basement.
2. Combine inpatient and emergency admissions at the present location of outpatient and emergency admissions and relocate outpatient admissions to the present outpatient receiving desk area.
3. Perform the three patient category admitting functions at three separate locations in a common area in the hospital basement.
4. Retain outpatient and emergency admissions at their present location in the basement and relocate inpatient admissions to a nearby location in the basement.

TABLE 7 Admission Record

								DISCHARGE DATE	TIME:	AM PM	NO. DAYS
THE McCULLLOUGH-HYDE MEMORIAL HOSPITAL (513) 523-2111 OXFORD, OHIO 45056					**ADMISSION RECORD**						

PATIENT INFORMATION	ADMISSION NO	ADMISSION DATE	TIME	ROOM NO.	BED	SERV. CODE	SERVICE	PHYSICIAN CODE	ADMITTING PHYSICIAN'S NAME	PRI.P	ADM.CLERK

PATIENT'S NAME (*LAST, FIRST, M*)	BIRTHDATE	AGE	SEX	M W S D ☐☐☐☐	REL. CODE	RELIGION	RACE	BIRTH PLACE

ADDRESS (*STREET, CITY, STATE*) — ZIP — AREA C — TELEPHONE NO.

NEXT OF KIN — RELATIONSHIP/ADDRESS — TELEPHONE NO.

PATIENT'S OCCUPATION — EMPLOYER — TELEPHONE NO.

EMPLOYER'S ADDRESS (*CITY, STATE, ZIP*) — HOW DID PATIENT ARRIVE? — PUBLICITY? YES ☐ NO ☐

ADMITTING DIAGNOSIS — PHYSICIAN

MEDICARE NO. SUBSCRIBER PLAN B — PAT. SOC. SEC. NO. — GUARANTORS PH. NO. — PRIV. SERV | ADM. DIA. | ADM CLASS | PLAC ACCD | DISC. — PREV. REC. NO

GUARANTOR'S NAME — RELATIONSHIP — ATTN: PHY. CODE — ATTENDING PHYSICIAN — GUAR. SOC. SEC. NO.

GUARANTOR'S ADDRESS (*CITY, STATE*) — ZIP — GUARANTOR'S OCCUPATION

BLUE CROSS NO. — SUBSCRIBER — CITY PLAN How Pd. — EMPLOYER NAME — REL | EFF. DATE

ACCIDENT DATE | TIME AM PM | TYPE OF ACCIDENT — EMPLOYER'S ADDRESS (*CITY, STATE, ZIP*) — PHONE No.

COMMERCIAL INSURANCE: — POLICY NO. — ADDRESS: CITY — STATE — ZIP

CASE NAME — CASE NO: — NUMBER — PROGRAM — COUNTY — STATE

CLAIM NO. — DATE OF INJURY — EMPLOYER AT TIME OF INJURY: — ADDRESS:

SPOUSE'S EMPLOYER, CARRIER & POLICY NO. — ADDRESS

NAME AT TIME OF ADMISSION — DATE — DISCHARGED WITHIN 60 DAYS FROM: — HOSPITAL/E.C.F. (NAME & ADDRESS) — WHEN?

DISCHARGE DIAGNOSIS:

SURGICAL PROCEDURES:

CONSULTATIONS:

DISCHARGE SUMMARY:

THIS IS TO CERTIFY THAT I HAVE REVIEWED THE CONTENTS OF THIS RECORD AND TO THE BEST OF MY KNOWLEDGE IT IS ACCURATE AND COMPLETE

713

FIGURE 1 **Locations of admitting and receiving areas**

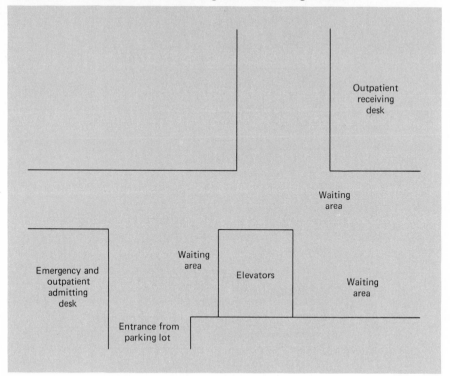

Hospital administration realized that there were a number of considerations that might be relevant for the best choice of locations for admissions for the various patient categories:

1. Combining inpatient, outpatient, and emergency admitting in a common location would allow personnel to be interchanged during times of peak loads for the various patient categories. It would centralize the admitting procedure at one location with the associated convenience of having all admitting paperwork in that one location. It would certainly be less confusing for patients in that all patients would report to a common location.

   There were some drawbacks associated with this merger. Although the necessary space was available, conditions would be more crowded than before, and there was some concern over a lack of privacy for patients being admitted. In particular, the administration felt that it would be desirable for inpatients to have a separate room in which to discuss the medical history required for admission. The other major

714

concern regarding the common location was the possible confusion and associated problems that might result if there was a backup of emergency victims waiting for treatment in the waiting room with the other patients.

2. If the inpatient and emergency admitting functions were combined at the present location of emergency and outpatient admitting and if outpatient admitting were relocated to the outpatient receiving desk, an employee would have to be assigned to this new outpatient admissions area to perform the admitting tasks. Since this task would not be a full time job, one area supervisor felt that some of the duties presently performed by technicians in the radiology lab could be done by the admissions person. These duties would include logging of lab work, filling out requisitions, and other such clerical work. This assignment would result in lab technicians being able to limit themselves to the technological aspects of their jobs and should result in some cost reductions from the radiology budget.

   There were some concerns about this alternative. Presently, lab people check on the accuracy of the information typed by the people in admissions. With this alternative, this particular check would be deleted. In addition, an extra person would have to be trained to perform all of the outpatient admissions work and there would be the same separation in the location of admission paperwork that exists at the present time. Finally, the merger of inpatient and emergency admitting produced the space, privacy, and confusion concerns that were associated with the first alternative, although to a lesser degree because of the elimination of one patient category.

3. Separation of the three admitting jobs to three separate areas seemed to satisfy all space concerns as there would be adequate space at each location for the particular admissions facility. In particular, the prospective inpatient admitting location included a large room with associated privacy and comfort for this function.

   There seemed to be disadvantages associated with this alternative. The admitting function with its associated paperwork would be completely dispersed into three separate locations. In addition, extra staff would probably be required. Finally, personnel could not be interchanged at peak times since it would be advisable to have all admitting stations continuously staffed.

4. The alternative retaining outpatient and emergency admitting at their present location and relocating inpatient admitting to a nearby location in the basement offers some advantages previously indicated for other alternatives. They include an admitting function which would

be more centralized than at present and a spacious area for inpatient admitting. A disadvantage would be the possible requirement for additional staff.

Mr. King, the hospital controller, considered these alternatives and wondered how he might choose the most favorable alternative. Hospital clerical staff wages were about $3 per hour with a 1.25 multiplier for the inclusion of benefits. The estimated time required by a clerk to process an admission form was 3 to 5 minutes. He wondered if there were some possible labor savings that might result from the adoption of a particular alternative. He was also concerned that there might be other viable alternatives that he had not considered. He also wondered if there was some additional information that might be useful in the decision-making process that could be easily obtained.

CASE DISCUSSION QUESTIONS

1. What queuing models could be used to analyze the problem?
2. What alternatives are financially attractive?
3. What are the non-financial considerations that should be considered?

CASE 9 MEDICAL ELECTRONIC INSTRUMENTS, INC.*

In April 1976, Fred Young, Product Manager for Non-Destructive Testing Products was considering the problem of releasing a new piece of non-destructive test equipment to the field sales and service organization of Medtronics.

Medtronics is a manufacturer of a wide variety of medical electronic equipment used in industry, hospitals and large clinics. Sales for 1975 exceeded $10 million, and at least a 20% increase was expected for 1976. The corporate headquarters and major manufacturing facility was located in Minneapolis.

Fred had recently received his M.B.A. degree in Marketing from the University of Minnesota. He felt that he could apply the techniques of operations research to his problem, particularly network planning.

The product to be released was a highly technical product which would be different in many ways from those the sales force currently handled. In order to make a major impact on the industry, Fred had decided to introduce the product at a major trade show, the National Convention of the American Society of Non-Destructive Testing, held Aug. 1–5 at San Diego. The product would be released to the national sales force immediately following the show.

There were many things to get done before this trade show. Fred was able to group these activities into nine major categories.

A. *Provide product training to the field sales force.* This activity included both lectures and hands-on equipment training in the use of the product. It would take approximately five days to train the sales force.

B. *Provide product training to the service force.* While it was essential for the sales force to possess product knowledge, a completely different training program had to be developed to teach the service force how to maintain the product. This training would also take about five days.

C. *Preparation of service kits.* Each serviceman must have a tool kit to service the new product, and be trained in its use. It would take about a day and a half to prepare these kits.

---

*Reproduced with the permission of the author Robert H. Collins, School of Business, Oregon State University.

D. *Preparation of Sales Aids.* Each salesman would receive a sales manual, plus assorted flip-charts, literature, product mock-ups, and visual aids to assist him in communicating with the customer. Sales aids must be prepared prior to the sales training program, and preparation would take about seven and a half days.

E. *Preparation of Warranty and Service Contracts.* As more industrial customers show reluctance to provide their own service, warranty and service contracts have become more important as competitive product features. Hence the sales force and the servicemen must be aware of them. It will take about five days to draw up these contracts.

F. *Designate Factory Support Teams.* Factory support teams act as a backup to the field sales and service force. It will take about one-half day to select these personnel.

G. *Preparation of Instruction Manuals.* Proper operation and maintenance by the customer is a major factor in ensuring product satisfaction, reducing warranty costs, and creating an overall favorable image for the manufacturer. Preparation will take about 25 days.

H. *Pre-Release Promotion.* Prior to the actual release of the product, promotion must be directed at potential customers. A combination of direct mail and trade advertising is used to create interest in the product, and announce Medical Electronics Instruments' attendance at the ASNDT trade show. It will take approximately five days to prepare this promotion.

I. *Preparation for the Trade Show.* It will take about six days to construct an effective exhibit.

Fred felt that a PERT chart would be of assistance in scheduling the many activities required to release his new product to the sales force. Therefore he summarized these activities, and completion times in the following chart.

CASE DISCUSSION QUESTIONS

1. Draw a project network (Pert chart) which depicts the logical sequence of events required to introduce Jim's new product.

2. What is the critical path, and how many days will he need to complete the project?

3. What is the probability that the expected critical path will be completed in 40 days. What is the probability the project will be completed in 40 days.

TABLE 1

Activity	Predecessors	a	m	b
Train Sales Force(A)	D, E, G	4.5	5.0	6.00
Train Service Force(B)	C, E, G	4.5	5.0	6.75
Prepare Service Kits(C)	None	1.0	1.5	2.00
Prepare Sales Aids(D)	F	5.0	7.5	10.00
Prepare Warranty/Service Contracts(E)	None	4.5	5.0	6.25
Designate Factory Support(F)	None	0.25	0.5	1.00
Instruction Manuals(G)	None	20.00	25.0	35.00
Pre-Release Promotion(H)	D	4.5	5.0	6.00
Prepare for Trade Show(I)	E, G, H	5.0	6.0	9.00
Attend Trade Show(J)	A, I	5.0	5.0	5.00

a—Most Optimistic Completion Time
m—Most Likely Completion Time
b—Most Pessimistic Completion Time

CASE 10 SYNERGISTIC SYSTEMS CORPORATION*

Mr. Norman Jenkins, manager of office equipment at Synergistic Systems Corporation, one of the top seven government contractors, was reasoning with Mr. George Wilson, manager of the contract typing pool. "George, I can't approve your request for a third copying machine just because you say you see typists waiting in line practically every time you're near your two machines. Back in 1966, I could have approved without question, but this is 1970. You know that we aren't doing as well these days due to the government cutbacks in aerospace spending. The word has come down from upstairs that we have to cut expenses wherever possible.

"As a matter of fact, we have been running a survey on usage of the machines in the building, hoping to reduce costs by eliminating unnecessary machines. Let me show you our results for your machines, George. This first table (Table 1) shows that you average 16.17 pages per contract. This second table (Table 2) shows that the average time between users arriving at the machines is 16.48 minutes.

"Previous surveys have shown that it takes one minute to make the required twenty copies of each contract page. Therefore, the average user should be on a machine 16.17 minutes. Since secretaries arrive to use the machine an average of 16.48 minutes apart, but only use the machine an

---

*Copyright © 1970 by the President and Fellows of Harvard College. Reproduced by permission. This case was prepared by Stuart I. Zarembo under the supervision of John S. Hammond.

TABLE 1 Pages per contract

Pages	Percentage of contracts	Pages	Percentage of contracts	Pages	Percentage of contracts
6	1	13	6	20	7
7	1	14	8	21	5
8	2	15	9	22	3
9	2	16	11	23	2
10	2	17	12	24	1
11	3	18	11	25	1
12	4	19	9		

average of 16.17 minutes, one machine should be adequate for your copying needs. Each machine costs us $110 per month or $5 per working day. How can I approve your request for a third machine with these facts in front of me? In fact, I was thinking of taking away one of your machines."

George Wilson puzzled over the tables a bit and then asked, "Why are all the times even numbers? Don't the users arrive 3 minutes apart, or 5 minutes apart?"

"Yes, but we found that it was convenient and accurate enough to record the information to the nearest two minutes. Anything up to 1 minute was recorded a zero, anything from 1 to 3 minutes was recorded as 2, etc. By the way here's the form we used to record the results," he added, showing Mr. Wilson the form shown in Figure 1. "We just used two of the machine columns in your case since you only had two machines, and we recorded 20 all the time in the number of copies column. We fitted a smooth curve to what we recorded on both the pages and time between arrivals."

TABLE 2 Time between arrivals

Time since last arrival	Percentage of arrivals	Time since last arrival	Percentage of arrivals	Time since last arrival	Percentage of arrivals
0	17	20	3	40	2
2	8	22	3	42	1
4	7	24	3	44	1
6	6	26	2	46	1
8	6	28	2	48	1
10	5	30	2	50	1
12	5	32	2	52	1
14	4	34	2	54	1
16	4	36	2	56	1
18	3	38	2	58	1
				60	1

FIGURE 1 Data sheet

Time of arrival	Number of pages	Number of copies	Machine 1		Machine 2		Machine 3	
			Time on	Time off	Time on	Time off	Time on	Time off

"Well, I don't really care how you recorded that data," said Mr. Wilson, "The important point is that secretaries are waiting in line and that's costing us money.

"You're familiar with our system of assigning each typist to only one contract at a time and having her make her own copies when she finishes the typing. The worst drawback of our present system is that the time anyone spends waiting to use a machine is wasted time, and women who type with the speed and accuracy that we need don't work for peanuts. The 15 secretaries who work for me cost us about $5 an hour each, including variable overhead, and that's $40 per working day. That's why I worry when I see them waiting in line at the machine."

Mr. Jenkins asked, "Why don't you hire someone just to make copies? You ought to be able to get someone to do that for only $2 an hour. You would save the time your typists spend making copies, and eliminate all waiting time, and still get by with only one machine."

"I fought that battle last year with Bob Johnson in Security. He agreed that we could save money by hiring someone just to run the copying machines, but he won't allow it. Most of the contracts are classified Secret or Top Secret, and he's scared stiff of what the government security inspectors will say about any procedure where extra personnel handle the documents," Mr. Wilson replied. "Now the problem is worse. With the aerospace spending cuts, we've got a hiring freeze. We wouldn't be allowed to hire a Xerox operator, even if we thought it was desirable."

"George, I understand your concerns, but I just can't help you when the numbers show that I should take a machine away from you rather than give you another one. Take this copy of our survey with you. If you can show me that I'm wrong, you'll get your machine."

Mr. Wilson folded the copy of the survey, put it in his shirt pocket and walked out dejectedly.

CASE QUESTIONS

1. Using the data as collected, determine if another machine can be economically justified by simulating 1 day for each machine configuration. Use the random numbers in Table 3.

2. What are the simulated costs for two machines and three machines?

TABLE 3 Random numbers

20 84 27 38 66	19 60 10 51 20	11 79 34 46 41	3 75 58 9 43
35 16 74 58 72	79 98 9 47 7	40 55 20 60 59	56 51 99 15 72
98 82 69 63 23	70 80 88 86 23	9 8 45 0 14	82 61 62 56 71
94 67 94 34 3	77 89 30 49 51	1 21 91 48 89	65 89 29 13 23
4 54 32 55 94	82 8 19 20 73	99 77 42 88 66	88 19 85 69 11
11 25 66 8 79	68 19 37 82 73	87 59 80 1 30	32 32 11 7 19
0 63 79 77 41	17 6 67 18 33	47 49 88 71 62	82 13 90 11 27
51 51 54 44 64	13 51 92 10 37	61 31 50 81 45	20 43 6 63 21
49 72 73 93 29	39 37 94 42 66	14 87 47 14 63	30 6 42 45 82
77 9 20 5 20	77 47 58 96 5	87 1 64 52 98	93 84 79 42 94
16 45 77 65 20	11 65 65 56 36	63 55 83 79 34	93 61 2 35 40
51 63 28 55 12	23 72 99 4 41	27 32 86 78 52	12 20 93 8 1
64 46 55 58 78	96 52 43 23 5	59 15 57 31 37	35 42 34 44 62
37 75 41 57 2	14 88 79 97 9	45 87 79 21 70	43 12 10 25 5
55 36 70 34 66	58 63 90 6 37	65 32 35 32 36	20 13 3 35 14
99 10 23 74 53	13 59 59 36 71	4 31 7 45 16	48 26 95 56 70
53 80 84 57 47	60 60 70 69 95	43 67 78 45 94	10 35 70 72 57
99 29 37 69 30	83 48 5 88 91	67 25 32 14 52	89 23 10 64 58
21 41 63 90 85	65 7 46 75 43	58 86 51 34 74	69 73 99 17 56
1 97 45 5 95	88 19 78 14 32	98 34 18 89 43	32 68 19 13 33
23 81 67 97 42	36 67 83 87 43	72 51 16 62 41	61 90 54 34 73
68 77 12 47 11	92 34 43 78 58	61 20 28 36 51	39 23 85 65 58
21 66 62 39 83	37 4 42 69 60	48 24 37 93 56	48 49 97 87 72
64 31 1 57 42	56 58 62 43 31	17 47 26 17 39	72 52 72 84 97
48 57 11 82 70	31 79 87 83 56	50 71 77 89 83	94 14 92 38 17
52 24 74 98 51	46 52 99 72 16	31 78 74 94 71	96 18 42 33 13
62 18 75 88 67	82 58 81 93 94	42 53 0 15 86	62 47 3 51 69

94	19	96	34	2		23	81	17	29	74		66	77	37	33	11		74	84	59	76	69
31	12	20	20	37		52	3	89	63	39		86	34	68	32	28		16	12	92	89	94
55	79	29	29	57		51	8	79	77	70		85	6	76	95	21		69	14	86	75	28
50	3	7	42	43		5	78	72	55	52		46	77	45	5	72		18	72	23	16	54
97	66	37	44	80		94	96	50	80	67		52	30	57	45	65		45	71	87	95	54
82	53	1	17	49		4	45	95	33	98		85	47	94	97	81		32	91	59	94	11
85	46	83	44	34		15	8	91	0	28		29	10	41	45	5		63	18	24	97	9
90	27	65	8	18		12	68	20	61	40		66	5	79	71	19		21	32	64	87	31
80	79	30	92	83		77	8	66	0	17		80	12	92	58	6		89	18	62	47	58
38	87	62	79	12		93	10	11	1	41		53	15	63	90	49		49	58	0	59	75
47	31	42	52	89		43	59	39	45	96		68	97	74	49	31		85	35	63	6	64
90	96	55	93	97		10	35	32	16	64		9	40	8	18	34		79	32	31	72	7
49	65	82	85	17		77	24	72	97	29		57	29	49	80	42		14	32	90	39	89

APPENDIX C
Areas of a Standard Normal Distribution

An entry in the table is the proportion under the entire curve that is between $z = -\infty$ and a positive value of z.

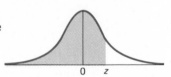

z	.00	.01	.02	.03	.04	.05	.06	.07	.08	.09
0.0	.5000	.5040	.5080	.5120	.5160	.5199	.5239	.5279	.5319	.5359
0.1	.5398	.5438	.5478	.5517	.5557	.5596	.5636	.5675	.5714	.5753
0.2	.5793	.5832	.5871	.5910	.5948	.5987	.6026	.6064	.6103	.6141
0.3	.6179	.6217	.6255	.6293	.6331	.6368	.6406	.6443	.6480	.6517
0.4	.6554	.6591	.6628	.6664	.6700	.6736	.6772	.6808	.6844	.6879
0.5	.6915	.6950	.6985	.7019	.7054	.7088	.7123	.7157	.7190	.7224
0.6	.7257	.7291	.7324	.7357	.7389	.7422	.7454	.7486	.7517	.7549
0.7	.7580	.7611	.7642	.7673	.7703	.7734	.7764	.7794	.7823	.7852
0.8	.7881	.7910	.7939	.7967	.7995	.8023	.8051	.8078	.8106	.8133
0.9	.8159	.8186	.8212	.8238	.8264	.8289	.8315	.8340	.8365	.8389
1.0	.8413	.8438	.8461	.8485	.8508	.8531	.8554	.8577	.8599	.8621
1.1	.8643	.8665	.8686	.8708	.8729	.8749	.8770	.8790	.8810	.8830
1.2	.8849	.8869	.8888	.8907	.8925	.8944	.8962	.8980	.8997	.9015
1.3	.9032	.9049	.9066	.9082	.9099	.9115	.9131	.9147	.9162	.9177
1.4	.9192	.9207	.9222	.9236	.9251	.9265	.9279	.9292	.9306	.9319
1.5	.9332	.9345	.9357	.9370	.9382	.9394	.9406	.9418	.9429	.9441
1.6	.9452	.9463	.9474	.9484	.9495	.9505	.9515	.9525	.9535	.9545
1.7	.9554	.9564	.9573	.9582	.9591	.9599	.9608	.9616	.9625	.9633
1.8	.9461	.9649	.9656	.9664	.9671	.9678	.9686	.9693	.9699	.9706
1.9	.9713	.9719	.9726	.9732	.9738	.9744	.9750	.9756	.9761	.9767
2.0	.9772	.9778	.9783	.9788	.9793	.9798	.9803	.9808	.9812	.9817
2.1	.9821	.9826	.9830	.9834	.9838	.9842	.9846	.9850	.9854	.9857
2.2	.9861	.9864	.9868	.9871	.9875	.9878	.9881	.9884	.9887	.9890
2.3	.9893	.9896	.9898	.9901	.9904	.9906	.9909	.9911	.9913	.9916
2.4	.9918	.9920	.9922	.9925	.9927	.9929	.9931	.9932	.9934	.9936
2.5	.9938	.9940	.9941	.9943	.9945	.9946	.9948	.9949	.9951	.9952
2.6	.9953	.9955	.9956	.9957	.9959	.9960	.9961	.9962	.9963	.9964
2.7	.9965	.9966	.9967	.9968	.9969	.9970	.9971	.9972	.9973	.9974
2.8	.9974	.9975	.9976	.9977	.9977	.9978	.9979	.9979	.9980	.9981
2.9	.9981	.9982	.9982	.9983	.9984	.9984	.9985	.9985	.9986	.9986
3.0	.9987	.9987	.9987	.9988	.9988	.9989	.9989	.9989	.9990	.9990
3.1	.9990	.9991	.9991	.9991	.9992	.9992	.9992	.9992	.9993	.9993
3.2	.9993	.9993	.9994	.9994	.9994	.9994	.9994	.9995	.9995	.9995
3.3	.9995	.9995	.9995	.9996	.9996	.9996	.9996	.9996	.9996	.9997

APPENDIX **D**

Selected Values of the Binomial Cumulative Distribution Function

$$F(c) = P(X \le c) = \sum_{x=0}^{c} \binom{n}{x} (1-p)^{n-x} p^x$$

Example If $p = .20$, $n = 7$, $c = 2$, then $F(2) = P(X \le 2) = .8520$.

n	c	0.05	0.10	0.15	0.20	0.25	*p* 0.30	0.35	0.40	0.45	0.50
2	0	0.9025	0.8100	0.7225	0.6400	0.5625	0.4900	0.4225	0.3600	0.3025	0.2500
	1	0.9975	0.9900	0.9775	0.9600	0.9375	0.9100	0.8775	0.8400	0.7975	0.7500
3	0	0.8574	0.7290	0.6141	0.5120	0.4219	0.3430	0.2746	0.2160	0.1664	0.1250
	1	0.9928	0.9720	0.9392	0.8960	0.8438	0.7840	0.7182	0.6480	0.5748	0.5000
	2	0.9999	0.9990	0.9966	0.9920	0.9844	0.9730	0.9571	0.9360	0.9089	0.8750
4	0	0.8145	0.6561	0.5220	0.4096	0.3164	0.2401	0.1785	0.1296	0.0915	0.0625
	1	0.9860	0.9477	0.8905	0.8192	0.7383	0.6517	0.5630	0.4752	0.3910	0.3125
	2	0.9995	0.9963	0.9880	0.9728	0.9492	0.9163	0.8735	0.8208	0.7585	0.6875
	3	1.0000	0.9999	0.9995	0.9984	0.9961	0.9919	0.9850	0.9744	0.9590	0.9375
5	0	0.7738	0.5905	0.4437	0.3277	0.2373	0.1681	0.1160	0.0778	0.0503	0.0312
	1	0.9774	0.9185	0.8352	0.7373	0.6328	0.5282	0.4284	0.3370	0.2562	0.1875
	2	0.9988	0.9914	0.9734	0.9421	0.8965	0.8369	0.7648	0.6826	0.5931	0.5000
	3	1.0000	0.9995	0.9978	0.9933	0.9844	0.9692	0.9460	0.9130	0.8688	0.8125
	4	1.0000	1.0000	0.9999	0.9997	0.9990	0.9976	0.9947	0.9898	0.9815	0.9688

Source: From Irwin Miller and John E. Freund, *Probability and Statistics for Engineers*, © 1965 by Prentice-Hall, Inc.

n	c	0.05	0.10	0.15	0.20	0.25	p 0.30	0.35	0.40	0.45	0.50
6	0	0.7351	0.5314	0.3771	0.2621	0.1780	0.1176	0.0754	0.0467	0.0277	0.0156
	1	0.9672	0.8857	0.7765	0.6554	0.5339	0.4202	0.3191	0.2333	0.1636	0.1094
	2	0.9978	0.9842	0.9527	0.9011	0.8306	0.7443	0.6471	0.5443	0.4415	0.3438
	3	0.9999	0.9987	0.9941	0.9830	0.9624	0.9295	0.8826	0.8208	0.7447	0.6562
	4	1.0000	0.9999	0.9996	0.9984	0.9954	0.9891	0.9777	0.9590	0.9308	0.8906
	5	1.0000	1.0000	1.0000	0.9999	0.9998	0.9993	0.9982	0.9959	0.9917	0.9844
7	0	0.6983	0.4783	0.3206	0.2097	0.1335	0.0824	0.0490	0.0280	0.0152	0.0078
	1	0.9556	0.8503	0.7166	0.5767	0.4449	0.3294	0.2338	0.1586	0.1024	0.0625
	2	0.9962	0.9743	0.9262	0.8520	0.7564	0.6471	0.5323	0.4199	0.3164	0.2266
	3	0.9998	0.9973	0.9879	0.9667	0.9294	0.8740	0.8002	0.7102	0.6083	0.5000
	4	1.0000	0.9998	0.9988	0.9953	0.9871	0.9712	0.9444	0.9037	0.8471	0.7734
	5	1.0000	1.0000	0.9999	0.9996	0.9987	0.9962	0.9910	0.0812	0.9643	0.9375
	6	1.0000	1.0000	1.0000	1.0000	0.9999	0.9998	0.9994	0.9984	0.9963	0.9922
8	0	0.6634	0.4305	0.2725	0.1678	0.1001	0.0576	0.0319	0.0168	0.0084	0.0039
	1	0.9428	0.8131	0.6572	0.5033	0.3671	0.2553	0.1691	0.1064	0.0632	0.0352
	2	0.9942	0.9619	0.8948	0.7969	0.6785	0.5518	0.4278	0.3154	0.2201	0.1445
	3	0.9996	0.9950	0.9786	0.9437	0.8862	0.8059	0.7064	0.5941	0.4770	0.3633
	4	1.0000	0.9996	0.9971	0.9896	0.9727	0.9420	0.8939	0.8263	0.7396	0.6367
	5	1.0000	1.0000	0.9998	0.9988	0.9958	0.9887	0.9747	0.9502	0.9115	0.8555
	6	1.0000	1.0000	1.0000	0.9999	0.9996	0.9987	0.9964	0.9915	0.9819	0.9648
	7	1.0000	1.0000	1.0000	1.0000	1.0000	0.9999	0.9998	0.9993	0.9983	0.9961
9	0	0.6302	0.3874	0.2316	0.1342	0.0751	0.0404	0.0207	0.0101	0.0046	0.0020
	1	0.9288	0.7748	0.5995	0.4362	0.3003	0.1960	0.1211	0.0705	0.0385	0.0195
	2	0.9916	0.9470	0.8591	0.7382	0.6007	0.4628	0.3373	0.2318	0.1495	0.0898
	3	0.9994	0.9917	0.9661	0.9144	0.8343	0.7297	0.6089	0.4826	0.3614	0.2539
	4	1.0000	0.9991	0.9944	0.9804	0.9511	0.9012	0.8283	0.7334	0.6214	0.5000
	5	1.0000	0.9999	0.9994	0.9969	0.9900	0.9747	0.9464	0.9006	0.8342	0.7461
	6	1.0000	1.0000	1.0000	0.9997	0.9987	0.9957	0.9888	0.9750	0.9502	0.9102
	7	1.0000	1.0000	1.0000	1.0000	0.9999	0.9996	0.9986	0.9962	0.9909	0.9805
	8	1.0000	1.0000	1.0000	1.0000	1.0000	1.0000	0.9999	0.9997	0.9992	0.9980
10	0	0.5987	0.3487	0.1969	0.1074	0.0563	0.0282	0.0135	0.0060	0.0025	0.0010
	1	0.9139	0.7361	0.5443	0.3758	0.2440	0.1493	0.0860	0.0464	0.0232	0.0107
	2	0.9885	0.9298	0.8202	0.6778	0.5256	0.3828	0.2616	0.1673	0.0996	0.0547
	3	0.9990	0.9872	0.9500	0.8791	0.7759	0.6496	0.5138	0.3823	0.2660	0.1719
	4	0.9999	0.9984	0.9901	0.9672	0.9219	0.8497	0.7515	0.6331	0.5044	0.3770
	5	1.0000	0.9999	0.9986	0.9936	0.9803	0.9527	0.9051	0.8338	0.7384	0.6230
	6	1.0000	1.0000	0.9999	0.9991	0.9965	0.9894	0.9740	0.9452	0.8980	0.8281
	7	1.0000	1.0000	1.0000	0.9999	0.9996	0.9984	0.9952	0.9877	0.9726	0.9453
	8	1.0000	1.0000	1.0000	1.0000	1.0000	0.9999	0.9995	0.9983	0.9955	0.9893
	9	1.0000	1.0000	1.0000	1.0000	1.0000	1.0000	1.0000	0.9999	0.9997	0.9990

Selected values of the binomial cumulative distribution function (*continued*)

							p				
n	c	0.05	0.10	0.15	0.20	0.25	0.30	0.35	0.40	0.45	0.50
11	0	0.5688	0.3138	0.1673	0.0859	0.0422	0.0198	0.0088	0.0036	0.0014	0.0005
	1	0.8981	0.6974	0.4922	0.3221	0.1971	0.1130	0.0606	0.0302	0.0139	0.0059
	2	0.9848	0.9104	0.7788	0.6174	0.4552	0.3127	0.2001	0.1189	0.0652	0.0327
	3	0.9984	0.9815	0.9306	0.8389	0.7133	0.5696	0.4256	0.2963	0.1911	0.1133
	4	0.9999	0.9972	0.9841	0.9496	0.8854	0.7897	0.6683	0.5328	0.3971	0.2744
	5	1.0000	0.9997	0.9973	0.9883	0.9657	0.9218	0.8513	0.7535	0.6331	0.5000
	6	1.0000	1.0000	0.9997	0.9980	0.9924	0.9784	0.9499	0.9006	0.8262	0.7256
	7	1.0000	1.0000	1.0000	0.9998	0.9988	0.9957	0.9878	0.9707	0.9390	0.8867
	8	1.0000	1.0000	1.0000	1.0000	0.9999	0.9994	0.9980	0.9941	0.9852	0.9673
	9	1.0000	1.0000	1.0000	1.0000	1.0000	1.0000	0.9998	0.9993	0.9978	0.9941
	10	1.0000	1.0000	1.0000	1.0000	1.0000	1.0000	1.0000	1.0000	0.9998	0.9995
12	0	0.5404	0.2824	0.1422	0.0687	0.0317	0.0138	0.0057	0.0022	0.0008	0.0002
	1	0.8816	0.6590	0.4435	0.2749	0.1584	0.0850	0.0424	0.0196	0.0083	0.0032
	2	0.9804	0.8891	0.7358	0.5583	0.3907	0.2528	0.1513	0.0834	0.0421	0.0193
	3	0.9978	0.9744	0.9078	0.7946	0.6488	0.4925	0.3467	0.2253	0.1345	0.0730
	4	0.9998	0.9957	0.9761	0.9274	0.8424	0.7237	0.5833	0.4382	0.3044	0.1938
	5	1.0000	0.9995	0.9954	0.9806	0.9456	0.8822	0.7873	0.6652	0.5269	0.3872
	6	1.0000	0.9999	0.9993	0.9961	0.9857	0.9614	0.9154	0.8418	0.7393	0.6128
	7	1.0000	1.0000	0.9999	0.9994	0.9972	0.9905	0.9745	0.9427	0.8883	0.8062
	8	1.0000	1.0000	1.0000	0.9999	0.9996	0.9983	0.9944	0.9847	0.9644	0.9270
	9	1.0000	1.0000	1.0000	1.0000	1.0000	0.9998	0.9992	0.9972	0.9921	0.9807
	10	1.0000	1.0000	1.0000	1.0000	1.0000	1.0000	0.9999	0.9997	0.9989	0.9968
	11	1.0000	1.0000	1.0000	1.0000	1.0000	1.0000	1.0000	1.0000	0.9999	0.9998
13	0	0.5133	0.2542	0.1209	0.0550	0.0238	0.0097	0.0037	0.0013	0.0004	0.0001
	1	0.8646	0.6213	0.3983	0.2336	0.1267	0.0637	0.0296	0.0126	0.0049	0.0017
	2	0.9755	0.8661	0.6920	0.5017	0.3326	0.2025	0.1132	0.0579	0.0269	0.0112
	3	0.9969	0.9658	0.8820	0.7473	0.5843	0.4206	0.2783	0.1686	0.0929	0.0461
	4	0.9997	0.9935	0.9658	0.9009	0.7940	0.6543	0.5005	0.3530	0.2279	0.1334
	5	1.0000	0.9991	0.9925	0.9700	0.9198	0.8346	0.7159	0.5744	0.4268	0.2905
	6	1.0000	0.9999	0.9987	0.9930	0.9757	0.9376	0.8705	0.7712	0.6437	0.5000
	7	1.0000	1.0000	0.9998	0.9988	0.9944	0.9818	0.9538	0.9023	0.8212	0.7095
	8	1.0000	1.0000	1.0000	0.9998	0.9990	0.9960	0.9874	0.9679	0.9302	0.8666
	9	1.0000	1.0000	1.0000	1.0000	0.9999	0.9993	0.9975	0.9922	0.9797	0.9539
	10	1.0000	1.0000	1.0000	1.0000	1.0000	0.9999	0.9997	0.9987	0.9959	0.9888
	11	1.0000	1.0000	1.0000	1.0000	1.0000	1.0000	1.0000	0.9999	0.9995	0.9963
	12	1.0000	1.0000	1.0000	1.0000	1.0000	1.0000	1.0000	1.0000	1.0000	0.9999
14	0	0.4877	0.2288	0.1028	0.0440	0.0178	0.0068	0.0024	0.0008	0.0002	0.0001
	1	0.8470	0.5846	0.3567	0.1979	0.1010	0.0475	0.0205	0.0081	0.0029	0.0009
	2	0.9699	0.8416	0.6479	0.4481	0.2811	0.1608	0.0839	0.0398	0.0170	0.0065

n	c	0.05	0.10	0.15	0.20	0.25	p 0.30	0.35	0.40	0.45	0.50
14	3	0.9958	0.9559	0.8535	0.6982	0.5213	0.3552	0.2205	0.1243	0.0632	0.0287
	4	0.9996	0.9908	0.9533	0.8702	0.7415	0.5842	0.4227	0.2793	0.1672	0.0898
	5	1.0000	0.9985	0.9885	0.9561	0.8883	0.7805	0.6405	0.4859	0.3373	0.2120
	6	1.0000	0.9998	0.9978	0.9884	0.9617	0.9067	0.8164	0.6925	0.5461	0.3953
	7	1.0000	1.0000	0.9997	0.9976	0.9897	0.9685	0.9247	0.8499	0.7414	0.6047
	8	1.0000	1.0000	1.0000	0.9996	0.9978	0.9917	0.9757	0.9417	0.8811	0.7880
	9	1.0000	1.0000	1.0000	1.0000	0.9997	0.9983	0.9940	0.9825	0.9574	0.9102
	10	1.0000	1.0000	1.0000	1.0000	1.0000	0.9998	0.9989	0.9961	0.9886	0.9713
	11	1.0000	1.0000	1.0000	1.0000	1.0000	1.0000	0.9999	0.9994	0.9978	0.9935
	12	1.0000	1.0000	1.0000	1.0000	1.0000	1.0000	1.0000	0.9999	0.9997	0.9991
	13	1.0000	1.0000	1.0000	1.0000	1.0000	1.0000	1.0000	1.0000	1.0000	0.9999
15	0	0.4633	0.2059	0.0874	0.0352	0.0134	0.0047	0.0016	0.0005	0.0001	0.0000
	1	0.8290	0.5490	0.3186	0.1671	0.0802	0.0353	0.0142	0.0052	0.0017	0.0005
	2	0.9638	0.8159	0.6042	0.3980	0.2361	0.1268	0.0617	0.0271	0.0107	0.0037
	3	0.9945	0.9444	0.8227	0.6482	0.4613	0.2969	0.1727	0.0905	0.0424	0.0176
	4	0.9994	0.9873	0.9383	0.8358	0.6865	0.5155	0.3519	0.2173	0.1204	0.0592
	5	0.9999	0.9978	0.9832	0.9389	0.8516	0.7216	0.5643	0.4032	0.2608	0.1509
	6	1.0000	0.9997	0.9964	0.9819	0.9434	0.8689	0.7548	0.6098	0.4522	0.3036
	7	1.0000	1.0000	0.9996	0.9958	0.9827	0.9500	0.8868	0.7869	0.6535	0.5000
	8	1.0000	1.0000	0.9999	0.9992	0.9958	0.9848	0.9578	0.9050	0.8182	0.6964
	9	1.0000	1.0000	1.0000	0.9999	0.9992	0.9963	0.9876	0.9662	0.9231	0.8491
	10	1.0000	1.0000	1.0000	1.0000	0.9999	0.9993	0.9972	0.9907	0.9745	0.9408
	11	1.0000	1.0000	1.0000	1.0000	1.0000	0.9999	0.9995	0.9981	0.9937	0.9821
	12	1.0000	1.0000	1.0000	1.0000	1.0000	1.0000	0.9999	0.9997	0.9989	0.9963
	13	1.0000	1.0000	1.0000	1.0000	1.0000	1.0000	1.0000	1.0000	0.9999	0.9995
	14	1.0000	1.0000	1.0000	1.0000	1.0000	1.0000	1.0000	1.0000	1.0000	1.0000
16	0	0.4401	0.1853	0.0743	0.0281	0.0100	0.0033	0.0010	0.0003	0.0001	0.0000
	1	0.8108	0.5147	0.2839	0.1407	0.0635	0.0261	0.0098	0.0033	0.0010	0.0003
	2	0.9571	0.7892	0.5614	0.3518	0.1971	0.0994	0.0451	0.0183	0.0066	0.0021
	3	0.9930	0.9316	0.7899	0.5981	0.4050	0.2459	0.1339	0.0651	0.0281	0.0106
	4	0.9991	0.9830	0.9209	0.7982	0.6302	0.4499	0.2892	0.1666	0.0853	0.0384
	5	0.9999	0.9967	0.9765	0.9183	0.8103	0.6598	0.4900	0.3288	0.1976	0.1051
	6	1.0000	0.9995	0.9944	0.9733	0.9204	0.8247	0.6881	0.5272	0.3660	0.2272
	7	1.0000	0.9999	0.9989	0.9930	0.9729	0.9256	0.8406	0.7161	0.5629	0.4018
	8	1.0000	1.0000	0.9998	0.9985	0.9925	0.9743	0.9329	0.8577	0.7441	0.5982
	9	1.0000	1.0000	1.0000	0.9998	0.9984	0.9929	0.9771	0.9417	0.8759	0.7723
	10	1.0000	1.0000	1.0000	1.0000	0.9997	0.9984	0.9938	0.9809	0.9514	0.8949
	11	1.0000	1.0000	1.0000	1.0000	1.0000	0.9997	0.9987	0.9951	0.9851	0.9616
	12	1.0000	1.0000	1.0000	1.0000	1.0000	1.0000	0.9998	0.9991	0.9965	0.9894
	13	1.0000	1.0000	1.0000	1.0000	1.0000	1.0000	1.0000	0.9999	0.9994	0.9979

n	c	0.05	0.10	0.15	0.20	0.25	*p* 0.30	0.35	0.40	0.45	0.50
	14	1.0000	1.0000	1.0000	1.0000	1.0000	1.0000	1.0000	1.0000	1.0000	0.9997
	15	1.0000	1.0000	1.0000	1.0000	1.0000	1.0000	1.0000	1.0000	1.0000	1.0000
17	0	0.4181	0.1668	0.0631	0.0225	0.0075	0.0023	0.0007	0.0002	0.0000	0.0000
	1	0.7922	0.4818	0.2525	0.1182	0.0501	0.0193	0.0067	0.0021	0.0006	0.0001
	2	0.9497	0.7618	0.5198	0.3096	0.1637	0.0774	0.0327	0.0123	0.0041	0.0012
	3	0.9912	0.9174	0.7556	0.5489	0.3530	0.2019	0.1028	0.0464	0.0184	0.0064
	4	0.9988	0.9779	0.9013	0.7582	0.5739	0.3887	0.2348	0.1260	0.0596	0.0245
	5	0.9999	0.9953	0.9681	0.8943	0.7653	0.5968	0.4197	0.2639	0.1471	0.0717
	6	1.0000	0.9992	0.9917	0.9623	0.8929	0.7752	0.6188	0.4478	0.2902	0.1662
	7	1.0000	0.9999	0.9983	0.9891	0.9598	0.8954	0.7872	0.6405	0.4743	0.3145
	8	1.0000	1.0000	0.9997	0.9974	0.9876	0.9597	0.9006	0.8011	0.6626	0.5000
	9	1.0000	1.0000	1.0000	0.9995	0.9969	0.9873	0.9617	0.9081	0.8166	0.6855
	10	1.0000	1.0000	1.0000	0.9999	0.9994	0.9968	0.9880	0.9652	0.9174	0.8338
	11	1.0000	1.0000	1.0000	1.0000	0.9999	0.9993	0.9970	0.9894	0.9699	0.9283
	12	1.0000	1.0000	1.0000	1.0000	1.0000	0.9999	0.9994	0.9975	0.9914	0.9755
	13	1.0000	1.0000	1.0000	1.0000	1.0000	1.0000	0.9999	0.9995	0.9981	0.9936
	14	1.0000	1.0000	1.0000	1.0000	1.0000	1.0000	1.0000	0.9999	0.9997	0.9988
	15	1.0000	1.0000	1.0000	1.0000	1.0000	1.0000	1.0000	1.0000	1.0000	0.9999
	16	1.0000	1.0000	1.0000	1.0000	1.0000	1.0000	1.0000	1.0000	1.0000	1.0000
18	0	0.3972	0.1501	0.0536	0.0180	0.0056	0.0016	0.0004	0.0001	0.0000	0.0000
	1	0.7735	0.4503	0.2241	0.0991	0.0395	0.0142	0.0046	0.0013	0.0003	0.0001
	2	0.9419	0.7338	0.4797	0.2713	0.1353	0.0600	0.0236	0.0082	0.0025	0.0007
	3	0.9891	0.9018	0.7202	0.5010	0.3057	0.1646	0.0783	0.0328	0.0120	0.0038
	4	0.9985	0.9718	0.8794	0.7164	0.5187	0.3327	0.1886	0.0942	0.0411	0.0154
	5	0.9998	0.9936	0.9581	0.8671	0.7175	0.5344	0.3550	0.2088	0.1077	0.0481
	6	1.0000	0.9988	0.9882	0.9487	0.8610	0.7217	0.5491	0.3743	0.2258	0.1189
	7	1.0000	0.9998	0.9973	0.9837	0.9431	0.8593	0.7283	0.5634	0.3915	0.2403
	8	1.0000	1.0000	0.9995	0.9957	0.9807	0.9404	0.8609	0.7368	0.5778	0.4073
	9	1.0000	1.0000	0.9999	0.9991	0.9946	0.9790	0.9403	0.8653	0.7473	0.5927
	10	1.0000	1.0000	1.0000	0.9998	0.9988	0.9939	0.9788	0.9424	0.8720	0.7597
	11	1.0000	1.0000	1.0000	1.0000	0.9998	0.9986	0.9938	0.9797	0.9463	0.8811
	12	1.0000	1.0000	1.0000	1.0000	1.0000	0.9997	0.9986	0.9942	0.9817	0.9519
	13	1.0000	1.0000	1.0000	1.0000	1.0000	1.0000	0.9997	0.9987	0.9951	0.9846
	14	1.0000	1.0000	1.0000	1.0000	1.0000	1.0000	1.0000	0.9998	0.9990	0.9962
	15	1.0000	1.0000	1.0000	1.0000	1.0000	1.0000	1.0000	1.0000	0.9999	0.9993
	16	1.0000	1.0000	1.0000	1.0000	1.0000	1.0000	1.0000	1.0000	1.0000	0.9999

n	c	0.05	0.10	0.15	0.20	0.25	0.30	0.35	0.40	0.45	0.50
						p					
19	0	0.3774	0.1351	0.0456	0.0144	0.0042	0.0011	0.0003	0.0001	0.0000	0.0000
	1	0.7547	0.4203	0.1985	0.0829	0.0310	0.0104	0.0031	0.0008	0.0002	0.0000
	2	0.9335	0.7054	0.4413	0.2369	0.1113	0.0462	0.0170	0.0055	0.0015	0.0004
	3	0.9868	0.8850	0.6841	0.4551	0.2630	0.1332	0.0591	0.0230	0.0077	0.0022
	4	0.9980	0.9648	0.8556	0.6733	0.4654	0.2822	0.1500	0.0696	0.0280	0.0096
	5	0.9998	0.9914	0.9463	0.8369	0.6678	0.4739	0.2968	0.1629	0.0777	0.0318
	6	1.0000	0.9983	0.9837	0.9324	0.8251	0.6655	0.4812	0.3081	0.1727	0.0835
	7	1.0000	0.9997	0.9959	0.9767	0.9225	0.8180	0.6656	0.4878	0.3169	0.1796
	8	1.0000	1.0000	0.9992	0.9933	0.9713	0.9161	0.8145	0.6675	0.4940	0.3238
	9	1.0000	1.0000	0.9999	0.9984	0.9911	0.9674	0.9125	0.8139	0.6710	0.5000
	10	1.0000	1.0000	1.0000	0.9997	0.9977	0.9895	0.9653	0.9115	0.8159	0.6762
	11	1.0000	1.0000	1.0000	1.0000	0.9995	0.9972	0.9886	0.9648	0.9129	0.8204
	12	1.0000	1.0000	1.0000	1.0000	0.9999	0.9994	0.9969	0.9884	0.9658	0.9165
	13	1.0000	1.0000	1.0000	1.0000	1.0000	0.9999	0.9993	0.9969	0.9891	0.9682
	14	1.0000	1.0000	1.0000	1.0000	1.0000	1.0000	0.9999	0.9994	0.9972	0.9904
	15	1.0000	1.0000	1.0000	1.0000	1.0000	1.0000	1.0000	0.9999	0.9995	0.9978
	16	1.0000	1.0000	1.0000	1.0000	1.0000	1.0000	1.0000	1.0000	0.9999	0.9996
	17	1.0000	1.0000	1.0000	1.0000	1.0000	1.0000	1.0000	1.0000	1.0000	1.0000
20	0	0.3585	0.1216	0.0388	0.0115	0.0032	0.0008	0.0002	0.0000	0.0000	0.0000
	1	0.7358	0.3917	0.1756	0.0692	0.0243	0.0076	0.0021	0.0005	0.0001	0.0000
	2	0.9245	0.6769	0.4049	0.2061	0.0913	0.0355	0.0121	0.0036	0.0009	0.0002
	3	0.9841	0.8670	0.6477	0.4114	0.2252	0.1071	0.0444	0.0160	0.0049	0.0013
	4	0.9974	0.9568	0.8298	0.6296	0.4148	0.2375	0.1182	0.0510	0.0189	0.0059
	5	0.9997	0.9887	0.9327	0.8042	0.6172	0.4164	0.2454	0.1256	0.0553	0.0207
	6	1.0000	0.9976	0.9781	0.9133	0.7858	0.6080	0.4166	0.2500	0.1299	0.0577
	7	1.0000	0.9996	0.9941	0.9679	0.8982	0.7723	0.6010	0.4159	0.2520	0.1316
	8	1.0000	0.9999	0.9987	0.9900	0.9591	0.8867	0.7624	0.5956	0.4143	0.2517
	9	1.0000	1.0000	0.9998	0.9974	0.9861	0.9520	0.8782	0.7553	0.5914	0.4119
	10	1.0000	1.0000	1.0000	0.9994	0.9961	0.9829	0.9468	0.8725	0.7507	0.5881
	11	1.0000	1.0000	1.0000	0.9999	0.9991	0.9949	0.9804	0.9435	0.8692	0.7483
	12	1.0000	1.0000	1.0000	1.0000	0.9998	0.9987	0.9940	0.9790	0.9420	0.8684
	13	1.0000	1.0000	1.0000	1.0000	1.0000	0.9997	0.9985	0.9935	0.9786	0.9423
	14	1.0000	1.0000	1.0000	1.0000	1.0000	1.0000	0.9997	0.9984	0.9936	0.9793
	15	1.0000	1.0000	1.0000	1.0000	1.0000	1.0000	1.0000	0.9997	0.9985	0.9941
	16	1.0000	1.0000	1.0000	1.0000	1.0000	1.0000	1.0000	1.0000	0.9997	0.9987
	17	1.0000	1.0000	1.0000	1.0000	1.0000	1.0000	1.0000	1.0000	1.0000	0.9998
	18	1.0000	1.0000	1.0000	1.0000	1.0000	1.0000	1.0000	1.0000	1.0000	1.0000

APPENDIX E
The Cumulative Poisson Distribution

$$P(r \leq r_0 \mid \mu)$$

μ \ r_0	0	1	2	3	4	5	6	7	8	9	10
0.02	980	1000									
0.04	961	999	1000								
0.06	942	998	1000								
0.08	923	997	1000								
0.10	905	995	1000								
0.15	861	990	999	1000							
0.20	819	982	999	1000							
0.25	779	974	998	1000							
0.30	741	963	996	1000							
0.35	705	951	994	1000							
0.40	670	938	992	999	1000						
0.45	638	925	989	999	1000						
0.50	607	910	986	998	1000						
0.55	577	894	982	998	1000						
0.60	549	878	977	997	1000						
0.65	522	861	972	996	999	1000					
0.70	497	844	966	994	999	1000					
0.75	472	827	959	993	999	1000					
0.80	449	809	953	991	999	1000					
0.85	427	791	945	989	998	1000					
0.90	407	772	937	987	998	1000					
0.95	387	754	929	984	997	1000					
1.00	368	736	920	981	996	999	1000				
1.1	333	699	900	974	995	999	1000				
1.2	301	663	879	966	992	998	1000				
1.3	273	627	857	957	989	998	1000				
1.4	247	592	833	946	986	997	999	1000			
1.5	223	558	809	934	981	996	999	1000			
1.6	202	525	783	921	976	994	999	1000			
1.7	183	493	757	907	970	992	998	1000			
1.8	165	463	731	891	964	990	997	999	1000		
1.9	150	434	704	875	956	987	997	999	1000		
2.0	135	406	677	857	947	983	995	999	1000		
2.2	111	355	623	819	928	975	993	998	1000		
2.4	091	308	570	779	904	964	988	997	999	1000	
2.6	074	267	518	736	877	951	983	995	999	1000	
2.8	061	231	469	692	848	935	976	992	998	999	1000
3.0	050	199	423	647	815	916	966	988	996	999	1000

The cumulative Poisson distribution (*continued*)

μ \ r_0	0	1	2	3	4	5	6	7	8	9	10	11	12	13
3.2	041	171	380	603	781	895	955	983	994	998	1000			
3.4	033	147	340	558	744	871	942	977	992	997	999	1000		
3.6	027	126	303	515	706	844	927	969	988	996	999	1000		
3.8	022	107	269	473	668	816	909	960	984	994	998	999	1000	
4.0	018	092	238	433	629	785	889	949	979	992	997	999	1000	
4.2	015	078	210	395	590	753	867	936	972	989	996	999	1000	
4.4	012	066	185	359	551	720	844	921	964	985	994	998	999	1000
4.6	010	056	163	326	513	686	818	905	955	980	992	997	999	1000
4.8	008	048	143	294	476	651	791	887	944	975	990	996	999	1000
5.0	007	040	125	265	440	616	762	867	932	968	986	995	998	999
5.2	006	034	109	238	406	581	732	845	918	960	982	993	997	999
5.4	005	029	095	213	373	546	702	822	903	951	977	990	996	999
5.6	004	024	082	191	342	512	670	797	886	941	972	988	995	998
5.8	003	021	072	170	313	478	638	771	867	929	965	984	993	997
6.0	002	017	062	151	285	446	606	744	847	916	957	980	991	996
6.2	002	015	054	134	259	414	574	716	826	902	949	975	989	995
6.4	002	012	046	119	235	384	542	687	803	886	939	969	986	994
6.6	001	010	040	105	213	355	511	658	780	869	927	963	982	992
6.8	001	009	034	093	192	327	480	628	755	850	915	955	978	990
7.0	001	007	030	082	173	301	450	599	729	830	901	947	973	987
7.2	001	006	025	072	156	276	420	569	703	810	887	937	967	984
7.4	001	005	022	063	140	253	392	539	676	788	871	926	961	980
7.6	001	004	019	055	125	231	365	510	648	765	854	915	954	976
7.8	000	004	016	048	112	210	338	481	620	741	835	902	945	971
8.0	000	003	014	042	100	191	313	453	593	717	816	888	936	966
8.5	000	002	009	030	074	150	256	386	523	653	763	849	909	949
9.0	000	001	006	021	055	116	207	324	456	587	706	803	876	926
9.5	000	001	004	015	040	089	165	269	392	522	645	752	836	898
10.0	000	000	003	010	029	067	130	220	333	458	583	697	792	864
10.5	000	000	002	007	021	050	102	179	279	397	521	639	742	825
11.0	000	000	001	005	015	038	079	143	232	341	460	579	689	781
11.5	000	000	001	003	011	028	060	114	191	289	402	520	633	733
12.0	000	000	001	002	008	020	046	090	155	242	347	462	576	682
12.5	000	000	000	002	005	015	035	070	125	201	297	406	519	628
13.0	000	000	000	001	004	011	026	054	100	166	252	353	463	573
13.5	000	000	000	001	003	008	019	041	079	135	211	304	409	518
14.0	000	000	000	000	002	006	014	032	062	109	176	260	358	464
14.5	000	000	000	000	001	004	010	024	048	088	145	220	311	413
15.0	000	000	000	000	001	003	008	018	037	070	118	185	268	363

14	15	16	17	18	19	20	21	22	23	24	25	26	27	28	29
1000															
1000															
1000															
999	1000														
999	1000														
999	999	1000													
998	999	1000													
997	999	1000													
997	999	999	1000												
996	998	999	1000												
994	998	999	1000												
993	997	999	999	1000											
991	996	998	999	1000											
989	995	998	999	1000											
986	993	997	999	1000											
983	992	996	998	999	1000										
973	986	993	997	999	999	1000									
959	978	989	995	998	999	1000									
940	967	982	991	996	998	999	1000								
917	951	973	986	993	997	998	999	1000							
888	932	960	978	988	994	997	999	999	1000						
854	907	944	968	982	991	995	998	999	1000						
815	878	924	954	974	986	992	996	998	999	1000					
772	844	899	937	963	979	988	994	997	999	999	1000				
725	806	869	916	948	969	983	991	995	998	999	999	1000			
675	764	835	890	930	957	975	986	992	996	998	999	1000			
623	718	798	861	908	942	965	980	989	994	997	998	999	1000		
570	669	756	827	883	923	952	971	983	991	995	997	999	999	1000	
518	619	711	790	853	901	936	960	976	986	992	996	998	999	999	1000
466	568	664	749	819	875	917	947	967	981	989	994	997	998	999	1000

APPENDIX F
The Chi-Square Distribution

Level of significance

Degrees of freedom	$\chi^2_{.995}$	$\chi^2_{.99}$	$\chi^2_{.975}$	$\chi^2_{.95}$	$\chi^2_{.05}$	$\chi^2_{.025}$	$\chi^2_{.01}$	$\chi^2_{.005}$	Degrees of freedom
1	.0000393	.000157	.000982	.00393	3.841	5.024	6.635	7.879	1
2	.0100	.0201	.0506	.103	5.991	7.378	9.210	10.597	2
3	.0717	.115	.216	.352	7.815	9.348	11.345	12.838	3
4	.207	.297	.484	.711	9.488	11.143	13.277	14.860	4
5	.412	.554	.831	1.145	11.070	12.832	15.086	16.750	5
6	.676	.872	1.237	1.635	12.592	14.449	16.812	18.548	6
7	.989	1.239	1.690	2.167	14.067	16.013	18.475	20.278	7
8	1.344	1.646	2.180	2.733	15.507	17.535	20.090	21.955	8
9	1.735	2.088	2.700	3.325	16.919	19.023	21.666	23.589	9
10	2.156	2.558	3.247	3.940	18.307	20.483	23.209	25.188	10
11	2.603	3.053	3.816	4.575	19.675	21.920	24.725	26.757	11
12	3.074	3.571	4.404	5.226	21.026	23.337	26.217	28.300	12
13	3.565	4.107	5.009	5.892	22.362	24.736	27.688	29.819	13
14	4.075	4.660	5.629	6.571	23.685	26.119	29.141	31.319	14
15	4.601	5.229	6.262	7.261	24.996	27.488	30.578	32.801	15
16	5.142	5.812	6.908	7.962	26.296	28.845	32.000	34.267	16
17	5.697	6.408	7.564	8.672	27.587	30.191	33.409	35.718	17
18	6.265	7.015	8.231	9.390	28.869	31.526	34.805	37.156	18
19	6.844	7.633	8.907	10.117	30.144	32.852	36.191	38.582	19
20	7.434	8.260	9.591	10.851	31.410	34.170	37.566	39.997	20
21	8.034	8.897	10.283	11.591	32.671	35.479	38.932	41.401	21
22	8.643	9.542	10.982	12.338	33.924	36.781	40.289	42.796	22
23	9.260	10.196	11.689	13.091	35.172	38.076	41.638	44.181	23
24	9.886	10.856	12.401	13.848	36.415	39.364	42.980	45.558	24
25	10.520	11.524	13.120	14.611	37.652	40.646	44.314	46.928	25
26	11.160	12.198	13.844	15.379	38.885	41.923	45.642	48.290	26
27	11.808	12.879	14.573	16.151	40.113	43.194	46.963	49.645	27
28	12.461	13.565	15.308	16.928	41.337	44.461	48.278	50.993	28
29	13.121	14.256	16.047	17.708	42.557	45.722	49.588	52.336	29
30	13.787	14.953	16.791	18.493	43.773	46.979	50.892	53.672	30

APPENDIX G
One-Tailed Table of Critical Values for the Kolmogorov-Smirnov Test

Values of $d_\alpha(N)$ such that $Pr[\max|S_N(x) - F_0(x)| > d_\alpha(N)] = \alpha$, where $F_0(x)$ is the theoretical cumulative distribution and $S_N(x)$ is an observed cumulative distribution for a sample of N.

Sample size (N)	Level of significance (α)				
	0.20	0.15	0.10	0.05	0.01
1	0.900	0.925	0.950	0.975	0.995
2	0.684	0.726	0.776	0.842	0.929
3	0.565	0.597	0.642	0.708	0.828
4	0.494	0.525	0.564	0.624	0.733
5	0.446	0.474	0.510	0.565	0.669
6	0.410	0.436	0.470	0.521	0.618
7	0.381	0.405	0.438	0.486	0.577
8	0.358	0.381	0.411	0.457	0.543
9	0.339	0.360	0.388	0.432	0.514
10	0.322	0.342	0.368	0.410	0.490
11	0.307	0.326	0.352	0.391	0.468
12	0.295	0.313	0.338	0.375	0.450
13	0.284	0.302	0.325	0.361	0.433
14	0.274	0.292	0.314	0.349	0.418
15	0.266	0.283	0.304	0.338	0.404
16	0.258	0.274	0.295	0.328	0.392
17	0.250	0.266	0.286	0.318	0.381
18	0.244	0.259	0.278	0.309	0.371
19	0.237	0.252	0.272	0.301	0.363
20	0.231	0.246	0.264	0.294	0.356
25	0.21	0.22	0.24	0.27	0.32
30	0.19	0.20	0.22	0.24	0.29
35	0.18	0.19	0.21	0.23	0.27
over 35	$\dfrac{1.07}{\sqrt{N}}$	$\dfrac{1.14}{\sqrt{N}}$	$\dfrac{1.22}{\sqrt{N}}$	$\dfrac{1.36}{\sqrt{N}}$	$\dfrac{1.63}{\sqrt{N}}$

APPENDIX H
Multiserver Poisson-Exponential Queuing System: Probability That the System is Idle, p_0

$\dfrac{\lambda}{s\mu}$	Number of Channels, s								
	2	3	4	5	6	7	8	10	15
.02	.9608	.9418	.9231	.9048	.8869	.8694	.85214	.81873	.74082
.04	.9231	.8869	.8521	.8187	.7866	.7558	.72615	.67032	.54881
.06	.8868	.8353	.7866	.7408	.6977	.6570	.61878	.54881	.40657
.08	.8519	.7866	.7261	.6703	.6188	.5712	.52729	.44933	.30119
.10	.8182	.7407	.6703	.6065	.5488	.4966	.44933	.36788	.22313
.12	.7857	.6975	.6188	.5488	.4868	.4317	.38289	.30119	.16530
.14	.7544	.6568	.5712	.4966	.4317	.3753	.32628	.24660	.12246
.16	.7241	.6184	.5272	.4493	.3829	.3263	.27804	.20190	.09072
.18	.6949	.5821	.4866	.4065	.3396	.2837	.23693	.16530	.06721
.20	.6667	.5479	.4491	.3678	.3012	.2466	.20189	.13534	.04979

$\dfrac{\lambda}{s\mu}$	Number of Channels, s								
	2	3	4	5	6	7	8	10	15
.22	.6393	.5157	.4145	.3328	.2671	.2144	.17204	.11080	.03688
.24	.6129	.4852	.3824	.3011	.2369	.1864	.14660	.09072	.02732
.26	.5873	.4564	.3528	.2723	.2101	.1620	.12492	.07427	.02024
.28	.5625	.4292	.3255	.2463	.1863	.1408	.10645	.06081	.01500
.30	.5385	.4035	.3002	.2228	.1652	.1224	.09070	.04978	.01111
.32	.5152	.3791	.2768	.2014	.1464	.1064	.07728	.04076	.00823
.34	.4925	.3561	.2551	.1821	.1298	.0925	.06584	.03337	.00610
.36	.4706	.3343	.2351	.1646	.1151	.0804	.05609	.02732	.00452
.38	.4493	.3137	.2165	.1487	.1020	.0698	.04778	.02236	.00335
.40	.4286	.2941	.1993	.1343	.0903	.0606	.04069	.01830	.00248
.42	.4085	.2756	.1834	.1213	.0800	.0527	.03465	.01498	.00184
.44	.3889	.2580	.1686	.1094	.0708	.0457	.02950	.01226	.00136
.46	.3699	.2414	.1549	.0987	.0626	.0397	.02511	.01003	.00101
.48	.3514	.2255	.1422	.0889	.0554	.0344	.02136	.00820	.00075
.50	.3333	.2105	.1304	.0801	.049	.0298	.01816	.00671	.00055
.52	.3158	.1963	.1195	.0721	.0432	.0259	.01544	.00548	.00041
.54	.2987	.1827	.1094	.0648	.0831	.0224	.01311	.00448	.00030
.56	.2821	.1699	.0999	.0581	.0336	.0194	.01113	.00366	.00022
.58	.2658	.1576	.0912	.0521	.0296	.0167	.00943	.00298	.00017
.60	.2500	.1460	.0831	.0466	.0260	.0144	.00799	.00243	.00012
.62	.2346	.1349	.0755	.0417	.0228	.0124	.00675	.00198	.00009
.64	.2195	.1244	.0685	.0372	.0200	.0107	.00570	.00161	.00007
.66	.2048	.1143	.0619	.0330	.0175	.0092	.00480	.00131	.00005
.68	.1905	.1048	.0559	.0293	.0152	.0079	.00404	.00106	.00004
.70	.1765	.0957	.0502	.0259	.0132	.0067	.00338	.00085	.00003
.72	.1628	.0870	.0450	.0228	.0114	.0057	.00283	.00069	.00002
.74	.1494	.0788	.0401	.0200	.0099	.0048	.00235	.00055	.00001
.76	.1364	.0709	.0355	.0174	.0085	.0041	.00195	.00044	
.78	.1236	.0634	.0313	.0151	.0072	.0034	.00160	.00035	
.80	.1111	.0562	.0273	.013	.0061	.0028	.00131	.00028	
.82	.0989	.0493	.0236	.0111	.0051	.0023	.00106	.00022	
.84	.0870	.0428	.0202	.0093	.0042	.0019	.00085	.00017	
.86	.0753	.0366	.0170	.0077	.0035	.0015	.00067	.00013	
.88	.0638	.0306	.0140	.0063	.0028	.0012	.00052	.00010	
.90	.0526	.0249	.0113	.0050	.0021	.0009	.00039	.00007	
.92	.0417	.0195	.0087	.0038	.0016	.0007	.00028	.00005	
.94	.0309	.0143	.0063	.0027	.0011	.0005	.00019	.00003	
.96	.0204	.0093	.0040	.0017	.0007	.0003	.00012	.00002	
.98	.0101	.0045	.0019	.0008	.0003	.0001	.00005	.00001	

APPENDIX I
Random Numbers

04433	80674	24520	18222	10610	05794	37515
60298	47829	72648	37414	75755	04717	29899
67884	59651	67533	68123	17730	95862	08034
89512	32155	51906	61662	64130	16688	37275
32653	01895	12506	88535	36553	23757	34209
95913	15405	13772	76638	48423	25018	99041
55864	21694	13122	44115	01601	50541	00147
35334	49810	91601	40617	72876	33967	73830
57729	32196	76487	11622	96297	24160	09903
86648	13697	63677	70119	94739	25875	38829
30574	47609	07967	32422	76791	39725	53711
81307	43694	83580	79974	45929	85113	72268
02410	54905	79007	54939	21410	86980	91772
18969	75274	52233	62319	08598	09066	95288
87863	82384	66860	62297	80198	19347	73234
68397	71708	15438	62311	72844	60203	46412
28529	54447	58729	10854	99058	18260	38765
44285	06372	15867	70418	57012	72122	36634
86299	83430	33571	23309	57040	29285	67870
84842	68668	90894	61658	15001	94055	36308
56970	83609	52098	04184	54967	72938	56834
83125	71257	60490	44369	66130	72936	69848
55503	52423	02464	26141	68779	66388	75242
47019	76273	33203	29608	54553	25971	69573
84828	32592	79526	29554	84580	37859	28504

68921	08141	79227	05748	51276	57143	31926
36458	96045	30424	98420	72925	40729	22337
95752	59445	36847	87729	81679	59126	59437
26768	47323	58454	56958	20575	76746	49878
42613	37056	43636	58085	06766	60227	96414
95457	30566	65482	25596	02678	54592	63607
95276	17894	63564	95958	39750	64379	46059
66954	52324	64776	92345	95110	59448	77249
17457	18481	14113	62462	02798	54977	48349
03704	36872	83214	59337	01695	60666	97410
21538	86497	33210	60337	27976	70661	08250
57178	67619	98310	70348	11317	71623	55510
31048	97558	94953	55866	96283	46620	52087
69799	55380	16498	80733	96422	58078	99643
90595	61867	59231	17772	67831	33317	00520
33570	04981	98939	78784	09977	29398	93896
15340	93460	57477	13898	48431	72936	78160
64079	42483	36512	56186	99098	48850	72527
63491	05546	67118	62063	74958	20946	28147
92003	63868	41034	28260	79708	00770	88643
52360	46658	66511	04172	73085	11795	52594
74622	12142	68355	65635	21828	39539	18988
04157	50079	61343	64315	70836	82857	35335
86003	60070	66241	32836	27573	11479	94114
41268	80187	20351	09636	84668	42486	71303
48612	62866	83963	14045	79451	04934	45576
78812	03509	78673	73181	29973	18664	04555
19472	63971	37271	31445	49019	49405	46925
51266	11569	08697	91120	64156	40365	74297
55806	96275	26130	47949	14877	69594	83041
77527	81360	18180	97421	55541	90275	18213
77680	58788	33016	61173	93049	04694	43534
15404	96554	88265	34537	38526	67924	40474
14045	22917	60718	66487	46346	30949	03173
68376	43918	77653	04127	69930	43283	35766
93385	13421	67957	20384	58731	53396	59723
09858	52104	32014	53115	03727	98624	84616
93307	34116	49516	42148	57740	31198	70336
04794	01534	92058	03157	91758	80611	45357
86265	49096	97021	92582	61422	75890	86442

65943	79232	45702	67055	39024	57383	44424
90038	94209	04055	27393	61517	23002	96560
97283	95943	78363	36498	40662	94188	18202
21913	72958	75637	99936	58715	07943	23748
41161	37341	81838	19389	80336	46346	91895
23777	98392	31417	98547	92058	02277	50315
59973	08144	61070	73094	27059	69181	55623
82690	74099	77885	23813	10054	11900	44653
83854	24715	48866	65745	31131	47636	45137
61980	34997	41825	11623	07320	15003	56774
99915	45821	97702	87125	44488	77613	56823
48293	86847	43186	42951	37804	85129	28993
33225	31280	41232	34750	91097	60752	69783
06846	32828	24425	30249	78801	26977	92074
32671	45587	79620	84831	38156	74211	82752
82096	21913	75544	55228	89796	05694	91552
51666	10433	10945	55306	78562	89630	41230
54044	67942	24145	42294	27427	84875	37022
66738	60184	75679	38120	17640	36242	99357
55064	17427	89180	74018	44865	53197	74810
69599	60264	84549	78007	88450	06488	72274
64756	87759	92354	78694	63638	80939	98644
80817	74533	68407	55862	32476	19326	95558
39847	96884	84657	33697	39578	90197	80532
90401	41700	95510	61166	33757	23279	85523
78227	90110	81378	96659	37008	04050	04228
87240	52716	87697	79433	16336	52862	69149
08486	10951	26832	39763	02485	71688	90936
39338	32169	03713	93510	61244	73774	01245
21188	01850	69689	49426	49128	14660	14143
13287	82531	04388	64693	11934	35051	68576
53609	04001	19648	14053	49623	10840	31915
87900	36194	31567	53506	34304	39910	79630
81641	00496	36058	75899	46620	70024	88753
19512	50277	71508	20116	79520	06269	74173

Answers to Selected Problems

CHAPTER 1

1. 26,365.64
3. 113
5. Stock 75
10. 13.33 ft. from origin

CHAPTER 3

3.1 $x_1 = 12$, $x_2 = 4$, Max value = 104

3.6 $x_1 = 150$, $x_2 = 644.44$

3.8 $x_1 = 35/91$, $x_2 = 45/13$, Max Value = 2485/91

3.12 $y_1 = 0$, $y_2 = 62.5$, $y_3 = 250$, Min value = 35,250

3.17   a) one   b) $x_1 = 1.75$, Max value = 8.75

3.18   a) $x_1 = 0$, $x_2 = 1$, $x_3 = 4$, $x_4 = 0$ b) yes   c) no   d) no

3.22   Produce 160 sq. yd. plywood; profit is $48,000

3.32 $x_1 = 1.50$, $x_2 = 4.57$; optimal design uses 250.24 sq. inches

CHAPTER 4

4.3   The dual, it has fewer constraints

4.6 $x_1 = 0$, $x_2 = 2$, Max value $= 16$; $y_1 = 2$, Min value $= 16$

4.9   a) $(-\infty, \frac{3}{2}]$ for S_1, $(-\infty, 2]$ for S_3 b) $[0,4]$ for x_1, $[-\frac{1}{5}, \frac{1}{2}]$ for S_2, $[6, \infty)$ for x_2 c) greater than \$7

4.11 a) resources 1 and 2   b) Either resource 1 or 2; both shadow prices are \$1   c) Resource 1 could be increased by 12, Resource 2 could be increased by 2, no limit on Resource 3

4.15 a) .74 gals. milk, .639 lbs. spinach per day, \$1.39, no.

b) vitamins C and D exactly, A and iron are overdoses

c) $[29.36, \infty)$ d) $c_1[.156, \infty)$, $c_2[0, \infty)$, $c_3[0, \infty)$, $c_4[0, 2.9]$

4.18 Constraints 2 and 3 are tight. Shadow price 1 is zero.

4.20 a) RHS 1 $[0,9]$ RHS 2 $[12, \infty)$ b) $y_1 = 1$, $y_2 = 1$
c) Cost range for $S_1(-\infty, 3]$ Cost range for $x_1[0,6]$
Cost range for $x_2[3\frac{1}{2}, \infty)$

CHAPTER 5

5.2   Two solutions are possible: Min cost is 304. One solution is $x_{11} = 11$, $x_{13} = 7$, $x_{14} = 2$, $x_{23} = 10$, $x_{32} = 13$, $x_{34} = 12$

5.3   VAM solution in 5.2 is optimal

5.6 $x_{12} = 600$, $x_{15} = 400$, $x_{23} = 1000$, $x_{24} = 100$, $x_{25} = 400$, $x_{31} = 800$, $x_{34} = 400$

5.10 1–1, 2–4, 3–3, 4–2

5.11 $x_{15} = 5$, $x_{27} = 7$, $x_{36} = 4$, $x_{47} = 2$

5.13 1, 5, 2, 3, 4, 1

5.15 1–x, 2–y, 3–Z

5.20 1-5, 2-2, 3-1, 4-3, 5-4, Min cost $= \$155,000$ If more than contract can be awarded to a bidder then 2–1, 2–2, 1–3, 5–4, 1–5, Min cost $= \$141,000$

5.21 Total cost with two factories is \$32,000 (transportation cost is \$12,000); total cost with three factories is \$35,750 (Transportation cost is \$14,750).

CHAPTER 6

6.1   Distance to node 2 is 5, node 3 is 4, node 4 is 3, node 5 is 14, node 6 is 13, node 7 is 26.

6.2   Arcs in tree are 1,4, 4,3, 3,2, 2,5, 2,6, 5,7   Length $= 35$

6.3   Max flow = 12

6.6   7,000 vehicles per hour

6.10   Yes, shortest route is now 1–5–7

6.14   Max shipment is 31,000 barrels.

CHAPTER 7

7.3   b) BDF   c) 12 days

7.5   d) 15.833 weeks   e) .267   f) .093

7.9   a) 15 days   b) $1275   e) $600

CHAPTER 8

8.3 $x_1 = 1$, $x_2 = 1$, $x_3 = 1$, $x_4 = 0$

8.5   a) 0–1 integer   b) mixed integer   c) linear   d) pure integer

8.7 $x_1 = 4$, $x_2 = 2$

8.9   The optimal purchase and storage strategy is to buy all 10 kits in November

8.10   63

8.14   path 1–2–5–7, distance 27

8.18   Run 25 T.V. ads

8.22   GPA = .000905 X + 2.598 where x = GMAT score

CHAPTER 9

9.1   a) $\frac{1}{16}$ b) $\frac{1}{16}$ c) $\frac{1}{2}$

9.3 $\frac{1}{2}$

9.6   a) $\frac{21}{39}$ b) $\frac{6}{39}$ c) .6   d) $\frac{5}{21}$

9.9   a) .08   b) .02   c) .18

9.13   a) .1204   b) .8541   c) less than .0001

9.19   .53

9.22   a) .1937   b) .2669   c) .0128

9.26   a) .25143   b) .74958

9.36   a) .007   b) .176   c) .068

CHAPTER 10

10.1   a) d_2 b) d_4 c) d_3

10.3   c) $16,666.50

10.6   c) buy 3 dozen balls early   EMV = \$301.70

10.10   c) Go without research

10.14   c) Take the test and do not drop no matter what

CHAPTER 11

11.1   \$483,750

11.3   \$501,250

11.5   \$501,350

11.8   \$533,383

11.21   b) \$78.135 per share   c) \$74.425 per share

11.23   \$1.16 per gallon

CHAPTER 12

12.4   3

12.8   a) .75   b) 3 minutes   c) 3 customers   d) .25

12.10   a) 11.76 minutes   b) Employ 2 repairmen

12.13 $Lq = 1.6308$ ships $Ws = 216.5$ minutes
$\rho = .625$ $P(0) = .375$
$Ls = 2.2558$ ships
$Wq = 156.5$ minutes

CHAPTER 13

Not Applicable

CHAPTER 14

14.3   a) 60   b) 4   c) 3 months   d) \$600

14.8   a) 45   b) \$1698.75

14.14   a) 27,576 trees   b) \$264,600

14.18   a) 122.4   b) \$4561.57

14.21   a) 10,000 lbs   b) \$54,848.00   c) \$17,000.00

CHAPTER 15

15.1 $\pi_1 = .25$
$\pi_2 = .25$
$\pi_3 = .50$

15.4 a) 20.6% paid, 47.7% delinquent, 33.9% bad debt

15.6 $12,528

15.10 a) Steady State probabilities are:

$\pi_1 = .769$
$\pi_2 = .154$
$\pi_3 = .077$

Since $\pi_1 > .7$, BIM will face an antitrust action.

b) In 2 years BIM's market share will be .726.

15.13 $1100.01 per month.

Index

S